STERLING SEAGRAVE

Dragon Lady

Sterling Seagrave, best-selling author of *The Soong Dynasty*, grew up on the China-Burma border, the fifth generation of an American family living in the Orient for nearly two centuries (his father was Dr. Gordon Seagrave, author of *Burma Surgeon*). As an investigative journalist in Asia, he contributed to many major newspapers and magazines. His other books include *Yellow Rain* and *The Marcos Dynasty*. He and his wife and collaborator, Peggy Sawyer Seagrave, live in Europe.

Dragon Lady

DRAGON LADY

The Life and Legend of the Last Empress of China

by

STERLING SEAGRAVE

with the collaboration of Peggy Seagrave

Vintage Books

A DIVISION OF RANDOM HOUSE, INC.

NEW YORK

FIRST VINTAGE BOOKS EDITION, SEPTEMBER 1993

Grateful acknowledgment is made to the following for permission to
reprint material: *Harvard University Press:* Excerpts from Hart's letters to
Campbell from *The I.G. in Peking*, edited by Fairbank, Bruner, & Matheson.
Reprinted by permission.
Mitchell Library, State Library of New South Wales: Excerpts from diaries
and letters of G. E. Morrison. Reprinted by permission.

Library of Congress Cataloging-in-Publication Data
Seagrave, Sterling.
Dragon lady: the life and legend of the last empress of China by Sterling
Seagrave with the collaboration of Peggy Seagrave.—1st Vintage Books ed.
p. cm.
Includes bibliographical references and index.
ISBN 0-679-73369-8 (pbk.)
1. Tz' u-hsi, Empress dowager of China, 1835–1908. 2. China—Empresses—
Biography. I. Seagrave, Peggy. II. Title.
DS763.63.T96S43 1993
951'.035'092—dc20
[B]   92-50582
CIP

Manufactured in the United States of America
10 9 8 7 6 5 4 3

For Peter and Dojean

"Future ages will hold the Empress Dowager in even greater horror than the Empress Wu."
                              —Alicia Little in the *Times* of London

"No one will ever understand what bungling there has been, and what culpability."
                              —Bertram Lenox-Simpson

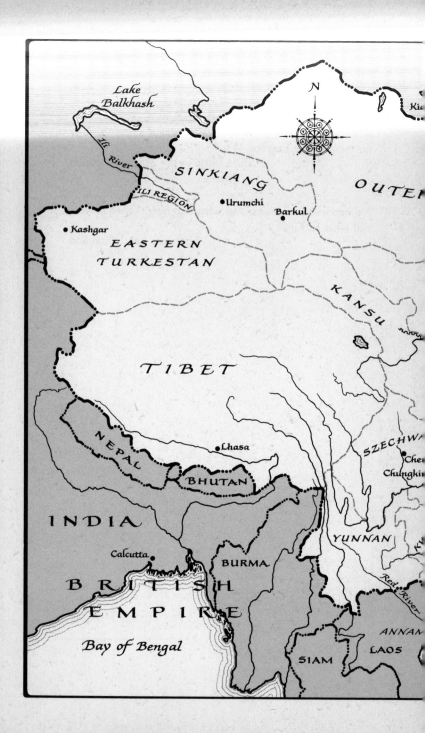

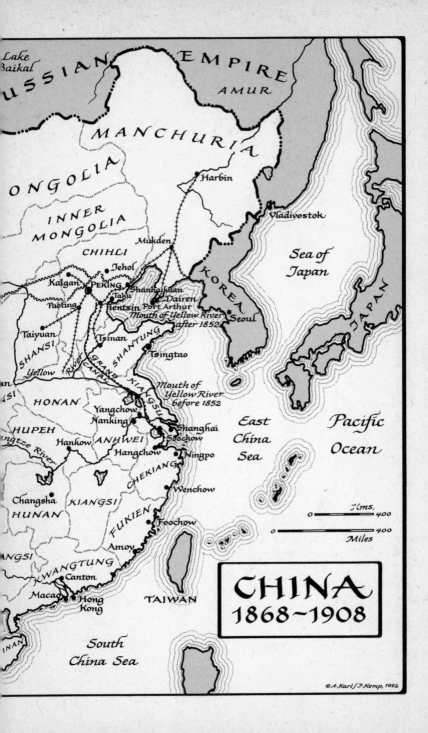

Lake
Baikal

RUSSIAN EMPIRE

AMUR

MANCHURIA

MONGOLIA

INNER
MONGOLIA

Harbin

Vladivostok

CHIHLI

Mukden

Jehol

Kalgan

PEKING

Taku

Shanhaikuan

Dairen

Sea of
Japan

Paoting

Tientsin Port Arthur

Mouth of Yellow River
after 1852

KOREA

Taiyuan

Tsinan

SHANSI

SHANTUNG

Tsingtao

Seoul

Yellow

River

GRAND CANAL

KIANGSU

Mouth of
Yellow River
before 1852

JAPAN

HONAN

Yangchow

Nanking

HUPEH

ANHWEI

Shanghai

Soochow

East
China
Sea

Pacific
Ocean

Hankow

Hangchow

Ningpo

CHEKIANG

Changsha

KIANGSI

Wenchow

HUNAN

FUKIEN

Foochow

Kms.
0 ——— 400

KIANGSI

Amoy

0 ——— 400
Miles

KWANGTUNG

Canton

Macao

Hong
Kong

TAIWAN

CHINA
1868~1908

HAINAN

South
China Sea

© A. Karl / J. Kemp, 1992

Contents

CAST OF CHARACTERS

Ababai son of Ching Dynasty founder, consolidated his domain

Lady A-lu-te Emperor Tung Chih's ill-fated bride

Bishop Johann Baptist von Anzer provoked Boxer reprisals

Benjamin Avery American minister

Ayaou Robert Hart's concubine, bore his first three children

Sir Edmund Backhouse genius, con man, pornographer, historian

Sir Henry Blake governor of Hong Kong at turn of century

Lady Edith Blake his wife

J.O.P. Bland Shanghai correspondent of the *Times* of London

Frederick S. A. Bourne British consul, Shanghai

Sir John Bowring governor of Hong Kong in Second Opium War

Hester Jane Bredon Lady Hart

Robert Bredon Hart's deputy at Customs and brother-in-law

Lily Bredon his wife

Juliet Bredon her daughter by another man

Byron Brenan acting British consul-general, Shanghai

H. H. Bristow student interpreter, started shooting Chinese

James Bruce, Lord Elgin British commander, burned Summer Palace

Frederick Bruce Elgin's younger brother, attacked Taku Forts

Henry Burgevine American soldier of fortune, fought Taipings

Anson Burlingame American envoy

Katherine Carl portrait artist

General Adna Chaffee U.S. commander, former Indian fighter

Auguste Chamot Swiss hotelier and adventurer

Chang Chih-tung Yangtze viceroy, rival of Viceroy Li

Sir Chang Yin-huan first Chinese knighted

Chao Shu-chiao Ironhat faction, headed Board of Punishments

Prince Cheng member, Gang of Eight

Chin Fei Emperor Kuang Hsu's Pearl Concubine

Prince Ching chief minister to Emperor Kuang Hsu

Ching Shou member, Gang of Eight

Valentine Chirol foreign editor, the *Times* of London

Dr. Chu Kwei-ting attended Emperor Kuang Hsu before his death

Prince Chuang Ironhat chief of imperial police, secret police

Prince Chun Hsien Feng's brother, father of Emperor Kuang Hsu

Prince Chun II brother of Emperor Kuang Hsu, father of Pu Yi

Duke Chung A-lu-te's father and member of Ironhat faction

Chung Li chief of Peking Gendarmerie, leading Ironhat

Henry Cockburn senior British legation interpreter

Edwin Conger American minister during Boxer crisis

Sarah Conger his wife

Baron Corvo Frederick William Rolfe, Edwardian pornographer

Charles Denby American minister

Dr. Dethève French legation doctor, examined Emperor Kuang Hsu

Gustav Detring Viceroy Li's German protégé at Tientsin

Prince Dorgon seventeenth-century Manchu regent who subdued China

Captain Charles Elliot British commander at Canton

Bishop Favier bishop of Peking

Charles Masson Fox Backhouse's cousin, patron of Baron Corvo

General Alfred Gaselee lifted the siege of Peking

Lancelot Giles British student interpreter

Charles ("Chinese") Gordon the legendary British officer

General Sir Hope Grant commander, 1860 punitive force to Peking

Dr. G. Douglas Gray British legation doctor

Baron J.B.L. Gros French envoy in 1860 punitive expedition

Karl Gutzlaff Prussian mentor of interpreters Lay and Parkes

Constantin von Hanneken Viceroy Li's German military engineer

Sir Robert Hart Customs chief

W. Meyrick Hewlett British student interpreter

Baron Edmund von Heyking German minister at start of Boxer conspiracy

Hiraoka Kotaro nominal head of Genyosha

Hirayama Shu Genyosha agent in Peking

Herbert Hoover in 1898 an aggressive mining engineer in China

Sir Robert Hotung rich Hong Kong comprador

Emperor Hsien Feng husband of Lady Yehenara

Hsu Chih-ching bureaucrat friend of Wild Fox Kang

Hsu Tung Grand Secretary, leading Ironhat mandarin

Hsu Ying-kuei president, Board of Ceremonies, Ironhat faction

Hung Hsiu-chuan emperor of the Taipings

Prince I member, Gang of Eight

Ito Hirobumi Japanese elder statesman, former prime minister

Dr. Huberty James eccentric professor at Peking University

Princess Jung An daughter of Lady Yehenara's rival concubine

General Jung Lu Tzu Hsi's lifelong ally, later prime minister

Kang I Grand Councillor and leading Ironhat mandarin

Kang Kuang-jen brother of Wild Fox Kang, one of the Six Martyrs

Kang Yu-wei charlatan, self-styled leader of reform movement

Baron Clemens von Ketteler German minister during siege

Kim Ok-kium murdered Korean exile leader

Emperor Kuang Hsu Tsai Tien, much-abused son of Prince Chun

Duke Kuei Hsiang Tzu Hsi's brother, father of Empress Lung Yu

Kuei Liang Grand Secretary, Prince Kung's father-in-law

Prince Kung Hsien Feng's brother, ruled China by coalition

Duke Lan son of Prince Tun, member of Ironhat faction

Horatio Nelson Lay aggressive British interpreter/negotiator

Bertram Lenox-Simpson China-born writer

Prince Li Grand Councillor and elderly Ironhat stalwart

Li Fei Hsien Feng's favorite concubine, Lady Yehenara's rival

Li Hung-chang viceroy, imperial China's great political boss

Li Lai-chung Shansi bandit, leader of Boxer hard core

Li Lien-ying Tzu Hsi's Grand Eunuch, a power behind the throne

General Li Ping-heng top Ironhat general, conceived Boxer plot

Liang Chi-chao propagandist, follower of Wild Fox Kang

General Liang Pi Japanese-trained Manchu, slain by Viceroy Yuan

Lim Boon-keng Singapore-based anti-Manchu propagandist

Commissioner Lin responsible for Barbarians in First Opium War

Lin Hsu reform adviser and one of the Six Martyrs

General Lineivitch Russian commander in 1900

Archibald Little missionary turned grasping Yangtze businessman

Alicia Little busybody, critic of Empress Dowager Tzu Hsi

Liu Kuang-ti reform adviser and one of the Six Martyrs

Frederick Low American minister

Empress Lung Yu Kuang Hsu's empress, niece of Tzu Hsi

Sir Claude MacDonald British minister during 1900 siege

Lady Ethel MacDonald his wife

Dr. W.A.P. Martin language professor, ex-missionary

Signor di Martino Italian minister

John Meadows Hart's first boss as acting consul in Ningpo

Queen Min doomed ruler of Korea

Miyazaki Torazo senior Genyosha agent in East Asia

George Morrison Peking correspondent of the *Times* of London

O. S. Nestegaard Norwegian missionary

General Nieh Shih-cheng moderate

Nurhachi Ching Dynasty founder

Okuma Shigenobu Japanese foreign minister

Captain Mortimer O'Sullivan British soldier of fortune, agent

Lord Palmerston British foreign secretary/prime minister

Harry Parkes British interpreter/negotiator

William Pethick American secretary to Viceroy Li

Stephen Jean-Marie Pichon French minister

Captain Poole British officer, led taking of Hanlin Academy

Pu Chun Prince Tuan's son, almost an emperor

Pu Yi Emperor Kuang Hsu's nephew, last emperor of China

Count Vasilevich Putiatin Russian envoy

Gilbert Reid American missionary, meddled in Chinese politics

Timothy Richard Welsh missionary, meddled in Chinese politics

Arthur von Rosthorn Austro-Hungarian minister

Lord Salisbury British prime minister

Marchese di Salvago-Raggi Italian minister

Sir Ernest Satow British minister to Tokyo and Peking

Admiral Sir Edward Hobart Seymour marooned in North China

Admiral Sir Michael Seymour his uncle; commander, Second Opium War

Telegraph Sheng head of Viceroy Li's Imperial Telegraph

General Sheng Pao Prince Kung's ally, arrested Gang of Eight

Colonel Shiba Japanese military attaché at siege of Peking

Polly Condit Smith American on holiday at siege of Peking

Herbert Squiers U.S. first secretary in Peking

Su Shun leader of Gang of Eight, tried to seize throne

Prince Su moderate, bullied out of his palace by Morrison

Sugimura Yotara Japanese envoy, helped murder Queen Min

Sugiyama Akira Japanese embassy chancellor, beheaded by mob

Sun Tzu master strategist/tactician, fourth century B.C.

Sung Po-lu bureaucrat friend of Wild Fox Kang

Boss Takee Shanghai godfather, outwitted by Viceroy Li

Tan Ssu-tung reform adviser and one of the Six Martyrs

Emperor Tao Kuang Hsien Feng's father

Captain von Thomann Austrian attaché at siege of Peking

Lady Susan Townley wife of British first secretary

Toyama Mitsuru godfather of the Genyosha secret society

Tsai Cheng son of Prince Kung

Tseng Kuo-fan first of the new Chinese warlords, Li's mentor

Prince Tuan son of Prince Tun, chief Ironhat leader

Prince Tun Hsien Feng's brother and rival

Prince Tun II son of Prince Tun, an Ironhat leader

Emperor Tung Chih Tzu Hsi's son

General Tung Fu-hsiang Muslim bandit-warlord, backed Ironhats

Empress Dowager Tzu An childless coregent with Tzu Hsi

Empress Dowager Tzu Hsi Lady Yehenara, survived to reign alone

Prince Ukhtomskii czarist conspirator in China

Hubert Vos portrait artist, admirer of Tzu Hsi

Sir Thomas Wade British minister at Tung Chih's death

Count Alfred von Waldersee German commander in chief 1900

Frederick Townsend Ward American mercenary, fought Taipings

John Ward American envoy

Wen Hsiang Grand Councillor, Prince Kung's ally

Weng Tung-ho chief tutor to Emperor Kuang Hsu

Wo Jen tutor of Emperor Tung Chih

Boss Wu Shanghai godfather, outfoxed by Viceroy Li

Empress Wu much-maligned empress of the Tang Dynasty

Yamagata Aritomo Japanese militarist/prime minister

Yang Chung-i imperial witch-hunter, Viceroy Li's point man

Yang Jui reform adviser and one of the Six Martyrs

Yang Shen-hsiu bureaucrat friend of Wild Fox Kang

Commissioner Yeh responsible for "Barbarians" in Second Opium War

Yu Derling a lady-in-waiting to Tzu Hsi

Yu Hsien Manchu governor, mass murderer of missionaries

Yuan Shih-kai Viceroy Li's protégé, briefly emperor of China

AUTHOR'S NOTE

In China there were only three reigning empresses over thousands of years:

Empress Lu in the Han Dynasty (206 B.C.–A.D. 220)

Empress Wu in the Tang Dynasty (A.D. 618–907) and

Empress Dowager Tzu Hsi in the Ching Dynasty (A.D. 1644–1911).

Dragon Lady

PROLOGUE

Flowers in the Back Garden

Each spring and autumn in Peking just before the end of the nineteenth century, when dust storms off the Gobi were not too severe, many of the foreign community—fewer than five hundred souls at the time, half of them missionaries—gathered on Wednesday evenings at six o'clock for a lawn party at the home of Sir Robert Hart, the "I.G." or Inspector General of Chinese Customs. A hundred men and perhaps thirty ladies came to hear Hart's brass band give a concert in the eight-acre Inspectorate garden. This was the social event of the week, and any distinguished strangers passing through Peking came as well. Ladies strolled under the lilacs, which hung over the paths in a purple mist in April, the scent of the lilacs mixing with their lemony cologne, rose water, and a German fragrance then fashionable called Rhine Violets. It was often hot, and the ladies came freshly scrubbed with Vinolia or Erasmic Herb Soap. The style-conscious wore silky lawn, in biscuit, rose pink, or soft green, adorned with ribbons and lace. To guard their complexions against Gobi grit they wore veils of white Russian mesh or tulle with pin spots; and fabulous hats of rice straw or blue harebell straw trimmed with velvet bows, ostrich plumes, osprey feathers, and lace. In rattan chairs grandes dames with upswept hairdos sat nibbling biscuits and watching children in knickers and pinafores dart among the bushes.

The diplomats talked shop; the missionaries looked disapproving; while the journalists up from Shanghai and Hong Kong drifted about listening for indiscretions. All classes and creeds were present, and the lions sipped tea with the lambs for the sake of hearing familiar Western tunes.

Here and there Chinese mandarins mingled with the "Foreign Devils," their hats and gowns decorated with the buttons, squares, and peacock plumes signifying high office. By far the most imposing were Viceroy Li Hung-chang and his protégé General Yuan Shih-kai.

Now seventy-six years old, Li Hung-chang was the richest and most powerful political boss in the empire; he controlled railways, telegraphs, mines, shipping lines, and had a private army and legions of secret agents. Many leading mandarins and Manchu princes had accepted money from the viceroy to bail them out of financial difficulties and were in thrall to him ever after. A deceptively kind looking man, standing over six feet four in thick-soled black satin boots, he had suffered a stroke that had partly immobilized his face and left him with a beatific smile—a dangerous man with a seraphic countenance. As it was still hot, Li wore a hat of woven bamboo covered with cream silk gauze, resembling a lampshade, decorated with a peacock feather fastened by a tube of Burmese jade. His robes were covered by a long silk coat, slit up the sides to allow horseback riding, embroidered front and back with a mandarin square emblematic of rank—in Li's case a white crane, for the first rank. His garments were tied at the waist with a leather belt from which hung purses and pouches holding fans, snuff, and a pocket spittoon that he reached for frequently and (clearing his throat and sinuses with a reverberating noise that sent shudders up the spines of all Europeans within hearing distance) spat into. Around his neck he wore a string of 108 beads like a Buddhist rosary, from which hung three strings of coral representing the Five Elements. Below them dangled a lollipop pendant of jade on its own cord, and the viceroy toyed with it in his left hand as he talked to Hart.

General Yuan was similarly dressed, but short and squat next to Li, beaming like Li's well-fed cat at a garden full of mice. Hart was always warning his Western colleagues that one day either Li or Yuan—or both—might stage a coup and seize power for themselves.

Noticeable for his absence was the urbane diplomat Sir Chang Yin-huan, the first Chinese to be knighted by Great Britain, who had learned to use a knife and fork while posted to the Chinese embassy off Dupont Circle in Washington, D.C. The ever popular bon vivant had recently been banished to faraway Sinkiang for his part in the failed reform movement of 1898. The edict referred to him as "crafty and inconstant."

Sir Robert said the mandarins came to his parties just "to get a sight of the two curios of Peking, the I.G. and his queer musicians." Fond of music, he had organized China's first brass band in the 1880s, into which he pressed Customs officers and their wives until they protested his tyrannical manner. He then hired Chinese and taught them to play Western instruments, including cornets, euphoniums, and a bombardon imported from England. The band played well under the direction of E. E. Encarnacao, a Customs employee from Macao. The fourteen uniformed musicians, all in their teens, had other full-time occupations: a barber played the flute, a shoemaker the cornet, and a tailor the drum. Every week they played Hart's favorites, "Nuit d'Amour," "When the Lights Are Low,"

"Gnomes Polka," and "American Barn Dance," mingled with tunes that were the rage in countries they had never seen. Hart was organizing a string orchestra as well for dinner dances he threw once a week, ending well after midnight.

Hart's house and compound were in the middle of Peking, on the edge of the legation quarter, near the rose-colored walls of the Forbidden City. It was bounded on the north by a Shaman temple, on the west by the sprawling gardens and palaces of Prince Su, on the east by the estate of Prince Yu, and was within a half mile of all the legations.

These magical gardens and artificial lakes behind tall walls made Peking very pleasant for those on the inside. The chief reminder that a real China lurked outside was the ever-present stink of human excrement. Out of the Forbidden City and through the legation quarter ran an open sewer that perfumed the air night and day, lending its unmistakable scent to tennis matches, soirees, and formal dinners in the legations, tainting the incense in Western cathedrals, and penetrating mosquito nets at night. In the dusty, teeming, clay-brick alleys of its Chinese City, children with slit pants squatted to relieve themselves in the middle of the road. In streets ankle-deep with nameless filth, smallpocked magicians, jugglers, and contortionists competed for coins with howling legions of leprous beggars. Atop city gates draped with banners, venereal soldiers in soupstained silks hawked and spat and shouted obscene advice to the ragged crowds below, cursing the bowels of the heavenly pig. There was no eluding the organic stink even in the quaint English tea garden of Sir Robert Hart, where it mingled with the bergamot in the tea.

In his mid-sixties, Sir Robert Hart was still vigorous after forty years in China. His hair was thin but dark, his beard neatly trimmed; he always wore a frock coat and tie, and a box of Shah brand gold-tipped Egyptian cigarettes lived in his pocket. He smoked a cheroot after breakfast and dinner, but since Lady Hart had taken the children back to England in 1881, he had taken up cigarettes to fight the solitude. At five feet seven he was every inch a "small, slender, ironclad autocrat."

In the absence of his family—it was eighteen years now—Hart entertained lavishly and often had houseguests with children; there were those who swore they had seen him playing blindman's buff with giggling girls out at the gazebo on the hill. But Hart formed no close friendships. At the height of his career he confided bitterly to his diary: "I am utterly alone and have not a single friend or confidant . . . there are spasms of loneliness which hit hard."

Hart was the only Westerner to enjoy daily contact with Manchu princes and senior officials of the court, making him the most influential and best informed foreigner in China. Since 1861 he had built a scrupulously honest, efficient Customs Service staffed mostly with foreigners, which produced a large part of the revenue that sustained the government of China. He was consulted by Chinese and foreign officials and was able to intercede discreetly on sensitive issues. As the I.G. he wielded immense patronage, but he resisted every inducement and practiced a painful discretion, to maintain his trust as an employee of the Chinese government and not an agent for England or any other power. He spent his whole life uncomfortably straddling a fence.

One of Hart's guests was Dr. George Ernest Morrison, Peking correspondent of the *Times* of London, who had first turned up at a garden party in the spring of 1897. He was a handsome, urbane man, with sloping shoulders, a big head, blue gray eyes, and a wandering smile. Morrison got along with everyone without revealing much about himself. He was a thirty-seven-year-old Australian knight-errant. Born and educated in Geelong, Victoria, the son of a Scottish immigrant, he had the lifelong wanderlust that was essential equipment in the Victorian Age, when reputations and fortunes were made on long-distance reconnaissance down the Nile, up the Irrawaddy, and across the Hindu Kush. At age eighteen Morrison walked alone across Australia, covering two thousand miles in 123 days. At twenty-one he led an expedition to New Guinea and nearly died from a spear wound; its barb was removed by a physician in Edinburgh, Scotland, where Morrison completed his medical training. Growing bored with being physician first to workers at a copper mine in Spain and then to a Moroccan sheik, he walked, rode, and paddled three thousand miles across China from Shanghai to Rangoon, publishing a memorable book about the journey in 1895. This brought him to the attention of the *Times,* who hired him to go to China. He was told, "When in doubt, consult Sir Robert Hart." This was not easy, as Morrison wrote to a friend: "Most of the men I see here frequently but I rarely meet the I.G. He has I know to be extremely cautious and guarded beyond measure in what he says."

Morrison was outside the normal pecking order. As Peking correspondent of the world's greatest newspaper and the only full-time resident journalist, he was a minister without portfolio. He listened with one ear to the secrets of the legations and with the other to the wooing of General Yuan Shih-kai. He could covet a knighthood and dream of running for prime minister of Australia while lying ingeniously and without remorse in his articles about China. His influence on history, deliberate and unconscious, altered the international equation for nearly a century afterward.

For a correspondent who spent twenty years in China and was known far and wide as "Morrison of Peking," a mastery of the Chinese language would seem fundamental, but Morrison lacked the will. He was always at the mercy of those who did speak it, with tragic consequences. He could never verify a story on his own and suffered occasional self-doubts: "I have blundered with misstatements," he wrote in his diary on January 7, 1899. "This causes me the most poignant regret." But vanity came to his rescue. After a puff about him was published by the *China Mail* in Hong Kong, Morrison wrote in his diary that it had been "written with my knowledge, such is fame." The article said: "Thanks to [Morrison], there is no journal in the world better informed on Chinese affairs, of the undercurrent that passes for politics in Peking." It was Morrison who provoked the statesman Lord Curzon to praise "the intelligent anticipation of events before they occur," which, wrote the *Times*, "was perhaps the most genuine tribute ever wrung from unwilling lips to the highest qualities which a correspondent can bring to bear upon his work."

What his editors did not know was that many of Morrison's articles contained distortions and inventions provided by his Chinese-speaking assistant and that Morrison himself kept a secret chronicle of events that was strikingly different from his newspaper accounts. As journalism's first China watcher, Morrison was responsible for many of the slanders and half-truths about China that persist to this day.

Morrison knew everyone at Sir Robert's lawn party and—thanks to an ear for scurrilous rumor, medical gossip, and sexual innuendo—kept a close tally of those, male or female, who had syphilis or gonorrhea, and was amused by the way the infections were passed around.

The senior legation residents were all there, including the mutton-chopped American minister, former cavalry officer Edwin Conger, and his painfully sincere wife, Sarah, a Christian Scientist who saw herself as a potential successor to the congregation's founder, Mary Baker Eddy. The Congers were drab, no-nonsense people, unlike Morrison's intimate friends Herbert Squiers, the elegant, ambitious American first secretary, and his wife, Harriet. Squiers spent all his spare time amassing an extraordinary collection of Chinese porcelains that was going to make him very wealthy. Harriet, who had come endowed with a sizable inheritance, had in tow one of her relatives from Boston, Polly Condit Smith, a jolly young woman who enjoyed Morrison's attention. He told his diary she was "fat and gushing," but Peking did not offer much choice.

Morrison was ambivalent about the British minister, forty-seven-year-old Sir Claude MacDonald, a tall, lean deerhound, with a magnificent waxed mustache and sorrowful eyes. He had seen military service in the Egyptian campaigns before being posted to Zanzibar and the Niger with the Consular Service. Nobody was quite sure how he had jumped from that obscurity to the top diplomatic post in China. Morrison joked that Sir Claude was promoted to Peking because the current prime minister, Lord Salisbury, believed that MacDonald had in his possession evidence to prove that Salisbury and Jack the Ripper were the same person. The very pretty Lady Ethel MacDonald, six years her husband's junior, was easily the most gracious and attractive Western woman in the capital.

Morrison did not like the French minister, Stephen Jean-Marie Pichon, a rotund former journalist with a walrus mustache who, unknown to his peers, slept in a nightshirt embroidered with red songbirds. Morrison, who despised the French, thought Pichon was spineless.

Signor di Martino, the Italian minister, was nervous and superstitious. He once refused to sign a diplomatic convention because he had seen a squint-eyed man on the street that morning. Morrison knew that di Martino kept a Japanese mistress out of sight at the Italian legation.

Also present was the choleric new German minister, Baron Clemens Freiherr von Ketteler, a Nietzschean superman doing his best to imitate Kaiser Wilhelm. He was accompanied by his pretty American wife, Maud, daughter of a Midwestern railway magnate.

In a wicker lawn chair nearby was twenty-five-year-old American mining engineer Herbert Hoover, who was working for a British company seeking gold-mining concessions in China. Seated by his bride, Lou, were Hart's brother-in-law Robert Bredon and his wife, Lily; her daughter by another man, Juliet; and Lily's current paramour, Bertram Lenox-Simpson, a chubby China-born Brit with a keen intellect whose continual wisecracking annoyed Morrison no end. Only twenty-two, Bertie spoke five languages, including Chinese, and was fond of riding, shooting, swimming, lovemaking, and food, in whatever order. Lily was a lively and good-natured woman from San Francisco, given to dressing like Marie Antoinette, even to gluing a beauty mark on her ample bosom. Morrison said that fat Bertie had put on Robert Bredon "the longest pair of horns worn by any cuckold in China!"

Missionaries were at the lawn party like mustard on a pork pie, among them the white-haired Welsh Baptist and political activist Timothy Richard—Morrison called him "very Welsh and not too bright"—and American Gilbert Reid. Richard and Reid were trying to subvert the Manchu regime by encouraging young radical Chinese reformers, several of whom as a consequence had just been beheaded, providing Reid and Richard with martyrs to champion. Here, too, was the eccentric Norwegian preacher O. S. Nestegaard, who was frequently seen parading around Peking in a white cutaway evening jacket and had scandalized the legations by exposing himself to the wife of the Russian minister.

Morrison detested missionaries. He had met a few he liked during his trip across China, brave people with good hearts, but they often caused more grief than good. One amiable Scot after seven years' work could claim only three converts, one of whom had since died. In a population of seven million friendly and peaceable Yunnanese, desperate for encouragement after years of famine, eighteen missionaries in eight years had converted only eleven souls; how long would it take to convert the rest?

Among the missionaries at Hart's party were the annoying Archibald Little and his indefatigable wife, Alicia, a leader of the antifootbinding movement, dressed in her usual mannish tweeds. Archibald had come to China as a missionary, then became an aggressive entrepreneur—Hart called him a "pushing Englishman." Morrison referred to Alicia as "that awful woman." While campaigning against footbinding she had lectured to five hundred college students in Hong Kong, showing them photographs of bare bound feet, and was mystified as to why they snickered, giggled, and laughed uproariously throughout. Although she published books about China, Alicia understood little about the country and failed to grasp the sexual role bound feet played in male fantasies. Showing Chinese students photos of bare bound feet—which they would not ordinarily see until they were married, and then only during sex with their wives or concubines—was like showing a gymnasium full of British schoolboys photos of bare pubes.

Because he disliked so many of the guests, Morrison spent most of the party huddled with two men, J.O.P. Bland and Edmund Trelawny Backhouse.

John Ottway Percy Bland, whom Morrison found useful but deeply annoying, was the thirty-five-year-old Shanghai correspondent of the *Times;* Bland could read and speak Chinese fluently and never let Morrison forget that *he* could not. Bland also served as secretary of the Municipal Council of the International Settlement in Shanghai, where he picked up a lot of dirt on the political doings of Manchu and Chinese alike, much of it biased and inaccurate. His private life was not happy, his wife being, as Morrison put it, a "faithless neurotic." Bland cut a dapper figure—his hair neatly parted down the center, his full mustache carefully scissored—and affected a nonchalant air in an expensively tailored hacking jacket and checked cravat.

Edmund Backhouse was a new arrival from London, a young linguist fresh out of Oxford who claimed to be fluent in ten or twelve tongues; a fragile-looking, vaguely handsome young man, resembling a night-dwelling spectral tarsier.

They were discussing Empress Dowager Tzu Hsi. Until the autumn of 1898 little had been known about her. Then, with the brutal crackdown on the burgeoning reform movement—leading to the exile of Sir Chang, the execution of Richard's and Reid's young martyrs, and the escape to Japan of the radicals Kang Yu-wei and Liang Chi-chao—a monstrous picture of the "Old Buddha" had begun to appear that confirmed everyone's worst suppositions and prejudices. In exile, Kang Yu-wei was now providing Westerners with shocking disclosures about the secret life of an evil tyrant.

Bland had the inside track, as he had been instrumental in Kang's escape to Japan by way of Shanghai and Hong Kong and had interviewed Kang extensively for articles that were adapted by all the major Western newspapers.

With the exception of Sir Robert Hart, who admired her greatly, Westerners in Peking or Shanghai really knew nothing about Tzu Hsi, or about the history of the Ching Dynasty, the inner workings of the Manchu court, or the hidden life of the Forbidden City. So for them as well as for newspaper readers far away this was their first "authoritative" glimpse of Oriental depravity at the highest level.

Kang was a self-styled reformer who would be unjustly celebrated in the West as the great hero of China's reform movement. In truth, there was little about him that was heroic, and his "authority" was entirely false, as more perceptive British diplomats in Shanghai had already discovered and confidentially advised their Foreign Office.

In Peking, however, Morrison, Sir Claude MacDonald, and the missionary community had all accepted Kang's story, believing that he knew the young emperor and the old dowager empress personally and was speaking from direct knowledge of their actions. Kang was merely a self-promoter and troublemaker who actually had been only on the periphery of the reform movement, plagiarizing the ideas of others and publishing them as his own. When Kang fled into exile, Bland and other journalists were taken in, calling him "the sage of modern China," giving worldwide credibility to his malicious anti-Manchu propaganda. Zealous but ill-informed missionary activists like Richard, Reid, and Alicia Little took up Kang's cause and repeated his slander as if it were gospel. At the height of the missionary era Kang's Western audience wanted so earnestly to see China transformed into a Christian utopia that they were susceptible to the blandishments of this bogus messiah. Riding a wave of credibility, Kang toured the world, milking donations as the self-appointed leader of the anti-Manchu movement, and eventually was beatified by American scholars as the man who would have brought China American-style democracy rather than a communist state.

From safety in exile Kang launched a poisonous campaign against the empress dowager, both in newspapers and in letters to all the diplomats in Peking. In them he insisted that the dowager was an evil hag who was keeping the young emperor prisoner, doping him on drugs and alcohol while plotting to depose him. After insisting that she had embezzled the imperial treasury, Kang turned to sexual slander, claiming that the dowager's chief palace eunuch really was not a eunuch at all but one of Tzu

Hsi's endless lovers and fellow conspirators. Kang called the dowager "the False Empress," a "depraved palace concubine," and repeatedly called her a murderess. Warming to his subject, he invented scandalous details of her life: "The False Empress has an illegitimate son called Chin-ming and she must mean to set him on the throne. . . . How can your honorable country consent to associate with a wanton false violent and poisonous person of this kind, a thief who deposes the Sovereign and usurps his Throne?"

Kang's vilification of Tzu Hsi might have faded away if the Manchu regime had not collapsed before his ink was dry. Some old China hands did see through his bombast. The missionary-educator Dr. W.A.P. Martin commented sourly to friends, "Kang Yu-wei has shown the cloven foot." But most of Kang's audience was left in no position to check his assertions. During the Boxer debacle in 1900, which signaled the beginning of the dynasty's death throes, Kang's allegations fueled a fresh attack on Tzu Hsi by Morrison and Bland, in close collaboration with Edmund Backhouse, the most ingenious of literary swindlers.

On his arrival in China in 1899, Backhouse, who soon had a fluent command of Chinese and Manchu, applied to join the Customs Service as an interpreter. After being turned down by Sir Robert Hart, he began translating Chinese news articles and official documents that Morrison used to compose dispatches to the *Times*.

Backhouse gradually became Morrison's unofficial editor and adviser, as a servant takes over his master. Growing weary of his post, Morrison became increasingly dependent upon Backhouse to report and write dispatches, many of them entirely fabricated, that appeared in the *Times* credited to Morrison.

Following Tzu Hsi's death in 1908 after reigning nearly fifty years, Backhouse announced extraordinary discoveries he said he had made among court archives and other manuscripts that fell into his hands after the Boxer Uprising, discoveries that confirmed Kang's image of Tzu Hsi as a wicked degenerate and brought to light extraordinary details of her past life: how she had disposed of rivals with poisoned cakes and how she had kept false eunuchs in the palace for her sexual amusement.

The moment was right for a complete review of her life by a Western authority, something scholarly, balanced, full of well-informed inside information on the secret machinations of the Manchu court. In 1910 Bland collaborated with Backhouse to produce what appeared to be just that: *China under the Empress Dowager*, a monumental history of Tzu Hsi's reign. This was followed in 1914 by *Annals and Memoirs of the Court in Peking*, which gave Westerners even more shocking details, from Manchu archives that only Backhouse had seen.

Their portrait of Tzu Hsi was of a ruthless, single-minded tyrant, an iron-willed, oversexed Manchu concubine who usurped power in 1861 to rule China with perversion, corruption, and intrigue for half a century, until her misrule caused the collapse of an empire that had endured more than two thousand years. Here for all to see was "that odious woman," as Morrison called her, "that awful old harridan," the wicked witch of the East, a reptilian dragon lady who had arranged the poisoning, strangling, beheading, or forced suicide of anyone who had ever challenged her autocratic control.

The greatest damage done by Backhouse was to make his portrayal of Tzu Hsi slyly pornographic, an approach that reveals both his cunning and his grasp of human nature. As a creature of depravity she was likened to Messalina, the degenerate wife of the Roman emperor Claudius, and was blamed for so corrupting the Manchu court as to render it incapable of resisting the aggression of the Foreign Powers in the closing decades of the nineteenth century.

Following these sensational disclosures, Backhouse became one of a handful of leading China authorities, and his collection of rare and ancient Chinese manuscripts formed a cornerstone of Oxford's Bodleian Library. His seeming authority was enhanced when, on the death of his father, Backhouse inherited the minor title of baronet, becoming Sir Edmund.

Both books were acclaimed by diplomats, scholars, and journalists alike for coming "as near as any book could to explaining the enigmatic character of the Dowager Empress Tzu Hsi." The *New York Times* said: "That the work is authoritative is indicated by the fact that it was compiled from the state papers and from the private diary of the Controller of the Empress's household, while even a cursory glance through its 525 pages shows its excellence of tone. . . . Probably no such collection of Chinese documents has ever before been given to the world, or one that better reflects the realities of Chinese official life." The *Spectator* agreed: "Rarely is a book written round state papers which is at once so sound in learning, so informing, and so fascinating to read as this." In its first eighteen months, the first book went through eight printings and was translated into several languages including Chinese, which made it a sourcebook for Chinese republican and communist scholars and propagandists as well.

Given these many endorsements, scholars and other authors over the decades have found it simpler to draw upon Backhouse and to overlook the evidence of contrary sources, among them firsthand letters and diaries of diplomats, military men, missionaries, business agents—and their wives—who lived in China and had infinitely better access to the empress dowager and her court than Backhouse ever did. After the Boxer Uprising in 1900 a number of books and magazine articles appeared, including narratives by Lady MacDonald; Sarah Conger; Lady Susan Townley, wife of the British first secretary; and American artist Katherine Carl, all of whom had actually met the dowager on more than one occasion. They are generally uncritical of Tzu Hsi and gave a remarkably sympathetic portrayal. The verdict of male reviewers has been that these appraisals were "uninformed" and trivial. However, in reexamining today these personal recollections of the dowager, we see that they contain many useful and refreshing insights into her character and events of the palace that *are* substantiated by official Western government documents and the private papers of diplomats and professionals who were in Peking at the time. One memoir denounced as a fraud again and again over the years— Derling's account of three years as one of Tzu Hsi's ladies-in-waiting— turns out not to be a fraud at all and contains many quotations that in substance are demonstrably accurate. The empress these books and articles portray was not a monster but an attractive woman full of recognizable quirks, and anxious to protect her status in an empire where women were treated like spittoons. These first-hand sources and many others dating back to the 1850s were simply ignored when it became fashionable and politically expedient in the atmosphere of the twentieth century to promote Tzu Hsi's evil caricature as a relic of the imperial past.

The biggest problem facing Western historians, biographers, and journalists who came on the scene after the death of Tzu Hsi has been to explain how she survived politically for nearly half a century. In keeping with Backhouse and Bland, they assumed a dark side to her character along the lines of the archetypal Western empresses, Catherine de' Medici and Catherine the Great. Many of these writers could rightfully claim formidable credentials as sinologists or Orientalists, diplomats or missionaries, military men or journalists. However, if pressed to document their statements about Tzu Hsi, it is now clear that not a single one could do so. When they cite any source at all for support, they cite each other, and collectively they all cite Edmund Backhouse. He, in turn, cites Chinese and Manchu sources that turn out to be counterfeit, inventions and forgeries he contrived with Chinese cronies.

Backhouse was able to draw brilliantly upon an ancient Chinese literary tradition of vilifying fallen emperors, empresses, and concubines with "secret" court histories that were largely or entirely fiction and allegory. Using this model, his bloodthirsty caricature of Tzu Hsi was a clever blend of Western fantasy and Chinese pornography going back many centuries to the Tang Dynasty. The best example is the defamation of the Tang empress Wu, who over a thousand years was systematically maligned by writers and dramatists in a manner strikingly similar to that used on Tzu Hsi.

In 1974, somewhat to Oxford's embarrassment and to the private dismay of China scholars everywhere, Backhouse was revealed to be a counterfeiter, a con man, and a complete fraud when Hugh Trevor-Roper published *Hermit of Peking: The Hidden Life of Sir Edmund Backhouse*.

Professor Trevor-Roper disclosed that Backhouse and his confederates had supported themselves in Peking by forging and selling Chinese literary "masterpieces," including the court papers and court diaries on which were based much of what he wrote about Tzu Hsi.

Although Trevor-Roper did not examine the consequences of the fraud, it followed that the two books Backhouse wrote in collaboration with J.O.P. Bland had to be intricate historical fabrications, since they were based on counterfeit material. However, the story Backhouse told about the dowager empress was so titillating, so full of scandal, sex, and evil, and was presented in such elegant and convincing detail that most biographers chose to overlook any doubts about authenticity. The image of Tzu Hsi had become so graven in stone that even Professor Trevor-Roper's book continued to refer to her in the same dark terms that Backhouse had coined. The con man had been exposed, but his counterfeit material was still bedrock scholarship.

Edmund Backhouse was the brilliantly flawed product of an unhappy childhood. Although his younger brothers became soldiers and admirals, Edmund was a bad seed, the despair of his mother and father. He particularly loathed his mother, Florence, conceiving a great pouch of venom he later vented on the dowager empress. At Oxford he squandered his inheritance trying to join Oscar Wilde's circle of homosexuals, then fled England and bankruptcy to appear in Peking one day early in 1899.

No one in China knew anything about him, least of all the great journalist Morrison. The last thing anyone suspected was that Backhouse was an extraordinarily gifted pornographer in the tradition of "Baron Corvo," who supported himself by writing "letters" describing his homosexual encounters, which were discreetly circulated and subsequently privately published by Edmund's cousin for the titillation of those of similar interests. Edmund had cut his teeth on such pornography as a child and adolescent and remained an energetic proponent of the art form all his life, which helps to explain the heavy underlying theme of sexual perversion that runs obsessively through his biographies of Tzu Hsi.

In April 1943 the seventy-year-old Backhouse entered the French St. Michael's Hospital in Peking, where he spent the last months of his life writing two additional manuscripts: "The Dead Past," his memoir of childhood, and "Decadence Mandchoue," an intimate recollection of his life in China.

The most curious sections of "Decadence Mandchoue" were passages describing what purported to be Edmund's long, raunchy love affair with Empress Dowager Tzu Hsi—literally, a love affair between biographer and subject. According to him, the affair began in 1902, when he was twenty-nine years old and Tzu Hsi had just turned sixty-seven. The liaison, he insisted, continued until her death six years later. He was still able to recall that he had had "many hundred (perhaps thousand) [*sic*] love affairs" with men and perhaps two hundred encounters with the dowager empress.

"Was I sexually adequate for her Majesty's overflowing carnality?" wrote Backhouse. "ALAS! I doubted it and wondered if I should develop the necessary timely orgasm to meet her unsated lust which would assuredly not have failed me, had another type of love been in question." He described one evening when he accompanied the dowager—who was, naturally, in disguise—to a homosexual brothel, where she commanded Edmund and the other patrons to "disport" themselves for her amusement.

Backhouse said his first orgy with Tzu Hsi took place at the Summer Palace. When he arrived he was instructed by Grand Eunuch Li Lien-ying about the dowager's sexual characteristics. Backhouse said Li confided that the dowager had an abnormally large clitoris, which she was in the habit of rubbing on the anus of her partner. "Li . . . anointed my secret parts . . . with the undiluted sandal-wood scent, he put a light cloak which reached as far as the thighs round me and summoned me to the Presence. Her Majesty's bedchamber was blazing with a score of lights; the spacious apartment was lined with a series of mirrors which reminded me of . . . Versailles. They all reflected my homely features red with passion. . . . Li accompanied me to the phoenix couch, and the Empress exclaimed: 'My bed is cold . . . now exhibit to me your genitals for I know I shall love them.' "

Backhouse said he was then required to perform oral sex on the elderly dowager, after which she got curious about him. Inserting her fingers into his anus she remarked, " 'Large anus: I'll warrant that it has seen service.' " To which Sir Edmund replied, " 'Yes, Your Majesty. . . . Innumerable as the hairs of the head.' " And so on page after page. These and many other similar passages reveal the obsessions of the man who took advantage of the gullibility of Morrison, Bland, scholars, and public the world over to bring off one of the greatest and most durable hoaxes ever perpetrated.

Even now, his reptilian image of the empress dowager is difficult to shake because it provides a satisfying justification for Western actions in China during the nineteenth and early twentieth centuries, actions that otherwise look foolish or outrageous.

For example, a reexamination of the celebrated Boxer siege of Peking's foreign legations in 1900—long blamed on the evil folly of Tzu Hsi—reveals that it was actually provoked by the bullying and hysterical behavior of Westerners, who shot hundreds of Chinese civilians, imperial soldiers, and mandarins *before* the siege began and brought the consequences down upon their own heads. Afterward Morrison produced a falsified historical record of the siege for the *Times* that was republished in various forms all over the world—while keeping a secret version in his private diary with the most embarrassing details, including the Western pillaging and burning of the great Hanlin Library, an atrocity that has always been blamed on the Chinese. History, once again, was the version of the victor.

Morrison's duplicity is deeply disturbing, but the Backhouse hoax is staggering. For most of this century, he is cited as the principal source for nearly all material written about the last years of imperial China, including not only popular biography but such basic scholarly works as Arthur Hummel's *Eminent Chinese of the Ching Period*, a biographical dictionary of Manchu China upon which all students and scholars depend. Backhouse renders many historical works suspect not only because he is a major source but because he caused much scholarly study to be undertaken during this century based upon assumptions that are now clearly false. All biographies and histories drawing upon the Backhouse fraud give a skewed picture of imperial China in the half-century preceding its downfall, and of much that followed.

A few younger scholars have begun making discoveries that explode prevailing myths about this period of Chinese history and about Tzu Hsi. But they are challenging an establishment of senior academicians whose works are thereby brought into question. Recent books on China make an obligatory reference to Backhouse as a suspect source but continue to adhere to his false portrayal of Tzu Hsi and her role in China's history.

Showing how the Backhouse hoax was created, and how it came to be accepted as the truth, requires going back to the beginning of Tzu Hsi's story, long before the scene of the crime, to reconstruct the truth piece-by-piece. This means reexamining the oldest clichés of the clash between China and the West, and about its conspiracies, murders, wars, and personalities. While this may seem to lead far afield, and many characters may seem minor, they are all part of the tapestry. Only by methodical reassembly of facts can we recognize history's real causes and effects. Readers will be rewarded by a new understanding of why the Chinese empire collapsed. Discovering the mischievous and paranoid forces at work backstage reveals Tzu Hsi's life in ways that mere biographical details cannot. So this is not a traditional biography, but an inquest into the hoodwinking of history. We are not in search of Tzu Hsi alone, but in search of a lost era for which she became a symbol. Call it an anti-biography. A full reevaluation must await fundamental research into the muddled archives in the People's Republic, which could take decades, or the release of Chinese documents seized by Japan in 1900.

Getting at the truth about Tzu Hsi is like removing overlays from a painting to restore the original; the truth emerges little by little. Sir Robert Hart was one of those rare Westerners in China who spoke the language, understood how things worked, and was patient and sympathetic enough to befriend senior officials rather than bully his way. Hart was born the same year as Tzu Hsi and during his half-century in China kept a meticulous diary of seventy-seven volumes, a unique and compassionate record of events and personalities, most of which remains unpublished. Hart's diaries and the unpublished diaries of Morrison and Backhouse, together with long-neglected letters and the personal papers of many others, help to scrape away the false overpainting, to reveal what follows.

CHAPTER ONE

Lady Yehenara

We do not even know her name. She was too private for that, and the world she lived in was uniquely designed to hide her behind multiple layers of court ritual and etiquette. Nobody ever spoke the name of the Son of Heaven or his wives, because they were demigods. She was born on November 29, 1835, the same year as Robert Hart, somewhere in China, but where exactly we do not know. Nor are we sure of her father's name or occupation, the name of her mother, or even the girl's milk-name, the name she was called as a nursing infant. She was an obscure daughter of an obscure Manchu officer and might have lived out her life in obscurity except that she was chosen to be one of the emperor's lesser concubines and had the good fortune to bear him his only surviving son. Thanks to Hart we know that she had three younger sisters and one brother who survived to adulthood. It is also a matter of record that she was fond of pretty clothes, Pekingese dogs, and chrysanthemums.

She stood about five feet tall, was strikingly pretty, slim and well proportioned, with delicate hands, arched eyebrows, brilliant black eyes, a high nose, full well-shaped lips set firmly above a strong chin, and a showstopping smile that men and women remarked upon even when she was in her seventies. Her jet black hair was brushed back from a broad forehead, and the only peculiarity in her appearance as a girl was a dot of red paint in the middle of her lower lip, a cosmetic touch common to all Manchu women. During her eight years as a concubine, her face was made up in a theatrical style, like a player in Peking opera. As a widow for the last forty-seven years of her life, she wore no cosmetics at all. Hart remarked, as did others who spoke Chinese, of her "sweet feminine voice," though it grated on the ears of foreigners who did not speak

Mandarin, a dialect that sounds guttural to the uninitiated, even in poetry or song. In old age, a minor stroke drew down her mouth on the left side, making her seem bitter or sullen when she was not.

She had only one husband and one son, but three thousand eunuchs waited on her. Upon her husband's death she reigned over China for nearly half a century—longer than any other woman ruler including Empress Wu more than a thousand years earlier and longer than all but a handful of male rulers through China's long history. There were only three reigning empresses over those thousands of years, and she was the last.

In 1851, when at age sixteen she was chosen to be an imperial concubine, she was referred to only as Lady Yehenara, from the name of her Manchu clan, the Yehe tribe of the Nara clan. Later, when she became an empress dowager and coregent of the empire, she was known by the title Tzu Hsi (which Westerners usually pronounced Susie), meaning Empress of the West, because she lived in pavilions on the west side of the Forbidden City.

The actual details of Yehenara's life to age twenty-one are so sparse that biographers and journalists found it necessary to invent them. After age twenty-one there are a few facts here and there, but the gaps continued to be filled with fiction. Scores of books, many by serious scholars, are gorged with lurid details, including seemingly authoritative tattle about her sex life, her plotting, and her murders. Peking was the political center of an ancient empire in which ambitious men engaged in a continual struggle for leverage and position, so she lived in a world of conspiracy and poisonings and forced suicides, but a careful reexamination of the evidence shows that she did not commit any of them.

Before we can make sense out of her muddled story, it helps to see some comic examples of how it came to be muddled in the first place:

By some writers we are assured that Yehenara was purchased in Canton as a sex slave for the emperor. Others portray her childhood as an Oriental version of the Little Match Girl: she used to sing in public, they say, while her sister passed the hat, in order to buy enough rice for her family, because her father spent all his money on opium and Chinese prostitutes. Others claim that her grandfather was a Russian "Foreign Devil." Such things happened often enough in feudal China, but there is no evidence to support any of these stories.

Among Western biographers it was Sir Edmund Backhouse who concocted most of the basic "facts" about Yehenara's childhood, along with most of the slander. "Her father Hui Cheng," he wrote, "held hereditary rank as Captain in one of the Eight Banner Corps. Considering the advantages of his birth, he was generally accounted unsuccessful by his contemporaries: at the time of his death he had held no higher post than that of an Intendant of Circuit. . . . in the province of Anhui, he died when his daughter was but three years of age."

There is no evidence whatever that this is true; however, new details were added as other biographers enlarged unabashedly upon the Backhouse legacy. Her father became a member of the Bordered Blue Banner. The family was not rich; "in China, that probably means her father was honest." Her father "was cashiered for deserting his post before the onslaught of the Taiping rebellion" when Yehenara was eighteen years old and already a concubine in the palace.

As for Yehenara's mother, about whom absolutely nothing is known, Backhouse states that she was "a lady of great ability and good sense, distinguished even amongst the members of a clan always noted for the intelligence of its womenkind." Another biographer assures us that Yehenara's mother was a great beauty, well preserved in middle age.

While there is no certainty even about the location of Yehenara's birth, no one paints a more poignant scene of her nativity than biographer Harry Hussey, who devoted a third of his book to this least known period of Tzu Hsi's life. Hussey depicted the marriage between Yehenara's parents as less than happy, due to the fact that her Manchu father was an opium sot who ran after small-footed Chinese prostitutes and had invariably bad luck at gambling tables. When he had exhausted the family's limited resources on the eve of Yehenara's birth, her mother convinced the kindly Mr. Wong, their Chinese landlord, to allow them to stay even though they could not pay the rent. The munificent Mr. Wong took such a liking to Yehenara's mother that he became a grandfather figure; Hussey referred to him thereafter as Grandfather Wong. It was Grandfather Wong who was present at the birth of Yehenara, not father Hui Cheng, who was out on the town.

A close friend of Grandfather Wong was Soothsayer Fu, who had a startling vision:

At the Hour of the Tiger, at the very time the little Manchu baby was entering this world, Fu saw a great flash of light. The gods pulled the curtains aside and gave the soothsayer . . . a glimpse into the future . . . he saw . . . the daughter just born . . . now grown into a beautiful woman, mingling with all the emperors and empresses as their equal. . . . The very power of his vision was too much for poor Fu's brain. He . . . fell to the floor [unconscious]. [This vision was confirmed when Soothsayer Fu examined the infant and spied a birthmark on her left breast.] Fu saw in the birthmark . . . the outline of a fox. He knew very well that "the mark of the fox" was the mark either of a good or evil omen. . . . He found an old Manchu prophecy . . . [that]

stated that [Manchu] rule . . . would someday be ended forever by a great woman of the Yehenara clan bearing the mark of the fox.

All biographers agree that Yehenara arrived in Peking somewhere between the ages of three and sixteen and in 1852 entered the Forbidden City as one of young Emperor Hsien Feng's concubines. None is certain how she got to Peking or where she came from, but all are willing to invent scenarios. Some claim Peking was her family home all along, or that she came to Peking only after her father's death, subsisting on the generosity of a wealthy relative named Muyanga. Most assert that she lived on Pewter Lane, the street of the tinsmiths, although "it is not certain which of the houses . . . was the home of the future Empress of China." All of this is sheer conjecture, presented as the truth.

In their 1910 biography Backhouse and Bland denounced certain versions of Yehenara's story as spurious, thereby enhancing their own believability.

The [spurious] story . . . was that when [Yehenara's] mother had been left a widow with a large family . . . they lived in the most abject poverty at the prefectural city of Ningkuo, where her husband had held office and died. Having no funds to pay for her return to Peking, she would have been reduced to beggary had it not been that, by lucky accident, a sum of money intended for another traveller was delivered on board of her boat at a city on the way [by Grand Canal to Peking], and that the traveller, on learning of the mistake and being moved to pity at the sight of the family's destitution, insisted on her keeping the money.

Although they claimed that this Good Samaritan account was counterfeit, it was "substantiated" in 1944 by Maurice Collis, the popular British biographer. Another writer tells how on this trip Yehenara met a pair of Western missionaries. She "did not like their ugly clothes, their harsh voices," he says, "but she did like their frank faces, their clean look, and their tall, slim bodies." He adds the original twist that her father was stationed at Wuhu, and when the Taiping rebels attacked, he fled with gold and silver from the town hall. "Apparently [he] was never brought to trial and many of the curious facts of this case were never proven."

Putting aside how Yehenara arrived in Peking, her biographers turn to how she came to be chosen as an imperial concubine and her preparation for life in the Forbidden City.

According to Backhouse, when the call went out for the selection of the young emperor's wives and concubines, Yehenara was on the list submitted by her clan. (Another writer maintained that she put her own name on the list.) Backhouse claimed that Muyanga, the Yehenara clan leader, had provided his eldest daughter as the emperor's first wife, but she had since died, and this gave Muyanga's clan first preference in nominating other candidates. Here Backhouse had the correct story but the wrong clan; it was the Niuhuru clan, not the Yehenara, that provided the original empress, who died and was replaced by another Niuhuru girl. She eventually became Dowager Empress Tzu An (Empress of the East).

Once nominated, Yehenara had no difficulty passing the preliminary verbal examination but next came a physical that tantalized male biographers. The most sensational account was written by a U.S. Army general, Frank Dorn, a linguist and specialist on China who served in Peking from 1934 to 1938 and was on the staff of General Joseph W. Stilwell during World War II; in retirement, Dorn wrote a book about the Forbidden City, with many details of Yehenara's private life. Dorn assumed that the passionate Yehenara had already lost her virginity and had to find a way to trick the palace examiners. He tells us exactly how Yehenara's physical proceeded.

On the day of her examination, [Yehenara] wore a pair of valuable jade bracelets. Wise beyond her years, she knew that when she lay on the couch in the examination room, the practiced hand of a midwife would discover in a second whether or not she was a virgin. When her turn came at last, she went into a theatrical tantrum and indignantly refused to be pawed over. As she did so, the story goes, she deftly slipped off the costly bracelets, and unseen by the eunuchs, dropped them into the eagerly waiting hand of the midwife. For an instant the two women's eyes met and locked in a glitter of mutual understanding. Finally, the elder nodded her head; and [Yehenara] was able to stand in line with the other selected maidens.

Having bribed her way into the imperial household with a couple of jade bangles, Yehenara had to gain the emperor's attention. According to most accounts, Emperor Hsien Feng squandered so much energy in brothels that he paid no attention to his concubines. Yehenara had to find some way to attract him. In one version the emperor encountered her in a garden, in another at a tea party. One biographer insists that she used a special perfume: "Manchu sources state without the slightest hesitation that [Yehenara] used more perfume than other women because she had the 'odor of the fox.' This apparently . . . marked her [as] a true member of the [Yehenara] clan." The writer adds coyly, "We have no accurate information on just how strongly the Empress smelled of a fox."

In a play about her life a British author outdoes the American general as a voyeur. Languishing in her bedchamber, Yehenara learns from eunuch Li Lien-ying (always degenerate and always poisoning people) that the emperor spends his time with prostitutes specializing in sodomy. Yehenara bribes the eunuch to bring the emperor by her pavilion. So that the eunuch understands her intentions, Yehenara reveals her plan explicitly. "Chinese girls [she says] . . . are not bothered with official dress. Let me show you what I mean." She kicks off her slippers and leans back, one leg to the ground, one leg on the bench, her gown loosened negligently. Li is quite startled but shows he agrees, and takes leave hurriedly. She calls after him in high spirits, "And I bet you could never tear yourself away from me if you were—if you were—not what you are!"

When the eunuch brings the emperor by in a sedan chair, Yehenara is lying on a couch playing a mandolin. "She alters her position so that anyone looking over the gate will have a good view of what she is taking care to show. She seems wholly absorbed in her playing. . . . Emperor Hsien Feng's voice is heard saying 'Halt.' " The emperor slips through a side door to confront her face to face. As she falls to her knees before the Son of Heaven, he stops her, saying, "You'll tire your legs by kneeling too much! And we need them for other purposes!" They spend the night making love in indescribable ways. From that moment, the emperor is the sexual prisoner of his concubine.

One of the best-known writers about China, Pearl Buck, portrays the first encounter somewhat differently, using as her dramatic device a heavy dose of Chinese aphrodisiac. (In Pearl Buck's case, the book is clearly identified as fiction.) After Yehenara is brought to the imperial bedchamber, she stirs the emperor's lust to a frenzy.

She knew now that this man was a weak and fitful being, possessed by a passion he could not satisfy, a lust of mind more frightful than lust of the flesh. . . .

"Bar the doors," the Emperor commanded.

So she barred the doors and when she turned to him again he was staring at her with fearful and unsatisfied desire . . . The ladies who lived in the Palace of Forgotten Concubines had told her . . . that if the Emperor delayed too long in his bedchamber, a powerful herb was mixed in his favorite dish which gave him sudden and unusual strength. Yet so dangerous was this herb that he must not be roused too far, for then exhaustion followed so extreme that it could end in death.

On the third morning, this exhaustion fell. The Emperor sank into half-fainting silence upon his pillow. His lips were blue, his eyes half closed, he could not move, his narrow face set slowly into a greenish pallor, which upon his yellow skin made him seem dead.

The result of this seventy-two-hour marathon, we are told, was that Yehenara became pregnant, and Emperor Hsien Feng became "an imbecile."

The next question to be considered by her biographers was, "But who in fact father[ed] this male baby, who only a few years later became the ruler of the Celestial Empire." Hsien Feng was already half paralyzed from debauchery, they claimed, so Yehenara did not give birth but bought a male baby from a Chinese woman and passed this child off as her own and Hsien Feng's.

Another writer adds that the mother of the infant was strangled by Yehenara's eunuch to insure silence. It did not occur to them that the Manchu were so paranoid about succession to the throne that a substitution would have been all but impossible, and Yehenara's pregnancy would have been monitored as closely as if she were the wife of the Prince of Wales. These anecdotes may seem silly but people believed them.

All these Western portrayals of Yehenara as a wicked manipulator originate with Sir Edmund Backhouse and depend on the assumption that Backhouse was telling the truth: that Yehenara was one of those brilliant, aggressive, and dominating characters who occur more often in literature than in fact, able to bribe her way with cheap bangles into the most inaccessible citadel on earth, there to take over everybody by the use of sex and guile; that she made a pawn of the emperor, suborned everyone else, and resorted spontaneously to murder to remove any obstacles. It is a very entertaining caricature, but it is completely phony.

The discovery that Backhouse was a con man who counterfeited his sources and concocted her legend makes it necessary to reexamine all the details. Every version of the legend that relies on Backhouse becomes equally suspect. So we must start from the beginning to see what Yehenara was really like and how the dramatic events in her life actually came about. Did she shape them, or did they shape her?

Looking back over the violent period in which she lived—a time of civil war, foreign invasion, palace coup and countercoup—it soon becomes apparent that other people committed the murders attributed to her. In some cases the culprits are identifiable, in others there are a number of obvious suspects, but Yehenara is not among them. One unexpected discovery is that Westerners mixed up Yehenara with other women, so some of the sensational allegations about her are the result of mistaken identity.

What was her real identity? She had two of them: one as a young girl in the palace when she was all but completely ignored as an insignificant ingenue from the provinces, the other after she gave birth to the only surviving male heir to the throne, which transformed her into a political factor. That was all yet to come.

As a girl new to the palace she was not a driven, homicidal character seeking victims but a reactive personality, by all indications a withdrawn, solitary, and pensive girl whose nature was to remain private, deeply submerged, and safely hidden, watching things happen and going along with them wherever possible. She was solitary because of a deep sense of melancholy and misfortune. She once explained, "I have had a very hard life ever since I was a young girl. I was not a bit happy when with my parents, as I was not the favorite. My sisters had everything they wanted, while I was, to a great extent, ignored altogether." As the eldest child she felt mistreated, neglected, and unloved and spent a lonely adolescence developing the curtains and masks that hide a clever but unhappy girl. This strong sense of personal tragedy, of being a victim of bad luck, remained with her all her life. Added to it in later years was the grief of a woman who was always left behind by her men.

Her chance to escape from this family misery came with the opportunity to enter the imperial household as a minor wife. She was fourteen when she was nominated as a candidate-concubine, sixteen when she was chosen, and eighteen when she completed the preparation. After this four-year ordeal, like an overfastidious finishing school, she was as subdued and careful as a girl entering the inner sanctum of any royal family in Europe. It was an exasperatingly artificial world of ritual where the only privacy was inside your head. Everyone watched her continually to see if she made a mistake. She had to seem gracious, pleasant, meticulously groomed, practiced in every tiresome detail of etiquette. She was submissive because that was expected of her. Beyond being attractive and obedient, she was a complete nonentity.

In the Forbidden City she came into contact for the first time with China's demigods, the celestial emperor and his Aisin Gioro clan of relentlessly conspiratorial and jealous half-brothers, the royal princes. Contrary to the legend she did not waltz in and vamp the emperor and his brothers. They all shared the traditional Confucian contempt for females, so her contact with them was limited. She was in regular contact only with the dowager empress, where she was only one in a cluster of girls.

Aside from the emperor's immediate family, the court consisted of ambitious political advisers, devious ministers of state, and generals who commanded armies that never saw battle. These were the high mandarins and feudal autocrats whose prejudices, paranoia, ignorance, and folly would dominate her entire life. In the future she would be shaped by them, not the other way around, shaped by powerful forces already at work, by great events and weak personalities, men and women already entangled in rivalries and conspiracies that were old and rancid before Yehenara was born. She was not the mastermind of tragic events but their victim.

Of her husband, Emperor Hsien Feng, the record is disastrous. Everything that happened to Yehenara was a consequence of Hsien Feng's caving in and the collapse of his reign.

On his father's side Emperor Hsien Feng traced his descent directly from the Ching Dynasty's founder, Nurhachi, who had prepared the way for the Manchu takeover from the exhausted Ming Dynasty.

The Ming was one of China's longest dynasties (A.D. 1368–1644), lasting sixteen rulers, including one who ruled twice, but later Ming emperors were incompetent, wasting their energies on pleasure, carried along by a brilliant administrative apparatus. By the end of the sixteenth century, the dynasty had lapsed into a coma, waiting to be pushed aside. The treasury was empty. Taxes became impossible, and traditional signs of misrule were everywhere—floods, droughts, and famines that showed the displeasure of heaven. Militarily the Ming were under pressure from the Mongols, the Japanese, and the Russians. Unable to face these challenges, the last four Ming emperors left affairs of state to favored eunuchs.

In desperation, the Chinese gentry began looking for an alternative to their Ming rulers. Traditionally, the gentry determined when a dynasty had forfeited the mandate of heaven, by transferring their loyalty to a new leader.

Salvation arrived in the form of the Jurched, a nomadic people from the cold high valleys and windswept grasslands northwest of Korea. Coming in contact with Ming frontier outposts, the Jurched settled down and adopted all but a few Chinese customs and institutions. They refused to bind the feet of their women, and Jurched men were distinguished by shaved foreheads, with a heavy braid of black hair like a rope down their backs.

Centuries passed while the Jurched clans fought among themselves, the main rivals being the Aisin Gioro and the Yehenara. Ming officials played them against each other, but this backfired. A Ming military commander encouraged a chief of the Aisin Gioro to attack his rivals, then betrayed him. The clan leader was tortured and burned to death. His murder started a bloodbath, ending in 1586 with the victory of twenty-four-year-old Nurhachi, the murdered chief's grandson. Nurhachi forced his rivals into line by military victories and political marriages. He cornered the market on furs, ginseng, and pearls, and cultivated the Ming emperors. In appreciation they allowed him to form a subordinate Jurched nation with himself as emperor. Nurhachi's other historic achievement was to organize a 7,500-man army in battlefield formations of 300 men each, identified by colored banners. In the manner of a military dictatorship, he used these Bannermen to administer his empire and to spy on his subjects. By the time Nurhachi was succeeded by his son, Abahai, the Jurched were pushing at the Great Wall, threatening to invade China itself.

Abahai was a master of indirection. He raised money for the assault on China by first conquering Korea. He used Korea's treasury to buy an alliance with the Mongol khans. They allowed Abahai's Banners to cross their territory to outflank the Ming at a weak point in the Great Wall. Breaking through, they advanced on Peking. A Ming general who rushed to the capital to defend it found that spies had already spread rumors that he was in league with Abahai. The Ming emperor, not a particularly bright fellow, arrested his own general, and Abahai's Bannermen entered Peking unchallenged and looted to their hearts' content. Before the Ming armies could rally, Abahai packed up his booty and went home beyond the Great Wall. He was not yet ready to confront the whole Chinese nation. Meanwhile he welcomed into his service Chinese scholars and officers who wished to defect, teaming them up with Mongol advisers, under the loose supervision of Manchu princes. This successful mingling of the three ethnic groups made the Jurched government seem less alien and more acceptable to the Chinese gentry. Abahai clearly had heaven on his side, and, as if to confirm this, in 1636 he declared the founding of the Ching (Pure) Dynasty, with himself as emperor, and the Jurched people were given a new name, with magical connotations of potency: *Manchu.*

Abahai did not live to see his plans of conquest fulfilled, but the stage was set. His heir, the child emperor Shun Chih, was only five years old, so two princes served as joint regents: Abahai's brother Dorgon and his cousin Jirgalang, both formidable characters. It was Dorgon who had the pleasure of collecting the family blood debt from the Ming.

Although schoolchildren the world over are told that 1644 is the year the Manchu conquered China, it was not conquest but treachery and came as something of a surprise. All the fighting was done for them by a Chinese bandit named Li. Li's stronghold at Shansi was within striking distance of Peking. As the Manchu Banners poised along the Great Wall, Bandit Li seized his chance and captured Peking for himself. It was April 1644.

The feckless Ming emperor, who earlier had arrested his own general, climbed to the pavilion on top of Prospect Hill behind the Forbidden City while bandits galloped through the dusty streets below, tied a yellow silk bowstring around one of the red lacquered beams, and hanged himself. So ended the Ming Dynasty.

Too late to save his emperor, a Ming general named Wu hurried in from the Great Wall to find Peking in chaos. To make matters worse, Wu's favorite concubine had been kidnapped by Bandit Li, who at that very moment was slaking his lust. The enraged general hurried back to the Great Wall, where he offered Prince Regent Dorgon and the Manchu Bannermen a deal: he would let them through the Great Wall as his allies, if they would help him liberate Peking, defeat Bandit Li, and recover his concubine. Dorgon agreed, and Bannermen poured through the Great Wall to confront the bandit army on the plains below.

In this freakish fashion, the Manchu found themselves in control of China without the need for conquest. Tactfully Dorgon maintained that the Manchu had not "invaded" Peking but had simply liberated it from bandits. However, they had no intention of leaving. In October 1644 the Manchu court was moved from Mukden to Peking, and the eight-year-old Ching Dynasty emperor, Shun Chih, ascended the dragon throne.

Once there, the Manchu had to secure their grip against a number of Chinese challengers—and did so with a reign of terror that depopulated large parts of the empire. Good and bad emperors came and went. Once the Manchu tyranny over China was established, the same rot set in that had corrupted the Ming Dynasty. By the start of the nineteenth century the Manchu emperors and their armies were weak and flaccid, and real power had slipped into the hands of bickering princes.

Yehenara's emperor, Hsien Feng, the seventh Manchu to rule China, was born in 1831 to Emperor Tao Kuang and an imperial concubine from the Niuhuru clan. Hsien Feng's mother died when he was nine years old, so he was put in the care of a concubine who had given birth to another male heir, later known as Prince Kung, who would play a major role in Yehenara's life. Prince Kung was the sixth son, two years younger than Hsien Feng. As children the two boys were very close; they practiced the martial arts together and competed in riding, archery, and lances.

Not all the royal brothers got along so well. The Manchu throne did not go automatically to the eldest son, so there was often a struggle over succession, which is why the princes were always bickering. The choice of heir this time had narrowed to Prince Kung, who was too fun-loving; Prince Tun, the fifth son, who was too angry and aggressive; and Hsien Feng, who was a complex mixture.

As a boy Hsien Feng was guided by his elderly tutor who had a shrewd grasp of human nature. According to tradition, it was this tutor who helped him rise above his brothers in his father's esteem. One spring, during a hunting trip in the desert at Jehol when Hsien Feng was fifteen years old, his tutor instructed him not to kill any game. If his father asked why, the boy was to say he had no heart to end life in the springtime when all creatures were meant to thrive. This explanation, when it was offered, so moved the emperor that he decided on the spot to make this son his successor. This angered and embittered Prince Tun, a proud and ambitious young man with a nasty temper.

To pacify Prince Tun who felt cheated of his birthright, the emperor gave him vast estates. In time Prince Tun became the leader of the most uncompromising antiforeign group at court, the Ironhat faction (after the helmets worn by leading Manchu nobles). His feud over the throne he passed down to his sons. Much of Yehenara's reign was spent warding off their plots. They were responsible for her worst crises. When the Boxer Uprising brought catastrophe in 1900 she found herself their hostage for a year in the wastes of Shensi. Their paranoia toward foreigners and their incompetence in carrying out their schemes was a major cause of the collapse of the dynasty.

Hsien Feng was nineteen when Emperor Tao Kuang died. Just before his father's death, the crown prince was married to a girl from the Niuhuru clan. It was customary for female cousins or sisters of the new empress to accompany her into her husband's household as secondary wives, wives-in-training, or handmaidens. Hsien Feng's first bride, Lady Niuhuru, had an eleven-year-old sister who was also pledged to him as soon as she reached puberty. If Lady Niuhuru had survived, she would have become the empress of China when Hsien Feng ascended the throne. But only a few months after the wedding she died of an unrecorded ailment, without bearing any children.

The court immediately became anxious. If anything happened to the new emperor, the absence of an heir could bring about a bloody game of musical chairs, as rival factions competed over the succession. But a new marriage could not be arranged immediately. Traditionally, a strict mourning period of three years followed the passing of an emperor; no new wife or concubines could be introduced to Hsien Feng's bed while he grieved for his father. These rules were so strict that any senior official who had a child born more than nine months after the death of an emperor would be dismissed from his post instantly. For the emperor himself to father a child during mourning would imply such a lack of filial piety that it would raise serious questions about his fitness to rule. Thanks to these restraints, Emperor Hsien Feng could not engage in sex until February 1853. But by then, a new harem would be waiting.

Competition for a place in the imperial harem was intense because life in the Forbidden City was much better than outside its gates. Nowhere were women treated with greater contempt than in a Confucian state. Chinese ideographs that include the character for "woman" mean: evil, slave, anger, jealousy, avarice, hatred, suspicion, obstruction, demon, witch, bewitching, fornication, and seduction. Confucius warned gentlemen against being "too familiar with the lower orders or with women." As the poet Fu Xuan wrote in the third century:

> *How sad it is to be a woman!*
> *Nothing on earth is held so cheap.*
> *Boys stand leaning at the door*
> *Like gods fallen out of heaven.*

Marriage in China was less of a union between man and woman than a contract of indentured servitude between a girl and her mother-in-law. A wedding was arranged by parents in an effort to advance themselves socially, politically, or financially. In traditional Chinese society a girl married into her husband's family and gave up all contact with her own parents. A bride was subservient to everyone in the new household but especially to her husband's mother, for whom she toiled without rest. Wife and mother-in-law were jealous rivals for the affection of the husband/son. Publicly a husband and wife were indifferent toward each other, never openly acknowledging the existence of the other. In private the wife would have to struggle to win her husband's respect, and only through her grown sons did she have any real hope of security. No wonder she then exhibited little affection toward her son's bride, and the cycle repeated itself.

A concubine was a serious and usually permanent member of a household. She was brought in to bear a son, after the first wife had failed, then remained as an assistant wife, with all the responsibilities and few of the privileges. Once the man lost interest, she was just another servant. In most cases she was purchased from her parents, so in fact she was a slave, though she could not be discarded without arriving at a settlement with her family.

On the other hand being chosen an imperial concubine was totally different; instead of being merely a love slave, she became a permanent member of the emperor's family enjoying both a luxurious life and great status. There was nothing demeaning about it; becoming an imperial concubine was an honor almost as great as being chosen empress and was coveted by the highest nobility. A girl who entered the Forbidden City as a concubine could end up empress by ordinary attrition. Life expectancy was short, for natural and unnatural reasons. So as fates go, to become an imperial concubine was infinitely preferable to being an ordinary Chinese wife.

By custom, the job of selecting the emperor's wives, concubines, and handmaidens fell to the empress dowager, in this instance Hsien Feng's stepmother. Drawing from a large pool of Manchu and Mongol debutantes, she went about choosing those who, in her opinion, would provide the best receptacles for the imperial seed. Manchu of all ranks, the emperor included, were forbidden to marry Chinese, so the selection of a new empress and concubines strictly excluded footbound Han Chinese girls. Imperial alliances were forged only among Manchu clans, between Manchu and their Mongol allies, and sometimes between Manchu and Muslim Chinese from the western provinces. All three—Manchu, Mongols, and Muslims—considered themselves Tartars, distinct from Han Chinese.

Contrary to Western fantasy, the dowager's selection was not based primarily on sexual attributes. Above all, the girls had to be levelheaded, amusing companions for the dowager herself, and only then appealing to the emperor. A girl need not be beautiful, but she should be pleasant, wholesome, well brought up, emotionally stable, small, plump, shapely, and—to nourish the emperor's maleness, or *yang*—she should be just reaching maturity, bursting with femaleness, or *yin*. Those with disheveled hair, long necks, protruding Adam's apples, irregular teeth, or a low, manly voice were eliminated automatically, because they were believed to drain a man's *yang* rather than strengthen it.

Imperial concubines were arranged in a hierarchy, and the ablest or most popular were given special recognition. They competed intensely for the favor of the emperor, or lacking that for the favor of the empress dowager. Whoever was the current favorite let it be known in a thousand ways, as her status was both obvious and implicit. If the emperor impregnated her, the future was secure. (If she failed, making beds in the Great Within was a much better life than she could find in the Great Without.) An imperial concubine's children enjoyed the same rank and rights as the children of the empress. And when an empress died, a favorite concubine could be the new empress. If she gave birth to a male heir, a concubine could become a full wife even if the empress was still alive. Great honors and privileges would be hers; she would be secure as no other woman in China, and the future would offer hope and promise. All she needed was a measure of beauty, courage, talent, ingenuity, persistence, and luck.

The Forbidden City—the Great Within—was a strange and difficult world, particularly for the women who lived there. Although as many as six thousand people sometimes occupied its precincts, after sunset only one of them was a mature male. During the day, outsiders entered on official business, but the only males allowed to remain inside its walls overnight were the reigning emperor and his unmarried sons under the age of fifteen. All the rest were "semi-men," the three thousand imperial eunuchs. The chief reason was to avoid any possibility of cuckoldry.

The Forbidden City was also the retirement home of all the widows and concubines of previous emperors. Twelve hundred years earlier, during the Tang Dynasty, the Forbidden City had not existed; in those days, with the capital at Sian, the concubines of dead emperors ended their lives in the company of nuns at Buddhist convents. But with the establishment of Peking as the capital and the gradual enlargement of the Forbidden City, these leftover women were consigned to small pavilions in the northeast quadrant to while away their lives in the Hall of Forgotten Favorites. Some were as young as fifteen when their emperor died, so time was their greatest burden. They lived in cubicles facing courtyards with twisted pine trees. In winter they made silk flowers for the branches, a pastime which speaks for their life as a whole.

The process of choosing a concubine for Hsien Feng had been set into motion years before his father's death. Word went out to Manchu families in all the provinces to nominate maidens. Months passed while the nominees were screened. In 1851, while the first year of official mourning for Tao Kuang was under way, the candidates were assembled in Peking. Those judged the most eligible, a short list of twenty or thirty, were taken to the Forbidden City for presentation to Hsien Feng's stepmother. Before meeting her, ladies-in-waiting, chief eunuchs, and court physicians administered examinations covering everything from social grace and conversational skill to physical inspections. Although Dorn and other biographers like to suggest otherwise, after more than two years of intense processing it is extremely unlikely that a girl who was not a virgin would have reached this stage. Only those who impressed the empress dowager's retainers were taken in for tea with the great lady. She then winnowed the group down to a handful she liked. These were to spend the next two years being prepared for the demands of palace life, one year at home, the second in the palace. One of those chosen in 1851 was sixteen-year-old Yehenara. After a year of outside preparation, she entered the Forbidden City in 1852, to spend another year learning court protocol within its rose walls.

Backhouse claimed that she was highly educated, that she "learned to paint skilfully and to take real pleasure in the art; she was an adept at the composition of verses. . . . At the age of sixteen she had mastered the Five Classics in Chinese and Manchu, and had studied to good purpose the historical records of the twenty-four Dynasties. She had beyond doubt that love of knowledge which is the beginning of wisdom, and the secret of power." By sprinkling his narrative with these occasional remarks about her high intelligence, Backhouse disarmed his readers while slyly preparing them for the wickedness to come.

According to the distinguished artist Hubert Vos, who painted her portrait in 1905 and saw a number of her watercolors, she was indeed a skilled painter, so in this detail Backhouse is correct. But his assertion that she could read and write and was educated in the classics by age sixteen contradicts palace records that describe the problems she had reading and writing documents in Chinese and Manchu. The truth is that as a young woman Yehenara did not know how to read or write either language, because it was not customary to teach girls to read and write. A Chinese biographer who understood this correctly maintained that Yehenara "was almost, if not quite, illiterate."

Yehenara's nomination was actually political. Imperial concubines usually were newly pubescent females drawn from families of Bannermen and nominated by the elders of each clan to gain political advantage. The chance to influence the imperial succession by bearing a male heir came only rarely, so every clan put forth its most promising maidens. Manchu succession struggles often ended in murder, so every way of influencing the outcome short of murder was taken very seriously. In terms of prestige, the Nara clan came third after the royal Aisin Gioro and the Niuhuru, and Lady Yehenara, as she was now called, represented one of the most aggressive of the four tribes that made up the Nara clan. The Naras had been in the forefront of harassing the Ming Dynasty at the end of the sixteenth century and, through a combination of military prowess, treachery, and the exchange of sisters and daughters, the Naras became linked to the ruling Aisin Gioro. A Yehenara girl was the mother of Nurhachi's favorite son, Abahai, the first emperor of the dynasty. Thus heredity was as important to Manchu matchmakers as it was to European royalty.

While she came from a powerful clan and had the political backing of its elders, little can be deduced about Yehenara's parents. Her father's name was Kuei Hsiang, not Hui Cheng, although a Westerner who only heard it spoken might spell the name phonetically as Hui Cheng. Yehenara's brother eventually was given the title Duke Kuei Hsiang; Manchu aristocrats often kept the same name as their forebears. Her father was not an insignificant character because he could trace his ancestry to the grandfather of Nurhachi, so he belonged to an elite group called the Imperial Alternates, to distinguish its members from the royals who had Nurhachi's own blood in their veins. Lady Yehenara was the first Imperial Alternate to enter an emperor's harem. One of her sisters later married Hsien Feng's younger half-brother, Prince Chun, the Seventh Prince, and her other two sisters married Manchu dukes. Yehenara may have had some influence on these marriages and probably arranged for her brother to become a duke. So she did well by her family, but no more than would a girl marrying into the Hapsburgs, the Romanovs, or the Windsors.

When official mourning for Tao Kuang finally ended, the younger sister of Hsien Feng's first wife took her dead sister's place as his primary wife, Empress Niuhuru. Along with her came the new group of concubines, including Yehenara. She was officially designated a concubine of fourth rank.

Ideally, in addition to the empress the harem was meant to include as many as three primary consorts; nine wives of the second rank; twenty-seven wives of the third, fourth, and fifth rank; and eighty-one concubines of the sixth through the eighth rank. Thus the proper number of imperial bedmates in theory was a grand total of 121 women. The depleted treasury of the later Manchu emperors meant they had to settle for one empress, two consorts, and eleven concubines. This was the case with Hsien Feng. While they were all at his sexual disposal, he was intended to have children with only the empress and two consorts. Rarely did the emperor bed any concubine below fifth rank, except as a warm-up, and the rest were just handmaidens.

Hsien Feng was supposed to play by certain traditional rules. These rules determined which concubine he could make love to and when and how, in keeping with ancient Taoist dogma about sex. Record keepers supervised an emperor's sexual contacts as if they were managing a stud farm. In earlier times, court ladies called *nu-shih* watched over every tryst to make certain that the ruler coupled with his various wives on the correct days, according to calendrics, and with the frequency established by the rites for each rank of concubine. They kept notes with red writing brushes, so these were the Records of the Red Brush. An emperor who did not assert himself could easily become a victim of this system, controlled by his servants.

According to Taoist theory, emperors needed as many wives and concubines as possible to maintain a balance between the life forces of *yang* and *yin*, to acquire the potency needed to father a Son of Heaven. Woman's yin essence, her fluids, were thought to be inexhaustible, while man's yang essence, his semen, was limited. To build up the emperor's yang required a great deal of yin. The best way for the female life force to transfer to the emperor was for him to engage in a lot of sex with his concubines, without ejaculating. While restraining himself, he must rouse his concubine to repeated orgasms. Taoists boasted that this exceptional self-restraint produced supernatural powers, although one suspects it took supernatural powers to show such self-restraint. The more women partners an emperor had, they said, and the more often, the better, so long as he restrained himself with every single one. A Chinese sex manual blandly asserts: "If in one night he can have intercourse with more than ten women it is best." (Taoist writers had an unusual sense of humor.) Sticking to the same woman was dangerous, because her vital essence would grow weaker, until she was no use at all. You must take your concubines like vitamins. Those of lower rank coupled with the emperor before those of higher rank, and much more often, to build up his yang for his monthly encounter with his empress.

Self-restraint is a basic part of Oriental philosophies. Success or failure in life, for a bandit or an emperor, depends on whether the force is with you, and rituals had to be observed to make sure it was. A good Confucian monarch should be a paragon of self-restraint. One sure way to avoid orgasm was prescribed by a Chinese doctor in the seventh century. At the last moment, "the man closes his eyes and concentrates his thoughts; he presses his tongue against the roof of his mouth, bends his back, and stretches his neck. He opens his nostrils wide and squares his shoulders, closes his mouth, and sucks in his breath." Failure occurred so often that physicians had to specify how many ejaculations a man could dare have without damaging his system: once every three days in spring, twice a month in summer and autumn, and not at all during the winter. One accidental orgasm in the winter was a hundred times more exhausting than one in the spring.

To make self-restraint easier, artificial devices were called into play, most effective being the sheep's eyelid. This curious object, kept in a tiny jade box by the emperor's bed, was a circle of finely tanned skin cut from around a sheep's eye, including upper and lower lids, eyelashes intact. After immersion in a cup of hot tea, it was slipped on like a soft ring, so that the eyelashes fanned out. With its help as a tickler, there was little difficulty generating all the yin an emperor could use from his concubines, and then some.

Monogamous Westerners imagined that with so many women available around the clock, the emperor of China suffered perpetual sexual fatigue, which explained why he was almost always, in their eyes at least, an imbecile. To Western minds in the nineteenth century concubines were no more than royal prostitutes like Nell Gwyn or Madame Pompadour, with nothing to do but groom their bodies for the next orgy. On the contrary, sex in the palace could be pathetically regimented.

According to Chinese sex histories, which are fairly consistent on certain points, eunuchs were responsible for prepping each concubine, assuring that she was suitably anointed and did not carry a weapon or poison. The designated concubine was undressed by eunuchs under the scrutiny of the chief. Chief eunuchs lived in symbiosis with the emperor, like a Victorian aristocrat with his manservants. Eunuchs helped all the ladies in the palace with their toilette, clothing, and coiffure; they were omnipresent and thus invisible. The concubine was wrapped naked in a red silk comforter embroidered with scampering dragons and phoenixes, and carried to the emperor's room. This was a holdover from the Ming Dynasty, when concubines had bound feet, making walking impossible once the feet were unbound for sex. On his carved blackwood bed she awaited whatever celestial fireworks were in store from the Son of Heaven. It was up to her to bestow the earthly delights.

After building himself up over a month with concubines, the emperor was to couple with his empress just once, when the best chance existed for her to conceive an heir to the throne. The Chinese believed that a boy would be conceived on the first or third day after a woman's period, a girl on the fourth or fifth, and none at all afterward.

If Hsien Feng had followed these rules strictly there would have been little fun and lots of squaring of shoulders and sucking in of breath. After being thoroughly spoiled during childhood, Manchu princes had little to do but break rules. By the time they reached puberty they had usually indulged in all manner of sexual experiments with favorite eunuchs or in Peking's male and female bordellos. Hsien Feng had been making the rounds with Prince Kung for years. In this taste for male and female brothels there are strong similarities between Hsien Feng and Queen Victoria's grandson "Eddy," Prince Albert Edward Victor, son of King Edward VII. While in England homosexuality was considered by commoners to be a crime against man, nature, and heaven, among China's elite homosexuality and bisexuality were no cause for raised eyebrows.

Because Hsien Feng broke the rules (he preferred one particular woman) we know a bit about his sex life and how Yehenara fit in, which is different from all the fiction.

Three years after his father's death, Hsien Feng asked his eunuchs to wrap up not Yehenara or the fourteen-year-old empress, but a concubine of the second rank called Li Fei. Second rank meant consort, a wife just below empress, considerably outranking Yehenara. When Li Fei was summoned, no Zen self-restraint was practiced, and she became pregnant almost immediately. She presented the emperor with his first healthy offspring. Unfortunately, it was a girl, named Princess Jung An, of no consequence in dynastic succession. Li Fei herself is obscure to history because she later disappeared. However, she is very important to the story of Yehenara because the identities of the two women have been mixed up, causing grievous damage.

When Li Fei's pregnancy became known, she was off-limits to the emperor. Custom required that she follow a rigorous prenatal regimen: associate with the right people, hear the right books being read to encourage right-thinking, and observe a strict code of good manners. She had to sit erect, with her seat and pillows arranged in a prescribed fashion; to abstain from strange foods; and to avoid unpleasant colors. If she failed to observe complete celibacy, the baby would be born with skin diseases. After the birth of the child, she was forbidden to have sex for another hundred days. Even hand holding was out of the question.

During the full year that Hsien Feng was barred from having sex with Li Fei, he began sampling some of the other maidens waiting impatiently for his attention and discovered Yehenara. The only surprise is that he did not take an interest in her sooner, for she had been waiting around the concubines' quarters for more than two years and was far from plain. Like all court ladies she was dressed in stiff and unrevealing silk brocade, lips dabbed with the red dot, and in the style for imperial concubines her face was brightly colored with powders, rouges, and tints as was sometimes the fashion in Greece and Rome and more recently at Versailles. At age twenty Yehenara was a beauty, with high cheekbones and brilliant black almond eyes tilted up a bit more than usual, and a slim and flawless figure.

Because she was overly serious she did not smile often, but when she did it was a smile of surprising warmth.

Other court ladies found her severe; she was spirited only with friends in private, laughing over board games or playing with the tiny Pekingese dogs that were the exclusive property of the imperial family. Unlike typical concubines glad to have the eunuchs relieve them of everyday chores, Yehenara craved involvement. In her responsibilities around the palace she showed energy and determination, impatience with others who were idle, and annoyance with the silliness of the concubines' quarters. She kept to herself, and after being stung by her temper the habitual clowns learned not to trifle with her.

When Hsien Feng noticed her the brooding ceased and she bloomed overnight like a willow too long without water. In that tiny world the shadows were deep and the emperor was the only source of light. His interest made her the new center of envy. She once remarked, "When I arrived at Court the late Emperor became very much attached to me and would hardly glance at any of the other ladies." This was true while it lasted, but Hsien Feng was as inconstant as springtime. His love affair with Yehenara began only after Li Fei became unavailable. It lasted only a few months, till she too became pregnant.

The pregnancy gave Yehenara security and acceptance in the imperial household. She was acknowledged as a full member of the emperor's family, no longer just a plaything. Women at court were more envious than ever. If she was successful in giving birth to a child that survived, even a girl, she was assured of status in perpetuity. If it was a boy, he would be a royal prince, and she would become a significant political factor.

From late summer 1855 until April 1856, while she was carrying her baby, Yehenara was sexually unavailable. In the meantime, Li Fei recovered from the birth of Princess Jung An, and to Yehenara's great disappointment recaptured Hsien Feng's full attention. To be jilted stung, reviving her sense of rejection. As she did all her life in times of crisis, she awakened at odd hours with sighs, pacing the tiny courtyards, unexpectedly weeping. Her romance had been brief, but it remained one of the two periods of joy in her life.

Her child was delivered on April 27, 1856, a boy, the first and so far only male heir. He was born at the Summer Palace in the outskirts of Peking, on Phoenix Island in Lake Kunming, the traditional setting for imperial nativities: a big, healthy boy destined to survive. While personal names in China were changed at whim, they had great importance to the palace for identifying children by generation. Hsien Feng and all his half-brothers had names beginning with I, as in I Wei, I Tsung, I Hsin, and

I Huan. All their sons were given names starting with Tsai, their grand-sons Pu, as in Pu Chun and Pu Yi. By this rule Yehenara's child was called Tsai Chun, but he is better known to history by his reign title, Emperor Tung Chih. (We will call him Tung Chih.)

For her part in producing the first heir to the throne, she was promoted to consort or concubine of the first rank, equal to Li Fei and second in prestige only to the empress. She was given the title I Kuei-fei, meaning Concubine of Feminine Virtue. The similarity between the titles Li Fei and I Kuei-fei makes it obvious for the first time why Yehenara was blamed in later years for things she did not do. A simple case of mistaken identity.

At twenty-one Yehenara had fulfilled her function as a brood-mare. As the birth of a son was the ultimate fulfillment for any Chinese woman, the birth of an emperor's son gave her the maximum status possible in China.

By this one stroke of biological luck Yehenara was elevated from total obscurity onto the political stage of China as a figure of unique importance to the survival of the dynasty. For the moment she had no power, political or otherwise, but she suddenly had presence. The mandarins who wielded real power at court took notice of her existence for the first time.

From this point on what she did or did not do took on a significance, or at least potential significance, that was completely lacking before. Her personality even underwent a change. What changed was her specific gravity, the way she was seen by other people, and the way she saw herself. Her political identity was yet to be shaped by disaster. However, like the young Queen Elizabeth I and the young Queen Victoria, the raw materials of certain traits were already visible, and one day these would influence her management of the imperial court.

She shared many qualities with Victoria in particular, including a sus-ceptibility to flattery that made her unable to see through the pretenses of courtiers; men who understood this took advantage and she was repeat-edly drawn into court intrigues that were not her invention or to her liking, notably the Boxer plot. Like Victoria she was a stickler for detail and etiquette and had a long memory for those she felt had slighted her, causing outbursts of temper or rage at servants or ladies-in-waiting, and at princes and ministers. The two women shared iron character and a sense of duty, but Yehenara was not as absorbed by trivia. As an old woman she was as stubborn and obstinate as Victoria and as burdened with protocol and puppy dogs, but while Victoria grew morbid, Yehenara merely deepened in melancholy.

The differences between her and Elizabeth I are striking. She was high-strung and energetic like Elizabeth, and might have excelled as a monarch under the right circumstances, but she was not similarly educated or brilliant at languages and geography, not as clever and as quick or as good a judge of men, which would be decisive in the successes and failures of these two monarchs. Unlike Elizabeth, Yehenara was not of royal lineage and arrived in the palace without valuable connections or family ties. She had no knowledge of the world at large, not even of the empire, and knew nothing of what went on outside the Forbidden City and the Summer Palace. Because she was a woman in a Confucian state, she was never permitted to travel in the provinces to learn about China firsthand. She was not permitted by her ministers to meet a foreigner until she was sixty-three. Of the three monarchs, Yehenara was the most manipulated because she was the most isolated. No breath of outside air ever blew into the Forbidden City, so she was completely dependent upon the information and integrity of her advisers and at the mercy of her viceroys. She was not allowed to select her ministers from the finest brains, and because of the tight grip of the Manchu clans she was too often the victim of the royal princes. She reigned so long that she suffered the folly of their sons as well. Ignorance was all around her, compounded by xenophobia, so her own innate intelligence was never given full play. She did share with Elizabeth an appearance of indecisiveness, in both cases born out of a desire to avoid conflict. Neither woman was indecisive by nature, but they learned to cultivate caution to such a degree that their ministers, particularly the firebrands at court, thought they were indecisive.

Because she was not schooled at all until she was tutored in the palace by scholars from the Hanlin Academy, Yehenara was entirely dependent upon her instincts and intuition. Until she was twenty-five she lived in total isolation, but after that her survival was threatened repeatedly. When an emergency put her at risk she reacted intuitively, becoming angrily aggressive in self-defense, the way a dozing housecat springs to life only to subside again into wary immobility. This resourcefulness produced the outstanding moments of her life. She once remarked, "As has always been the case in emergencies, I was equal to the occasion."

Appropriately for a devout Buddhist she consciously tried to emulate the Buddha's serene watchfulness. Sir Robert Hart and others who understood more about her situation in Peking confirm that this was her real nature, and it is for this reason that she came to be called "the Buddha" and later "the old Buddha," terms the Chinese, including court ministers, used affectionately and in admiration. It was only at the time of the Boxer Uprising in 1900 that Westerners who misunderstood her role began using the term "Old Buddha" abusively, and it took on a pejorative sense.

These were traits that developed in the second phase of her life, after the birth of her son brought an end to her isolation. But they did not really become visible until the court fled from Peking to escape capture by the Allies in 1860. Fear combined with emergency produced a resourceful woman of great tenacity. But that was yet to come.

If she hoped the birth of a son would reclaim her lost place in the emperor's affections, she was wrong. At a time in his life when Hsien Feng was increasingly overwhelmed with problems, he was anxious to lose himself in revelry. Yehenara was too intense and serious. Li Fei was gay and lighthearted.

She was not the only one spurned. Although tradition required the emperor to spend one night a month with Empress Niuhuru, thanks to his grand passion for Li Fei he had no yang left to make the empress pregnant. Self-restraint was not one of Hsien Feng's cardinal virtues. According to his critics he had few virtues, cardinal or otherwise.

As a romantic, Yehenara was disappointed, but as a mother all seemed well. "I was lucky in giving birth to a son," she remarked once in unconscious understatement. "But after that, I had very bad luck."

The death in 1856 of the empress dowager altered the precedence of women at court. Hsien Feng's empress now became the head of the household. She was two years younger than Yehenara and never produced a child, but as empress she was in a unique position as the legal or official mother of the heir apparent. Yehenara was only a surrogate mother and had little to say about raising her own child. The job of breast-feeding the boy was given to wet nurses, and palace eunuchs looked after the child around the clock. Yehenara's contact with her son was limited to ceremonial calls on auspicious occasions determined by astrologers. The shaping of a potential emperor was too important to leave to his illiterate mother. This created friction between the two women, and Yehenara later said frankly, "I had . . . quite a lot of trouble with [Empress Nuihuru] and found it very difficult to keep on good terms with her."

In time a second son was born to Hsien Feng but died in infancy. Some sources say this was the second child of the favorite, Li Fei, and give the birthdate as 1859.

By the beginning of 1860, Hsien Feng could no longer cope with the problems confronting him. Misfortune was coming in great waves. Events outside the palace of which Yehenara knew nothing were about to sweep over them, leaving everything she knew destroyed or damaged. She would become a refugee, fleeing. Long afterward, when she was the only one left of Hsien Feng's wives and concubines, she was universally blamed by Westerners for provoking all the grief and destruction, for causing Hsien Feng's foolishness, for vamping him, for exhausting him sexually, for making him unable to face the invasion of China by the Foreign Powers in 1860, and finally for turning him into a drug addict, a drunken sot, and an imbecile. The rest of her life she had to live with attacks on her reputation that were the result of Hsien Feng's infatuation with a different woman and the inability of Westerners to distinguish between them.

During his reign, no Foreign Devil was sufficiently informed to know which concubine was the emperor's favorite or for that matter who the empress was. Until 1860 there were no Western diplomatic missions in Peking. After that date even Robert Hart was not absolutely sure which concubine was which. Nobody knew their real names, and the titles were easy to confuse. Was it Li Fei or I Kuei Fei?

What caught Western fancy was the idea that the emperor of China had been made witless by too much fornication, so any woman who participated must be depraved. The sad truth is that Hsien Feng needed no help falling apart. His father had already buckled under the strain of simultaneously trying to crush the Taiping Rebellion and to ward off the Foreign Devils.

CHAPTER TWO

Foreign Devils

When all the myths are stripped away it was the deliberate mischief of a handful of Englishmen that led to the humiliation and death of Emperor Tao Kuang and his son, Emperor Hsien Feng, so that for the first time in more than a thousand years China's throne passed into the hands of a woman. The success of this mischief popularized a peculiar Western state of mind toward China that encouraged Backhouse and many others to misrepresent the facts and falsify the record, for which we are still paying the price.

While Great Britain was approaching the zenith of its power at the midpoint of the nineteenth century, China had sunk to its weakest point since the Manchu took control in 1644. Corruption was epidemic, and Emperor Tao Kuang's reluctance to act ruthlessly was seen as weakness, inviting more abuses. In the south, Western traders at Canton and Macao flouted the law, smuggling in massive quantities of cheap Indian opium, driving a spike into the heartwood. Opium became a symbol of China's sovereignty and whether foreigners could violate that sovereignty at whim; the fact that corrupt Chinese and Manchu officials participated in the trade did not make the issue less real. It became a game among Westerners to provoke the Chinese at every turn and, when the Chinese struck back, to demand concessions from local mandarins. If concessions were not forthcoming, gunboats were called in; China found itself at war over issues that were trumped up and incidents that were greatly exaggerated or entirely imaginary. Many Westerners built successful careers out of bullying the Chinese, among them George Morrison of the *Times* and Sir Edmund Backhouse. But among the first to perfect the technique were consular officers, who took advantage of the long delay in communications in the age of sail to bring down armed confrontations without the sanction of their home governments. The leading advocate of this school of diplomacy was Queen Victoria's foreign secretary and prime minister, Lord Palmerston, whose foreign policy was based on collision. London in the nineteenth century was far removed from the scene of action. Palmerston and other prime ministers had to depend upon—or take advantage of—the gut instincts and quick decisions of consular officials at the sharp end of the stick, many of whom were ambitious merchants acting only temporarily as consuls, untrained in the traditions and trade-offs of diplomacy. These acting consuls knew that for political reasons their government usually would feel obliged to endorse actions taken in the heat of the moment. In the politics of collision, rude surprises were grasped as great opportunities, and armed force was used to guarantee the outcome, while the public at home was led to believe it was all part of a grand design.

Bullying over opium smuggling and deliberate lying by acting consular officers brought about the Allied invasion of North China in 1860, when young Emperor Hsien Feng fled with his family into the Tartar wastes beyond the Great Wall and the magnificent Summer Palace was put to the torch. So opium politics ultimately put Yehenara on the throne.

To control opium addiction, the Manchu had established a government monopoly in 1729, levying such high taxes that the drug was restricted to a privileged few. British merchants saw a huge potential market among the poorer people of China by dumping Indian opium there at a very low price. This caused an explosive spread of addiction in China, undermining family life and further weakening the government. Eunuchs in the emperor's own household became addicts. By 1839, annual imports had jumped to 3.6 million pounds. All the tea in China could not pay for it. Chinese silver reserves evaporated, and commodity prices shot up.

No foreigner seriously believed that the Manchu had the strength of character to take drastic action. So everyone was surprised when Emperor Tao Kuang decided to close down the foreigners' opium trade. Canton was then the only port open to Western merchants, who were allowed to reside there only during the trading season, from November to May, keeping their permanent establishments downriver at Portuguese Macao. Tao Kuang, a tall, gaunt figure with a bald head and a morose, bony face, had reached the end of his patience and moaned aloud, "How, alas! can I die and go to the shades of my imperial fathers and ancestors until these dire evils are removed!" In March 1839 the law arrived in Canton in the person of Commissioner Lin. As viceroy of Hupeh and Hunan provinces Lin had ordered that any smoker who refused the cure had part of his upper lip cut off, to prevent him from using a pipe. Lin began gently by appealing directly to Queen Victoria on moral grounds. He wrote her:

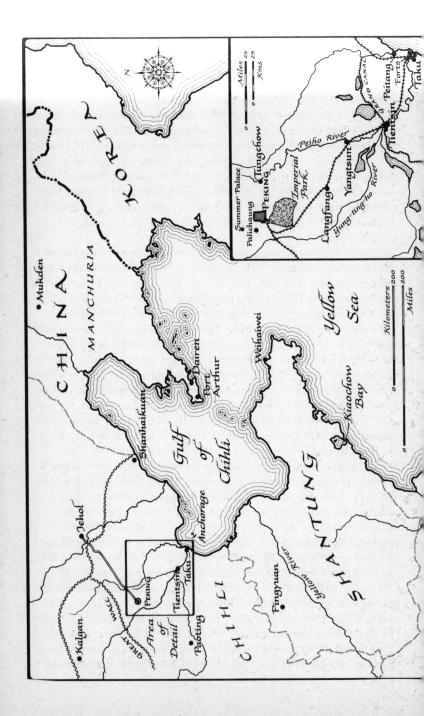

After a long period of commercial intercourse, there appear among the crowd of barbarians both good persons and bad ... there are those who smuggle opium to seduce the Chinese people and so cause the spread of the poison to all provinces. Such persons who only care to profit themselves, and disregard their harm to others ... are unanimously hated by human beings. Having established new regulations, we presume that the ruler of your honorable country ... must be able to instruct the various barbarians to observe the law.

There was no reply.

Lin advised the foreign traders in Canton that opium was an illegal commodity and requested the surrender of their opium stocks and a pledge to abstain from the trade in the future.

Captain Charles Elliot, charged by his government with overseeing all aspects of trade by British merchants in and around Canton, attempted to smuggle out one of the three major opium traffickers, Lancelot Dent, head of Dent & Co., but the Chinese blocked their escape by constructing barriers across the river. Elliot capitulated and delivered 20,283 chests of British-owned opium, but he accused Lin of "unjustifiable imprisonment of the whole foreign community in Canton."

Elliot was now permitted to leave for Macao, taking all Englishmen who had not already gone. They petitioned Lord Palmerston, then foreign secretary, to strike back and to demand indemnity for their opium, reminding him that the trade had been endorsed by the British government.

Danish, German, American, and Spanish captains signed Commissioner Lin's pledge and entered Whampoa to trade freely in other goods, but Captain Elliot, in a rage, tore the document to shreds. Hereafter, he announced, all British vessels would discharge their cargoes at Macao. When Lin replied by prohibiting all commerce at Macao as well, British captains traded directly with Chinese smugglers offshore.

Tension was aggravated by a drunken brawl in which a British sailor murdered a Chinese civilian and injured several others. Elliot paid hush money to the surviving victims for a statement that it was all an accident and staged a mock trial that found the killer innocent. He and his mates were shipped to England and set free, and Elliot told the Chinese that he was unable "to discover the perpetrators of this deed." Clearly, Elliot was a man of flexible ethics.

Unfortunately, China misunderstood the special relationship that existed between private British traders and the government in London. Parliament was under strong pressure from business interests at home to go to war over this affront to free enterprise. Peking also underestimated the military power of England and the destructive force at her command, primarily in the form of modern cannon.

The Foreign Office had another motive for war: it wanted to force direct official intercourse with the court in Peking, which the Manchu had consistently refused.

Canton was blockaded by British men-of-war. When Lin protested, the *Volge* and *Hyacinth* opened fire, and the First Opium War was on.

In London, William Gladstone denounced the attack in Parliament: "A war more unjust in its origin, a war more calculated to cover this country with permanent disgrace, I do not know and have not read of. The British flag is hoisted to protect an infamous traffic; . . . we should recoil from its sight with horror."

To China's surprise, the British did not pursue the attack on Canton but sailed up the coast to capture Tinghai at the mouth of the Yangtze, where the defenders were unprepared. Some ten thousand seasoned British troops were deployed against Chinese forces who had no experience fighting anyone but themselves and no acquaintance with modern cannon. Other battles followed at Canton, Ningpo, and other ports, until Peking gave in.

The Treaty of Nanking was signed under duress on August 29, 1842, aboard the H.M.S. *Cornwallis*. A turning point in the history of China, it opened five Treaty Ports to foreign trade; ceded Hong Kong to Great Britain; paid $6 million indemnity for opium destroyed by Commissioner Lin, $3 million for debts owed to British traders by Canton merchants, plus $12 million indemnity to England for the cost of the war. (Two years later, France and the United States demanded and obtained similar Treaty Port concessions.)

The Manchu were defeated but not convinced. The emperor's militant advisers, known to their enemies as the Gang of Eight, still felt secure in Peking; they could go on surrendering small pieces of China for many years. But it was all too much for Emperor Tao Kuang. He had neglected domestic problems and civil war in order to deal with the Foreign Devils, only to fail in both. His mother, one of the few human beings he felt close to, then died. The spirit went out of Tao Kuang, and his health gave way. He dressed in sackcloth and spent the next twenty-seven days pining beside his mother's corpse. Refusing food and taking only small amounts of water, he slipped away after her into the other world.

He was succeeded by his nineteen-year-old son, Hsien Feng. On Hsien Feng's head and the heads of his empress and concubines, Yehenara among them, still greater disaster would fall.

From the outset Westerners judged Hsien Feng to be either an incompetent playboy or an idiot, lacking even his father's honorable motives.

Whether this was due to his youth and inexperience or to the isolation in which he had been raised, he was unfit to steer the ship of state at such a crucial time. He seemed to have no grasp of the situation and to be indecisive at all the critical moments.

What they were in no position to see was that Hsien Feng was completely in thrall to the Gang of Eight, the group of militant councillors he had inherited from his father. They, not he, directed China's actions.

Each emperor appointed a group of conservative advisers to counsel his heir, among them hard-core Manchu grandees known as the Ironhats, typically the most reactionary men in the hierarchy. The Ironhat faction at court was dominated at mid-century by four Manchu nobles: Su Shun and his half-brother Prince Cheng, Prince I, and Ching Shou. They were generals of the Manchu armies and extremely antiforeign. These four powerful nobles controlled the emperor's four Grand Councillors, and together they made up the Gang of Eight.

Su Shun was the prime mover in the clique and the most powerful man in Peking next to the emperor himself. Bold and ambitious, he was sixteen years older than Hsien Feng, the right age and temperament to impress the young emperor. He began his career as a minor aristocrat of lowly tenth rank, but he enjoyed the protection and sponsorship of his half-brother, Prince Cheng, the most powerful of the Ironhat princes. It was Prince Cheng who introduced Su Shun to the emperor and insinuated him into the inner circle, where he gradually made his manipulative personality felt. By his mid-thirties Su Shun was in charge of all the imperial playgrounds, including the Sea Palaces, the Summer Palace, and the "hunting lodge" at Jehol. Promotions came thick and fast. He was appointed to the Grand Secretariat, raised to deputy lieutenant-general of the Banners, and attained one of the most feared positions in China: president of the Censorate, the ideological watchdog of the state bureaucracy, a post that enabled him to extort money through fear. In 1859 he became president of the Board of Revenue, putting his fingers in every rice bowl. He ingratiated himself into the emperor's private life, becoming the imperial pimp and binding Hsien Feng to him by common sexual adventure. Encouraged to indulge himself, the unwary young emperor became physically wasted and mentally erratic. Su Shun's enemies believed that he was deliberately trying to destroy the emperor's health to make Hsien Feng more malleable.

Su Shun had enemies for many reasons. He was brusque, offensive, draconian, quick to punish, maintaining a reign of terror in which the slightest violation of Confucian etiquette could be used to destroy you. His own behavior was far from correct. During a scandal over missing treasury funds, his Board of Revenue was burned down to destroy the evidence. At the imperial examinations he permitted a number of failed candidates to pass, in return for bribes. These exams were the only way to get civil service appointments, so they were an ideal means of patronage. Many men spent their entire lives trying to pass the full cycle to make their way to the summit. Despite his relatively humble beginnings, Su Shun was amassing a large fortune.

In 1854, after a decade of calm following the First Opium War, Britain began pressing Hsien Feng with new demands: the extension of its trading rights, the revision of existing tariffs, the establishment of a British legation in Peking, the opening of the northern port of Tientsin to trade, the right of foreigners to purchase land in the interior of China, and the full legalization of the opium trade. The French, Russian, and American governments joined in these demands, and deadlines were set for China to meet.

Hsien Feng's response was to turn all foreign dealings over to the Chinese military governor in Canton, an ill-tempered fat man named Yeh. The son of a village apothecary, Yeh had risen through sheer ruthlessness to become governor-general of the southern provinces of Kwangsi and Kwangtung, including Canton. Ordered to stamp out the Taiping Rebellion there, he made his reputation by slaughtering a large part of the population of South China, on the presumption that most peasants were antigovernment and therefore rebels. He wiped out whole towns, boasting that he had killed more than seventy thousand "rebels" in less than six months.

In Canton, Yeh refused to meet foreign envoys, ignored their demands, and tried to reduce contact with any Westerners to zero. He was matched in sheer bloodymindedness by his Western counterparts, Sir John Bowring and Harry Parkes. Bowring, in his sixties, was a man of ability, but deeply conceited, without any comprehension of political principles on the grand scale. He was a published author and former member of Parliament, forced by financial necessity to take up a diplomatic career; in 1849 he served as consul at Canton and in 1854 became governor of Hong Kong. As a child he had dreamed that the king appointed him the first ambassador to Peking; as an adult he felt a craving to realize the dream, no matter what the cost to others. Despite repeated warnings from his prime minister not to resort to force in China without prior approval from London, which could take nine months, Bowring gratified his ambition by plunging Great Britain into another war with China over an entirely fictitious dispute.

Bowring's compulsion to compel China to grovel was shared by his subordinate, Harry Parkes, a young interpreter temporarily serving as Britain's acting consul in Canton. Parkes was twenty-six years old, of ordinary height, olive complexion, with blond hair and whiskers; his nervous eyes and twitching mouth revealed great tension. He built his legendary career (as an admiring biographer put it) "mainly by never giving in, never allowing himself to be slighted, but always resolutely maintaining the dignity and honor of his country before the Chinese." Parkes became a symbol of everything China detested in Westerners.

Their excuse to drag Emperor Hsien Feng into war was a rotting hulk in Canton. The *Arrow* was a lorcha, a Portuguese hull with a Chinese junk rig and sails. She had seen better days and was now owned by a Chinese smuggling boss resident in British Hong Kong. In order to develop trade in the Crown Colony, Sir John Bowring granted licenses to Chinese vessels indiscriminately, allowing smugglers and pirates to operate under the British flag. These boats—in Chinese called "scrambling dragons"— carried on a brisk opium trade while flying the Union Jack, becoming a great annoyance to the Chinese government. To protect her from seizure by Chinese coastal patrols, the *Arrow* had been registered in Hong Kong on September 27, 1855, but her license expired a year later on September 27, 1856. The owner neglected to renew her registration. The *Arrow*'s crew was Chinese, but a gin-soaked Irish skipper had been hired to give the lorcha an authentic foreign appearance. On the morning of October 8, 1856, eleven days after her right to British protection ended, she was anchored in the Pearl River while her Irish skipper was "breakfasting with a friend" on another ship in the harbor. The *Arrow* was boarded by four Chinese officers and sixty marines looking for a notorious pirate, easily recognized by his red turban and his missing front teeth. A man fitting that description had been seen aboard the *Arrow* that very morning. Although he was no longer on board, the entire Chinese crew was arrested.

The Irish skipper swore to Harry Parkes that the *Arrow* was still under British registry and had been flying the Union Jack when boarded. The Chinese denied that there had been a flag at her mizzen, which was confirmed by other European captains in the harbor. Even Sir John Bowring secretly expressed doubts: "It appears," he said, "on examination, that the *Arrow* had no right to hoist the British flag; the license to do so expired on the 27th of September, from which period she has not been entitled to protection." He concealed this from the Chinese, consoling himself that by their ignorance of the facts the Chinese forfeited any claim to be legally in the right.

Harry Parkes was neither a British diplomat nor a civil servant. He was only an interpreter, serving temporarily as an acting consul. Yet he decided entirely on his own that this was a clear case of Chinese troops violating British sovereignty and insulting the British flag. He went to the Chinese naval vessel in the harbor to demand the release of the *Arrow* crew. The commander refused. Parkes later complained to Commissioner Yeh that while he was aboard, the Chinese marines threatened him with violence. (Accustomed to getting his way, Parkes tried to free the sailors with his own hands and was struck by a Chinese officer. He told friends that the marines "laughed at me . . . threatened me with violence, and I was actually struck one blow, though to this circumstance I have never made official allusion, as I wished to keep every personal feature out of view.")

Nursing a bruised ego, Parkes pressed his case relentlessly to Commissioner Yeh, insisting wrongly that the *Arrow* was entitled to British protection, that any British ship in Chinese waters was still "on British soil," with full extraterritorial rights. Joining in the charade Bowring instructed Parkes to demand "an apology for what has taken place and an assurance that the British flag shall, in future, be respected." Two weeks later Yeh freed all twelve crewmen but refused to apologize. Parkes turned the argument over to the Royal Navy, bringing about the so-called Arrow War.

Gunboats under the command of Admiral Sir Michael Seymour bombarded Canton for six days, pausing only on Sunday out of Christian piety. Out of a sense of brotherhood American ships joined in the bombardment. The Chinese fired back at the American ships and one sailor was killed, so Commodore Armstrong decided to teach the Chinese a lesson by storming the forts guarding Canton and obliterating them with fifty-pound kegs of gunpowder.

William Gladstone again spoke out angrily in Parliament: "You have turned a consul [Harry Parkes] into a diplomatist, and that metamorphosed consul is forsooth to be at liberty to direct the whole might of England against the lives of a defenceless people." Lord Palmerston's government—he had become prime minister in 1855—was defeated on the issue in Parliament and elections were called, but, thanks to a great dose of jingoism in the press, the public was roused to a froth and Palmerston was returned to power, vindicated. Capitalizing upon his electoral victory, he dispatched a punitive expedition to China headed by James Bruce, Lord Elgin. (It was his father who removed most of the sculpture from the Parthenon, lost half of it at sea, and sold the rest to the British Museum.)

Recognizing a splendid opportunity, France jumped in, using as her excuse the unrelated murder some months earlier of an obscure missionary who had been working deep in the interior in violation of Chinese law. French expeditionary forces embarked under the command of Baron J.B.L. Gros, a diplomat of thirty years' experience.

Elgin was instructed to obtain reparations for injuries to British subjects during the recent bombardment of Canton; to get compensation for British expenses throughout; to secure the right of periodic visits by a British minister to the court at Peking; and to demand the extension of trade rights to Tientsin in the north and to cities along the Yangtze and other great rivers in China's interior. The French government gave Baron Gros similar instructions.

Although in his black frock coat the stubby Lord Elgin bore a strong resemblance to a cigar butt, he was a man of intelligence and sensibility. Above his boiled collar was a kind countenance wreathed by white mutton-chops. In his late forties, he was still young enough to be considered a potential prime minister, although as governor of Jamaica and governor-general of British North America he had been criticized for being too good-natured and conciliatory. Conscious of the need to correct this soft image—and aware of public outrage over atrocities being committed upon English men, women, and children during the Sepoy Mutiny, which was being put down in India at that very moment—Elgin resolved to take a very hard line with China. In effect, the Chinese would be made to pay for the fiendishness of the Indians.

America sent an observer, and Russia jumped in as well. The czar's envoy was Admiral Count Vasilevich Putiatin, whose secret instructions were to mediate between the Manchu and the Europeans "so as to prevent the fall of the dynasty and the shifting of the political gravity from North China to South China," a shift that would benefit the British and French at the expense of the Russians.

The envoys of Britain, France, the United States, and Russia gathered off Canton aboard men-of-war. On December 12, 1857, Lord Elgin and Baron Gros sent simultaneous notes to Commissioner Yeh. In "calm and dignified language" they demanded the execution of treaty obligations at Canton, right of entry to the port, and compensation for losses to date. Yeh was given ten days to think it over. A line of British men-of-war took up positions in front of the town.

"I never felt so ashamed of myself in my life," Elgin wrote in his diary. "I feel I am earning for myself a place in Litany, immediately after plague, pestilence, and famine." But he did not shirk his duty.

The Chinese refused to bend to the Allied demands, and after long bombardment Canton fell two days before New Year's 1858. The city was "a scene of great desolation," all destroyed on the phony excuse of the good ship *Arrow.* An occupation government was set up, dominated by Harry Parkes, who became the absolute warlord of Canton for the next three years.

Once Canton was secure, the Allied force sailed north to Taku to press the issue directly on the emperor in Peking. Under the influence of Su Shun, who controlled all information reaching the throne, Hsien Feng still believed that the Allies were coming to beg favors from him, so he instructed his negotiators to toy with the "barbarians."

Lord Elgin, frustrated by these evasive tactics, gave orders to take the Taku Forts by force. Tartar cavalry were arrayed outside the forts, wearing fantastical costumes but armed only with bows and arrows. The military state of the country, Elgin wrote, was so pitiful that "twenty-four determined men, with revolvers and a sufficient number of cartridges, might walk through China from one end to another."

Taking advantage of the fact that the fortress guns were anchored in place, Allied gunboats moved in under their range and made quick work of the defenders. Seizing the initiative, Elgin and Gros gave orders to take the nearby city of Tientsin as well; with its capture, they were only seventy miles from Peking. Panic-stricken by the enemy advance, the emperor dispatched new negotiators, including the elderly Commissioner Kiying, who had negotiated the earlier Treaty of Nanking.

By now Lord Elgin had grown accustomed to playing the Harry Parkes role of "the uncontrollably fierce barbarian." He instructed his subordinates to follow suit, because the "stupid" Chinese "never yield anything except under the influence of fear." Unless the Chinese met his demands now—and were quick about it—they were to be in no doubt that the British would march all the way to Peking.

He left negotiations to his younger brother, Frederick Bruce, and to twenty-six-year-old interpreter Horatio Lay, "the most crafty of the barbarians," who had been brought along precisely because of his appetite for hectoring. (Harry Parkes could not be in two places at once.) With his fluency in the language, Lay could keep Elgin informed of what the Chinese were really up to, and deal with them accordingly. When the half-blind Commissioner Kiying addressed the Allies with his customary blend of patronage and conciliation, which had always worked in the past, Lay cut the old man short and waved under his nose a copy of a secret memorial Kiying had written to the throne, which had been found when Canton fell. In it Kiying boasted of being able to manipulate the barbarians by "caressing" and "restraining" them. "We have to curb them by sincerity," he had written.

When Lay read this aloud, old Kiying burst into tears and fled the room, humiliated. He was taken in chains to Peking, where he was ordered to commit suicide; he did so by swallowing poison.

Emperor Hsien Feng was now advised by his negotiators that the capture of Kiying's secret files spoiled everything. "The traditional methods have been seen through. Our techniques of control are lost." On June 25, 1858, they said Lay "came to headquarters with a self-made treaty of fifty-six articles and pressed Your slaves to agree to it. His pride and anger everyone with eyes could see. Not only could there be no discussion but not even one word could be altered. The gunboats were close by and if we let him leave, Your slaves certainly had no assurance it would not cause a rupture." The result was the Treaty of Tientsin, signed grudgingly by the Chinese negotiators.

The treaty opened to foreign trade ten new ports along China's rivers, allowed foreign travel in the interior, granted freedom of movement in all of China to Protestant and Catholic missionaries alike, limited tariffs on foreign imports to 2.5 percent, and promised the payment of six million taels of silver in reparations to Britain and France. (With the tael measuring one and one-third ounces of silver, this added up to eight million ounces of bullion.) And from now on Westerners were permitted to import and sell opium.

Emperor Hsien Feng approved the Treaty of Tientsin under duress because it was the only way he could get the Foreign Devils to leave North China and stop threatening Peking, although they would be back in a year's time to get final ratification. Meanwhile the emperor ordered the Mongol general Seng-ko-lin-chin, his foremost military commander, to repair the Taku Forts and get ready to defend them.

In June 1859, when it was time to exchange ratifications of the treaty, the Allies returned under the leadership of Frederick Bruce, with thousands of soldiers and many ships of the line.

General Seng advised the foreign envoys that it was forbidden to enter the Peiho River by way of Taku. The emperor's personal wish was that they should "anchor their vessels of war outside the bar, and then, with a moderate retinue, proceed [overland] to the capital for the exchange of treaties." This was not a deliberate provocation. There was another harbor in the mouth of the Peitang River just to the north, where they were invited to land. The American envoy, John Ward, agreed to this request and took the overland route, and his treaty was ratified without incident.

Although the Chinese position was correct, for a third time British representatives in the field began hostilities against China upon an issue in which they were technically in the wrong, and lacked London's sanction. Disregarding the emperor's not unreasonable instructions, Frederick Bruce ordered an attack on the Taku Forts.

"It grieves me," wrote the missionary-linguist W.A.P. Martin at the scene, "to see the more enlightened party so continually in the wrong." On hearing of the attack, Lord Malmesbury, then the British foreign secretary, wrote in his journal: "Accounts from China are very sad; and if true, Mr. Bruce is to blame."

General Seng had done much to improve the Taku Forts; defenses were now well constructed, and this time the Chinese had blockaded the Peiho River with iron chain instead of bamboo. Bruce ordered Admiral Sir James Hope to clear the blockade; at low tide on June 25, 1859, some six hundred marines and engineers were dispatched across the broad mudflats to remove the obstructions. While they struggled waist-deep in the mud, the Taku Forts opened fire, with surprising accuracy. More than fou[r] hundred men in the landing force were killed, and Admiral Hope w[as] severely wounded.

Stunned by the defeat, Frederick Bruce withdrew the Allied force [to] Shanghai. For a change, the Chinese had won. In Peking the Manch[u] were jubilant. The successful repulse of the British at Taku convince[d] them of their renewed military prowess. But it was a victory they woul[d] soon regret.

In London the press howled for vengeance. The public was inflame[d] by business interests who saw an opportunity to teach China a lesson [it] would never forget. Englishmen were assured that their defeat in th[e] Peiho delta mud was the result of a treacherous ambush by the cunnin[g] Mongol, General Seng, and that the Taku cannon had been manned n[ot] by "stupid Chinese" but by skilled Russian artillerymen. Once again Lor[d] Elgin was ordered to head a new punitive force to China, to bring th[e] young emperor to his senses. A personal apology was demanded fro[m] Hsien Feng, along with a heavy indemnity for the loss of soldiers, sailor[s] and ships. The French again sent Baron Gros.

Elgin's second punitive expedition to China set out in the summer [of] 1860. This time the Allies did not approach the Taku Forts directly. The[y] landed without opposition three miles up the coast at Peitang, then a[t]-tacked the forts from the rear. When the forts surrendered, the Alli[es] again occupied the city of Tientsin. By August 1860 the British an[d] French armies had reached Tungchow at the head of the Grand Cana[l,] only five miles east of Peking. The Manchu protested every step [of] the way.

At this moment Emperor Hsien Feng and his family were not in th[e] Forbidden City but at the Summer Palace in the northwestern outskirt[s,] under the protection of the Imperial Guards. The foreign invasion [of] North China had caused the court to polarize into two distinct faction[s.] The more powerful were the Gang of Eight and their supporters, th[e] Ironhats, who still refused to compromise, no matter what the cons[e]-quences, urging withdrawal into the interior of China if necessary. The[y] formed an iron ring around the emperor, isolating him from other adviser[s] and even from members of his own family. The Gang of Eight wante[d] Hsien Feng to take his empress, his consorts, and his concubines—includ[-]ing Yehenara and her son, the heir apparent, who was now four year[s] old—out of Peking to the imperial retreat at Jehol 110 miles north, beyon[d] the Great Wall. The Gang of Eight would of course accompany them [to] Jehol and would go on making decisions for him. There the court woul[d] be safe from barbarian treachery until this confrontation was settled. Th[is] would free General Seng's army to concentrate on exterminating th[e] Foreign Devils around Peking.

Opposing the Gang of Eight was a more pragmatic group of Manchu princes and Chinese officials who realized that only a negotiated settlement would rescue the regime from disaster. Given the Manchu's long-standing prohibition against the formation of any factions, cliques, or political parties, these pragmatists were in constant jeopardy. They were not yet in a position to do more than present their opposing views circumspectly and submissively, or risk immediate execution. They were led by the emperor's favorite half-brother, Prince Kung, who urged Hsien Feng to remain at hand to oversee the resolution of the crisis. If the emperor was present, his decisions could be implemented immediately; if he was at Jehol, each decision would be delayed for days.

While Hsien Feng waffled, slow but steady progress was being made in talks between Manchu negotiators and Harry Parkes, who was acting as spokesman for Lord Elgin. But on August 18, Parkes discovered a Mongol army of some twenty thousand men taking up battle positions between him and Peking. When he protested, Parkes and his companions were taken hostage.

Emperor Hsien Feng had flip-flopped once again and decided to go to Jehol, leaving the field clear for a military showdown, which he was certain his armies would win. This nullified all the points of agreement so far reached by Parkes, infuriating Lord Elgin. He instructed the British commander, General Sir James Hope Grant, to march his troops on to Peking: "the bad faith of the Chinese releases us from any obligation to restrict our advance" and "the safety of Mr. Parkes, and of those who are with him, will be best consulted by a forward movement." It is curious to hear Lord Elgin condemn the Manchu throne for "bad faith" when the Arrow War and all its grotesque consequences resulted directly from the lies Parkes and Bowring had told about the *Arrow.* Allied artillery immediately began pounding the Mongol positions. Towering Irish chargers bore down on the tiny Mongol horses, knocking them aside, while grapeshot fired at belly level decimated horse and infantry. The Mongols were swept away like crumbs from a table.

News of the defeat galloped everywhere. Nearby at the Summer Palace the court ladies were in a state of wild alarm. There was hasty packing of hundreds of carts filled with the wardrobes and personal effects of the empress, the consorts, the concubines, and the families of senior officials. Many treasured items—the majority of the contents of the palaces—had to be left behind. It would take the better part of a week to reach the relative safety of the Great Wall, so there was no time to waste. Imperial Guard regiments hurried off with their quartermasters to clear the road for the emperor's sacred chariot. Stones had to be swept off the royal way, and the surface had to be dusted with egg-yolk yellow chalk. Emperor Hsien Feng ordered his half-brother Prince Kung to remain in Peking and look after things: "You are appointed to stall for time and are to communicate with the Barbarian chieftains in your name only." Kung was to be assisted by his father-in-law, Grand Secretary Kuei Liang, and Grand Councillor Wen Hsiang.

At sunrise on September 21, while the emperor and his court were still packing, the Allies advanced along the Grand Canal to Palikao, where the French army found their stone bridge blocked by massed Mongol cavalry. A grisly battle followed in which a thousand Mongols died. In the five battles the Allies had fought so far, they had lost only twenty men.

If they had proceeded around the capital to the north, in the direction of the Summer Palace, they could have cut off the emperor's escape and captured the entire court, but Elgin did not know this. He ordered a halt to await the arrival of siege guns coming upriver from Tientsin, which would take a week. The walls of Peking were eighty feet thick.

In the darkness before dawn on the morning of September 22, 1860, Emperor Hsien Feng and his great entourage—including the Ironhats Prince I, Prince Cheng, and Su Shun; the empress; consorts; concubines; Yehenara and her son—left the Summer Palace in sedan chairs and carts drawn by mules, headed for Jehol in a procession five miles long. They were preceded and followed by a brigade of Imperial Guards, wagon trains, and three thousand eunuchs, all decorated in silks and satins, flags, banners and bunting, as if they were off to a picnic.

Elgin's forces remained at Palikao for nearly two weeks while Prince Kung, the new chief negotiator, did what he could to delay. When the siege guns arrived at last on October 5, the Allies heard a false rumor that the emperor was still at the Summer Palace. It was agreed that the Allies would advance separately around the north side of Peking, to rendezvous the following day at the Summer Palace to capture whoever was there. The British were delayed fighting off harassing Mongol cavalry, so the French went on ahead.

The next day, October 7, Elgin discovered where the French were. "We hear this morning that the French and our cavalry have captured the Summer Palace of the Emperor. All the big-wigs have fled."

The Summer Palace was a sprawling complex of pavilions scattered over thousands of wooded acres beside Lake Kunming, in the hills northwest of the capital. While the Forbidden City in the heart of Peking was the base of dynastic power, the Summer Palace was the imperial residence and the real seat of government for six to ten months of the year. For nearly a thousand years, fleeing the grit and heat of Peking summers, emperors had come to Lake Kunming to conduct their business and pleasure. This had been Yehenara's home the past three years. At the Summer Palace, the strict and suffocating routines of the Forbidden City were greatly relaxed. Here, as a young concubine and later as empress, she would slip away to the palace kitchens to prepare dishes of hard-boiled spiced eggs. She spent hours tending her garden and took pleasure in sending gifts of food and flowers to her friends and favorites. In the afternoons there were elaborate excursions on the lake, as twenty-four eunuchs pulled the oars to propel the imperial barge, while small boats followed behind, bearing sweetmeats, water pipes, and a portable stove to make tea.

The first of these summer palaces was built in the twelfth century; other ornate pavilions, gardens, and fishponds were added during the Yuan and Ming dynasties, hidden in groves among the hills, connected by meandering footpaths. In the eighteenth century this labyrinth of palaces was expanded at colossal cost by Emperor Chien Lung, until there were hundreds of pavilions covering thousands of acres. At his command, they were filled to overflowing with treasures and works of art from throughout the empire. By the end of Chien Lung's reign, the Summer Palace dwarfed in size and splendor any other royal residence on earth. Unlike Versailles, which was a statement for all the world to see, the Summer Palace was a secret place until the arrival of the French and British armies in 1860, which explains their complete astonishment.

The French had reached the Summer Palace at dusk on October 6, and were immediately set upon—*attacked* is too strong a word—by a small group of eunuchs left to protect the deserted estate. Making quick work of the eunuchs, the French broke through the outer gate, and in the darkness the Collineau brigade occupied the first court, having no idea what to expect next. The place was silent and apparently empty. Inner gates were barricaded and guarded for the rest of the night.

At dawn on October 7 the French were stunned by the sight of what lay before them. At that moment the British Dragoons galloped up and joined the French generals in the contemplation of this extraordinary scene. The magnificence of the Summer Palace was almost beyond description. Count d'Herrison, secretary to the commander of the French forces, who accompanied the generals and colonels on their tour of the grounds, described the personal quarters of the emperor:

The walls, the ceilings, the dressing tables, the chairs, the footstools are all in gold, studded with gems. Rows of small gods in massy gold are carved with such wonderful skill that their artistic value is far beyond their intrinsic worth. In a room adjoining the throne room were gathered all the articles for the daily use of the Son of Heaven, . . . his tea service, his cups; his pipes—the bowl of gold or silver—the long tubes enriched with coral, jade, rubies, sapphires, and little tufts of many colored silk; his ceremonial chaplets of rows of pearls as large as nuts. . . . Involuntarily we spoke in low tones, and began to walk on tiptoe on seeing before us such a profusion of riches for the possession of which mortals fight and die, and which their owner had abandoned in his flight as indifferently as a citizen closes the door of his house. . . . All was so natural, so familiar, so commonplace to him that he did not even try to save these treasures.

The main hall of the imperial library measured 40 feet tall, 30 wide, and 120 long, lined with a priceless collection of manuscripts.

The French commander, General Cousin de Montauban, ordered that no one enter the palaces, but the temptation was too much. His soldiers pushed their way in.

"Soldiers buried their heads in the red-lacquered chests of the Empress," said d'Herrison, "others were half-hidden among heaps of embroidered fabrics and silk, still others were filling their pockets, shirts and kepis with rubies, sapphires, pearls and pieces of crystal." Drawers were forced open with bayonets to disgorge piles of jewelry and precious gems. Soldiers picked up enameled snuffboxes, porcelain vases, brilliant cloisonné, jade carvings, rosewood tables, graceful bronzes, chests of carved cinnabar lacquer, jeweled music boxes, an unbelievable number of mechanical toys and clocks, which began a discordant symphony. What could not be carried off was smashed, stabbed, or shot. A French officer wrote his father, "Nothing like it has been seen since the barbarians sacked Rome."

The British Dragoons joined in. They were so staggered by the incredible amounts of gold that one officer wrote in his diary, "We could not believe it was genuine so threw most of it away, a bad job for ourselves."

The vanguard of the British main force arrived late on October 7 to find the Summer Palace a scene of utter chaos. Before everything was completely gone, British, Irish, Welsh, and Scots sprinted through the grounds, some dressed in women's silk gowns, scooping up whatever remained.

At 5:00 P.M. Lord Elgin arrived. "Alas!" he sighed. "Such a scene of desolation. . . . There was not a room that I saw in which half the things had not been taken away or broken to pieces. . . . Plundering and devastating a place like this is bad enough, but what is much worse is the waste and breakage. . . . War is a hateful business. The more one sees of it the more one detests it." Especially, he might have added, those wars that are started over false issues.

CHAPTER THREE

The Palace Coup

While the French and British armies frolicked in the secret gardens of the Summer Palace, Emperor Hsien Feng and his court traveled seventy miles into the sun-scarred hills northeast of Peking, paused at the Great Wall, then descended forty miles into the deserts to safety in the imperial retreat at Jehol. In all, the journey took ten days, and while it was done in high anxiety, it was also done in high style; they looked nothing like refugees. The imperial household rode in gaily decorated wagons, chariots, and sedan chairs, festooned with bunting, banners, and plumes. Every Manchu prince had a retinue of horsemen, each company uniformed in bright silks identifying his household. Yehenara and her son, emperor and empress, Li Fei and other court ladies, and the chief eunuchs, all rode in palanquins carried by teams of eunuchs or borne by mules, many of the women weeping through the days. The road before them was swept with feather brooms and sprinkled with yellow chalk. Every stone was removed to keep the bearers from stumbling. The four-year-old heir apparent rode the entire distance with the empress or his wet nurses rather than with his mother. Behind them an unending stream of heavily laden wagons shrieked and groaned through the autumn days. Along the way a number of strategically placed small palaces served as way stations. They reached Jehol on October 2.

The imperial "hunting lodge" at Jehol was neither rustic nor small but a city of palaces, halls, pavilions, lakes, gardens, supporting facilities, and residential areas for staff and families, with a permanent population of nearly half a million. Everything the court could possibly want was here, including troupes of clowns and jugglers.

Jehol was first developed by Emperor Kang Hsi in 1677 as a military base from which to dominate Mongol lands to the northwest. His grandson, the extravagant Emperor Chien Lung, greatly enlarged the retreat into an imperial playground five miles in circumference, with fanciful palaces set in pine-forested hills around a lake. By 1790 he had added thirty-six new buildings, including theaters for Peking opera. Chien Lung spent half of each year amusing himself in Jehol, and it was there that he received the first British envoy to China, Lord MacCartney, in 1793. To save money, Hsien Feng's father, Emperor Tao Kuang, ended the practice of spending whole summers there.

The main palace was a cluster of pavilions for formal audiences. Nearby was the Hall of Refreshing Mists and Waves, the emperor's bedroom. Hsien Feng often languished there, dictating memos to Prince Kung in Peking.

To the east was a smaller palace, the Pine and Crane Chambers, where the empress was housed with the favorite Li Fei, Yehenara, and eleven other concubines who had fled with them. The emperor's son had the run of the place, dressed in imperial yellow silks, black pigtails over each ear. At age four he was learning his first nursery rhymes, the Chinese equivalent of Western alphabet poems. His half-sister, Princess Jung An, was a year older, and the two were playmates, completely indulged by their wet nurses. It was not unusual for imperial children to continue sucking at the breast until they were eight years old. In Jehol the two children were blissfully unaware that their world had been turned upside down.

A third group of palaces, called Wind from the Valleys, overlooked the jet black lake. Here Hsien Feng came to brood on the scenery. Rising out of the firs in the distance were green and red Chinese pagodas, and the yellow tile roofs of Tibetan Lamaist monasteries. Close by was a three-story theater where Hsien Feng and his eight councillors spent much of their time watching performances, munching melon seeds, and drowning their sorrows.

For contemplative moments there was a building housing a copy of *The Complete Library of the Four Treasuries of Knowledge,* an opus of 38,304 volumes that took 160 scholars eight years to produce. Only seven copies had been made; one of the seven had just been destroyed when Allied troops looted the library at the Summer Palace.

The emperor and his ladies remained at Jehol for the next fourteen months. Their flight from Peking has been called an act of cowardice, "an open confession of utter despair," and the climax of "one of the most melancholy decades in Chinese history." Historians, Chinese and Western, blame Hsien Feng. "The timid and dissolute emperor . . . characteristically suggested that he should march out of Peking as though he intended to take personal command of his armies, but then ride away to the safety of his palace at Jehol. In the end, he hurriedly went north without even this pretence at resistance." This was not a great moment in China's history, to be sure, but it was not a great moment in the history of the West either.

There is still disagreement about Hsien Feng: Was he good or bad, bright or stupid, determined or irresolute, desperate or cowardly, incompetent or ill-advised? One Chinese historian scoffed that he was "dreaming as usual and wasting time in sighs . . . [a] weakling Emperor, fearful of his personal danger." Another argued more fairly that he "was in fact an unusually good Confucian monarch—that is, before his personality began to disintegrate under the pressure of internal rebellion and foreign invasion and he devoted himself almost entirely to becoming an expert on the Peking opera."

Among Lord Elgin's officers Colonel Garnet Wolseley concluded: "After a childhood passed in the seclusion of such palaces . . . it is scarcely to be wondered at that the royal heir should grow up into an indolent, dreamy, and impractical manhood." However, Lord Elgin himself mused that Hsien Feng "is not such a fool as people suppose."

Yehenara's biographers usually state flatly that this was the moment she became a decisive or pivotal force in the government of China, that the emperor was completely in her thrall. The biographers Bland and Backhouse tell us: "In the records left by chroniclers and diarists of that time [1850s] it is generally noticeable that the Emperor's opinions and doings are ignored and that all the business of the Imperial City and the Empire had come to depend on the word of [Yehenara] . . . particularly remarkable when we bear in mind that she was at this time only a concubine." They claim it was now that she began her career as a murderess, insisting that a "Decree was put out by [Yehenara] offering large rewards to any who should slay the barbarians." Nothing could have been further from the truth.

Hsien Feng was spending all his time at Jehol drowning his sorrows with Su Shun and other members of the Gang of Eight or with Li Fei. Yehenara saw him only in groups. Whether Li Fei played a manipulative role is open to conjecture. She may have been the inspiration for the notion that one of Hsien Feng's concubines was dominating him, re[...] him memorials and helping him draft edicts, but it is not at all cer[...] she could read and write. Su Shun would have found ways t[...] to her interference immediately, unless he was using Li F[...] a means of controlling the emperor, which is at least pl[...] at which Hsien Feng disintegrated at Jehol suggest[...] doing much to hold him together and, given the [...] ing, may have been doing just the opposite. [...] of the situation when he was alert, as su[...] Prince Kung in Peking. But these peri[...]

and it is obvious that there was a systematic campaign to destroy him. Su Shun, the man closest to the emperor, was most to blame for encouraging him to squander what remained of his energy and wits, and his motive is self-evident. When the emperor died, Su Shun intended to take power for himself as regent behind a new puppet ruler.

All the court ladies at Jehol had been through an ordeal. The Allied invasion and march on Peking had caused panic among them with reports of the approach of a barbarian horde drunkenly raping and looting every town and village on the way from Tientsin. Yehenara's own misery and fear of capture by the barbarians was made worse by her imagination, because she had never actually seen a Foreign Devil. Escaping from the Forbidden City to the Summer Palace, she had the momentary reassurance of being in a place she had come to regard as her real home, the quiet pavilions on the edge of Lake Kunming, the gardens and hidden lotus ponds and miles of cleverly contrived footpaths with arched bridges over brooks full of flashing golden carp. Then they were fleeing from the Summer Palace as well, leaving behind nearly everything worthwhile. Worst of all her tiny lion dogs, each with its own bright ribbon tied with a pearl clip. The eunuchs had snatched them away to throw down wells rather than let them be captured by the Foreign Devils and eaten. She had wept all the way to Jehol.

Jehol had brought a chilling discovery. As Yehenara watched the emperor disintegrate, she found herself unable to do anything for him because of the hostile vigilance of the Gang of Eight. If he died her world would be in jeopardy. She had been safe inside the magic circle of the imperial household, secure as the mother of the heir apparent but otherwise left to her own devices. At Jehol she was conscious for the first time of being surrounded by conspirators. To be sure they had been all around her in the Forbidden City and at the Summer Palace, but until Jehol she [...] The Grand Secretaries, Grand [...] had been so much furniture— [...] a troupe of thespians forever [...], and procedure prescribed for [...] was this layer of etiquette, and [...]cution that their real motives [...] Only a practiced ear could [...] in filigree, an idea hidden in [...]ades memorizing the past to [...] most devious made it to the [...]. It was natural for an inex[...]ed, and she had only superfi[...]own together by the escape

She was galvanized by a discovery reported to her by the eunuchs, whose omnipresence in the palaces made them exceptional eyes and ears. Patrolling one night through the empty courtyards of the main palace at Jehol, they heard sounds and came upon a disturbing scene: Su Shun was sitting on Hsien Feng's throne—in his hand one of the emperor's own porcelain dishes bearing the five-clawed dragon design—eating with imperial gold chopsticks a meal served by his own chief eunuch. They were stunned: no man but the emperor was allowed in the palace precincts after sundown; this particular chamber was the emperor's private world and nobody would dare to touch the imperial porcelain on pain of beheading; only a maniac would seat himself upon the Dragon Throne. They observed this behavior by Su Shun on many occasions and it became a central point of the official indictment of him later.

It was then that Su Shun's real purpose became clear to Yehenara for the first time. She was stricken with a sense of dread, the realization that she was helpless, unable to do anything for her husband, her son, or herself. From that night her life at Jehol was changed. Her efforts to gain access to Hsien Feng to tell him what the eunuchs had seen were always blocked by guards posted by the Gang of Eight, who insisted that the emperor was too ill to see anyone but his ministers.

If Su Shun secretly coveted the throne, the continuing sickness of Hsien Feng was deliberate, and her life and the life of her son were in jeopardy. The shock of fear electrified her, and fear for her own survival and the survival of her son caused her to think. Her political education finally had begun. What she did not know was that others shared her suspicions and were already quietly preparing to take action.

During the emperor's protracted absence from Peking, Prince Kung became China's surrogate ruler. Being forced to deal directly with the French and British matured and strengthened him and overcame that mixture of fear and loathing that immobilized other Manchu aristocrats; he was a man energized and awakened by mortal danger. Not only did he have to deal personally with the Foreign Devils, but he was repeatedly made aware by them of his deficiencies, a novelty for a Manchu prince. Robert Hart noted, "The prince is not very clever; neither is he as yet well up in foreign politics or political economy: but he is well intentioned, and is anxious to do what is right, if he could only know what *is* right and be allowed to do it. He has a great deal to contend with, being in many measures by the anti-foreign ministers, amongst the emperor's chief favorites, who have his Majesty's ear at Jehol."

Two years younger than the emperor, Prince Kung had qualities missing from Hsien Feng's character his Manchu and Chinese contemporaries showed unusual tact and imagination for a Manchu prince accustomed to having every whim fulfilled without hesitation. He believed that at this point the greater danger to the dynasty came from the civil war brought about by the Taiping Rebellion, not from the invasion of the Foreign Devils, and argued that it would be wise to come to terms with the West, so the government could concentrate its energies and resources first on defeating its internal enemies.

Kung was an oddly attractive man, with penetrating eyes and a diffident swashbuckling manner, but at the same time he was private and self-contained. No Westerner other than Robert Hart ever became close to him. He lived in a palace on a small lake near the Forbidden City, one of the Sea Palaces. Its Garden of Moonlit Fertility was the home of cranes, parrots, and hawks. Gold and black carp darted through its ponds and waterfalls, the water supplied by a blindfolded donkey turning a water-wheel. Among its pavilions was a temple for fox fairies, magical and dangerous creatures able to change into beautiful women and seduce unwitting males into joining nocturnal adventures. Kung's wife was the daughter of Grand Secretary Kuei Liang. She and four concubines bore him nine children.

During the first five years of Hsien Feng's reign, Prince Kung had served as senior prince on the Clan Council and as comptroller of the Clan Court, the two organs supervising the conduct of all Manchu. These posts gave him the leverage he needed to rally the Manchu nobility for an eventual showdown with the Gang of Eight.

In working out a new relationship with the Western Powers, the prince was helped by his father-in-law, Grand Secretary Kuei Liang, who had dealt with the "barbarians" previously in Canton and Tientsin, and by Wen Hsiang, a Manchu official from a poverty-stricken family who had risen to Grand Coun... h merit and integrity. Because of his impoverished... ng was more realistic than other Manch... nselves to have limitless power.

...le matters quickly in Peking, Prince ...nsibilities ducked by the Gang of ...the Allied armies were looting the ...teria. Without bothering to get ...Grand Councillor Wen Hsiang ...y to feed and pay the Peking ...cy commission to handle civil ...ay police security around the ...armerie. With General Seng ...er to Manchu officers whom ...Sheng Pao, who stood by ...inese mandarins also came

...ght and
...ng opposed
...whom are the
...nd are with him at
...pund
...ce Kung had many of the
...whom he was regarded by he
...While he was a playboy, he
...ter.
...ries as a snob and a playboy, he

to his aid. His difficulties were not just with the Allies but with great numbers of civilians fleeing the city in fear and confusion, leaving homes and stores open to Chinese looters. For his own safety he slept in a different house every night.

When the Allies were finished looting the Summer Palace, Lord Elgin gave Prince Kung an ultimatum to release Harry Parkes and his party within three days, or they would attack Peking itself. The prince had already decided to release Parkes, but this new threat made him dig in his heels, and he sent Elgin a note deploring the looting and demanding reparations. When he refused to surrender one of the gates of Peking, the Anting Gate on the north side, the British prepared to take it by force. Sappers were given the task of setting up a siege gun battery. The bluff worked, the gates swung open, and Peking surrendered.

On the occupation of the capital, the emperor sent urgent orders to Prince Kung to sign a peace agreement quickly and to exchange ratifications of the Treaty of Tientsin so that the Foreign Devils would stop where they were. To stall any longer might bring them to Jehol.

Harry Parkes and his companions were freed. This was a grim moment for China because Parkes was outraged by the minor indignities he had suffered during his confinement (his hair was pulled) and was determined to have some spectacular revenge. He spent several days closeted with Lord Elgin, persuading him to exact historic retribution. When Elgin discussed the question with Baron Gros, they could not agree on whether to burn down the Forbidden City or the Summer Palace. Gros preferred the Forbidden City, because it was a comparatively small area and its destruction would be visible to everyone. But Elgin perceived that the Summer Palace had a special place in imperial affections. Harry Parkes convinced him that its destruction would be a gesture the Manchu would never forget. Furthermore, after the Allied looting of the Summer Palace, burning it to the ground would erase the evidence, defining its destruction to future generations as an act of punishment rather than wanton vandalism. Only Parkes knew to what extent it was revenge for the phony *Arrow* incident—or for his vanity?

"Upon the 18th October," Colonel Wolseley recalled, "the 1st division . . . set fire to all the royal palaces which lay scattered about in that neighborhood. Throughout the whole of that day and the day following a dense cloud of black and heavy smoke hung over those scenes of former magnificence."

The destruction was completed by Royal Engineers, among them Lieutenant Charles Gordon, who placed explosive charges in many of the pavilions. Over the thousands of acres of gardens, the only building that survived relatively intact, due to inexplicable oversight, was the Pavilion of Precious Clouds, high on a hill above Lake Kunming.

Prince Kung bitterly protested the burning, but the next day he acceded formally to all the demands of the Allies. China was prostrate and had no choice but to do what it was told. The Convention of Peking included the emperor's apology for the treachery of his troops the previous year when they successfully defended the Taku Forts against the unwarranted British attack ordered by Frederick Bruce.

With the signing of the convention, the ratification of the Treaty of Tientsin, and the burning of the Summer Palace, the Allied armies withdrew, leaving the Manchu to settle their own differences.

To smooth future relations with the West, Kung proposed the creation of a special office to handle all contacts with the Foreign Powers. China had never before needed an office of foreign affairs because she had never recognized another state as an equal. It would have the drab name Tsungli Yamen (General Management Office). Prince Kung became its chief, essentially China's foreign minister, a position he occupied for the next twenty-three years. In a typically reasonable memorial to the emperor in January 1861, he explained: "If we do not restrain our rage but continue the hostilities, we are liable to sudden catastrophe . . . we should act according to the treaties and not allow the foreigners to go even slightly beyond them. In our external expression we should be sincere and amicable but quietly try to keep them in line. Then within the next few years, even though occasionally they may make demands, still they will not suddenly cause us a great calamity."

Here was a necessary job, not a popular one. To negotiate with Foreign Devils implied collaboration and treason, so officials of the Yamen were assumed to be flatterers and traitors. While Westerners thought they were dragging their feet, Chinese thought they were selling out. Ministers and employees of the Yamen came to be called "devil's slaves."

Kung did everything he could to downplay the Yamen. Its first offices were in the same Buddhist temple in northwestern Peking where Parkes had been kept, "a dirty, cheerless, barren building . . . in an infamous state of repair." Its officials all had other jobs and came to the Yamen only in the afternoons. Their workload was excessive and proved fatal to several. Wen Hsiang, complaining in his diary of exhaustion, said he felt like "a donkey with a heavy load and a tight collar."

For all its failings, the Yamen gave Prince Kung his own domain and enabled him to build a broader base against the Gang of Eight—a struggle for power that would soon reach a climax.

The emperor's long absence at Jehol was provoking scandalous rumors about how he was spending his time. Lord Elgin heard that Hsien Feng was marrying his fourth wife, while the *New York Times* savored the news that he had taken with him thirteen concubines. The Chinese themselves said he was cavorting with female impersonators in the theater at Jehol.

Lady Yehenara was never mentioned. When the emperor wanted female company it was always Li Fei.

The scholarly debate over Hsien Feng's personal failings diverts attention from the tragedy inflicted on China by the Allies and from the power struggle behind the scenes. Prince Kung continually pressed his half-brother to return to Peking: the longer the Gang of Eight kept him at Jehol, the longer Su Shun could decide policy without interference. But even after the French and British armies had gone, Hsien Feng announced that he was not coming back till spring.

There was more to this delay than cowardice. Some diplomats fatuously attributed it to the old audience controversy. It was a fundamental part of etiquette in China that anyone coming before the emperor had to kowtow, touching his forehead to the floor nine times, even members of his own family (except his mother and father). In the eighteenth century, Emperor Chien Lung had jokingly excused Lord MacCartney from performing the ritual on the condition that MacCartney refrain from kissing his hand. As Chien Lung's jest made clear, kneeling and touching your forehead to the floor was no more debasing than kneeling to kiss the unwashed hand of a monarch or pope. For diplomats to refuse to observe Chinese court etiquette signified their contempt, so emperors since Chien Lung had refused to hold audiences until the etiquette was followed. On March 25, 1861, foreign ambassadors would take up official residence in Peking for the first time, as one of the concessions exacted by Lord Elgin. They would be entitled to an occasional audience with the emperor, raising once more the problem of how to conduct an audience when Western envoys still refused to kowtow.

But this was not why Hsien Feng failed to return. At age twenty-nine his health had taken a sudden plunge. Years later Yehenara explained: "During the last year of his reign the emperor was seized with a sudden illness." His collapse began soon after their arrival at Jehol but was kept secret by the Gang of Eight, who posted guards to seal off the emperor's Hall of Refreshing Mists and Waves. His return was postponed repeatedly until April 1861, then canceled altogether. An edict said only that "further information . . . will be issued in the coming fall."

Simply put, the young emperor was crushed with mortification. He had failed himself, his country, and his ancestors. Because of his inadequacy, the barbarians had not been content to force their treaty terms but had looted and obliterated the greatest collection of treasure in the empire, destroying countless ancestral relics and prized objects left to Hsien Feng as a legacy by his forebears. For the only time in the history of the Manchu Dynasty, the imperial household had been violated, and the guilt was his alone to bear.

His own father had been driven to fatal despair by less trying circumstances, pining away by his mother's coffin. In 1861 all signs indicated that Hsien Feng might be the last of his dynasty, the greatest Manchu failure. Under the circumstances, any number of ailments that might otherwise have been minor, including those arising from excessive use of alcohol, could be fatal. Rather than restrain him, Su Shun was helping the process along.

Early in August 1861 Hsien Feng suddenly went into crisis. On the verge of death, he seemed strangely unaware of what was coming, for according to Su Shun he made no preparations for the transition to his heir.

The incumbent emperor had the sole right to designate one of his sons as his successor, or in rare cases a brother or nephew. But nobody missed a chance to interfere, least of all the royal princes and their allies. There were many legitimate ways to do so. On the death of an emperor, if there was no designated heir, the empress dowager had the right to choose among qualified candidates, in consultation with senior members of the ruling house. In an emergency, high officials of the court could decide. History had shown that nothing would stop determined princes from taking advantage of these various means, and if everything else failed they would resort to murder and even serial murder.

China had a long history of quarrels between princes, armed revolt, deposition, restoration, redeposition, murder, and usurpation. The Manchu were no exception, and all nine Manchu emperors rose to power out of succession crises. To steal the throne for himself, the tyrannical Yung Cheng (A.D. 1678–1735) substituted his name for that of the rightful heir, then after becoming emperor, killed or imprisoned his brothers to keep them from interfering. In a fit of paranoia he then introduced a system by which the name of the designated heir must always be placed in a sealed box to be opened only after an emperor's death, as a way to confirm that the presumed heir was not an impostor, as Yung Cheng himself had been. Normally, emperors had many sons, so the sealed box was to avoid fraternal bloodletting. Never before in all the generations of Manchu monarchs, however, had there been an emperor with only one surviving son. The situation in Jehol was unique. Theoretically, Yehenara's child was the only legitimate successor, but that was now in grave doubt.

If Su Shun was to be believed, Hsien Feng was too far gone to resolve the issue of succession verbally before his death, and nobody would know until after he died whose name, if any, he had placed in the sealed box. Su Shun seemed to be preparing the court for the revelation that the sealed box would be found empty.

Yehenara was therefore in great danger. Her position as mother of the heir apparent, which once had meant security and prestige, could mean her murder if Su Shun planned to block her son's succession. It would simply be reported that she was overcome by grief at Hsien Feng's death and committed suicide after taking the life of her little boy.

If she was going to do something it would have to be soon. But what could she do and who could she turn to in the midst of the enemy camp?

Women were not supposed to meddle in state affairs but did. Empresses or dowager empresses often tried to influence the choice of a successor or tried to rule as regents for a child, in order to gain personal power or to thwart a rival. Of the first 180 emperors of China, 78 initially required the help of a regent, often the dowager empress. These women were therefore in as much danger as the royal heirs. Empresses had been forced to commit suicide in order to keep their sons off the throne, and sons had died very suddenly of smallpox (always rampant in China) to make way for their rivals. In many of these cases it is difficult to tell where mischief ended and fear began.

Su Shun had three choices. If he coveted the throne for himself, as implied by what the eunuchs had seen in the empty throne room, then on Hsien Feng's death he could declare himself emperor and prepare to defend his position. Or he might name a Manchu puppet, hoping to split the opposition and rally dissidents to his side. In either scenario Yehenara and her son were doomed.

She could take no comfort from the possibility that Su Shun might choose a third alternative: to let Yehenara's child succeed to the throne but usurp for himself the role of regent to rule behind the throne. This choice was the least likely, because Su Shun had announced already that Hsien Feng had not designated his son as his heir.

A straightforward coup was certain to be challenged. His safest course was to rule behind a figurehead. A puppet of his own choosing would allow him to bargain with the royal princes. Prince Tun and Prince Chun were already in Jehol, possibly for that reason. Twenty-year-old Prince Chun was one of the militant Manchu nobles who backed Su Shun's policy of defying the Foreign Devils. Not especially bright, his loyalties were divided; he had recently married one of Yehenara's younger sisters, a shrill neurotic, so he might resist the idea of deposing Yehenara's child, his nephew by marriage and by blood, seeing more to be gained by keeping the nephew in place.

Prince Tun, who thought he had been cheated of the throne, was one of the princes most hostile to foreigners. He would shed no tears over Hsien Feng's passing, but he would go along with Su Shun's palace coup only if one of *his* sons was promised the throne or he himself was named Prince Adviser. Even the ambitious Su Shun might balk at saddling himself with a perpetually angry and violent alcoholic whose followers included some of the most ruthless generals in China.

Prince Kung remained a question mark far away in Peking.

Nobody in Jehol could be certain of the emperor's exact condition because of the tight security that the Gang of Eight had established around the Hall of Refreshing Mists and Waves. Yehenara's attempts to visit Hsien Feng continued to be thwarted. Tight censorship also was evident in Su Shun's official transcript of court affairs leading up to the night Hsien Feng died:

> The Summer Palace at Jehol was usually beautiful but the summer heat made His Majesty's life unbearable. His health deteriorated from the middle of the sixth month [according to the Chinese lunar calendar]. . . . Although his health improved temporarily in the early days of the seventh month, his condition deteriorated steadily afterwards . . . suddenly, after supper . . . on the fifteenth of the seventh month, His Majesty fainted. The court officials were hurriedly called to the palace and took turns attending the emperor. His Majesty did not regain consciousness until the early hours of the sixteenth; when His Majesty felt a bit better, he summoned all the court high officials to his bedside. . . .

According to Su Shun, and to fleet-footed eunuchs who saw to it that the news was spread immediately to the adjoining palaces, with what might be his last gasp the dying emperor had appointed the Gang of Eight as a Council of Regency before sinking back into a coma, leaving the whole matter of succession unresolved. Su Shun therefore ordered the sealed box opened and discovered that the emperor had not designated an heir in the customary fashion—the box was empty.

Hearing this, Yehenara was shocked into action. Until then she had not known what to do, but this confirmed her worst fear: Su Shun intended to push her son aside. She was risking everything, but in a matter of minutes or hours her husband would breathe his last and the chance to act would be gone forever.

According to her own account, she found her son, tore him away from his wet nurses, picked him up, and hurried to the Hall of Refreshing Mists and Waves. In the past she had always been turned back by the guards on standing orders that the emperor was too ill to see anyone but his ministers. Now, when it was evident that Hsien Feng was very close to death, the guards acted instinctively in letting the mother of the Crown Prince rush the boy to his father. They would have stopped her if she had come alone, but they were in awe of the five-year-old Son of Heaven.

The emperor's bedroom was filled with officials including Su Shun and his cronies, but they were too startled to interrupt her as she strode directly to the ornate blackwood bed, holding her son in front of her like a battering ram, and in a clear voice spoke to the pale figure under the coverlet.

"What is to be done about your successor to the throne?"

Appearing to be asleep or unconscious, Hsien Feng made no reply. Frantic that it might already be too late, Yehenara thrust the boy onto the bed, and raised her voice.

"Here is your son!"

Hsien Feng's eyes opened, resting on the boy. There was absolute silence in the chamber as his lips moved.

"Of course," he said weakly, "he will succeed to the throne." Then added, "His mothers will be his regents."

These were the last words he spoke, for a few minutes later he was dead.

From the clamor in the room, Yehenara's bold gamble had succeeded. Recalling the confrontation years later, she said, "I would not wish anyone to experience what I passed through at that time. . . . I naturally felt relieved when this was settled once and for all." It was the first major crisis in her life and one she had met with daring assertion, moving so swiftly that she acted virtually without thinking. Intuitively she had grasped the principle that for a woman in the Manchu court, survival required audacity.

Su Shun was livid with rage. By muttering these last words in the hearing of so many officials, Hsien Feng had stymied his plot to place a substitute on the throne. Su Shun would never forgive Yehenara for this. He was now obliged to make do with this concubine's child. But he was absolutely not prepared to accept Hsien Feng's final order that the boy's two mothers would act as regents.

When mother and child had been surrounded by admiring courtiers and escorted out of the chamber so that the emperor's body could be attended to, the Gang of Eight conferred secretly, then called a meeting to announce that they were abiding by the emperor's earlier designation of them, not the two women, as a Council of Regency for the child, giving each of them the rank of Special Regent. This designation made while the emperor was fully conscious, they said, took precedence over words mumbled only half-consciously moments before he died. No mention was made at the meeting of any role for the two mothers. As a Council of Regency, they would rule for the boy emperor until he came of age and be guided by their own judgment. In response to a challenge from officials who had been in Hsien Feng's bedroom during Yehenara's dramatic showdown, Su Shun declared flatly that the Council of Regency would not be subservient in any way to the widowed empress or the mother of the boy.

This caused a stir among the mandarins, princes, and military officers present, but nobody was immediately sure what precedent to follow. It had been nearly two hundred years since the last regency. There was no one alive with experience in managing such a procedure. With the Gang of Eight firmly in charge in Jehol and the area ringed by their troops, nobody was inclined to challenge them. The meeting adjourned with the princes and officials dispersing in clusters to discuss these contrary developments. For the next twenty-four hours everybody including Prince Tun and Prince Chun was scuttling from meeting to meeting, debating what was proper and correct (as opposed to their own ambitions, which they kept to themselves). Meanwhile the Gang of Eight set about shaping matters to their own liking and testing the water.

Cautiously at first they referred to themselves on official papers as "princes and ministers assisting in state affairs." Growing bolder, they changed their joint title to read "princes and ministers of the Grand Council." Of the eight, only four were properly Grand Councillors. By assuming these titles, the other four including Su Shun himself were improperly appointing themselves to the Grand Council. These were appointments only an emperor could make.

The backlash over Su Shun's refusal to elevate the two women was the beginning of a peculiar Manchu battle over etiquette, in which propriety provided the daggers. Rather than striking directly at the Gang of Eight and trying to block their grab for power, which could quickly become bloody, Manchu house rules allowed court officials to raise questions of etiquette that would accomplish the same end by tripping up Su Shun. In Jehol they all knew that the emperor's last words had appointed the two mothers as regents, and they all knew that the Gang of Eight were carrying out a palace coup by naming themselves regents. Their protests, carefully couched in the most oblique and obsequious language, were directed at honoring the emperor's last wish and observing tradition by elevating the two mothers of the new emperor. Su Shun found himself in an awkward position, facing a stone wall of fastidious mandarins and oafish princes all trying to outdo one another on the subject of virtue. It was only a Manchu parlor game but a potentially deadly one where the punishment for a violation of propriety could be decapitation or worse. Since Emperor Jung Cheng, a police state had existed under the Censorate, a reign of terror built on strict observance of propriety. Treason could be found in the most banal misstep, with the yellow silk bowstring awaiting anyone denounced. Su Shun had used this technique for years to terrorize his political enemies or to extort bribes and payoffs, so he knew how easily the tables could be turned on him.

Accustomed to getting his way by stealth, he decided to take evasive action, requesting a private meeting with the widowed Empress Niuhuru. Using all the guile at his disposal, he praised her extravagantly and explained that after regrettable delays caused by the emperor's death it was to be announced officially that she was the empress dowager of the empire. He asked her in return to cooperate with the Council of Regency by keeping one of the two imperial seals and using it to endorse the edicts and decrees the Council would issue in behalf of the boy emperor.

Empress Niuhuru, an amiable twenty-four-year-old, had lived in the palace since she was fourteen but had only a rudimentary grasp of the intricacies of government and no experience of intrigue. She was no match for Su Shun and found herself agreeing, whereupon Su Shun hurried off to call another meeting.

When the court was assembled, he announced that Empress Niuhuru was officially declared empress dowager. He reaffirmed that the Council of Regency alone would be responsible for drafting all edicts for the child, but with the full cooperation of the empress dowager. Every edict would bear two imperial seals, one at the beginning, the other at the end. One seal was in the hands of Su Shun, the other in the hands of the new empress dowager. He made no reference to the boy's natural mother, Yehenara.

Immediately there was another ripple of protest. Several officials challenged the propriety of completely excluding the boy's mother from this process, particularly in view of the emperor's last wishes. Opponents of Su Shun had found an issue to rally around.

Grudgingly, he sent a message demanding a private meeting with Yehenara. It is possible to reconstruct what happened next because the broad outlines are to be found in official versions of events published later. On his way to the meeting in the Pine and Crane Chambers, it was Su Shun's plan to offer Yehenara the title of empress dowager but to withhold the seal for his own use. He assumed that becoming a full empress dowager would placate her and mollify his critics.

When she came into the room her appearance had changed dramatically. The painted concubine dressed in iridescent silks had been replaced by a freshly shriven young Buddhist nun. Immediately after her husband's death, Yehenara had scrubbed off all traces of make-up and dressed in coarse white sackcloth, the first stage of traditional mourning in China. As prescribed, her luxuriant black hair was wrapped in strips of white cloth. She came to the meeting with Su Shun in a state of extreme agitation. Before he could say a word, she demanded that he immediately do what was correct in obedience to the late emperor's final wishes, declare her co-empress dowager and co-regent with Empress Niuhuru, and abandon his attempt to usurp the regency.

Su Shun was completely unprepared for this plain-speaking frontal assault. He had intended to beguile Yehenara as he had Empress Niuhuru, but the impertinent concubine had chosen confrontation instead. Unaccustomed to anything but compliance in women, he was momentarily speechless.

Because so many officials had heard Hsien Feng's last wishes Yehenara was more angry than afraid. Several senior mandarins had come to see her since then, to pay their respects to the mother of the new emperor as was customary following an emperor's death. They had made their support for her very clear. None of them wanted trouble with the Gang of Eight, but their encouragement gave her the will to stand up to a traitor trying to make a pawn of her child.

Su Shun counterattacked. Astounded that any woman would attempt to intimidate him, he raged at her, and told her that Empress Niuhuru had already agreed to cooperate with him and had already been proclaimed the sole empress dowager. He insinuated that the empress despised her and would never share power with a concubine.

Trapping him in his own words, she reminded him that he was speaking to the mother of the new emperor, not to a concubine. It would be prudent to show humility toward her or risk insulting the emperor himself, not only before the court but in the eyes of officials and gentry throughout China.

The rebuke stung Su Shun deeply. If he was afraid of anything it was that his many enemies would gang up on a violation of etiquette. They might differ about everything else but unite around some imaginary insult to the dragon throne. For the time being Su Shun had the advantage and intended to keep it, but Yehenara had reminded him of the need to be cunning even with concubines. He stormed out of the room.

Yehenara immediately hurried to see Empress Niuhuru to tell her what had occurred. She explained how the Gang of Eight was attempting to seize power and how Su Shun was trying to sow discord between the two of them, to set them against each other. They were both in great danger, as was the boy. Their best protection was to guard each other from the intrigues of the Gang of Eight.

Alarmed by Yehenara's warnings, the empress agreed to join forces against the Gang of Eight. In her own grief she had not realized what Su Shun was up to. When a new emperor was chosen it was customary for his natural mother to be elevated to the position of empress dowager, even if she was no longer living. It was only proper that Yehenara should be accorded the same recognition, and Niuhuru would immediately summon Su Shun to make her position clear.

The following morning, August 23, 1861, the court at Jehol was assembled and Su Shun announced without expression that Lady Yehenara, known as I Kuei Fei the Concubine of Feminine Virtue, was now elevated to the rank of empress dowager with the widowed Empress Niuhuru. The two women would not be involved in decision-making or in drafting edicts, but as ceremonial figureheads, each would retain one imperial seal, to be applied at the beginning and end of each decree as a purely symbolic gesture. Henceforth, Empress Niuhuru would be known as Empress Dowager Tzu An, Empress of the East, for her designated palace in the Forbidden City, and Lady Yehenara would be called Empress Dowager Tzu Hsi, Empress of the West.

Nobody was satisfied because Su Shun's compromise still failed to address the central problem: Hsien Feng had designated the dowagers as regents not the Gang of Eight. Again fear kept them from doing more than protest mildly.

Su Shun believed that this arrangement with the two women ultimately would prove to his advantage. The use of the seals by both dowagers would disguise his role in drafting the edicts. But he was mistaken. He and his cronies had unwittingly created a problem for themselves. They failed to anticipate that the two women, thinking independently, might wish to do more than decorate the edicts with the seals. Legally, they now had it within their power to withhold the seals if they did not approve of a particular edict or if they had a headache. And, to Su Shun's dismay, this was exactly what happened.

Meanwhile his enemies in Peking launched their counterplot. At the urging of Prince Kung, the dowagers began to receive encouragement from powerful mandarins throughout the empire. Steeped in Confucian tradition, they believed that the dowagers fulfilled much more than a merely ceremonial function; these women were an important part of the imperial chain of command. Learning of the death of Hsien Feng, these scholar-officials did what tradition said was correct under the circumstances: they wrote memorials to the new emperor by way of the dowagers instead of through Su Shun. General Seng, for example, wrote directly to the dowagers, addressing the child emperor. In so doing, he and other powerful military and civil officials went on record that the dowagers were the proper guardians of the emperor, custodians of the imperial seals, and caretakers of the state. General Seng's acceptance of the dowagers' authority, totally omitting any reference to the self-styled regency of the Gang of Eight, helped to create a situation of utmost delicacy in Jehol. As Yehenara had warned Su Shun, if he insulted her he insulted the emperor and that would almost certainly prove fatal. As the most powerful general in North China, Seng's support of the ladies implied military backing, if such was needed. The Gang of Eight had been too clever, unintentionally letting their success or failure turn on two obscure women. They would regret it bitterly.

In Peking, Prince Kung had been shocked by the news of Hsien Feng's death and angry that he was not named regent or at least Prince Adviser to the child emperor. He put his own scheme in motion quickly, for he knew that if they were given the opportunity the Gang of Eight would try to make him a scapegoat for the Allied occupation and the destruction of the Summer Palace. Kung tightened security in Peking and instructed his supporters and advisers to be even more discreet than usual: Su Shun had many spies in the capital. With the help of scholars at the Hanlin Academy, Kung sent letters to distant provinces mustering support.

Having repeatedly been refused permission to visit his brother in Jehol during the last ten months of his life, Prince Kung now had a legitimate excuse to go, as he was required by court etiquette and Confucian ethic to pay his respects to the emperor's remains, a request Su Shun could not refuse. On September 5, 1861, the prince set out from Peking with only a few bodyguards, to avoid arousing suspicion. He made the long trip without stopping and went immediately to the funeral hall where Hsien Feng's body lay in state, attended by high-ranking mourners. Also there were the dowager empresses, Tzu Hsi and Tzu An. They were hardly prepared for what followed.

As Prince Kung entered, dressed in white sackcloth, and saw the corpse of his childhood comrade his eyes filled with tears, and he broke down. The court records describe how "No sooner had he approached the body . . . than he wept. Everyone seemed moved by his visible grief. Everybody who served in the Hall also wept. No one had mourned Hsien Feng's death as obviously as Prince Kung."

His grief had an impact on Tzu Hsi in particular. Throughout her life, during the anniversary of the month of Hsien Feng's death she would become deeply distressed and withdraw from her duties. She closed down the palace theaters, refused to gamble, and threatened any who laughed in her presence. Dressed all in black (the color of secondary mourning), down to black handkerchiefs, she spent the whole of the month weeping, never ceasing to mourn her young husband even as an old woman. She did not share history's appraisal of him as a failure.

After recovering from his grief, Prince Kung requested a meeting with Su Shun and his top cronies, Prince I and Prince Cheng, along with the two dowagers. As Kung knew from his own spies at Jehol—among them the disgruntled Prince Tun and the disillusioned Prince Chun—the Gang of Eight were too busy, so he was left alone with the dowagers without seeming to have sought to see them in secret. They talked for over an hour, and Kung enlisted them in his conspiracy to topple Su Shun.

Kung also had time to see his brothers. The seventh prince, Prince Chun, was already disillusioned with Su Shun's dictatorial behavior. When Chun was excluded from secret discussions, he offered to spy for Prince Kung. The eldest of the royal half-brothers, Prince Tun, was disappointed by the pickings at Jehol, so he turned against Su Shun also and was now collaborating secretly with Prince Kung's coalition. For the only time in their lives, the royal princes stopped feuding and cooperated, with stunning results.

For the remainder of his stay at Jehol, Prince Kung was circumspect about what he said and did, attending all the funeral ceremonies and observing every detail of mourning protocol. Not once did he or his brothers protest the self-appointed regency of the Gang of Eight. He took pains to be cordial to Su Shun and his associates, and they were disarmed by his apparent lack of hostility. He kept his stay brief and returned to Peking on September 11 to huddle with his own partisans. They had not been idle during his absence. Within three weeks of Hsien Feng's death, they were ready to begin the next phase of the conspiracy.

Suddenly, high officials began sending memorials to Jehol petitioning the two dowager empresses to take over the direct administration of the empire as regents as ordered by the late emperor, in place of Su Shun and his group. Two Grand Secretaries, a Censor, and others joined the call for a female regency.

The first and boldest of these memorials attracted wide attention. It strongly supported the right of the dowagers and condemned the exclusion of Prince Kung from the list of special regents. It would be "more appropriate and convincing," it said, to choose one or two senior members of the Imperial Clan as regents or advisers to guide the child emperor and the dowager empresses on national affairs.

Furious, the Gang of Eight drafted a decree in the young emperor's name reprimanding those who had shown the temerity to propose a female regency. When the dowagers were told to apply their seals to this decree, they refused. This strategy had been the primary reason for Prince Kung's meeting with the two women during his visit to Jehol, when they made common cause. He needed their help with the seals in Jehol so that when he applied pressure suddenly from Peking the Gang of Eight would find itself caught in a squeeze.

Su Shun retaliated by withholding imperial household funds, but the dowagers were stubborn. He cut off all food and drink to the Pine and Crane Chambers and starved the two women and their entourage of court ladies and eunuchs until finally, after going hungry for the better part of a week, they capitulated.

As issued in language stylized to sound as if it came from the five-year-old boy, Su Shun's decree reveals the seriousness and the foolishness of the Gang of Eight: "There has never been in our nation's history an empress dowager's regency. . . . His Majesty, the late Emperor Hsien Feng, willed and appointed eight special regents to assist me. . . . Therefore, the suggestions in the memorial . . . are absurd. . . . These cannot be accepted, and should never be repeated." This was followed by two more edicts from Jehol: the emperor's body would be taken back to Peking by procession leaving Jehol on October 26, and the new emperor would be enthroned in Peking on November 11.

As far as Su Shun was concerned, unaware of the net now being cast around him, the matter of the regency was settled and he could return to Peking without any challenge to his absolute control. He summoned to Jehol the viceroy of Chihli, the province surrounding Peking, for a report on road security and instructed him to provide the court with two hundred carts for the return journey. There would be two separate processions. The first to depart would include the dowager empresses and the young emperor. Tradition required that the new emperor must be in Peking first to greet his father's remains. Later, Su Shun would leave Jehol with Hsien Feng's body in a grand funeral cortege. As a normal precaution against bandits, Su Shun assigned bodyguards of his choice to accompany the dowagers and the boy emperor, along with two leading members of the Gang of Eight.

When news of the forthcoming processions reached Peking, Prince Kung dispatched to Jehol his own military escort for the ladies, under the command of his most trusted general, Sheng Pao, the imperial commissioner responsible for maintaining peace and order in Peking. This rank entitled him to enter Jehol freely, to "aid the imperial return."

Sheng Pao arrived in Jehol on September 18, 1861, and with Su Shun's permission paid a brief courtesy call on the dowagers and the child emperor, normal practice for a high official or military commander. His circumspect behavior and lavish courtesy relieved Su Shun of any suspicion, and Sheng Pao's name was removed from the list of people being kept under strict surveillance. Prince Chun acted as a secret conduit for verbal messages from the dowagers to General Sheng Pao and from the general to Prince Kung in Peking.

When preparations for the court's return were complete the winding road south from Jehol through the Great Wall again became a mass of trooping colors. The dowager empresses, Tzu An and Tzu Hsi, left first with the child emperor and various officials, proceeding at a fast pace set by General Sheng Pao and his well-armed cavalry. Su Shun and his contingent followed more slowly, escorting the imperial coffin in a traditional funeral procession, stopping each night at palaces along the way.

The object was to lure the Gang of Eight back to the capital. So long as they remained in Jehol, they were protected by a military force loyal to them. If they could be obliged to leave their remote sanctuary, they could be intercepted as they passed through the narrow mountain defiles south of the Great Wall.

Pressing ahead, General Sheng Pao and the dowagers made the ten-day journey in only six days, arriving in Peking on the morning of November 1, three days ahead of the funeral procession. All around the capital, Prince

Kung had posted large numbers of troops, seeming to be part of the color guard greeting the court.

When Tzu An and Tzu Hsi reached the Forbidden City, they were met by Prince Kung, Grand Secretary Kuei Liang, Grand Councillor Wen Hsiang, and others. The following day a decree was issued in the name of the child emperor, sealed by Tzu An and Tzu Hsi, removing the Gang of Eight from all political office and ordering their arrest while an investigation of their loyalty to the throne was carried out. Orders were issued for the imprisonment and trial of every member of the Gang of Eight "of whose unscrupulous duplicity, corruption and arrogance, with undue assumption of power, there was abundant proof."

Two of Su Shun's circle who had escorted the empresses to Peking ahead of the rest, Prince I and Prince Cheng, were immediately taken into custody. The others, still two days away, were charged with "subversion of the state" and mishandling of foreign affairs (meaning the Allies' invasion). The edict that had been issued on the eve of Hsien Feng's death assigning the Gang of Eight the powers of regency was declared a forgery, amounting to subversion of the state.

Prince Kung sent General Sheng Pao out with a strong force of cavalry to intercept the others. They took the Gang of Eight by surprise at the town of Panpitien below the Great Wall. Prince Chun, who was traveling with the funeral cortege, then revealed his part in the plot and was given the honor of personally arresting Su Shun.

In an empire where government customarily moved at a glacial pace, the treason investigation was concluded with extraordinary speed. Imperial decrees of November 3 and 5 were directed solely at Su Shun, and no words were minced. He was called a traitor, a usurper, a bribe-taker, and was accused of having a "generally unspeakable wickedness," covering any judicial oversights. He was stripped of all titles and honors, his properties in Peking and Jehol were confiscated, and a search began for the hidden treasure he was believed to have. Although a sentence had not yet been passed, edicts warned people not to attempt to conceal any of his treasure, or they would suffer the "same punishment which is to be inflicted upon Su Shun."

The precise crimes of the Gang of Eight were published in an edict of November 8:

On the day of [Hsien Feng's] death, these ... traitors claimed to have been appointed to a Council of Regency, but, in fact, His Late Majesty, just before his death, had commanded them to appoint us [the dowager empresses] Special Regents, without giving them [the Gang of Eight] any authority whatsoever. ... This title [of Special Regent] they proceeded to arrogate to themselves. ... Moreover, they disobeyed the personal and express orders given them by the empress dowagers . . . they openly asserted at an audience their claim to be the Special Regents and their refusal to obey the empresses. . . . As to Su Shun, he insolently dared to seat himself upon the imperial throne. He would enter the palace precincts unbidden, whether or not he was on duty. He went so far as to use the imperial porcelain and furniture for himself. He also demanded an audience with the empresses separately, and his words when addressing them indicated a cunning desire to set one empress against the other, and to sow seeds of discord.

The only question remaining was punishment. As princes of the blood, Prince I and Prince Cheng were permitted to commit suicide. Lesser members of the Gang were deprived of all rank and honor and were sent in disgrace to distant provincial exile in the western deserts. The only member of the Gang not punished was Prince Kung's brother-in-law, Ching Shou. It has been said that he was spared because of this family connection, but the real reason is that he was Prince Kung's mole within the Gang of Eight. He was rewarded rather than punished, keeping his dukedom and holding various high positions until his death in 1889.

Su Shun's fate was a matter for special consideration because he had personally insulted, bullied, and starved both dowager empresses, who were hardly going to let that pass. In the edict of November 8 issued by the empresses, he was said to deserve lingering death by slow dismemberment, the Death of a Thousand Cuts. This is a classic form of execution practiced by every dynasty in China's history and was a routine method of torture used by Dominican monks in Europe during the Inquisition, so while it is chilling evidence of Tzu Hsi's capacity for sustained anger, it was not at all exceptional in cases of high treason. She probably chose it as the most frightful execution from a list read to her, for she would have had no more acquaintance with beheadings and torture than any of the other court ladies.

After long debate in the Clan Court, it was resolved that "to preserve the dignity of our imperial family," Su Shun was simply to be decapitated. Where, of course, was another matter.

Ordinarily, a man of Su Shun's stature would not have been beheaded in public in the usual place, Peking's vegetable market on Greengrocer Street. This was done to disgrace him further, apparently at the insistence of the two dowagers, who wanted him shamed for all to see. Su Shun had said and done much at Jehol to earn their loathing. He paid for it when, before a large crowd of street rabble, his head rolled among the cabbages. It was Bland and Backhouse who fifty years later invented the "real reason" for the execution of Su Shun. It was not because he had committed treason and staged a palace coup, they claimed, but because he had turned down Tzu Hsi's sexual advances, telling her plainly "that too many men had known her charms for him to wish to make one of that great company."

Although anti-Manchu propagandists later insisted that Tzu Hsi was the mastermind behind everything that unfolded, there is no evidence that either of the empresses at this time was more than a participant in a much larger power struggle centered on Prince Kung and Su Shun. Bland and Backhouse wrote that "she put into execution the bold plan which defeated the conspiracy and placed her at the head of China's government." Not so. By themselves, the women had been at Su Shun's mercy.

Prince Kung might have sent emissaries to consult the two women and to get their secret cooperation before he himself enlisted them during his visit to Jehol. But an assertion like Backhouse's that "Prince Kung . . . at this time was in secret correspondence with [Tzu Hsi] whom [he] . . . had already recognized as the master-mind of the Forbidden City" is the nonsense of a man obsessed with women as demon manipulators. Neither dowager could read or write, so they could hardly have carried out secret correspondence with Prince Kung or the much broader campaign of furtive correspondence needed to rally support from governors, viceroys, and other high officials throughout the empire. What took place was the performance of a large and well-rehearsed orchestra, not a solo on a single stringed instrument.

Bland and Backhouse promoted the absurdity that Emperor Hsien Feng remained at Jehol in order to keep Tzu Hsi—then merely a helpless Yehenara—away from her real lover, the Manchu general Jung Lu, in Peking. Others insist that Yehenara alone persuaded Hsien Feng to flee to Jehol, so it was her fault that the Summer Palace was destroyed, an assertion that does a great disservice to the memory of Sir Harry Parkes. A British author declares flatly: "In 1861 [Yehenara] destroyed the emperor by poison." Knowing nothing of Manchu paranoia about tight supervision of palace medicines, he claims she had charge of the emperor's drugs and increased the dosage with the help of her perennial co-poisoner, the always-evil eunuch Li Lien-ying. One Western writer, adding his own embroidery, said Su Shun persuaded the emperor to sign a secret decree ordering Yehenara to commit suicide on his death. He fails to explain why Su Shun did not make use of it, but he claims it was never seen by anyone because it was stolen by her. Another version of this fiction claimed that the dying Hsien Feng gave Empress Tzu An a secret decree to protect her from Yehenara, "which she was only to use in case of extreme emergency." In it the emperor supposedly wrote that Yehenara was "crafty and hard," and if she caused trouble Tzu An had full power to have her executed. No such decree ever surfaced, even during periods when the two dowagers were supposed to have fallen out. On the other hand Li Fei did vanish immediately after Hsien Feng's death, which opens up avenues of speculation about her real part in all this. Unaware that Yehenara/Tzu Hsi was illiterate, others repeat the bromide that she spent many hours reading the dying emperor official papers and advising him what to do and could do this because she had cast a sexual spell over him, when, in reality, his constant companion to the end was her rival Li Fei. These writers generally agree that Yehenara was behind all the tragedies that struck the Ching Dynasty for half a century from the time she first entered the Forbidden City. It is a very simplistic view of history.

In 1861 the real struggle was between the Gang of Eight and the rival coalition of Manchu nobles and senior Chinese government officials led by Prince Kung. Su Shun lost the struggle not because of convenient poisonings and sexual frenzies by a Manchu Lady Macbeth but because he was outmaneuvered by Kung. And Prince Kung was only doing what previous emperors had shown was absolutely necessary to a healthy reign: purging all rivals who covet power. He needed the dowagers in the short term to pinch Su Shun in a forceps; in the longer term he needed them as symbols of legitimacy in the transfer of authority back to the traditional power centers he and his associates controlled in Peking.

Yehenara started the trek to Jehol as a frightened refugee from the Summer Palace holocaust, a position as innocent as that of the fifteen-year-old Lady Jane Grey during the Tudor succession crisis of 1553. In Jehol, she was surrounded by conspiratorial, unscrupulous courtiers who would stop at nothing to gain control of the throne and who would not hesitate to make use of her or anyone else in the process. Had she, like Grey, shown a willingness to cooperate passively with the conspirators instead of being hostile toward them from the outset, Su Shun would have jumped at the chance to make her and her son part of his conspiracy, and she would have become one of the targets of Prince Kung's countercoup, ending up beheaded like Lady Jane. Instead, acting entirely on her own in the midst of the enemy camp, she took the dangerous but correct path of insisting on her son's succession and pressing for her own acknowledgment as dowager empress. To her credit, she defied Su Shun before she was approached by Prince Kung and became aware of the larger conspiracy he represented. Her initiative at Jehol provided the foundation for her reputation in China of having great strength of character and for the esteem in which she was held by Chinese scholar-gentry over the coming decades. She earned the grudging respect of men who, being Confucians, found it difficult to respect a woman on any terms.

The fate of Li Fei remains a mystery. Since she was at the emperor's side to the end, she may have been the real inspiration for the persistent mythology that one of the emperor's concubines helped him to his doom.

Could she really have persuaded Hsien Feng to flee Peking, to hide in Jehol till the Foreign Devils were gone, and then to drown himself in drunken revelry? If anyone led him astray it was his chief adviser, Su Shun, who may or may not have enlisted Li Fei's help. We may never know, for by suicide or murder the mother of Princess Jung An disappeared.

In an urgent dispatch to Washington reviewing the dramatic turn of events at Jehol and Peking, the first American minister to reside in Peking, Anson Burlingame, advised the secretary of state that "there has been a court revolution at Peking in which the old Council of Regency was overturned and all its members put to death or banished or degraded. The Dowager Empress [Tzu An] has been declared Regent and Prince Kung . . . is her chief Minister."

The American minister was not aware that there were *two* dowagers in the palace. In reporting from China, such mistakes were the rule rather than the exception. As the consort I Kuei Fei, Yehenara was confused with Li Fei. Now that she was to be called Tzu Hsi why not confuse her with Tzu An? Burlingame's mistake has since been topped many times over. When she died in 1908 after reigning for nearly half a century, even the usually scrupulous *New York Times* could not get it right, referring to Tzu Hsi throughout its obituary as Tzu An. And more than eighty years after this obituary gaffe, scholars at Harvard's East Asian Institute continue publishing books in which there is only one dowager empress—Tzu Hsi—as if Tzu An had never existed.

CHAPTER FOUR

Behind A Gauze Curtain

Prince Kung's coup was concluded by the enthronement of the five-year-old emperor in the Hall of Grand Harmony. A new reign was declared, and the boy was given the title Emperor Tung Chih, meaning both Return to Order and Joint Control—signifying a new period of government by coalition. This was in part a political hedge designed to avoid two problems: a true regency and direct rule by women.

The coalition was being extremely careful to stress the temporary nature of the role the dowagers were playing for the boy emperor. In a male-dominated Confucian society delicate sensibilities were involved. By their choice of the reign name Tung Chih the coalition members were harking back to an ancient precedent, attempting to reassure supporters who were horrified by the prospect of female rulers. Although there was no Salic law in China, excluding females from succession to the throne, there was an unwritten prohibition: a woman absolutely must not become monarch. Even the idea was considered dangerous. During the Sung Dynasty (A.D. 960–1279), when the death of an emperor led to the possibility of an empress regent, scholar-officials insisted that all edicts issued by her should bear the word *tung,* meaning "together with, jointly," in order to emphasize that it was the emperor, no matter what his age or condition, who remained the ruler, not his mother.

Under the Manchu, the title of regent had taken on the ugly connotation of usurper. In all the years of the Ching Dynasty there had been only one official regent—Dorgon, who exercised absolute power for six years after the Manchu gained control of China in 1644. When he died very suddenly (possibly murdered), his enemies vilified him so thoroughly that his image, and the image of a regent, never recovered. So in 1861 nobody wanted a true regency if it meant another Dorgon.

Direct rule by women was even more frightening. There had been female regencies in China before, but only for very brief episodes when it was necessary to dethrone an emperor, to enthrone a prince, or to announce surrender to an enemy. On those occasions, an empress mother or a widowed empress was asked to assume authority as regent temporarily, purely as an emergency measure. The most famous case was that of the Empress Lu in 170 B.C. She set the precedent for an empress dowager to issue imperial edicts in her own name and herself named two successors to the dragon throne. She was said to have poisoned one of them when he became contrary. In 74 B.C. the powerful General Huo Kuang raised an empress dowager to the role of regent temporarily, in order to dethrone Prince Chang-i. Twelve hundred years later, in 1127, the Sung emperors were captured and taken away by the Jurched Tartars; the puppet who ruled in their place, not wanting to assume the throne himself, promoted an imperial consort to regent and had her proclaim a prince as emperor, founding a new Southern Sung Dynasty. Traditionally, therefore, female regents appeared only momentarily, when they were needed as a figurehead or as a cat's-paw for a powerful man operating behind the scenes, or for a powerful clan or faction needing a gauze curtain to hide its political moves. Such was the case with Prince Kung's coalition and the two dowager empresses.

Something just short of a regency was needed. The backing of a number of powerful Manchu and Chinese clans, viceroys, governors, and generals had given Prince Kung the leverage he needed to overthrow the Gang of Eight. For his coalition to seem legitimate it needed to have the dowagers as figureheads but without vesting absolute power in them. Power would be shared among the members of the coalition.

To win support, Prince Kung and his allies launched a propaganda campaign in which they referred to the helplessness of the "orphan and widow[s]," the "tender age" of the emperor, and the "hazardous and troublous times and situations." Every effort was made to press home the point that until the emperor came of age, the government of China would be conducted not by a single man—a reference to Su Shun, to Dorgon, and to other usurpers of the past—nor by a single woman.

Prince Kung's detractors, among them his jealous older brother Prince Tun, continued to prey on ancient fears of the danger of women meddling in politics. The eldest prince was always a spoiler. He had dreamed of a larger role for himself in the dynasty's affairs and had been soured by disappointment. Prince Kung managed to keep him at bay, and Tun never held a prominent post in the administration; however Tun did represent a dark force leading the ultra-conservatives, and through his personal alliances with Chinese and Tartar generals, had to be reckoned with. Over the years, Tzu Hsi often sided with Prince Tun when least expected because she felt at the time that his position was the correct one on a

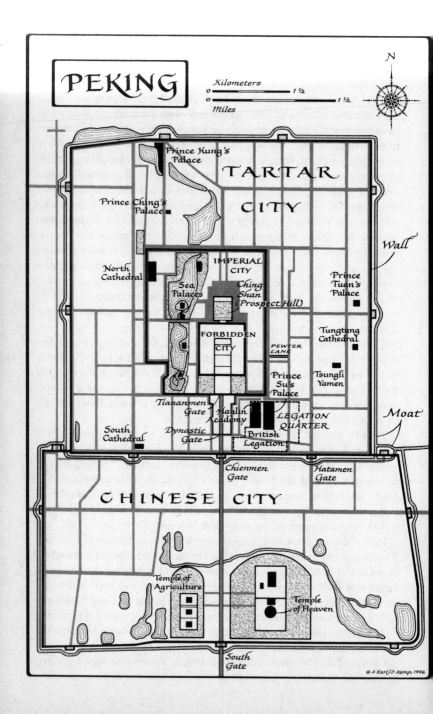

particular issue, however unpopular it might be with the moderates. Her occasional support surprised Tun as much as it did his enemies. But it established a bond between them that helped to balance the continuous rivalry of the royal princes. Later, his sons would use this bond to insinuate themselves into Tzu Hsi's inner circle.

In educated Confucian society, dark warnings were always circulating about the troubles that came when concubines were allowed to interfere in matters above their station, particularly in politics. This fear had been incubating for more than a thousand years, and Prince Tun revived it continually.

Everybody knew about the most celebrated concubine in Chinese history, Yang Kuei-fei, adored by the Tang emperor Hsuan Tsung (A.D. 712–756). Her patronage raised so many of her relatives to high positions that factional strife broke out at court, leading to the An-Lushan Rebellion. When the emperor had to flee for his life, his bodyguards insisted that his concubine be turned over to them, and they strangled her.

The only instance in more than a millennium in which a woman had achieved absolute power in China was also during the Tang Dynasty—the notorious Empress Wu (A.D. 625–705). Like Tzu Hsi, Wu began as a concubine and ended an empress. In Wu's case she became not just a reigning empress but China's absolute monarch. She did not take power suddenly by palace coup but through a long drawn-out process during which she had ample time to develop her political skills, to learn protocol, to learn to read and write, and to cultivate powerful courtiers. In this respect alone, Wu was much better prepared than Yehenara was in 1861 when she abruptly became Empress Dowager Tzu Hsi, so there is little similarity between the two women.

It was the fear of another Empress Wu that was making the Confucian gentry, as well as many Manchu princes, nervous about Tzu An and Tzu Hsi. There are only a few hard facts about this extraordinary woman, Wu, and over the centuries they have been overlaid by a mass of delicious or slanderous anecdote, concocted by authors of "secret histories." These so-called histories blend fiction and fact to make entertaining reading, much of it hilariously erotic or pornographic, in the tradition of Chinese sex novels. They really are not histories at all, but Westerners have often made the mistake of taking them literally. There are also many Empress Wu jokes and sly insinuations that can be made about any woman simply by likening her to Empress Wu. Peking operas have fantastic villains modeled on Wu. Like a witch or a vampire, she has been invoked to frighten every Chinese child: if you don't do this or that, Empress Wu will get you. Poor Wu.

According to these secret histories, during her teenage years as a concubine in the bedchambers of Emperor Tai Tsung, Wu had become a sex fiend and a witch—or fox, which in China means the same thing. Before he died, they say, she seduced his spineless heir, Crown Prince Kao Tsung. According to one chronicler, Wu surprised the young prince while he was changing his clothes and debauched him on the spot. When she was retired to the convent with all the other spent concubines on the death of her emperor, it was just a matter of time until the young heir came to see her, and brought her back to the palace to comfort and guide him.

Conservative statesmen were said to have been shocked that the paramour of the father was now the paramour of the son. It had the stink of incest. They tried to block Wu's rise. One by one she disposed of all her female rivals. The legitimate Empress Wang was in Wu's way, so she was doomed. According to legend the foul deed was done in the year A.D. 654, when Wu bore the young emperor a daughter. She invited Empress Wang to come see the baby. After the empress finished paying her respects, Wu supposedly suffocated her own infant; moments later Emperor Kao Tsung walked in. Wu burst into tears, crying that the empress had just been there. The emperor was enraged; he accused Empress Wang of murder and witchcraft and had her imprisoned in a tiny chamber on the palace grounds. Its doors and windows were bricked up, and there was only a small opening through which food was passed. Wu was promoted from concubine to empress in her stead.

One day, as the emperor passed Wang's cell, his former empress called out plaintively, begging him to name her prison the Court of Remembrance. When Empress Wu heard of this, she ordered the prisoner beaten to death. The executioner then cut off the lady's hands and feet and threw what remained into a brewing vat. All very colorful.

To show that this cruelty was characteristic of Empress Wu, the secret historian tells about another unfortunate, a comely niece who briefly turned the foolish emperor's head; Wu put ground glass in her food.

The young emperor exhausted his wits in wild bouts of fornication with Wu. (In secret histories the Chinese were always witless from too much sex, so there are obvious parallels to the stories about Hsien Feng.) Chroniclers savored these orgies, dwelling on sexual details that nobody could have witnessed and in the process becoming inconsistent. They lost track of which character was abusing whom. One author said that Wu did not hesitate to "abase her body and endure shame in order to conform to the emperor's will." She subjected herself to sexual ordeals, says the chronicler, not because she was a nymphomaniac but because she realized that the throne of China could be hers alone, if she could perform sexual murder. Wu arranged to have large mirrors installed around the imperial couch, and the young emperor performed stunts with her in front of them, sexual acrobatics such as Shooting the Arrow While Galloping, described as follows: "While the woman lies on a table or any other high object, with her legs apart . . . the man runs toward her from some distance and aims at entering her at the first try." He spares us the bruising consequences of failure.

Other Wu-games required additional partners. In Twin Dragons Teasing the Phoenix, the besotted emperor and one of his courtiers simultaneously assaulted Wu's Jade Gate and her Flower-in-the-Back-Garden—a difficult trick even for a team of contortionists, but easy enough in a Chinese secret history.

During these busy days and nights, Wu somehow found time to bear four sons and another daughter. Despite the orgies that were alleged to have taken place continually, there appears to have been no question about the paternity of her children, because all of them were acknowledged as the seed of the emperor. Perhaps this, as much as anything else, shows the discrepancy between fact and fantasy in the Wu legend.

Wu thrived, but the emperor grew sickly, and by the year A.D. 660 he was a vegetable, dependent on her to manage state affairs. Of course, it was a well-known principle of Taoism that a man who did not restrain himself during sexual encounters dissipated his life force, while the female partner grew stronger. Thus writers were able to draw a clear moral from the pathetic example of Emperor Kao Tsung. Wu caused the emperor to fail in his responsibilities as a monarch. She had to be seen as a demon in order to explain her phenomenal energy and accomplishment. In a Confucian society, great energy and talent were normal for men, abnormal for women.

When the shriveled emperor finally expired in A.D. 683 the throne went to Wu's eldest son, whose young wife foolishly attempted to take her mother-in-law's place in power. Angered, Wu deposed her first son, replaced him with her second son, then became impatient and seized the throne for herself.

As sole ruler, Empress Wu no longer had to contend with female rivals for an emperor's affection. But as a lifelong debauchee she did have trouble providing for her own gratification. The commentators insist that she acquired a number of lovers—"white faces," as Chinese gigolos were known, because of their use of cosmetics. These lovers were provided by enterprising pimps among her equerries.

In A.D. 697 after ruling China one way or another for nearly forty years, Wu, now a feeble old lady of seventy-two, fell under the spell of two Rasputins, half-brothers named Chang who came to the court as musicians and mesmerized the elderly empress with flattery and sensual entertainment.

Opposition to the Changs became intense. The old empress allegedly silenced the most outspoken of the critics, her nineteen-year-old grandson, by having him flogged to death.

Using this appalling deed to justify their actions, a group of ministers and generals staged a palace coup, executed the Chang brothers, and forced the old empress to relinquish power to the crown prince.

Once the throne was taken away from a woman and returned safely to a proper Son of Heaven, harmony was restored to the empire. Wu withdrew to a secluded palace where eventually she died, leaving Chinese history an irresistible target for defamation.

How much of her legend is true cannot be established after more than a thousand years, during which the records have been purged and rewritten many times. But because of the strict privacy surrounding the throne, only a few details of Wu's life were ever known with any certainty in the first place, just as in the case of Yehenara/Tzu Hsi. The embroidery and slander all came years later, when nobody really cared what the facts were, preferring to be entertained.

Despite her largely fictional nasty reputation, historians have had to acknowledge that Wu governed China with great character, courage, skill, efficiency, and administrative ability. China's culture flowered as never before or since. The list of the Tang Dynasty's achievements during her reign and immediately following it dwarfs the accomplishments of all but a handful of China's male rulers over thousands of years. Had she been a man, Wu would certainly have been acknowledged as one of the empire's greatest sovereigns. But for a woman to achieve such things unquestionably would require sinister gifts, including witchcraft, abnormal sexual prowess, and a knack for poisoning.

"The hen does not announce a new day," says one proverb that captures the Confucian state of mind. A verse from *The Book of Songs*, assembled by the sage, admonishes:

> *A clever man builds a city*
> *A clever woman lays one low . . .*
> *For disorder does not come from heaven,*
> *But is brought about by women.*

So it was largely a wish to avoid the Empress Wu association that led Prince Kung to set up a novel coalition in 1861, with the two dowagers serving only as temporary ceremonial regents. If its durability is any measure the coalition was a success. At a time of imminent disaster, China really needed greatness, to be sure, but in the absence of greatness, durability was the next best thing. The structure of the coalition was summarized by the *New York Times* on March 29, 1868:

Since the coup d'état . . . the supreme Government has been vested in the two Empress Dowagers as Regents. . . . Prince Kung, the chief actor in the coup, [was named] Prime Minister and made President of the Great Council . . . whose function is to advise the sovereign in all public matters. . . . The highest in rank and most powerful boards or officers in the empire are the Ministers of the Presence, the Great Council and the Grand Secretariat. The Ministers of the Presence are properly a portion of His Majesty's household, and not a part of the State machinery. They are always, however, persons of the highest rank, and as they have always the ear of the Emperor, their power is very great, especially when the sovereign is weak or inexperienced. Their private influence with the sovereign frequently overrides and neutralizes the . . . Great Council. It is said to do so at the present time. There are six or seven Ministers of the Presence, of whom Prince Kung's younger brother, the seventh prince [Prince Chun], is said to be the chief. . . . The Great Council is . . . the real governing power in the empire. . . . Government action is taken either on the direct action of the Emperor or his immediate advisors, or on memorials presented by the high authorities at the Capital or Provinces. In ordinary cases . . . the memorial is forwarded through a board of registration to the office of the Grand Council where it is used and suggestions are made, or the draft of a decree drawn up for action thereon. This is laid before the Throne, and, if approved, is sent to the Grand Secretariat to be copied and dispatched.

There is no suggestion here of tyranny by any single woman; those allegations all came later.

In 1869, eight years after Su Shun's execution, the two dowagers were appraised by one of the empire's most perceptive statesmen, the scholar-general Tseng Kuo-fan, of whom we shall hear more. Tseng was brilliantly educated and a shrewd judge of humanity. Because of his exceptional competence he had risen to an unusually high station for a Chinese under Manchu rule. As he was not a Manchu, his survival at the top depended upon his endless vigilance and cunning. In 1869 he was summoned to Peking and while there had four separate interviews with the dowagers. Emperor Tung Chih, who was by then thirteen years old, was also present. Tseng's miniature portrait of the leading figures in Peking is probably closer to the truth than anything that appeared subsequently:

The ability of both dowager empresses is anything but exceptional. At audience, they had not a single important word to say. The emperor was young and quiet, thus making any guess [about his ability] impossible. The state of affairs hinged entirely on the grand councillors like Prince Kung, Wen [Wen Hsiang], and Pao [Pao

Yun], whose power surpassed that of [the emperor]. Prince Kung is extremely intelligent but lacks the steadfastness to be able to persevere in any view for any length of time. Wen Hsiang is upright, yet suffers from narrow-mindedness, and he fails to look to others to complement himself. Pao Yun is an object of criticism on the lips of many. The rest are more mediocre—truly a cause for great concern.

Tseng was perplexed to discover that Tzu An and Tzu Hsi made no deep impression on him and that they were ill at ease in his presence. He had expected the dowagers (perhaps one more than the other) to be shrewd and aggressive, especially in view of their role in outwitting Su Shun and the Gang of Eight at Jehol. After eight years as figureheads of the coalition he had assumed that the two women were skilled politicians and clever manipulators. Because the survival of men at court depended on guile and a mastery of manners, everyone presumed that the dowagers were endowed with similar survival skills. What deceived Tseng was the mask Tzu An and Tzu Hsi wore during all but the most informal audiences to guard their positions from criticism. Both empresses had been thoroughly schooled about the sensitivity of men to any appearance of slyness and cunning in women, so while the men at court sought to project an image of high intelligence, a woman's intelligence required her to hide it and to appear bland and unthreatening.

Tzu Hsi appreciated that her job at court was to be a mediator and arbiter on all issues. Success depended upon being seen as a paradigm whose only interest was to help the ministers determine the best course. In the early years she avoided pressing a view of her own.

As the fulcrum in a scale, she provided the stable point on which all state policy was to be weighed. This process involved a certain amount of theater; like priests in a temple everyone had to take the ritual very seriously. As a child she had hidden behind many gauze curtains. As empress dowager Tzu Hsi still tried to appear impassive, serene, and benign in the manner of the Buddha. She had matured since the crisis of 1860–1861, and restraint had turned her melancholy into the beginnings of wisdom. Eventually she would become an institution, surrounded by ministers who had grown up after Jehol and who treated her like an oracle, expecting her to take positions on all matters. Now in her thirties the mask she wore convinced Tseng that her impassivity was a sign of weakness and ignorance. The importance of Tseng's perception historically is that Tzu Hsi was not seen as threatening, manipulative, or sinister by one of the shrewdest men in China.

While it was judged to be mediocre, the coalition nevertheless continued to function for the better part of forty-seven years. There was no one in Peking, as Tseng said, "who could be looked upon as leading or guiding the central administration." The chief objective of the coalition was to avoid catastrophe and meanwhile to find small ways of improving the situation. Not a magnificent policy, perhaps, but in China it had been a long time since magnificent policies had brought anything but disaster.

General Tseng's evaluation that Tzu Hsi was not threatening or manipulative stands in stark contrast to that made retrospectively by Western scholars. Bland and Backhouse, the false biographers, turned Tseng's portrait of Tzu Hsi completely around: "The infinite resource, indomitable courage and personal influence of the Empress Dowager, Tzu Hsi, undoubtedly rescued the dynasty at a crisis which, but for her, would have brought the Manchus' rule to an end with the flight and death of her husband, the Emperor Hsien Feng."

Between the appraisals of Backhouse and Tseng there is such a gulf of deliberate malice that it tells us volumes about the person making the appraisal. The judgment of Backhouse is typical of historians because to this day they all depend on Backhouse, while Tseng's firsthand appraisal has been forgotten. Much is to be learned about China and about the West by discovering why the false image persists while the true is ignored. Fantasy that is self-serving is irresistible.

Although proponents of female conspiracy theory insist that Tzu Hsi was a match for Empress Wu in every sinister detail, real similarities are not easy to find (though they are easy to insinuate). Tzu Hsi may have shared Wu's ambition and vitality, perhaps some of Wu's temper, but her rise in 1861 was only to the ceremonial edge of power and was engineered by other ambitious people, all of them men. For years afterward she remained only a ceremonial figure, and when her power eventually did increase, it was attrition and longevity that transformed her into an institution. It is not an invidious comparison to say that in this respect she was more like Queen Victoria than like Empress Wu.

Tzu Hsi's participation in events in Peking was not seen as sinister at the time by Westerners or by Chinese, outside of a small circle of archreactionaries suspicious of all women. There was apprehension among Confucian gentry about the *idea* of a female regency, as we have seen, but this did not fix on Tzu Hsi in particular, any more than it fixed on Tzu An. Few people outside the court had more than a dim idea who Tzu Hsi was. Outsiders knew of her only as the young mother of the boy emperor.

The dowagers, while still only in their mid-twenties, were complete novices in matters of state. Their training since childhood had suited them only for childbearing, flower arranging, and music and had not included the study of government or the classics. They were dependent upon Prince Kung, the Grand Councillors, and the unofficial Ministers of the Presence led by Prince Chun. Even after they began learning to read, neither Tzu An nor Tzu Hsi could comprehend official documents, because they were written in Manchu, while they were being taught to read Chinese. Translations into Chinese had to accompany each document, so the two women would understand the gist of what they were approving. (Even then, their ability to read more than a few hundred characters in Chinese at that early point has never been established with any certainty.) Neither woman had learned enough about protocol to be able to dictate imperial edicts much less write them. So intense was the etiquette of the court that the bureaucratic machinery would have frozen, unless senior officials spoke and acted for the ladies. No evidence has come to light that anyone other than Prince Kung, and later Prince Chun, ever played such a role. We do know that tutors were assigned to read to the dowager empresses daily from the classics and to teach them to read and write, and both women eventually took delight in being able to brush auspicious characters onto scrolls, which they presented as gifts.

Neither woman had a firsthand knowledge of events outside the Forbidden City, except what she saw through the curtains of her sedan chair as she passed in her processions on visits to the imperial tombs. Tradition required that all houses along the route be shuttered and all citizens remain behind locked doors on pain of death.

The two attractive young empresses did occupy an exalted position at court, not because of their individual power, their personal charisma, or their political acuity but because exaltation was required by Confucian etiquette.

Thanks to two thousand years of tradition, it was the office the dowagers occupied that had status, not the two women themselves. Tradition guaranteed a dowager empress an impregnable place in the court no matter what her personal qualities. Being of an older generation, she took precedence over the new emperor in all matters of protocol. When the emperor visited a dowager, he could not even sit down until she asked him to. Using protocol, a dowager could, in an emergency, overrule the emperor, but she would do so only if she could reasonably expect the support of court officials. In this way a dowager theoretically could act as a check on the powers of the emperor if he made unwise decisions. In practice such an event was exceedingly rare. It happened to Tzu Hsi only once, in the autumn of 1898.

Real power remained in Prince Kung's hands. True, all documents or memorials from the provinces and the military were sent to the two empresses, as figureheads. But we know that these documents and memorials were then sent on immediately to Prince Kung and the Grand Councillors, who studied each issue and drew up various options on which they based their recommendations. The dowagers then gave the emperor's ceremonial approval to the recommended option, by applying the two imperial seals. In the first years of their modified regency, they were not entitled to do more.

When the dowagers attended audiences with their councillors and ministers, they sat behind a silk gauze screen, whether the young emperor was present or not. Westerners who heard about this procedure thought this veil was somehow sinister, but it was nothing more than observance of the traditional segregation of men and women among the higher classes in China. In private homes similar segregation occurred. In this way women were able to participate in family life (or in court life) without seeming to be physically "present," which would have disturbed the sensibilities of Confucian males. Few foreigners in China would have known this, because they did not have access to the private lives of the higher classes. On those rare occasions when Westerners *were* invited into an upper-class or gentry household, only men were present, the women invisible.

Little historical background was understood by Westerners in China, who were dependent upon what they could learn from Treaty Port compradors or hired interpreters, who were themselves ill-informed and far from disinterested. Such people filled in the gaps in their knowledge with colorful inventions, because it was important to *seem* to know what was going on. Over drinks at the Long Bar in Shanghai or gossiping at the new racetrack, they mingled misinformation and supposition and passed it on by letter, diary, memoir, travelogue, diplomatic report, and journalism to the far corners of the earth, where it was accepted as fact.

It was only natural for Europeans to think about the two dowagers in European terms. In the West the most powerful dowager queens were both Catherines: Catherine de' Medici, Catholic regent of France from 1560 to 1574, whose bloody reign of religious repression culminated in the St. Bartholomew's Day massacre of Protestants in August 1572. And Russia's Catherine the Great who, with the help of her lover, murdered her imbecile husband the emperor and reigned alone for thirty-four years. Both were dowagers in a Western sense, "a widow holding property or a title from her deceased husband." However, the Western word "dowager" is not identical to the Chinese word "*t'ai,*" and this contributed to misunderstanding of Tzu Hsi's position. The Western term "dowager empress" implied that a royal but otherwise ordinary woman had risen above her station to execute total power in a state. Thus the term took on an exaggerated significance when it came to be applied by Westerners to Tzu Hsi and reinforced their supposition that she had acquired the title by cunning. However, being Oriental and a woman, she was also, by the measure of many Victorian men, incapable of great ability. Thus in the same breath they would assert that she was both cunning and stupid, one of the oxymorons typical of the age.

About Tzu An we know virtually nothing, except the few details already related about her Niuhuru clan, her birth, and her entrance into the imperial family following her sister's death. In all affairs requiring the attention of the dowagers, particularly the education of the young emperor, she took precedence over Tzu Hsi. Although she was two years younger, she had been Hsien Feng's empress, so she came ahead of Tzu Hsi in processions, in receipt of honors, and in homage. Typically she is depicted as meek and mild, retiring, conciliatory, and good-natured. But there is little evidence even of this. There are certain episodes in which Tzu An is said to have exhibited temper and willpower. She could be adamant and forceful in pressing her own views. So the picture of her as a nice simple girl was exaggerated later to build up the contrast between her and Tzu Hsi. Most scholars fail to even mention her.

Since childhood Tzu Hsi had lived under one matriarch or another: her own mother, then her mother-in-law, then Tzu An. If she felt resentment toward her coregent, it is hardly surprising. The self-styled reformer Kang Yu-wei and biographers Bland and Backhouse exaggerated this animus to suggest that Tzu An was good and kindly and looked after the infant Tung Chih, while Tzu Hsi was a self-centered young woman who neglected her son, encouraged him to gamble and drink and to waste his time, while she had affairs with actors and sham eunuchs, in the manner of Empress Wu. As we shall see, this simply is not true.

Tzu An was the legal mother of Emperor Tung Chih and head of the imperial household; it was her prerogative to decide the upbringing of both Hsien Feng's children, in consultation with Prince Kung. Emperor Tung Chih and his sister, Princess Jung An, were taught to obey Tzu An, to answer her summons immediately and never to dispute her decisions; she, not Tzu Hsi, decided their punishment if they misbehaved. If Tung Chih was not disciplined it was Tzu An's fault. The two dowagers issued orders jointly as required of them by the coalition, but in domestic matters and child-rearing Tzu An had precedence. This was why Tzu Hsi "found it very difficult to keep on good terms with her." This is an important point, because of the extraordinary tragedy that was unfolding with the boy.

Tzu An was absolutely hidden from curious eyes. There is no convincing record of any Westerner's ever seeing her in person. Only after her death was a portrait painted for the ancestral hall in the Forbidden City. The idea of a portrait from life was abhorrent to the Chinese. Artists were never permitted to view the remains, especially in the case of the imperial family. Instead the painter used a book containing every conceivable shape of face, eye, lip, and ear. The family chose nose number 12, mouth number 18. All such portraits were done full-face, devoid of expression or shadow, only the costume suggesting the status of the man or woman represented.

The portrait of Tzu An shows a slight figure seated stiffly on a throne, burdened by a spike hat adorned by two phoenixes made of pearls, wearing a high-collared Manchu robe and a short cape of imperial yellow silk that flared at the shoulders. She has a slim nose, small mouth, and a slight pointy chin, and her expression is dreamy and absent.

The only photographs we have of Tzu Hsi were taken when she was old and exhausted. They have the stark, desolate quality of nineteenth-century frontier photographs, which made even the eyes of children look dead, their features flaccid. Fortunately, Tzu Hsi broke with tradition and gave permission for two Western artists to paint her portraits in 1903 and 1905, and they perceived much more than the glass plate negatives.

One, Hubert Vos, was working in the palace on a realistic portrait of Tzu Hsi at age seventy when he was instructed to eliminate the realistic details. His shrewd response was to start over with a parallel portrait of the way she must have looked as a woman of twenty-five. The result is a sort of Manchu madonna, a young woman of strikingly pretty features, slender hands with jewel-encased fingernails, and the dot of red paint that Manchu women wore on their lower lip. No Westerner had ever seen her in person at age twenty-five.

Aside from her rare expeditions to the imperial tombs in the hills outside Peking, Tzu An lived the rest of her life in the Forbidden City. Tzu Hsi spent the better part of fifty years inside its walls. Only the dusty winds of the desert penetrated. Behind a broad moat the walls rose thirty-five feet, extending two and a half miles around the 250-acre enclosure, hiding scores of pavilions and palaces. The inner spaces of the forecourts were awesome. Above them rose three great audience halls, standing on huge slabs, the beams and tile roofs intricately decorated in reds, greens, blues, and yellows. Behind these ceremonial buildings stood the Gate of Cloudless Heaven, which was the final barrier. Here the Imperial Guard took over from the normal palace guard. This gate led to the Inner Courts and the private world of the imperial family, a labyrinth of courtyard after courtyard, growing ever smaller till they became the tiny cribs of retired concubines, who lived out their lives here.

Tzu Hsi's official residence was in the inner courts of the western section—hence the name Empress of the West—guarded by the Gate of the Culture of Characters. Her pavilion had high pink walls inset with small windows. Its courtyards were filled with flaming pomegranates, sweet-scented acacia, blossoming peach, plum, and cherry trees, and late-blooming chrysanthemums. Caged birds were everywhere, their songs filling the air, and Pekingese lion dogs appeared and disappeared on urgent missions, pursued by eunuchs with braided queues flying. Her pavilion contained a low blackwood throne where the young woman received ladies of her retinue or the boy emperor when he came to visit.

Her apartments were sparsely furnished by Western standards, with cushioned benches, low tables, and stiff rosewood chairs. The windows were curtained with blue silk and were open even in the coldest weather.

Her bedroom had an elaborately carved blackwood alcove bed, or *kang*, with three tall sides and the fourth side open. Its platform was laid with a thick felt pad and three softer padded mattresses covered with yellow satin brocade. Everything was imperial yellow, the sheets yellow silk, the bed curtains yellow brocade, the coverlet a yellow satin quilt embroidered with gold dragons and blue clouds. A great many embroidered pillows were strewn about, but she preferred one stuffed with tea leaves, which were believed to be good for the eyes. Another pillow was stuffed with dried flowers and herbs. Over the top of the bed the frame of carved wood was hung with tiny silk drawstring bags filled with musk. While she disliked other perfumes, she was fond of musk, which inspired her critics to spread the rumor that she "smelled of foxes." And foxes were supernatural. Like many Manchu women she smoked a water pipe, sipped honeysuckle tea during the day, and drank a cup of hot sugared water before bed.

In later years she moved across the Forbidden City to more secluded quarters, identically furnished. There a small private grotto adjoined her bedroom, behind sliding panels. At one end of it was a large rock with a yellow cushion; beside this stood an incense burner for moments of meditation. Hidden tunnels connected her palace to others in the Forbidden City. They existed long before Tzu Hsi was born, but on showing them to a visitor she remarked, "I don't . . . talk about these places . . . people might think that they were used for all kinds of purposes." (General Dorn, for one, imagined them to be the settings of trysts and murders.)

She had no privacy unless she demanded it. Attendants were ever-present: two handmaidens in her bedroom, two eunuch guards in the antechamber, four more by the red lacquered doors, a dozen others within call; six more ladies waited patiently in rooms on either side of the courtyard.

New handmaidens were chosen for these duties every spring, when the daughters of the lowest of Manchu families were brought to the Forbidden City. Head eunuchs picked those they thought would please the two dowagers. In the palace these handmaidens all wore blue silk gowns, their hair parted at the side and braided in a single long queue, tied with red silk cords. The girls, ages ten to sixteen, remained in imperial service for ten years, then were given a pension and a wedding trousseau. A few remained their entire lives, keeping house, overseeing new handmaidens, or directing the work of lower eunuchs.

Customarily, emperors and mandarins rose between midnight and 3:00

A.M. to begin their duties. Tzu Hsi's breakfast was a bowl of hot milk and lotus root porridge, followed by an elaborate toilette. After bathing, she tied on a soft cotton flannel bib or apron, followed by a pair of silk pantaloons tied with a drawstring, then a flannel camisole. On top of this underwear, a maid helped her slip on one of hundreds of silk or satin gowns that she wore casually around the pavilion.

It was a eunuch, not a handmaiden, who dressed her long black hair. Parting it in the center, he brought it low at the back of her ears, braided it, and made the braid into a knot on the top of her head, to form the base for the Manchu headdress, secured to the knot with long pins. Tzu Hsi was particular about her complexion. As a widow she was no longer permitted to use cosmetics, not even the dab of red on her lip. Instead she paid careful attention to her grooming, which included removing all facial hair by pulling twisted threads.

As a woman of relatively humble origins, anxious to look the part she was playing, she was fastidious about clothing and jewelry. Over the decades she accumulated three thousand boxes of "everyday" accessories, from gold bracelets set with pearls and jade to a string of pearls fashioned into plum blossoms, and a stork hairpin of pearls, silver, and coral. Most of these were gifts from admirers—mandarins or wealthy gentry seeking her favor. To display as many of their gifts as possible, she changed clothes and accessories several times a day, depending on official functions.

Preparing for an audience took hours. A typical audience costume was a yellow satin gown embroidered with pink peonies, and a headdress with flowers on each side made of pearls and jade, with a jade phoenix in the center. Over her gown she wore a cape covered with thirty-five hundred pearls the size of canary eggs. The cape was made in a fishnet pattern and was joined with two pure jade clasps. As accessories she wore pearl bracelets, jade bracelets, and several jade rings. For thousands of years it had been customary to let some nails grow long. On the little and ring fingers of Tzu Hsi's right hand were gold fingernail protectors three inches long; on the left hand, two protectors made of jade. The rest of her fingers and her thumbs were kept trimmed. Her shoes were decorated with tassels of pearls and embroidered with tiny pieces of different colored jade.

When all was ready, she was carried in a sedan chair borne by eight eunuchs to one of the great audience halls. The head eunuch walked on her left and a second chief eunuch on her right, each with a steadying hand on the chair poles. Four eunuchs of the fifth rank walked in front, and twelve of the sixth rank followed behind. Each carried something: handkerchiefs, clothes, shoes, combs, brushes, powder boxes, perfumes, pins, black and vermilion ink, yellow paper. Bringing up the rear were six handmaidens, each carrying something—a dressing room on legs.

When the boy emperor was in a good state of mind, he was placed on a throne on a raised platform in the front of the audience hall, and the two dowager empresses sat on thrones behind him, hidden by the gauze curtain. When the tedious ceremony became too much for the boy, he sat on the lap of one of the empresses, or was excused from the audience hall altogether. Ministers and officials, after performing the ritual kowtow, presented their petitions and memorials, along with the option chosen by them, and awaited the pronouncement of the two women. Except in the most unusual circumstances, it is a matter of record that the women replied, "We leave it to you," meaning that the ministers should take the course of action they had already decided was best. This procedure helped to maintain the appearance that the empresses were actively involved in decision making, which was of great importance in a country where ceremony was more important than reality. When official business was completed, the empresses returned by sedan chair to their respective palaces and changed into simpler clothes. The rest of the day was taken up with the education of the young emperor or with finding their own amusements. Tzu Hsi typically examined gift baskets of flowers and fruit sent by courtiers and looked over new bolts of silk presented as gifts. She was fascinated by such trivia, but her main loves were her pet lion dogs and her gardening. Several of the palace eunuchs were expert breeders. Tzu Hsi's pets, most of them black, lived in their own pavilion, with marble floors, and were taken for daily walks and given regular baths. She had a particular favorite she called Shadza, meaning "Fool," and had flowers tied into his hair. Flowers crowded her chambers, her loge at the palace theater, and her audience halls. She had eunuchs place fresh flowers in her coiffure, winter and summer. Courtiers sent her baskets of blooms every day from the gardens on their estates. She spent hours folding and cutting origami or twisting blades of grass into rabbits and birds. In truth there was not much else for her to do. She was a bird in a cage. Her main function in life had been to produce an heir to the throne, and that she alone had done. Now, aside from seeing to his education, which was largely in the hands of Tzu An and others, she only had to help sustain the status quo at court, by performing her ceremonial functions.

As she tended her flowers, a tutor or an educated eunuch read from ancient Chinese history, poetry, and lore. Sometimes she became impatient with dull passages and had the reader skip ahead. She took daily walks around the Forbidden City, even in the rain, a habit that annoyed court ladies whose silks, like those of the eunuchs, became drooping rags.

When all other distraction failed, Tzu Hsi was fond of a board game played with dice on a large square covered with white silk and painted with fantastic designs, representing the Earth and Fairyland. The object was to get an ivory chessman into Fairyland.

When she was pensive she called for brush and ink and practiced brushing large ideographs on four-foot-long scrolls. At other times she painted watercolors of flowers. These she gave to courtiers to show her approval.

Meals were taken wherever she happened to be. Her ladies brought a portable table with dried fruits and nuts as an appetizer. About one hundred fifty tiny dishes, each different, were then placed in long rows, all served in yellow bowls with silver spoons, ornamented with green dragons or the ideograph for Long Life. A eunuch brought a white jade pot of honeysuckle tea, and another brought slim gold chopsticks. Both eunuchs knelt on the floor, holding up trays with offerings of pork, mutton, fowl, and vegetables. Pork was served as meatballs; sliced with bean sauce or fish sauce; chopped with bamboo shoots; cooked with cherries or onions, with cabbage, with turnips; or minced with pancakes. Rice was part of the menu, but Manchu, like many northern Chinese, preferred bread: baked, steamed, fried, or stuffed as dumplings. Face made it necessary for the imperial kitchens to serve an empress very elaborate meals twice a day, but the plates were tiny, no more than demitasse saucers, and Tzu Hsi ate little from them, the rest going back to the eunuchs, who grew fat.

Her life followed this pattern for forty-seven years, from the time she was widowed in 1861 until her death in 1908. But instead of being remembered, as are so many of Britain's monarchs, for a wholesome love of dogs, flowers, and fancy clothes, she became notorious for her supposedly insatiable carnal appetites, and this infamy has been enlarged upon by biographers and historians ever since. None of them seems to have given serious thought to the fact that the original accusations made against her are all traceable directly to anti-Manchu propagandists who were actively attacking her during her last decade, from 1898 to 1908. Because the Ching court foolishly made no effort to refute these allegations, they became accepted as fact.

In 1901 a wealthy Singapore-based Chinese propagandist, Lim Boon-keng, published a book that contains all the basic fabrications. He charged that as a young concubine Yehenara had "exhibited her charms to a mighty concourse of eunuchs. . . . It was noticed that the eunuchs were mostly young men with fine physique and comely features. . . . The idle and curious, finding nothing more profitable to do, counted the number of young persons who entered the palace, became Court attendants, and then disappeared. Where had they gone? . . . gossip spread like wildfire that young servitors of the Court suffered from sudden deaths within the walls of the Imperial City." So most of Tzu Hsi's eunuchs were not eunuchs at all, but her lovers. As she used them up, she had them killed.

This basic theme was expanded greatly by Backhouse and Bland in their two biographies of the dowager, which appeared soon after her death. As

Western "experts" on China they carried more weight with Western readers than Lim Boon-keng. In their first book Bland and Backhouse touched only lightly on the secret life of the dowager, which they described as the "merry round of an Oriental Trianon." They did insinuate an element of sexual depravity by including in the book a long chapter about the imperial eunuchs and Tzu Hsi's relationship with them: "It was common knowledge and the gossip of the tea-houses, that [the chief eunuch's] lightest whim was law in the Forbidden City. . . . Under these circumstances it was only natural, if not inevitable, that unfounded rumours should be rife in exaggeration of the real facts, and so we find it reported that [the chief eunuch] was no eunuch, and . . . that [Yehenara] had been delivered of a son of which he was the father."

Having planted the idea of an illegitimate child fathered by a eunuch, Backhouse and Bland went on to expand this theme in their next book. According to an "authentic" Chinese source they quoted, the father of this illegitimate child was either the sham chief eunuch or a Peking restaurateur, both of whom were murdered by Tzu Hsi. But after publishing this canard Bland and Backhouse ultimately rejected both explanations and instead identified General Jung Lu as the father of Tzu Hsi's imaginary bastard child. Quoting "An Anhui Official," they asserted that in early 1881 Tzu Hsi was confined to her rooms for two months and "it was generally believed that she gave birth to a child, of whom Jung Lu was believed to be the father."

Bland and Backhouse claimed that as a girl in Peking there was "among her youthful playmates . . . a kinsman, Jung Lu. . . . By common report she had been betrothed to him from birth." There is no evidence of any kind to support this. Jung Lu came from a different clan, so if he was a cousin it was of the most distant variety. We can only be certain that he was one of her closest friends and supporters in later years, when he was one of the leading moderates in the government. Nevertheless, an Italian biographer describes their romance as being "In oriental form and in an oriental setting . . . the old, old story of Lancelot and Guinevere."

Slandering Tzu Hsi became a literary game over the decades. Many years later, General Frank Dorn gave the story new gloss and authority: "She contrived many a rendezvous with Jung Lu that were completely private. The ground beneath the Great Within was honeycombed with tunnels. . . . Jung Lu used one of these secret routes . . . that terminated under Tzu Hsi's antechamber, which could be reached by a stairway. . . . A bolted trap door hidden by a rug opened into Tzu Hsi's room."

Once, Dorn said, an attempt was made to assassinate Jung Lu in the tunnels. But the sturdy Manchu drove his dagger into the heart of his assailant and fought off others who pounced on him from the inky darkness. Hearing the sounds of violent struggle under the floor, the dowager "shuddered with fear." But Jung Lu survived; they made love that night, and the dowager became pregnant. Having been a widow for a number of years, the difficulties of concealing the pregnancy and avoiding a ruinous scandal would have been insurmountable for anyone but her. According to Dorn, she established a guest in her apartments, a younger sister who feigned pregnancy. When Tzu Hsi's daughter was born, the infant was passed off as her sister's child, and was taken by Jung Lu to his own palace, where she was raised with his other children.

It is an amusing idea, and one might wish for her sake that her life had been just such a burlesque filled with Florentine intrigues and Viennese frivolity, because the truth is melancholy. Stripped of the gaudy overpainting, her real character was too guarded, somber, and tragic. Under those layers of historical graffiti was a spirited and beautiful young woman trapped in a losing proposition: a dutiful widow who would have been executed in a flash if she had been promiscuous; a jilted wife who helplessly watched her husband go mad; a hopeful mother whose only son was a clown who would be murdered in gothic circumstances; a figurehead empress who lost three emperors to conspiracy; a frightened matriarch whose reputation was destroyed as she presided over the decline of a bankrupt dynasty.

CHAPTER FIVE

Two Men on a Horse

While the Forbidden City wrapped Tzu Hsi and Tzu An in an unreal world, the empire outside its walls was in the final agonies of the great Taiping Rebellion—the bloodiest civil war in human history, with a death toll of twenty-five million people. Many of the audiences attended by the dowagers, and the edicts to which they put their seals, concerned desperate measures to suppress the Taiping rebels. With the armies of Britain and France no longer threatening the regime and the Gang of Eight out of the way, Prince Kung made a radical change in Manchu policy and put unprecedented military power in the hands of a Han Chinese. For two centuries Manchu rulers had deliberately avoided doing this, for fear that once a Chinese had his own army he would turn on his alien masters. Since 1644 no Chinese had been allowed to raise his own troops, and not one Chinese commander who had shown himself to be exceptional had died in bed of old age; all were assassinated, beheaded for imaginary violations of etiquette, forced to commit suicide, or fragged—hit by friendly fire. But in 1862, at Prince Kung's urging, the two dowagers put the fate of the dynasty in the hands of Tseng Kuo-fan, the man who later judged them both to be unexceptional, and left the resolution of the Taiping Rebellion to him. In doing so, they unwittingly set in motion precisely those subversive forces that their ancestors warned would bring about the dynasty's humiliation and collapse. Tseng himself would not turn on them, but one of his protégés—the incomparably cunning Li Hung-chang—would be launched on an extraordinary career in which he would become the real power behind the throne, leaving Tzu Hsi presiding over an increasingly empty shell.

It was a sweet-and-sour solution, but something had to be done. During the first half of the nineteenth century one peasant rebellion after another had risen against the Manchu's incompetent and often brutal administration. The Taipings were only the latest, but they were successful where others had failed. Since 1850 they had swept through province after province, defeating all the Manchu forces that Emperor Hsien Feng sent to block them. In desperation, the Gang of Eight put ruthless men in charge at provincial and local levels, men who resorted to mass extermination campaigns: whole Chinese communities in the south were liquidated down to women and children. It was a time of great misery, compounded by drought, famine, and flood. In disgust and desperation, the suffering countryfolk joined the Taiping ranks. Their emperor, Hung Hsiu-chuan, and his disciples provided the kind of organizational genius, inspirational framework, and manic dedication that was needed to bind these diverse elements into a huge army of half a million men. They established their capital at Nanking, where they threatened to overrun the heartland of China.

They saw themselves as Christians, intent upon establishing a Heavenly Kingdom of Great Peace (Taiping). Hung Hsiu-chuan was not a little bit mad. He had failed four times to pass the Confucian civil service exams and as a result was blocked from becoming one of the scholar-gentry. Hung's third failure took place in Canton, where a Chinese Christian gave him a tract called *Good Works to Admonish the Age,* full of Biblical exhortations and Old Testament history. Hung was in a deep depression when he read the tract and immediately decided he was the younger brother of Jesus Christ and would establish a new dynasty in China. Soon he had a hard core of disciples whom he appointed princes of the Heavenly Kingdom, including a charcoal maker, a rich scholar, and an odd-jobs man. They proved to be remarkably competent military commanders, compared to the Manchu.

The Taipings rejected everything the Manchu had introduced, from ideas to costumes. Taiping men wore their hair long and loose instead of in a Manchu queue, so they were called Long-haired Bandits, or simply Long Hairs. They gave rights to women to take civil service exams and to become state officials. What the Taipings advocated, so strangely modern and utopian, threatened not only the Manchu but the whole system of Confucian social order that was the glue binding China together. Because they challenged Confucianism itself, they were strenuously opposed by China's Confucian elite. As Tseng Kuo-fan explained:

. . . the bandits . . . taking their clue from the outer barbarians, venerate the religion of God. From their bogus lords and ministers, down to their soldiers and mean people, all are called brother. Farmers are unable to freely cultivate in order to pay taxes, as they call all the fields the fields of the Heavenly King. Merchants are unable to freely trade in order to seek profit, as they call all the merchandise the merchandise of the Heavenly King. Scholars are unable to recite the Confucian Classics, as they have other theories of a so-called Jesus and the New Testament. All of China's several thousand years of propriety, morality, and social relationships, of literature and law, are suddenly dragged in the dust and utterly destroyed.

Now in his early fifties, Tseng was the son of a minor member of the Hunan gentry. His father had passed a civil service exam only after sixteen tries, but Tseng himself proved to be unusually bright, quickly reaching the top *chin-shih* level, equivalent to a doctorate from Oxford. In acknowledgment of his rare gifts he was appointed to Peking's elite Hanlin Academy, where he proved to be that rarest of creatures, a virtuous man. Tseng looked less like a warlord than he did a venerable sage. At five feet nine inches he was strongly built, with a broad chest and square shoulders but with a large head exaggerated by the Manchu fashion of shaving the brow and braiding the hair in a queue down the back. He wore a full beard that hung over his chest, adding to the impression of great sagacity. His sad hazel eyes were keen and penetrating, and his mouth was tightly compressed into thin lips. The overall impression was of strong will, high purpose, great dignity, and total self-possession. He was not a man to be trifled with.

Tseng was first given an ambiguous military command by the Gang of Eight when the Taipings swept into Hunan Province in 1852. Tseng happened to be there at the time, on leave from the Hanlin, mourning the death of his mother. Su Shun insisted that he put his mourning aside in the interest of the empire, and raise a local army to beat the Taipings back. Tseng did so but found his hands tied in a hundred ways. Su Shun refused either to make his appointment formal with an edict from Emperor Hsien Feng or to give him the authority he needed to raise local taxes to pay his men. This was a typical bit of Manchu treachery. Without a formal appointment, the Han Chinese Tseng could at any time be judged to have overstepped his authority, and be executed. The Gang of Eight wanted him to stop the Taipings, but they were afraid to give him any real power. After gaining control of China, Manchu emperors jealously prohibited even their own brothers from holding independent commands. A private Chinese army would pose an even greater danger to Peking. In fighting the Taipings this proved to be self-defeating. Manchu armies repeatedly failed. Tseng was the first to achieve a progression of victories over the rebels. Nevertheless, he was hamstrung by Su Shun in every way. (Despite this, Tseng found ways to give his men good wages regularly—a rare thing in China in any age—supplemented with "virtue money" to keep them from bribes and extortion. His Hunan Army became the first self-respecting government military force the empire had seen in centuries and won battles as a result.)

In 1860, when the Taipings completely destroyed the Manchu armies besieging them at Nanking, Su Shun reluctantly made Tseng president of the Board of War and viceroy of the war-torn provinces of Kiangsu, Anhwei, Kiangsi, and Chekiang. But the Gang of Eight never gave anything with one hand without taking it away with the other. They assigned the Mongol prince Kokorchin as Tseng's deputy, putting a spy at his elbow and making any independent decisions impossible. Tseng was more hobbled than before.

Prince Kung's coup in 1861 changed all that. The prince immediately granted Tseng all the independent authority the Gang of Eight had deliberately withheld.

Kung grasped that the Taipings were the greatest threat to the dynasty's survival so he negotiated a settlement with the Foreign Powers to free his government and his generals to deal with the rebels. One of his first steps after toppling the Gang of Eight was to get behind Tseng completely. With the support of Tzu Hsi and Tzu An, Prince Kung was successful in persuading the Manchu leadership to change its policy regarding Chinese military leaders. If the Taipings were to be defeated, the Manchu needed the help of men like Tseng. In doing so, Kung sealed the fate of the Taiping movement, but he also brought into existence the prototype of a new strain of Chinese warlords.

From this point on the coalition would carefully encourage certain Chinese to play a larger role in the empire's defense. They would be watched closely, but no longer would they be hobbled. This change of policy was one of the boldest actions of the imperial government in the last half of the nineteenth century, but it heightened Manchu fears of an overthrow. Tseng himself had to be endlessly careful not to panic his patrons.

Now Tseng feared more than ever for his own safety, writing to his brother early in 1862, "During the past few months, there has been a startling change in Peking. When the Empress Dowagers became co-regents new policies were inevitable and have already been felt. Everyone, including foreigners, was shocked by all these changes. Recently, I have received in quick succession some fourteen imperial orders and edicts. I think that I have been given too much power, and my position is so high as to become unstable and even dangerous."

Prince Kung and the dowagers were taking a calculated gamble. They knew Tseng well and believed they could rely on him. They were right up to a point for it was not Tseng himself who took conspiratorial advantage of this unprecedented opportunity.

Tseng's greatest skill lay in his ability to select clever subordinates and to employ them in espionage and intrigue, in the manner of a chess grand master. His military organization included a personal secretariat, or *mu-fu*, private individuals of scholar-gentry stock, who served as his tax collectors, commissary managers, and secret agents. Although he was himself stern and ascetic, he often chose talented eccentrics, men of action, and sometimes men of genius.

His ablest protégé was Li Hung-chang, then only a young Chinese scholar. Li had all his master's cunning but none of his scruples. He was remarkable for his looks if not his virtue, standing six feet four, with a full mustache and black almond eyes that were as warm as a pawnbroker's balls. He was disarmingly handsome, with an expression of such utter sincerity that he inspired immediate confidence. If you felt compelled to entrust him with the orphanage strongbox, it would be there when you returned, although in the meantime Li would have invested its contents at 300 percent and pocketed the difference. Absolutely ruthless, calculating, and mischievous, he was destined to become the most powerful Chinese political boss the empire had ever seen. But while General Tseng was his lord and master, Li served his apprenticeship patiently and well, for as the proverb goes: When two men ride on horseback, one must always sit behind.

Li was born twelve years before Tzu Hsi, in 1823, to an upper-class family in Anhwei Province, just west of Shanghai, one of the strategic provinces commanding the lower Yangtze. He did brilliantly in his studies, becoming a Hanlin scholar at age twenty-four and a Hanlin compiler at age twenty-eight, preparing decrees and edicts for the emperor. He showed a rare talent for mincing words, applying knowledge and talent the way a butcher wields a filleting knife. For such a young man Li had an unusual grasp of how things really worked in China and no qualms whatever about clawing his way to the top.

It was at the Hanlin Academy that Li and Tseng first established their master-pupil relationship. In 1853, when Tseng took on the task of organizing the Hunan Army to fight the Taipings, Li left government service to return to his native province of Anhwei as a private employee of the governor. It was the first calculated step in a master plan.

So long as he remained in the civil service, Li could not be assigned to his home province. By taking a private post with the Anhwei governor he sidestepped this barrier and was able to begin building a power base on his home turf before he was thirty. With the governor's approval, by June 1853 he had a thousand fighting men under his command, ostensibly to fight the Taipings and other rebels and brigands; they were really Li's personal army. Many of his officers were former outlaws, and Li used them to enlist other bandits and ruffians to expand his fighting force into a new Anhwei Army.

In strong contrast to General Tseng's Hunan Army, mostly salt-of-the-earth farmers commanded by true scholars, Li's men were mercenaries, misfits, and con men, who normally filled the ranks of secret societies and outlaw gangs. Those officers who held scholarly degrees had bought them. Li and Tseng were different generations. Tseng resisted the changes being introduced to China through the Treaty Ports, while Li adapted to them and made them serve his purpose. He was willing to compromise with vested interests at any time and never railed against bribery or corruption. Li understood the dangerous times in which he lived and knew that only venal men could extort the money he needed to support his troops—and to pay his own salary. "I am the son of a poor man," he protested slyly, "with the reputation of suddenly possessing immense wealth." In 1859, after helping to liberate his hometown from the Taipings, Li joined Tseng, becoming his personal secretary. In return he had a valuable inside look at the political gamesmanship of a warlord's field command. Tseng sent him on missions as a secret agent and debriefed him personally on his return, giving him pointers and showing much appreciation for Li's wiles, especially his ability to see into the hearts of the men with whom he dealt. But Li's gargantuan conceit made the headquarters of the Hunan Army "too shallow a beach in which to harbor so large a ship."

Tseng decided to give the younger man an assignment equal to his craftiness. From Nanking the Taipings had been waging successful campaigns in Kiangsu Province, near Shanghai. The terrain was flat, green, and agriculturally rich, crisscrossed by canals and dappled with lakes. Silkworm country. A fine place for ambushes.

General Tseng appreciated that the only way to defeat the Taipings was to cut the rebel taproot by destroying their main base at Nanking, where Emperor Hung had his throne. But Tseng was continually diverted by having to provide relief for other cities and towns.

With the fall of Soochow, in southeastern Kiangsu Province, its wealthy gentry fled to Shanghai and pressed Tseng urgently for help, approaching him literally in tears. "Cease your crying," he exploded. "Although I am not able to send my main army, I shall send a 'surprise' force."

The surprise force was Li Hung-chang, with handpicked elements of his private Anhwei Army of roughnecks. He was to liberate Soochow and rescue Shanghai, the city of evil—and, while he was at it, lighten its pockets and make himself its warlord.

Running the Taiping blockade on the river with fast steamers, Li arrived in Shanghai early in April 1862. Here was a ripe fruit waiting to be plucked and eaten. Shanghai was the Big Lichee, China's party city, a Sodom and Gomorrah of refugees and international scalawags. Its Chinese population, fewer than five hundred souls in 1852, had soared by 1860 to the half-million mark, as rich and poor fled the Taiping advance. In gold rush style, Shanghai swarmed with deserters, adventurers, and seamen from foreign naval and merchant fleets.

Beneath the strumpet's skirts there was an ongoing struggle for control of the city and its fabulous revenues, with local bosses fighting off the refugee Soochow-gentry who were trying to get a piece of the action.

The men who controlled Shanghai experienced a collective frisson of dread at Li's arrival. They knew the city was not really threatened by the Taipings, because they were secretly supplying the rebels with goods and weapons. They feared that Li would put his heavy thumb on their scales, and they would be fleeced by a new master of the art.

Li had sufficient military force and imperial authority to do just that. General Tseng had arranged with the dowager empresses for Li to be appointed governor of Kiangsu, one of the two provinces butting up against the Treaty Port (the other was Chekiang). The incumbent governor, Hsueh Huan, refused to give up a life of pleasure in Shanghai to attend to his military responsibilities against the Taipings; instead, he employed a gang of vagabonds to harass merchants, loot foreign ships, and murder all who protested. This gang numbered only a few thousand men, but the governor claimed that they were really an anti-Taiping militia of fifty-five thousand volunteers, which allowed him to pocket the salaries of the ghost soldiers. General Tseng likened him to a Chinese peasant who saw a rabbit kill itself by running into a tree and thereafter spent his days by the tree convinced that he had discovered an effortless way to bag game.

It was in this manner that Li Hung-chang came to head one of the empire's richest provinces at age thirty-one. His hostile reception in Shanghai confirmed that the city had much to hide, particularly the Treaty Port compradors who grew fat on cumshaw payoffs as go-betweens for foreign merchants. The top bosses were Wu Hsu and Takee, who had been using Governor Hsueh as their bagman. Prosperous bankers on the surface, they were actually arms merchants, swindlers, and extortionists, running protection rackets and fake charities, including a fund for homeless refugees underwritten by Western merchants. Boss Takee had been comprador for the opium traders Jardine Matheson and spoke English like a pimp. The bosses employed a small army of foreign mercenaries trained in rapid-fire rifles and artillery who posed an obstacle to Li's plan to make his own private army the sole defense of the city and thus gain control of its flourishing protection rackets.

Under existing treaties it was illegal for Chinese to hire foreign mercenaries, but on the pretext of pirate suppression, Boss Takee had hired an
American freebooter called "Admiral" Gough. In the crew of Gough's
steam-driven gunboat, the *Confucius*, was a twenty-nine-year-old American, Frederick Townsend Ward, a wild man with thick raven tresses over
his shoulders, who was bent on self-destruction.

Born in Salem, Massachusetts, Ward went to sea as a boy, then became
a hired gun in the California goldfields and in the illegal coolie trade
between China and Mexico. This brought him to Shanghai, where he
intended to offer his services to the Taipings at a price; instead, he became
the head of Boss Takee's army of mercenaries. In less than three years the
penniless drifter had hundreds of thousands of dollars and more power
than he could handle. Together with his second-in-command, North
Carolinian Henry Burgevine, they recruited waterfront scum, deserters,
and Filipino cutthroats, who were paid by Boss Takee with money ex-
torted from merchants' associations.

After a few weeks' drill with Sharp's repeating rifles and Colt revolvers,
Ward's gunslingers set off to recapture Sungkiang, twenty-five miles
southwest of Shanghai. Ward led them dressed in a Prince Albert frock
coat, armed only with a walking stick and a Manila cheroot. Camped
before Sungkiang on their first night out, they drank so much whiskey
and made so much noise that all surprise was wasted, and the next day they
were driven off by the Taipings and fell back in disgrace to Shanghai,
where most of the men collected their paychecks and deserted.

Vowing revenge, Ward recruited a second army, staged a surprise
attack, and captured Sungkiang. Encouraged, he went on to attack the
Taiping stronghold of Tsingpu, where he lost all—artillery, gunboats, and
provision train—and was gravely wounded. Shanghai's English-language
newspaper, the North China *Herald*, no great admirer of Ward's, reported: "The first and best item . . . is the utter defeat of Ward and his
men before Tsingpu. This notorious man has been brought down to
Shanghai, not as was hoped, dead, but severely wounded in the mouth,
one side and one leg. . . . The force is now disbanded."

Ward disappeared for eight months; when he returned, his mouth
wound had given him a sinister look and a speech impediment. He tried
to recruit tars from Royal Navy vessels and was arrested by Admiral Sir
James Hope and locked in a cabin aboard the warship *Chesapeake*. That
night Ward squeezed through a porthole and was rowed away by
friends in a sampan. A deal was then struck with Admiral Hope that
Ward would keep hands off sailors of the Royal Navy and instead recruit a Chinese force to be commanded by Europeans, with discreet
British assistance.

Ward soon had five thousand Chinese soldiers dressed like French-

Algerian Zouaves, in green turbans and knickerbockers. His officers were American soldiers of fortune, in it for the gin.

Just before Li arrived in Shanghai, Ward and this big Chinese force made a good show with the naval support of Admiral Hope, taking the Taiping city of Kaochiao. For this the dowagers bestowed Chinese citizenship upon Ward, with a third-rank mandarin's button and the military rank of colonel. Optimistically, they renamed Ward's force the Ever Victorious Army. Ward consolidated his business relationship with Takee by marrying the boss's daughter. Together he and Takee bought two American-built gunboats and ran a lucrative business chasing Yangtze River pirates and taking over their smuggling operations.

When Governor Li disembarked with his twenty-five hundred troops from Anhwei, marching through Shanghai in simple rural peasant dress, people laughed. They were used to the flash and color of Ward's foreign legion. Li retorted: "Is it more important that the troops be smartly dressed than that they be able to fight?"

Li was impressed by Ward's weapons, if not his uniforms, and set about equipping his own braves with Sharp's rifles. He moved circumspectly, not accosting Boss Wu and Boss Takee directly, but gradually and patiently replacing their appointees with his own men.

Li cultivated Ward, and by the end of 1862 their armies were fighting side by side. Yet behind the pretense of cooperation, each resented the other deeply. "The Devilish governor [Li Hung-chang]," wrote Ward to American envoy Burlingame in Peking, "has fastened on to all the Revenue here and not withstanding that I have done all the fighting . . . they actually owe now 350,000 [taels of silver] to me and my friends for advances made on account of wages etc."

Only days after this denunciation, Ward was watching from a hill as his men attacked a town northwest of Ningpo when he was shot in the back. He died that night. It was not the hand of Providence that removed this impediment from Li's path but friendly fire. Fragging rivals became one of Li's signatures.

Instead of disbanding the Ever Victorious Army, which was sanctioned by the dowagers, Li appointed as the new commander Henry Burgevine, Ward's second-in-command, a man of "large promises and few works" who was certain to fail. So that nobody misunderstood whom to blame for Burgevine's failings, Li made Boss Wu his co-commander and gave Boss Takee the burden of paying the army's wages. They had no choice but to destroy one another, which they quickly did.

By now Li's control of Shanghai was so complete that merchants were no longer willing to meet Takee's demands for money. Takee in turn refused to pay Burgevine from his own coffers. One night, leading a few armed men, the angry Burgevine barged into Takee's residence, knocked the banker to the floor, and made off with all his silver bullion. Li immediately put a reward on Burgevine's head, describing him as a "shady character." On his recommendation the dowager empresses ordered both Boss Wu and Boss Takee degraded, removing Li's chief rivals with a few strokes of the vermilion brush. That was how Li did things, setting up his enemies to self-destruct or calling in a little friendly fire.

There was still the matter of the Ever Victorious Army, now Li's own toy. To command the force Li sought a foreigner of established reputation. The British government offered him the service of Lieutenant Charles Gordon, on loan from the Royal Engineers.

Nearly three years had elapsed since Gordon had helped blow up the Summer Palace. He was now thirty years old, still in the early stages of his legendary career. He had served in the Crimea and the Second Opium War and had gone to Peking with Lord Elgin, collecting his share of loot and sending imperial sables, jade, vases, and enamels to his sisters and mother. Since then Gordon's unit had been assigned to improve defenses for the International Settlement in Shanghai, which made his selection to head the Ever Victorious Army convenient as well as fortuitous.

Gordon was an exotic whose pale gray eyes had stared too long at things others could not see. In Shanghai he strode about in riding boots, baggy britches, and a frock coat, chain-smoking cigars. He carried only a wand of victory as he watched from low hills the action of his troops. He lived on raw eggs, sucking a dozen at a time, and carried a pewter teapot of boiled water, pulling from the spout. Although his sex life was uncertain, he had a fondness for children and rescued many orphans from the Taiping havoc. In Shanghai he had six young Chinese boys for servants.

Gordon was not impressed by the Ever Victorious Army. His first task was to whip it into shape. He dismissed opium smokers, abolished bounty payments for the capture of towns, eliminated looting on pain of death, and prohibited liquor in camp.

Meanwhile, the American, French, and British ministers, feeling that Burgevine had been a victim of Governor Li's intrigues, pressured Prince Kung to see that Burgevine was reinstated. Li was angered by this interference and briefly contemplated buying Burgevine off, but it proved unnecessary. Running low on funds, Burgevine defected to the Taipings. The dowager empresses immediately withdrew his honorary Chinese citizenship. Captured by Li's troops in a Taiping stronghold, Burgevine was "accidentally drowned."

The Taipings were on the defensive now. Li intended to liberate Soochow, one of their remaining strongholds, where forty thousand Taiping troops were garrisoned. Gordon's Ever Victorious Army did badly at Soochow, but, thanks to quarreling among the Taiping leaders, the city fell unexpectedly on December 5, 1863. Gordon's men were accused of looting, murder, and atrocities, so he withdrew his army to camp else-where, leaving behind, in the care of Governor Li's officers, several cap-tured Taiping princes for whom he had great admiration. These Taiping princes had surrendered on the understanding that Gordon would protect them and that they were to be given high ranks in the government army. In Gordon's absence Governor Li invited the rebel princes to a dinner party and as an appetizer had them all beheaded.

Stunned, Gordon demanded Li's immediate arrest, trial, and execution for war crimes, or he would resign himself and defect to the Taipings. As a constant reminder of Li's "premeditated treachery" Gordon kept the head of one of the princes under his bed. He would dig it out, like Hamlet with the skull of Yorick, to reflect upon the rottenness of all things Chinese, and would roam through his camp with a revolver, threatening to kill Li on sight.

Prince Kung and the dowager empresses, regarding Gordon as a public hero in the fall of Soochow, sent him a present of 10,000 taels of silver wrapped in captured Taiping battle flags. This infuriated him even fur-ther, and he refused the honor. Gordon explained that the only thing he really coveted was an Imperial Yellow Riding Jacket exactly like the one Li wore. Designating a field marshal, this was the highest military award the Manchu gave; Gordon's having one presumably would put Li in his place. The dowagers sent him one. Gordon came closer than most people to understanding Li's cold-blooded nature. He had also heard the persist-ent rumor that Li cherished secret ambitions for the dragon throne. But soon afterward, Gordon left China.

He was not present when the Taipings were finally defeated at Nan-king on July 19, 1864, in another of those mind-boggling rapes for which Nanking is remembered. The failed Confucian scholar and founder of the Heavenly Kingdom of Great Peace, Emperor Hung, by his own account one of the brothers of Jesus Christ, died a month before the city fell, from a lingering illness attributed to poison. General Tseng's brother, Tseng Kuo-chuan, was the man in charge of the final carnage, described in official reports: "Smoke and flames from the burning buildings filled the city . . . several hundred female attendants in the palace hanged themselves in the front garden, while the number of rebels that were drowned in the city moat exceeded 2,000. We searched the city and in three days killed over 100,000 men . . . not one of the rebels surrendered. Many rebels (men and women) gathered together and burned themselves." Travelers to the area months later described a killing ground "white like snow with skulls and bones." The dogs were fat.

Peking was well pleased. The Taiping Rebellion was over. Tzu An and Tzu Hsi handed out honors like party favors, even to those who had not participated. General Tseng Kuo-fan was created a marquis; his brother was made an earl. Governor Li also was made an earl.

At age forty-one Li was in absolute control of Shanghai and now was named viceroy of the whole Yangtze basin, China's heart and soul. It had taken him only ten years to get the wealth and power that really mattered. The Manchu had only the illusion of empire. For the moment Li was content to let them keep the throne. Success was a dangerous thing, as Marquis Tseng continually reminded him. Baited traps were everywhere.

Tseng wrote his brother: "Looking back in our history, I have found that no one, however successful, escaped troubles, even disasters, both political and personal. They are difficult to avoid. I am writing to you, my brother, in hope that we can be especially prudent that we do not fall into any traps." Perhaps he was recalling a moment at the height of the siege of Nanking, with one hundred thirty thousand men under his and his brother's command, when he received a tiny slip of paper with a secret message: "Your Excellency has already the entire southern half of the country in your hands, do you have any further idea?" Tseng turned white with rage and fear.

Foreigners were speculating openly that the Manchu could be over-thrown at any time by Tseng or Li, so both men developed a peculiar gait while they walked the line. As though dancing a minuet, Tseng would move ahead, then humbly step aside to let his protégé take over, then move ahead again, and once more step aside. Each time he stepped aside, Tseng did so with self-deprecating melodrama, claiming that he was too old, too fuzzy, too ill, too clumsy, to handle so much responsibility.

With the Taipings out of the way, the next military challenge was the Nien secret society operating southeast of Peking, in Shantung and north-ern Anhwei provinces. Suppressing the Nien rebels had been the job of the Mongol general Prince Seng, who had tried earnestly but unsuccess-fully to defend Peking against Lord Elgin's armies in 1860. General Seng was expected to destroy the Nien rebels and also to serve as a shield to protect Peking from any Chinese commander rash enough to turn on his masters and strike at the capital. But in 1865, while he was in hot pursuit of a Nien band in Shantung, General Seng was ambushed and slain. It was almost certainly friendly fire, which had served Li so well in the past and would again in the future. The Mongol prince was fragged to get him out of the way. In addition to his own forces, he had been commanding troops on loan from Tseng Kuo-fan and Li Hung-chang, which put them conve-niently within his defensive perimeter.

Indeed, Seng's murder removed a major obstacle to Li's ambitions. Seng had been the only non-Chinese general that Prince Kung and the dowagers could rely upon consistently, a hardworking man who kept his soldiers in hand, paid his own way, and won the respect of the people. Seng's virtue was an impediment to Li. He was given a state funeral in Peking.

His murder left the Manchu more dependent than ever upon Li and Tseng. Marquis Tseng was appointed to take the Mongol's place with supreme military control of North China. He turned over control of South China to Li.

Immediately the minuet had to be danced again, for once more Tseng became the target of criticism for overreaching himself. He responded with loud complaints that he was too old and tired, and in ill health. Humbly he asked to be permitted to resume his old post down south in Nanking and recommended Li as his successor in North China.

This display of excessive modesty endeared Tseng to the court, so instead of letting him retire they made him viceroy of Chihli, the province surrounding Peking, the top provincial post in China. Whoever was viceroy of Chihli was effectively next in power after the boy emperor and Prince Kung.

Once again, Tseng performed his curious minuet, going off to nurse his failing health while recommending Li as his successor. In March 1872 he died peacefully in bed at age sixty-one, the first Chinese general to do so since the Manchu came to power two centuries earlier.

In his place Li was made viceroy of Chihli and chief military commander of the capital region. At age forty-nine he was the youngest and most powerful governor-general in China, viceroy of the empire—the man Prince Kung and the dowagers would have to rely upon in a crisis. From then on Li became the invisible partner in the coalition. While the dowagers reigned, Li ruled.

CHAPTER SIX

Life in a Yellow Mist

I n the absence of a true Manchu strongman, the survival of the Ching
Dynasty ultimately depended upon doing a good job raising Tzu Hsi's
son, the young emperor Tung Chih. Whether he took an active role
or remained only a figurehead was less important than that he *appear* to
be an ideal Confucian Sage-King. In China so much depended upon
appearance that the Heavenly Mandate itself was at stake, and the dynasty
could rise or fall depending upon the behavior of a teenager. Despite the
best efforts of Tzu Hsi, Tzu An, and Prince Kung, it all went terribly
wrong. The short, tragic life of Emperor Tung Chih skewed the delicate
balance of the coalition and brought Tzu Hsi one step closer to reigning
alone.

Traditionally, age fifteen was the earliest that a boy emperor could be
recognized as an adult and assume the throne with all its powers. At the
time of the coup of 1861, Tung Chih was five years old; thereafter, Tzu
Hsi had little to do with her son's upbringing. As in the Japanese system,
the daily routine of raising a young emperor was the jealously guarded
prerogative of the imperial household agency. Only Tzu An, his official
mother, had influence here. During the next ten years specially chosen
tutors had to mold Tung Chih's character and cultivate his thinking, to
prepare him for great responsibilities.

The job of prepping Tung Chih for his imperial role was given to the
fifty-seven-year-old Mongol scholar Wo Jen, acclaimed as one of the three
most virtuous men of the empire. He was also one of the most powerful.
In addition to his post as chief tutor, he was also president of the Censorate, the ideological watchdog of the regime; chancellor of the Hanlin
Academy; and secretary of the Board of Revenue. Nobody challenged Wo
Jen on anything. His uncompromising and dogmatic pursuit of Confucian righteousness was not confined to his supervision of Tung Chih. As

the high priest and moral policeman of the court during the next nine years, he made it his job to bring the dynasty as an institution back to "propriety and righteousness" from the follies of "power and plotting," even if the patient died from the cure.

Nobody seemed to doubt that Tung Chih could be infused with Confucian virtues and schooled to sagacity. It was part of the Chinese state myth that this was possible. If he fell short on any count, the princes and the Grand Councillors assumed they would guide his decisions, as they did now with Tzu An and Tzu Hsi, seeing to it that the options presented to him were well considered and correct. How wrong they all were.

In recent centuries the Confucian system had not been particularly successful in shaping its rulers; nobody approximating its ideal had appeared in generations. Many thought the problem had begun only recently with Hsien Feng or Tao Kuang or with Chia Ching, who preceded Tao Kuang. But it was the great emperor Chien Lung, ruler from 1735 to 1796, who had made it fashionable to be outwardly correct and inwardly corrupt. As a young ruler Chien Lung had shown exceptional ability, but in his middle years he deviated from Confucian virtues, becoming self-indulgent and eccentric, and as an old man he foolishly relinquished power to his lover and favorite, the manipulative Ho Shen, encouraging others by his example to be equally two-faced during generations to follow. All good Confucians talked about a dramatic return to the cardinal virtues but failed to bring it off. Succeeding emperors Chia Ching and Tao Kuang had not been up to the job, and Hsien Feng had broken under the strain.

As to their spartan military virtues, these had been sabotaged even earlier by Chien Lung's father, Emperor Yung Cheng, in the late 1720s. To protect himself from his ambitious sons and nephews, he forbade princes to hold any military or administrative posts, giving them little alternative but to spend their lives as idle playboys. Thereafter, like many upper-class Europeans of the day, the education of Manchu princes was restricted to effete studies of etiquette and the classics. They received no practical training in the daily management of the nation or in the proper exercise of power. So when one of these princes succeeded to the throne as the new emperor, he was completely dependent upon his advisers. Realizing the advantage this gave them, ministers and advisers made no effort to enlarge the knowledge of their sovereign and instead used strict observance of tradition as a way to stifle any curiosity or hunger for knowledge. Tzu Hsi was never encouraged to travel throughout the empire or to inform herself about foreigners and their ideas. Her nephew and successor Emperor Kuang Hsu was the first to insist on being provided with translations of Western magazines and books.

When Tung Chih's tutors set about molding him into a monarch, they were blinded by what they wanted to believe. They saw themselves as brilliantly virtuous and intended to remake Tung Chih in their own image. Even General Tseng was convinced that the moral character of the new emperor would ultimately determine whether China was revitalized, although he meant something more wholesome than the stilted and narrow-minded training that Tung Chih actually received. The emperor, Tseng said, must set a perfect moral example, which would lead to the empire's being perfectly governed, just as day follows night. Tseng regarded moral suasion as "the primary instrument by which the ruler accomplished his duty of maintaining the security of the entire society." The only way to achieve this was for the young emperor to devote himself to the study of the past, to find exemplary monarchs on whom to model himself.

At first Prince Kung supervised Wo Jen's efforts to educate the boy. The prince strongly believed that Tung Chih must be taught new ways to handle the Foreign Powers. It was essential for him to learn all he could absorb about countries and people outside the Middle Kingdom, their geography, their societies, their political history, their laws, and the rules of warfare observed by them. But Wo Jen blocked every effort to introduce a modern curriculum. Wo Jen shared a bias common among Hanlin scholars that their ancient privileges would be jeopardized if new foreign ideas took hold; instead of becoming masters of those ideas, they tried to ignore them. Wo Jen gained the support of the empress dowagers by flattery, which was something that the spirited Prince Kung simply was not able to do. (Although the dowagers owed much to Prince Kung, they were often offended by his brash and arrogant manner; Kung was the only man in a position to scold, chide, or belittle them.)

Although he aspired to be perfect, Wo Jen was given to self-important poses. He made a public display of frugality, but others knew better. Leading scholars sponsored clubs or societies to surround themselves with fawning toadies. Wo Jen began a club called the Bran Eating Society, whose members had to eat bran instead of white-milled flour, to display their mastery of self-denial. His neighbors could not help noticing that when Wo Jen was alone, his kitchen produced the most succulent aromas. Perhaps it was inevitable that his efforts to make Tung Chih into a Sage-King would produce exactly the opposite.

Each day he and his assistants met the boy at a pavilion called the Heng-te Tien. The basic lessons were the same as for all upper-class children. At age three Tung Chih had been taught twenty-five ideographs that read, in part, "Work well to attain virtue, and you will understand propriety." Heady stuff for a three-year-old. Once he recognized the characters, he was taught to write them. An ideograph was first outlined with vermilion ink on a single sheet of yellow paper, and the boy filled it in. Eventually, he had to brush each character himself. When he could control the brush, he memorized the *Primer of One Thousand Characters*, a poem of two hundred fifty lines in which no ideograph was repeated. At age seven he was taught the Four Books and the Five Classics, which form the basis of Confucianism. This was done almost entirely by rote memory. With an open text before him, Tung Chih parroted Wo Jen as he followed the text with a finger and repeated phrase for phrase. Even the dullest student was able to memorize some of the classics in this fashion. Mastering all the classics normally took until age fifteen, when a successful boy would have committed to memory 431,286 characters—not a system for the fainthearted, or for the imaginative. Because Tung Chih was so troublesome and willful, it appears that Wo Jen eventually resigned himself to giving him a quick-study course, intended to provide only a superficial knowledge.

An effort also was made to teach the boy calligraphy. One of the traditional marks of special favor that an emperor could bestow was a scroll bearing a good-luck message. But Tung Chih proved to be a bad student in all subjects. Luckily, the Hanlin scholars who drafted imperial edicts could brush a variety of calligraphic styles, so they were able to counterfeit good-luck scrolls that were passed off as the young emperor's own work. This set the standard for a life of deception.

Inattentive students, or those who amused themselves by playing with toys hidden in their sleeves, were ordinarily scolded or hit with a stick on the palms and thighs. In the case of Tung Chih this posed a problem. The body of an emperor was sacred, even when he was a brat, so discipline had to be applied indirectly. Tutors and palace eunuchs alike had to exercise great restraint, and Tung Chih became accustomed early to getting away with everything.

Mrs. Anson Burlingame, wife of the U.S. minister, heard of these difficulties in the Forbidden City and wrote to her sister that "Prince Kung has charge of the young emperor's education, and gives out that it is sometimes difficult to make his majesty attend to his books, on account of his [Kung's] being deprived of the means of chastisement usual to youth of less august rank (which, I suppose, we should vulgarly call a 'good spanking!')." When all else failed, the dowagers might order a eunuch to tweak Tung Chih's cheek.

Tzu An and Tzu Hsi were novices in government and had no idea how to instill discipline in the boy emperor. In the Forbidden City, where every whim could be gratified furtively, discipline was his biggest problem. Eventually a contributor to the *New York Times* was able to write: "He is said to be childish in his tastes and amusements, and if this be true, surrounded as he is by all that is calculated to foster idleness and sensuality, the prospect of the future before him is not encouraging."

Pleasure was his greatest danger. When the Manchu first took up residence in the Forbidden City, they fell into an ecstasy from which they never escaped. Pu Yi, the last Manchu emperor and a cousin of Tung Chih, wrote poignantly of his own rapture: "Whenever I think of my childhood my head fills with a yellow mist. The glazed tiles were yellow, my sedan-chair was yellow, my chair cushions were yellow, the linings of my hats and clothes were yellow, the girdle around my waist was yellow, the dishes and bowls from which I ate and drank, the padded cover of the rice-gruel saucepan, the material in which my books were wrapped, the window curtains, the bridle of my horse . . . everything was yellow. This . . . made me feel from my earliest years that I was unique and had a 'heavenly' nature different from that of everybody else."

To escape this yellow rapture required inspiration and guidance, but Wo Jen was a self-satisfied Confucian automaton capable of inspiring neither. His tedious carping on morality was guaranteed to inspire the opposite. Prince Kung, who had thrown off the suicidal trance in his own life, might have been able to discipline Tung Chih had he had complete authority, but he was busy with affairs of state, and his own sons were almost as bad. Eventually, when Kung tried to straighten out Tung Chih at age nine, it was already too late.

Unwisely, the emperor's supervision during off-hours had been left to the palace eunuchs, the "foul fraternity." There is no certainty when the imperial household first employed eunuchs; the practice of castrating and emasculating prisoners of war goes too far back. Eunuchs were part of Chinese rule as early as 1100 B.C. Two thousand years later, when the Ming Dynasty was founded, its victorious troops swept through the provincial strongholds of adversaries, seizing, emasculating, and castrating every male in sight, old and young. Many thousands were deformed in this fashion. Those victims who were unusually talented or fortunate were able to gain employment in the Ming imperial service.

Most eunuchs in Tung Chih's day were volunteers, men who sought employment by these desperate means. The specialists who performed the surgery were called "knifers"—a hereditary occupation. Before the cutting, bandages were twisted as tourniquets around the lower part of the patient's belly and the upper thighs to prevent excessive bleeding. The genitals—"Thrice Precious"—were numbed by a hot sauce of chili peppers. The candidate, heavily drugged on opium, reclined on a wooden bed while one apprentice supported him with an arm around the waist and two others held his legs apart. After asking one last time if the patient had changed his mind, the "knifer" took a small curved knife and, seizing the Thrice Precious in one hand, with one stroke sliced them off as close to the belly as possible to avoid leaving a stump, which was considered bad form. The job done, a tiny pewter bung was jammed into the urethra and the wound covered with rice paper soaked in cold water, and bandaged. The dazed patient was made to walk around to prevent the formation of fatal blood clots. For the next three days he was not allowed anything to drink, nor could he urinate. When the bandages were removed and the bung jerked out, urine spurted like a fountain, a sign that all was well. Complete healing took three months, after which the eunuch was ready to seek work. His shriveled Thrice Precious were preserved like figs in a jar so he could verify his sterility and so they could be buried with him when he died, his shade flitting away all of a piece. (Similarly, when a man was decapitated, his head was sewed back on before burial—if he had friends or relatives to do it.) Most eunuchs were inconvenienced by no longer being able to control their bladders. Bed-wetting was common, and they were constantly dribbling in their clothing; hence the Chinese expressions the "foul fraternity" and "he stinks like a eunuch."

On the other hand, many eunuchs thereby gained entry to powerful households where, having lost interest in earthly delights, they were able to manipulate their masters and grossly enlarge their personal wealth, even usurping titles to great estates. At various times in China's history, particularly in the late Ming Dynasty, palace eunuchs became so powerful that nothing could be done without their approval.

The most notorious of these "semi-men," as they were called by a Jesuit in the seventeenth century, was Wei Chung-hsien, a favorite of Ming emperor Hsi Tsung. Wei secretly kept a concubine, whom he savored in other ways, and wanted a son so badly that he conducted a far-ranging search for any medicine that could restore his procreative powers. A doctor told him that if he extracted the brains from seven living men and ate them, his genitals would return to their original state. Wei procured seven criminals, had their heads split open, the pulsing brains scooped out, and devoured the revolting mess. (It is not recorded whether the experiment was successful.)

Despised for their own sakes as well as for their inclination to be malicious, the palace eunuchs formed a secret society of man-made hermaphrodites, like acolytes in an underground church. Some were all too eager to make themselves available to their masters as sexual objects.

The interference of eunuchs contributed to the downfall of the Ming Dynasty, which ushered in the Manchu era. Since then, strict controls had been introduced to keep them from meddling in political affairs. Nevertheless, they were everywhere in the Forbidden City, and nothing could be done without their involvement. They were like ants at a picnic, utterly insignificant but omnipresent.

Eunuchs were responsible for looking after umbrellas and stoves, delivering edicts, leading officials to audiences, receiving money and tribute grain, keeping watch for fires, chasing mice, tending books in the library, pressing the yellow silk riding jackets granted to field marshals, flogging offending serving women, singing falsetto opera, tending concubines, standing vigil on all comings and goings, and keeping flies off the dried fruit. They were strictly graded, and each member of the imperial family was entitled to a certain number, depending on rank. Imperial princes and princesses each were entitled to thirty; hereditary princes, twenty; nephews of the emperor, twenty; grandsons of the emperor, ten; great-grandsons, six; great-great-grandsons, four. Salaries were low, chief eunuchs getting twelve taels of silver a year and perks, including kickbacks and illegal extras like the proceeds from the sale of stolen household effects, art objects, or jewels. All chief eunuchs and many head eunuchs had their own kitchens, and some had their own households and families, complete with maidservants.

Humbler eunuchs had an extremely hard life; they ate poorly, were beaten and left in the end with nothing for their old age. If they were driven out of the palace for some mistake, they were reduced to begging and starvation. Inside the Forbidden City they lived their lives like monks, in tiny cells in two alleyways behind the Mind Nurture Palace. Although at times they were honest and virtuous and a great support to their sovereign, they were also the shadows in the yellow silk and could lead an unwary young emperor to anything he wished, and much he did not.

They waited on Tung Chih when he slept, washed, emptied his bowels, dressed, and ate. They joined him on walks and at his lessons; they told him stories. They fed him and wiped him. They picked his flowers and his nose. He gave them petty rewards and ordered nasty beatings. They never left him for a single moment. They taught him much that was good and much that was bad. Where other children had dolls and invisible friends, the emperor had eunuchs. They were his slaves. But he was also their slave.

They dressed him in gowns of twenty-eight styles, each ordained for a different purpose and a different day of the lunar month. He was accompanied everywhere by a large retinue, eunuchs in front to sound his approach, eunuchs on either side advancing crabwise to ward off dangers, more eunuchs behind with tea sets and cakes and sweets and medicines—potions of lampwick sedge and chrysanthemum, essence of woundwort, pills to Rectify the Vapor, Six Harmony Pills for Stabilizing the Center, Gold Coated Cinnabar to relieve "heatiness," Fragrant Herb Pills, Omnipurpose Bars, colic medicine, antiplague powder, Three Immortals Beverage for indigestion, and, if all else failed, an imperial chamber pot.

Tung Chih was utterly idle. He breathed, and the air he breathed was perfumed. He showed no incentive, no "potential for classical studies." Before age nine he discovered that for the Son of Heaven there were more interesting things than calligraphy. He began engaging in sexual experiments with his eunuchs, and since everyone was desperate to please him, his choice of intimate companions—eunuchs and otherwise—was limitless.

Prince Kung reproved Tung Chih on more than one occasion for behavior leading to rumors that he was "always fooling around with eunuchs." Unfortunately, Kung lacked the authority to enforce his will upon the child. Who spanks the Son of Heaven?

In April 1865 a power struggle broke out between Prince Kung and the nine-year-old boy.

Despite the widespread support that Kung had received during the Jehol coup and the general acknowledgment of him since then as the acting ruler or prime minister of China, his power base was shaky. This was partly his own fault, a consequence of his personality. He was, after all, a Manchu prince, spoiled, arrogant, impatient, and quick to anger. He rushed political decisions, showing indifference toward Manchu and Chinese conservatives alike. Since the coup, Kung had been a continual target of criticism by the court conservatives. His efforts to promote Western learning and to strengthen foreign ties had offended many of the old guard, especially Wo Jen. As early as the fall of 1864, three years after the coalition gained power, censors were memorializing the throne, criticizing Kung's leadership. In February 1865 they warned him against a tendency to be insatiable, complacent, arrogant, dominant, and selfish. Wo Jen, as president of the Censorate, was behind the campaign.

Prince Kung was indeed extravagant in his personal habits. He lived in an opulent lakeside palace, making him a target of envy and gossip, and by all accounts Prince Kung did live well. As a snob and a former playboy, he could not avoid making his arrogance apparent in his everyday manners, even the insolent way he sat in a chair. It was difficult for him to feign the kind of deference that was owed to the two dowagers by court etiquette.

A man who had been coddled since birth, Kung never appreciated Tzu Hsi's solitude and craving to be loved and admired. Had he been more perceptive and less insolent she would have been his ally for life. But their petty disagreements left them both vulnerable to the conspiracies bubbling in the court. Nor was he especially concerned about the effect his manner might have. Both dowagers had been stung by Prince Kung often enough that they too were eager to teach him a lesson.

On April 2, 1865, an edict fired Prince Kung from all his imperial offices and his job as Prince Adviser to the emperor. The edict, issued under the young emperor's name, said:

> . . . knowing he had the power to control the government, Prince Kung . . . exploiting my youthfulness often . . . tried to dominate me.

He tried to create misunderstandings between me and the . . . dowagers. Also, during the daily audience, Prince Kung has always been haughty and behaves insincerely. Unless these actions are publicly revealed, they will surely jeopardize my rule, especially when I come of age and assume my power from the . . . dowagers. This is indeed a serious matter. [Kung] has assumed a dictatorial tone, and attempted to sow dissension in the imperial family—a charge which we cannot investigate at present.

It was Tung Chih's first lesson in the exercise of imperial power. He had defied his uncle with the support of his mothers and the approval of Wo Jen. In a government filled with ambitious men, a nine-year-old has surprising leverage if he is an emperor.

Others rallied to Kung's support, among them Prince Chun, who was called in on April 3 to help in the conduct of daily audiences. Chun felt that the punishment went far beyond what the young emperor or the dowager empresses should be allowed to do to any Imperial Clan prince. After all, the dowagers were only intended to be window dressing. If they got away with this, other princes, including himself, would not be safe. He urged the empresses to call a Clan Council to review the charges. When the meeting commenced the next day, April 4, 1865, attendance was carefully weighted in Kung's favor.

Bowing to the collective will, the emperor issued another edict in which Kung was scolded for violations of etiquette but was judged to be a trustworthy ally of the throne. He was restored to his post as chief of foreign affairs but was still barred from his role as Prince Adviser and head of the Grand Council. Prince Chun and others were not satisfied, and memorials poured in to the throne on Kung's behalf. A month later he was grudgingly restored to Grand Councillor, but not Prince Adviser; the nine-year-old was stubborn. The crisis seemed to have passed, but the supervision of Tung Chih was now turned over to Prince Chun, the new Prince Adviser, a man who was easy to fool.

By the time he was fourteen, Tung Chih was the subject of a growing public scandal. He was known to be slipping out of the Forbidden City to find forbidden fruit in the wine bistros, theaters, and brothels of the Tartar and Chinese cities. On these sexual forays his behavior was so wanton and indiscreet that even Wo Jen was forced to accept the situation. He warned Tung Chih that a recent fire in the Forbidden City was a portent from heaven and that the boy should mend his ways, or at least be more circumspect. Wo Jen's admonitions were ignored, and when he died two years later, Tung Chih's behavior quickly deteriorated further. Wo Jen's experiment in creating a Sage-King was a miserable failure. The leading Confucians had failed in raising her son, and Tzu Hsi was at a loss what to do next. She was not ignorant of his conduct, but she was not yet willing to jeopardize her relationship with the boy by openly siding with Prince Kung against him. She valued family loyalty to the point that at times she was irrationally convinced that Tung Chih was just going through a rebellious adolescence. She was his mother, even if he was a bad seed.

On many of his adventures, Tung Chih was accompanied by his first cousin, Tsai Cheng, a son of Prince Kung. Tsai Cheng was two years younger than the emperor, but he could come and go as he wished so long as he avoided his father's wrath. At the age of twelve he knew his way around Peking's male and female brothels. He was later blamed for encouraging Tung Chih's sexual misconduct, but it seems to have been the other way around.

It was the fastidious but world-wise Robert Hart, long resident in Peking, who recorded astonishing details of Tung Chih's frenzied sex life. "He appears to have been living awful fast," Hart wrote with dismay in his diary. "Women, girls, men and boys—as fast as he could, one after the other. He sent for 60 boys to Soochow: the [local officials] received a [sacred edict] and asked the Governor-General what to do: the Governor-General would give no advice—except not to notice it—thinking it evidently too bad; foiled there the youth got 60 boys at Peking, all of whom were castrated (as the story goes) and it is from them probably he has got some horrid disease." A Western physician confided to Hart that Tung Chih had been treated for syphilis since before he turned fifteen.

It has been alleged by various Western and Chinese sources that Tung Chih's father, Emperor Hsien Feng, also indulged in homosexual liaisons. But bisexuality was a fact of life in Peking long before the Manchu came to power. The Han Dynasty (206 B.C.–A.D. 220) gave the language a euphemism for homosexuality, "the cut sleeve," because one emperor, rather than disturb his sleeping favorite who was lying on part of the imperial gown, cut off his sleeve when he had to get up to attend an audience. Another emperor supposedly shared the favors of a concubine and her brother, who was a eunuch. It was the height of fashion to be gay during the Sung Dynasty (A.D. 960–1279). And under the Mings many outstanding scholars and poets kept handsome boys to look after their books. The Manchu adopted these fashions as well.

A Chinese novel that appeared in 1852 provides a vivid picture of Peking at the time Tung Chih was born. Aside from male and female brothels, the novel describes scholars frolicking in their gardens with painted boyfriends from the theater. Peking opera houses were traditionally home to transvestites who served in their off-hours as prostitutes, many owing their success onstage to after-hours patrons. Though they were celebrated in their own circles, the general population despised them, particularly those who played the subservient sexual role, who were contemptuously referred to as "rabbits."

Female prostitutes, especially those with upper-class clientele, threw "flower banquets," dinner parties to which guests would take their favorite prostitute of either sex. Officials with a reputation for being especially "pure" were popularly believed to insist upon only virgin prostitutes, and it was considered the summit of good taste to provide such men with girls of ten or eleven or younger, purchased from their parents, to deflower over a good bottle of wine. Officials who were less fastidious satisfied themselves with their favorite eunuchs.

Writing in 1910, Tzu Hsi's biographers Bland and Backhouse claimed that a secret diary of a chief eunuch told the following details about Tung Chih's escapades: "The young Emperor was in the habit of visiting the theatres and brothels of the Chien Men quarter in the company of a eunuch . . . it became a matter of common gossip in the capital that the Son of Heaven was frequently mixed up in drunken and disreputable brawls. . . . In the day time he would frequent, incognito, the book and picture shops . . . to purchase lewd carvings and paintings of the kind to which the dissolute patricians of Peking have always been partial."

It was hardly necessary for Tung Chih to go in search of pornography. His great-great-grandfather, Emperor Chien Lung, like others before him, had commissioned many pornographic works of art, which were available from the storerooms of the Forbidden City. The imperial library included *The Art of the Bedchamber*, *Important Guidelines to the Jade Room*, and *Secret Dissections of Health Maintenance*. The last included advice on how a man could increase the size of his "turtle." It prescribed holding the testicles in one hand while rubbing the belly clockwise with the other hand exactly eighty-one times; then reverse hands and repeat the process. This was followed by beating the penis repeatedly against either leg: "whacking the turtle." With patience and perseverance, the tome advised, practitioners were assured of "an increase in all dimensions."

These manuals asserted that the mythological Emperor Huang Ti (supposedly born in 2704 B.C.) became immortal after having intercourse with twelve hundred women, a goal pursued by many since then with less salutary results. In the midst of this marathon, the emperor was supposed to have been instructed by Lady Purity in nine basic methods, with such names as The Dragon Turns, The Tiger Slinks, The Monkey Wrestles, The Cicada Clings, The Phoenix Hovers. Instructions included exact positions, depth of penetration, and numbers of thrusts, concluding, "Pause after every nine thrusts and do not thrust any more after you have done so eighty-one times."

From Robert Hart's diary we do know with some certainty that Tung Chih was provided early on with a very young girl to initiate him into heterosexual pursuits, apparently in an effort to draw him away from his homosexual fixation. This inspired rumors years later that Tung Chih had produced a son by this girl. The infant reportedly fell into the hands of the Russians, and czarist agents were trying to use the "pretender" for leverage in one of the periodic Chinese succession crises.

All attempts to control Tung Chih having failed, the Grand Council reached a collective decision that it was time for him to be married; perhaps he would stay at home if he was provided with an empress, several consorts, and a few concubines. Wedding plans had been rumored for a year or more when it was announced that the marriage would take place on October 16, 1872.

He was given no voice in choosing empress or concubines. His official mother and his real mother, Tzu An and Tzu Hsi, made these decisions, guided by the Clan Council. An announcement appeared in the Peking *Gazette* on March 12, 1872:

> A benign Edict has with profound respect been received from their Majesties Tzu An (The Benevolently Tranquil) the Empress Dowager, and Tzu Hsi (The Benevolently Happy) the Empress Mother . . .
>
> We have . . . selected the daughter of Chung, a member of the Imperial Academy and Reader to his Majesty, whose [Mongol] family name is A-lu-te; She being accomplished, cautious, correct and sedate, we decree shall be Empress.

The bride, two years older than Tung Chih, was called by her clan name, Lady A-lu-te. She was of Mongol descent, with royal blood on her mother's side. In 1852 Emperor Hsien Feng had sent her paternal grandfather at the head of a force of Bannerman to suppress the Taipings. Failing (like many others) to do so, he was degraded and his property confiscated. The buildings eventually occupied by the foreign ministry, or Tsungli Yamen, were once his Peking residence. His son, Chung Chi, father of the future empress, redeemed the family by serving brilliantly against the Taipings on his own initiative. This brought him to the attention of Prince Kung, who assigned him to assist in directing police patrols around Peking during the Western invasion in 1860. By 1865 Chung Chi had risen to head the Peking Gendarmerie and that same year passed with first honors the highest examination, placing him in the Hanlin Academy. He was assigned as a reader to Tung Chih in the Forbidden City, where the dowagers took a liking to him and to his daughter. The family was restored to grace, and Chung Chi was made a duke of the third rank, Duke Chung. He was to play an important role in later events in Tzu Hsi's reign.

The mother of the future empress was a daughter of Ironhat Prince Cheng—one of the Gang of Eight and half-brother of Su Shun—who had been ordered to commit suicide after Prince Kung's coup. It was said that this relationship to the Gang of Eight was not held against the girl, but it may have been one of her greatest assets. For while her father's bond to Prince Kung satisfied the pragmatists at court, her mother's link to the Gang of Eight pleased militant conservatives. This was a conciliatory gesture. Prince Kung's coalition was not without its enemies, particularly the Ironhats, who hoped eventually to install a new emperor of their own choosing. One way to placate them was to guarantee that Tung Chih's male offspring would be descended from both ends of the political spectrum. The choice of a Mongol girl was not unusual, since intermarriage between Tartars was encouraged to bind the Manchu-Mongol alliance.

The key to the selection of A-lu-te was the eldest royal prince, Prince Tun, responsible for the dynasty's dealings with Mongol and Muslim frontier areas. While Prince Kung had been busy with the Taiping Rebellion in the south and the development of Tseng Kuo-fan's army to defeat them, Prince Tun had been overseeing a campaign to put down Muslim uprisings in the western provinces of Shensi and Kansu. Tun's alliances with Mongol and Muslim tribal leaders enlarged his power base as leader of the Ironhats. Everyone was lobbying Tzu Hsi and Tzu An in behalf of their favorite candidate for empress, but ultimately Prince Tun won their endorsement of A-lu-te, cementing his bond with Mongol hard-liners.

The dowagers also chose Tung Chih a secondary consort and principal concubines, whose appointments were also announced in the *Gazette* of March 12, 1872:

The daughter of Feng Hsiu, a Secretary of the [Board of Punishments] whose [Manchu] family name is Fu Cha, we decree shall be His Majesty's Hui Fei or Intelligent Consort [First Concubine].

The daughter of Chung Ling, a Prefect whose [Manchu] family name is Ho She Li, we decree shall be His Majesty's Yu Fin or Lustrous Consort [Second Concubine].

The daughter of Sai-Shang-Ah, lately a Lieut. Genl. whose [Mongol] family name is A-lu-te, we decree shall be His Majesty's Hsun Sin or Generous Consort [Third Concubine].

This Generous Consort was an aunt of the empress-elect, and both girls were referred to similarly by clan name, as Lady A-lu-te. Thus if the empress failed to conceive a male heir, another girl from the same clan might succeed, assuring the clan double the chance of being embodied in the next emperor.

The prospective empress spent a year at a palace outside the Forbidden City, to learn court etiquette. There were many preliminary ceremonies, including the presentation of betrothal gifts. The first gift included two horses with saddles and bridles, eighteen sheep, forty pieces of satin, and eight rolls of silk, escorted to the bride's residence by royal princes. A fortnight later, gifts of greater value were sent, including 100 ounces of gold, 10,000 ounces of silver, two horses and bridles, and various gifts of cash and clothing for her parents and siblings.

Meanwhile an elaborate bridal sedan chair was prepared in the Palace of Cloudless Heaven, draped in scarlet and gold, and adorned with four silver phoenixes on its corners. This Phoenix Chair was then taken with great ceremony to A-lu-te's home along with the bride's traditional scarlet trousseau, escorted by princes and incense bearers, eunuchs, chamberlains, and a bodyguard.

Two days before the wedding, two ministers from the Tsungli Yamen called on foreign envoys at their legations to request that they and their nationals remain indoors at the designated time. The envoys felt insulted and gathered that evening to compare their outrage. Nonetheless they complied, and apparently not one among them peeked at the procession bearing the empress-elect to the palace.

This procession left the bride's home at 3:00 A.M., the hour judged by soothsayers to be auspicious. Lady A-lu-te, swathed in red silk, her face hidden by a veil, remained invisible inside her ornate palanquin. With much dignity the Phoenix Chair and the bride were carried into the Forbidden City and into the Palace of Cloudless Heaven, where princes of the blood stood waiting with their wives, court officials, groups of ladies-in-waiting, and eunuchs.

The moment arrived when A-lu-te was to emerge from her chair, but custom required that she could descend only in the presence of women and eunuchs; all princes and male officers of the court withdrew. A-lu-te was assisted from the Phoenix Chair by eunuchs and ladies and was escorted to the Palace of Earthly Peace next door, where her sixteen-year-old lord and master stood waiting. They drank a nuptial cup and ate sons-and-grandsons fertility cakes, then went alone into the bridal chamber, thirty feet square and empty except for a dragon-phoenix couch filling a quarter of the space. Everything—ceilings, bed, pillows, flowers—was red. In China, red is the color of hope.

It hardly seems necessary to dwell upon the plight of the virginal bride, Empress A-lu-te, who was making her first acquaintance with the bisexual and syphilitic Tung Chih.

The wedding over, a quarrel immediately broke out over dismantling the coalition. Tung Chih was impatient to be rid of his Prince Adviser, Prince Chun, and his two imperial mothers, and to run the empire his own way. But the dowagers stood firm, and the date for the boy's accession to the throne remained set for four months later, on February 23, 1873. Some thought this was strictly a dispute between mothers and son, the mothers not wanting to be pushed aside; others suspected that the Manchu nobility feared their interests would be in jeopardy when this boy took over. Nobody wanted Tung Chih to gain complete control, and certainly not sooner than necessary. The Clan Council pressed the dowagers to stand up to the boy, something neither woman had shown an inclination to do previously.

The U.S. envoy, Frederick Low, reported: "The Ministers of the Yamen are reticent upon the subject; they profess to have no knowledge of the reports. . . . The subject is however discussed with freedom by the lower officials, and the report generally believed by all classes."

When Tung Chih did succeed to the throne, on February 23, 1873, the foreign community was in a tizzy over what gifts to send, finally settling on uncontroversial mirrors in blackwood frames, inlaid watches, and musical clocks.

The day after Tung Chih was enthroned, the legations made a written request for an audience. It had been eighty years since a Western emissary had been received by an emperor, when Chien Lung saw Lord MacCartney. After all these years there was still an impasse over protocol, mostly having to do with kowtowing and not letting Foreign Devils into the Forbidden City. The court stalled on various pretexts until a scholar suggested that if the audience was staged outside the Forbidden City, in a pavilion set aside for repulsive contacts, it might be tolerable. At last all points were agreed, and the foreign envoys attended a dress rehearsal in full regalia.

When the audience took place on Sunday, June 29, 1873, the whole affair—concluding a silly disagreement over etiquette so profound that blood had been shed, careers destroyed, and palaces burned—was finished in half an hour.

The Japanese envoy, being a full ambassador, was received first and alone; after him the other envoys in a body, all ministers plenipotentiary. They found the young emperor seated on a throne, upon a dais ten feet square, raised three feet above the ground, surrounded by a railing. This put his head well above those of the envoys, although he was seated and they were standing. Tung Chih was a small, reed slim, delicately boned young man with an almond-shaped head, whose features looked as if they had been painted on by a miniaturist. Near him stood Prince Kung, as chief of foreign affairs, with two other princes and two Ministers of the Presence. On either side, extending from the dais to the front corners of the hall, were double rows of court officials. Outside on the terrace stood thousands of mandarins in shimmering silks. The envoys, all in formal diplomatic uniforms with sashes, medals, white gloves, gilt buttons, and hats or helmets, advanced one step and placed their credentials on a yellow table between them and the emperor; the latter bowed slightly in acknowledgment, without expression. Prince Kung knelt to receive Tung Chih's reply, after which he advanced toward the envoy and said, "His Majesty expresses the hope that the Emperors, Kings, and Presidents of the States . . . are in good health; and . . . trusts that all business between foreign ministers and those of the Tsungli Yamen will be settled amicably and satisfactorily." The audience was over. To say it was an anticlimax overlooks the great excitement of the Western participants, all of whom took pains to hide it.

Later, when this excitement subsided, the legations let it be known that they were not at all happy about being received outside the Forbidden City in a building reserved for tributary states; this became their new ax to grind, remaining a burning issue for the next twenty years.

Tung Chih had more important things on his mind. After only six months of marriage and concubines, he began slipping out of the Forbidden City again and started throwing faun orgies in the arcadian ruins of the Summer Palace. Fascinated by the ruins, he dipped into the treasury to begin repairing them, on the pretext of providing a retirement home for the dowagers.

His ministers opposed the reconstruction as far too expensive. Nevertheless, they all chipped in money, including Prince Kung, to begin clearing debris at the site. Tung Chih appropriated huge sums to begin the work. He became so involved that he neglected all other duties, ignoring urgent memorials from officials throughout the empire, even missing daily audiences and important ceremonies. As one Chinese critic put it, "His performance in government fell short of even minimal expectation." Here was no Sage-King.

Gossip about his sexual conduct was reaching such intensity that the Grand Council and the Clan Council became outraged. The most damning criticism was a memorial written by Prince Kung himself on August 27, 1874, a furious attack on the emperor, charging:

> . . . you consider work too burdensome, not engaging in serious discussion with the censors . . . spending too lavishly. . . . There is a widely circulated rumor in and outside the court that you are always fooling around with the court eunuchs and indulging in personal pleasures. I know that this is not true; yet Your Majesty has to behave carefully to avoid this kind of talk, which can be dangerous. . . . Especially in recent months, many memorials and petitions to you from various officials have never been read or transmitted to your

advisers or other high officials. This is indeed serious, for Your Majesty has simply blocked the channel.

Two days later, on August 29, at a special audience of officials called to discuss the problem, Tung Chih was confronted by two of his uncles, Prince Kung and Prince Chun, and other Grand Councillors. Prince Kung insisted upon reading his memorial aloud, embarrassing Tung Chih further. The eighteen-year-old emperor stormed out of the meeting.

On September 9, 1874, another audience was called to review the situation. This time Prince Kung had two imperial tutors, Li Hung-tsao and Weng Tung-ho, to give added support to his argument. The upshot was that Tung Chih agreed to abandon the Summer Palace project and to trim his sails. But the furious emperor then stunned the assembly by announcing that Prince Kung would be degraded immediately, along with his son, Tsai Cheng, apparently for not keeping his lip buttoned. Two days later Prince Chun, Grand Councillor Wen Hsiang, tutor Li Hung-tsao, and six others were also dismissed from office. In effect the entire cabinet was fired, precipitating a crisis.

Tung Chih had alienated the Grand Council and the Clan Council, outraged a slew of Manchu princes and nobles, and offended any number of viceroys, governors, and provincial officials. Government was paralyzed. Under pressure from the Clan Council, the two dowagers intervened. No description of their confrontation with Tung Chih survives, but his decrees sacking everybody were reversed. Prince Kung and his son were restored to grace, as were the others.

For once the dowagers had taken Kung's side against "their" son. When they acted together, Tzu Hsi and Tzu An apparently did have some control over the headstrong young emperor.

There is no record of what was being said about the September crisis in various quarters. This complete absence of information suggests that chronicles deliberately were not kept because tempers were much hotter than we imagine. For within weeks Tung Chih's reckless living suddenly and fatally caught up with him.

On December 9, 1874, reports came out of the Forbidden City that the emperor was gravely ill. He was said to have been stricken by smallpox, presumably contracted somewhere outside the Forbidden City. The dowagers were called in, and their ceremonial regency was reinstated. The new American minister, Benjamin Avery, reported:

On or about [December 9] . . . His Imperial Majesty (who is at no time robustly vigorous, being small of stature and delicate looking) was taken ill with the smallpox, which is generally very prevalent in

Peking . . . This . . . has been followed by a Decree, dated [December 18] . . . stating that the Emperor has concluded to relieve himself for a while of the cares of State and has delegated to the Empress Dowagers the temporary direction of affairs. This decree has been thought to indicate the serious illness of the Emperor, used to foreshadow a change in the government; but so far as I can learn his illness is not serious or threatening, and he is simply taking a prudent precaution. Prince Kung . . . is generally regarded as most likely to succeed him, in the event of his death.

Although Prince Kung might again become prime minister, there was no way he could succeed to the throne, short of another coup d'état. In order to carry out the ceremonial obligations of ancestor worship, the throne had to be passed to the next generation after Tung Chih, posing a complex problem if the emperor died, since he had not yet produced an heir. But Avery's report is interesting for its suggestion that the illness was being used to cover a forthcoming and premeditated change in the government.

Even before Tung Chih's illness suddenly became fatal, there had been hot debate over how to fill the unexpected void at court. Some kind of mechanism must be put in place to enable the government to function in the absence of a monarch. Not everyone was happy with the prospect of letting Prince Kung resume his domination of the coalition. If there was to be a peaceful change, here was the opportunity. Surprisingly, the hard-drinking curmudgeon Prince Tun persuaded the ladies to come out of retirement and resume daily administration of the government. Tung Chih was finished, and the throne would soon be empty, reopening the question of succession. By putting the dowagers back in charge, rather than Prince Kung, Prince Tun hoped to give himself an edge in the selection of a successor, improving his chances of forcing through the nomination of one of his sons. He had spent his life trying to get control of the throne.

On January 9, 1875, Robert Hart noted in his diary: "Emperor seriously ill . . . doctors differ: [the emperor's own physician] says he must take medicine—outside doctors say he requires tonics." Two days later, January 11, Hart wrote: "Call from Dr. Andera. He says it is syphilis and not smallpox that the Emperor is ill of."

Whichever it was, smallpox or syphilis, tonics were no cure. The following day, January 12, Tung Chih died. He was only nineteen years old.

There was a collective sigh of relief.

Tzu Hsi was always reticent about her son thereafter, rarely mentioning him. If, as she said, there had been only two moments of happiness in her life, her romance with Hsien Feng and giving birth to Tung Chih, the second had ended as sadly as the first. Her son was out of control before he was ten years old so that not even his royal uncles, Prince Kung, Prince Tun, or Prince Chun, could rein him in. Tung Chih had always been careful to be filial and obsequious to Tzu An and Tzu Hsi. His behavior around them was exemplary, so they were deceived, and their experiences with Tung Chih were completely different from what others saw and heard. If Tzu Hsi had wanted to raise him differently that would have been difficult because she could have been overruled by Tzu An who was the absolute authority on all domestic matters. As his mother Tzu Hsi defended him vigorously at first, but eventually she was faced with overwhelming evidence that her son was a monster. She never revealed whether she thought his death was arranged. She wept when he died, but not for simple sorrow.

Instead of a peaceful retirement, the shaken dowagers found themselves in the middle of a crisis over the naming of Tung Chih's successor. He had not placed the name of an heir in the sealed box and had delegated affairs of state directly to his imperial mothers, rather than to Empress A-lu-te or to one of the royal princes. The coming months would be filled with more intrigue and murder than usual.

CHAPTER SEVEN

Suicide of a Phoenix

Chinese history is full of bloody power plays, such as the time the last ruler of the Tang Dynasty, Emperor Li Tsu, was guest of honor at a banquet where all nine of his brothers were murdered one after the other by the host, warlord Chu Chan-chung. Over dessert Li Tsu finally agreed to abdicate, bringing the glorious Tang era to an ignominious end. His brothers might reasonably have preferred a quicker decision, but political murder is the last way to communicate with the deaf.

Scholars who have reexamined Chinese palace records recently dispute the theory that Emperor Tung Chih died from syphilis, although they concur that he was living a life of debauchery. The documents in question, covering the last thirty-six days of his life, indicate that, officially at least, he died of smallpox. There were those in 1875, and later, who maintained that Tung Chih was deliberately infected by a handkerchief tainted with the virus. Smallpox had been epidemic in China for generations. Usually the virus was contracted by inhalation, and there were celebrated cases of people being murdered by contaminated handkerchiefs.

A diagnosis of smallpox in official documents hardly puts to rest the judgment of contemporary foreign medical observers in Peking, based on inside information in the medical community, that Tung Chih had contracted syphilis at least four or five years earlier, and that the disease had advanced to such a point that he died of its effects. Given the primitive state of medical knowledge in China at the time, and the political sensitivity of diagnoses affecting the sacred person of the Son of Heaven, court physicians may have been far from certain, or reluctant to say what they knew. After several years without treatment, syphilis progresses to its third, or tertiary stage, in which half the cases are incapacitating or fatal. Any part of the body can be affected, including the brain, the nervous system, and the arteries, producing insanity, paralysis, and death. In advanced cases of tertiary syphilis, it is not unusual for eruptions like measles to appear, followed about two years later by eruptions like smallpox; hence the customary European reference to syphilis as "the pox." So, while court records may identify the young emperor's fatal illness as smallpox, it is possible that they were mistaken or hiding what they knew, and that the boy died of terminal syphilis. Or, was it murder?

Smallpox and syphilis are not mutually exclusive. The eruption of syphilis pox would have provided an ideal cover for the introduction of a hanky tainted with smallpox virus, as a means of quickly ringing down the curtain on Tung Chih's sorry reign.

Exactly what killed him is less important than the timing and the political circumstances. Tung Chih had turned out badly, and had offended a lot of powerful people, so the assumption of regicide is a natural one; indeed, foul play was widely suspected at the time, reaching the ears of the legations. Before the year 1875 was out, the *New York Times* labeled the emperor's death "mysterious," although the editors did not elaborate.

Motive was everywhere, for there were many who had reason to loathe and despise Tung Chih, especially after his political confrontations with Prince Kung in August and September 1874. Wo Jen's experiment in raising him had been a disaster, for Tung Chih had turned out to be the opposite of a good Confucian monarch. The fate of Prince Kung's coalition was at stake, and the prince himself had suffered acute embarrassment and loss of face at Tung Chih's hands, adequate cause for homicide throughout the Orient. More important, the continuation of Manchu rule in China (uncertain at best) was at risk with Tung Chih on the throne, which opens the short list of suspects to any number of grandees including the Ironhats, Prince Tun, and Prince Chun, both hoping to supersede Prince Kung as the de facto regent.

Regicide is an art. The surgical removal of adversaries, generals, and emperors had been cultivated and refined for thousands of years. In his treatise on the subject in the fourth century b.c., the sage Sun Tzu revered subtlety and indirection in political murder above all, commending the elimination of an enemy without any hint of discord.

Help with the finer artistic details was always available. Each faction had its capable backstage partisans, foremost among them Viceroy Li Hung-chang, who was maturing into an *éminence grise* on the order of Cardinal Richelieu, and who had shown himself willing and able to use murder as a purgative whenever the need arose, and without losing his good humor. Prince Kung had come to depend upon Li for a great variety of secret services, and in return Li enjoyed the prince's continuing patronage. After his phenomenal success against the Taipings, and in restoring the Yangtze basin to government control, Li became Prince Kung's secret partner in the coalition. In the crisis of 1875 we know that the prince relied on Li's cleverness and ingenuity to make the difference in any showdown over the succession.

Twenty-five years after Tung Chih's death, when it became fashionable to blame Tzu Hsi for all the malicious or sinister things that happened in Peking, the self-styled reformer Kang Yu-wei claimed she had poisoned her own son with the smallpox hankie in order to regain the throne for herself. As motives go this is highly unlikely. Because she had borne an heir to the throne, she already enjoyed absolute prestige, and she showed no appetite for administrative detail. Empress dowager was as good as it got. The rest is fantasy. No evidence exists of any serious disagreement between mother and son. Her indulgence of Tung Chih, and Tzu An's, was as much to blame for his lack of self-discipline as the blindness of his conservative tutor, Wo Jen. The likeliest poisoners were those who had something to gain or to avenge.

The boy's assassination removed an embarrassing problem, as did the killing of Caligula, although Tung Chih's transgressions were only of the same nature and not yet of the same magnitude. Among the princes and ministers, nobody showed any surprise that Tung Chih's collapse in December turned out to be fatal in January, as if they were all in on it. Conspiracies over the succession began the minute he collapsed and went on building during the month he lay in his deathbed. The moment his death was confirmed the rival princes and clan leaders were plunged into secret meetings lasting twenty-four hours, for which they thought they were well prepared. As it turned out, none of them was as well prepared as Viceroy Li, who played a decisive role without even being present.

As in past succession crises, this dynastic summit was dominated by the royal princes, for the choice would be made from their Aisin Gioro clan. Once again it boiled down to a test of cunning between Prince Kung and Prince Tun.

By tradition the throne had to be passed down a generational ladder, from one rung to the next, so each emperor could perform rituals venerating his predecessor as an ancestor. In 1875, by this rule, the throne should have gone to a son or a nephew of Tung Chih. However this time the roulette was more complicated than the succession struggle of 1861, for Tung Chih was the only Manchu emperor in ten generations to die without a legitimate son to succeed him. If we believe some sources, he failed to designate a successor of any kind.

At this time there were only two princes available in the next (Pu) generation: Pu Hsi, who was in his twenties, and Pu Lun, an infant born two months before Tung Chih's death. Both were disqualified because, according to the peculiarities of Manchu genealogy, they belonged to outer rings of the royal family. Their unsuitability made it necessary to break all the generational rules to find a candidate elsewhere, starting with the royal princes themselves. There were five surviving brothers of Emperor Hsien Feng: the eldest, Prince Tun (the Fifth Prince), Prince Kung (the Sixth Prince), Prince Chun (the Seventh Prince), and two younger brothers, the Eighth and Ninth princes, who had little leverage because they lacked significant power bases. Of the five, the natural leaders were Prince Kung and Prince Tun.

For twenty-five years Prince Tun, an ill-tempered, hard-drinking, bull-headed reactionary, had nourished a grudge. He was only six days younger than Emperor Hsien Feng so he felt he had been cheated out of his birthright, that he should have been emperor. His claim may actually have been stronger than that, for according to intelligence obtained by the British legation Prince Tun was really several days *older* than Hsien Feng. But his father, Emperor Tao Kuang, had tried to neuter his ill-tempered son by downgrading his precedence at court, calling him fifth-born instead of fourth-born, and then by giving Tun in adoption to an uncle. This unusual step legally removed the prince from the succession, unless all his brothers should die childless before him. That rankled deeply, causing the bitter lifelong feud between Prince Tun and Prince Kung, and lay behind the vengeful ambitions of his sons. Prince Tun was now the leader of the anti-foreign Ironhat faction once led by Su Shun and the Gang of Eight. They quarreled continually with Kung's more pragmatic followers over compromises and concessions to the Foreign Devils. They could not agree on anything, whether it was Manchu privileges, titles and estates, or who would dominate the Clan Council, the Clan Court and the throne.

If the rules of succession were going to be broken, well-informed circles in Peking expected Prince Tun, Prince Kung, or Prince Chun to succeed directly to the throne by palace coup. Of them, Prince Kung was the popular favorite, but Prince Tun had the support of powerful conservatives and the backing of some very truculent Chinese and Tartar generals.

Other courtiers argued that the three princes would not risk a direct grab for the throne, but would put forth their sons as stalking-horses.

While Prince Kung's eldest son, Tsai Cheng, was vulnerable to criticism on moral grounds because he had participated in Tung Chih's notorious forays through Peking brothels, Prince Tun's three boys—Tsai Lien (later Prince Tun II), Prince Tuan, and Duke Lan—were the dynasty's leading hotheads. The selection of any of Tun's boys would cause alarm in the legations.

Prince Chun was the only ranking royal prince with a son so young his character was unformed, a three-year-old who could be put on the throne as a compromise and groomed for the job. His mother was a younger sister of Empress Dowager Tzu Hsi. The boy's chief disadvantages were that foreigners regarded his father as the dumbest Manchu royal, a "man of violence," and his mother was a shrieking neurotic.

Despite the boy's suitability, Prince Chun did not seek his nomination. Through his corps of spies, Viceroy Li discovered that Prince Chun had been bought off, and had agreed to back Prince Tun's bid to put one of his sons on the throne. To outwit them, the wily viceroy and Prince Kung came up with a clever scheme of their own. Minutes after Tung Chih's death Prince Kung visited Tzu Hsi in private and persuaded her that her sister's boy was the best solution, a far better candidate for emperor than any of the other possibilities, including his own sons and those of Prince Tun. Tzu Hsi liked the boy and, having just lost her own son, readily agreed with the prospect of having her sister's child in the palace. Tzu An also was persuaded. Since the object of Li's stratagem was to catch the reactionaries off guard, the decision was not discussed with the boy's father. At Prince Kung's urging Tzu Hsi sent two trusted courtiers, diplomat Chang Yin-huan and General Sheng Pao, to her sister's palace to bring the child on a visit to the Forbidden City. The two dowagers then summoned a Clan Council on the pretext of asking for advice.

At this dynastic summit, etiquette obliged all the princes to feign disinterest. Nobody could ask for the nomination for his son, yet nobody could decline it. As the council convened Prince Kung took them off guard by announcing that he was removing himself, his sons, and all other members of his family from the running. This put the other princes in an awkward position, for now they had to pretend to resist nomination, too.

The succession in 1875 was probably the last chance Prince Tun would have to win control of the throne through his sons, yet protocol prevented him from opening his mouth except to give advice. As a tense silence settled over the assembled princes, Tzu Hsi looked around and said: "As none of you will speak, will you hear me?" They remained mute. "I'll adopt a child," Tzu Hsi said, "the son of the Seventh Prince."

"The Fifth Prince [Prince Tun] about jumped off his feet," Robert Hart wrote in his diary, "the Sixth [Prince Kung] looked annoyed—but the Seventh [Prince Chun, after muttering a Manchu oath in astonishment] said . . . 'That will do.' "

Although this council was held in secret, the American minister learned that Tzu Hsi "who is credited with much force of character" rose and went from the chamber, then "suddenly appeared with her little nephew, exclaiming authoritatively, 'This is your Emperor!' "

The whole scene, Hart concluded wryly, had been carefully staged. As a master of stagecraft, Li understood them all very well. Tzu Hsi had been coached to repeat her bold performance at Hsien Feng's deathbed in Jehol. Prince Tun was outraged because he assumed that he had been betrayed by his younger brother. Prince Chun was astonished yet had no choice but to accept the great and unexpected honor. He was chagrined that Prince Tun regarded him as a traitor, completely unprepared for the responsibilities now thrust upon him, but protocol gave him no alternative.

"Between ourselves," Hart wrote, "Prince Kung is *stronger* than ever, and with his previous experiences I fancy his coming ten years of office will show good results." At age forty-two, the prince was in his prime.

After the council meeting, protocol required that Prince Tun and Prince Kung call on their younger brother at his home. Usually Prince Chun came out of his palace to greet them. This time he did not. They were told that he had fainted and was lying down. When they were taken to his bed, he said dazedly, "What difficulty this puts me in, where am I?" After paying his respects tersely, Prince Tun left in a cold fury.

Some have taken the Seventh Prince's startled outburst of cursing in the council and his fainting spell afterward as evidence that he was worried about what would happen to his son in Tzu Hsi's clutches. It would be a mistake to credit Chun with too much concern for his son's welfare. He had a history of terrorizing his children, and a close study of his wife produces the interesting discovery that she was a child-abuser whose sons usually expired in infancy. This boy was lucky to escape.

Within twenty-four hours of Tung Chih's death it seemed to be all over when a decree in the names of Tzu An and Tzu Hsi proclaimed that the late emperor's three-year-old cousin, Tsai Tien, would be the new emperor, under the name Kuang Hsu, meaning "Glorious Succession." This was followed by an edict from the infant himself announcing that his adoptive empress mothers would continue their ceremonial regency during his minority. The matter was closed. Prince Kung's coalition would remain in power, and the dowagers would apply the imperial chops to all decisions. The uncharacteristic speed of these edicts suggests great urgency. But it was not over.

To forestall the confirmation of Kuang Hsu, Prince Tun and his faction startled everyone by revealing that the newly widowed Empress A-lu-te was pregnant and they intended to back the succession rights of her child. The whole debate was reopened. Intense quarreling resumed among the princes and there was an outbreak of saber-rattling.

If, as Viceroy Li hinted to Robert Hart, the dowagers and Prince Kung had known beforehand that Empress A-lu-te was pregnant, then their selection of Kuang Hsu was deliberately rushed to prevent the Ironhats from using her child to keep the succession open.

An emergency meeting of princes and clan elders was convened in Peking, this time including ministers and viceroys as well. Counterattacking, Prince Kung's loyalists pointed out that there was no way to be sure

A-lu-te would have a son and the throne would remain dangerously empty for many months until the sex of the child was known; if it turned out to be a girl the long delay was a complete waste. This argument did not sway the Ironhats.

Matters were suddenly reversed again when news came that Empress A-lu-te had just attempted suicide by swallowing gold powder and was only saved by the quick action of her servants. The young empress remained desperately ill for two-and-a-half months before she finally succumbed, either to the original dose or following the administration of a coup de grace. During that period, Prince Tun was in a rage and China was on the verge of civil war. Troop movements were reported, there were rumors of rioting in Peking, and palace coups were said to be imminent.

Ominous rumblings were conveyed to the *New York Times*, which reported on January 31, 1875: "It is rumored that disturbances have taken place in Pekin, growing out of the question of the succession to the throne." And on February 12: "Telegrams from China say that a civil war in that country is considered imminent." Again on February 13: "A feeling of uncertainty prevails with regard to the succession to the imperial throne. Although the son of Prince Chun has been elected . . . it is thought possible that this arrangement may be disturbed."

These troop movements and street riots were Prince Tun's way of bringing pressure on the Clan Council to delay the acceptance of Kuang Hsu as the new emperor. Tun's previous attempts to outmaneuver Prince Kung had failed, so he resorted to muscle by bringing into Peking groups of wild Muslim Chinese horsemen from Kansu Province, former bandits allied with the Ironhats. They thundered through the dusty alleys and went on a rampage in certain parts of the city, provoking the rumors of civil war or a military takeover of Peking. Prince Tun could pass off the troublemakers as cavalry rioting for back pay, but nobody was fooled. There was also violence by street rabble, supporting Prince Tun's contention that citizens were outraged by the way Kuang Hsu was chosen from outside the proper generational line of succession.

The American legation reported: "Within the past month a Grand Council convoked by Prince Kung and his associates of the Tsungli Yamen and consisting of eight other Princes, sundry Nobles, and Mandarins, has been in session deliberating on affairs of the Empire. All efforts to ascertain positively the objects of this unusual convocation, and the subjects discussed have been fruitless."

In the absence of a record of the secret discussions, a review of the sequence of events is provocative: Tung Chih had died suddenly, probably a victim of regicide. On January 14, only two days after her husband's death, Empress A-lu-te's pregnancy was disclosed to Robert Hart by

Viceroy Li, along with the news that she had tried and failed to kill herself. News of this attempted suicide was withheld from the public for weeks while secret negotiations went on over the succession. These discussions ended suddenly on March 27, 1875, when the death of Empress A-lu-te was finally announced, attributed only to "serious illness." Her heir to the throne died with her, leaving the Ironhats bereft of a candidate. At that point Prince Tun reluctantly agreed to go along with the succession of Kuang Hsu. Everyone went home.

The *New York Times* reported in May 1875, two months after her death was revealed: "The circumstances of [A-lu-te's] death have aroused general suspicion concerning its cause, and there is but little attempt to conceal the belief that the fear of complications in case her expected child should be a son led to the sacrifice of her life."

The story implied that her death was ordered for political reasons, or, as Robert Hart put it, "the poor girl had to die." Ordered by whom? Viceroy Li told Robert Hart that she had tried to kill herself by swallowing gold leaf, a common method in China for murder, not suicide, because gold works relatively slowly and ends in agony. For suicide, opium was much preferred. A-lu-te was twice a victim: A bungled first attempt that failed to block news of her pregnancy, and two months later a murder that worked.

The succession struggle of 1875 was turning into murder by musical chairs. Both Hart and the newspaper reports imply that A-lu-te died to keep the birth of a son from interfering with the succession of Kuang Hsu, in which Prince Chun, Prince Kung, Viceroy Li, and others had the most to gain. Kuang Hsu was the only way they could block Prince Tun.

Curiously these men with the most to gain were not suspected or blamed. Instead, historians assert that Tzu Hsi did it, she forced the girl to kill herself because she feared she would lose her preeminence at court to the young empress. China scholar Arthur Hummel tells us that A-lu-te committed suicide "being the sole remaining protest she could make against the cruelties of her mother-in-law," a statement Hummel bases on Bland and Backhouse, who claimed that A-lu-te starved herself to death as a way of protesting her treatment by Tzu Hsi. The entire soap-opera scenario was a Backhouse invention.

On the contrary, no evidence has come to light that she mistreated A-lu-te in any way. It was Tzu Hsi who chose A-lu-te as her son's empress; if she had a son the boy would be Tzu Hsi's grandson, and his birth would reconfirm her status at court and give her security for another generation. So whether A-lu-te's child or Kuang Hsu became emperor, Tzu Hsi would continue preeminent.

What conclusively rules out a poisoner's role for the dowager empress is something nobody has ever remarked upon. All people closely connected with her son were being eliminated. In addition to Tung Chih himself and then Empress A-lu-te, before the year 1875 was out, his half-sister, Princess Jung An, was also dead. Within forty-eight hours of Tung Chih's death, Tzu Hsi herself became a target. About the same time A-lu-te was first stricken, Tzu Hsi collapsed and stayed desperately sick during the rest of the 1875 succession crisis. Her illness was diagnosed as a severe liver ailment (one effect of poisoning with toxins or heavy metals including gold). She remained an invalid, with occasional remissions, for the next eight years, until 1883. During that period her absence from court functions is fully documented and her death was rumored or expected on a number of occasions. On March 29, 1875, for example, two days after A-lu-te's death was made public, the American legation reported: "The Empress Dowager [Tzu Hsi], the more influential of the two Regents, is also very sick." (There is no mention of Tzu An's being sick at all during these years.) And later: "[Tzu Hsi] has been so ill for months that her death has been daily expected and several times reported on the streets."

If there was a conspiracy to murder Tung Chih, to dispose of his pregnant empress, to get rid of Princess Jung An, and to poison Tzu Hsi as well, why was one of the victims blamed for the plot? Historian Immanuel Hsu tells us that "the dowager . . . did little to help [Tung Chih] recover, but everything to hasten his end." The *Encyclopaedia Britannica* remarks that his death "was hastened, according to the gossip of the day, by the machinations of his mother." There was no such gossip, except as invented many years later by Kang and Backhouse. John Fairbank tells us in *China: Tradition & Transformation*, that Tzu Hsi "according to legend even encouraged [Tung Chih] in a life of excess that brought on his death."

Who did poison all the members of Tzu Hsi's immediate family? Unquestionably Prince Kung had the strongest motive, but he would not have dirtied his hands. In Viceroy Li he had the practiced scalpel to perform the secret surgery, if necessary the sledgehammer. Despite his great charm, Li was a dangerous man who never hesitated to take such initiatives. Prince Kung need only express the wish to be rid of Tung Chih; Li was quite capable of taking it from there. While Tung Chih had caused the prince serious trouble and embarrassment over the last ten years, Kung's exasperation may have carried over to Tzu Hsi for not taking a firmer hand with her son and intervening in the prince's behalf. The timing of Tzu Hsi's own sudden illness is too odd to have been coincidental. Once inspired to remove Tung Chih, Li might well have decided that it made sense to eliminate everyone connected to him as a general purgative to improve the health of the sick dynasty. As any serial killer will concede, murder stimulates the appetite. Whoever made the arrangements, somebody was determined to kill Tung Chih, his empress, his mother, and his half-sister, as if to clear the banquet table hastily for the next customers—as in that celebrated party a thousand years earlier when Emperor Li Tsu dined with warlord Chu Chan-chung, and all nine of his brothers were murdered between soup and nuts. Although Tzu Hsi barely survived the banquet of 1875, she got stuck with the blame anyway.

CHAPTER EIGHT

"Our Hart"

Robert Hart doubtless knew a great deal more about the death of A-lu-te than he dared commit to his diary or confide to colleagues. This painstaking discretion was one of the reasons why, for nearly half a century, he retained the trust of Prince Kung and Tzu Hsi as head of the Imperial Customs Service. Hart was in a better position than other Westerners to know what was going on behind the scenes, and at no time during those years did he show any inclination to regard Tzu Hsi as conspiratorial, sinister, or manipulative. Only strong-willed and hot-tempered.

He concluded, for example, that Tzu Hsi was responsible for some of the harsh punishment meted out after the Gang of Eight were condemned. He wrote in his diary for January 9, 1875, that Tzu Hsi was "the clever woman" while Tzu An was "the amiable one." When Su Shun was beheaded he said, "It was [Tzu Hsi's] doing: she has temper—but she has also ability."

Before he was thirty, an age when many men still wonder what lies ahead, Robert Hart already had become the most influential Westerner in China and the chief source of revenue for the imperial government, good reason for both Tzu Hsi and Prince Kung to call him "Our Hart." From the day of his first appointment as Acting Inspector General of the Customs in June 1861, when he was only twenty-six, he had thrown himself into straightening out the mess existing at the Treaty Ports in the collection of foreign customs duties. (Domestic Chinese customs duties were not his concern.) He proved to be a man of great energy, doggedness, shrewdness, and business acumen. He took his new post very seriously, attended to minute details himself, worked long into the night, and brooked no nonsense from his employees. He was not a cynic like Viceroy Li—the other mainstay of the coalition—but a puritan. He became intimately acquainted with Manchu princes and mandarins, and his unpublished letters and diaries remain the most reliable source on the real nature of Tzu Hsi.

He first arrived in China in 1854, between the Opium Wars, a boy of nineteen assigned to the British consulate in the busy river port of Ningpo. A slender, clean-shaven young Ulsterman, his curly hair already thinning on top, there was a look of fierce intensity in his eyes but none of the bullyboy bluster so common among Foreign Devils along the China coast.

He must have smelled Ningpo long before he saw it, as the brigantine *Erin* eased around a bend in the greasy Yung River. Ningpo was the main port of Chekiang Province, connected to Shanghai, Soochow, and Hangchow by a network of waterways spreading hundreds of miles around the yawning mouth of the Yangtze River. It was the lower terminus of the Grand Canal, which linked dusty Peking in the north to its rice bowl in the south. Teeming with humanity, the town squatted with its pants down on a fork of the muddy Yung, sixteen miles from the ocean. Its shabby appearance hid a thriving commercial center, dominated by native bankers who kept their gold and silver out of sight. Local sampans fished the tidelands, fresh produce flowed from the surrounding delta, the hills provided lumber for busy mills, and merchants wove cotton, built ships, dried and salted fish, and produced cheap goods for export. The conservative native banking families of Ningpo had grown up from running pawn shops, and they controlled the lifeblood of the community. Raw sewage ran out of every pore. The city was protected by the garbage-strewn river, and by walls and moats built in the tenth century, during the Tang Dynasty. Although ships had to sail upriver to reach her, the inland location sheltered Ningpo from the direct blast of typhoons and discouraged casual attacks by enemy squadrons. Since the fifth century, it had been easier and safer to sail in to Ningpo and offload cargo than to sail up the pirate-infested Yangtze to Nanking. Ships from Japan, Korea, Taiwan, and the Philippines came here, along with coastal traders from Fukien and Canton. The Portuguese had arrived in 1545, followed by the Dutch and the British. In recognition of Ningpo's importance a mandarin customs agent presided over a large office in town, and imperial army and navy forces were based here to chase pirates from the waterways.

The noisy business district along the main east-west street was a jumble of storefronts and noodle shops hung with glazed duck carcasses. Crowded together were dry goods, job printers, and bakeries. Pharmacies sold roots and herbs, powdered deer antlers, withered frogs, and snake glands. Each narrow alley was the center of a different industry, this one bamboo, that one lanterns, all packed into a ghetto less than a mile and a half across. On the riverbank where foreigners lived there were a few Western merchants and two consuls, one British, one Portuguese, who had the job of seeing that their nationals paid customs duties to the Chinese government and did not get in trouble.

Ningpo was to be Hart's home for four years, doing clerical chores for the British consulate while learning to speak, read, and write Chinese. For companionship there were two dozen missionaries, mostly earnest young men and their wives, plus the odd spinster missionary or underage daughter. Life was dull. But Robert Hart was in need of a quiet life. He had sinned and was paying the price of remorse.

He was from Portadown, County Armagh, a small town near Belfast in Northern Ireland, born February 20, 1835, just nine months before Yehenara. He was the first child of Henry Hart, a reborn Christian and manager of a distillery who had suffered a brush with the bottle and then chosen the straight and narrow. Robert was raised a strict Wesleyan when this meant twice-daily readings of the Scriptures. Money was to be saved, not frittered away. Life was all work and pleasure was sinful.

By age fifteen Robert had passed the entrance examination for The Queen's College in Belfast, full of "young men of narrow means and broad ambitions." Hart stood out, and won a scholarship for a year of postgraduate work in modern languages. At that moment the British foreign secretary was looking for a way to solve the chronic shortage of interpreters in China. After the opening of the Treaty Ports there was a sharp increase in the demand for interpreters and translators at Britain's new consular offices, while the existing staff were whittled away by disease, climate, and promotion. Hong Kong governor Sir John Bowring suggested building the Consular Service by taking on promising young linguists from colleges, sending them directly to China and immersing them in language study while employing them as clerks in the Treaty Ports. In Belfast thirty-six students submitted their names, but the nomination was given to Hart, without examination. He received £100 for travel expenses and an annual starting salary of £200, plus the following advice from a foreign office official: "Never venture into the sun without an umbrella, and never go snipe shooting without top boots pulled up well over the thighs."

The appointment to China rescued him from an embarrassing situation. College had liberated him from small-town scrutiny, and he had enjoyed a series of infatuations with middle-class young ladies intent upon marriage. What they could not provide, Hart and his chums found among the professional ladies in Belfast pubs, one of whom gave him something to remember her by.

Luckily, Hart's infection was soon healed in Ningpo, whether by his morning readings of the Bible and his nightly bouts of anxiety, or by his first six months of abstinence. By Christmas 1854 he was once again chafing for female companionship.

His boss, Acting Vice-Consul John Meadows, was an offbeat character, a self-proclaimed freethinker, a tall bearded man with gray speckled hair and wild blue eyes—"quite like those of a maniac." Meadows was having Chinese shipwrights build him a small sailing vessel, on which he planned to live when he and the Consular Service parted company, which was not far off.

Meadows had "gone native" and taken a Chinese mistress, who lived with him in one wing of the consulate. Hart was charmed by "Mrs. Meadows" and observed that his boss treated her with all the respect and courtesy the missionaries lavished on their own Western wives. Passing her one evening, he noticed that she seemed depressed and "I happened to have a pretty rose in my buttonhole which I handed to her as I walked past. I then cut some roses in the consulate, and returned and gave them to her."

These innocent encounters with a pretty Chinese girl were in sharp contrast to Hart's workdays, which were occupied helping Meadows collect customs duties and deal with smugglers, pirates, shipments of opium, and sensitive negotiations with mandarins and river police. Western ship captains resented paying customs and preferred illegal activities like opium smuggling, or carrying contraband into port under cover of their foreign flags.

The Portuguese consul, Marques, was a swarthy, ill-tempered little man, with long black hair, gold-rimmed spectacles, and a protruding tooth that did not prevent him from playing a *fado* on his harmonica. Marques turned a blind eye to the evasions of his countrymen and helped them set up a convoy business, providing armed Portuguese lorchas to guard Chinese merchant ships against pirates, in return for protection money, which Marques shared. The pirates struck back by chasing the lorchas into the river at Ningpo, where the Portuguese fled ashore to seek refuge. A few sought sanctuary at the British consulate, beating frantically on the gates. Meadows refused to let them inside, for this would imply collusion. The Portuguese were dragged into the paddy fields and beheaded. Incidents like these taught Hart much about the ruthlessness of men on both sides of the China coast trade.

He had been in Ningpo for only two months and his Chinese lessons were not far advanced, but he was determined. He met an American Presbyterian missionary, W.A.P. Martin, with whom he became lifelong friends. Martin chose to live not with his fellow Protestants across the river but in a ghetto of the old city. His rapport with the Chinese and his command of their language impressed Hart and encouraged him to master both Mandarin and Ningpo dialects and to grasp the rules of Chinese etiquette that determined the success or failure of all official and social contacts in the Middle Kingdom. Hart had engaged a Chinese tutor for seven dollars a month—"a queer looking old fellow . . . he can let down the corners of his eyes and the corresponding corners of his mouth in a most peculiar manner." But he needed more help than this. "The language is so very peculiar—so much omitted that is expressed in our language, and so many words brought in merely to turn a sentence well, that it is very laborious work indeed to get along." To take the pain out of learning, his Chinese tutor suggested that Hart might buy a concubine and study the local dialect with her. "Here is a great temptation," wrote Hart. "Now, some of the China women are very good looking: You can make one your absolute possession for from 50 to 100 dollars and support her at a cost of 2 or 3 dollars per month. . . . Shall I hold out—or shall I give way?"

By early May he had a sleep-in dictionary, his concubine, Ayaou. He had just turned twenty; Ayaou was barely past puberty but was wise beyond her years. Thanks to her his life settled into a quiet routine and he was able to get on with his consular duties and his Chinese studies, quickly becoming fluent in Mandarin and Ningpo dialect.

His liaison with Ayaou lasted for a decade. By the time he was thirty she had borne him three children, all of whom lived to maturity.

From his first days in China, Hart had taken offense at the way Westerners casually abused the Chinese. In Hong Kong, while on an evening stroll with a Mr. Stace, he was shocked at the man's behavior: "He rather surprised me by the way in which he treated the Chinese—pitching their goods into the water and touching them up with his cane." Many of his peers used rude and aggressive tactics for their amusement and to get their way in business and pleasure. Such failings were typical of interpreters for the Consular Service; they were expected to be linguists not diplomats, because the "close attention indispensable for a successful study of the Chinese language warps the mind and imbues it with a defective perception of the common things of real life."

Hart's nearest contemporary among the British interpreters in China was Horatio Nelson Lay, attached at the time to the Shanghai consulate, who had worked for the British superintendent of trade in Hong Kong since he was fifteen. At first Hart was charmed. Lay's self-confidence as a hard-living, hard-drinking ruffian and womanizer impressed him. But he soon saw through Lay's bluster: "He treats the Chinese in so insulting and unkind a manner as to irritate me very much."

Like the formidable Harry Parkes, Lay had learned how to bully the Chinese from the grossly obese, wild-eyed Prussian adventurer-missionary-interpreter Karl Friedrich August Gutzlaff, whose impact on history, mainly for the worse, has never been fully appreciated. Gutzlaff's over-bearing influence on Lay, Parkes, and other impressionable young En-glishmen led to catastrophic confrontations for nineteenth-century China, including the Arrow War, the burning of the Summer Palace, and other calamities that were a direct result of their hot heads and swollen vanities.

Gutzlaff was a German Lutheran who made a living on the outer fringes of the missionary craze in Asia, taking up first one job then an-other, as his purse required.

He was a short, squat figure, so fat that he waddled, "the clothes that for shape might have been cut in a village of his native Pomerania ages ago; [a] broad-brimmed straw hat; the great face beneath it, with that sinister eye!" The son of a tailor, Gutzlaff was first apprenticed to a girdle maker in Stettin. A poem he wrote in praise of the king of Prussia won him admission to a Berlin school for missionaries. A Dutch missionary society sent him to Siam, where he learned Chinese and married a wealthy English woman just before she died, inheriting a large sum. Putting down the cross, Gutzlaff bought passage on a junk to China, where he signed on as an interpreter aboard the East India Company vessel *Lord Amherst* investigating the potential for illicit trade along the coast. Trading any-where but Canton was strictly forbidden, but Gutzlaff bribed local manda-rins to break the law. His ability to bluster and intimidate Chinese in their own language and his skill at offering them inducements earned him a steady job with the British government as an interpreter during the First Opium War. The British were so pleased that they made him Chinese secretary to the new government of Hong Kong, where thanks to Bow-ring he began teaching his bullying techniques to others.

At age fifteen Horatio Lay and his thirteen-year-old brother, George, were sent to China by their mother to be taken in by Gutzlaff. They were sons of a British consular officer in China whose premature death at his post in Amoy in 1845 had left the family destitute. Horatio found Gutzlaff impossibly offensive, but he had nowhere else to turn. To escape, he learned Chinese as fast as he could, foregoing a normal Victorian educa-tion, living like a pauper, looking after his brother and ever conscious of his mother's plight. He had no time for normal adolescent pastimes and developed no social graces. Despite these failings, Lay became exception-ally fluent in Chinese and was promoted over his seniors as the interpreter attached to the new British consulate in Shanghai. He jumped at the chance to become the Shanghai customs inspector in May 1855, at a hand-some salary of £1,450 a year, three times his pay from the Consular Service.

Lay carried out his new responsibilities ruthlessly, exposing both Chi-nese and Westerners who were indulging in smuggling, fraud, and fal-sification of documents. The Manchu were delighted and rewarded him handsomely. "Lay is the most crafty of the barbarians," observed one mandarin approvingly. "We must continue to hold him responsible for all the barbarians."

Still only twenty-three years old, Lay was riding high, single-handedly supporting his widowed mother and three siblings in England. But having so much authority at such an early age, combined with avarice, soon turned him into a tyrannical, domineering bully just like Gutzlaff.

The Treaty of Tientsin permanently changed the lives of Hart and Lay, when the Manchu government extended the Inspectorate of Customs from Shanghai to all the other Treaty Ports. This new Chinese Customs was to be headed by a foreigner, chosen by the Manchu, who would be known as the Inspector General of Customs, "the I.G." To everyone's surprise, the Manchu chose Lay for the job. They had mixed feelings about him, but his work for Lord Elgin badgering their most astute negotiators had earned their grudging respect. Lay was put in charge of collecting duties on all foreign trade for the whole China coast and for choosing the other foreigners who would perform customs house duties in all the Treaty Ports. In June 1859 he hired Robert Hart away from the Consular Service and made him deputy commissioner of Customs for Canton.

From Belfast to Ningpo had been a great leap for a young man. By comparison, Hart's transfer from British to Chinese government service was like passing through a looking glass. The rapidly expanding Customs provided great opportunities for an ambitious young man with a gift for the language and a sensitivity to Chinese attitudes and culture.

Fate then intervened. After being knifed by an assailant in Shanghai, Horatio Lay did not recover fully and decided to take a long leave of absence in 1861 to regain his health. It was an awkward moment to leave, since China was hard-pressed to pay the heavy indemnities the Allies demanded after seizing Peking. Foreign Customs duties were one of the few ways Prince Kung's Tsungli Yamen could raise the money. Despite a personal invitation from the prince to come first to Peking, Lay left abruptly for England, causing a serious affront. Before leaving, however, Lay ordered Robert Hart to go to Peking in his place.

It was in the early summer of 1861 that Hart made this first trip to Peking, in the midst of the crisis over the Gang of Eight that brought Prince Kung, Tzu Hsi, and Tzu An to power. Hart was thrust unexpectedly into close contact at the Tsungli Yamen with the prince, who was surprised to find one barbarian who was both courteous and cordial. The results were astonishing. "The prince himself became friendly and courteous in the highest degree," reported the British minister at Peking, "and the impression produced by Mr. Hart's honesty and frankness was so favourable, that he was urged strongly to remain at Peking to assist the

Chinese Government . . . Prince [Kung] always speaks of him as 'our Hart,' and the common answer to any suggestion which appears reasonable but difficult of execution is 'We could adopt it if we had one hundred Harts.' "

Prince Kung was then only twenty-eight years old, two years older than Hart, and was dealing for the first time with the maze of foreign political and economic affairs. Hart found him to be a bit unsure of himself, a somewhat timid young man who feared that his contact with foreigners would make him fatally vulnerable to his conservative Manchu and Chinese opponents. To limit his direct dealings with Westerners, Kung had already tried unsuccessfully to persuade the throne to give the job of supervising foreign customs to Wo Jen's Board of Revenue rather than to his Tsungli Yamen. With Hart he was stiff and dignified at first, but he began to relax when he found that Hart had an intimate knowledge of the treaties and the ports and could provide facts and figures to back all his recommendations, details that enabled the prince to guard his back from enemies.

Entirely on his own, Hart was evolving a personal approach that would make him unique among prominent foreigners in China. Gradually, Chinese and Manchu alike would respond to his flexibility and perception, giving him access to officials, to ruling princes, in time even to the imperial household. He alone would be permitted to join them in thousands of hours of conversation over the years.

Hart recounted these early experiences with Prince Kung to a medical officer at the British legation, David F. Rennie, who jotted down the anecdotes after dinner each evening. "The prince put a long series of questions to [Hart] on custom-house matters," wrote Rennie, "and remarked that [Hart] must think him almost childish asking so many and such apparently simple questions; but the truth was that, until lately, he was totally unacquainted, not only with these special matters, but with business matters generally, having had, until recent events compelled him to assume his present responsibilities, but little to attend to beyond amusing himself." Hart was impressed by the prince's efforts to understand: "Strange to say, the prince perceives the advantage which is likely to accrue to trade from low duties, while the more experienced and astute [Wen Hsiang] cannot see this, and stoutly holds out for high duties."

When Rennie's account was published, Hart was shocked, vowing never again to reveal any of his private discussions or personal perceptions of China's rulers. Prince Kung was also alarmed, so Hart took a lifelong vow of silence to protect himself and the prince from further indiscretions. Because of this vow, we have to read between the lines in his unpublished diaries to assemble the multitude of Hart's perceptions into the rare picture that emerges of the Manchu leadership at unguarded moments.

Sometimes Hart arrived early at the Yamen to find the prince alone, reading dispatches. This gave them time for friendly chats about such things as cannibals and horses—and time for Prince Kung to marvel over the wonderful invention of pockets in Hart's clothing. Manchu men carried their personal effects—fans, tobacco, pocket spittoons—in small pouches hanging from their belts. When Wen Hsiang would join them later in the day, Hart would be amused to hear the two Manchu agree that there was hardly an official in the Chinese government whom they would trust and how fortunate they were to have foreigners in their employ "whose reports they can trust as being in accord with facts."

Hart was shrewd but forthright in cultivating the Manchu, while they were busy cultivating him. They never had any doubt about what Hart wanted and where he stood. As early as 1861 Prince Kung observed that what made Hart exert himself in their behalf was "his covetous anxiety for the extremely large salary of the Inspector General." This was easier for the prince to understand than the more complex cravings of Lay and Parkes, for whom money was muddled with glory and malice. Gradually Hart became Prince Kung's private adviser on everything under the sun. "I saw [Prince Kung] frequently—in fact," Hart said, "whenever I wished to do so, and was in constant attendance at the Foreign Office."

Lay meanwhile was still officially Hart's boss and still pushing as hard as ever. Returned from England, Lay now conceived a plan for an imperial Chinese navy to defend the coast and to enforce Customs duty collections. He received permission from the throne to purchase a fleet of steam gunboats in Europe, with British crews. But Lay, always a man of bluster, went too far when he demanded that he be placed in charge of the fleet, as China's Lord High Admiral. In this role Lay would take orders only from the emperor, with no Manchu or Chinese official as middleman. Doubtless this made sense to an Englishman, because it assured that the navy would not be used as a pawn by local mandarins. But Lay's plan interfered with the schemes of Viceroy Li Hung-chang, who preferred a navy that he alone would control and manipulate. The viceroy scuttled Lay's fleet by hiring away the British crews and stirring up his fellow governors along the coast, all of whom had ambitions for their own naval squadrons. This was the end as well of Lay's brief career as the I.G. of Chinese Customs. He was paid off grandly by the Manchu, leaving China with the handsome sum of nearly 21,000 taels of silver in severance pay. Robert Hart immediately inherited his job as the I.G.

Under Hart the Customs became an honest, efficient civil service, staffed primarily with foreigners. He would tolerate no bullying Harry Parkes or Horatio Lay on his team. Westerners who worked for him— French, Russian, German, English, and American—were expected to show respect for their host country: "The Inspectorate of Customs is a

Chinese, and not a foreign Service, and as such it is the duty of each of its members to conduct himself towards Chinese, people as well as officials, in such a way as to avoid all cause of offence and ill-feeling." A British consul complained that the Customs officers were "much more Chinese, many of them, than the Chinese themselves."

Hart thereafter provided no less than one third of the entire revenue of the imperial government. His Customs also ran the Imperial Post Office. Salaries and other earnings in the Customs far exceeded what was paid in the Western diplomatic services. With the low cost of housing, food, and servants in China, a careful man could save half his wages and plan an early retirement. The Chinese Customs became one of the most attractive careers a man could have in the East. Members of Parliament and peers of the realm began pestering Hart to hire their children or the children of relatives. Hart's own relatives nagged him pitilessly. Over the years he prudently took on a certain number of well-connected nominees and through this judicious patronage was soon building himself a useful constituency in London and other capitals.

By 1866 his control of Customs was total. He was the only man in the Customs Service recognized by the Chinese government and alone was responsible for its operations. He was given an allowance by the government and was accountable to no one but himself for its expenditure.

There were times when he grew weary, disgusted, ill, or lonely, but each time he was about to resign and go home he reminded himself of "the difficulty likely to be caused by my withdrawal at a time when I alone held the threads of several unfinished experiments." "I want to make China strong," Hart wrote, "and I want to make England her best friend."

His main enemies were his own countrymen—chiefly British merchants, who wished to make their fortunes as fast as possible and go home. "We are not out here for our health," they were fond of saying. They objected to any controls that interfered with profits.

Some British ministers at Peking resented Hart; others stayed amicable, valuing his insights, his intercession at court, or his ability to arbitrate a sensitive matter completely behind the scenes. Although he was in love with China and had great hopes for his future there, he never went native. His suits, shirts, shoes, socks, topcoats, and underwear all came from home. So did his candy, his alcoholic beverages, and the sheet music he played on his violin. He ordered everything from British catalogues.

In late 1865 Prince Kung granted Hart leave for several months to go home on urgent private affairs. It was his first time back to England in nearly twelve years. His urgent private affairs were named Anna, Herbert, and Arthur Hart.

He had maintained his Chinese mistress, Ayaou, since 1855, and they now had three children: Anna, born in late 1858 or early 1859; Herbert, in

1862; and Arthur, in 1865. Many years later, when he was an old man thinking about posterity, Hart went back through his diaries and purged most of the references to his love affair with Ayaou, so there is no record of what became of her. All we know is that she vanished from his life in 1865, apparently dying in childbirth after delivering her third child. Hart took the three children to England, placed them with a family, and provided financially for their schooling and maintenance until they reached maturity. He never saw them again.

Although he rarely mentioned Ayaou even obliquely, Hart never forgot her. In a letter written ten years later, in 1875, he described her as "one of the most amiable and sensible people imaginable," while casting himself blackly as "a fool."

The other matter of urgent personal business that obliged him to ask Prince Kung for home leave that year was that Hart had determined to find and marry a proper wife. He was free to do so, since the death of Ayaou, and as he confided to his diary, "I feel rather lonely, and I wish very much I had a wife." By then he was making £4,000 a year, a handsome salary even in London.

He sought a wife as straightforwardly as he had bought a concubine. Arriving back in Northern Ireland, he became acquainted with Hester Jane Bredon, the daughter of his family doctor, and five days later proposed marriage. Hessie was a prim, severe girl of eighteen, a model of Victorian fustiness in overdecorated velvet, with a measuring eye for the main chance. What Hart was after was not a grand passion but a Victorian marriage, one that would suit his station. Their courtship lasted three months. When they were married on August 22, 1866, she was only nineteen to Hart's thirty-one, but that was a suitable spread for a man already making a great name for himself in the East.

Hessie spent the next ten years with him in China, during which she lost her first baby by miscarriage, then gave birth to a daughter, Evey, and a son, Edgar Bruce. Her life in Peking was as pleasant as it could be anywhere under the British Raj. There were Hart's parties, and when she went to pay calls on the ladies of the legations she traveled in a green sedan chair carried by four men.

The Harts were compatible if not adoring, and Robert was proud of Hessie and the children. As in many such colonial marriages the children were a convenient and proper reason to separate before the marriage went sour. In 1876, her duty fulfilled, Hessie took the children and went back to England, to begin enjoying the fruits of her labor, as the wife of the famous I.G.

Hart was still living at the time in the Peking suburbs, in a Chinese house he had renovated to please Hessie. In 1877 the Manchu court gave him permission to move to a new location on a corner of Marco Polo

Street near the legations, to facilitate his Customs business. There he built a new house, a Western-style villa set in a big garden, with offices and individual cottages for his staff. Hart's house was laid out in a letter H, with drawing rooms, a billiard room, his cluttered private office, and a reception room for Chinese guests. Like most other residences in Peking, the compound was surrounded by a high wall.

When he made a trip to Europe in April 1878, he and Hessie were reunited briefly. Their last child, a girl he nicknamed Nollie, was conceived. Hester came back to Peking with him, and Nollie was born there on November 1, 1879. No longer intrigued with life in the mysterious East, Hessie again took the children and returned to Europe in 1882. The Harts were separated for the next twenty-four years. Always discreet, he never explained this separation and stayed in touch faithfully by mail. Ever careful with money, he was becoming a wealthy man and provided a luxurious life for Hessie in England and on the Continent. It was what she had always wanted, and he had not let her down.

The two most important servants of the dragon throne now were complete opposites: Viceroy Li Hung-chang and Robert Hart, the most powerful Chinese political boss and the most influential Westerner. They developed a close working relationship but remained aloof personally. When the viceroy was in Peking, Hart made it a habit to see him as often as he could, in the evenings about 10:00 P.M., and stayed late, chatting into the small hours. In Hart's diaries, Li is mentioned again and again as a source of valuable inside information. He admired the simplicity with which Li ran his household; the viceroy served Hart a plain table, usually fish, chicken, and a large bowl of rice. When Hart commented favorably upon this to a member of the Yamen, remarking how he disliked the waste that so often accompanied the multiplatter banquets of the rich, word immediately got back to Li. The next time Hart arrived, there was an elaborate meal of more than sixty dishes, from shark fin soup to lichees. Never a big eater, Hart was obliged to sample every course, while Li took great pleasure in his discomfort, remarking deadpan, "You shall not have the chance to go away again and say that you have been fed like a coolie in my house."

He saw Li at his best and at his worst. It was Robert Hart who was called in to mediate the angry dispute between Li and Charles Gordon in 1864—over the beheading of the Taiping princes—during which Gordon gave him a critical analysis of Li's treachery and ruthlessness.

Hart was wary of Li, but he did not allow himself to be discouraged by the many instances of cynicism and perfidy in the regime. Professionally he respected the viceroy, a respect that matured as both men grew to old age in the harness. "Li is not bad," Hart said, "but his surroundings are very objectionable—lots of ability, but no honesty or veracity."

For all his corruption, dishonesty, and opportunism, Li was a man of action, extraordinarily competent at everything he set his mind to. He became personally involved in the most routine and boring tasks, pouring energy into finite detail. Other Chinese officials might bask in the sun, avoiding any form of labor, but Li was a human dynamo, and this was something the Ulsterman admired. "He wants occupation," Hart once noted, "and the others are glad to let him handle such nasty work."

All his adult life in China, Hart remained stubbornly optimistic that his efforts and those of other men of good will would eventually win through and set China firmly on the road to reform and modernization. After his first ten years in Peking he wrote to a friend, "I do think the big ship is coming round at last and heading in the right direction."

In 1885 Hart was offered the post of British minister to Peking. When he cabled news of the offer to his wife, Hessie, she urged him to turn it down. He was grieved by the dilemma this put him in. How much he longed for the "sentimental glitter of ending [his China career] at the Legation."

The opportunity to become the British minister arose with the unexpected death of the incumbent, none other than the turbulent Harry Parkes, now Sir Harry, the originator of the tragic Arrow War, who as a young man had caused Hart both envy and dismay: "What self-assertion that man has got, and how much fortune favors him!" Hart was so tempted by the opportunity to succeed Sir Harry that he had already drafted a farewell address to the Customs Service. His plan called for his brother James to succeed him. But James's failings—mostly the result of alcohol—were obvious to others: "The Yamen thinks him a little too fond of fun." Viceroy Li was pressing for his own man to succeed Hart as I.G.

The viceroy's choice was Gustav Detring, a shrewd and tenacious German with curly black hair, a neatly trimmed Vandyke, and coolly perceptive eyes framed by pince-nez, who had come to China some twenty years earlier. Hart had hired him in 1865, noting that "he seems a pleasant, intelligent young fellow: but he lisps somewhat, and will always speak Chinese with an accent." By 1872 Detring had risen to become a commissioner and six years later was appointed to Tientsin, where he became a private adviser to Li. Contrary to Hart's normal practice of rotating his men, as a favor to the viceroy he allowed Detring to remain in Tientsin for a full twenty-seven years. As confidential consultants to the Chinese government, Detring and Hart sometimes found themselves about to collide.

Hart feared that with Detring as I.G. the Customs would become the personal preserve of Li. As with everything else Li touched, it would become contaminated and would be used to funnel money into Li's coffers instead of into the national treasury. He complained to a friend that a

Customs Service dominated by Li would be "so maimed . . . as to end its usefulness if not its days." The only way to thwart Li was for Hart to refer the Detring matter directly to the empress dowager. Tzu Hsi decided she would prefer "Our Hart" to remain as the I.G.

The wish of the dowager made up Hart's mind, and he announced that he would remain in his post. For the next twenty-three years he labored on, the only Western man to portray Tzu Hsi consistently as a woman and not a monster.

CHAPTER NINE

A Hostage to Etiquette

Kuang Hsu was only three years old when he was brought into the Forbidden City in 1875 to live with his official mother Tzu An and his aunt Tzu Hsi. Confused and frightened, he had trouble adjusting, and his transformation into the Son of Heaven was not easy. Robert Hart wrote in his diary:

> [Prince Kung] looks after the Emperor himself—telling him what to do and generally taking care of the child. The [child's father, the Seventh Prince,] was not there: he's ill and grieves for the boy who, too, on his side is not happy at all. His mother and nurse and another woman [came] to pacify him; but were turned out; again the nurse was sent in; but [Tzu Hsi] sent her out again in an hour: the Empress Dowager [Tzu An] . . . is determined the lad shall forget all his former condition and grow up a completely palace-born lad.

Later medical reports show that by the time he was a young adult Kuang Hsu was severely traumatized and at times could hardly function. The vital question has been how much of this was inflicted in the Forbidden City. Scholars have been unanimous in supposing that before he came to the imperial palace Kuang Hsu was a normal—if high-strung—little boy who was deeply upset by being wrenched out of the family nest, deprived of a wholesome childhood, and then tormented by "the evil murderess" Tzu Hsi until he was a human wreck, living a virtual prisoner in the palace until he died—either murdered by Tzu Hsi or on her orders. This is the version of Kuang Hsu's story that was invented by the self-styled reformer Kang Yu-wei as a means to discredit the empress dowager. Do-gooders like Alicia Little then rushed to circulate Kang Yu-wei's version as the truth, and nobody ever saw fit to stop the giddy tale-spinning of this claque of ill-informed bigots. Bland and Backhouse invented more grim details. The truth about Emperor Kuang Hsu is dramatically different and much more interesting.

At age three Kuang Hsu was almost spastic with tension, already so overwrought that he had a severe speech impediment, the result of child abuse by his real mother, Tzu Hsi's sister.

Kuang Hsu's mother was described graphically by another member of the family, who later became Emperor Pu Yi: "She was a devout Buddhist and would not go into the garden in the summer, saying she was afraid of trampling any ants to death. Yet although she was so benevolent towards ants, she was merciless when it came to beating servants. It was said that the incurable facial tic of one of the family's eunuchs was the result of the flogging she once had given him." Kuang Hsu had four siblings by his mother, but three died in infancy, evidently of abuse and malnutrition. Their mother, wrote Pu Yi, "never allowed her children to eat their fill. . . . [Her] fourth son died of malnutrition before reaching the age of five." She tyrannized her children, even disapproving of smiles and laughter. " 'Why are you laughing? Have you no manners?' "

Even Kuang Hsu's half-brother, Pu Yi's father Prince Chun II, did not escape the damaging influence of Tzu Hsi's sister. Like Kuang Hsu, he stammered all his life, at times to the point of incoherence.

The image that emerges is of a shrieking harridan and child-beater who, after shaking and pummeling her infants into a choking and stammering terror, then locked them up in closets until they wept themselves to exhaustion. Little wonder that Kuang Hsu was already a nervous wreck when he was brought to the imperial palace to be a surrogate emperor.

Tzu Hsi pushed for her nephew's selection as the new emperor in part to rescue him from his mother's abuse. Tzu Hsi would certainly have known about the deaths of Kuang Hsu's siblings, and he was the only living male blood relative of her next generation. When Kuang Hsu's mother and wet nurse came to the palace to "pacify" the child, a prospect that might well make us shudder, it was Tzu Hsi who immediately made them leave. Some historians suggest that it was Tzu Hsi's intervention that had made it possible for her sister to marry Prince Chun. However, by her own admission, Tzu Hsi did not get along with any of her siblings and was apparently horrified by this sister's treatment of her children.

The boy's severe agitation was made worse during his formative years in the Forbidden City, not by Tzu Hsi but by the suffocating schooling he was given in toadying and in exaggerated Confucian court etiquette by chief tutor Weng Tung-ho. He was thrust into the deformed environment of the Forbidden City, where he became a hostage to etiquette, strictly

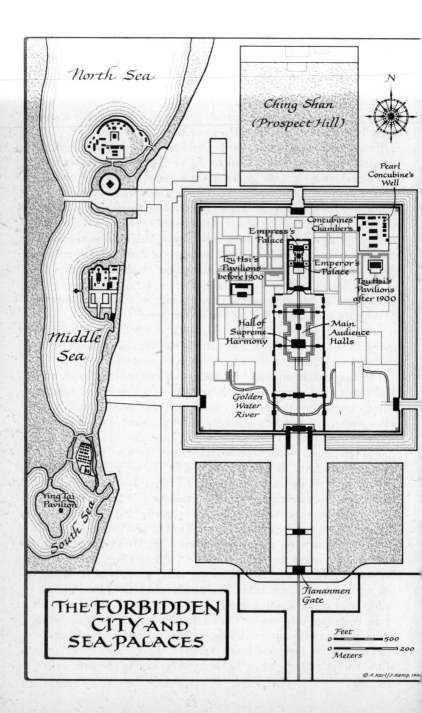

North Sea

Ching Shan
(Prospect Hill)

N

Pearl
Concubine's
Well

Concubines'
Chambers

Empress's
Palace

Tzu Hsi's
Pavilions
before 1900

Emperor's
Palace

Tzu Hsi's
Pavilions
after 1900

Middle
Sea

Hall of
Supreme
Harmony

Main
Audience
Halls

Golden
Water
River

Ying Tai
Pavilion

South Sea

THE FORBIDDEN
CITY AND
SEA PALACES

Tiananmen
Gate

Feet
0   500
Meters
0   200

© A. Karl/J. Kemp, 1992

supervised by overly fastidious tutors, put continually on the defensive, and drilled by his chief tutor to be abjectly fearful and submissive toward Tzu An and Tzu Hsi.

In raising the ill-fated Emperor Tung Chih, the empress dowagers and the palace tutors had been too indulgent—with disastrous results. Now, although Kuang Hsu had been rescued from the persecution of his biological mother, his tutors were going to overcompensate and make him pay for Tung Chih's misbehavior by being smothered in strict conformity.

Tzu An, the higher ranking of the two dowagers, took charge of the child. All else aside, Tzu Hsi was too sick with her liver ailment to be much involved. Until he was nine years old, all decisions about him were the primary responsibility of Tzu An, his father Prince Chun, and his chief tutor Weng Tung-ho.

The palace eunuchs went to work on the child to make certain he was different from Tung Chih, and different he was. No longer was the Son of Heaven to be punished with a mere pinch on the cheek. The new American minister, Charles Denby, reported: "He is said, whether justly or not I do not know, to be passionate and self-willed. Stories are told of his having destroyed in fits of passion foreign clocks and watches of which he has great numbers." His mother's crudely effective method of dealing with children who threw temper tantrums continued to be used on Kuang Hsu at his father's insistence after he moved into the Forbidden City. The chief eunuch would exclaim, "The Lord of Ten Thousand Years has fire in his heart. Let him sing for a while to disperse it." Howling, tiny Kuang Hsu would be locked in the small, windowless closet where his chamber pot was kept, and no matter how much he wailed, screamed, kicked or implored, nobody paid attention. Only when he stopped "singing" would they let him out. These periods of miserable solitude had their effect, making him deeply melancholy and introspective. Unlike Tung Chih, Kuang Hsu was a very impressionable, sensitive child, with a fragile ego.

When he balked at his long hours of monotonous study or tedious official ceremony, he was threatened with retribution by the Thunder God. On cue from a tutor, eunuchs in another room crashed and banged as if the Thunder God was next door ready to take vengeance. From this Kuang Hsu developed a lifelong fear of thunder and loud noises, adding fits of panic to his already heavy burden. When he reached puberty these fits became so severe that he was literally immobilized with fear for days.

He did not escape his mother entirely. In keeping with her rules, even in the palace Kuang Hsu was forced to be frugal in his meals. Denby reported: "The diet of the emperor is vigorously prescribed. . . . Should he desire to partake of any article not on the menu, the Board having charge of the Imperial table must be consulted before he is supplied." To compensate for the boring diet, the boy stuffed himself. When he did, two eunuchs grabbed him by the ankles and turned him upside down, banging his head on the floor "to settle his stomach." Tzu Hsi later commented to a palace lady-in-waiting that when Kuang Hsu was brought to the palace "he was so thin and weak. His parents seemed to be afraid of giving him anything to eat." But she was too ill during this period to intervene regularly on the boy's behalf.

Tzu An's heavy ceremonial commitments left the child at the mercy of the eunuchs much of the time. When they thought they could get away with it, they were extraordinarily malicious. They withheld from the dowagers information about his health, which was always delicate, so his health did not improve; mischievously, they dressed him in excessive layers of clothes, so he was bound up like a doll in a straitjacket; they teased and tormented him in countless small ways. Once permitted to discipline the child, they went too far, producing in Kuang Hsu a lifelong fear of servants. He once wrote an essay arguing that eunuchs were a source of great evil, asserting that the "downfall of the Tang [Dynasty] was induced exclusively by the [perversities of the] eunuchs." When he reached maturity, he made them suffer the consequences. Against them the gravest charge he made was of flagrant irreverence toward the Son of Heaven, punishable by execution. Like Tzu Hsi, who was sensitive about real or imagined slights, as an adult Kuang Hsu could not tolerate the eunuchs' slightest disrespect. When they made him furious, he ordered them beaten. They responded by spreading gossip in the teahouses, which reached the ears of the court's detractors, who passed along these tales to missionaries and journalists. Jade chopsticks were not the only things eunuchs stole from the imperial family; face could be stolen as well.

Inevitably, the extreme secrecy of the Forbidden City helped provoke these silly rumors. The dowagers were obliged to address the issue with an edict on June 11, 1878, when Kuang Hsu was six years old, "for the re-establishment of order and the stamping out of false rumors and floating gossip." In the edict the ladies said memorialists were complaining: "For the last month or more rumors have been rife, and more than one wild and weird story has been spread abroad, causing much fear and trepidation as it is bandied about from mouth to mouth."

One rumor, published in the Chinese newspaper *Empire*, claimed that Kuang Hsu was a pretender and that he had two pupils in each eye. The newspaper suggested that the dowagers had substituted one baby for another, as part of a wicked Manchu plot. After the story appeared, the publisher of *Empire* was said to have committed suicide; whether willingly or unwillingly is not clear. The rumor about Kuang Hsu's being a changeling matured over the years, eventually becoming part of the mass of slander against Tzu Hsi. It was a useful device for those who chose to challenge her legitimacy along with the legitimacy of the emperor. To imply that he was not a genuine royal was useful for rival Manchu factions, particularly the Ironhats, who wanted the throne for their own descendants. By 1900 the most popular version of this slander was that Tzu Hsi gave birth secretly to a child after a long love affair with General Jung Lu. First the offspring was said to be a girl; later this tale merged with the changeling story and the illegitimate child became a boy, who was secretly substituted for Kuang Hsu.

If the emperor's speech impediment had been widely known outside the palace in the late 1870s, such a rumor would never have gained currency. As it was, his father, Prince Chun, eventually became Prince Adviser to the throne, so the notion that another child was substituted for his own is silly. He may not have been the brightest Manchu prince, but he could recognize his own son.

Tutor Weng was a man whose loyalty was beyond question but whose misguided influence on Kuang Hsu has yet to be fully understood. He had suffered during his own childhood because of the persecution and degrading of his father by the Gang of Eight. In 1861, when Prince Kung's coalition took power, Weng's father was restored to grace; Weng himself, having attained the highest honors in the imperial examinations, was appointed a lecturer in the classics to the two dowagers. In their presence he was obsequious and servile, in order to protect and improve his position at court. Because he fawned over the two ladies continually and was always pressing other officials to flatter them and shower them with gifts, he was rewarded by the grateful dowagers with lavish privileges and was eventually raised to the supreme post of Grand Councillor. After Tzu An's death, he became the most outspoken supporter of Tzu Hsi, always rushing to her defense. Once, when the irritable Prince Tun criticized Tzu Hsi's leniency in judging a high-level bribery case, Weng rebuked him. "Prince Tun is amiss in his words. Ever since the beginning of the empress dowager's administration behind the curtains, everything has been settled solely in the interest of justice and impartiality." Such blatant sycophancy might seem to reflect badly on Tzu Hsi's judgment, for tolerating among her ministers somebody who was so excessively servile. However, protocol in the court made this kind of language typical. Ministers vied with each other to be elaborately gracious and to top each other in expressions of their admiration for the ruler. It was all part of the Confucian game, and not all that different from the baroque flattery of European courts.

Tzu Hsi did, for the most part, exhibit a strong sense of justice in her dealings with people, as long as she understood the situation. Unfortunately, her craving to be liked, and her vulnerability to flattery made it impossible for her to see into the minds of her manipulative courtiers.

Weng's absolute mastery of Confucian ritual and protocol made him unassailable in his official posts, while his toadying to the dowagers made him utterly secure in his private life.

In his tireless efforts to make Kuang Hsu ever more submissive and filial toward Tzu An and Tzu Hsi, Weng greatly overdid it. During official discussions he would pause to remind the young emperor of his obligation to refer all matters to the dowagers and prodded him while at it to make elaborate displays of sincerity.

The result of all Weng's brainwashing was that in the presence of the dowagers Kuang Hsu became transfixed. When he reached puberty he seemed on the surface to have a pleasant, friendly relationship with his aunt, but he was secretly so tense in her presence (and in the presence of women in general) that he suffered involuntary ejaculations. Of course this had a devastating effect on his self-esteem. At the time he did not realize that these orgasms were caused by a congenital defect. Medical reports after 1898 show that he was so tense he became impotent; he was unable to make love or to father a child. The French physician who examined him concluded that this grew out of a kidney ailment that was not recognized or treated by palace physicians and was aggravated by his extreme tension.

Here was a severely abused child who was suddenly made emperor of China, with all that entailed in exaggerated ceremony and artificial manners, only to discover as he grew up that he had a medical disability, an illness that made him impotent and subject to involuntary orgasms. All those who saw Kuang Hsu and his aunt together observed that she behaved in a kindly way toward him; she was even present during his medical examination by the French doctor, when Kuang Hsu spoke frankly about all these physical problems including his orgasms, something he could not have done if he was mortally afraid of her. Intimidated by the grande dame as he was intimidated by all women, yes, but not terrified. Only when he was able to fall asleep did he relax.

There was a positive side to his years of suffering. For the first time the education of an emperor of China was broadened to include more than just the Confucian classics. Wo Jen, the imperial tutor who had blocked all of Prince Kung's attempts to introduce Western ideas during the childhood of Tung Chih, had since died. Kuang Hsu's tutors, for all their faults, taught him Western subjects and Western concepts, as Charles Denby reported: "The emperor has been carefully educated after the Chinese fashion, [but] books from abroad [also] have been translated for his instruction." Later, "His intellect is supposed to be good." And again, ". . . the emperor has commenced the study of the English language. Two students of the Tung-wen College are his teachers. They attend him every morning at one o'clock. . . . It is said that he has a remarkable memory and is learning fast." The Tung-wen College was an interpreters' school established as an adjunct to Prince Kung's Tsungli Yamen. Robert Hart had arranged for his friend, the missionary-linguist W.A.P. Martin, to head its foreign staff.

To his everlasting credit, Kuang Hsu began to demonstrate as he grew up a dedication and commitment to the role of emperor that must have gratified the dowager empresses. As he entered his teens, he also showed a natural inclination to be an ascetic, preferring a monkish life of self-denial and solitude. Unlike Tung Chih, he exhibited no desire to cavort with the eunuchs and no interest in slipping out of the palaces. Kuang Hsu was never at ease in company; he ate his meals alone, a self-made prisoner in a world of warped protocol. A hostage to etiquette.

Like Hamlet he was of two minds about everything. He aspired to be decisive, but he was indecisive. He wanted to emulate the warrior kings of the past, but he was physically frail. He wanted to lead, but he could only follow, always waiting for someone to show him the way. Although he was slight of build, dainty, with delicate facial features, and was never in robust health, he was neither cowardly nor cringing; he braved the elements, taking long walks in the snow while refusing any cover or protection from his eunuch entourage. He once made a cryptic remark suggesting that like Tzu Hsi he considered the falling snow a way to hide himself from the people who were constantly surrounding and scrutinizing him. Like all Manchu princes he had daily lessons in the martial arts, including Wushu (erroneously called Kung Fu in the West), swords and staffs, falconry, and firing a compound Mongol bow while galloping on horseback. He recorded a few small administrative victories as well: as he grew up he began keeping careful watch on the much-abused imperial household budget, eventually cutting allocations by a third. No small feat.

From 1875 to 1881 Tzu An was not ill for even a day. Without warning early in April 1881 she collapsed. An edict reported that "the benign lady was suddenly taken ill. A decoction of medicine was immediately given to dissipate the ailment . . . but unexpectedly on the following day the sickness rapidly grew dangerous, respiration was hindered by copious generation of phlegm and the case became urgent and desperate. Between the hours of 7 and 9 P.M. [she expired]." She was forty-four when she died.

Inevitably, jaded Peking buzzed with the usual conspiratorial talk of murder and intrigue. The American legation reported: "Vague rumors of plottings in the Palace are afloat, but as yet they are but rumors and not worth repeating." With the senior of the two dowagers now dead and with Tzu Hsi's long debilitating illness, this would have been an opportune moment for a coup. Despite rumors, nothing developed. In 1910 the biographers Bland and Backhouse, never ones to ignore a rumor, wrote simply: "Tzu An fell ill of a sudden and mysterious sickness." They went on to assert: "It is very generally believed, and was freely stated at the time, that . . . Tzu Hsi brought about the death of her colleague."

There is nothing whatever in the record to support this statement. In 1914, four years after the Ching Dynasty had fallen from power, the same two authors discovered "evidence" that "Tzu Hsi made up her mind to kill [Tzu An]." The foul deed, they said, was accomplished with poisoned cookies. She did it, they said, because Tzu An had discovered Tzu Hsi in bed with an actor. This is absurd not only because it smells but because at the time Tzu Hsi was still an invalid. It was two more years before she began to recover.

Nonetheless, more than sixty years later, in *Eminent Chinese of the Ching Period,* Arthur Hummel noted under his entry for Tzu An: "Rumors spread that she had been poisoned by Tzu Hsi." He neglected to point out that these particular rumors did not spread until more than a quarter century after Tzu An died. Immanuel Hsu tells us in *Modern China* that Tzu An was "reputedly poisoned by Tzu Hsi." Reputed by Edmund Backhouse. The truth is, she died of viral flu.

The death of Tzu An left the ailing Tzu Hsi the sole dowager empress and the sole female regent. The imperial family and its undertakings were her responsibility exclusively for the first time. She was the matriarch now. It would be up to her to patch up quarrels between competing princes and factions at court.

Winning over the sole dowager empress became a vital part of court politics. Major decisions continued to be made by court officials and were then presented to her for approval. But as time passed, her approval took on a significance of its own. They made her an institution.

She was now forty-five years old. Kuang Hsu was nine. Much has been written to suggest that there was serious discord between Tzu Hsi and her nephew during this period, but it was not apparent to Robert Hart or to the astute envoy Charles Denby. Without identifying his source, Denby wrote that Kuang Hsu was known to be "devoted to her," as well he might have been.

Robert Hart commented on the matter in a letter in 1886: "The Emperor went to the Temple of Heaven yesterday and returned to the Palace this morning. He is said to be a bright, handsome youth, and this act brings him nearer the day when he'll be his own master. How wonderfully the Empress [Tzu Hsi] has held out and how well she has worked—Regent during two long minorities."

Until Kuang Hsu reached manhood, Tzu Hsi would be seen by the outside world as the true ruler of China, while in fact it was Prince Kung who had always bound the coalition together and made it work, with the support of Viceroy Li and others.

By 1884 Prince Kung had effectively ruled China for twenty-three years. Only three Manchu emperors had ruled longer than that (Chia Ching being only a powerless figurehead during his first years on the throne), and no regent or adviser had ever enjoyed such a prolonged period of control.

Only a year after Tzu Hsi recovered her health and while Kuang Hsu was still gasping for air in his yellow silk cocoon, the Manchu court became involved in a new power struggle that brought Prince Kung's benign rule to a sudden end. As in the Jehol coup of 1861 and the succession crisis of 1875, it was a tug-of-war between Kung's coalition of pragmatists and the leading Manchu reactionaries, the Ironhat faction. A new generation of hotheaded Ironhats had risen to positions of power by 1884, backed by Chinese officials who were equally hostile toward foreigners. Kuang Hsu and Tzu Hsi were caught in the middle.

Several leading reactionaries had been untouched by the purge of the Gang of Eight: Prince Tun, the Fifth Prince; Prince Chun, the Seventh Prince and the father of Kuang Hsu; and Duke Chung, the father of Empress A-lu-te. As Prince Chun's role at court increased with the maturity of his son, his followers multiplied and the leverage of hardliners increased. Sniffing victory, they began to chip away at Prince Kung's authority, waiting for the right opportunity to dislodge him. They were afraid to move too fast. While they were jealous of Prince Kung, they were not afraid of him. But they hated and feared his ally Viceroy Li.

Being a realist, Li was less interested in who sat on the throne as emperor than in making sure that Prince Kung remained chief minister, in a position to protect Li's many profitable enterprises. In return for Li's support over many years, the prince had seen to it that the viceroy was given unique privileges. By 1878 after six years as viceroy of Chihli Province, the choicest post in the empire, Li was technically overdue for rotation to another part of the empire. But thanks to Kung's intervention, Li continued to hold the Chihli post until 1895—twenty-three consecutive years, giving him unprecedented opportunity to increase his wealth and clout. He was always a dangerous adversary for the Ironhats to take on, and it was Li who foiled their previous power grab in 1875. But even a man as cunning as Li made mistakes through greed and accident that left his vulnerable underbelly exposed to attack.

When he was first made viceroy of Chihli, Li had established a "new" army with the support of the throne. Using his private Anhwei Army as a nucleus, Li reorganized the northern military forces and combined them with his own under the name Peiyang (Northern) Army. By amalgamating these forces with the laudable objective of modernizing them, he gained control of a much larger force and put the field commanders under direct obligation to him rather than to the throne. As viceroy he could also pay their expenses from the provincial treasury, instead of from his own coffers.

Chihli protected Peking from foreign invasion, in theory if not in practice. The provincial capital, Tientsin, was the port of entry for shipments of tribute rice from the south. Diplomatically it was a second Peking: most foreign nations set up consulates in Tientsin, where Li maintained his official residence. He owned much of the city, having grabbed all the property he could when he first became governor-general. Ever acquisitive, he took over property throughout the empire, squeezing it from enemies, taking it in compensation for unpaid loans. He owned mansions in Peking that he picked up when Chinese or Manchu officials defaulted on secret deals. As the richest man in China, Li found ways to dispense patronage to the highest Manchu nobility, many of whom were cash poor, living on imperial allowances. He was always lending money to spendthrift Manchu nobles, then calling in the debts when they were on their uppers. Since he was inventive and discreet, rather than brutal and obnoxious, he was feared more than despised.

Li had almost total control over the development and exploitation of North China's resources. Whenever Li put together deals involving Chinese and foreign investment, he kept a chunk of stock in the venture, sometimes sitting as chairman of the board or putting in a surrogate. In this way he retained control of the Soochow, Shanghai, and Nanking arsenals; mines in Shansi and Shantung; coal and iron mines in Chihli. He saw to the construction of a three-mile-long railroad, the first in China, at the Kaiping mines in 1878; the construction of telegraph lines in Chihli; the building of cotton mills in Shanghai; the promotion and founding of the Tientsin Military Academy and Torpedo School.

One of his most successful ventures was the China Merchants Steam Navigation Company, which he established in 1872. Until that time, tribute rice was carried north in junks owned by former pirate syndicates now subsidized by the central government. Foreign steamships were coming into use and were being chartered for the first time by Chinese merchants. Li proposed that Shanghai businessmen underwrite the cost of building a fleet of steamships from scratch, which would then be chartered by the central government to carry the tribute rice. Part of the deal was that the company would be run by men personally selected by Li. Thereafter he held a monopoly on all tribute rice shipments, as well as control of the steamship fleet, and all of this done with others' money.

As Superintendent of the Northern Ports, he was responsible for seeing that the tribute rice was protected at every stage of its journey from the south. Li garrisoned his own army units as "grain troops" along the route from the paddy fields downriver to Shanghai. Local officials had to provide up to a third of local taxes to support Li's troops. By these methods he sought to control everything from beginning to end: he was able to pressure merchants to start a venture, to extort funds to maintain it, to control large blocks of its stock, to administer it through puppets, to guard it with his own troops, and to oblige others to pay for the soldiers' maintenance. Such men, the sage Sun Tzu would remark, are a joy to their sovereign.

Li's soldiers also supervised the transportation of salt to Peking, allowing him to oversee the salt monopolies that were one of China's major sources of tax revenue. In sum Li had become so involved with the basic necessities of life that by 1875 the Manchu were completely dependent upon him for their survival. Since Li cloaked all his deals in secrecy and had his loyalists planted everywhere, it was impossible to remove him from power or to assassinate him, without jeopardizing the state itself. The strangler fig was now supporting the host tree.

Li engineered deals, negotiated treaties, dispatched armies, and saw to it that the heart of the empire was administered, policed, spied upon, goaded when necessary, and that foreign interests were stroked or kept at bay. None of this pleased the Ironhats. They distrusted his deals with foreign governments, they knew he was being enriched by commercial contracts and huge foreign bribes, they resented being patronized by him, and they reasoned with some justice that it was only a matter of time before Li staged a palace coup and put himself on the throne. Robert Hart, who knew him well, often voiced fears in his diary that Li could strike at any time.

The crisis that served in 1884 as an excuse to bring Prince Kung down began when France seized the ancient Chinese tributary states of Tonkin, Annam, and Cochin in Indochina and began probing up the Red River and the Mekong, challenging China's hegemony along her southern border. While Paris made warlike noises, well-armed French naval squadrons plied the South China Sea. Prince Kung, recalling vividly the Allied seizure of Peking in 1860, tried to appease France and to negotiate a settlement, with the help of Viceroy Li. This effort at appeasement only incensed the patriotic Ironhats further.

To succeed against Prince Kung and Viceroy Li, the Ironhats needed strong Chinese support. Joining them in their conspiracy was the Pure party, a Chinese pressure group led by the foxy Chang Chih-tung, viceroy of the southern provinces of Kwangsi and Kwangtung, bordering on Tonkin. Both the Pure party and the Ironhats opposed any deal with Foreign Powers and advocated immediate war with France. Viceroy Chang, a nimble opportunist, and others banded together to flatter and boost the emperor's father, Prince Chun, encouraging him to play a larger role in his son's government; they built the Pure party around him and through him gained access to the young emperor and to Tzu Hsi.

Kung's success as leader of the coalition was built on compromise and concession. Now, more and more people were attacking him as a vacillator, procrastinator, and appeaser. He was harried first by one clique, then another. Believing the reports of his envoy in Paris and Robert Hart's assessment of the situation, Prince Kung felt that France could be brought to a compromise settlement. He dispatched Li Hung-chang to arrange it. When Li's settlement turned Indochina into a joint protectorate of China and France, the Pure party attacked both Prince Kung and Viceroy Li as "traitors." This became a rallying cry for the Ironhats. The throne was flooded with well-orchestrated memorials denouncing the two men.

Faced with growing dissension in the court, Tzu Hsi and Kuang Hsu capitulated and ordered Prince Kung to step down. The edict of dismissal cleared Prince Kung of the charge of treason. He was accused only of arrogance, nepotism, and inefficiency. They were all guilty of them.

Backhouse's version of these events is slightly different. According to him, Kung was dismissed because Tzu Hsi "believed that the Prince was intriguing against her with the young Emperor." Backhouse slyly added that she also believed that Prince Kung was "responsible for a recent memorial, in which several Censors had roundly denounced her for depraved morals and boundless extravagance." (Backhouse invented both the intrigue and the critical memorial.)

To save his own skin in 1884, Viceroy Li switched sides at the last moment, withdrew his support from Prince Kung, and gave it instead to Prince Chun and the Ironhats—taking his enemies completely by surprise in the best tradition of Wushu. They fumbled their daggers without spilling a drop of Li's blood. Kung's place as chief minister was taken by the emperor's father, Prince Chun. Foreign relations were placed in the hands of forty-eight-year-old Prince Ching, a man with no identifiable scruples. (Prince Ching came from a family with a long history of greed and manipulation. He had a reputation for dealing under the table, accepting bribes, and catering to the bad tempers of reactionaries.)

Once Prince Kung was out of office, back tending his fox-fairy garden, the Ironhats and their Pure party allies turned their attention again on Viceroy Li. Before they could remount their attack, the quarrel with France in Indochina boiled over into war. Previously the Ironhats had been able to blame failure on Prince Kung and his henchman Li. Now they found themselves alone responsible for winning a war. By the time they sorted out their order of battle the French were in firm control of Indochina. Chagrined, the Pure party had to appeal to Viceroy Li in his role as top diplomatic negotiator to rescue China's chestnuts from the fire.

To everyone's astonishment, after Prince Chun was confirmed as chief minister at court he became much more reasonable. The reality of running the empire made political extremism attractive only to those on the outside. Once inside, problems looked different. The Seventh Prince found himself performing the same balancing act his half-brother had carried on for more than twenty years.

Chun also discovered that he was neither willing nor able to restrain Li's appetite for power. The prince had no taste for dealing with foreign governments and foreign banks, and he had no stomach for the kind of tedious attention to detail that made Li a great administrator. So within months after Prince Kung's fall, Li magically reemerged as China's real ruler behind the scenes—treasurer, home minister, foreign minister, chief of intelligence, minister of transportation, minister of communication, and superintendent of trade. Some of these jobs he performed publicly, because he was instructed to do so by the throne, but many of his dealings were secret, carried out by his private staff of *mu-fu*, numbering in the hundreds. As an insurance policy he sent an unending stream of gifts to Prince Chun and to the empress dowager, which they found difficult to resist, as Li had intended. However, Li's efforts to win over Emperor Kuang Hsu proved to be his one great failure in a lifetime of success.

Kuang Hsu turned fifteen in 1887 and by tradition should have been married, thus preparing him for his accession to the throne a few months later. Both ceremonies were delayed for two years. It is usually said that this was because Tzu Hsi refused to relinquish power, but the sad truth is that Kuang Hsu was not ready. Early that year his father fell seriously ill. It was Prince Chun, not Tzu Hsi, who made the decision to postpone the handing over of power, then led the effort to persuade Tzu Hsi to remain as regent for several more years. The delay gave her extra time to choose Kuang Hsu's wife and concubines. She chose her extremely homely but sensible niece, daughter of Tzu Hsi's brother, Deputy Lieutenant General Kuei Hsiang; she would be called Empress Lung Yu. The empress-elect was three years older than Kuang Hsu, severely bucktoothed, plain as a jackrabbit, and twice as thin. As Kuang Hsu was Tzu Hsi's nephew this was a marriage of first cousins, not unusual in European aristocracy but potentially dangerous genetically. Because of Kuang Hsu's medical problems, it did not matter.

Many writers have criticized Tzu Hsi's selection of her nephew as emperor and her niece as empress. She already had all the power so she simply wanted, like any monarch, to gather around her what family she could as companions for her approaching old age. Those who watched them together in the palace say she seemed genuinely fond of Kuang Hsu and Lung Yu.

As imperial concubines, she chose two sisters from the Tatala clan. The girls were favorites of the emperor's senior tutor, Weng Tung-ho, whose suggestions carried weight with Tzu Hsi. The first, called Chen Fei or

Pearl Concubine, was ambitious, had a natural sparkle and pretty features; her sister, called Chin Fei or Lustrous Concubine, was rotund, with a placid but almost lifeless expression. One may have been chosen because she was bright, vivacious, and physically attractive, the other because she was not intimidating. Kuang Hsu was to do his duty with one of them, if at all possible.

Trouble developed immediately. Neither the empress-elect nor the young emperor was happy about the arrangement. Lung Yu, evidently a girl of strong character, was said to be stubbornly opposed to the whole idea from the beginning, and was forced into it by her family. Kuang Hsu reportedly refused even to see the bride, much less to consummate their marriage. Nevertheless, the ritual wedding ceremony took place on February 26, 1889.

The week after his wedding Kuang Hsu, now in his seventeenth year, assumed the throne. That same day, March 4, 1889, Tzu Hsi gratefully retired from the regency. The fifty-four-year-old empress dowager assumed that she could at last return to a simple life at the Summer Palace, leaving behind court strife and politics. To mark her retirement, she handed out awards to a great many people. Robert Hart in particular had reason to celebrate: "The Emperor is marrying; the Empress Dowager after two Regencies extending over about thirty years, is retiring to private life. Half a dozen important edicts are issued thanking all who had worked during the Regencies—living and dead, and one edict . . . praises me and my work, and [has] given me the very first (Cheng) rank from three generations back! From the foreign standpoint nothing could be more whimsical—from the Chinese, nothing could be more honourable." The Ancestral Rank of the First Class of the First Order for Three Generations meant that the honor was retroactive, bestowed on his ancestors rather than on his descendants, the only time in history that the honor was conferred on a foreigner.

Tzu Hsi demonstrated with this award that she was prepared to break with tradition from time to time despite the opposition of her ministers. Some of her courtiers were scandalized that a Foreign Devil now outranked most of them and their ancestors. The throne had not made such a gesture of support for a barbarian since the reign of Emperor Kang Hsi one hundred fifty years earlier when favored Jesuits were rewarded with mandarin rank. Tzu Hsi's recognition of Robert Hart and the approval it implied of the work he was doing was a major step in the direction of much-needed reforms in the Chinese government. Hart represented the kind of revolutionary change required to make the bureaucracy efficient. Ironically, Tzu Hsi had never been able to meet Hart and talk with him face-to-face because of the hidebound constraints of etiquette. Thirteen more years would pass before she was able to break those rules and arrange a private audience. In the meantime, this gesture was the only way in which she could express her approval in public.

Theoretically, Kuang Hsu was now the autocratic ruler of the empire; in fact, he was only a puppet of the system. Throughout his reign he was never in charge, except for a period of months in 1898. During the first part of his reign his decisions were guided by his tutor Weng Tung-ho, by Prince Kung, then by his father, Prince Chun. On the death of Prince Chun in 1891, Prince Ching, a cat's-paw for Viceroy Li Hung-chang, began advising the emperor. Kuang Hsu was always the object of manipulation; he never asserted himself in the way Emperors Kang Hsi and Yung Cheng had, by ruthlessly purging potential rivals, and he paid the terrible price. Admittedly, Kuang Hsu was still a youth. When he found the long hours of official duty taxing, he was known to slip off the throne and sneak behind the gauze curtain for a smoke.

The low comedy to which the Manchu government had sunk by this point was illustrated by its handling of the severe drought that racked the great North China plain in the summer of 1890. Robert Hart wrote about the young emperor's role. "The Emperor and Court . . . took to praying hard for rain, and we not only got it but 'caught it!' Now they are praying for fair weather, but not hard enough! We have had lakes in the city . . . rivers in the streets—swimming baths in the courtyards—shower baths in all the rooms."

At age nineteen Kuang Hsu held his first audience with the foreign ministers, on March 5, 1891, their first audience with an emperor since their perfunctory meeting with Tung Chih in 1873. Said the perceptive Denby of Kuang Hsu: "He has the appearance now of a delicate youth. He is small and thin and gives no promise of possessing physical strength. He is pale and intellectual looking. His eyes are large and black and his face smooth and hairless."

The envoys noticed his speech impediment and other odd traits they did not fully understand. As Denby put it, "He has a hesitation in his speech, and . . . he speaks slowly and with difficulty. While ordinarily quiet in his disposition, he is said to be very obstinate." But, Denby went on, everyone had high hopes for the boy: "Railroads, the electric light, physical science, a new navy, an improved army, a general banking system, a mint, all in the bud now, will soon be in full flower. . . . The reign of the young emperor will be the most memorable epoch in Chinese history."

Denby was right, it would be memorable, but not for railways and light bulbs.

It was Kuang Hsu's fate to be confronted three years later at age twenty-two with the empire's worst military debacle since 1860 when the Sino-Japanese War broke out in the summer of 1894. For Tzu Hsi the war meant yet another emergency at court in which she would be called upon to intervene. Her importance to the dynasty as an arbitrator had steadily increased over the years as those who had managed court business and affairs of state died or were dislodged by political enemies. It was Tzu Hsi's fate to have survived them all. Now, on the eve of her sixtieth birthday, the Japanese crisis—not her "insatiable" personal ambition—propelled her back onto center stage.

CHAPTER TEN

The New Ironhats

For years Japan had been attempting to undermine China's position as overlord of Korea. If the Japanese gained control of the Korean peninsula, they could threaten Peking, posing the gravest danger yet to the continued existence of the Ching Dynasty—a dynasty whose survival now depended upon an uncertain and impotent young emperor and an aging dowager who knew little of the real world. Much turned on how Viceroy Li handled Japanese provocations.

Korea was vulnerable because its ruling family was split by a long-running feud, in which agents of China, Japan, and Russia meddled at every opportunity. Twenty years earlier, in 1873, the strong-willed Korean regent, Taewon-gun, father of the feebleminded King Kojong, was forced to step down, giving way to Queen Min and her ambitious clan. Tokyo took advantage of this domestic quarrel to dispatch a fleet of warships and forced Korea to open herself to Japanese trade. This alarmed Peking, which saw any Japanese gain as a Chinese loss.

In 1882, in a Japanese-backed attempt to depose Queen Min and restore the old regent, a mob attacked the palace in Seoul and the king and queen barely escaped with their lives; several Korean court ministers were hacked to pieces. The resulting chaos provided China with an excuse to intervene, and Viceroy Li sent his most promising and conspiratorial protégé, twenty-three-year-old Yuan Shih-kai, with four thousand men to be stationed in the peninsula. Yuan (whom we first encountered at Robert Hart's lawn party) was the viceroy's chief agent in Korea for the next twelve years, a man of guile, swagger, and boundless ambition, with great appetites for women, food, money, and power.

After Yuan's arrival, China and Japan took turns backing rival factions in Seoul. In 1884 Korean radicals staged a coup. The plotters were funded by Tokyo and were supported by an elite force of Japanese secret agents, former samurai, disguised as Koreans. Although this coup was quickly put down by Yuan and his Chinese troops, one of the coup leaders, Kim Ok-kium, escaped to Japan, where he became a gadfly continually annoying China.

To avoid having the Korean situation grow into a full-scale military confrontation, Viceroy Li signed a pact with Japan's prime minister, Ito Hirobumi, called the Li-Ito Convention, which kept the cork in the bottle for the next ten years, while both countries continued their Korean intrigues under the table. During this period the Chinese tried repeatedly to have the Korean troublemaker Kim Ok-kium extradited from Japan, but the Japanese refused to cooperate. Yuan dispatched assassins to kill him, but Kim was protected by members of Japan's Dark Ocean society, the Genyosha, an ultranationalistic secret organization of Japanese military officers and underworld gangsters. Eventually, however, Kim allowed himself to be persuaded by the Chinese ambassador in Tokyo that if he went secretly to Shanghai, where he would be safe in the International Settlement, a deal could be arranged whereby Kim would head a new government in Seoul. He was surprised at a Japanese-owned hotel in the International Settlement in Shanghai in March 1894 and shot dead. His murder had been arranged through collusion involving Viceroy Li in China, General Yuan in Korea, and the Chinese ambassador in Japan.

After the murder the viceroy sent his personal thanks to the Chinese ambassador: "His murder has now provided a timely solution. I have received a letter from Yuan Shih-kai saying that the Korean court was dancing for joy and . . . that he was deeply obliged to you for your assistance in luring [Kim] to China."

It was premature to dance for joy. The assassination of Kim was the catalyst that brought about the disastrous Sino-Japanese War of 1894–95. Kim's close ties to the Genyosha enabled the Japanese secret society to use his murder as an excuse to agitate for war. Senior officers of the Japanese foreign ministry and army general staff, particularly the hawk Yamagata Aritomo, believed that Korea could be taken militarily, but they knew that Prime Minister Ito would not cooperate unless the crisis was pushed to the brink. The vice chief of the Japanese general staff secretly advised the Genyosha to "start a conflagration"; then it would be his "duty" to "go and extinguish the fire." The Genyosha were happy to oblige.

Starting a fire in Korea was easy. The Korean peasantry were so downtrodden that many sought refuge in a religious sect called Tonghak. Genyosha agents provoked the Tonghak into armed revolt against the Korean rulers. Both China and Japan sent troops to intervene. Frightened of what they had started, the Tonghak peasantry laid down their torches, but the fire was already out of control.

Yuan was given only fifteen hundred Chinese troops as reinforcements, but the Japanese military deliberately sent inflated reports of their numbers to Prime Minister Ito, so in response Tokyo dispatched eight thousand men. The Japanese army poured into Korea to extinguish a fire that they themselves had lit. Once on the peninsula in strength, the Japanese insisted on setting up a joint commission to reform the Korean government, a pretext for imposing joint rule.

With war now seemingly inevitable, Yuan slipped out of Korea secretly on July 17, 1894, bound for Tientsin. He was not prepared to sacrifice himself to a lost cause at this early stage in his career.

On July 25, 1894, spies informed the commander of a Japanese naval squadron that more Chinese troops and ammunition were being sent to Korea aboard a chartered British ship, the S.S. *Kowshing,* sailing out of Port Arthur. The Japanese squadron intercepted the *Kowshing* and demanded that she follow, but the Chinese refused to obey. Immediately, the Japanese fired two broadsides and a torpedo point blank, sinking the *Kowshing* with everyone aboard. Those who did not drown were machine-gunned as they clung to bits of wreckage.

In Peking, Robert Hart despaired over the news: "China is keeping quiet for a day or two to see what England will do, and also to give time for the joint endeavor of England, Russia and Germany . . . to persuade or force Japan to put out the war torch. But in a day or two if waiting shows no promise of being rewarded, China will herself act: and I fear only disaster will follow. The Japs will win everywhere at the start and China in a funk will cave in." How right he was.

Unknown to Hart, Japan already had obtained England's promise not to interfere, and Russia followed suit.

Since the fall of Prince Kung the Ironhats were in a dominant position in Peking, occupying many of the senior posts around the throne. So at the urging of these bellicose advisers, Tzu Hsi and the inexperienced Emperor Kuang Hsu were committed to war. Both Manchu and Chinese officials were contemptuous of the Japanese, referring to them in diplomatic correspondence and imperial decrees as "dwarf-pirates" and "dwarf-bandits." Times had changed, however. Since the Meiji Restoration in 1868, the Japanese had begun to industrialize and to arm themselves for an all-out assault on the balance of power in East Asia. Hart was one of the few onlookers who grasped that China was way out of her depth. Most Westerners assumed that in the long term China would defeat Japan by sheer force of numbers. They failed to grasp that the Japanese were extremely serious about everything they did, while China could barely coordinate its right and left hands to thread a needle.

When the war began the senior imperial tutor, Weng Tung-ho, master of empty ceremonies and consummate toady, was named to the Grand Council and appointed special consultant to the throne to advise the emperor on how to run the war. This was like appointing a dancing instructor as general of the armies. Weng knew absolutely nothing of war; it was characteristic of him to posture and vacillate. This he did, urging both war and peace, on alternate days of the week, with drastic consequences. Terrible losses piled up for China, while Peking showed itself unable to stand fast and unable to back out.

During the crisis Tzu Hsi, who also knew nothing of war, was consulted constantly and was expected to mediate between war party and peace party, and to do so had to return to the Forbidden City from her retirement at the Summer Palace. The burden of arbitration was left to her, not because she had any competence in military matters but because nobody else had any competence either. Her role as ceremonial arbiter had become so habitual that Emperor Kuang Hsu was often bypassed completely in the decision-making process. To avoid insulting either the emperor or the dowager, it was decided that henceforth all documents for the throne would be submitted to both Tzu Hsi and Kuang Hsu simultaneously. They worked together in Tzu Hsi's office on pretty Ying-tai island, in one of the lakes beside the Forbidden City, in a pavilion built long ago by Emperor Chien Lung.

Tzu Hsi had learned a few lessons in common sense, which she tried to impress upon her quarreling ministers. Two weeks before China's declaration of war, she had cautioned that their policy decisions must not be misunderstood. They must be firm and decisive (which they were not). The Ironhats were as certain they could defeat Japan in 1894 as the Gang of Eight had been convinced they could defeat Lord Elgin in 1860. As the war went terribly wrong, they played upon Tzu Hsi's fears that Manchu ancestral burial grounds and Peking itself might be violated by the "dwarf pirates." This alone was enough to get her behind their saber rattling. She thought she could count on Viceroy Li, who ultimately controlled both the army and the navy through surrogates. Her experience had been that Li could work miracles.

It would take more than a miracle. China's navy consisted of different fleets ruled by overlords in various coastal provinces, each with his own parochial interests. One of the largest, the Fukien naval fleet, had gone to the bottom in 1884 during the war with France over Indochina. That embarrassment had put Peking under intense pressure to rebuild, modernize, and centralize the navy. Li, as the most powerful official on the coast, had been agitating for a central navy for years and without blushing put his own name forward to head it. An Admiralty Board was set up under Prince Chun, Prince Ching, and Viceroy Li. It was an empty gesture from the beginning, because parochialism continued to maintain four separate fleets in four parts of the coast, but the Admiralty Board provided a new and golden opportunity for patronage and malfeasance. Li directly ran the

Northern Navy and the Northern Army, and contracted with foreign firms to build fortified harbors, including major bases at Port Arthur in Manchuria and Weihaiwei on the Shantung peninsula. He purchased ships from British and German builders and by 1890 had some twenty-five vessels, including nine modern warships. He also arranged for loans from foreign banks to start a naval academy. But modern ships and ordnance were useless in the wrong hands.

The Admiralty Board remained only a princely pork barrel. Prince Chun, as chairman of the board, requisitioned the funds Li had borrowed for the naval academy and used them to build motor launches for the amusement of the court at the Lake Palaces in Peking and on Lake Kunming by the Summer Palace. The emperor's father was in a position to demand money from Viceroy Li at any time, in exchange for not interfering in his affairs. Other Admiralty funds were used by Prince Chun and Prince Ching to shower gifts on the empress dowager, underwriting lavish and unnecessary projects designed to please her, in order to win her support in policy debates.

Prince Chun had made extravagant plans to complete the restoration of one wing of the Summer Palace as Tzu Hsi's principal residence in retirement, and put the arm on Li for the necessary funds. Li had his own private way of dealing with importuning princes. Instead of going to foreign banks for a loan, Li launched a discreet money-raising campaign disguised as a secret navy defense fund drive. Wealthy gentry and rich officials in every province were squeezed to contribute on the understanding that it was for the benefit of the dowager empress. It was later said that Tzu Hsi squandered all the money set aside for the improvement of China's navy to build a Marble Barge on Lake Kunming, a charge that has been repeated dogmatically in both popular and scholarly works. The truth is that the Marble Barge was built by Emperor Chien Lung a century earlier, not by Tzu Hsi, and after being defaced by the Allies in 1860 it was restored cosmetically on the orders of Prince Chun as a way to flatter her. Tzu Hsi certainly benefited from its restoration, because she liked to visit the barge and to admire its murals (which were defaced again by the Allies in 1900). But the idea that China lost the war with Japan because she misappropriated the navy's budget to build the barge is ludicrous. While the dowager was certainly aware that great sums were being lavished by Prince Chun and others on the restoration of the Summer Palace, there is no evidence that she had any idea where the funds originated. The only people in a position to expropriate navy funds, secret and otherwise, were Viceroy Li and the two senior ruling princes because they *were* the Admiralty Board.

Li's main navy base was at Port Arthur, at the southern tip of Manchuria. A German army engineer was given responsibility for the fortifications, and what had once been a junk haven was turned into a model big-ship port, dredged to a uniform depth of twenty-five feet. Towering bluffs and more than forty modern guns guarded its entrance. With a dockyard, machine shops, warehouses, a railroad, electric lighting, and a torpedo depot, it was China's finest port facility.

Across the Gulf of Chihli was the excellent harbor of Weihaiwei, on the tip of Shantung peninsula, with three fortified islands across its entrance. Li also fortified the anchorage at Dairen and built forts along the coast. He was trying not to rely exclusively on the navy. In the 1890s faith in steam-powered warships was not yet universal.

Although it had yet to be tested in battle, Li's Northern Navy got good press. Shanghai newspapers praised his "powerful ironclads" and "swift torpedo cruisers." He sent his six best warships on goodwill voyages, including a visit to Japan in 1891, where Japanese agents had a chance to study them closely and to plant subversives in their crews.

American minister Denby was effusive, saying, "There can hardly be a doubt now that the [Northern] squadron alone is quite capable of coping single-handed with any other fleet at present stationed in East Asiatic waters."

To the contrary, like Chinese soldiers dressed in tiger-stripe uniforms, Li's navy was hopelessly unprepared for the real thing. It was over with astonishing speed. By September 1894, only a month into the war, Hart was writing that "Li's boasted fleet, fortifications, guns, and men all proved below what was properly expected: just now the difficulty is munitions—the southern fleet has only 25 rounds per gun, and, as to the northern fleet, they have no shells for the Krupps, and no powder for the Armstrongs." Even worse, Hart said, "some very big folk are making money out of every disaster." He meant, among others, Li's entire venal clan, who were profiteering on the war by supplying defective ammunition to Li's own ships.

On September 17, in the mouth of the Yalu River, the Japanese destroyed half of Li's vaunted navy in a single afternoon, without serious damage to even one of their own ships, the most significant naval victory since Nelson crossed the T at Trafalgar. Hart groaned that "the coast is now literally clear and Japan can land men and march on Peking."

When news of the disaster reached Peking, Tzu Hsi was stunned. Nothing she had been told by her ministers had prepared her for the shock of real events. She canceled all plans for the celebration of her birthday that November. By Chinese reckoning it would be her sixtieth birthday, one of special significance, and elaborate plans had been made long before the war. The huge sum of ten million taels of silver had been allocated by the government to pay for ceremonies and festivities, and more than one million taels had already been received from wealthy gentry as birthday gifts for her. The figures are deceptive, because they give the impression that all this money would be spent on the dowager when in fact much of it was to pay for public events, and much of the money would be embezzled in traditional fashion as it made its way up and down the pecking order; large amounts would vanish as tips and payoffs to underpaid officials clinging to every rung of the bureaucratic ladder, and Tzu Hsi herself would be expected to bestow the rest in generous amounts to favorite princes, courtiers, viceroys, governors, mayors, magistrates and other officials, and distinguished gentry in all provinces who had performed special services over the years. Her sixtieth birthday, in other words, was an excuse for the Grand Council to requisition great sums of money and then make it all disappear. Her insistence upon canceling the celebration annoyed a great many nobles, gentry, and functionaries who had been expecting sensational handouts.

After the Yalu River disaster Emperor Kuang Hsu tried to rebuke Viceroy Li through his aunt. The viceroy was deprived of all his honors, including his prized double-eyed peacock feather and the yellow silk field marshal's riding jacket that he had earned in the Taiping campaigns. Kuang Hsu wanted to go all the way and sack and degrade Li, but Tzu Hsi stopped him from becoming carried away. It was sufficient punishment to cause the viceroy extreme loss of face by withdrawing his favorite honors. Anything more would be rash. For the time being, Li was allowed to retain all his offices, including viceroy of Chihli and chief of the Northern Army and Northern Navy.

Everybody was afraid of what Li might do in revenge, so mandarins at all levels took pains not to be identified with these punitive orders. This made it all the more obvious that the edict of punishment was not a collective decision, but originated at the top. The feather and yellow jacket had been bestowed upon Li many years earlier by Tzu Hsi at the urging of Prince Kung. She was the only one who could take it back. So the edict was a clear statement that the dowager empress herself was incensed at the mishandling and humiliation of the navy.

Emperor Kuang Hsu had wanted to take this opportunity to eliminate Li as a threat to the regime. The Ironhats also saw this as the chance of a lifetime to bring Li to his knees. But they all failed to grasp what Tzu Hsi understood perfectly well. As the invisible partner of the coalition government and the richest and most powerful man in China, Li was too important and valuable to destroy without crippling the government as well. The dowager seemed to be the only one wise enough to keep a moderating hand. She also knew that if Li got sufficiently angry he might decide to strike back by seizing power for himself. (At that moment Robert Hart was musing sourly, "I should not be surprised if either Prince Kung, or Li, or the two in company, settle matters by a coup d'état.")

Despite his inherent duplicity and corruption, the dowager appreciated Li as an exceptional man, brilliant, far-seeing, energetic, and efficient. Nobody could have prevented a war that Yamagata and the Genyosha were determined to bring about, no matter what ruse or provocation they required. Nor, once war began, could Li have done anything to prevent the destruction of his prized fleet and fortifications, for China had not yet developed a military competence equal to its new hardware. Faced by frighteningly aggressive Japanese commanders, more than one of Li's captains had "showed the white feather" and either ran or was destroyed. Those who stood their ground and tried to fight found they had been provided with dud ammunition, supplied by members of Li's own family. Nevertheless, only a fool would believe that Li had countenanced such folly.

He seemed to know all along that he would be blamed for the war. He began early making provisions for his family, dividing his favorite properties among them and turning much of the rest into cash. If he were charged with treason and found guilty, not only would his life be forfeit but his properties as well. His heirs would be lucky to escape with their lives. At least he could make certain the survivors would be rich.

Tzu Hsi's restraint in her handling of Li demonstrated genuine statesmanship, which she now repeated. Twelve days after Li was reprimanded, Prince Kung was called out of retirement by Emperor Kuang Hsu at Tzu Hsi's urging and once again was given the job of rescuing China from disaster. Kung had been tending chrysanthemums in his garden for ten years, nursing grievances against the men who had done him in, those who had removed him from leadership of the coalition, and had become a bit rusty, but he had the experience, the instincts, and the stature that Prince Ching lacked. He was given responsibility for the Board of War, the Admiralty Board, the Tsungli Yamen, and, ultimately, the Grand Council as well. Despite the many efforts to portray Tzu Hsi as a gullible stooge of the hotheaded Ironhats, here she was only weeks out of retirement restoring the pragmatic leader of the moderate coalition.

Even with Prince Kung back in charge, by the end of October, Hart saw little hope: "Here everything is as bad as bad could be—there's no head—no strong man: past misdoings have bred present impotency." Emperor Kuang Hsu was reduced to clutching at straws. On Prince Kung's advice he called in Constantin von Hanneken, the German army engineer who had supervised the fortification of Port Arthur in 1881. The emperor agreed to make von Hanneken commander in chief of China's armies, "with ample funds and ample power," in hope that under the leadership of a Western general and officer corps another Ever Victorious Army might turn the tide against Japan. The results might have been salutary if the plan had been carried out. But the very next day the indignant Ironhats, blinded by their xenophobia, persuaded Kuang Hsu to reverse himself and cancel the von Hanneken plan. "Had it been done," Hart wrote, "China would have been safe and Japan would have eventually had to pay her an indemnity. But vacillation. . . . It's deplorable. . . . One day a force of 100,000 with 2500 foreign officers is authorised, and the next countermanded, and indemnity offered! It's shocking—the flabbiness and want of backbone."

Prevented by his Ironhat advisers from acting upon any sensible advice, Emperor Kuang Hsu in a desperate effort to force his own commanders to fight, stripped them of titles and rank but allowed them to remain in the field, on the understanding that they would be beheaded if they lost a battle. The choice was hardly theirs to make. Impregnable Port Arthur was captured in November 1894. The Japanese then easily took the fortified harbor at Weihaiwei in Shantung. Securing its guns, they sighted them on the Chinese ships in the anchorage below and finished the work begun at the Yalu. The balance of power in Asia was decisively altered.

Rather than surrender, Admiral Ting Ju-chang and his subordinates committed suicide. In this way they redeemed themselves and saved their families from death and confiscation of their estates. There were said to be three ways in China to avoid something unpleasant: the first was to plead illness; the second, to flee the country; the third, to commit suicide. Robert Hart had described the amiable Ting as a mere figurehead: "He never saw a ship before, and [was] selected chiefly because he has some modesty and good sense, and will not himself order the men to furl the pumps, shiver the gangway or heave the funnel."

With the fall of Weihaiwei, the war was essentially over. By the end of February 1895 the Japanese were in possession of the whole of Korea and Manchuria's Liaotung peninsula, and the Chinese were suing for peace.

Peking tried through various intermediaries, including American diplomats, to reach an accommodation with Japan. Having a much more realistic idea of how things worked, Tokyo refused to negotiate except with the disgraced Viceroy Li. Accordingly, on February 13, 1895, Li was relieved of his duties as viceroy of Chihli and appointed to head the peace talks. That settled, Japan agreed to discuss a treaty. It was perfectly clear to Li that Emperor Kuang Hsu and the Ironhats planned to make him their scapegoat.

"Peace can only be got by great sacrifices," Hart wrote, "and the man who has to sign them away has a very ungrateful task before him—the nation will execrate him and the government at least pillory!" Hart was right, but Li got spectacular revenge during the Boxer crisis, five years later.

Li arrived at Shimonoseki, Japan, on March 19, 1895, with an entourage of 135. Five days later, leaving one of his negotiating sessions with Prime Minister Ito, Li was shot in the face by a "fanatic" in the pay of the Genyosha, a superficial wound with the bullet only grazing his left cheek. This worked to China's advantage, as the shooting increased the international outcry for Japan to moderate her demands. It was announced that the empress of Japan herself prepared bandages for Li.

The terms agreed to on April 17 included the cession to Japan in perpetuity of the island of Taiwan, the Pescadores, and Liaotung peninsula; the opening of seven Chinese ports to Japanese trade; the payment of 200 million taels, with permission to occupy Weihaiwei harbor until this indemnity was cleared; and recognition of the "full and complete autonomy and independence of Korea," which meant relinquishing it to Japan.

Though he had seen it coming, Hart was shaken by China's defeat: "I am afraid we are tinkering a cracked kettle." Privately he began to speculate about how soon the Manchu would be doomed by their own incompetence and intransigence. As he confided to a friend in 1895, "I fear, as far as the dynasty is concerned, it is hopeless: in ten years' time revolution will do the trick." It took sixteen. On the other hand, he had confidence in the Chinese people and was convinced that eventually they would emerge as a great power.

Kuang Hsu's ultimate reaction to the defeat was not to seize this moment to reassert his imperial prerogatives, an opportunity his ancestors Nurhachi or Dorgon or Kang Hsi or Yung Cheng would never have missed. Instead, he fell into a deep funk, announcing that he wished to abdicate. Prone to fits of despair, he sat on his throne weeping and declaring openly, like the unfortunate Emperor Tao Kuang during the First Opium War, "How can I bear to remain as the master?"

It was time for bold action, not for despair. Conspiracy was in the air. The news that Kuang Hsu wished to retire to a life of contemplation whetted the appetites of the imperial princes who coveted the throne—or the shadows immediately behind it. "There is something curious going on in Chinese circles," Hart observed, "and a coup d'état will not astonish me: people are ranging themselves, some behind the Emperor—others behind the Empress Dowager, and it looks as if one of these illustrious personages would have to push the other to the wall presently."

The only audacity in Kuang Hsu's generation (perhaps the only virility as well) was concentrated in the brash and aggressive sons of Prince Tun, the most prolific of Prince Kung's brothers who fathered eight sons before his death in 1889. Of them, the three eldest were inflamed by Manchu patriotism and obsessed with conspiracy. Upon their father's death they began to flex their own political muscles, and by the time of the Sino-Japanese War they had risen to the leadership of the Ironhat faction. Tsai Lien, the eldest and inheritor of his father's title, was now Prince Tun II and the heir to great estates; next came Prince Tuan and Duke Lan, dashing, arrogant, ambitious, and impatient troublemakers who had no sympathy for the weak, hesitant, stammering, androgynous Kuang Hsu. They were all cousins of the emperor and like young Plantagenets, saw this as a license to scheme on the throne for themselves. Together with their brooding and contrary Ironhat cousin Prince Chuang, they were throwbacks to the violent feudal days of Dorgon and Nurhachi. Too sheltered and spoiled during their childhood to have any knowledge of the hardships of real life, they believed in Taoist magic, consulted soothsayers daily, and saw themselves as legends in the making. If they could somehow gain the throne they believed they could turn fortune around and restore the ancient glory and isolation of China simply by murdering or expelling every last Foreign Devil and Japanese "dwarf bandit," an undertaking that would have intimidated anyone still in touch with reality. At this moment of defeat by Japan and national disgrace, such a grandiose ambition had an intoxicating effect on the Ironhats and their followers, who were happy to blame Emperor Kuang Hsu for everything. Forgetting the lesson of Lord Elgin (perhaps never having heard of him), they believed that the Foreign Powers, once expelled from China, would never return.

Prince Tuan and his brothers were motivated largely by a feudal craving for vengeance. Long ago their late father had narrowly missed becoming emperor in place of Hsien Feng. And if Prince Kung and Viceroy Li had not blocked their way during the succession crisis of 1875 following the death of Emperor Tung Chih, one of these brothers, or one of their sons, would now be sitting on the dragon throne instead of Kuang Hsu. They believed that their family had been cheated repeatedly of its imperial birthright, a mistake they intended to correct.

Although he was not the eldest, the brash, swaggering, and insolent Prince Tuan was their natural leader. Now in his mid-thirties, he was technically too old to covet the throne for himself unless it could be encouraged to fall into his hands, but if Kuang Hsu abdicated, Tuan had a son waiting in the wings, Pu Chun, and with his son on the throne the prince would rule through a regency. Pu Chun, although not very bright, was in the proper generation to succeed Kuang Hsu.

Before he began to assert himself in the early 1890s Prince Tuan had been a relatively obscure young prince whose chief claim to fame was that he had married a niece of Tzu Hsi, a daughter of the dowager's brother Duke Kuei Hsiang. This gave him privileged access to the empress dowager as a member of her family, and allowed Tuan to cultivate her and to gain her ear whenever he wished. His wife was a sister of Kuang Hsu's empress, so he had the run of the palaces. Prince Tuan promoted his son to Tzu Hsi at every opportunity, and as he grew out of infancy Pu Chun became as fat, sleek, and confident as a muskrat, with an insolent manner appropriate to an aspiring heir apparent.

Like many other members of the closed-minded Manchu nobility, Prince Tuan avoided contact with foreigners and was adamant in his views. Diplomats thought the Ironhats were stupidly narrow minded, and identified them in official reports as "the reactionaries gathered behind the empress dowager." This made her seem to be the leader. Although Tuan flattered her and made use of the family tie to gain leverage, the Ironhats were by no means the dowager's "gang," nor was she in any sense their patron. As empress dowager, Manchu rules required Tzu Hsi to consult the royal princes as well as her cabinet ministers. In the previous generation, among the royal brothers only Prince Kung, Prince Tun, and Prince Chun had been energetically involved in decision-making. Of the three only Prince Kung was still alive so she had no choice but to consult the next Aisin Gioro generation, in which only a few princes showed an active interest in policy-making. While Prince Kung's fun-loving sons had an aversion to politics, Prince Tun's ill-tempered brood were obsessed with power to an unwholesome degree, particularly the singleminded Prince Tuan. He was doggedly persistent. As a royal prince and first cousin of the emperor, he became a fixture in the court and the audience chambers. He haunted the Summer Palace and sought out the dowager empress continually, presenting gifts, pressing his attentions and gradually making himself a part of her daily consultations. At first his close attention and tenacity did not seem ominous.

She was impressed by Tuan's exuberance, hardly surprising for a woman surrounded all her life by timid eunuchs and pandering mandarins. The prince's aggressiveness, if a bit frightening, was at least dashing and positive. She did not realize until it was too late that he was slowly taking her over. Later, she had reason to regret being so unwary, as she found herself a prisoner of his private security forces.

While the prince did not have a master strategy, a plan did exist in broadest outline. Tuan and his associates were quietly gathering into their hands all of the instruments of security and control, including the best brigades of the Banners; the best elements of the Chinese armies; the headquarters of the secret police, national police, and Peking Gendarmerie; the vital boards that controlled revenue and finance; the Board of Punishments; the Censorate; and viceroys and governors of strategic provinces. In 1893–94, when the armed forces were reorganized on the eve of the war, Prince Tuan was promoted to adjutant general of the Banners, the pivotal post that had been held by Su Shun and his cronies in the Gang of Eight. Tuan was then given the privilege of forming his own personal force, which he named the Marksmen for the Tiger Hunts (Husheng Corps). This was composed of ten thousand Manchu between the ages of twenty and thirty-five who were the pick of the leading Banner forces. While the Manchu Banners might be useless as a fighting force, barely competent to carry out ceremonial functions, there were in the ranks some talented younger men. For the Marksmen of the Tiger Hunt, Prince Tuan recruited the best soldiers from the White, the Yellow, and the Bordered-Yellow Banners. They were drilled by Western methods and trained in the use of modern weapons including Sharp's repeating rifles and Krupp rapid-fire artillery pieces.

The implication of the name and the ultimate purpose of this new army were not immediately apparent to the foreign community. Tiger was the euphemism the Ironhats employed as a code word for the Foreign Powers. Since there were no elephants in China, tigers were the largest animal that could threaten the ruling dragon. General Li Ping-heng, a seasoned Han Chinese commander from southern Manchuria whose exceptional honesty and dislike of foreigners made him an idol to the young Ironhats, warned of how the Great Powers had "Tiger Eyes." Li Ping-heng was a bitter enemy of the policy of foreign appeasement long identified with Prince Kung and Viceroy Li. He believed that Chinese armies could win if they were properly led, which was nevertheless a very large "if" indeed. During the Sino-Japanese War he protested: "The Powers are watching with a tiger's voracity. Their moves [in the future] will depend upon how we conclude the war with Japan. . . . If the generals, viceroys, and governors are strictly ordered to fight to the death, the Japanese will collapse within half a year." Easier said than done. Orders to fight to the death would never change the army's ancient tradition of running when the first shot was fired, as Li Ping-heng would eventually discover to his terminal dismay. China's quiver was full of bent arrows. Yet this tough talk from a man they hero-worshipped made a deep impression on the Ironhats. Naturally enough, they felt that everything wrong could be put right if the throne adopted their point of view.

The Ironhats were misguided because their experience with military operations was primarily in western China against poorly armed Muslim rebels. In those Tartar wastelands, armies under the command of General Tso Tsung-tang pursued a scorched-earth policy in which nobody was left alive. Soldiers and officers were dealt with so harshly that there was never any attempt at rebellion or mutiny. Troops knew better than to run away; they would be tracked down and mutilated. These methods were different from those in North China where generals commanded political armies, not slaughter machines. Political armies were never bloodied, so they were not prepared for the brutal determination of Japanese soldiers conditioned to fight or face beheading. General Li Ping-heng might be right in principle, but when it came to commanding political armies he would turn out to be disastrously wrong.

In the atmosphere of danger, Prince Tuan persuaded Tzu Hsi that his personal army could provide a significant improvement in palace security. Aside from the Imperial Guards, who had charge of the palace gates and other bodyguard duties, after 1894 Prince Tuan's Tiger Hunt Marksmen formed the innermost ring of protection around the throne, guarding the dragon's lair. The second ring was the Peking Field Force, under the chief minister, Prince Ching. The third ring, commanded by Jung Lu, was the Military Guards Army, the best-trained force in the capital region. Jung Lu, the lifelong friend of Tzu Hsi, was responsible for the protection of the throne as chamberlain of the Imperial Guards, and for the security of the capital as head of the Peking Gendarmerie. But his exclusive control of palace security was being penetrated and undermined by Prince Tuan's changes. By catering to the whims of the pushy prince and letting him have his way with the Tiger Hunt Marksmen, Tzu Hsi unwittingly allowed him to slip inside Jung Lu's magic circle. Before long, the prince would begin to flex his muscles, using his security men to spy upon and intimidate members of the imperial household, and eventually even to bully and threaten the dowager empress, until she found herself a virtual hostage.

Prince Tuan's secret weapon was an alliance he had with the ruthless Muslim Chinese general, Tung Fu-hsiang, commanding an army of 12,000 cutthroat Muslim braves recruited from the wilds of Kansu, who were now camped in the imperial park south of the capital. Tung was a former bandit chief who established a merciless reputation during the great Muslim rebellion against Manchu rule between 1863 and 1878. In the first six years of the rebellion, Tung and his father led their men to one bloody victory after another over the Manchu and Chinese armies sent to suppress them. In his early thirties at the time, Tung was not only a shrewd military strategist, he was also an excellent businessman, and in 1869 he struck a rich bargain with the Manchu government. He would betray his own people and go over to the government with his entire army in exchange for being allowed to keep all the lands and properties he could seize from his former Muslim allies. Each time he defeated or captured a rival rebel leader, Tung would take possession of all his palaces, properties, and treasure. He did such a thorough job of stamping out Muslim resistance that at the end of the rebellion in 1878 the Manchu gave him a hereditary rank. By then Tung was a very rich and powerful man; as warlord of Kansu Province his influence covered a much greater area stretching all the way from the mountains west of Peking to the cold high deserts along the Russian border. The alliance with Tung gave the Manchu peace on their western frontier, and they were able to call upon the venal general to carry out brutal suppression campaigns whenever necessary. General Tung and his unwashed paladins could be had for a price but the unwary soon discovered they were masters of blackmail and ransom.

It was Prince Tun who pushed through the secret alliance with Tung during the Muslim rebellion. At the time, Prince Kung had persuaded the Clan Council that in order to suppress the Taiping rebels, he should be allowed to build up Tseng Kuo-fan and his army of Chinese mercenaries on a scale that the Manchu had avoided since gaining control of China. Taking advantage of this radical change in policy, Prince Tun had argued for and been given the same license in the western provinces, ostensibly to bring an end to the Muslim revolt. Through the Chinese General Tso Tsung-tang, who served as his agent, Prince Tun agreed to the deal proposed by Tung Fu-hsiang to betray his fellow Muslims in return for control of the territory and property of his victims. A bond was forged between him and Prince Tun that was periodically reinforced by the payment of huge bribes from the imperial treasury. It was vital for the Muslim warlord to have an influential advocate at court and it was always useful for a prince to have firepower handy to press home his point of view in family quarrels. At Prince Tun's death in 1889, this bond was transferred to his sons.

Although tacitly under the overall military control of chief of staff Jung Lu, General Tung owed his personal loyalty only to Prince Tuan and made it his duty to look after Prince Tuan and his brothers as if they were his own children. His desert stronghold provided them with a vast military base far in the interior of China. From Kansu and Shensi, Prince Tuan and his brothers could call in elements of General Tung's Muslim cavalry whenever they wished to intimidate enemies at court. Their father had done exactly this during the succession crisis of 1875. Tung's army of former bandits was unusually effective as a political weapon because his men had a reputation for being ruthless and sadistic, waging genocide rather than war. The mere appearance of a troop of General Tung's cavalry was enough to cause panic among Chinese and Westerners alike. It was only necessary for Prince Tuan to have Tung's cavalry trot up and down the streets of Peking. In the politics of terror they were a useful weapon for an ambitious prince.

The Ironhats were thus secure in the knowledge that whenever General Tung's Kansu horsemen were camped on the southern outskirts of the capital, his military support could tip the balance their way in the event of a sudden putsch or coup d'état.

Jung Lu recognized the threat Tung posed to the dynasty, and to get him out of Peking, dispatched Tung to Shensi in October 1895, to help suppress an isolated Muslim uprising. Tung did such a thorough job of wiping out the insurgents that foreigners were told "his name strikes terror today in every Chinese heart."

While Tung was thus occupied elsewhere, danger came unexpectedly from Korea once again. In Seoul the Japanese carried out a bloody coup deposing Queen Min in favor of the former regent. On October 7, 1895, Japanese-trained battalions, accompanied by Japanese policemen in civilian clothes, forced their way into the quarters of the queen. After murdering two of her ladies-in-waiting, they cornered Queen Min. When the Minister of the Royal Household tried to shield her, a Japanese swordsman lopped off both his hands. The defenseless queen was then stabbed repeatedly, carried outside, thrown still alive on a pile of firewood, doused with kerosene, and torched. Tokyo denied responsibility, but the deed was planned and executed by its embassy personnel in Seoul. Tokyo recalled Sugimura Yotara, secretary of the legation, and the rest of the staff and in a show trial found them all innocent. However, Sir Ernest Satow, British minister in Tokyo, investigated and concluded that there was "no doubt about the murder of Queen Min by two Japanese of whom one was [Sugimura]."

Queen Min's grisly murder shocked Tzu Hsi; her fear of being similarly attacked led her to encourage the Ironhats further. Prince Tuan tried to take advantage of his new leverage to bring the court under his complete control. But his lack of sophistication and lack of political experience enabled more urbane and experienced mandarins, liberals and moderate conservatives alike, to talk circles around him. So while the leverage of the Ironhats grew as they gained control of more instruments of power, they failed to gain a mastery of policy debates and were never certain of winning on any issue. This frustrating standoff had the result of making them despise their adversaries even more.

Although familiar with Tung Fu-hsiang's nasty reputation, the foreign community in Peking knew little about the Ironhats or about Prince Tuan until 1900, and was slow to appreciate the significance of this new power bloc of militant, anti-foreign princes. Western diplomats saw them only as "the gang of reactionaries gathered behind the dowager." To give them their due, the Ironhats were right to fear that China was about to be pulled apart and eaten by ravenous foreign tigers, unless drastic steps were taken. Japan's easy victory in Korea and its annexation of Taiwan confirmed their worst fears. One after the other China had lost Nepal, Burma, and Indochina; Korea and Taiwan were gone; and Manchuria now hung in the balance. Pieces of the coast had been bitten off around each Treaty Port. One of the latest concessions to the Japanese had been to allow them to build factories in the Treaty Ports, a right that was demanded in turn by all the other Foreign Powers under provisions of most-favored-nation status. This brought about an international stampede for mineral rights and associated privileges in China during the rest of the 1890s; a scramble for concessions that many Chinese saw as rape.

There was little China could do to resist. Her navy had been destroyed, her army shattered, and the indemnities she was forced to pay to Japan created a financial emergency that made it necessary to disband tens of thousands of soldiers, who were left with no means of supporting themselves other than banditry. If the Ironhats were going to kick out the hated Foreign Devils, it would require more than Prince Tuan's Tiger Hunt Marksmen and Tung's Muslim cavalry. General Li Ping-heng had an ingenious idea for raising a huge grass-roots army and was already at work on the scheme.

While the Ironhats conspired to seize power, a curious phenomenon occurred. Fragile and uncertain Emperor Kuang Hsu, at last shaking off the funk of defeat, tried to respond to the challenge facing him by firing his advisers and taking a bold initiative, in the manner of a proper Sage-King.

CHAPTER ELEVEN

The Wild Fox

C hina's defeat by Japan also galvanized other ambitious men who saw that the time had come for change if China was to survive into the twentieth century. They disagreed sharply with the reactionaries on the form those changes should take. Reactionaries wanted to restore the empire's glorious isolation by tightening traditional controls and expelling all foreigners and their influences. Reformers wanted to abandon the old system and modernize the government, as Japan had done so successfully since the Meiji Restoration. A clash between them was inevitable if the young emperor failed to handle these opposing forces with tact and ingenuity. He would need to keep his aunt, the empress dowager, firmly on his side throughout.

What neither of these factions knew was that Viceroy Li was planning to avenge himself by setting them at each other's throats. Thanks to Li's manipulations the Ironhats became embroiled in conspiracies that ended in disaster for their rivals in the great reform crisis of 1898. During the reign of terror that followed, those reformers who escaped punishment sought someone to blame. The dowager empress had been the figurehead of the regime far longer than many of the reformers had been alive, so she became the focus of their vengeance, the target of an extraordinary outpouring of slander making use of the international press. Before the year was out, her image was changed into that of a bloodthirsty tyrant. The demonizing of Tzu Hsi had begun.

Robert Hart smelled trouble but had difficulty figuring out what was afoot. People were allying themselves with rival factions. "It . . . looks like a lot of quicksilver on a flat surface with little curleycues cutting across to join large ones and these again splitting up and forming new centres without seeming rhyme or reason! . . . It's like the man with the three thimbles and the pea: you see the pea for a moment and you then swear it is under such a thimble—and lo it's not!"

Some of the conspiracies Hart heard about involved foreigners. A British adventurer, Captain Mortimer O'Sullivan, became thick with the Education Movement, a group of disenchanted Hanlin scholars who were secretly seeking help from British and American missionary activists in Peking. "One of their ideas," Hart reported, "is said to be to poison the Emperor and put another youngster on the throne!" There were other unsettling rumors: "Gossips circulate the story that the reputed son of the last Emperor Tung Chih was brought back yesterday by Prince Ouchtomsky and will be put on the throne. Kuang Hsu . . . of course will resign when the true heir appears."

Hart's "Prince Ouchtomsky" was Prince E. E. Ukhtomskii, an agent of the Czar who promoted the idea of a fundamental kinship between Russians and Asians. In 1896 he accompanied Li Hung-chang to celebrations in St. Petersburg of the recent coronation of Czar Nicholas II.

With his usual cunning Li had turned the St. Petersburg trip to his advantage. He and diplomat Sir Chang Yin-huan concluded a secret treaty that gave Russia control of the Liaotung peninsula in Manchuria, to stymie Japanese designs on the same area. During these negotiations, the Russian finance minister, Count Witte, paid Li a bribe of a half-million rubles and Sir Chang a bribe of a quarter-million to arrive at terms acceptable to St. Petersburg. From Russia, Li traveled on around the world for a year, meeting Kaiser Wilhelm, Queen Victoria, and President Grover Cleveland. In America newspapers called him China's greatest statesman. To avoid being poisoned by agents of his enemies back home, Li never ate a meal during the trip, no matter where he was being entertained, unless it was prepared by his own cook, who accompanied him wherever he went. On his return to Peking, his reception was frigid, and he was assigned to work in the Tsungli Yamen—a serious comedown. Because of their secret association, Ukhtomskii's plot to put a pretender on the Manchu throne may have been worked out in connivance with Li, who was seeking ways to destroy his enemies at court and regain his lost preeminence in China.

Other conspirators were also at hand. Hart observed that "Yuan Shih-kai . . . will not be last in the race should a scramble for the throne come about." Although General Yuan was Li's well-fed house cat and chief mouser, he was consumed with ambition of his own. So long as Li remained strong, Yuan would not dare to act independently, but when the aging Li passed from the scene, Yuan would be set to pounce.

Aside from the danger of a palace coup or a revolution from the streets by anti-Manchu elements, there was also the threat of interference by the Foreign Powers. Many thought the gravest danger came from Japan.

Tokyo's long-term strategy was to bring about the downfall of the Manchu emperor *and* the Russian Czar, leaving the Meiji emperor unchallenged in East Asia. Japan had already succeeded in displacing China in Korea and Taiwan and was making inroads in Manchuria. Japanese agents were also busy in Mongolia and the Shantung peninsula, in Peking and Tientsin. It is little wonder that the Ironhats were alarmed.

But Japan was not the only aggressor. In the south, France had carved off Indochina, while Great Britain had seized Burma and made it part of British India. Diplomatically, Britain and the United States were making a halfhearted effort to shore up the administration, to keep the Russians from gaining advantage, but the meddling of British and American journalists, adventurers, merchants, and missionaries was eroding the regime's foundations. Their none-too-subtle encouragement of reformers fed Ironhat suspicions that the reform movement was actually an international plot, linking Britain and America with Japan.

Hart took no comfort from the fact that Prince Kung was once again chief minister, for his old friend's abilities were diminished by ill health and personal problems. Kung was now sixty-five years old; this was his swan song. Hart said he spent most of his time and energy avenging himself on the people who had ousted him in 1884. After months of illness Prince Kung died in May 1898, removing his stabilizing influence just when it was needed most.

Kung had been one of the most important figures in the empire since 1860. After enlisting Tzu An and Tzu Hsi in his plot to wrest power from the Gang of Eight, Kung's great achievement had been to bind together a failing dynasty, to disguise its rot by various ruses and concessions, until the brain-dead patient was kept alive only by the life-support system of the Chinese bureaucracy. Kung had made repeated efforts to groom new emperors—first Tung Chih, then Kuang Hsu—and in both cases had been disappointed. The gene pool of the Ching Dynasty was drying up. Once great warriors, their legs had gone, and they could no longer sit a horse.

The prince's death left Emperor Kuang Hsu on his own for the first time in his life. Up to this point, he had always been under the influence of a senior adviser: first Prince Kung, then his father Prince Chun, then Prince Ching and imperial tutor Weng Tung-ho, and finally Prince Kung again.

At age twenty-six, Kuang Hsu was still an innocent young man, earnestly seeking ways to correct the ancient corruption and abuses of power that were the underlying causes of China's weakness. Unlike Prince Tuan's clique, who remained closed-minded, Kuang Hsu had benefited from some Western education. He had Western books and articles translated for him and studied the Japanese experiment with modernization to discover how an island nation of "dwarf pirates" could turn itself, practically overnight, into a world power. If it was possible for Japan, so it could be for China.

Kuang Hsu craved to infuse new blood and new ideas into his anemic administration. Early in 1898 he opened the subject of reform to general discussion by inviting all citizens to send him memorials directly, bypassing the watchdogs of the Censorate. Previously the right to memorialize the emperor had been reserved to those of high rank. In response to the emperor's appeal there was a rush of memorials denouncing the old and espousing the new. This time the critics were not China's hidebound scholar-gentry, usually careful to keep their complaints to themselves, but a group of freethinkers and bohemians known as the *ming-shih,* or scholar-celebrities. Many *ming-shih* seized the opportunity of the emperor's appeal to tell him bluntly what they thought was wrong and how to fix it. Instead of announcing their opinions and ideas in wine gardens, they became political activists. One of their targets was the emperor's Grand Council. While he was surrounded by dogmatic Grand Councillors such as Weng Tung-ho, Kang I, and Prince Li, the *ming-shih* asserted, it was impossible for the emperor and his people to engage in a constructive dialogue about ideas. These Grand Councillors were either Ironhats or their followers. The chief function of an Ironhat, like any other helmet, was to deflect enemy blows; but it also had the function of deflecting alien ideas. If Kuang Hsu wanted new ideas they would have to come from the outside, from the *ming-shih.*

The backbone of any Chinese government was the scholar-gentry, which provided the base of talent for national, regional, and local administration. Dynasties rose and fell, but the imperial bureaucracy survived more or less intact. As men passed the civil service exams, became functionaries, and moved up the ladder through the system, they acquired perks and wore cap-buttons and other badges of rank announcing exactly what privileges they were due. In a culture that venerated old age, a white-haired grandfather was nevertheless expected to give up his chair to a young scholar.

Inevitably, many candidates failed their examinations; others scorned the system and refused to participate. From these ranks came the *ming-shih.* They prided themselves on pursuing moral and intellectual perfection in their own way. Except in certain instances they refused government service and believed that they fulfilled an important social role by examining the problems of China from a different perspective, giving them valuable insights. Some *ming-shih* were men of means, able to maintain schools of followers, but most had only their wits and talents and depended upon wealthy patrons for their survival. They were cultivated by straitlaced counterparts in the bureaucracy who passed along their unorthodox opinions and gossip to higher authorities, keeping the regime informed of dissent, scandal, and conspiracy. As one might expect in such a situation, the ranks of the *ming-shih* were full of spies and informers.

Among the *ming-shih* also was a subculture of scholars who had gone feral, iconoclasts who disregarded the rules or broke them deliberately. These were "wild foxes," a term that in China implied abnormality, mischief, and the supernatural. Such people were only one step removed from "fox fairies," magical creatures able to change their form and to appear and disappear at will.

In previous decades the *ming-shih* had been content to debate issues in an amiable fashion over wine and noodles. After the defeat by Japan, the more daring among them began pressing their ideas in memorials to officials with access to the emperor. Their message was not merely that the Manchu had to change but that the Manchu had to reform. Old power blocs like the Ironhats had to go, the suffocating civil service exam system had to be abandoned, and China had to awaken and strengthen herself to take her proper place in the world; this was like urging the Vatican to ordain women priests and to promote contraception. Bolder *ming-shih* made the drastic proposal that China should become a constitutional monarchy based on the Japanese model—and should invite the hated Japanese to show them how.

In an effort to make the idea of reform seem more palatable, the more prudent *ming-shih* put forth a milder program whereby the Confucian code of social ethics would remain in place and China would borrow only certain measures from Western science, technology, and economics that would strengthen China. This was only a vague platform, but after centuries of rigid thought control no one was prepared for the fear and anger these proposals would arouse, and the heads that would roll.

Despite their classical education, and in many cases their brilliance, the scholar-celebrities and wild foxes ignored an important historical lesson: scholars were always viewed by the Manchu as subversives. The Ching Dynasty was founded on military power and political alliances purchased with someone else's money; after gaining control of the Chinese empire by accident, they had secured their position by slaughtering resistance and sustained themselves by witch-hunting and the persecution of heretics. After washing off the lingering smell of horse sweat, the Manchu had cloaked themselves with borrowed Confucian virtue and styled themselves the saviors of Confucian civilization, which had been nearly extinguished—they said—by the corruption of the Ming emperors. Since then Chinese scholars who had dared to criticize the Manchu had been ruthlessly purged, their heirs and relatives beheaded, their ancestral tablets destroyed. The Confucian system was turned by the Manchu into an exercise of form and style without substance, and its practice became a ritual of survival. Breaches of etiquette were punishable by death, not really what the ancient sage had in mind.

Intolerance of scholars was nothing new in China. The first emperor of the Han Dynasty (206 B.C.–A.D. 220) showed his contempt by ripping a hat off a scholar and urinating in it. But the Manchu turned Confucianism from a code of ethics into a system of thought control. Official periodic reviews of written history and literature were pressed on scholars under the pretense of bringing together great works of art, but with the real purpose of screening out anything critical or disagreeable and then burning it. Scholarship was especially dangerous under emperors Yung Cheng and Chien Lung, both of whom indulged in mass censorship and vivisection of intellectuals. That great "art patron" Chien Lung destroyed some twenty-six hundred titles. Since then scholars in China had learned to avoid such dangerous subjects as politics and economics; instead they fell into boring rhapsodies of textual criticism and philological study. The Manchu book burners and witch-hunters were still very much in power in the 1890s, not as individuals but as an implacable institution.

The *ming-shih* were not well equipped to challenge it. Chinese writers depicted the *ming-shih* as men of superior intellect but inclined to petty chatter and sensual indulgence. When they were not busy reciting poetry or discussing fine points of Confucian reasoning over bowls of wine, they frequented flower boats, brothels, and playhouses. A day at the theater could start at noon and not end till evening. Accompanied by flutes, gongs, and drums, tragedians would strut and squeak in falsetto Peking opera, while the audience drank tea, munched gourd seeds, and ate fried melon rind. Female roles were played by young men who minced about the stage on tiptoe with the swaying grace of lotus-footed maidens.

Despite their frivolous pursuits, the *ming-shih* included sincere men who saw Emperor Kuang Hsu as China's bright hope. Clinging to the outer fringes were opportunists and self-seekers. The noisiest and brashest of them was the wild fox Kang Yu-wei, the man who would begin the systematic slander of Tzu Hsi.

Kang was a Cantonese whose father had died of tuberculosis when the boy was ten, leaving his schooling to his paternal grandfather, a teacher and minor official. The boy showed a flair for discussion, debate, and self-promotion. His only prominent ancestor was a great-granduncle who served briefly as an acting governor of Kwangsi during the suppression of the Taiping Rebellion. This granduncle returned to their ancestral village in the mid-1860s and set himself up in a cottage with a large library and a spacious garden where he entertained cronies. Little Kang hung around the house, and his precociousness and theatrical posing made him a toy for the older men. He mimed their manners and cultivated their air of superiority. In return they made much of him, telling him he was destined to be a great sage like Confucius.

Unfortunately he believed them. He became so convinced that he was one of the chosen that he grew lazy and contrary, behaving so erratically that local folk thought he was mentally ill. In his craving for the limelight he began doing things to shock and offend local custom, in order to gain notoriety.

Kang gradually matured into a moonfaced little dumpling, with pouting lips bracketed by wisps of mustache, projecting an air of profound self-satisfaction. He wrote that even at age eleven he had a "knack of directing the affairs of men." He thought Heaven had entrusted him with a historic mission. He told people that when he was born "crimson fire entered the house at midnight, and I began my life."

An admiring biographer who knew him personally acknowledged: "Modesty and humility . . . were not among his virtues. . . . Haunted by no intellectual perplexities, he seldom paid serious attention to diverging opinions held by other men." In his conceit Kang saw himself as a fearless crusader, while he was really only an exploiter, ready to take credit for other people's ideas.

At age nineteen, he had an opportunity to take the first set of imperial civil service exams but put it off. For the next eleven years he wandered around, going first to Hong Kong, where he was astonished by "the elegance of the buildings of the foreigners, the cleanliness of the streets, the efficiency of their police." His next stop was Shanghai.

Although vainglorious, Kang was not a prig. He appreciated the finer things in life and liked to enjoy himself. In addition to a village wife he eventually acquired two concubines, one a girl of seventeen purchased when he was fifty years of age. Picking up an assortment of Western ideas, he dreamed of establishing a free-love utopia in China where "all men will give their sexual desire free play. . . . There will be men who enjoy homosexual relationships. . . . There will be no reason to prohibit such relationships, if they are not the result of coercion." In 1882 he went north to Peking, where he flunked his first exams. After six years of "self-education" he returned to Peking in 1888, at age thirty, to sit once more for the examination. Again he failed. This time he hung around to make the acquaintance of the Peking *ming-shih* and their wealthy sponsors, among them imperial tutors Weng Tung-ho and Li Hung-tsao, both archconservatives with a secret taste for naughtiness.

Kang was a newcomer to this bohemian underworld and an outsider in his quaint attitudes, but he was quick to improvise. As he moved along the outer fringe of this exciting milieu, he realized that much of its fascination came from the flash of leading members, men who had achieved celebrity and political influence because of their novel ideas, flamboyant style, and personal audacity. Kang resolved to make himself over into just such a creature and to climb upon the political stage himself. He began by addressing a memorial to the dowager empress and Emperor Kuang Hsu, advising them that a crisis was coming when it would be necessary to stop abuses of government. This was not original in idea or content, for Kang simply rewrote a memorial written by a friend employed as a Censor. He had embarked on what was to become a lifelong habit of plagiarism. Without a sponsor he had no way to deliver the memorial, so he put it away, to be dug out many years later for inclusion in his autobiography as "evidence" of his early commitment to reform.

Although Kang liked to see himself as a natural leader of the *ming-shih*, they saw him as neither a serious scholar nor an original genius, only a poseur. Ignored by the intelligentsia, he returned to Kwangtung, where he joined a circle of local scholars debating the classics, espousing as his own some of the heretical views he had overheard in Peking and Shanghai. This made him seem exotic and avant-garde, so he began to acquire a tiny provincial following of admirers. With his usual exaggeration he declared them an "academy," with himself as sage-teacher.

Among his "students" was a bright young journalist named Liang Chi-chao, a gifted writer who lacked the panache to make his own way, and attached himself to Kang. Together, Kang's pupils rummaged through the gossip of previous centuries, writing essays on eccentric themes. Eventually, in 1891 Kang himself produced a treatise that he plagiarized from the work of his pupils, as a college professor might publish a book based on essays written by his students, without crediting them. It was titled "The Forged Classics" and argued that the original Confucian texts had been altered hundreds of years after the death of the sage, to suit the needs of the state. This argument had been going on for centuries and was nothing new. But under the Manchu thought-police debate on such matters had been stifled and the controversy largely forgotten. By seizing upon it, dusting it off, and presenting it as his own original argument, Kang showed the cunning that would enable him later to dust off the pornographic "secret histories" of the "murderous" Empress Wu a thousand years earlier, and use them as inspiration in vilifying Tzu Hsi.

In a society taught to believe in the purity of ancient learning, Kang's restatement of the old argument about the altered Confucian texts was startling. His main contribution was to publish openly what the *ming-shih* usually had the sense to discuss only among themselves. Like fundamentalist Christians or Muslims, ardent Confucians preferred to believe that the classics were authentic in every detail. Many men had lost their heads for suggesting otherwise.

Kang's treatise ignited a raging controversy not for what it said but for having said it. He immodestly proposed that China's salvation lay in following his own interpretation of the sage from "untampered" texts. In his new notoriety he was dubbed a naughty "wild fox" by no less than the Confucian dancemaster, imperial tutor Weng Tung-ho. Kang's scandalous treatise was brought to the attention of the throne. Powerful patrons of the *ming-shih* had to intervene to save him from punishment although the printing blocks used to print his pamphlet were ordered destroyed. Notoriety brought him instant celebrity and automatic entrance into the coveted ranks of the *ming-shih*.

That did not help him pass the civil service exams. He sat for them again in 1894 and failed. The following spring he returned to Peking for a last try. This time he passed, just barely. But ever after he boasted that by all rights he should have scored first. His poor showing qualified him only for a lowly clerical job in the Board of Works. Insulted, he did not bother to show up for work. As Kang later put it in his autobiography, "I was not going to bend my back for . . . rice."

He was rescued from reality by the Sino-Japanese War. Scholars and students, objecting to the peace terms dictated by Japan, circulated petitions in an attempt to stop the throne from accepting. Some of these petitions were forwarded to Emperor Kuang Hsu. Kang later claimed, falsely, that he was active in these efforts, but he only capitalized on the petition campaign by writing an essay about it, once again piggybacking the work of others. He intended to send his essay to the emperor, but it was rejected by the bureaucrats he hoped would pass it up the line. Nevertheless, Kang paid to have tens of thousands of lithographic copies of his essay published by a vanity press in Shanghai. They sold well, and through little effort of his own he became identified with the reform movement. Encouraged, he revised his essay and this time couched it in more modest terms of postwar reconstruction. Echoing many others, he argued that China needed to improve her military capability, to centralize her currency and banking system, to expand her railroad and steam navigation, to develop her mines, and to organize a postal service. In Peking his memorial was added to a pile of essays that the emperor circulated among provincial officials for their comment. Governors paid little attention to Kang's paper, but he had tasted glory.

Until the end of 1898, Kang never once attacked the dowager empress, but afterward he claimed to have been her critic all along. For example, he wrote that it was Tzu Hsi who forced Kuang Hsu to accept the Japanese treaty terms, under the influence of chief eunuch Li Lien-ying: "The empress dowager, who always heeded [his] advice, therefore casually consented to the cession of Taiwan" to Japan. Nobody challenged this absurd statement, so it became part of his eventual indictment of her.

Searching for ways to attract more attention, he joined one of the reform discussion societies that were then the rage and went to Shanghai to organize a provincial branch he could dominate. His satellite group published a newspaper that Kang insisted on dating with the year 2737, counting from the death of Confucius instead of the year of Emperor Kuang Hsu's reign. This violation of established custom was considered so deliberately offensive that it was nearly treasonous, and the society had to disband in both Peking and Shanghai. Such petty outrages were all that Kang had achieved to date (it would be two more years before he began his attacks on the dowager empress), but he now saw himself as a cult leader, a self-appointed sage. He let it be known that he was engaged in a monumental reevaluation of Chinese history and Confucian ethics.

In 1897 he published a book called *Confucius as Reformer*, perversely arguing that the sage did not favor the status quo but change, which was inevitable. Critics wondered whether Kang was really a wild fox, a genius operating by his own rules, or only a publicity hound exploiting others' ideas to shock and offend in a desperate attempt to advance his career.

That year, when Germany occupied Kiaochow, on the Shantung peninsula, under the pretext of putting down anti-Western agitation by local troublemakers, Kang dashed off a memorial to the throne urging modernization of China to thwart foreign incursions. Experts and intellectuals like himself, he said, should be given access to the throne to help the emperor make wise decisions. When officials refused to pass on his memorial, Kang had it published in a Shanghai newspaper and arranged a private printing. He was becoming adept at exploiting the press in the Treaty Ports for self-promotion and propaganda in a country where newspapers were still rare and Western-style printing of books and pamphlets was just becoming established as small missionary presses were becoming commercial concerns.

Kang heard that a conference was to be held in Sweden to discuss international peace through disarmament and persuaded a friend in the Censorate to put his name in nomination as a delegate. In due course he was summoned to the Tsungli Yamen for an interview in January 1898. Four senior officials of the Yamen sat in on the interview: former viceroy Li Hung-chang; imperial tutor Weng Tung-ho; the Manchu security chief, General Jung Lu; and Sir Chang Yin-huan, a former ambassador to Washington and London.

Kang had blundered into the big league. These four enormously powerful men, representing various blocs, were to play important roles in the tragic events of the months to come, in which the earnest young emperor would become the victim of a Byzantine intrigue and the innocent heads of genuine reformers would roll. Kang was completely unaware of the significance of this occasion, but it was the turning point in his life.

With the exception of the ambassador, a patron of the *ming-shih* who knew Kang as a party guest in Peking, the Yamen ministers had gathered not to conduct an interview but to have a close look at a potential troublemaker, as if examining a bug under glass.

"Sir Chang," as he was called in the legations, was the first Chinese to be knighted by Great Britain and was Peking's first international playboy. He also had the odd distinction of being the man who had carried the wailing infant Kuang Hsu from his home to the Forbidden City in 1875. At age sixty-one he was still a gay blade. In his youth he had failed the imperial exams but had purchased sufficient rank to make his way, and with a mixture of guile and talent became the military secretary to Li Hung-chang's brother, which started him on the path to glory. Given the job of collecting revenues, he increased them so dramatically that Li rewarded him with a job in the Tsungli Yamen. As an outsider who never passed the exams, his rapid rise provoked jealousy. Nonetheless he was appointed minister to the United States, Peru, and Spain from 1885 to 1890, spending most of that time in Washington, D.C., where he entertained lavishly in the Chinese legation off Dupont Circle. On his return to Peking he became an intimate of Grand Tutor Weng, both serving as patrons of the *ming-shih*, spilling a little wine as friends of the arts. This influence paid off when Chang was sent to Queen Victoria's Diamond Jubilee, where he was knighted. As China's most Westernized mandarin, he enjoyed unusual access to Emperor Kuang Hsu, satisfying the young man's curiosity about the West. Because of his gregarious personality Sir Chang was often at odds with Li Hung-chang, but the two collaborated on the secret treaty with Russia, both coming out of the deal with fattened purses. It was Sir Chang who had arranged Kang's interview at the Tsungli Yamen.

During the interview the disarmament conference in Sweden was never mentioned. Kang spent the whole time haranguing the four senior officials on his favorite subjects of reform and the advantages of constitutional monarchy. Tutor Weng found Kang's behavior arrogant, Li thought he was offensive, and General Jung Lu (no man to mince words) simply disliked him.

A few days later, again thanks to Sir Chang's influence, Kang was invited to prepare a paper summarizing his outspoken ideas on reform for the emperor's consideration. In this new memorial Kang repackaged the idea then gaining popularity among celebrities in Peking, that China should emulate Japan and should follow the same steps the Meiji regime had taken to modernize and strengthen itself. For good measure he threw in a few other borrowed ideas: the abolition of corruption, the setting up of an office in the palace to coordinate the introduction of reforms, and the creation of an "avenue of opinion" so memorials could be sent directly to the throne without first being intercepted by bureaucrats.

Kuang Hsu had been taking a great interest in the reform movement, personally reading *ming-shih* memorials as he sought a solution to China's predicament. There is no evidence that he found what Kang had to say exceptional in any way. His were among the many memorials the emperor was reading and sending to his viceroys and governors for comment. However, Kang later claimed that Kuang Hsu decided to launch his reform program only after reading Kang's *Study of the Reforms in Japan.* According to Kang, the emperor sent a message to the empress dowager saying, " 'I have no desire to be the ruler of a state that will collapse. If you do not return my powers to me, I shall abdicate.' " At this point, the empress dowager gave her consent, according to Kang's version of the story. There is no evidence whatsoever to support this scenario. Tzu Hsi had not taken the emperor's powers away in the first place and was at this time back in her retirement at the Summer Palace. The assertion that she had usurped her nephew's powers could only have been made by someone truly ignorant of how things worked, or mischievous, or both. Like just about everything Kang ever wrote about her, this story depended on the reader's being unable to check his assertions.

To everyone's great surprise, on June 11, 1898, with the approval of the empress dowager, Emperor Kuang Hsu issued his first reform decree, urging princes, officials, and commoners alike to strive to learn useful knowledge without sacrificing basic Confucian moral teachings. This was the beginning of the Hundred Days Reform. Over the next 102 days, the emperor issued some fifty reform edicts affecting government administration, military development, industry, education, and international relations. Each of these edicts was issued by Kuang Hsu himself, without reference to his Grand Councillors, and only after consulting Tzu Hsi, whom he visited every few days at the Summer Palace. Any disagreement between them was resolved before Kuang Hsu's final draft was published. Obviously, she had abundant opportunity to interfere beforehand had she wanted to. She did not know how to fix China and merely hoped that the young emperor would gradually find his own way. Unfortunately, instead of going slowly and cautiously, Kuang Hsu moved ahead so quickly that he frightened the entrenched mandarins, censors, and Ironhats alike, who protested to the empress dowager with growing alarm. But she did support Kuang Hsu's program of reform steadfastly over the next three months, and lost confidence only when the Ironhats presented her with contrived evidence of conspiracy. The American minister, Charles Denby, praised the empress dowager's role, saying: "It will not be denied by anyone that the improvement and progress [in China] . . . are mainly due to the will and power of the Empress Regent."

Coming as they did at a time of great uncertainty about the competence of the government and the steadiness of the emperor, these unilateral decisions by Kuang Hsu provoked a much more violent backlash than was justified. His reforms were modest in themselves but taken together they were revolutionary in spirit and were seen as dangerous by the Ironhats. The emperor had not yet decreed a radical change in governmental form, but it was apparent to the hard-liners that he was moving rapidly in that direction. What frightened them most was that his edicts were bypassing the traditional *cordon sanitaire* imposed on the throne by the princes and advisers to the throne, challenging the preeminence of the Manchu grandees and breaking their grip on censorship and procedure maintained for generations since Emperor Yung Cheng.

Kuang Hsu had indirectly raised the specter that the form of government might change, whether by peaceful transition to constitutional monarchy, as outwardly adopted by Japan, or by the neutralization of the grandees and their replacement by a republican regime. The Ironhats had every reason to feel paranoid. The defeat by Japan frightened them. There was insurrection in the countryside, in the widespread revolt of the underground Society of Elders and Brothers (Kolaohui), and in Shanghai and Canton the republican movement was gaining momentum with Japanese encouragement.

Among the Ironhats there were those in favor of an immediate preemptive strike, a palace coup to replace Kuang Hsu with Prince Tuan's son. Others warned that the best way was to win over the empress dowager, who might be persuaded to intercede and resume the regency. The question was how.

CHAPTER TWELVE

The Puppet Show

Kuang Hsu launched his reforms by sacking people who had abused and humiliated him, or interfered too much in his decisions.

First to be fired was Grand Councillor Weng Tung-ho, his former grand tutor. Not the least of Weng's sins had been to give the emperor bad and contradictory advice on the conduct of the war with Japan. Weng had occupied a position of trust for so many years that he took for granted his influence over the young emperor.

Weng was the archetypical Confucian bureaucrat, all manners and no substance, who fawned on the dowager empress and made common cause with the Ironhats. He was one of a group of weathercock mandarins who pirouetted with every political breeze. Now sixty-eight years old, Weng was concurrently a member of the Grand Council, president of the Board of Revenue, member of the Tsungli Yamen, and an Associate Grand Secretary, a key man at court and a sorry comment on the state to which China had sunk. Although his tutorship of the emperor had ended two years earlier, in 1896, Weng still had daily access to Kuang Hsu as a Grand Councillor and was usually present at audiences. As much as anyone, he was responsible for aggravating Kuang Hsu's nervous condition, keeping the emperor an emotional cripple by continually making him uncertain of his own judgment, discouraging him from asserting himself, and fostering in him an exaggerated filial piety, bordering on paranoia, toward his aunt. Outsiders assumed that a tyrannical Tzu Hsi kept the emperor under her thumb, but the available evidence suggests otherwise. Courtiers like Weng set an exaggerated style of groveling to advance their careers and used their influence over the emperor during his childhood and adolescence to instill dread. When the opportunity came, the emperor struck back at Weng, not at his aunt.

At a meeting of all the Grand Councillors early on June 15, 1898, Weng annoyed the emperor by continually and tediously urging caution, insisting that Tzu Hsi be involved in the reform process at every step, down to the selection of reform officials. Behind this tiresome display of veneration for the dowager was Weng's attempt to block the reforms by tying the emperor's thumbs behind his back with red tape. Although he was among the most prominent patrons of the *ming-shih*, the ever cautious Weng, sensing trouble ahead, had begun to distance himself from the reform movement as it gathered momentum in the first half of 1898. If it was going to come to a showdown between the reformers and the Ironhats, there was no doubt on which side he would be.

The emperor had endured Weng's dogged interference for many years and his patience now snapped. After a respite he summoned a second meeting of the council, specifically excluding Weng. This meeting ended with the emperor's going against the advice of all his remaining councillors and peremptorily ordering Weng's dismissal.

Quite the opposite story was told by Backhouse and Bland, who insisted that Weng was fired by the dowager because he was leading the emperor down the road of reform—a persistent piece of disinformation that most scholars still subscribe to, despite contrary evidence given by Hart and others. At the time Weng was fired, Tzu Hsi was at the Summer Palace unaware of the proceedings and was only informed later.

The suddenness of Weng's removal, and the fact that it was ordered without first consulting the empress dowager, served notice that Kuang Hsu finally had come of age. This alarmed Prince Tuan's faction, which included the remaining members of the Grand Council and other powerful officials at court. Generations had passed since an emperor had actually ruled on his own; in the meantime real power had been in the hands of courtiers heading cliques like the Gang of Eight, or the coalition of the late Prince Kung.

The death of Prince Kung and the firing of Tutor Weng left only four Grand Councillors. Kang I, one of Prince Tuan's most powerful allies, easily dominated the other Grand Councillors, including the illustrious but fuzzy-minded Ironhat, Prince Li. These were not men of imagination. Kang I was powerful not because he was a great statesman but because he was self-righteous, hostile, inflexible, and opposed to change of any kind, which in the conservative Manchu court meant upright and trustworthy. Rather than smooth things over as Prince Kung might have, Kang I persuaded other officials that the emperor had acted impetuously and was not to be trusted without a guiding hand. If Kuang Hsu could not arrive at decisions by consensus (which meant giving way to the collective judgment of his elders), it might be necessary to remove him from the throne. Prince Tuan's son, Pu Chun, was conveniently at hand to succeed him.

Here, unexpectedly, was an opportunity to impeach Kuang Hsu. To do it, the hard-liners would have to be extremely circumspect. First, they would have to persuade the aging dowager to resume her regency, then ease Kuang Hsu out.

If we must look for a precise date when fatal reaction to the reforms began, it was the date of Weng's firing, June 15, 1898, four days after the start of the Hundred Days Reform. Four days later, Robert Hart heard the first rumblings of a coup plot. Tutor Weng's "fussy conservatism" had caused him to lose his job, Hart said. And that had stirred up "a palace plot to put power [back] in the Empress Dowager's hands."

Putting power back "in the Empress Dowager's hands" is an expression that is easily misunderstood. She had never attained absolute power, merely ceremonial position. When the Manchu talked of "returning her to the throne" it did not mean "to power," because power remained exclusively a privilege of the princes, grandees, and high mandarins, the retention of which is what this quarrel was all about. She was once again needed as a figurehead to lend the appearance of legitimacy to those who would really be wielding power. Prince Kung had been the first to make use of Tzu An and Tzu Hsi in this manner in 1861 and again in 1875. Now Tzu Hsi was needed by the Ironhats for the same purpose.

George Morrison, Peking correspondent for the *Times* of London, received a letter about this palace plot from A. E. Hippsley, one of Hart's employees in the Chinese Customs in Tientsin. "The Edicts of the 15th (dismissal of Weng Tung-ho) constitute a coup d'état," Hippsley wrote Morrison grandly, meaning that Kuang Hsu had tried to kick out all the reactionaries. "Indeed, the Empress Dowager is reported to have said that . . . the Emperor whose administration has already brought China to the verge of ruin, can no longer be entrusted with the conduct of affairs and that she must resume the reins. There was even, I am told, talk of . . . dethronement of the Emperor."

Hippsley was distorting inside gossip and feeding these distortions to the foreign press. He worked for Gustav Detring, head of Customs in Tientsin, who had spent his entire career in Viceroy Li's pocket, so Detring may have put him up to writing this disinformation to Morrison. There were many occasions when Li, the master of conspiracy, had people write letters to journalists, send telegrams, or leak information long before events occurred, as a way of helping them to happen. A prime example was when one of Li's men leaked to the Shanghai press news of an assassination that did not take place till days later. Hippsley wrote his letter to Morrison on June 20, 1898, only five days after Weng's firing. For a lowly Customs official writing from Tientsin, he seemed to know a great deal about what was happening behind the scenes many miles away in Peking, including several things that were not true: that the empress dowager said the emperor could no longer be trusted and that she must resume the reins.

It will be demonstrated that Tzu Hsi did not reach such a conclusion till three months after Hippsley wrote his letter. The record shows that Tzu Hsi became seriously alarmed only in mid-September, after Prince Tuan's faction deliberately provoked and frightened her with help from an unlikely quarter.

She may have been disturbed by Kuang Hsu's dismissal of Weng in such a peremptory manner, given the tempest he stirred up, but there is no evidence that she was enraged or even angry. Distressed, yes. As Robert Hart explained to Morrison, the whole matter of Weng's firing came down to a question of tact, etiquette, and delicacy, points about which the empress dowager was extremely sensitive. "Pity," said Hart, "[that] the Emperor did not go about it more gently!" Tzu Hsi's nephew continued to visit her at the Summer Palace in the days and weeks to follow; there is no record of their quarreling, and there was no interruption in her evident approval of his reform edicts. (When the crisis was over, most of his reforms were kept in place.)

The day after Weng's dismissal from the Grand Council, June 16, Wild Fox Kang had his one and only interview with the emperor, arranged by Sir Chang. Before the meeting, both General Jung Lu and Grand Councillor Kang I, having judged Kang to be a man of only superficial talent, suggested giving him a job as an ordinary secretary in the Tsungli Yamen, where his fascination with foreign ideas might be put to some practical use. While this would have been charitable, Kang fantasized that when he met the emperor at last, Kuang Hsu would appoint him imperial adviser on all reform matters, a Grand Councillor for Reform, had such a post existed.

The interview was brief and inconsequential. All the emperor was prepared to offer Kang was the aforementioned clerical job in the foreign office. This was little better than Kang's original assignment at the Board of Works. To salve his ego he convinced himself that the emperor had been misled by his conservative advisers and so failed to realize that here was a man of unusual ability.

Immediately after the disappointing interview, Kang complained to Sir Chang, then rashly spread the word around *ming-shih* circles that he had been sabotaged by the emperor's advisers. He was being kept under surveillance, so retaliation was swift. The Ironhats, still miffed over the dismissal of tutor Weng, tried to even the score by striking at Kang's patron, the high-living Sir Chang. On June 21 Sir Chang was impeached for taking bribes, specifically the Russian rubles he had received secretly from St. Petersburg. Despite the seriousness of the charges, Kuang Hsu let the amiable Sir Chang off with a wrist slap. The Ironhats took the emperor's leniency as a direct affront and complained to Tzu Hsi. After the harsh treatment of Grand Councillor Weng, this leniency did anger the dowager, who had always adhered to a policy of being conspicuously evenhanded, because harmony was one of the few antidotes to intrigue.

Mounting a counterattack, the Wild Fox's friends in the Censorate jointly accused another leading reactionary, the president of the Board of Ceremonies, Hsu Ying-kuei, of being mediocre, arrogant, and domineering. Hsu struck back, bypassing the Censors and going straight to the heart of the problem, labeling Kang Yu-wei a troublemaker, a licentious miscreant, and a bogus expert in Western matters. Like hounds baying on the hunt, other conservative officials made similar attacks on the Wild Fox over the next three weeks. They all regarded Kang as a self-seeking troublemaker with a big mouth. So far this was only a battle of words, but it polarized the debate into two distinct camps, the reformers versus the reactionaries, with Kuang Hsu and the empress dowager caught in the middle. This played into Kang's hands, as he was becoming increasingly identified with genuine reformers who would have been better off without him. Association with Kang was going to become fatal.

Moderates at court who heretofore may have favored, or at least not opposed, the idea of reform now began to identify reform with the reckless and offensive behavior of Wild Fox Kang, a complete outsider who had simply attached himself like a leech to the reform movement. At the same time, Kang helped matters along by falsely identifying himself to foreigners as the actual leader of an unofficial reform party, boasting that he knew the emperor intimately.

Meanwhile real alarm was growing among conservatives that there might actually be something more sinister afoot. A number of Westerners were showing exaggerated enthusiasm for Kang and the prospect of radical changes in the regime and were encouraging dissidents at the Hanlin Academy and in other government agencies. Manchu agents reported that British and American missionaries and English adventurers with military backgrounds were secretly agitating in favor of a constitutional monarchy. It was known that the legations used people like these when they did not want to be connected directly with subversive activities. There was also a heightened level of activity at the Japanese legation and a flurry of comings and goings by suspected agents of the Genyosha in Peking and Tientsin. Alarmed by these reports, the already paranoid Ironhats became convinced that the reform movement might actually be cover for an armed overthrow, supported by the Foreign Powers. As a precaution, it was decided to beef up security forces in Peking.

One of the men the Wild Fox was abusing loudly and often during his round of *ming-shih* drinking parties was General Jung Lu, who had been one of the senior officials to interview Kang at the Tsungli Yamen. He was a professional policeman, an attractive man with a well-tended beard and an undeserved reputation for having little imagination. As a young officer Jung Lu had been a good-natured swashbuckler. At age sixty-two he had matured into a man of dignity and prudence, the only Manchu everyone could trust. He had always been close to Tzu Hsi and is usually said to be her cousin, although he was not a member of her clan. Jung Lu could trace his ancestry back to Nurhachi's most distinguished general. Ever since, emperors had heaped posthumous titles and ranks upon this illustrious predecessor, so Jung Lu enjoyed an unusual status in Peking and his loyalty to the dynasty remained beyond question. Since 1888 he had served as chamberlain of the Imperial Guards. After the defeat by Japan he was made an Associate Grand Secretary and president of the Board of War and was appointed to the Tsungli Yamen to watch over other ministers. The security of the court, and of the regime as a whole, were his main concerns, but he was also responsible for keeping an eye on the ambitious military men assigned to modernize China's armies. With the dowager empress in retirement, an uncertain young emperor on the throne, and hotheaded Ironhats spoiling for revenge, Jung Lu was keeping a busy vigil. It was up to him to block any uprising.

Jung Lu recommended that General Yuan Shih-kai be given command of the New Army, numbering seven thousand men. Unlike the old Anh-wei and Hunan armies, which were privately raised and financed by Tseng Kuo-fan and Li Hung-chang to fight the Taipings, the New Army had been raised and financed by the central government. It was trained by the German Constantin von Hanneken and equipped with Western weapons. As commander of the New Army, General Yuan came under Jung Lu's direct control. He still owed loyalty to his lifelong patron, Li Hung-chang, but could play games on a much larger board. General Yuan and this force were headquartered at Hsiaochan, near Tientsin, where they were the first line of defense against foreign invaders.

As the Hundred Days Reform got under way, Kuang Hsu again pro-moted General Jung Lu, this time to Li Hung-chang's old posts of viceroy of Chihli and Superintendent of Trade for the Northern Ports. This brought all military forces in North China under the command of the most reliable Manchu. In addition to the New Army under General Yuan, Jung Lu became commander in chief of three other national armies: the forces of generals Sung Ching, Tung Fu-hsiang, and Nieh Shih-cheng, all strategically positioned around Peking. Jung Lu's headquarters were in Tientsin, but by 1898 it was possible to travel by train from Peking to Tientsin in several hours.

Of these four armies, all but one were under the personal command of a Han Chinese general. The Manchu were all aware of the possibility that in a crisis Han forces might rebel, so the Ironhats were partial to General

Tung Fu-hsiang, the former bandit whose army of wild Muslim-Chinese horsemen and braves from Kansu Province was brought into the imperial hunting preserve on the southern outskirts of Peking on orders from Prince Tuan, on what was described as a routine drill with new Western rifles. Because of their different ethnic background, these Tartar forces would have little hesitation to fire on Han Chinese.

As a further precaution against trouble, Jung Lu's old job of commandant of the Peking Gendarmerie was given to another of Prince Tuan's supporters, the policeman Chung Li, and his gendarmes were reequipped with new foreign rifles and machine guns. Three Manchu Banners and an artillery and musketry battalion were ordered to reinforce the Summer Palace. Grand Councillor Kang I was made adjutant general of the Scout Division of the Banners, and Jung Lu's Peking Field Force was rearmed with modern breechloaders.

Anyone noticing these extraordinary changes might fairly have wondered what was going on. The establishment was bracing itself, but for what?

By mid-July—one month into the Hundred Days—conservative opposition to the emperor's reforms had hardened, and indirect attempts were being made by Prince Tuan's allies to persuade the dowager to come out of retirement. One of her ladies-in-waiting cried on her shoulder; her husband, a member of the dowager's clan, had been dismissed from the Board of Rites by the emperor. Next, a delegation jointly headed by a Manchu and a Mongol complained to her quaintly that Kuang Hsu was violating the laws of the ancestors (by doing something innovative). Tzu Hsi did not let either appeal goad her into interfering.

These efforts were led by Grand Councillor Kang I. What most upset Kang I was that he and his three fellow Grand Councillors were now in danger of being fired themselves. The emperor had decided to appoint a group of young reform advisers. Conservatives feared that it was just a matter of time before these reform advisers would displace the Grand Council. In an effort to discredit all reformers and dissuade the emperor from his plan, the conservatives launched a new attack on Wild Fox Kang. He became the target of a rush of memorials criticizing as heresy his interpretation of Confucius and accusing him of "ideological sedition." His friends in the *ming-shih* were alarmed. Kang's efforts to draw attention to himself were provoking trouble for all of them at a time when the emperor's newborn reforms ought to be nurtured. One of the Wild Fox's friends in the Censorate wrote a formal petition imploring the emperor to have Kang sent to Shanghai to run a reform newspaper with government support, an excuse to get him out of Peking. The emperor readily agreed. But Kang dragged his feet; he and his disciple, journalist Liang Chi-chao, boasted about leaving momentarily to take up the "imperial commission," but stayed into September to make the most of their grand exit.

Assuming that the matter of Kang had been dealt with, the emperor went ahead and selected four young men, all Chinese, to serve as his reform advisers and made them responsible for supervising the implementation of all reform edicts. These men—Tan Ssu-tung, Yang Jui, Liu Kuang-ti, and Lin Hsu—were empowered to offer advice to the emperor and to draft his reform edicts, thus preempting the Grand Council, while also bypassing the Censorate and the Hanlin Academy. Under this arrangement not only the Ironhats but the Manchu as a whole would remain in the dark about the emperor's reform edicts until they appeared, which would allow them no time to prepare countermoves.

Here was the breaking point.

Three of these reform advisers were promising protégés of Viceroy Chang Chih-tung, who had risen to power on the coattails of the Ironhats as head of the conservative Pure party but who had since become independently wealthy brokering joint ventures with Western companies in provinces he controlled. Since the downgrading of Viceroy Li, Chang Chih-tung had become the most influential Chinese viceroy. When the emperor let it be known that he was looking for talented young reform advocates to serve as consultants in the palace, Viceroy Chang quickly recommended his favorites.

The most appealing was Tan Ssu-tung, himself a wild fox, a twenty-three-year-old Hunanese scholar-adventurer. As a boy he showed brilliance in his studies, but he also had a fondness for swordplay. His father, a widower, became governor of Hupeh in 1889, which gave his son obvious advantages. After failing five times to pass the civil service exams, however, Tan gave up trying and damned the system for the way it blocked gifted men from entering the mainstream. He started his own reform society and traveled to Peking hoping to meet other iconoclasts, including Kang Yu-wei. He missed him but became acquainted instead with Kang's follower, Liang Chi-chao. Meanwhile, in an effort to get his son back on the traditional path, Tan's father got him a job as a petty bureaucrat, purchasing the necessary rank. Tan refused, calling it "a beggar's livelihood." He craved to break free (as his father put it), "as much as birds and animals seek to break out of their cages." He accepted an offer from the progressive governor of his home province to help introduce reforms there and was not in Peking when the Hundred Days began. As a charismatic leader of the Hunan reform movement he was an attractive choice for the emperor's inner circle of new advisers.

Tan's big disadvantage was his innocence of the realities of power, which made him vulnerable to seasoned manipulators. This innocence was evident in his susceptibility to Japanese blandishments. Tokyo was watching developments in Peking with keen interest. At the beginning of 1898, some months before Tan was chosen for the palace job, three officers of the Japanese general staff came to China, ostensibly to see Viceroy Chang about organizing a new army in Hunan and Hupeh provinces that would be given modern training by Japanese advisers. While they were in Hunan, the Japanese officers cultivated young Tan, suggesting a secret alliance between China and Japan. Not only would China learn how to modernize and strengthen herself by the example of Meiji Japan but Tokyo would show her how—secretly, so that the Manchu grandees would not be alarmed needlessly. They assured Tan that Japan was motivated only by altruism. Unfortunately, Tan was taken in.

So when he took his place as one of the emperor's new reform secretaries, Tan vigorously pressed the idea of inviting senior Japanese to take up residence in Peking as personal consultants to the Ching emperor. To give the Ironhats their due, this scenario does seem harebrained considering the murderous role the Japanese had played in bringing "reform" to Korea. But Tan was young.

The emperor also chose two older advisers, scholar Yang Jui who, like Tan, was the chairman of the reform society in his home province, Szechwan, and another Szechwanese, thirty-nine-year-old Liu Kuang-ti, who had been working for the Board of Punishments.

The fourth and last of the emperor's new advisers was Lin Hsu, a young Fukienese scholar who was the chairman of the reform society in his province and a onetime follower of Wild Fox Kang.

Two days after the new advisers were installed, and after listening at length to their suggestions, Emperor Kuang Hsu decreed another round of purges. Surprising the legations, he fired both Sir Chang and the great Li Hung-chang from the Tsungli Yamen, along with two other Yamen ministers identified with Li. At first appraisal this seemed to bring Li's long career to an end. But it was never wise to underrate Li, especially when his back was to the wall.

White-haired, grandfatherly Li Hung-chang was now seventy-five and had recently been dealt one embarrassing blow after another, causing him catastrophic loss of face and revenue. He was being used as a whipping boy for the mistakes of the Manchu and as a scapegoat for the failure of the Chinese system.

Although Li was no longer a viceroy, he was still the most powerful man in China. His protégés included generals, admirals, governors, police chiefs and magistrates, heads of Chinese banks and corporations, shipping magnates, chiefs of posts and telegraphs, leaders of sects and triads, and godfathers of the new Chicago-style underworld syndicates like the Green Gang taking hold in port cities along the coast and rivers. Through these protégés and through his many connections with Western diplomats, businessmen, and journalists, Li continued to have incomparable leverage. Through them he would now strike back. At his age he had little time, so he could not rest until he had regained his lost face.

Cultivating Morrison of the *Times*, but only through third parties such as Detring, Li began a calculated image-building campaign. He made it a point to be seen in as many gatherings of foreigners as possible, including Robert Hart's lawn parties. Hart observed: "The great man dines out when asked, and he was at [Sir Claude] MacDonald's Fancy Dress Ball on New Year's Eve—very much out of place, with his pocket spittoon well to the front always!" Nobody was sure what Li was up to, so they badly underestimated the wily old man. In a matter of weeks he would begin to turn the tables, and reformers and Ironhats alike would pay dearly. The innocent Kuang Hsu was completely unprepared for the great wave of conspiracy and treachery about to engulf him.

Li had negotiated his secret deal giving Russia control of southern Manchuria as a means of blocking the further advance of Japan. But Kuang Hsu now wanted Japanese help and had installed his own pro-Japanese kitchen cabinet of young reformers who immediately pressed him to get rid of Li and all other officials they saw as pro-Russian. They did not grasp that Li's connivance with Russia was only a matter of expediency. As China's brain and nervous systerm, his real ambitions went far beyond kickbacks and bribes. Greedy and self-serving as he was, Li embodied much that was wise and brilliant in Chinese character. The Manchu might have been hanging from their red lacquered rafters many years earlier if Li had not protected them from their own monumental incompetence. In doing so, Li was ruthless and murderous to be sure, but he had resisted more than one chance to seize the throne for himself. Unlike lesser mortals he understood that chairman of the board was better than emperor. Kuang Hsu might have been wiser to give Li all the power and prestige he wanted in return for his help. This was what Prince Kung and Tzu Hsi had done. Instead, the emperor had acted rashly and turned his most ingenious civil servant into his most cunning adversary. Hereafter Li would make it look as if the Ironhats were causing all the trouble. But in the puppet shows of 1898 and 1900 the strings were all controlled by Li.

Through his own spies, augmented by czarist intelligence, Li had already discovered that Kuang Hsu was contemplating a secret pact with the architect of the Meiji Restoration, Ito Hirobumi, who had been prime minister during the Sino-Japanese War and was now an elder statesman. Ito was about to arrive in China on what was to be portrayed as a private visit. He would actually be in Peking to discuss becoming a special consultant to Emperor Kuang Hsu on restructuring the Chinese government—without the prior approval of the Grand Council or the Clan Council. As a realist, Li opposed any deal that would put Japanese officials in the Forbidden City and allow Japanese agents to permeate the Chinese bureaucracy. Li's Russian friends were equally alarmed, and were pressing him to block the Japanese initiative.

As the young emperor's latest victim, Li found himself in strange company: the very Ironhats who had so recently conspired against him at the end of the Sino-Japanese War. If he informed them of the secret deal to be made with Ito, it would provoke their paranoia and confirm their worst fears. He knew that Prince Tuan and his followers were maneuvering themselves into positions of greater control over police, military, revenue, and control organs; he was well informed of their ambitions for the throne and their long-term plot to expel all foreigners from China. Once again Li found himself in the position of being able to act as a catalyst or spoiler. For a mind as happily devious as Li's, it was entirely possible to set both groups of his enemies—Ironhats and reformers—upon each other then sit back to harvest the consequences.

In Tientsin, on September 11, 1898, Viceroy Jung Lu welcomed Ito Hirobumi to China, and the two had what was called a cordial meeting. On his arrival in Peking by train a few days later, Ito had a private talk with his old adversary Li Hung-chang and met officials of the Tsungli Yamen.

Now nearly sixty, Ito was an impressive and unusually urbane figure in the crumbling, parched alleys of Peking. His neatly trimmed spade beard and mustache were pure white against a ruddy complexion, and he carried himself with the regal bearing of a samurai, although he was dressed in a beautifully tailored three-piece suit, like a British investment banker. Here in the rundown capital of the effete Ching Dynasty was the author of the Meiji constitution.

On the face of it, Ito's constitution had restored to the emperor of Japan the authority that had been suborned for centuries by the xenophobic shoguns and had introduced a semblance of basic civil rights and the beginnings of what seemed to be democratic institutions. In reality the Meiji emperor was now merely in the thrall of a different group of power brokers: industrialists, militarists, and expansionists who had used the cause of modernization and reform to sweep away the old feudal power blocs and replace them with new ones. The obvious similarities to the situation in Peking were not lost on the Manchu grandees anxiously clinging to power in China, who were eager to see their authority increased, not reduced. Following the Japanese model would consign the Ironhats to the dustbin.

The emperor and the reformers saw only what they wanted to see. For the idealistic Kuang Hsu, the Meiji example appeared to promise a restoration of the emperor's preeminence as chief executive with new instruments of administration modeled on the Japanese parliament, where much of the day-to-day government in Japan seemed to be vested in delegates of the people. (This was true only in appearance, as Ito's expensive suits only looked as though they were cut on Savile Row.) Kuang Hsu apparently imagined that this renaissance was a simple matter of firing all the reactionaries who stood in the way and installing a new group of progressives. He failed to grasp that the Japanese parliament was controlled behind the scenes by political bosses like militarist Yamagata Aritomo and the godfathers of the Genyosha, who together had brought about the Sino-Japanese War despite Ito's good intentions.

Ito himself was no threat to China. He was a moderate, opposed to hawks like Yamagata. Although Ito was said to have had a secret audience with his own emperor before leaving Tokyo for Peking, it seems that he made the trip not as a provocateur but as a wise man earnestly seeking to help. There is no evidence linking him to Japanese intrigues simultaneously under way in China, which were set in motion by Yamagata and the Genyosha. Reports of Japanese secret agents attempting to agitate the reform crisis in Peking are borne out by Genyosha archives. The Genyosha provided a means of running secret agents in China without coming under official scrutiny in Tokyo, while maintaining deniability in the field. Wherever they were carried out, Genyosha assassinations, kidnappings, and extortion were abetted by Japanese army and naval forces, diplomats, and commercial representatives of Japan's great trading houses, the zaibatsu. From time to time even Ito made use of the Genyosha (as he would once again during this visit to Peking), but it was Yamagata's dream (not Ito's) to breakfast on Korea, lunch on Manchuria, then banquet on China as a whole.

Yamagata, a former prime minister and defense minister who was about to become prime minister again in the autumn of 1898, had a long history of gaining his objectives by unconventional means, employing irregulars in wartime and secret agents in peacetime. He was the leading promoter of Japanese expansion, one of the inner circle of the Meiji emperor, and lord protector of the Genyosha. As early as 1879, to facilitate the subversion of China, he had set up a spy network there under cover of a chain of pharmacies with the trade name Halls of Pleasurable Delights, run by Genyosha agents. They traveled the countryside as salesmen, dispensing telini fly and other aphrodisiacs, *rin-no-tama* bells, and pornographic pictures of the sort the Genyosha boss, Toyama Mitsuru, particularly enjoyed. These potent drugs and erotic pictures were used to cultivate and then subvert local gentry as they became addicted. The Genyosha's nominal head, Hiraoka Kotaro, became so familiar to Peking officials that he was labeled "Tokyo's unofficial ambassador."

The anxiety caused among the Ironhats by the arrival of Ito was the signal for Li Hung-chang to begin his revenge. He made use of one of his henchmen, a Chinese security man named Yang Chung-i, whose daughter was married to Li's grandson. Yang was one of the most zealous ideological snoops in the Censorate, the agency responsible for policing China's bureaucracy as well as for calling the emperor to task when that was appropriate. Like the Hanlin Academy, the Censorate employed people of divergent views, even a few dissidents who supported Wild Fox Kang. The most dangerous Censors were sharp-eyed secret policemen and self-appointed bluenoses, continually pointing fingers at ideological backsliders and potential traitors. Yang fell into this latter category. He was a watchdog for the archconservatives, a protégé of the Manchu security chief, Jung Lu, but his main loyalty through marriage was to Li.

Immediately after Ito's arrival in Peking, Censor Yang drafted a lengthy memorial at Li's instigation alerting the empress dowager to a number of alarming developments, including the assertion that the emperor had engaged none other than Wild Fox Kang as a secret adviser, and urging Tzu Hsi to intervene and resume without delay her position as regent.

What Yang was proposing was nothing less than the impeachment of Emperor Kuang Hsu, so it became a very delicate matter to find a high official prepared to deliver such an explosive document to the dowager. Nobody was to know that Li was behind it. First, Yang took his memorial to Viceroy Jung Lu. After reading it, the cautious Jung Lu refused to participate and instructed Yang to show it to Prince Ching next. Prince Ching also was reluctant to become involved, as the situation had not yet reached terminal crisis. Surely somebody else could be found. For the next two days Yang (and Li) held back.

By far the most mischievous of Li's proxies, of course, was General Yuan Shih-kai, who now began to play a characteristically treacherous role. On September 14, the day Censor Yang composed his inflammatory indictment, the emperor had the first of two private audiences with General Yuan, supposedly to discuss problems of reforming the army. Since his hasty return from Korea on the eve of the recent war, Yuan had been put in overall charge of the program to retrain China's armies in Western skills and weapons. This caused many people, including the radical reformers, to mistake him for a liberal. The thirty-nine-year-old general was a man of many faces and, like Iago, could be extraordinarily charming. Kuang Hsu was easily persuaded that Yuan was on his side, prepared to put his New Army behind anything the emperor chose to do. Two days later Yuan was informed that the appreciative emperor had appointed him vice-president of the Board of War.

It was announced that the emperor was to hold a formal audience with Ito in the Forbidden City on September 20, which would be attended by the empress dowager, Prince Ching, and many other senior officials. What none of the emperor's critics yet knew was that in the meantime Kuang Hsu planned to confer in secret with the Japanese statesman on September 18, and to make him an offer that (had they known) would have astounded and infuriated the old guard. Kuang Hsu was certainly aware that his actions were provoking a backlash and must have been informed of gossip that the Ironhats were plotting a preemptive strike. As Robert Hart's diary makes absolutely clear, such dangerous talk had been in general circulation in Peking, Tientsin, and Shanghai since only a few days after the emperor had fired Grand Councillor Weng three months earlier. Under the circumstances it would only have been natural for Kuang Hsu to ask General Yuan whether he could be counted on to back the throne in an emergency. Assuming that Yuan was the liberal he pretended to be, he was the key to blocking any Ironhat coup attempt. But Yuan's expressions of loyalty were never sincere. Loyalty to anyone but Li was against his nature. So from the moment he asked for Yuan's help, the emperor's fate was sealed.

CHAPTER THIRTEEN

The Betrayal

Wild Fox Kang later claimed that on the very day the emperor saw General Yuan, the fourteenth of September, Kuang Hsu wrote Kang a secret message, saying that his (the emperor's) life was in danger. This was the same day that Censor Yang drafted his indictment to the empress dowager, so in principle the emperor *was* in danger. Kang claimed that the message, in the form of a secret decree, was sent through an intermediary and did not reach him until four days later, on September 18, the day the emperor had his second meeting with General Yuan.

There are a number of reasons that Kang's story is peculiar. It had been two full months since the emperor authorized Kang's departure for Shanghai to take up editorial duties there, but the Wild Fox was still in Peking, making the rounds of *ming-shih* parties, spreading rumors, slandering the old guard, and piling faggots on the fire. Meanwhile conservative officials in the provinces appealed to the emperor to order the beheading of Wild Fox Kang and his sidekick, Liang Chi-chao, as heretics and troublemakers. Recklessly, Kang boasted at parties that he and his younger brother, Kuang-jen, had secret nightly audiences with the emperor. Had that been the case, no secret message would have been required. These stories, which if they were true reflected badly upon the emperor's judgment, reached the ears of officials who despised Kang as a self-seeking charlatan. If nothing else, Kang's big mouth was jeopardizing the whole reform movement, proving him to be a fool as well. When Kuang Hsu visited his aunt at the Summer Palace on September 16, he heard from her about the boasting of the Wild Fox. The following day, September 17, he issued a public decree ordering Kang to leave immediately for Shanghai, making the important point in it that he had met Kang only once, to discredit the idea that Kang had influence over him and had been seeing him secretly. Kang claimed that he was at a party at an imperial Censor's house drinking wine and enjoying a concert when this decree was published. The first he knew about it, he said, was when he saw the decree posted in the streets. Taking it lightly, he made no immediate arrangements to go. For the next four days, he continued doing what he had been doing all summer: visiting friends, attending dinner parties, stirring the caldron.

Early in the morning on September 18, Kuang Hsu had his second private meeting with General Yuan, this time at the Summer Palace. According to Yuan, during this interview he accepted the appointment as vice-president of the Board of War. But that was the topic of least significance. Kuang Hsu now took the general into his confidence on a matter of great secrecy: the emperor intended to proceed with his reform program at any cost and would hold a secret meeting with Ito in the Forbidden City in a matter of hours, that very day, and none of the old guard would be informed, including the Grand Councillors, the Tsungli Yamen, and the empress dowager. At his secret meeting with Ito, Kuang Hsu intended to ask the Japanese statesman if he would accept a post as a special consultant in Peking, a post that could be construed as putting a foreigner in control of the entire administrative machinery of China, with the emperor's personal authorization to make changes similar to those Ito had introduced in Japan.

When Yuan left the Summer Palace in the predawn darkness with his bodyguard in tow, he was only a short distance from the entrance to Prince Ching's suburban estate. He made his way there in the gloom and by prior arrangement found Prince Ching and Li Hung-chang waiting expectantly for him. Although there is no record of what was said during this conspiratorial meeting, from what followed it is evident that Yuan betrayed the emperor by telling Li and Prince Ching what Kuang Hsu had confided to him minutes before in strictest secrecy. Li was accompanied by his henchman, Censor Yang, the secret policeman from the Censorate, who had with him the draft of his memorial to the empress dowager. That indictment could now be revised and updated, and there should no longer be any difficulty persuading the Ironhats themselves to present it to the dowager collectively.

Soon afterward, answering an urgent summons, Prince Tuan, Duke Lan, and the rest of the Ironhat leadership arrived and were briefed by Prince Ching and Censor Yang. (In the meantime Li and General Yuan, who were anathema to the Ironhats, made themselves scarce.) Prince Ching then called a full Clan Council. After deliberating and preparing their case, they went in a group the short distance to the Summer Palace to inform Tzu Hsi of the latest developments and to ask her formally to resume her regency—that is, to let them resume power behind her skirts.

Specifically, they told her that the emperor was holding a secret audience at that very moment with Ito, and that the emperor intended to propose a Sino-Japanese alliance in which Ito would be brought in to head the government of China, a calculated exaggeration. This would endanger all of them. In particular, they said, it would jeopardize Tzu Hsi's position as the retired empress dowager, an argument certain to alarm her. They need hardly remind her of the fate of Korea's Queen Min, stabbed and roasted to death in a spectacular fashion by Genyosha assassins to clear the way for the Japanese takeover in Seoul.

The men confronting Tzu Hsi in the audience chamber adjoining her retirement quarters on Lake Kunming were young firebrands, complacent grandees, and old professional politicians. They had in common a cynical self-interest that made it easy to manipulate the sixty-three-year-old woman. After some confusion and uncertainty on her part about what they were up to, they had Tzu Hsi's undivided attention.

If China followed in the footsteps of Meiji Japan, they told the dowager, Manchu control would end, power would be transferred to the irresponsible demagogues of new Chinese political parties no better than the troublemaker Kang Yu-wei or the republican gadfly Sun Yat-sen, and the foolish emperor would become at best a mere figurehead. It would mean the end of the world they had known.

The principal spokesman during this momentous visit to the dowager was Li's provocateur, Censor Yang, whose moment had come at last. Tzu Hsi listened to him at first with her usual mask of composure firmly in place, then anger flared up in her eyes and she interrupted him peremptorily and ordered Yang to read his entire memorial aloud.

Yang began reading by reminding her of the many conspiratorial activities of the *ming-shih* over the years and described Kang Yu-wei's recent unwholesome influence. Kang, he said, had wormed his way into the inner courts of the Forbidden City, not physically but through intermediaries. Under the influence of Kang and the *ming-shih*, he said, the emperor was being persuaded to dismiss men of experience. In effect, Kuang Hsu was taking the advice of this troublemaker and his associates, placing them in a position tantamount to Grand Councillors, in violation of ancient practice. Now, he said, Kuang Hsu wanted to put Japan's Ito in a position second only to the emperor himself, as a de facto prime minister of China, to dictate how China was to be ruled and by whom.

Tzu Hsi again interrupted the Censor's reading. If there was ever an occasion when her celebrated temper was visible to all, this was it. Yang was accusing an emperor of treason, which was grave enough. But in this case the emperor was a boy she had rescued from her sister's clutches, an abused child she had sheltered and protected as a substitute for her own dead son, a boy put at such a disadvantage by chronic illness that he would never be able to defend himself adequately against his royal cousins. As throwbacks to their rude tribal origins in eastern Siberia, Prince Tuan and his followers had been pursuing Kuang Hsu like a pack of wild dogs tormenting a crippled pony until they could pull him down. What none of them understood was that after her own son's death, Kuang Hsu had become her son reincarnated. Tzu Hsi had always been gentle and maternal toward him. The two lived in symbiosis in the palaces, virtually as mother and child. In edicts Kuang Hsu often referred to the two of them as mother and son, sometimes calling her his imperial mother, sometimes just mother. Someone else might have been able to listen in silence to the indictment, but Tzu Hsi realized with growing anger that they were trying to get her to destroy her adopted child. With the anger came fear.

She demanded to know what evidence Censor Yang had to support these charges. While Yang admitted that some of these charges were based on hearsay rather than hard evidence, there was reason to believe that Kang Yu-wei and others in the reform movement were involved in a deliberate conspiracy influenced and supported by Japan, with the collusion of Great Britain. Yang was not arguing against reform itself, he assured her, but against letting these important changes be decided by wild foxes and dwarf bandits.

This startling accusation, backed by imperial clansmen she had always relied upon for guidance, was designed to give Tzu Hsi no real alternative but to come out of retirement and resume the regency. Even so, she told the Clan Council that she refused to be rushed into an immediate decision; but September 18, 1898, saw a fateful shift of balance in Peking.

Tzu Hsi was not unaware of what her nephew had been doing, at least until his secret meeting with Ito. The Summer Palace was only six miles from the Forbidden City. During the Hundred Days, Kuang Hsu had made more than ten trips to visit his aunt, and she had made several return visits. They were not isolated from each other, except in the imagination of the Western legations and the missionary community, who were poorly informed but thought otherwise. During these visits the dowager had ample opportunity to hear directly from her nephew what he was doing, what reforms he was introducing, and whom he was dismissing from office. There is no record of Tzu Hsi's intervening in any manner during these visits, no record of her ordering her nephew to do anything differently. Up to this point she was not opposed to any of his reforms. She may never have interfered at all if Prince Ching, Prince Tuan, and other conservatives had not gone to extraordinary lengths to persuade her, spurred on by Li through his surrogates. The text of Yang's indictment makes it obvious that Tzu Hsi herself was not the one initiating action, no matter how often she was later blamed. Li was the instigator, manipulating the Ironhats and the Clan Council.

Tzu Hsi had not been expecting trouble. In retirement she had fallen into pleasant routines at the Summer Palace. A highpoint in her life was the arrival of a huge pitted boulder, resembling a meteorite and taller than a horse, a gift from a provincial official for the garden in her small courtyard. But today the crafty conspirators of the Clan Council had caught her off guard and completely bowled her over. She was overwhelmed by the indictment against her nephew, but she was being manipulated. While some of the charges were nonsense and others were greatly exaggerated, there were some that were deeply disturbing, particularly those insinuating a secret relationship between Kuang Hsu and Wild Fox Kang, and a secret conspiracy with Japan. At this point she could not be certain that the insinuations behind the charges were true. She would need to brood about them, while fending off pressures to act.

The indictment was not as disturbing to her as its potential effect. Each charge could be dealt with individually, but not the ultimate implication that Kuang Hsu was incompetent and could not be left alone to run the empire. This was an admission that had hovered over the court for years, since it had first become apparent to the princes that Kuang Hsu's chronic illness had damaged his confidence. He would never develop the assurance he needed to dominate his rivals and take command. Nothing brought out the Manchu bloodlust faster than the discovery that a rival was defenseless.

As the matriarch of the dynasty Tzu Hsi's responsibilities were weighing heavily upon her. Once proud of her energy and the force of her will, she had grown tired. Still a handsome woman in her early sixties, her body had thickened. In repose, her face was drawn and severe, although when she smiled her face still lit up the way it had as a girl. But behind her infrequent smile was a deep pool of melancholy. For nearly forty years she had been alone in the midst of a great crowd. She had lived through the Allied invasion of 1860 and the destruction of the Summer Palace, the death of her husband and the crisis at Jehol, the decline and murder of her son and the succession crisis of 1875, her eight years of near-fatal illness, and the humiliating defeat of the Sino-Japanese War. The war had revealed the incompetence of everyone in Peking including herself. During her first years as dowager empress she had relied on Prince Kung until their friendship was soured by the behavior of Tung Chih and Kung's careless insolence. In the absence of a vigorous and commanding presence on the throne, an emperor who could pull the dynasty together, they had put a woman in charge, and she had to rely too on lesser men. In any crisis, she had sought help from Viceroy Li. But the war had shown even the crafty Li to be a rotten log. There was nobody she could count on any more. Perhaps there never had been.

Her husband had died convinced that the disasters of his reign made him the greatest failure the dynasty had ever seen. In the years since then she had discovered that Hsien Feng was wrong. The disasters continued decade after decade, and might go on forever. Her life had been spent stubbornly warding off the dynasty's collapse, hoping that the quarreling princes and mandarins would find common ground. Instead of reviving the dynasty's fortunes and building toward a rebirth of China, they were more sharply divided than ever. All that interested them was infighting. The prospect of Kuang Hsu's becoming the latest victim of this family disease was too alarming for her to deal with hastily. She would have to begin her own discreet investigation.

She had outlasted two emperors, and it now looked as if she would outlast three.

While this indictment was under way in the dowager's quarters at the Summer Palace, three separate telegrams arrived from Viceroy Jung Lu in Tientsin, warning that seven British warships had appeared unannounced off the Taku Forts, a remarkable and unusual occurrence that aroused immediate alarm. This was later explained by the British legation as "purely coincidental," a routine cruise up the Gulf of Chihli, but such things are rarely coincidental. The supposition that Britain had joined Japan in a plot connected to Ito's visit already had been strengthened by the appearance in Peking of the meddlesome missionary and political activist Timothy Richard.

Richard was a well-connected representative of the London Missionary Society who had come to China first to work in the arid Shansi region west of Peking. Unable to cope with the horrors of rural famine, he suffered a nervous breakdown, only to discover that he had a natural gift for dealing with the *ming-shih* dilettantes of Shanghai and Peking. Richard set himself up as their pipeline for Western learning. He was responsible for translating into Chinese a number of books that influenced the reformers. None of this was done exclusively for altruistic reasons; Richard had a keen eye for politics and was doing everything he could to cultivate dissident Hanlin scholars who were interested in reform only as a political tool. Richard and others in his group rashly encouraged the *ming-shih* to believe that the conservative establishment in China could be displaced as easily as Liberals replaced Tories in England, with a new world there for the taking. He and his circle failed to comprehend the extreme importance of indirection in China; nearly a century later and under an outwardly different political system, events in Peking's Tiananmen Square in 1989 again demonstrated that grand assumptions about easily displacing the entrenched authority in China can produce tragic consequences. But the young radicals of 1898 were similarly flattered and misled by Western attention, and through them Richard gained disproportionate influence in reform circles. He became publicly identified with Wild Fox Kang when he hired Kang's closest follower, journalist

Liang Chi-chao, as his Chinese secretary, a move that in Manchu eyes positively linked the British government with the lunatic fringe of the reform movement.

Helping Richard was the American Presbyterian missionary Gilbert Reid, who pushed the idea that Christianity should marry with Confucianism. The two men fancifully styled their movement the Mission Among the Higher Classes in China.

Always watching new arrivals in Peking, Sir Robert Hart observed that Richard was not a man without personal ambition. Many foreigners were attempting to put themselves in a position to influence China. Hart concluded that Richard was not likely to be the one: "The Hanlin [scholars] who follow Reid and Richard are found to be doing so with a political object, and are using the two R's instead of being used by them. . . . Richard is an enthusiast and more inclined to believe his hopes than his eyes. Worthy people both, but the idea of their reforming China, remodeling its institutions, and in short, carrying on its government, is too delicious!"

Also involved with Richard and Reid was the British soldier of fortune Captain Mortimer O'Sullivan, who had come to China privately, bearing letters of introduction from senior figures in the British government. Since then, he had busied himself intriguing with the same dissident Hanlin scholars that Reid and Richard were cultivating. Because of his military background, his previous service in South Africa during the Boer War, and his impressive connections in London, O'Sullivan could easily be mistaken for a secret agent.

A few days before the British warships appeared off Taku, Richard had arrived in Peking from Shanghai. According to Richard, he was invited by Kang to go to Peking "and be one of the Emperor's advisers." That he was taken in by Kang's posturing was nothing new: Richard had told readers of the North China *Herald* three years earlier that Kang was "the sage of modern China."

Richard's sudden appearance in Peking, his ties to the suspicious Captain O'Sullivan, and his mysterious comings and goings at the British legation added to the Ironhats' conviction that a conspiracy was under way involving Britain and Japan with the reformers, a fear that seemed to be borne out by the unexplained appearance of the British fleet.

Unaware of what was unfolding at the Summer Palace, Emperor Kuang Hsu held his secret audience with Ito on September 18 at the Forbidden City and ironically had his offer rejected. Ito's private diary, actually written years later for public consumption, discreetly avoids mentioning any activities in Peking on September 18, 19, 21, or 22 and only emphasizes his formal audience on the twentieth with the emperor, the empress dowager, and other courtiers. However, Sir Ernest Satow, the astute British minister to Japan at that time, advised Lord Salisbury in London that Ito did see Emperor Kuang Hsu privately on the eighteenth, two days before the formal audience. (Satow added his acute perception that the preemptive strike now being planned by the Ironhats behind the skirts of the empress dowager had been engineered by Li Hung-chang.)

If the emperor was expecting Ito to offer any instant solutions to China's problems or to volunteer his own services to clean out the Augean stables, he was greatly disappointed. In the absence of any record of the secret discussion between Kuang Hsu and Ito it is revealing to examine the strong views the Japanese statesman had expressed during a conversation a few days earlier with Morrison of the *Times*. According to Morrison, Ito said he despaired of reform in China:

> . . . there is no statesman, no man willing to take responsibility, no man standing out boldly and conspicuously before his fellows. Edicts decreeing reforms are being issued by the Emperor in profusion but they are never acted upon. An imperial ordinance that the officials shall be virtuous, upright and incorruptible cannot transform men who are hopelessly corrupt with the corruption carried to them by hereditary transmission through hundreds of generations. China must revise her revenue—She can do so by . . . decreasing or abolishing the expenditure now amounting to some 3,000,000 [pounds sterling] per annum absorbed by the vast hordes of Manchu retainers dependent upon the Court. To do this most easily and effectively the removal of the Court from Peking would be wise. No reform of the Court is possible so long as the Emperor remains [surrounded by them] in Peking.
>
> China must have an army and viewing the hopeless corruption of the people the army must be foreign drilled and foreign officered—and this must be done by officers from England and Japan. Events must bring closer together England, Japan, and China. Russian aggression. . . . No one can foresee where it is going to end. . . .
>
> The Censorate must be abolished. The Censorate is the root of all evil and of all corruption. The harm that it has done in checking all efforts at reform is infinite. No system is more rotten. Censors are unpaid, they all live by blackmail. Threats of impeachment will wring money from the most flint-hearted mandarin, the man impeached is he who has not squared the censors.

Given his strength of character, Ito must have been equally candid in his advice to Kuang Hsu: cancel all Manchu perks, move the capital away from Peking, put the armies under foreign command, and abolish the Censorate. Any one of these acts could easily prompt a palace coup or outright regicide. Presumably Kuang Hsu as planned asked Ito to take on the burden of reforming the Chinese government, as a special adviser, but it seems that Ito agreed to do no more than consider the proposal and respond in due course, which at that crucial moment was tantamount to "no." He had every reason to doubt whether the young emperor could mount the tiger, much less ride it.

This same day, while Ito met secretly with the emperor and the Iron-hats and Censor Yang were trying to persuade the reluctant dowager to intervene, Wild Fox Kang claimed he was finally given the emperor's secret appeal for help, which supposedly had been dispatched four days earlier. He said he discussed with his friends what action they should take, and they decided that the emperor's young reform secretary Tan Ssu-tung should go to see General Yuan at his headquarters near Tientsin, and seek his aid. Indeed, when Yuan reached his headquarters in the late afternoon, after betraying the emperor, he found Tan waiting anxiously to see him. There are two versions of what transpired, one from the unreliable Kang Yu-wei, the other from the unreliable Yuan Shih-kai, but they give essentially the same story with different trimmings.

Kang, writing only a few months after the event, claimed that Tan's visit to General Yuan was entirely the result of the secret communication from the emperor, which he said read as follows: "My position is threatened, I order you and the others of the same mind as you to devise plans secretly to save me." On receiving this, Kang said, they asked Tan to persuade Yuan to go to the aid of the emperor. "We asked him to lead several hundred determined men to escort the emperor, to ascend the Meridian Gate, to kill Jung Lu and to destroy the conservative faction."

According to Kang, Yuan told Tan: "To kill Jung Lu would be as simple as killing a dog. But all the officers in my camp are his men, and the guns, bullets and powder are all under his control. Moreover, [my headquarters] is more than [sixty-five miles] from the capital by railway. I fear that before my troops can reach the capital, news may leak out. However, if during the imperial review of troops at Tientsin [planned for October] the emperor should enter my camp, I can then, on the emperor's orders, kill the rebellious ministers [Prince Tuan's Ironhats]."

Tan was completely taken in by the wily general's expressions of loyalty to the emperor. According to Kang, the young man left Yuan's headquarters with the impression that the general was with them and would shield the emperor, although not by an immediate strike. Kang boasted that Yuan was "one military commander on our side [who was] well disposed toward the emperor." Kang's follower Liang Chi-chao also praised Yuan as a man of courage who was loyal to the emperor and who "knew the ruthlessness" of the empress dowager. It was only much later that it dawned on the Wild Fox that Yuan had played them all for fools.

In his own version, published ten years later, in 1908, Yuan said Tan told him he had a secret decree from the emperor ordering Yuan to arrest and kill Jung Lu and to surround the Summer Palace.

Yuan stalled and stammered, protesting that he could not simply take the young man's word for it. When Tan pressed him for an answer, saying he would come back with an order in the emperor's own Vermilion Pencil, Yuan objected, "No, nothing should be put in writing. There must be no mandate in the Vermilion Pencil. Please allow me time to think. I shall let you know within two or three weeks." (Yuan knew, of course, that the Ironhats would strike much sooner.)

Tan countered: "His Majesty wants this to be done quickly. We must come to a decision tonight so that I can report back to him. In fact, I can show you a mandate in the Vermilion Pencil now." Yuan claimed that what Tan showed him was merely a copy written in black ink and that its contents were vague and indirect, not demanding the palace coup that Tan proposed. He said it read: "We have resolved to reform, but the old ministers are reluctant to lend their support. We cannot force the pace, lest Her Gracious Majesty, the Dowager Empress, be displeased. We hereby command [the four reform advisers] to find a better approach."

This is very different from Kang's version: "My position is threatened, I order you and the others of the same mind as you to devise plans secretly to save me."

General Yuan reassured Tan without committing himself, promising only that "I will risk my life for my Emperor and my country." The young reformer returned to Peking convinced that the general was on their side.

There has been a lot of controversy ever since over these messages. The whole matter turns on whether or not the emperor's secret communication was authentic, and if so, what really was the wording? Scholars who have examined Kang's holographic copy of the "secret decree" have pronounced it a counterfeit.

If the secret edict was a fake, it may have been forged at the order of Li Hung-chang, backdated to September 14 and delivered to Kang on the morning of September 18, to put the final nail in the coffin of the reformers and to force the Ironhats to make their move without further stalling. Forgery is an ancient and hallowed craft in China, and many Hanlin scholars were trained to emulate the emperor's calligraphy in order to prepare greetings for the new year and commendations for imperial honors. All Li needed to begin the violent backlash was "proof" that the reformers actually were conspiring to stage an armed revolt, with or without the help of the Japanese and British. One of the most celebrated devices of the sage Sun Tzu was to plant counterfeit messages to provoke enemies into ill-considered actions. In this respect a counterfeit appeal for help from Kuang Hsu would have the same effect as a real one.

Li had agents among the reformers who were in a position to deliver such a phony appeal for help. Tan had not seen the emperor for several days, because Kuang Hsu was visiting his aunt at the Summer Palace, returning to the Forbidden City only for his secret meeting with Ito. Thus there was no way for Tan to authenticate the secret message, unless he was prepared to wait for the opportunity. Being gullible, the reformers may never have suspected a counterfeit because they already believed that the emperor was in danger, and they had long dreamed of an armed showdown in which the dowager's "gang" would be imprisoned, killed, or put to flight.

In neither Yuan's nor Kang's version is the dowager mentioned as a target, only her "gang": the old guard. The Wild Fox's friends liked to portray Tzu Hsi as the chief obstacle to reform and to imply that Kuang Hsu was desperate to be rid of her. In fact, in an authenticated message that Kuang Hsu wrote to one of his reform secretaries, Yang Jui, he made it clear that he wished to take a conciliatory approach to his aunt, so that reforms could continue and personnel changes could take place without offending her.

General Yuan stuck to his original schedule. He had been sent to Tientsin to investigate the appearance of the British fleet and was to return to Peking the following night to report to the emperor. At 5:00 P.M. on the nineteenth he boarded the evening train for Peking, and in the early hours of the twentieth, before the formal Ito audience, he entered the Forbidden City for his third private interview with Kuang Hsu that week. After reporting on the officially declared innocence of the British fleet, Yuan later claimed, he sought to warn the emperor of the danger he faced from the Ironhats and cautioned him to go slow. No other account of their conversation exists. Wild Fox Kang asserted afterward that the emperor gave Yuan a secret edict during this meeting, but he did not know the contents. In an atmosphere so thick with duplicity and lying, it would be interesting to know Kuang Hsu's side of the story, but this remains a mystery.

General Yuan's quick trip to Peking allowed him to consult again with Li. Thereafter the general returned to Tientsin and went directly to Viceroy Jung Lu to betray the emperor again, telling Jung Lu about Tan's visit and the scheme of the reformers to seize power in the name of the emperor. Yuan treated it lightly, making it seem comic and adolescent, as if the reformers were needlessly worried about the emperor's being deposed. Yuan told Jung Lu that he had been asked to protect the emperor, to dispose of Jung Lu, and to arrest the Ironhats.

According to a member of the viceroy's staff, Jung Lu hurried to Peking, but he arrived at the Summer Palace too late in the evening to see the dowager, who was asleep, and gave the information instead to Prince Ching, on his promise that he would tell Tzu Hsi the next morning. The viceroy then returned to Tientsin.

There was nothing criminal in what Tan had suggested. The emperor was in power legitimately, and Tan was one of his officials. Whether or not reactionary Manchu princes approved of Kuang Hsu's reforms and his plans to involve Ito, these were nonetheless legitimate actions by the ruler of China. For any clansmen to interfere was criminal conspiracy, unless the emperor had been impeached successfully. In the face of such a criminal conspiracy, it was entirely legitimate for the emperor and his loyalists to take drastic countermeasures. Technically, at this point the Ironhats were in the wrong.

On the other hand, the clansmen shared the conviction that they had entrusted power to Kuang Hsu on the assumption that he would maintain things as they were, ruling by consensus, and would not make changes without consensus just because he believed changes should be made. Right or wrong, they were convinced that he was about to sell out China to the Japanese. They believed that they had every right to remove him from power and to restore the previous state of affairs, putting the empress dowager back in her old figurehead role and installing a more reliable puppet in the form of Pu Chun, Prince Tuan's son. In their minds this was not so much a coup as a rescue operation. Finally, their actions would not be criminal if they could enlist the empress dowager to lend legitimacy; she could be construed as outranking the emperor, and she would not actually depose him but merely resume her role as his tutor in good government, meaning that he would need her endorsement of all decisions.

Tzu Hsi still was undecided. There is no evidence that she was as agitated as the Ironhats. She had never completely relinquished power; technically she still had the right of veto over any of the emperor's decisions. But in her retirement she had insisted on this privilege less and less, until she had stopped exercising her veto at all. On his own volition the emperor continued to refer most of his decisions to her as a courtesy. Although her critics in later years contended that she craved to regain power, how this could improve her situation is hard to conceive. She had reigned longer by this point than any other woman except Empress Wu, and longer than most emperors, Manchu or otherwise. In her semiretirement she continued to enjoy all the benefits of power, whether at the Summer Palace or in the Forbidden City. All she had really relinquished was administrative detail, which anyone in her position would be reluctant to resume.

However, on September 19, she traveled incognito into Peking from the Summer Palace, avoiding the usual ornate procession, to attend the formal audience for Ito the next day. She was greeted by the emperor, but according to palace records only a few officials knew she was in the Forbidden City. She settled into her old pavilion but stayed out of sight. During the formal Ito audience the next day she remained invisible, as was the custom, behind a gauze screen. Among the spectators at the audience were Prince Ching and a number of Manchu dignitaries and high officials, plus a large number of court eunuchs. After an exchange of greetings, Ito was invited to take a chair, and a brief conversation followed.

Kuang Hsu: "At the present time reform is pressed upon our country by necessity. We are willing to hear an opinion expressed by your Excellency, and we request your Excellency to tell our princes and great ministers of the Tsungli Yamen in detail the process and methods of reform, and give them advice."

Ito: "I have reverently received your decree. If your princes and great ministers will make inquiries, your alien minister, in accordance with what he has actually seen, will certainly sincerely explain to them whatever is beneficial to your honorable country."

Ito planned to remain at the Japanese embassy for the next week or two, and Chinese government ministers could solicit his views there. It was an anticlimax. There was no dramatic announcement.

After the audience Ito was honored with a banquet. When the formalities ended, Kuang Hsu wished him a safe journey back to Japan. Tzu Hsi did not return immediately to the Summer Palace but remained at her quarters in the Forbidden City, apparently continuing her own investigation into the warnings of the Ironhats. Only after the Ito audience did she summon General Yuan to her pavilion to hear his account of the reformers' preemptive strike plot. He arrived, as ordered, on the twenty-first. After listening to his version of the affair, she called in Prince Ching and Grand Councillor Kang I for a discussion. It was only at this meeting that she made her final decision to resume control. Evidently she was persuaded at last that Prince Ching and the others were right and that Kuang Hsu had at the very least exhibited bad judgment and had relied upon men who were encouraging him to take precipitous actions. At the same time, the aggressive hostility of the Ironhats had to be taken into account. There was only one way to prevent trouble from either extreme, radicals or reactionaries, and that was by placing herself back in the role first chosen for her by Prince Kung many years earlier, as the ceremonial regent of a coalition of factions, protecting Kuang Hsu, not deposing him.

If she had any doubts about whether the Ironhats were exaggerating the danger, on the day of the Ito audience one of Wild Fox Kang's associates, Yang Shen-hsiu, openly memorialized the throne proposing an alliance of

China, Britain, and Japan. Censor Sung Po-lu, another friend of Kang's, made the same recommendation the next day in another memorial. He also proposed that Kang should be made the emperor's chief aide to work out the details and that Li Hung-chang should be called in to consult with Ito, along with missionary Timothy Richard. The inclusion of Li in this proposal was a transparent attempt to make it seem balanced and reasonable. These memorials were badly timed, for they helped to convince Tzu Hsi that the point had come to intervene.

At a critical moment like this the character of a monarch—or of any man or woman, for that matter—is put to the test. In their youth, the dynamic Emperor Kang Hsi or his ruthless son Yung Cheng would have risen to the occasion and put all their enemies to flight. Kuang Hsu, for all his admirable and sympathetic qualities, was never cut out for such a dominant role. He had been burdened with physical, medical, and emotional problems since childhood and was not up to the task of routing the Ironhats, winning over the Clan Council, or convincing his aunt that she should stick to her retirement and leave the business of governing the empire to him. Not the least of his disadvantages was his speech impediment, which in such a moment rendered him completely inarticulate. His aunt had only to explain that the entire Clan Council was opposed to his independent actions and had insisted upon her resuming daily supervision of the administration. The Clan Council was the highest authority in Manchu China, and the emperor was dependent upon its approval and support. An emperor could overrule the council only if he felt that he had sufficient personal authority to take power into his own hands. This might have been the case with Kang Hsi or Yung Cheng, or even with Chien Lung, but it was certainly not the case with the hesitant Kuang Hsu. The tragedies that followed have to be seen as brutal excesses committed by the Ironhats as they took advantage of being temporarily in the dominant position.

While there is no record of what transpired between the dowager and Kuang Hsu, it was a sad moment for both of them. The edict of September 21, written by the emperor, stated his position (and the dowager's) quite clearly.

The affairs of the nation are at present in a difficult position, and everything awaits reform. I, the Emperor, am working day and night with all my powers. . . . But, despite my careful toil, I constantly fear to be overwhelmed by the press of work. . . .

Moved by a deep regard for the welfare of the nation, I have repeatedly implored Her Majesty to be graciously pleased to advise me in government, and have received her assent.

This is an assurance of prosperity to the whole nation, officials and people.

Just as he had on China's defeat by Japan in 1895, Kuang Hsu then fell into a deep despair. He went into seclusion in the Ying-tai pavilion on an island in the lake called the South Sea next to the Forbidden City. His disappearance from the court for the next three days, while he regained his composure, caused the legations to believe rumors that the emperor had been deposed and murdered. This provided Wild Fox Kang with a sensational opportunity. Kang maintained that Tzu Hsi had imprisoned, tortured, and killed her nephew for having dared to think of reforming the government. One especially durable rumor said the emperor was not dead but a prisoner ever after in the Ying-tai pavilion. Three bridges originally led to the island. By 1898, however, only one footbridge still stood, so it was pointed out that the emperor could be guarded easily. Another rumor, heard by Sarah Conger, wife of the American minister, was that the emperor had tried to escape from the island prison. Kang Yu-wei claimed that several reformers, led by Tan Ssu-tung, had planned to climb the south wall of the palace enclosure to rescue Kuang Hsu with Japanese assistance in the form of a man named Prince Big Sword the Fifth, but failed. Amazingly, this fable of the emperor's imprisonment is adhered to by almost every prominent twentieth-century China scholar. Of course, the emperor was neither dead nor imprisoned and had been back at work for some time. The Ying-tai pavilion was the office he had always shared with Tzu Hsi when they worked together. It is a matter of record that there was an interruption in his routine of only three days, evidently caused by dismay and disillusion, not by torture and imprisonment. He had always been a prisoner of the system. Backhouse and Bland greatly exaggerated this three-day retreat, claiming that the emperor remained a prisoner of Tzu Hsi for the rest of his life; scholars who have subscribed to this Backhouse myth have done so in the face of overwhelming evidence to the contrary.

Tzu Hsi returned to the Summer Palace, apparently as depressed as her nephew by the experience, leaving the Ironhats free to persecute their enemies. Confusion on their part over who was involved in the reformers' plot led to a rash of arrests. On September 21, the same day the emperor announced Tzu Hsi's return to the regency, an edict was issued accusing Wild Fox Kang of "ganging up with others for clandestine purposes" and "influencing court decisions with devious views." This wording was surprisingly mild, given General Yuan's statements that Kang and his friends had been plotting to murder Viceroy Jung Lu and to stage an armed takeover. Kang's arrest was ordered. His younger brother also was to be taken into custody.

As Kang had left for Tientsin by train the day before, on his way at last to Shanghai, he could not be found in his usual haunts. His brother was apprehended at the Nan-Hai Social Club, sitting on a chamber pot.

"Kuang-jen was at the time in the toilet and he could have escaped," wrote Kang, "but the head servant, who bore a grudge against Kuang-jen . . . showed the officers where to find him."

A dispatch arrived from Viceroy Jung Lu on September 23, saying that his investigators had confirmed the broad details of the reform plot and he would bring this information with him on his next trip to Peking. Acting on the strength of this message and under strong pressure from Prince Ching and Grand Councillor Kang I, the dowager ordered the arrest of Tan Ssu-tung and six others. Kang's associate, the journalist Liang Chi-chao, also was being sought.

Emperor Kuang Hsu had pulled himself together by the early morning hours of September 24 and resumed his customary reading and making notations on memorials from officials, working with his aunt in the Ying-tai pavilion, passing the more sensitive decisions on to her. He also went back to sitting beside her at official audiences, a practice he continued for the rest of his life. Despite the provocative rumors sweeping the legations, he had not been physically abused or removed from power. He had only been obliged to function once again as he had for years, under his aunt's supervision. Unfortunate and sad, to be sure, but hardly sinister. Meanwhile, the Ironhats were out hunting for heretics.

The day the emperor returned to work, September 24, more arrests followed. Most prominent was former ambassador Sir Chang Yin-huan, who had sponsored Wild Fox Kang in Peking and frequently entertained him, and two lesser officials who allegedly had connived with Kang to present his memorials to the emperor. When the soldiers arrested Sir Chang, they ransacked his house, apparently searching for Kang. The emperor's four reform advisers, Yang Jui, Lin Hsu, Tan Ssu-tung and Liu Kuang-ti, were also taken into custody. Yang Jui was still in bed when the police arrived, and he was manacled and dragged away in his underpants. Suspecting nothing, Lin Hsu went to the Forbidden City to attend to his duties as usual and was placed under arrest. When word reached Liu Kuang-ti of the order for his arrest, he turned himself in. Tan himself made no effort to evade arrest.

The charge against the four reform advisers at this point was merely that they were suspected of "liaison" with Wild Fox Kang. The other three men arrested, including Sir Chang, were accused of "collusion" with Kang. Their trial on these relatively mild charges was to begin three days later on September 27. By the time the trial began, however, under extreme pressure from the Ironhats the charges were upgraded to sedition.

The Ironhats were flexing their muscles and enjoying the exhilaration of power. They had the upper hand and saw this as an opportunity not to be wasted. Why let these radicals off lightly? Better to make a brutal point that would discourage others.

The trial was being conducted in the main hall of the Board of Punishments. On September 28, after only one day, the proceedings were halted. A decree had been delivered from the palace ordering the summary execution of six of the prisoners. The edict was signed by Emperor Kuang Hsu.

At 4:00 P.M. Kang Yu-wei's brother, Kuang-jen; his friend, Yang Shen-hsui; and the four reform secretaries—Tan, Yang, Lin, and Liu—were taken outside and beheaded. They became known as the Six Martyrs of the Hundred Days.

According to Kang Yu-wei's account: "There was a crowd of onlookers. Kuang-jen was the first to be executed. He looked about as if to say something, but there was no one near to whom he could speak. The other five men in turn went calmly to their death." When Kuang-jen was beheaded, he was wearing only a short jacket. According to Kang, a family servant found some proper clothing, sewed the head back onto the body, purchased a coffin, and buried him beside the Temple of Kuan-yin, the goddess of mercy. But all of this appears to be another of Kang's inventions; according to the North China *Herald*, no one was bold enough to claim Kuang-jen's body, and it was dragged away by the executioners the following day and thrown into an open pit that served as a common grave for paupers and criminals.

Kuang-jen had studied medicine for three years under the American surgeon John C. Kerr and had been unhappily employed in a minor civil service job in Chekiang Province for one year before giving it up to devote himself full-time to his older brother's political organization. According to one of Kang's biographers, Kuang-jen had held meetings in 1896 with the republican revolutionary Sun Yat-sen at the Pin-fang Restaurant in Hong Kong, to work out cooperation between the groups led by Sun and Kang. From the viewpoint of the Manchu court, Sun's group was distinctly subversive, and anyone having dealings with it was liable to decapitation.

An edict was published, after the fact, explaining the court's abrupt decision to execute the six, who were now being labeled rebels and traitors: "Immediately memorialists declared that if there was any delay in this trial there was great danger of riot. We meditated carefully on the investigation [by Viceroy Jung Lu] of the said rebels. Their crime was great, without precedent and they must not escape the net of the law. If they were permitted to speak, they would involve many others; therefore We could not await the report from the Board of Punishments, and yesterday We decreed that the guilty persons be immediately executed."

Involving "many others" alluded to the growing number of moderates in the government who were sympathetic to the reform movement. They included the cosmopolitan officials of the Tsungli Yamen, many of whom had been diplomats posted abroad, and the wealthy and powerful patrons of the *ming-shih* intelligentsia. If the trial had gone on, many of these enlightened scholar-officials might have been named and exposed to attack by the Ironhats. To save themselves they would have to counterattack, which could bring about the fatal confrontation between moderates and reactionaries that Tzu Hsi had worked so hard to avoid. The Ironhats, revived by the ambitions of Prince Tuan, were out for blood. The prince was applying direct and indirect pressure on Tzu Hsi to behead the small group of reformers he had arrested. Typical of Tuan, he became carried away by the obvious, failing to see that if he kept the prisoners alive and forced them to implicate others, he could cause his enemies much greater long-term damage. By giving in to his demands for the beheading of the Six Martyrs, Tzu Hsi and Kuang Hsu postponed a much greater tragedy, applying a painful tourniquet to avoid a fatal hemorrhage.

According to the court records, "someone warned that if there were any delay, something untoward might happen," including riots in the streets. Fear of riots in Peking did not refer to crowds of citizens demonstrating in favor of the reformers, but to General Tung Fu-hsiang's Muslim-Chinese troops now camped in the southern outskirts of Peking, who would gallop through the streets to intimidate the throne and force it to order the executions. The day after the executions, in the imperial hunting preserve, Tung's men attacked picnicking staff of the British and American legations in a clear warning not to meddle further.

So it seems that Kuang Hsu and Tzu Hsi were forced to have the reformers executed to avoid having the Kansu cavalry run amok. Doubtless their rampage would have been portrayed as a spontaneous outpouring of popular displeasure at the pampering of these radicals. Three weeks later, Tung's men attacked and beat up a group of foreign engineers and Britons from the Peking legation at the railway station, and the diplomatic community howled in dismay, demanding that Tung be ordered out of Peking. Unwilling to risk armed confrontation with the notoriously independent general, the government solved the problem by making a generous "contribution" to Tung, and he obediently withdrew with his troops to Kichopei, eighty miles east of Peking. For the time being, Tung had fulfilled his mission in providing muscle for the Ironhats during the Hundred Days, and threatening to riot if the martyrs were not beheaded as the Ironhats demanded. He could afford to take some time off. Just offstage, he waited patiently for Prince Tuan's signal to return to Peking for the next stage in the campaign to exterminate the Foreign Devils.

Sir Chang was saved from beheading by the intervention of the Western legations. Sir Claude MacDonald and other ministers appealed directly, as did Ito, who was still in Peking. It was decided that the ambassador would have all his property confiscated and be sentenced to exile in remote Sinkiang Province. An edict stated that "his actions were deceitful, mysterious, and fickle, and he sought after the rich and power-ful." When they heard that Sir Chang would be banished, Morrison of the *Times*, Hugh Grosvenor of the British legation, and others plotted to kidnap him on his way to exile and bring him into the legation. When Sir Chang learned of their plan, he sent word to Morrison that he had no desire to interfere with the course of imperial justice. Two years later, he was murdered in exile, apparently by one of General Tung's hired guns on orders from Prince Tuan.

One other reformer who had been arrested was spared both execution and banishment. Seventy-two-year-old Hsu Chih-ching, who had submit-ted some of Kang's memorials to the throne under his name, was merely jailed in Peking. Thirty other men were arrested, imprisoned, dismissed from office, held under house arrest, banished, and had their families arrested as well, as the Ironhats continued their purge. Of these thirty, five had not participated directly in the reform movement but were only relatives and friends of the reformers. For a time it was feared that two hundred more would be arrested, mostly members of the reform societies and newspaper editors who had advocated reform. But the purge abruptly stopped.

Historians, in reviewing the Hundred Days, are almost unanimous in damning the empress dowager as a villain of immense power, dedicated to evil (reform, by definition, always being good). Bland and Backhouse falsely claim that there was continual strife between the dowager and Kuang Hsu over reform. "The issue of reform now became a power struggle between the emperor and the empress dowager, and the conflict was sharpened after the death . . . of the emperor's mother, the dowager's sister, who had served as a cushion between the two." (The power strug-gle was, of course, with the Ironhats, not with Tzu Hsi, and Kuang Hsu's mother was the one chiefly responsible for his being at a terrible disadvan-tage from earliest childhood.)

Others go on to assert: "In short, as his program [of reform] unfolded, the emperor found himself at war with the whole establishment, not least with . . . the Empress Dowager." (She stayed out of it till the very last day and in fact had supported his reforms till then.) "The Empress Dowa-ger found her entire world threatened by Kang Yu-wei's attack on those twin pillars of her regime, classical learning and organized corruption." (This is a complete misrepresentation.) In his book *China since 1800*, John A. Harrison asserts that Tzu Hsi became "as early as 1865, the greatest source of power in China" and concludes "the empress demonstrated not only her hatred of reform but also of China." (Both statements are absurd.) Fairbank tells us that at the end of the Hundred Days Reform, Tzu Hsi "executed the radicals she could catch." (She seems to have had little, if anything, to do with it.)

Many of Kuang Hsu's summer edicts were allowed to stand, especially those providing for more effective administration of military, industrial, and commercial affairs, and for expansion of the nation's school system. The reforms that were rescinded were those the Ironhats were most afraid of—the ones that tried to open up the existing political system. The treatment of the reformers, the arrests and executions, had the effect not of purging China of reform but of making its advocates more cautious.

In an edict of November 16, 1898, the dowager clearly stated her own intentions and her policy on reform:

> Laws and institutions are not bad when they are first established, but as time goes on defects accumulate, making it necessary to change them in order to meet the requirements of the time. . . . Day and night I labor arduously in the Palace. . . . A moment does not pass that I do not think about planning for self-strengthening. . . .
>
> Although the customs and governmental systems of Western countries differ in more than one way from those of China, their methods and techniques . . . are, as a rule, capable of [helping a country] to attain prosperity and strength. . . . If we can select what are good among these and apply them, putting them into use one by one, we shall be able to achieve the desired results promptly and consistently.
>
> It is feared, however, that persons of shallow thinking interpret Our intentions wrongly, imagining that the Government has decided to follow the beaten path and is no longer concerned with far-sighted plans. This would be entirely contrary to Our intention to . . . achieve good administration.

Henry Cockburn, the Chinese secretary of the British legation in Peking in 1898, assessed the situation at court as follows:

> I think it is fairly evident that the Emperor got carried away by visions of a new China, renovated by his hand, and that . . . he did not understand the difficulties in his path. There was more excuse for him than for [his reform advisers], for he has had no experience of the outer world. They moved him, I imagine, much as the agitator at home [in England] moves the mob; the mob believes that the day is coming when the pint pot shall hold a quart. The Emperor's visions of the future were higher doubtless and less selfish, but hardly less impractical.

Cockburn's informed appraisal was unusual. Most authorities pronounced Tzu Hsi's return to power "brutal," and usually state incorrectly that she "abolished" all reforms. Historians speak of her "tormenting . . . the wretched Kuang Hsu." "For the rest of his life, Kuang Hsu lived in abject submission to his aunt." This is a gross exaggeration. He was always submissive toward her, submissive by nature but also submissive by choice; his deteriorating physical and emotional state made him increasingly dependent upon his aunt. He was not her prisoner. At the Summer Palace for much of the year he lived in pavilions next door to hers, and she was continually fussing over him, urging council ministers to find better doctors to treat his chronic illnesses, which were becoming worse. Kuang Hsu's real attitude toward Wild Fox Kang and the derailing of the reform movement is revealed very clearly in an edict he wrote in 1901, after three years of reflection:

> Since 1897 and 1898, specious arguments have been rampant, which erroneously draw a line between the new and the old. The calamity brought about by the traitor Kang was ever more serious than that caused by the [Boxer siege of the legations in 1900]. . . . The traitor Kang's talk of "new institutions" amounted to playing havoc with the institutions, not to reforming them. The said traitor and his associates took advantage of Our illness secretly to develop seditious schemes. We therefore earnestly entreated the Empress Dowager to guide the administration. . . . [She] has no objection to reform. [However,] in modifying laws and regulations We do not intend to sweep away everything old. . . . That mother and son hold one and the same conviction should be seen by all . . .

Two women who had a chance to observe Kuang Hsu almost continually at close range for a period of many months after the Hundred Days found him shy and sad, his lifelong personality traits. Kuang Hsu was then living in the partly restored Summer Palace on Lake Kunming, in pavilions adjacent to Tzu Hsi's quarters and as elegant and luxurious as hers. There he led his own life, occupied with his studies, reading a lot, studying English, and learning to play the piano. He showed no interest in his empress or concubine but had a great fondness for children. "He had but few favorites in the Palace, and quite ignored the pretty young girls and women of Her Majesty's entourage." He fulfilled court obligations reluctantly. Bored by audiences, he would slip away at the first opportunity, pacifying himself with endless cigarettes. Neither observer saw evidence that the emperor felt any animosity toward his aunt. "Their relations, though rigidly formal . . . seem to be most friendly. If there is any feeling on his part as to the check on his Government received by the 'coup d'état' of 1898, he does not seem to feel that Her Majesty is responsible for it." Sir Robert Hart had mixed feelings about the outcome of the crisis:

The situation here has changed in a twinkling . . . the Empress Dowager having thrust the Emperor into the background and assumed the reins of government: but I fear it is the pro-Russian party [Li Hung-chang] that is winning, and that the deposition (almost) of the Emperor is [Russian minister] Pavloff's reply to Li Hung-chang's expulsion from the [Tsungli] Yamen! . . . It is rumored that the Emperor had taken to Ito and that this had much to do with the Empress Dowager's sudden attack: the old lady had been perfectly quiet—too quiet—for weeks and doubtless all that occurred was thought out and prepared by herself and party. She is a wonderful woman and she has bowled over the Emperor by as astounding a coup d'état as the one with which she placed him on the throne.

The real victor in the collapse of the Hundred Days was Li Hung-chang. His motives were serial: to displace an emperor who had rashly caused him loss of face and fortune, to reestablish Tzu Hsi as the central arbiter in the government in hope of regaining his titles and privileges more easily through her, and ultimately to push his Ironhat enemies into a crisis so severe that they would self-destruct. As he had in the past, Li would manipulate the crisis to make matters as bad as possible. When he was called in to rescue the dynasty, as he always was, his price would be steep, and it would have to be paid before he would act. Simple extortion, raised to a fine art. This is precisely what happened in 1900.

Because his behind-the-scenes help to the Ironhats had been decisive, having General Yuan betray the emperor to them and Censor Yang present their argument skillfully to the empress dowager, Li was soon restored to the rank of viceroy. This time he was posted far away to be governor-general of the southern provinces in Canton, where the Ironhats thought he would be less of a threat. As usual they were wrong. Li had only begun his revenge. He would need two more years to finish.

In the months to come, believing that they were now almost in complete control of the court, Prince Tuan's group began to prepare for the day when they would expel all foreigners from China. These preparations manifested themselves in a great variety of ways, all of them misunderstood by the legations and only vaguely grasped by the missionaries. Prince Tuan, a man obsessed by glory and careless about how he got there, was becoming the supreme authority in Peking through fear. He arrogated to himself the role of special adviser to the empress dowager. Tzu Hsi was blundering ever deeper into Tuan's trap by revealing her own deep indecision. For some years she had misjudged him, assuming that he was just the most energetic of the younger generation of royal princes. Now his dynamism was beginning to look more like paranoia, and his security forces in the palace were acting less like protectors and more like turnkeys.

CHAPTER FOURTEEN

The Fugitive

While bloody reprisals were under way in Peking, Wild Fox Kang was eating steamed pork-filled dumplings with his fellow steerage passengers aboard the British ship *Chungking* wallowing down the China coast toward Shanghai, totally unaware that he was the object of a spreading manhunt. Although he later boasted that he was on his way south on a secret mission for the emperor, this was not borne out by his behavior.

He had left Peking aboard the morning train to Tientsin on September 20, after a last round of late-night farewell parties. As a self-indulgent man he took a first-class compartment to himself, reached Tientsin in the early afternoon, found a hotel, and the next day boarded the P&O Line steamer *Chungking*. Because of crowding, he could not get good accommodations and had to travel in steerage, with fellow passengers reeking of vomit. After a voyage of three days the ship crossed the broad estuary of the Yangtze and entered the mouth of the smaller Whangpoo River to approach Shanghai harbor. As the ship crept toward the shabby suburb of Woosung, and its overpowering stink of human feces, a fast launch came alongside; a few minutes later Kang was approached at the rail by J.O.P. Bland, the Shanghai correspondent of the *Times*. Bland, his skin pink with sunburn and his hair slicked down with lavender-scented pomade, held out a photo, looked at it and then at Kang, and asked, "Is this a photograph of you? Did you kill anyone in Peking?"

Bland was on a mission for Acting British Consul-General Byron Brenan, to intercept Kang. In Peking, Timothy Richard had rushed to the British legation, where in a state of near hysteria he urged Sir Claude MacDonald to help rescue Kang from Chinese justice. Instructions were wired to British consulates along the China coast to be on the lookout for Kang and to rescue him before he was arrested by the imperial authorities.

But these messages did not reach the Shanghai consulate till after Brenan was galvanized into action on his own by the excitement of the local Chinese authorities. Brenan wrote MacDonald on September 26, 1898, describing the bizarre situation:

On the morning of the 23rd I received a letter from the Taotai [in effect the mayor of Shanghai] informing me that he had received secret instructions to arrest [Kang Yu-wei] on his arrival at Shanghai. The Taotai at the same time sent his Secretary to inform me that the Emperor was dead, and that Kang was accused of having given His Majesty certain drugs which proved fatal. The Taotai requested that I should have all British ships arriving from Tientsin searched, and that I should instruct the municipal police [of the International Settlement] to watch the different wharves as the steamers arrived. To facilitate identification, he [the Taotai] sent a photograph of Kang Yu-wei, and he added that a reward of 2,000 dollars would be paid for his arrest. In the course of the morning the British steamship *El Dorado* arrived, and as she was entering the anchorage she was stopped by an official Chinese launch, and an Inspector of the Chinese river police in uniform (a British subject) boarded her and searched the vessel for Kang Yu-wei. As this was done without a warrant from me, and without my permission in any way obtained, I complained to the Taotai of this illegality. . . .

In the course of the day (23rd September) I received numerous messages from the Taotai and other officials to the effect that Kang Yu-wei was known to be coming by the steamship *Chungking* due on the 24th. The Chinese detectives and policemen were in a high state of excitement at the prospect of gaining the 2,000 dollars, and I feared that on her arrival the vessel would be rushed by a crowd of Yamen runners [from the mayor's office].

The fact that the *Chungking*'s wharf is on the French Settlement, made it difficult for me to take measures for the steamer's protection. After the previous day's experience in the case of the *El Dorado*, I also had misgivings as to the action the Chinese authorities might take before the vessel entered the harbour limits, so I decided that the best course was to intercept the steamer outside Woosung. I did not wish any officer of this Consulate to be openly connected with the transference of Kang Yu-wei from one steamer to another, so I accepted the offer of Mr. J.O.P. Bland's services. As he speaks Chinese well, he was a very suitable person to employ for the purpose.

Early on the morning of the 24th, Mr. Bland went out in a launch some miles outside Woosung, and intercepted the *Chungking*. With the aid of the photograph which the Taotai had given me there was no difficulty in finding the man. He was absolutely unconscious of any impending danger, and it was not until he was shown the . . . application for his arrest that he realized his perilous position.

Bland showed Kang the decree from the Shanghai Taotai charging that he had "poisoned the emperor by administering red pills to him" and ordering that he was to be "secretly arrested and executed on the spot." Bland told him of the arrest of the reformers, including his brother; Kang broke into tears. When he had composed himself, he gave Bland copies of five secret decrees he claimed were given to him by the emperor. Bland explained that he had been sent by the British consul who "knows that you [Kang] are a loyal subject of the emperor and could not have committed this crime. So he has specifically instructed me to come with a warship to rescue you. You must come with me immediately to the launch. There is not time to lose because the circuit intendant of Shanghai is coming to search this ship."

It has always been assumed that the Taotai concocted the charge of regicide in order to guarantee that people would turn in Kang, although the reward was sufficient incentive. What is overlooked is that the Taotai was one of Li's men, a wealthy merchant from Ningpo whose career had been advanced by Li and whose government post had come to him through Li's patronage. He was a crony of Li's most important protégé in Shanghai, Sheng Hsuan-huai, known to Westerners as "Telegraph Sheng" because he was head of the imperial telegraph network, a private corporation set up by Li; Telegraph Sheng was a primary source for Western journalists of false and alarming stories about events in Peking. By spreading news that the emperor had been poisoned, the Taotai and Telegraph Sheng contributed to the widespread impression in Shanghai, Hong Kong, and the outside world that the Manchu government was on the verge of collapse—an impression that Li was craftily promoting at every opportunity in order to create such a crisis that his enemies would be confounded and he would be recalled to duty.

In the absence of solid information from Peking, reports from Shanghai were circulating around the world that Emperor Kuang Hsu had been overthrown in a violent coup by the Manchu princes. Newspapers everywhere printed wild reports, including a howler in the *New York Times* that Empress Dowager Tzu Hsi and former Viceroy Li Hung-chang were married the morning of September 22 and fled to Tientsin by train, blowing up the railway tracks behind them to prevent pursuit.

Most of these deliberately provocative reports were first published in the mosquito press of Shanghai or were spread at the popular Long Bar and in other Western drinking establishments along the Bund, the bustling city's immaculate Victorian riverside promenade where signs prohibited dogs and Chinamen.

In only a few decades, Shanghai had grown from a ramshackle village of coastal pirates and pig farmers into a busy international city guarding the Yangtze estuary, commanding all trade for a thousand miles upriver into China's still-mysterious interior. Whitewashed colonial buildings now lined the Bund, the headquarters of major trading houses like Jardine Matheson, Russell & Company, and Dent & Company. Here canny merchants from Edinburgh or Boston bid against Persian and Sephardic Jews, and ruined their livers drinking the nights away with small-footed Chinese prostitutes in huge brothels run by the Green Gang. The detritus of their sins piled up in the streets and was washed by rains or swept by coolies into the river where (if you made the mistake of looking too closely), you could make out each morning the arms and legs of dead babies tangled with the corpses of dogs and giant bandicoot rats, floating away with the rotten fruit and inksmeared balance sheets on the high tide of empire. Among the steamships, clippers and decrepit junks crowding the waterfront were five dismasted cargo hulks with corrugated iron roofs, holding the opium reserves of the great trading houses. The Bund was now paved, and pansies bloomed in the shade of the broadleafed sycamores lining the riverbank, and beyond in the quiet street wiry rickshaw pullers trotted past Sikh traffic policemen in starched khaki shorts and turbans. Some things never change no matter how big a city grows, and from across the river in the unspeakable slum called Pootung came the everpresent nosewrinkling stink of fermenting pigshit, a constant reminder that Shanghai would always be a town of pig farmers at heart.

The inflammatory rumors about the emperor, originated by Li's proxies, were aggravated by a telegram from Peking sent by Kang's follower Liang Chi-chao informing his supporters in Shanghai that he was alive and well and stating flatly that the emperor had been killed. The British consul-general, Brenan, believed the rumor and cabled the news of the murder to Lord Salisbury. The next day the story was published by Shanghai's North China *Herald*, giving it additional credence among whites, most of whom shared the paper's conspicuous loathing for all things Chinese.

From that moment on (as Li had shrewdly foreseen) the story took on a life of its own.

The *New York Times* ran the harrowing headline: CHINESE EMPEROR KILLED—MAY HAVE BEEN TORTURED—SOME THINK HE WAS POISONED BY CONSPIRATORS. The accompanying story said that while the death of the emperor was "confirmed," reports differed as to the means employed "in his taking off." In one version he died by poison, in another by strangulation, while a third stated "he was subjected to frightful torture, a red-hot iron being thrust through his bowels." Manchu sources (read Li's Shanghai proxies) also had "confirmed" that the emperor was poisoned by little red pills given to him by reformers, while the reformers retorted that the little red pills had been given to the emperor by unspecified people in the Forbidden City.

Nobody informed Kuang Hsu that he was dead. However, by the time Kang arrived in Shanghai and was intercepted by the gullible Bland, an atmosphere of great sympathy existed among Westerners both for the Wild Fox and for the poor "dead" emperor.

Brenan's letter to MacDonald said that Bland wasted no time.

In a few minutes [Kang] removed himself to the launch, and he was then conveyed [by Bland] to the Peninsula and Oriental steamer *Balaarat*, then lying outside Woosung. Her Majesty's [warship] *Esk* as a measure of precaution, had been sent down to Woosung, and those on the *Chungking* jumped to the conclusion that Kang Yu-wei was taking refuge on the English gunboat, so that when the *Chungking* arrived at Shanghai the detectives and officials on the look out for Kang Yu-wei were informed that he was on board the *Esk*. That evening and all next day I received many inquiries from the officials as to [Kang's] whereabouts, but after a time they seemed to perceive that the refugee had found a safe asylum. . . .

During the *Balaarat*'s stay at Woosung I was somewhat anxious lest some Chinese hireling, stimulated by an offer of a large reward, should make an attempt on Kang Yu-wei's life, but the precautions taken by Captain Field, of the *Balaarat*, were complete, and an armed sentry stood outside his cabin-door night and day.

This was elegant treatment indeed for the moonfaced self-promoter whose reckless behavior had done so much to excite the Ironhats, doom the reformers, humiliate the earnest young emperor, and set reform back beyond recall.

While the *Balaarat* was at Woosung, British consul Frederick S. A. Bourne visited Kang in hope of eliciting some valuable information, but he later advised the Foreign Office that Kang knew nothing of what was happening in Peking and was only pretending to have an inside track. Kang, he said, had only the shallowest grasp of court dealings, "repeating what he has read in the way of wide political speculation." This was one of the few accurate observations any Westerner made but was overlooked in the almost hysterical rush to boost Kang and condemn "the dowager and her gang."

Bourne's astute perception of Kang as a mere mountebank did not stop

Bland from making extravagant use in the world press of Kang's mixture of hearsay and fiction, which suited Bland's racist and political prejudices perfectly. He took what Kang told him, mixed it with his own hugely erroneous assumptions, and sent the following dispatch to the *Times*:

> He informed me that he left Peking . . . in compliance with a secret message from the Emperor warning him of his danger. He further stated that the recent events were entirely due to the action of the Manchu party, headed by the Dowager Empress and Viceroy Jung Lu, and including all the high Manchu officials. The latter were displeased by the Emperor leaning toward the Reform Party, and decided to restore the regency of the Dowager. The Dowager Empress's party is bound by an understanding with the Russians whereby the latter, in consideration of the support of Russian interests, undertake to preserve Manchuria as the seat of the dynasty and to maintain Manchu rule in China. . . . The present movement is entirely Manchu. . . . The influence of Li Hung-chang is now subordinate to that of Jung Lu and is likely to decrease.

This was just the sort of thing Victorian England liked to hear, having spent the better part of the nineteenth century fretting about Russia's territorial expansion. But Bland mixed up his players as usual and gave Tzu Hsi, Jung Lu, and the Ironhats credit for a magic trick only Li could perform.

"Kang Yu-wei," Bland went on, "urges that England has an opportunity to intervene and restore the Emperor to the throne. . . . He also observes that unless protection is afforded to the victims of the coup d'état it will be impossible henceforward for any native official to support British interests."

On September 27 Kang's steamer sailed for Hong Kong, in company with the warship *Esk*. One of Kang's fellow passengers on the voyage was the shrewd Henry Cockburn of the British legation in Peking, who was on his way to England. He interviewed Kang Yu-wei at length between Shanghai and Hong Kong and like Consul Bourne was not impressed with the Wild Fox or his assessments of the court. He concluded that as a source of information Kang was useless and deserving only of ridicule. Unfortunately Cockburn's views were reserved to the Foreign Office. Regarding Tzu Hsi and her chief eunuch, Li Lien-ying, Cockburn wryly reported to Sir Claude MacDonald that Kang threw out dark, veiled hints that "this man Li and the Empress Dowager are on closer terms than divorce courts consider satisfactory."

The world press announced the emperor's death again and again during the first two weeks after Tzu Hsi resumed her regency. Some newspapers said a grandson of Prince Kung had succeeded to the throne on October 1. The *New York Times* heaped praise on this young man it called Prince Yin, described as "good-looking, intelligent . . . decidedly pro-foreign." Englishmen who had met Yin, the paper said, "declare he will not be a puppet like his predecessor."

Puppet was not a very gracious epitaph for Emperor Kuang Hsu, the hopeful reformer who so recently had been the darling of the diplomatic community and journalists. Worse was to come.

Kang's steamer, the *Balaarat*, arrived in Hong Kong the evening of September 29, and he was greeted by the colony's wealthiest Chinese comprador, Ho Tung (later Sir Robert Hotung), accompanied by the colony's administrator, Major General Sir Wilsone Black, and by police superintendent Francis H. May, all anxious for a glimpse of this odd fish.

Thanks to extraordinary British prescience, Kang's wife, his concubine, and his daughters, who were living in South China, were all able to flee to Macao and thence to Hong Kong; his mother was spirited directly to Hong Kong, and his brother's widow and daughter arrived three days later. This was highly irregular and adds to the impression that Britain was more deeply involved than has ever been acknowledged. When the Kang family were found to have escaped, all their property was confiscated. The Wild Fox complained that even distant relatives were put upon by "unscrupulous men who quickly seized on the occasion to carry out their nefarious schemes. Many of my relatives suffered from their extortion."

Even instant heroes can be a nuisance. Being a Chinaman, Kang posed awkward problems for the British authorities. It was unthinkable to keep him on ice in government buildings, or in their own homes, which is why the wealthy Ho Tung was brought in. Generously, the comprador arranged for the Kangs to move into his mansion and gave them several thousand dollars for pocket money. Other wealthy Chinese contributed to these funds. Kang's "dramatic escape" and putative friendship with the "slain" emperor had made him an overnight celebrity. He was feted by the biggest Chinese tycoons in the Crown Colony.

Despite such generosity, hospitality, and thoroughly British attention to every domestic detail, Kang was anxious to move on. He saw the Japanese as his real allies. He had already contacted the Japanese consul in Shanghai, who wired Tokyo that Kang wanted to settle in Japan. By October 9 he had a formal invitation from the one-legged foreign minister, Okuma Shigenobu, along with assurances that he would not be troubled by the Chinese diplomatic mission in Tokyo.

Now that he was being acclaimed by Westerners far and wide as the sage of modern China, Kang repaid his British hosts by putting himself at the disposal of journalists. He gave his first long exclusive interview to the *China Mail*. His sponsor and host, Ho Tung, identified only as "a well-known comprador," served as English translator. After some throat clearing in which Kang explained that he had been depressed by news of the beheading of his brother and the emperor's rumored murder, Kang "thanked the British people for the kind protection they had afforded him and for the interest the English people were taking in the advancement of the political and social status of China and the emancipation of the emperor." Then he launched into a vicious attack on Tzu Hsi:

> Since the Emperor began to display an interest in affairs of State, the Empress Dowager has been scheming his deposition. She used to play cards with him, and gave him intoxicating drinks in order to prevent him from attending to State affairs. For the great part of the last two years the Emperor has been practically the figurehead against his own wishes.
>
> You all know that the Empress Dowager is not educated, that she is very conservative, that she has been very reluctant to give the Emperor any real power in managing the affairs of the Empire. In the year 1887 it was decided to set aside Taels 30,000,000 for the creation of a Navy. . . . The Empress Dowager appropriated the balance of the money for the repair of [the Summer Palace]. . . .
>
> She has never seen many outside people—only a few eunuchs in the Palace and a few Ministers of State who have access to her.

Presenting himself as an insider, Kang turned to sexual innuendo. "There is a sham eunuch in the Palace who has practically more power than any of the Ministers. Li [Lien-ying] is the sham eunuch's name. He is a native of Chihli. Nothing could be done without first bribing him. All the Viceroys have got their official positions through bribing this man, who is immensely wealthy. Li Hung-chang is not to be compared with him." (To suggest that anyone in Peking was wealthier than Viceroy Li was absurd, but Kang's audience was in no position to check his assertions.)

Enlarging upon his authority, he claimed that he had seen Tzu Hsi himself. "She is of medium height and commanding presence, rather impetuous in manner. She has a dark sallow complexion, long almond eyes, high nose, is fairly intelligent looking and has expressive eyes." There is no evidence that Kang ever saw the dowager, even at a distance. Even Sir Robert Hart had never seen her. At the time Kang had his one brief audience with Kuang Hsu in the Forbidden City, the empress dowager was at the Summer Palace.

Pleased by the response to this first major interview, Kang wrote to the various Western ministers in Peking, urging them to save the emperor. In similar letters to Edwin Conger and Sir Claude MacDonald, Kang called the dowager "the False Empress," a "licentious and depraved palace concubine," a "usurping, murderous thief," "a wanton, avaricious old woman," and "the scourge of the people." This was the first time such slurs were voiced and marks a dramatic turning point in the life of Tzu Hsi and the history of imperial China. From 1898 on black propaganda would displace truth. Warming to his subject, Kang listed scandalous details of her life, adapted liberally from the gossip he had heard at *ming-shih* drinking parties. "The False Empress has an illegitimate son called Chin-ming and she must mean to set him on the throne. . . . How can your honorable country consent to associate with a wanton false violent and poisonous person of this kind, a thief who deposes the Sovereign and usurps his Throne?" (By this point Tzu Hsi had herself been China's sovereign in one manifestation or another for thirty-seven years, and had neither deposed Kuang Hsu nor usurped the throne.)

Kang reminded the ministers that "the False Empress Dowager is conservative, ignorant, violent and profligate. She poisoned our Empress, [Tzu An] the consort of Hsien Feng, our empress [A-lu-te] the consort of Tung-chih, the latter dying of rage and grief in consequence." (The death of Tzu An had occurred seventeen years earlier, allowing ample time for any rumors of poisoning to develop, but this is the first time on record that the charge was made. Kang also garbled the death of A-lu-te, asserting that Tung Chih had died of rage and grief after his wife was poisoned, when in fact he died before her. He obviously knew nothing of Tzu Hsi's also being poisoned.)

"Now," he went on, "in combination with one or two traitorous statesmen, she has secluded our emperor and is secretly plotting to usurp his throne, falsely alleging that she is counselling in government. . . . All the scholars of my country are enraged that this meddling palace concubine should seclude [the emperor]. . . . She has appropriated the proceeds of the Good Faith Bonds to build a . . . Palace at Tientsin to give rein to her libidinous desires. She has no feelings for the degradation of the state and the misery of the people."

It was all rubbish, but Westerners had little knowledge of China and did not know what to believe. Even those Westerners long resident in Peking knew nothing about the inner workings of the court, the actual life of the Forbidden City, the authentic history of the Ching Dynasty or its true ups and downs since the two dowagers were appointed ceremonial regents in 1861. Even in the legations few grasped that there had once been two dowagers.

In Hong Kong, Kang went to see Miyazaki Torazo, who had supported Sun Yat-sen financially since the mid-1890s, as a front man for the Genyo-sha. Kang, aware of Miyazaki's connection to the underworld, and failing to grasp that his real enemy was Prince Tuan, appealed to him to help murder Tzu Hsi. He told Miyazaki "that the empress dowager was the only obstacle to reform in China, and expressed a desire to eliminate her by hiring some Japanese soshi [assassin]." Miyazaki felt that this was a business that one of Kang's ardent young followers, not a Japanese, should take care of and told Kang as much. The next day a nervous young man chosen by Kang to undertake the murder came to Miyazaki to ask for help and to make a tearful farewell.

Over the next eight years Kang initiated a number of plots to assassinate the dowager. One of his friends sent to Peking to kill her became so enraptured with the wine and the flower girls that he squandered his budget for the mission. Another of Kang's assassins was arrested and put to death. Neither the empress dowager nor the emperor ever forgave Kang for his slander or his murder plots. Kuang Hsu, far from being under torture in a Manchu dungeon, issued a number of edicts condemning Kang, which speaks for itself.

Sir Robert Hart wrote that "the old lady is furious over the Kang Yu-wei affair—which one can't wonder at, and that worthy is being interviewed at Hong Kong and his sayings are published and doing international harm."

Sir Claude MacDonald and other European ministers in Peking were very susceptible to what they called "this Shanghai rumor," that the emperor really might be a prisoner or suffering physical abuse. Anxious to reassure themselves, the legations took advantage of an edict issued by Kuang Hsu on September 25, at the end of his three-day retreat. The edict spoke of his long-standing ill health, which had not been relieved by the treatments of imperial physicians, and requested: "Should there be any persons, either in the capital or the provinces, who are skilled in the treatment of disease, let the officials at once recommend them to the throne." The legations collectively pressed the Chinese government to allow a Western doctor to examine Kuang Hsu, assuming he was still alive. It was made clear that only such a medical checkup would clear the air of the corrosive rumors and restore British and international confidence in the regime. As a qualified physician, George Morrison tried to get the assignment for himself; it would have been an incomparable scoop. He claimed to be the senior medical doctor in Peking at that moment, but he was turned down by Sir Claude, who said Morrison would be inappropriate because he was the *Times*'s correspondent. Another private British physician, Dr. Curwan, was rejected because he was a close friend of Kang Yu-wei and Timothy Richard. Sir Claude decided finally on the French legation physician, Dr. Dethève, on the grounds that he was the only medical man in Peking attached to a diplomatic mission at that moment, the British legation's doctor being on leave.

Dr. Dethève visited Emperor Kuang Hsu on October 18, 1898, accompanied by Prince Ching and an interpreter from the Italian legation. If the dowager was indeed a committed xenophobe, if she hated her nephew Kuang Hsu and wished him dead, if she was the all-powerful demon portrayed by Wild Fox Kang, she would never have agreed to such a revealing examination by a foreigner. She was in fact present throughout, making the frankness of the medical interview that followed all the more illustrative of the emperor's open relationship with her. First of all, of course, Dr. Dethève discovered that Kuang Tsu was indeed alive, not a prisoner, and had been neither tortured nor poisoned. Physically, the emperor apparently was afflicted with Bright's disease, a kidney ailment, Dethève concluded, and suffered a number of secondary effects brought on by that illness. Mentally, he was a mess, but whether any of his neuroses could be blamed upon the dowager or anyone else, or simply upon genetics, his own mother's abuse, and his peculiar education in the Forbidden City, is a matter for conjecture.

Dethève's medical report, written in French, was sent to all the legations and was immediately forwarded by them to their home governments. Although it was very intimate, because of the personal nature of its observations, its substance was soon leaked to the public and became the inspiration of ruinous gossip in China, in Europe, and in America, destroying what little was left of Kuang Hsu's shattered image. The report is extraordinarily graphic and revealing:

At first glance, [his] state is generally feeble, terribly thin, depressed attitude, pale complexion. The appetite is very good, but the digestion is slow. . . . Vomiting is very frequent. . . . Listening to the lungs with a stethoscope, which His Majesty gladly allowed, did not reveal indications of good health. Circulatory problems are numerous. Pulse feeble and fast, head aching, feelings of heat on the chest, ringing in the ears, dizziness and stumbling that give the impression that he is missing a leg. To these symptoms add the overall sensation of cold, in the legs and knees, fingers feeling dead, cramps in the calves, itching, slight deafness, failing eyesight, pain in the kidneys. But, above all these are the troubles with the urinary apparatus . . . His Majesty urinates often, but only a little at a time, in 24 hours the amount is less than normal. His Majesty stresses his ejaculations, which come at night and are always followed by voluptuous sensations. These nocturnal emissions have been followed by the lessening of the faculty to achieve voluntary erections during the day. After having considered these different symptoms, I have come to the conviction that the illness is due to a lesion on the kidneys, which in Europe is called Nephritus, or a chronic inflammation of the kidney. In this illness, the blood, in passing the kidney, deposits products which are . . . poisonous to the organism. When the kidney does not pass these products with the urine, because of a lesion on the organ, the same products are carried by the blood to different organs, accumulating and causing troubles, like those described. It is necessary to give a regime which does not require the kidney to work hard. . . . The best regime is a regime of milk only, without other foods. It consists of taking milk, cow or human, three or four litres a day, in which is dissolved 50 grams of lactose (milk sugar). The regime should be followed for several months. For medication, the powder of digitalis has real use. The pain in the kidneys can be calmed by massages and cupping. . . . As for the involuntary ejaculations, this indicated the general enfeebled condition, in particular of the muscles of the lower back. . . . This is my humble advice, which I submit to His Majesty with the great hope that I have given some relief.

That Kuang Hsu was able to speak with such openness in front of Tzu Hsi is astonishing indeed and should put to rest any notion of a wall of hatred and mistrust between them. The report concluded with Dethève's judgment, "Not in immediate danger." Medically, he meant.

The biggest problem, Dethève felt, was that the emperor's illness made sexual intercourse impossible, and without sex there would be no heir to the throne. Kuang Hsu also suffered from sudden involuntary ejaculations during the working day when he was under emotional stress, one of the side effects of his kidney ailment and nervous tension. He could not make love to his empress or to his concubines even if he was attracted to them, which he was not. For dignity's sake he could not put himself into such a circumstance with any woman. He would remain childless but the presence of the empress and concubines would serve as a continual reminder of his impotence. The awareness of these inadequacies had not prevented Kuang Hsu from showing real strength of character in firing Weng Tung-ho from the Grand Council and launching the Hundred Days Reform. He might have prevailed over the Ironhats and brought about dramatic changes in China had he not been at such a terrible physical and emotional disadvantage.

Dr. Dethève did not express an opinion about the emperor's psychic state. Another Western physician reviewing the emperor's symptoms later summed up Kuang Hsu's condition as neurasthenia, aggravated by his malfunctioning kidney, which Webster's defines as "an emotional and psychic disorder that is characterized by impaired functioning in interpersonal relationships and often by fatigue, depression, feelings of inadequacy, headaches, hypersensitivity to sensory stimulation (as by light or noise), and psychosomatic problems (as disturbances of digestion and circulation)." All of these symptoms had been associated with Kuang Hsu since childhood, which goes a long way toward explaining why the Iron-hats had him at a disadvantage.

So it is possible to draw some simple conclusions. Whatever his original mental condition as an abused child—producing his stammer—it had been made worse by his upbringing in the Forbidden City under the continual nagging and faultfinding of Tutor Weng, among eunuchs who goaded the boy maliciously. It was Weng who made the boy grovel in subservience to his aunt. He reached maturity only to discover that all he had been told about his responsibilities as emperor were lies and that in reality he was only a rubber stamp for the claque of reactionary princes and mandarins who held collective power behind the throne.

In Russia, the fact that the only son and heir of Czar Nicholas II had hemophilia would be a closely guarded state secret. But Kuang Hsu's poor mental and physical health became common knowledge, through the negligence or contempt of the legations. The uproar created by Dr. De-thève's medical report coincided with a series of secret Clan Council meetings in the autumn of 1898 at which the Ironhats succeeded in press-ing for the secret designation of an heir to the throne. The Ironhats now had the upper hand, having terrorized all moderates into silence by their brutal handling of the reformers, so they thought this the right moment to put forward their candidate.

Sir Robert Hart learned that "six youths are under inspection in the palace and it is said one of them will be Emperor before the end of the month." The rivalry among the princes to have their own candidate chosen was intense, but over quickly. Unlike the succession crisis of 1875, this time the candidates were all properly from the next generation, princelings of the Pu nomenclature. Pu Lun was rejected for reasons of his bloodline and his father's conspiracy in 1860 with the Gang of Eight, the same reason he had been rejected in 1875. A number of other boys received inadequate support. A dark-horse candidate was suggested, a son of Prince Ching, but he was disqualified for being outside the immediate imperial family. The choice fell, inevitably, to the son of Prince Tuan, twelve-year-old Pu Chun. Although Pu Chun's selection was supposed to be "secret," Morrison heard rumors that the choice had been made as early as October 12 (two weeks after the Six Martyrs' beheading).

There were good reasons for keeping the choice of Pu Chun secret temporarily. A public announcement would be taken by the legations and the outside world as confirmation of a conspiracy to replace Kuang Hsu, generating even more diplomatic hostility. While Pu Chun's selection was kept secret, it was known to all within the court and had the effect of making Prince Tuan even more of a power behind the throne.

Other concessions to the Ironhats were wrested from the empress dow-ager that autumn. The North China *Herald* reported on October 31, 1898, that she had bestowed upon Prince Tuan and his elder brother, Prince Tun II (Tsai Lien), the Shangfang swords, which gave them the right to decapitate anyone, anytime, anyplace, regardless of rank or dignity. This was an ancient privilege, rooted in antiquity, that made them chief body-guards of the throne, but in the wrong hands it also had the effect of making Prince Tuan chief justice and chief butcher. For someone like Tuan the right to behead anyone who disagreed was normal. A more ominous signal could hardly have been sent, but Morrison and the lega-tions failed to take notice, so fixated were they on the dowager herself as the villain.

For the first time since the Jehol Coup, nearly forty years earlier, power was becoming concentrated in the hands of the most aggressive, chauvin-istic, and narrow-minded faction at court. Although there were still many moderates in the government who disagreed with the Ironhats, there was great personal danger in offending the princes of the Shangfang swords. Tuan's men were all over the city, spying and informing.

Curiously, Tuan was virtually unknown to the foreign community. Had they been paying attention during the Hundred Days, they would have seen Tuan and his brothers reveal a violent opposition to reform. There had been continual rumors about his plots to murder or depose the emperor. It would be a mistake to regard him only as a vengeful and demented man consumed by personal ambition, coveting absolute power for himself and the throne for his son. Tuan seems to have been a genuine patriot, albeit a superpatriot, whose sincerity was never in question. He had all the makings of a Homeric hero, including a fatal flaw. He was dashing, personable, impressive, and a natural leader among his peers. His father, the first Prince Tun, was similarly imposing but dangerous when drunk. In their own eyes the primary policy issue for the Ironhats was to restore Manchu supremacy in China by expelling the foreign intruders who had caused the empire nothing but humiliation.

The flaw that made Prince Tuan and the Ironhats dangerous to others and to themselves was their deliberate withdrawal from reality, their absolute refusal to acquaint themselves with foreign people or foreign ideas, foreign guns and foreign armies—all the while foolishly assuming that under their leadership their armies would fight rather than run and the Chinese people would rise up in unison to throw the foreigners and their armies into the sea. They failed to recognize that evolution had passed them by, the world had changed, their enemies had superior weap-ons, the rules of the game were altered. Ultimately their refusal to contem-plate these changes would end in disaster. They still believed in magic, and magic was going to let them down.

Although Tzu Hsi also had no real experience of foreigners she decided to launch her own public relations campaign by inviting the ladies of the foreign diplomatic corps to tea, an unprecedented event. Nobody would be expecting to find the emperor at the tiffen as well. The legations would be reassured to see that Kuang Hsu was alive and reasonably well, the ladies would observe that there was nothing but affection between the dowager and her nephew, and foreigners in general would be won over by a demonstration of imperial goodwill. It would be the first time any foreign woman had ever seen Tzu Hsi. She had received Prince Heinrich of Prussia six months earlier, in the middle of May 1898, at a formal audience with Kuang Hsu in which she did not stay behind the gauze curtain, the first time she had ever been seen by a foreign male. Prince Heinrich, then in China as admiral of the German Fleet on a tour of the China Station, was the Kaiser's brother and a grandson of Queen Victoria, a figure who fascinated Tzu Hsi, which probably explains why she broke with tradition. Weng Tung-ho was disgusted by this breach of etiquette and complained bitterly to her about this meeting with a Foreign Devil. However, she had decided to satisfy her curiosity about Westerners, even in this small way. It was a revolutionary step for any upper-class Chinese woman, especially the empress. She never moved quickly in such matters. Nine years earlier, she had created a great stir in the court for investing Robert Hart with mandarin rank. It had taken this much time for her to take the next step. Encouraged by that experience she was ready to break with tradition again.

It was unheard of for a Manchu empress to entertain foreign ladies, so she had to go against her Grand Councillors in setting it up. The party was arranged for December 13, 1898, in the Winter Palace, one of the Sea Palaces next to the Forbidden City. American minister Edwin Conger had misgivings, for he had just been deluged with letters from Wild Fox Kang portraying Tzu Hsi as a scheming, blood-soaked murderess, but Conger said he hoped that "some good may result therefrom." He told the State Department that "when it is once known by the Chinese people generally that the Empress Dowager is herself willing to see and entertain foreigners, some of their antipathy [toward foreigners] will be allayed." Mrs. Conger's houseboy was very excited.

There was obfuscation on both sides, which annoyed Robert Hart: "First they were not ready the day H.M. wanted them to appear—then when the second appointed day came round they could not go because they could not decide on one interpreter, each wanting her own (except Lady MacDonald)—then another difficulty came up as the Secs' wives and Ministers' daughters claimed to belong to the diplomatic corps and insisted on being received." In the end the official party included only the wives of the ministers of Great Britain, Russia, Germany, France, Holland, America, and Japan.

Lady MacDonald was equally frustrated:

The Empress was very curious to see us, but her Councillors objected strongly to this new and pro-foreign move, and tried in many ways to block our Audience by conceding as grudgingly as possible the stipulations made by our respective husbands that we should be received with every mark of respect. Some of the stipulations which we ladies insisted upon seemed exacting even to our husbands, and Prince Ching said laughingly to [Sir Claude] at one of the meetings, that foreign wives seemed almost as difficult to please as Chinese. The negotiations lasted for about six weeks but we stood firm on all essential points and finally woman's curiosity proved stronger than man's opposition. . . . Four European Interpreters and two Chinamen . . . accompanied us to the Palace.

At ten o'clock on that cold morning a mounted Chinese escort sent by the Tsungli Yamen went to each legation to accompany the ladies and interpreters to the British legation, as Lady MacDonald was the most senior. Each lady was in a sedan chair and had five chair-bearers and two mounted attendants, or *mafoos*. When they reached the first gate of the Sea Palaces the ladies had to leave their chairs, bearers, attendants, and escorts and were taken inside the park to an elegant railroad coach that had been presented to China by France. Lady MacDonald noted that the cars were "gorgeously upholstered and hung with mirrors, but the sun of years had told on the purple silk hangings, and the cushions were worn and shabby." Mrs. Conger described the events: "We entered this car, and eunuchs dressed in black pushed and hauled it to another stopping place, where we were received by many officials and served with tea. . . . After a little rest and tea-sipping, we were escorted by high officials to the throne-room. Our heavy garments were taken at the door, and we were ushered into the presence of the Emperor and Empress Dowager."

Leading the procession, Lady MacDonald found the dowager waiting in a room that was small "and except for some magnificent wood-carvings and several mirrors unfurnished; a hideous European carpet of antediluvian pattern covered the stone floor, and innumerable glass chandeliers and Chinese lanterns hung from the roof." Even more interesting were the people in the room: "It was crowded with gaudily-dressed and gaily-painted ladies-in-waiting, pink and yellow were the predominating colours, their cheeks and lips vying with their petticoats. Many officials were also present and I fancy to most of them, and to all the ladies, we were objects of considerable interest; the ladies had never seen their foreign sisters at such close quarters before, and many of them had never seen us at all."

Tzu Hsi was sitting on a dais behind a long, narrow table decorated with fruit and flowers "watching our entry with the keenest interest," noted Lady MacDonald,

and no less keenly did we look at this formidable lady to whom is imputed such an iron will and unbending character. Though over sixty she is still a young-looking woman with jet black hair and kindly dark eyes; in repose her expression is stern, but when she smiles it lights up and all traces of severity disappear; her face is not of the ordinary Chinese or Manchu type, and she might in another part of the world pass for an Italian peasant. In stature she is short and slight . . . her hands and feet are small and well formed, the greatest disfigurement from our point of view being the two gilt nail protectors. . . . In front of the table behind which her Imperial Majesty was installed, and a little to one side, sat the Emperor. It was a pleasurable surprise to us all to find him taking part in the Audience, as we were told only the Empress was to receive us. A sad-eyed delicate-looking youth showing but little character in his face, he hardly raised his eyes during our reception.

This was the first time the emperor had been seen by a foreign woman, so they stared at him in fascination, knowing from their husbands or from legation gossip every detail of his medical condition, making him extremely uncomfortable. It was also the first time Kuang Hsu had ever seen Western women, except at a distance. To Oriental eyes the legation ladies presented a truly formidable picture. Aside from the wife of the Japanese ambassador, who wore a fine embroidered silk kimono and obi, the ladies were all dressed in what each regarded as the summit of good taste for her country and time—which is to say the height of La Belle Epoque, the Victorian age, the Gay Nineties, and so forth—each of them done up like a Tiffany lamp, corsets cinched tight, hats like chef salads with ostrich plumes. They looked like nothing so much as a group of fabulous operatic divas in full costume, ready to sing arias from Verdi and Puccini. In the poorly heated palace they were all freezing. Easily the most attractive was pretty Ethel MacDonald, a tall, graceful woman in her early forties whose golden curls and demure intelligence did much to soften the impression that they were attending a state funeral.

Sarah Conger, a dour Christian Scientist dressed all in black, recalled how they "stood according to rank (longest time in Peking) and bowed. Our first interpreter presented each lady to Prince Ching and he in turn presented us to Their Majesties." Lady MacDonald then read a short address in English on behalf of the ladies: "We rejoice that Your Imperial

Majesty has taken this first step towards a personal acquaintance with the ladies of Foreign nations. We venture to express this hope that your august example will be followed by the ladies of China, and that the peoples of the East and West will continue to draw nearer to each other." The dowager responded through Prince Ching. Listening to her, Lady MacDonald decided that Tzu Hsi had "a harsh voice, disagreeable to listen to and talks in a louder key than is usual for a Chinese lady," though the other ladies found her voice melodic and pleasant.

> Another low bow on our part, then each lady was escorted to the throne where she bowed and curtsied to the Emperor, who extended his hand to each. We then stepped before Her Majesty and bowed with a low curtsy. She offered both her hands and we stepped forward to her. With a few words of greeting, Her Majesty clasped our hands in hers, and placed on the finger of each lady a heavy, chased gold ring, set with a large pearl. After thanking Her Majesty, we backed from the throne and took our places as before. Again we bowed low and backed from their Imperial presence.

The ladies were then escorted to a banquet hall, where they were entertained by Prince Ching and five Manchu princesses. Lady Mac-Donald observed that "Prince Ching was in the room but did not share our tiffin, he sat gravely smoking cigarettes and watching the party." By Chinese etiquette this was a normal separation of the sexes. After dining, the ladies went to another room for tea and cigarettes, during which Lady MacDonald noted that "the Palace ladies thawed somewhat, allowed us to admire and examine their pretty dresses, and in turn felt the materials of our dresses." The diplomats' wives met the dowager again, and Mrs. Conger commented: "She was bright and happy and her face glowed with good will. There was no trace of cruelty to be seen." The other ladies commented on her "charming" smile. After this renewal of greetings, the entourage moved to the palace theater for a variety show lasting an hour. When it ended, they joined the dowager a last time for a tea ceremony that amounted to a peace offering. "When tea was passed to us she stepped forward and tipped each cup of tea to her own lips and took a sip, then lifted the cup, on the other side, to our lips." It horrified her ministers and the princes to see her bestow this exceptional honor on Foreign Devils. Each guest was again presented with gifts.

The Western press found the whole episode disgusting, offensive, and farcical. Morrison's foreign editor at the *Times*, Valentine Chirol, wrote his correspondent: "I feel very strongly about exposing the representatives of refined European womanhood to the ribald jests of Palace Eunuchs and the offensive curiosity of Chinese Mandarins, who will of course represent the ceremony as a great kowtow before the Empress and the Empress' party. However, the thing is done and there is no good kicking against accomplished facts."

Morrison reported to the *Times* that "Her Majesty was especially gracious to Lady MacDonald, and once while conversing with her patted her playfully on the cheek."

Sir Claude MacDonald reported enthusiastically to the Foreign Office that "the Empress Dowager made a most favorable impression by her courtesy and affability. Those who went to the Palace under the idea that they would meet a cold and haughty person of strong imperious manners, were agreeably surprised to find Her Majesty a kind and courteous hostess, who displayed both the tact and softness of a womanly disposition."

Later, when she published a thoughtful appraisal of Tzu Hsi in a British journal, Lady MacDonald provided a very unusual and important insight into the dowager's nature:

> I should say the Dowager-Empress was a woman of some strength of character, certainly genial and kindly . . . this is the opinion of all the ladies who accompanied me. I was fortunate in having as my interpreter the Chinese Secretary of our Legation [Henry Cockburn], a gentleman of over twenty years' experience of China and the Chinese; he speaks and writes the language well, and is possessed of great ability and sound judgment. Previous to our visit, his opinion of the Dowager-Empress was what I may call the generally accepted one. My husband had requested him to take a careful note of all that passed, especially with a view of endeavouring to arrive at some estimate of her true character. On his return he reported that all his previously conceived notions had been upset by what he had seen and heard, and he summed up her character in four words, "amiability verging on weakness!"

Cockburn had expected to find a calculating, reptilian woman with a heart of ice, capable of poisoning sons and lovers, and ordering false eunuchs to poke hot irons up the young emperor's backside—all of which had been attributed to her in recent weeks in newspapers around the world. Instead he found a sad and uncertain woman anxious to be liked, a woman afflicted by a lifelong tristesse who was increasingly stricken by her inability to control events. As she saw her reputation being ruined, she was trying to fight back by winning over the ladies of the legations, which struck Cockburn as the sheer folly of weakness.

This was precisely the same experience and identical conclusion reached by the wily Tseng Kuo-fan (an exceptional judge of character by all accounts) when he first met Tzu Hsi twenty-nine years earlier. He called her ability "anything but exceptional" and observed that she "had not a single important word to say." Hardly what one would have expected of an evil Empress Wu.

What was behind this fragile façade, seen through by the first of the new Chinese warlords and mentor of Viceroy Li on the one hand and Cockburn, who would have been the MI6 resident in Peking had MI6 existed then?

Tzu Hsi's weakness in managing the court may be traceable to her feelings of parental rejection and worthlessness as a child. Her husband had rejected her to return to Li Fei. Her son had rejected her to pursue a suicidal sex life. She was forever seeking reassurance from her courtiers, making her an easy mark for calculating princes. As a manager of people she was no match for Tseng Kuo-fan or Li Hung-chang. She could not anticipate trouble and steer around it. She waited it out, avoiding action, hoping matters would work themselves out. She was no master of realpolitik, and was repeatedly confronted by dilemma. She could never stop the incessant intriguing of the princes. There were only three times in her life when she had taken dramatic action, in each case frightened by great danger: in 1861, in 1875, and in 1898. Each crisis could have led to a coup, so her steps were taken in desperation, not because she had a grand strategy. After each emergency she withdrew, rearranged her gauze curtain, and settled back into her role as mediator and empress mother. If she had a guiding political philosophy it was to avoid tragedy, and in that she failed not once or twice but continually.

Although Tzu Hsi was assigned any number of perverse characteristics by people who knew nothing of her—and scholars who should have known better—the simple truth is that she was as unremarkable as drinking water. The rest is all nonsense, slander, and mischief, motivated by greed, racism, sexism, and plain everyday wickedness. That is why any study of her must really be a study of those who demonized her. Drinking water, of course, is only unremarkable until you need it.

CHAPTER FIFTEEN

Poisoned Pen

The manhunt in Peking for journalist Liang Chi-chao was abandoned when he made a successful escape to Japan, to rendezvous with the Wild Fox. An edict ordering his arrest and immediate beheading employed an ideograph depicting a little animal with short legs, riding on the back of a wolf; the wolf (or wild fox) was Kang Yu-wei. Liang, the little animal riding around on Kang's back, was still in Peking when the city gates were closed to prevent his escape. He sought refuge at the Japanese legation. The only senior foreign diplomat in town during the crisis (the rest were on holiday at the ocean or in the hills) was the acting Japanese ambassador, busy playing host to Ito Hirobumi. On Ito's orders, Liang was given immediate sanctuary.

Ito remained in Peking for another week, till September 29, during which he had many discussions with Liang and heard of the arrest, trial, and beheading of the Six Martyrs who had been Ito's outspoken champions at court. Meanwhile, there was a citywide dragnet for Liang. At Ito's command, Liang was disguised as a Japanese and spirited off to Tientsin by a secret agent of the Genyosha named Hirayama Shu. Reaching the anchorage at Taku, the secret agent and the Japanese consul at Tientsin put the fugitive safely aboard the gunboat *Oshima*. Coded orders arrived by telegram directly from Japan's Foreign Minister Okuma, and the *Oshima* weighed anchor and steamed out to sea, only to be intercepted by a Chinese naval vessel. Viceroy Jung Lu's agents had been watching the Japanese closely, but not closely enough. Chinese marines boarded and demanded Liang's surrender; the Japanese captain refused. Remaining out of sight in his cabin, Liang scribbled what he believed to be his last letters to family and friends. But his luck held. The marines returned to their own ship empty-handed, and the *Oshima* resumed her voyage.

In Japan the Kobe *Chronicle* revealed on October 22 that the *Oshima* was bringing "a very valuable present." Compared to Kang Yu-wei, perhaps he was. The two men were a Chinese spin-off of Boswell and Dr. Johnson: Kang performed, while Liang took notes. Until this point the journalist had been a comparatively insignificant character, an idea man for Kang, a creature—as the ideograph implied—whose own legs were too short for strutting. He lacked Kang's aggressiveness, preferring to achieve his purposes indirectly through his writings. The Japanese rescue propelled Liang onto the world stage and turned him into one of the most effective black propagandists of his day, master of the poisoned pen. His main target was Tzu Hsi.

If his legs were short, his talents were long. For the son of a Kwangtung farmer he was exceptionally bright. At age nine he was writing thousand-character essays and inhaling the alkaloid verses of Tang poet Li Po. He passed his *shu-jen* exams when he was only sixteen. But he despised arbitrary formality, complaining: "One might not know there was anything in the universe but commentaries and fine style." In 1890 he tried to pass the metropolitan exams in Peking and failed. On his return to Canton he met Kang Yu-wei, became one of the first students at Kang's "academy," and then one of its teachers. He tried three more times to pass the exams, in 1892, 1894, and 1895, when Kang squeaked by but Liang failed again and gave up trying.

By then Liang had made one of his most important foreign contacts, becoming Chinese secretary to missionary Timothy Richard. It was a stroke of fortune to fall into Richard's orbit, and vice versa. Liang helped Richard appeal to the *ming-shih* and to get close to the conspiratorial wing of the Hanlin Academy. In return Richard advanced Liang's career by building his image among foreigners as one of the bright young reformers who would lead the New China.

With this encouragement Liang became a contributor to a number of reform newspapers and magazines. On the strength of his writings he was invited in 1897 by Viceroy Chang Chih-tung's crony, the governor of Hunan, to serve as chief lecturer at a newly established Academy of Current Affairs in Changsha, one of the hotbeds of reform. There he joined others of like mind in organizing a reform society and became friends with Tan Ssu-tung, who would become the emperor's favorite reform adviser and one of the Six Martyrs.

Just before the Hundred Days Reform, Liang went to Peking to help Kang push at the doors of the Forbidden City. Through the intervention of Sir Chang, Liang was granted an audience with the emperor soon after Kang's own and, having made a better impression, was rewarded with a much better job than Kuang Hsu had offered the Wild Fox: he was put in charge of the new government translation bureau, although he did not read or speak any foreign language. Liang worked quietly in the background till tragedy struck in September, when Ito saved him from the executioner's harvest.

The gunboat *Oshima* put in at Miyajima, on the Inland Sea, where a member of the Japanese foreign ministry was waiting to take Liang to prearranged lodgings in Tokyo. At the end of October he was joined there by the Wild Fox, escorted from Hong Kong by Miyazaki Torazo.

Several months earlier the Japanese had provided sanctuary also to the leader of the Chinese republican movement, Dr. Sun Yat-sen, following the failure of his rebellion in Canton, and had arranged for Sun to have comfortable quarters in Yokohama. Although the egos and politics of Kang and Sun were incompatible, the Genyosha served as a bridge between them.

Japanese intellectuals, politicians, and leaders of the Genyosha saw Kang and Liang as valuable pawns in their long-term strategy to expel Western colonial powers from the Orient, particularly Russia, and to bring all of East Asia under Japanese influence. In this scheme the Genyosha was a dangerous partner. Ten years earlier, when the Genyosha thought Count Okuma Shigenobu was being too liberal with foreign governments, he lost a leg to a would-be assassin. Now Foreign Minister Okuma and the Genyosha were again collaborating, this time to sponsor Kang's anti-Manchu propaganda and Sun's republican intrigues.

On his arrival in Japan, Kang was presented as an expert source, a court intimate, and a favorite of the Chinese emperor. He told everyone he had been rescued from certain death by the quick action of Timothy Richard and Sir Claude MacDonald, aided by British consular officials in Shanghai and Royal Navy vessels, which made him sound much more important than he was. He boasted that he had been vetted personally by a correspondent of the *Times* of London, J.O.P. Bland, who had confirmed to the entire world that he, Kang, was a great intellectual and an honest reformer.

From then on the inflated publicity of Kang that was in general circulation around the world greatly distorted his influence upon the revolutionary movement in China and caused him to be taken seriously by Western governments who might have shied away had they known the truth. Nearly everyone was taken in.

From 1898 to 1900, foreign newspapers favoring reform in China eagerly and uncritically republished the propaganda that Kang and Liang were busy contriving. The basic source was Liang's magazine, *China Discussion*, subsidized by the Japanese, which began publication in Yokohama on December 23, 1898, three months after he was smuggled out of China. Articles first published in *China Discussion*, giving a false or distorted version of events and personalities in Peking, were extracted and republished by Liang in a collection entitled *Account of the Coup d'Etat of 1898*.

The book was revised and reprinted in Shanghai and Yokohama in 1899 and became the accepted version of the Hundred Days, the bible of the reform movement.

English-language newspapers in China—such as the North China *Daily News* and its weekly edition, the North China *Herald* (published in the Shanghai International Settlement where they were not subject to Manchu censorship)—adopted the false version put forth by *China Discussion*. The *Herald* frequently printed translations of articles by Kang and Liang, presenting them as authoritative, and thereby made them palatable to newspapers in England and America. Viewpoints expressed in the *Herald* were rarely attributed to Kang or Liang by name, but the similarities are so striking that it is evident they sipped from the same cup. Editors of the *Herald* did not hide their dislike of Tzu Hsi or their support for the reform movement, of which Kang was now the self-styled fountainhead. What the *Herald* printed in Shanghai was relayed by Bland to the *Times* in London, then picked up by the *New York Times*, the two papers that served as journals of record throughout the English-speaking world. (Bizarre reports about the dowager are easily traced from local newspapers in America to the Chicago *Tribune*, from there to the *New York Times*, then to the *Times* of London, to the *Herald* in Shanghai, and finally to Liang's *China Discussion* in Yokohama.)

Liang's anti-Manchu magazine naturally was popular with overseas Chinese. One article that appeared in March 1899 singled out Tzu Hsi, Jung Lu, and Kang I as the architects of China's doom. "Maybe," wrote Liang, "they will come to realize the dilemma they are in, and then they will certainly change their ideas. I say: a tortoise cannot grow hair, a rabbit cannot sprout horns, a cockerel cannot lay eggs, and a withered tree cannot produce blossoms, because it is not in their nature to do so. Concern has to exist in the heart. . . . Now all Tzu Hsi knows is a life of pleasure-seeking, all Jung Lu knows is lust for power, have either ever spared a thought for the good of the country?" Then Liang added, "They are so stupid that they would die before coming to their senses." He heaped praise on Emperor Kuang Hsu. "Heaven gave this saint to save China. . . . Although he has been imprisoned and dethroned, luckily he is still with us, Heaven has not yet abandoned China! Fellow countrymen, strengthen all with resolve, spend all effort in the emperor's cause!" (By this time Liang was well aware that Kuang Hsu had not been imprisoned or dethroned.)

Despite the efforts of imperial authorities to intercept copies of the magazine, they were circulated widely inside China. High officials, including the once avid supporter of the reformers Viceroy Chang Chihtung, read the magazine and were outraged; Chang warned the Tsungli Yamen that it was corrupting the minds of the people. Grand Councillor

Kang I is said to have presented a copy to Tzu Hsi, and she was "very angry." By any measure it was treason. An edict appeared in February 1899 offering a prize of 100,000 taels of silver for delivery of Kang and Liang "dead or alive." It was signed by Kuang Hsu.

Unfortunately for them, the ingrown Manchu had no comprehension of international propaganda and how to exploit or combat it outside China. They were slow to react, and never seemed to grasp the profound and long-lasting damage that was being done to them through newspapers, magazines, and books printing statements that could be challenged or disproved. In the imperial hierarchy Viceroy Li was the one notable exception, and he would continue to use propaganda and manipulation of the press with stunning effect during the Boxer Uprising, but again Li's victims were the Manchu. Ultimately the whole legend of Tzu Hsi turns on black propaganda, and lying became the chief weapon in the reduction and downfall of the dynasty. How different matters might have been if the Manchu had recognized this danger; but they were strangely blind to it, still frozen in the ways of previous centuries, like the terra-cotta army guarding the tomb of Emperor Chin Shih Huang-ti, buried for thousands of years in splendid tight formation.

Viceroy Chang Chih-tung, who had been the patron of three of the Six Martyrs, was one of those who went after the bounty. He worked tirelessly to have Kang and Liang expelled from Japan. He sent assassins posing as students to Tokyo. Striking back in *China Discussion*, Kang and Liang denounced Chang as a "weathercock mandarin" and a reactionary who had known in advance about the Ironhat plot against the reformers and had gone along with it. After only a year of publication, the journal's printing plant in Yokohama was mysteriously destroyed by fire.

Not surprisingly, the Japanese soon tired of playing host to the blowhard Kang. He had been a houseguest of Foreign Minister Okuma for only five months when Okuma persuaded him to make a fund-raising trip to Europe or North America. Kang did not go empty-handed; Okuma and the Genyosha greased his path with at least nine thousand dollars in pocket money, and he sailed for Canada in March 1899. He was unable to visit the United States because American immigration officials required a voucher from the Manchu government, so he went to British Columbia, where he was taken seriously by Canadian officials and his pockets were filled by overseas Chinese merchants. He went on to London, where Sir Charles Dilke, leader of the Liberals, brought up for debate in the Commons the idea of British intervention in China because Tzu Hsi was "corrupt and besotted." The Conservatives (aware of their own diplomatic reports) retorted that Kang himself was guilty of "injudicious conduct."

Accustomed to living well on others' money, Kang soon ran through his reserves and settled in Singapore, where Lim Boon-keng, a rich and well-educated transcultural, paid his bills. Kang had to do something decisive soon or fade into oblivion; Lim's associates in Singapore were willing to back an armed uprising. With this exciting prospect Kang collected $300,000 from overseas Chinese, who wanted to guarantee the goodwill of any new regime. As a target he chose the city of Hankow in Hupeh Province, where the Genyosha had set up one of their Chinese drugstore chains as a front for secret operations. Since then many Hankow gentry and merchants had been subverted so Kang assumed it would be easy to carry out a revolt with their support.

From the start the plot went awry. Supplies and military goods to be smuggled into China from Japan, through a dummy hardware company in Hong Kong, never arrived. The Hankow contingent rebelled ahead of schedule and the plot was exposed. This pratfall cost Kang much of his financial support. Still in Singapore, he became convinced that Sun Yat-sen had sent an assassin after him. He decided to take a vacation in Darjeeling with his younger daughter and his concubine. There in the Himalayan hill resort he rented a house and lived for years on money that had been donated for the Hankow uprising.

In Japan, meantime, the small animal who rode around on Kang's back was doing somewhat better. Liang, the more subtle and discreet of the two men, was able to avoid offending his Japanese hosts and continued his propaganda efforts with their help. He took pains to cultivate Count Okuma, giving him receptions and banquets.

By then Liang and Kang had developed an international readership with an endless appetite for new details about the evil Manchu empress. Until 1898 few people had been aware of her existence; now she was becoming one of the most sinister figures in Chinese history. In the United States this was boosted by the recurring phenomenon of the Yellow Peril, provoked by white politicians, labor organizers, religious fundamentalists, and landgrabbers. Combined with male fantasies about a woman ruler in an Oriental empire, this produced an odd visceral chemistry. The notion that the corrupt Chinese were dominated by a reptilian woman with grotesque sexual requirements tantalized American men.

For inspiration Liang and Kang dug deeper into the historical gossip of the Peking literati, who were so fond of likening Tzu Hsi to that familiar personification of evil, Empress Wu. Westerners unacquainted with the tradition of Chinese secret histories failed to recognize that much of what Kang and Liang were publishing about Tzu Hsi had been said before about Wu. One of their most popular themes was how Tzu Hsi, having murdered so many of her rivals, set out to poison Emperor Kuang Hsu. This theme was repackaged especially for the British audience by Kang's host in Singapore, Lim Boon-keng, who wrote under the name

Wen Ching, since "the reach of the Manchu knife is long." Not long enough.

George Morrison, who had the pleasure of dining with Lim in 1901, described him as "somewhat bumptious." Bland also was acquainted with Lim and influenced by him. He was described by Reginald Johnston, later the British tutor of Emperor Pu Yi, as a "distinguished" Chinese. In the 1890s he was one of the Malay peninsula's most influential men, the son of wealthy Singaporeans of Fukienese ancestry. Educated at the prestigious Raffles Institution in Singapore, he was the first Chinese in the colony to win a Queen's Scholarship, using it to study medicine, like Morrison, at the University of Edinburgh. After five years in Great Britain, including a year at Cambridge, he returned to Singapore in 1893 to start a medical practice and enter politics, helped along by his ability to be engaging in the five principal tongues of the island—Fukienese, Cantonese, Malay, English, and Tamil. In 1895, at age twenty-six, he was named to Singapore's Legislative Council. The following year, when he married the daughter of an associate of Sun Yat-sen's, Lim began publishing anti-Manchu propaganda.

His chief asset was the ability to move back and forth between cultures, turning Chinese ideas into colloquial Western journalism. His vehicle was the English-language magazine of which he was a founder, *Straits Chinese*, which tirelessly pushed the cause of overthrowing the empress dowager. When the saintly moonfaced Kang visited Singapore, Lim stuck with him around the clock.

Lim wrote a series of his own articles as Wen Ching for the Singapore *Free Press* about the tragedy of the Hundred Days Reform and the evil nature of Tzu Hsi, elaborating upon Kang and Liang's raw material. These were collected and published in book form in London under the title *The Chinese Crisis from Within*. In its preface Lim disclaimed any originality. He was indebted to friends, "some of whom have had very exceptional facilities of acquiring accurate information." However, he had to allow these well-placed friends to remain anonymous. To put his British readers at ease, Lim assured them that he had written these articles only for his "amusement."

He began with a brief summary of the career of Kang Yu-wei, referring to him as the "Nestor of Reform." "As far as the Chinese of today are concerned," he said, "the historical works of Kang Yu-wei mark the commencement of a new epoch in their intellectual history."

Turning to his main theme, he told Britons that Tzu Hsi was "vivacious, fiery, and high-spirited." As a young woman, she had distracted Emperor Hsien Feng from his duties as monarch. "While he was caressing the petulant [Yehenara], the Taiping rebels were capturing city after city, and the 'red-haired devils' were marching on his capital." Lim claimed that before Tzu Hsi's son died, Emperor Tung Chih actually had chosen an heir, one of the young Manchu princelings, but Tzu Hsi had selected Kuang Hsu instead. This "adopted child" of Tung Chih was still alive, Lim asserted, and was "one of the few liberal-minded and progressive princes of Pekin."

Taking up the question of whether Tzu An's death had been the result of foul play, Lim said, "The Chinese story is that she partook of some favourite [delicacy] specially prepared for her by [Yehenara's] relatives. She was seized with agonising pains soon after, and before the Court physicians could arrive she had expired." Why this had never before been reported Lim failed to explain.

Next he turned to sex in the Summer Palace. One fake eunuch, he said, was never enough for Tzu Hsi. Like Messalina and Catherine the Great, she wanted them by the bushel. "The young [Yehenara] exhibited her charms to a mighty concourse of eunuchs!" The real reason she dressed in elaborate costumes, he said, was to please her love slaves. "Proud of her charms, she spared no expense to set them forth. . . . After the death of her husband, she was obliged to exhibit her beauty to vulgar eyes within her palace."

To titillate his Victorian audience he confided that under ordinary circumstances there would not have been much risk of love play with an emasculated eunuch, but Tzu Hsi's chief eunuch, Li Lien-ying, was a fake. Li "had evaded the customary barbarity, and grew up to be the favourite chamberlain of [Yehenara]."

Lim revealed that Li Lien-ying ordered fancy Paris fashions from Shanghai so that he and Tzu Hsi could dress in these costumes and act in plays. "How charming for an Empress to act the slave and a chamberlain the slave's lover!" (As in all effective propaganda, there was an element of truth: Tzu Hsi often staged "amateur theatricals" in which she and her court ladies dressed in costumes, and sometimes the chief eunuch was obliged to join them; a photograph from 1903 shows one such stage set, with her chief eunuch looking extremely uncomfortable.)

Warming to his subject Lim said, "It was noticed that the eunuchs were mostly young men with fine physique and comely features. . . . The simple-minded folks of Pekin recognised amongst the eunuchs of the Western Palace the faces of many young men who shortly before were students preparing for their examinations." After brief periods of service, he said, these young men would suddenly disappear, the victims of "sudden deaths within the walls of the Imperial city."

The lasting image of Tzu Hsi with which Lim wished to leave the reader was of a poisonous and malevolent ruler: "She . . . did not hesitate to repeat in almost every detail the crimes and intrigues of Catherine de' Medici."

Lim's attacks were racist as well. Many upper-class Han Chinese re-garded the Manchu as an incorrigibly corrupt race, as is implicit in some of his remarks: "But what can you expect of a young Manchu female trained in the polluted and licentious seraglio of the dissolute Emperor Hsien Feng?"

While these allegations of sexual misconduct were amusing and stimu-lating to Western readers in an age of prudery, for Chinese and Manchu a widow's chastity was no laughing matter. In the dowager's case chastity was the bottom line. If she could be shown to have had affairs since the death of her husband, then she forfeited all rights to her exalted position. In previous generations, had such conduct been proved, she would imme-diately have been put to death. There is no reason to believe that had changed.

Tzu Hsi was widowed at the age of twenty-six. Since she lived until she was seventy-three, could she have remained absolutely celibate those forty-seven years? On the basis of evidence presently available, no one knows. The allegations are just fiction. More than any other member of the imperial family, she had to be scrupulous about appearances. She was more vulnerable than most women to attacks on her character, no matter how indirect. Her power at court was based primarily upon fulfilling her ceremonial role as the ultimate arbitrator, which required the *appearance* of absolute virtue. She was under constant observation by thousands of eunuchs like flies on the walls of the Forbidden City and Summer Palace: any deviation from virtue would have been reported immediately to real or potential enemies. Her legitimacy was sensitive simply to rumors of sexual license. She was surrounded by endlessly conspiratorial princes and mandarins and ubiquitous Censors ready to denounce anyone for a bribe or squeeze. It was therefore in self-defense alone that she was so strict about observing proper form and was angered by any slight directed at her. So it was only natural for her detractors to use sexual slander.

Proof was another matter. For example, had she carried on a love affair and become pregnant, as Kang's circle liked to assert, her many attendants would have known, because she was bathed and dressed by them every day of the week. For such a large number of eunuchs and maidservants to have kept such a secret in a place like the Forbidden City, in an atmosphere of profound corruption handed down as the heritage of thou-sands of years, is inconceivable.

For all its pomposity, the slander of Kang and company was just frivo-lous drinking-party character assassination typical of the *ming-shih*, not the sort of deadly serious charge that an ambitious Tudor courtier would have used in an attempt to bring down a queen. Westerners had no way of knowing the difference.

The clincher is that if the Gang of Eight or the Ironhats had ever been able to provide genuine evidence of her sexual misbehavior to the Clan Court, they could have swept Tzu Hsi out of the palace and put their own choice on the throne. So the idea that she romped with hundreds of false eunuchs, dropping babies here and there, is laughable.

Kang's slander in 1898 was the first time anyone had made such allegations about Tzu Hsi. When the American envoy, Charles Denby, completed a close study of her reputation nine years earlier in 1889, he wrote to Washington: "She has shown herself to be benevolent and economical. Her private character has been spotless."

Why then did this garish cartoon drawn by Kang and Liang, and put into urbane English by Lim, become the basis of every major biography of the dowager empress from that time on? In a word because it was so satisfying. Lim firmly fixed the idea that blame for all of China's ills, past and present, could be laid at the feet of this monster. No crime was too frightful, no conspiracy too bizarre, no murder too hideous. By universal agreement the woman who occupied China's dragon throne was indeed a reptile. Not a glorious Chinese dragon—serene, benevolent, good-natured, aquarian—but a cave-dwelling, fire-breathing Western dragon, whose very breath was toxic. A dragon lady. That explained everything, and justified everything.

It was now up to the professionals—Morrison, Bland and Backhouse—to turn this Chinese mudslinging into more elegant and pernicious "authenticated" history, adding many ingenious journalistic fabrications of their own, and in the process to help topple the dynasty.

CHAPTER SIXTEEN

The Sly Pornographer

Morrison had been in Peking a bit more than a year when the Hundred Days Reform collapsed. Even experienced Peking residents were caught off guard by the sudden violent crackdown, trying to grasp what had happened and what Kang's role had been. Robert Hart was practically alone in remaining calm and unflappable.

For most of that summer and during the bloody martyrdom of September, Morrison had been hunting snipe in the Yellow River delta or pursuing romances at secluded holiday homes in the Western Hills beyond Peking. When he returned he knew little of the events leading to the arrest and beheading of the Six Martyrs and was trying to catch up by interrogating his sources, all of them full of conspiracy theories. As the Peking correspondent of the *Times* of London Morrison had to kick the mud off his Wellies and perform an act of clairvoyance, in order to emerge overnight in the role of seer, able to declaim eruditely and at length about all aspects of the supposed coup and its players.

Morrison knew zero about Kang. This obscure character had appeared from nowhere to be spoken of as the leader of the Reform party, a prominent intellectual of the New China, an intimate of the young emperor, a close comrade of the Six Martyrs, the foremost enemy of the empress dowager, a celebrity in Hong Kong, a friend of Japan, a Chinese Messiah. At least that was what the more gullible Westerners in Peking were saying.

Assuming that Bland might know more than he did, Morrison wrote to his colleague in Shanghai asking about Kang's importance. His question reveals how little he knew. "Do you consider it conceivable that it was because simply he was a peaceful academic non-militant reformer that Kang Yu-wei stirred up this bitter revolt of the Empress Dowager and the subsequent spilling of blood?"

Bland was hardly in a position to set Morrison straight, having been the first to make Kang an international celebrity with his own grossly biased and inaccurate articles in the *Times*. Kang's mixture of hearsay and fiction suited Bland's anti-Manchu prejudices perfectly. Instead of becoming suspicious like Henry Cockburn and Frederick Bourne, Bland had flatly accepted what Kang told him and added to it his own erroneous assumptions about the empress dowager. So Bland's effort to enlighten Morrison had the opposite effect, filling the senior correspondent's head with false premises and reinforcing his own innate bias against Tzu Hsi. Morrison jumped to a conclusion that reveals a fundamental flaw in his thinking. He reasoned correctly that the crackdown on the reform movement, the shunting of Kuang Hsu to the sidelines, the return of the empress dowager, and the selection of Pu Chun as heir apparent, were all parts of a single conspiracy. But he identified this conspiracy with Tzu Hsi rather than with Prince Tuan and his Ironhats. Knowing nothing whatever about these obscure royals, and failing to understand that Manchu princes had a long history of intervention, Morrison saw them as no more than Tzu Hsi's "gang," and believed that she alone was behind the "dethronement" of Kuang Hsu and his reduction to a vegetable. "The best solution . . . now," Morrison wrote in a letter, "is the death by no means improbable of the Empress Dowager." He was satisfied that she was the cause of all this misery and that her murder would be liberating. Morrison persisted in this dogmatic view despite the evidence from Dr. Dethève that nobody had done anything wicked to Kuang Hsu, nobody had tortured him or kept him prisoner, his problems were all medical (with secondary psychic effects); his aunt might be, like Queen Victoria, an intimidating figure in the broadest sense, but the French physician had observed that she was genuinely anxious about her nephew and obviously was no threat to him in his own eyes. Although a doctor himself, and intimately informed of Dethève's analysis, Morrison detested Tzu Hsi the way he detested the French, irrationally. So his fixation on Tzu Hsi as an ogre made him misunderstand what was really happening. He failed to recognize Prince Tuan and his allies for what they were: a separate and dangerous political force rapidly moving into position to inflict appalling damage on China in one of the great false-steps of the age. Unprepared for what was afoot, Morrison misread all the signals and blundered backward into greatness.

This fixed idea became fundamental to all Morrison's subsequent reporting about China and the empress dowager over the next decade. While he would shift his personal political support discreetly from Viceroy Li to General Yuan, in harmony with British policy, he never reappraised his condemnation of Tzu Hsi. In Morrison's mind the only good dowager was a dead dowager. Between the lines the *Times* heartily endorsed this view.

Sir Robert Hart had taken to Morrison when they first met in 1897, as one clever but solitary romantic will take to another, but a coolness developed as Hart began to perceive Morrison's underlying cynicism, his contempt for the Chinese and their culture, and the ease with which he adjusted his ethics to advance his career. After Morrison's manipulative role in the Boxer affair in 1900 the two men rarely spoke.

Along with many other imperialists Hart had known, Morrison failed to grasp that the Western medicine they were forcing down China's throat was killing the patient, and they were neither willing nor able to alter the prescription; better to strap the old man down till he stopped kicking. England's reluctance to overextend herself by simply annexing China encouraged among Britons there a feeling of regal restraint and smug self-satisfaction, bolstered by an equal unwillingness to let Japan or Russia take over. As a journalist obliged to make sense of such ambiguities Morrison found it much easier to fix all blame for events in China on the stubborn, unsophisticated dowager empress, who understood little of the hopelessness of the situation.

At a time when precious little was known about China and few people had any experience of its perilous interior, Morrison seemed an ideal choice for the *Times*'s Peking correspondent. He was then thirty-six years old, tall, husky, broad shouldered and handsome, with more than his fair share of audacity. He was a marksman, a competent horseman, and he had walked and ridden across China to the northern border of Burma, a journey others had attempted only at their peril, usually being murdered along the way. For Morrison the dangers and glories of long-distance reconnaissance were a lifelong habit, and his combination of intelligence, charm, daring, and agreeable writing style won him the enthusiastic confidence of his peers. Because he felt imperial contempt for those he wrote about he never bothered to learn Chinese. Not even a Chinese-language expert like Henry Cockburn was free of these Victorian vices; when he left his Peking post in 1906 after ten years in China, Cockburn boasted that not once during all that time had a Chinese other than his servants ever set foot in his house.

Morrison's disdain for the language put him at the mercy of interpreters, translators, and intermediate sources. There was no way he could report or verify a story on his own. The *Times* had hired Morrison knowing that he did not speak Chinese; to be fair, gaining a mastery of the language would have required years of effort. Neither he nor the *Times* considered this a serious deficiency. As in the Consular Service, learning languages was for the lower orders. No real gentleman would have the time to waste on foreign tongues, and there were more than enough menials to handle that sort of thing. Morrison was there to report on affairs affecting British interests in China. As coadvocates of British imperialism the question of China's best interests simply did not occur to either Morrison or his editors. They were in lockstep with Whitehall.

When he first arrived in Peking, Morrison depended heavily on "the all-knowing" William Pethick, the American secretary of Viceroy Li, who passed on secret information. Morrison was always hurrying off by train to Tientsin to see Pethick. This explains the speed and accuracy of some of his early scoops. Sir Robert Hart was not aware that Pethick was feeding Morrison inside information about Li's dealings with the Russians and complimented the journalist on his "skill in extracting the truth from the evidence." If Hart had known, he could have warned Morrison that Pethick was not a disinterested or objective source but a singularly dedicated agent of Viceroy Li, who was in turn an extraordinarily gifted manipulator of the press. Morrison was being fed good information a lot of the time by Li and Pethick to win his confidence and to shape his attitudes, so that he and his newspaper could be subtly influenced. Li had other journalists he could use for outright lies or for shock effect. Morrison and the *Times* were special.

For day-to-day tittle-tattle about the Chinese and what they thought, Morrison simply relied on his landlord and houseboys. He had few opportunities to meet Manchu and Chinese on the inside track. Surprisingly, despite his dependence on Pethick (or perhaps because of it), he met Viceroy Li only once. He almost met Prince Ching by accident when the prince mistook his house for the Belgian legation.

What George Morrison needed was a reliable source, an assistant in Peking. For his first eighteen months he was constantly struggling with this problem. His was a lonely job, made lonelier by his private nature and by the urgent need to seem lucidly informed about everything.

It was ironic, then, that of all the Westerners in China he ultimately chose to put his trust in twenty-five-year-old Edmund Trelawny Backhouse. Edmund gratified many of Morrison's cravings at once: for intellectual companionship, for witty interpretation or translation, and for an inside track to the darkest secrets of the Manchu court.

They first became acquainted when young Edmund appeared at one of Hart's weekly lawn parties early in 1899. Backhouse, who had studied at Oxford and had a good command of Chinese, applied to join the Customs Service. Sir Robert wrote: "A very good candidate has come to Peking—a Mr. Ed. Backhouse—(with letters from Lord Salisbury, Duke of Devonshire, and Mr. Chamberlain) a son of a Director in Barclay & Co.'s, who knows Russian and Chinese and is aged 25; he would be a very desirable addition, but I can't afford it." The Customs Service was overburdened with staff.

A week later Edmund was taking breakfast with Morrison, who raved in his diary: "E. Backhouse to breakfast, scholar Winchester. Son of man whose portrait in *Vanity Fair* recently. Speaks, reads and writes Russian, Modern Greek. Knows 2500 Chinese characters . . . French, Spanish, Italian, German. Gifted man." They met frequently after that, for breakfast or dinner. For Morrison, tired to death of Peking routine, it was a stimulating change of pace.

Edmund Backhouse was extremely shy and ingrown, a gentle-faced and sensitive white mouse. He was ill suited to the manly legation antics of pony racing and picnics and had rented a house outside Peking, in the hills. The two men took a long donkey ride together that day to escape the city's dust and heat. It became a regular thing for Morrison. He would leave Peking at 9:00 A.M. and ride out into the hills to Edmund's cottage, to take tiffin together. They had much in common: both were bachelors with intellectual pretensions, interested in books and manuscripts, obsessed with sexual peccadillos of every sort, and both pretended to be stuck in Peking. At thirty-seven Morrison was old enough and experienced enough to see himself as the younger man's patron and what he needed more than a wife at that moment was a helpful ward. Edmund was the perfect foil, his shyness hiding extraordinary scholarship. Both were flattered by the other's attention.

Edmund revealed very little about himself. He said he was from a family of Lancaster Quakers who by the nineteenth century owned a family bank, and had interests in collieries and railways. His father, Jonathan, broke with his family's strict Quaker heritage by marrying into an Anglican family in Cornwall; his bride was Florence, the daughter of Sir John Salisbury-Trelawny. After the marriage, he sold the family banking business to the Barclays and became a director of Barclay Bank, living the life of a country squire. He was politically active and in due course was made a baronet for his services to the Liberal Unionist party.

Edmund was their eldest son. His siblings did well; two brothers became admirals, while a third was a successful soldier, and his sister, Harriet, married the lord-lieutenant of a shire. Edmund was educated at Winchester and went on to Merton College, Oxford, where he read classics and began studying Asian and European languages. A natural mimic, his literary and linguistic skills bordered on genius. He did not learn foreign languages the hard way, by toil and diligence, but picked them up spontaneously, through a quirk of memory and a gift of eye, ear, and tongue. In addition to English he eventually claimed to speak eleven languages: Chinese, Japanese, Mongol, Manchu, Russian, Greek, Pali, German, French, Italian, and Danish, most of which he claimed he could also read and write.

Morrison was not by any means naïve; he was, in fact, a harsh judge of character. He warned the *Times* that "we have had in our employ out here one man who was tried for arson, there not being sufficient evidence to convict him of murder which he had undoubtedly committed: another who had done seven years imprisonment, and a third [who had] been sentenced for embezzlement." It was not easy to find "good help" and good stringers in this part of the world, and this was one reason he was so pleased with Backhouse.

Edmund immediately began to translate Chinese news articles and official documents that Morrison used to compose letters and telegraphic dispatches to the *Times*. At last Morrison had his own Peking assistant, legman, interpreter, and expert on Manchu esoterica.

Thanks to their collaboration, Morrison was able to stop relying so heavily on Pethick and Bland, and his ability to interpret events in China was greatly improved by daily access through Edmund to court documents and Chinese newspapers. Unlike Pethick and Bland, who held strong political views, Backhouse seemed utterly aloof, correct and courteous in all things. He was the perfect amanuensis, even graciously drafting portions of Morrison's articles for him, particularly those having to do with court customs and personalities. Edmund had the peculiar ability to change himself at a moment's notice into whatever Morrison wanted. That he might also be insane did not become apparent until much later. Morrison never hired Backhouse formally nor paid him for his work. Edmund was well off, receiving some three hundred pounds sterling a year in remittances from his father, not an inconsiderable sum at the time, especially in China where a man could live very well on that provided he was prudent. As a correspondent of the *Times* Morrison was making only £500 a year when they met, from which he also had to pay professional expenses, including dinner parties for legation friends. This collaboration in which money played no part may have been suggested by Edmund to ingratiate himself, as he had been accustomed to doing at Oxford. However, Morrison did repay him with gifts, loans, and by entering into book-buying deals in which he acquired what he thought were valuable Chinese books and manuscripts from or through his brilliant young friend.

Since arriving in Peking, Morrison had begun collecting rare Chinese books and manuscripts, along with books about China in English and other languages, building a library that could be sold someday to pay for his retirement. Since he could not read Chinese, he relied on Backhouse to help him select ancient manuscripts. Morrison was investing serious money based on his friend's recommendations. Only Edmund was certain of their provenance.

The relationship was cordial, even affectionate. They would sit up late into the night, Backhouse translating documents and Morrison turning them into dispatches. Edmund's letters to Morrison breathe loyalty. "My Dear Morrison, Many thanks for your note, please don't bother to get me any chocolate as I don't want any." "My Dear Morrison, Very many thanks for the jam you have kindly sent. Please let me pay for it when I see you."

Backhouse made it a point to be in Peking whenever Morrison was away and kept his friend and patron supplied with the background and scuttlebutt that are a foreign correspondent's stock-in-trade. He became Morrison's eyes and ears: "My dear Morrison, Thank you very much for your exceedingly kind letter. . . . I hope you have had a pleasant time at home, and that you will come back looking much better than when you went away. I was lunching at Bishop Scott's the other day, and he was speaking of the murder of Brooks in Shantung. . . . He does not seem very well satisfied with the efforts made so far to capture the murderers."

Edmund was sharing his home outside Peking with G. P. Peachey, a student interpreter forced to resign from the British legation following a misplaced romance. Inspired by reading about Morrison's trek across China a few years earlier, Backhouse and Peachey set off together for Mongolia, not to return to Peking until June 1900.

While Backhouse was a timid recluse who avoided legation life, Morrison was drawn to it like a tomcat. He was fascinated and at the same time repelled by his compatriots, for most of whom he felt contempt. Peking was a backwater, and as such collected its share of human debris. On the one hand Morrison needed a continual flow of information from his peers in the legations, and on the other he craved female admiration in a capital with a limited supply of Western women. "The only maidens who ever show any fondness for me are the elderly rejects with yearnings and false teeth, who suffer from indigestion, with clammy hands and . . . [are] quite unsuitable for marriage." He protested that he had tried everything from masturbation to whorehouses and was bored with the former and wary of the latter. As a doctor and a journalist he took careful note of those in the Western community who were currently suffering from syphilis or gonorrhea. Enough of the men consulted him informally so that he knew more than he should about the women. "G. came in smelling of chloroform. He has had a bubonic swelling in his groin and been under . . . treatment . . . and is getting better. Some Chinese lady gave him this present."

A string of inconsequential love affairs was meticulously catalogued in his diaries. One was with "Maysie," the golden-haired daughter of a millionaire American senator. Traveling the Far East with a chaperone whose duties were nominal, "Maysie" bestowed herself upon Morrison and many others. Her candor and his excitement fill three pages of his diary.

Accustomed as long as she can remember to play with herself every morning even when unwell, even after passing the night in bed with a man. Seduced by . . . a doctor in the French restaurant in San Francisco known as the Hen and Chickens or Poultry or some such. Pregnant. . . . Went to Washington got out of difficulty . . . slept constantly with Congressman Gaines. . . . Four miscarriages. "Kissed" [Morrison's euphemism for cunnilingus] all the way over in the *Siberia* after leaving Honolulu by [the captain]. Had for days in succession by Martin Egan. . . . Mrs. Goodnow had told [Maysie] that once kissed by a woman she would never [again] wish to be kissed by a man. Her desire now is to get a Japanese maid to accompany her back to America and to kiss her every morning.

The sex life of Peking fascinated him, and he made frequent vulgar entries in his diary. "Lunched with Simpson to meet Bredon [Hart's brother-in-law] a gentleman for whom he has much sympathy and has decorated with the longest pair of horns worn by any cuckold in China!" "Dined with Bredon family party. Lily [Bredon] and Hebrew Simpson [his slurring reference to Bertram Lenox-Simpson] who is suffering very badly from syphilis. . . . Lily has syphilis presumably." "Mrs. Hill has had most of the men here. Likes nothing but to be between the sheets with a man." "Lucy [Gray, wife of the British legation doctor] says next to being an actress she would like to be an independent fast woman changing her lovers every 10 days." "F. and Mrs. J. P. Grant: They were . . . in bed when J. P. came in: 'Get out Sir! How dare you come in you little bald headed scoundrel,' [said F.] His language simply paralyzed Grant." "Jamieson tells me that [the American minister's] stenographer has gone and married an American hooker and has been transferred to Manila in consequence." "Madame Legendre [wife of a French author and doctor] when in Peking was bitten by a dog that has since developed rabies. She has to undergo Pasteur treatment at Tomsk. And what about Casenave [Maurice Casenave, French diplomat] people are now asking?"

He was a voyeur entranced by lesbianism: "She doesn't like men but when she loves women, she loves beautiful women." "She was a notorious lesbian who was expelled from the Presbyterian Ladies' College." "I see that Mrs. S and she have recognised each other and furtively I find them together." "Perhaps she employs the Japanese [maid] to suck her as do so many women of evil instincts."

Sir Robert Hart unwisely chatted with Morrison about his private life, and Morrison kept tabs in his diary: "I.G. till very late being enamoured of Mrs. Key." "Dined with the I.G. and saw his sex mania for young girls."

While Morrison kept Backhouse amused with the latest legation gossip, Edmund responded in kind with exotic tales of Manchu decadence, gleaned from his acquaintances in the *ming-shih*. The tantalizing charges of sexual misconduct made against the dowager empress by Wild Fox Kang intrigued both men, and once Edmund perceived Morrison's fascination with the presumed dark side of the dowager he exerted himself to dig up and recount more sensational accusations.

Outwardly, Backhouse looked as innocent as an acolyte and was so carefully mannered and meek that his behavior at times seemed masochistic. This was his way of hiding his real nature, which was so wildly outrageous that he had been forced to keep it submerged like Renfield's hiding his appetite for flies and roaches. Edmund's hands were well shaped and feminine, with long tapering fingers, but they moved nervously with excitement or tension as he talked late into the night. His most remarkable features were his eyes, which almost gave him away. Their expression changed constantly, turning instantly from scholarly meditation into a frenzy of religious ecstasy, then into the exuberant lust of a young satyr, then narrowing into the greedy cunning of an obscene old roué as he warmed to his erotic accounts of the empress dowager's performing in orgies with her false eunuchs.

With Morrison the sharp-eyed professional Edmund was always careful to make it clear that these were stories he heard from well-placed sources among the *ming-shih*, Chinese and Manchu scholars with jobs at court or responsibilities in the palace who knew about such things firsthand. Since arriving in Peking he had mingled with the *ming-shih*, frequenting their favorite theaters and wineshops and, thanks to his language skill and similar sexual tastes, becoming accepted by the more eccentric elements. Through them Backhouse claimed access to secret, high-level Chinese sources that corroborated Kang's charges of sexual misconduct by the dowager.

The *ming-shih* gossips and secret-history writers were not the only source for dowager slander. Morrison and Lim Boon-keng were friends who had attended the same medical school; Lim filled Morrison's head with dowager abuse. From various clues it seems that Backhouse knew Lim also but did not get along. After Lim provided Backhouse with much of his original material for attacking the empress dowager in his biography, Backhouse turned on him and denounced Lim as a pretentious Oriental overstuffed with Western education:

Drawing on a typically Babu store of "Western learning," this writer compares the empress to Circe, Semiramis, Catherine de Medici, Messalina, Fulvia, and Julia Agrippina; quoting Dante and Rossetti to enforce his arguments, and leavening his vituperation with a modicum of verifiable facts sufficient to give to his narrative something of vraisemblance . . . his work is almost valueless.

There was no way that Lim or anyone else could compete with the eloquent Backhouse when it came to poisoning the dowager's reputation and slyly filling in the pornographic details.

What nobody knew was that Edmund was the product of a bizarre and miserable childhood that would have made fascinating study for a Freudian psychiatrist. He complained bitterly that "my childish years were ideally unhappy, for I was born of wealthy parents who had everything they wanted and were miserable. . . . I heard not a kind word nor received a grudging dole of sympathy but hate and hate alone throughout the live long days, the while [my mother] mocked my childish tears." "Her rages," he said, "were veritable cataclysms." His father once thrashed him, and his younger brother Roger "was always very rude to me."

They all hated him because not only was Edmund a liar, a cheat, and a thief, but at the same time ostentatiously homosexual, a combination that seems to have been a bit more than his parents could handle. None of these attributes was unusual among his contemporaries, singly or in combination, but Edmund had the additional disadvantage of being functionally insane. He was brilliant but highly unstable, a true exotic with an extraordinary fantasy world and long bouts of psychotic depression.

At age eight he was sent to St. George's, Ascot, a school run with excessive passion by the Reverend Herbert Sneyd-Kynnersley, who relished beating bare buttocks. There the already fey Edmund was taught to be a perfect gentleman and a compliant catamite of one upperclassman after another. He went on to Winchester, where he was judged by his contemporaries to be a liar, a thief, and unaccountable. At Merton College, Oxford, he failed to complete his studies, squandering his inheritance desperately trying to become part of Oscar Wilde's circle of homosexuals, and being scorned and used by them. He confided to Morrison only that he was a friend of Alfred Douglas, whose seduction by Wilde and subsequent love affair had been one of the great scandals of London in 1895.

After a severe nervous breakdown during his last term, Edmund suddenly dropped out of Oxford in the summer of 1895 and fled England, ducking £23,000 in unpaid bills and escaping an embarrassing scandal. He was forced to declare bankruptcy to dodge his debts, leaving his father to face the creditors. The debts were eventually cleared to rescue the family name, with payment of only a tenth of the claims. Edmund's whereabouts during the next three years remain a mystery, but he eventually made his way to China, arriving in Peking early in 1899.

With the final settlement of his debts that year, and his father's unwillingness to continue supporting him in style, Edmund became a remittance man, paid not to return home. He was obliged to seek fame and fortune by his own devices. The lack of a more agreeable financial settlement with his father was a bone that he gnawed on all his life.

When Edmund saw Sir Robert Hart about employment with the Customs Service, Hart noted that he carried with him letters of recommendation from various peers of the realm. It is uncertain how he might have obtained such letters, or whether they were genuine. Whatever the case, in his unpublished memoirs written in the last year of his life he described a love affair he claimed to have had with a prime minister in the 1890s.

> He took me into his beautiful library and showed me Napoleonic literature with broadsheets and caricatures, letters to Marie Louise from the emperor, and to Pope Pius VII. Among his trophies in his study were two Eton birch rods decked in the light blue colours of the school, reminiscent of boyhood floggings. It has been said that he enjoyed reciprocal flogging like Swinburne . . . but he never suggested the procedure in his intercourse with me. My readers will agree that, when a young man is privileged to have sexual intercourse with a Prime Minister, any proposal regarding the "modus operandi" must emanate from the latter and as far as I was concerned, it was the case of being "le locature" (the tenant as the Frenchman wittily put it) and passivity was the invariable order of the day.

If nothing else, Backhouse was a clever raconteur.

These unpublished memoirs are part of a pornographic literary tradition on which Edmund had fed deeply as an adolescent, typified by the *Venice Letters,* a collection of letters written to Edmund's cousin, Charles Masson Fox, by an eccentric Englishman named Frederick William Rolfe, who used the pseudonym Baron Corvo. Rolfe was a drifter who made his living as a writer, painter, musician, photographer, schoolmaster, student priest, and male prostitute. He planned a career in the Catholic church but was judged unsuitable because he spent his time photographing young Italian boys dressed only in loincloths, and ran up huge debts. He settled in Italy, where he became dependent upon the kindness of strangers, sponging off lovers and patrons the rest of his life. When he wore out his welcome he repaid his benefactors by threatening embarrassing lawsuits to extort more payments. He was a prominent eccentric in Venice, living in an old palazzo on the Grand Canal, traveling to parties reclined on a leopard skin in a gondola manned by four oarsmen. It was there that he met Edmund's cousin, Charles Masson Fox, and struck up an arrangement. Afterward Rolfe and Fox began a curious correspondence of which only Rolfe's letters survive, eventually published privately as the *Venice Letters.* They vividly describe a rampage of erotic adventures Rolfe claimed to have had with a number of boys and men. In return for these letters Fox sent Rolfe money, usually in very small amounts of several pounds at a time. Fox and his circle in London and Cornwall were thus provided with freshly written pornography for their amusement.

As a boy Edmund Backhouse spent time with his grandparents in Cornwall, where he fell into the company of his cousin Charles, seven years his senior. It is uncertain whether Edmund ever met Rolfe, but he was immersed from an early age in the privately circulated homosexual pornography of which Corvo is just one example.

Whatever his quirks and perversities, Edmund was a born storyteller who found his metier unexpectedly in imperial China on the eve of revolution, slyly mingling pornography and journalism like a child stirring nightsoil for fertilizer. Throughout his life he seemed to experience exquisite satisfaction in relating mischievous tales of Tzu Hsi's feminine perversity to anyone who would listen. In his early days in Peking he would embroider upon a scandalous tidbit picked up from the *ming-shih* and float the rumor with Morrison and others. The gossip would percolate through the legations, gaining widespread acceptance. Edmund would then corroborate and enlarge upon his rumor with the discovery of new "facts." He became fascinated by the Chinese tradition of secret pornographic histories and biographies and began collecting them to stir into his repertoire. As he became more proficient with Chinese materials, he produced phony "official" documentation (diaries and memorials), critiqued his own counterfeit sources, pointed out the flaws in others' theories (such as Lim's), and led his credulous audience to the inescapable conclusion that only Backhouse was correct.

Edmund's counterfeit version of events inside the Forbidden City developed extraordinary complexity over the years. He started with a mildly suggestive picture of "an Oriental Trianon" and then went on to build an entire secret world of false eunuchs and orgies, bastard children, murdered concubines, on a scale comparable to Jonathan Swift but deliberately made believable. His historical caricature of Tzu Hsi grew to include the whole range of nymphomania, debauchery, perversion, and homicide associated traditionally with Empress Wu. Many of these allegations were first printed in the *Times* without attribution to Backhouse; newspaper readers assumed that these were well-researched, well-founded facts or inside knowledge coming straight from the pen of the well-known George Morrison. The truth, of course, is that Backhouse made up these stories and provided them as "informed gossip" to Morrison, who unwarily passed them along in dispatches to the *Times*. Newspapers around the world then adapted these stories, giving them currency far and wide. When the time came for Backhouse to publish his own biographies of the dowager, he often credited the *Times* as his authoritative source to back up assertions that he said were made by Chinese officials or that he had discovered in secret Manchu diaries. It was all an elaborate exercise in scholastic flimflam that only a man of extraordinary patience and wit could have sustained.

Westerners in Peking, including Morrison and Hart, always were pointing out what a blessing it would be to have an insider's view of what was really going on in the Manchu court. Although Backhouse did not contract with Bland to collaborate on their first book till after Tzu Hsi's death in 1908, it seems that he actually began composing many years earlier, perhaps as early as 1900, inspired by Wild Fox Kang and Lim Boon-keng. All the time he was chatting with Morrison late into the night and noticing his friend's fascination with the dowager's presumed secret life, Edmund was busy conceiving his masterpiece. The notion of blending a scholarly Western biography with Chinese pornographic fiction suited Edmund's eccentric tastes, his sense of humor, his prodigious literary talents, and his genius at mimicry—and represents his great contribution to literature: the hoax of the demon dowager. Beginning with the secret histories of ancient kingdoms, he resolved to create a "secret diary" supposedly kept by a former senior official of Tzu Hsi's own household. Originally he contrived the diary in English, plagiarizing freely from Chinese and Western sources. Portions of it were then translated into Chinese and copied out in ideographs by Edmund's cronies, using a running script appropriate to a diary. It is extraordinary that his co-author Bland never sought to look closely at Edmund's source materials; when others tried to examine them later, Edmund explained that they had been lost, stolen, sold, or destroyed by fires that conveniently wiped out his "collection" periodically.

His two biographies of Tzu Hsi written with Bland made their intricate pornography palatable to Westerners by describing an "alien" way of life no reader was expected to condone. Readers were justified in examining these "shocking" revelations because Edmund presented them as fragments of the secret diary of a high Manchu court official, to be read with clinical detachment like a zoologist's report on the repulsive behavior of a distant species of orangutans.

As scholarly works the books are elegant examples of Edwardian prose. The reader is constantly comforted by the air of authority and the clever use of rhetorical devices. Once you realize that what you are reading is *not* true but part of an intricate hoax, that cleverness is multiplied.

In all Edmund Backhouse spent nearly forty-five years in Peking, much of the first half devoted to his studies and falsifications of the Manchu court, much of the second half to encouraging others to do the same. Eventually his sanity became less and less secure, and in his final months he revealed himself in two exuberant and deranged memoirs bearing a strong resemblance to the *Venice Letters*, but far superior in scope and imagination. The most curious sections of these manic memoirs are the passages describing Edmund's purported love affair with Tzu Hsi. Although these manuscripts have never been published or closely studied by most China scholars, nothing else so clearly exposes his madness, and this is his undoing.

"My intercourse with Tzu Hsi," wrote Backhouse, "started in 1902 and continued until her death. I had kept an unusually close record of my secret association with the empress and others, possessing notes and messages written to me by Her Majesty, but had the misfortune to lose all these manuscripts and papers."

The extravagance of this wanton sexual burlesque with the dowager and the grotesque details of their encounters make it painfully apparent that they are the inflamed sexual fantasy of a mind completely unhinged. What began many decades earlier as ingenious, mischievous satire—disguised as history—now degenerated into lunatic graffiti.

How did Backhouse bring off his hoax in the first place? What led generations of China scholars to take him seriously? The answer is collusion. Of course Backhouse had help from George Morrison who gave him his start, and from J.O.P. Bland who was so gullible he believed everything he was told by Kang Yu-wei and Backhouse as long as it was anti-Manchu. Thanks to Morrison and Bland, all the basic Backhouse inventions about Tzu Hsi were published in the *Times* as a matter of record, a record that Backhouse could cite for authority without revealing that he was citing himself. But in their encouragement of Backhouse, Morrison and Bland were not alone. As foreign correspondents they were only the sharpened end of a state of mind. There was collusion in Western prejudices about China—readers wanted to believe such things. In Peking at the turn of the century it was the style; just about everybody was falsifying the record. Take for example the many ways the Boxer siege was falsified by Morrison and others to pin the blame on Tzu Hsi.

CHAPTER SEVENTEEN

Weed People

The Boxer Uprising and the so-called "'siege of the legations" in 1900 have always been portrayed as parts of a lunatic plot backed by empress dowager Tzu Hsi and as a prime example of Chinese treachery. Few events in Asian history are more familiar to Westerners and more misunderstood. Everything about it is wrong. In the past the Boxers were thought to be a mass movement growing out of China's traditional secret societies, martial artists who rose in rebellion against the Manchu but were diverted into fighting Foreign Devils instead, leading to the famous siege. This was not the case at all. In recent years a reappraisal of the Boxers has shown them to be a largely spontaneous grassroots phenomenon of peasants made invulnerable by magic—not so they could overthrow the Manchu regime but to attack the hated Chinese Christian converts they blamed for their misery and to expel all foreign missionaries from China.

If the Boxers were not rebelling, were they part of a conspiracy against foreigners backed by Tzu Hsi? And did the siege actually happen the way we are told—brave Western defenders holding off waves of maddened Boxers in red headbands until they were rescued by an international expedition from eight nations? Or was this all buncombe contrived to hide blunders, advance careers, prevent the discovery of profound crimes, and put the blame on Tzu Hsi? Here again the legend is completely false.

While it is now certain that there *was* a conspiracy in which the Boxers originally were intended to play an important part, most of them knew nothing about it, and Tzu Hsi was as much its victim as Emperor Kuang Hsu. More disturbing is the discovery that the celebrated siege was greatly exaggerated, if not entirely imaginary. It did not happen the way we are told; the definitive account published in the *Times*, it turns out, was deliberately falsified from beginning to end by Morrison, who kept a secret and entirely different chronicle of events in his diary. Most of the killing before and during the siege was carried out by Westerners, not Chinese. The empress dowager's military commanders spent most of the siege trying to stop the shooting (not the other way around), and to cap it all the Boxers played no part in the siege whatever. They were not even in Peking at the time.

While the legations themselves provoked the crisis, wildly overreacted, and then lied ingeniously to cover it up, the real manipulator behind the scenes was Viceroy Li Hung-chang, whose role in the whole affair has never been seen before. It was Li who craftily goaded the Foreign Powers into intervening in China militarily by spreading completely false accounts of horrifying Chinese atrocities to newspapers in the West, as part of his continuing effort to undermine the Ironhats and to regain his lost prestige. The Allied commanders, under orders to exploit the situation, started a shooting war with China not to rescue the legations but to seize as much territory as possible before the empire fell apart, which they expected at any moment. Far from being an example of Chinese treachery, therefore, the Boxer affair is a monument to Western hypocrisy.

To begin at the beginning, there was a conspiracy afoot. It was devised by the Ironhats, but no conspiracy is absolute or predestined; chance and opportunity play major roles in the most determined plan. The Ironhats were incompetent when it came to putting grand strategies into practice; they had no clear-cut idea how to proceed and merely moved forward with the changing situation. All they knew was that they wanted to remove all foreigners and foreign influences from China and to turn the clock back to past glory.

The idea of adopting the Boxers to create a secret irregular force, then using this deniable medium to drive the foreigners out, seems to have occurred first to the most experienced military commander in the Ironhat faction, General Li Ping-heng. In the past, rural uprisings in China had always been subversive, challenging the authority of the Manchu regime. The violence southeast of Peking in the 1890s was different. It was directed at foreign missionaries or their local converts and was in no way anti-Manchu. With the right encouragement and discreet guidance it could become a mass anti-foreign movement across North China without seeming to have any connection to the Manchu regime. Western outrage and military reprisals could be avoided by placing all the blame on the Chinese peasantry. Or so the Ironhats thought.

It all started in Shantung Province, the province southeast of Chihli that juts out into the China Sea. Western Shantung was a densely populated, desperately poor agricultural region, flat, hard, treeless, and saline, leached out by the droughts and floods of the Yellow River, "China's Sorrow."

Here men were driven to banditry by natural disasters and calamities caused by Foreign Devils, including the massive unemployment of bargemen on the Grand Canal brought about by the introduction of steamships and railways. Many of these men joined the secret societies and bandit gangs that were part of Shantung's unruly border region, smuggling salt and opium or preying on travelers. This was China's Sherwood Forest, the setting for the great novel of brigands and superheroes, *Water Margin*, and other romantic epics acted out by wandering troupes or puppeteers at village fairs and temples. The disintegration caused to Shantung by the Sino-Japanese War, the financial crisis that followed and disbandment of penniless soldiers, added to the misery of countryfolk so that by 1895, following another bad harvest, they were in a state of insurrection.

Out of a total population of over four hundred million, only a tiny fraction of rural Chinese in the 1890s had ever seen a white man. Villagers were by nature open and friendly toward strangers, but in times of crisis there was a dread of foreign things. Western missionaries and their converts were thought to pollute the air and to disturb the *feng-shui* spirits that inhabit all things. Good luck could be attained only by making the *feng-shui* happy. Foreign houses and buildings, particularly churches with tall spires, were thought to irritate the spirits, as did telegraph lines and railway tracks that cut through ancestral burial grounds. When spirits were annoyed, there were disasters. When foreign engineers or missionaries were annoyed, there were diplomatic protests. The idea that foreigners were disrupting Chinese society by introducing alien drugs and alien religion, along with foreign products, was a powerful propaganda weapon. Thirty years earlier Prince Kung had told the British minister, "Take away your missionaries and your opium, and all will be well."

By 1870 some two hundred fifty Catholic missionaries could claim a Chinese flock of four hundred thousand. The three hundred fifty Protestant missionaries, who spent the greater part of their time quarreling among themselves, could claim only six thousand converts. As they moved ever deeper into the interior, starting schools and churches, orphanages and clinics, the missionaries came into direct conflict with gentry and villagers, interfering with traditional practices and injecting politics of a new and alien variety. In western Shantung, where the population was so poor that there were few gentry, the conflict was between villagers and Christian converts. Missionaries forbade their converts to take part in any form of ancestor worship or to contribute financially to rituals and festivals that in a village were the only distraction from a life of toil. This set Chinese Christians apart and increased the burden on everyone else. Anxious to save souls and to keep account books, missionaries often were satisfied with converts who were the dregs of society—freeloaders referred to contemptuously by Chinese as "Rice Christians"—and uncharitably demanded preferential treatment for them in lawsuits and disputes over land.

At Ningpo, where Robert Hart had his first job in China, nearly all the Protestant Chinese converts were in the direct employ of the missionaries who had "converted" them. By professing Christianity they got jobs and job security.

By the 1890s resentment of these Rice Christians and their missionary sponsors was being deliberately provoked by clever, widely distributed anti-Christian propaganda, given away free to customers of pawnshops in the provinces of Kiangsi, Hupeh, Honan, Hunan, Shantung, and Chihli. A number of pamphlets portrayed the private lives and religious practices of Christian missionaries in a way guaranteed to incense Chinese readers. Robert Hart described one pamphlet as "very clever . . . a queer mixture of truth and error. . . . It is evidently the work of a well-read man, and I have no doubt but that the literati have it, and many more like it, on their shelves." It accused Christians of indulging in incest, sodomy, emasculating little boys, and using magic to accomplish perverted ends. These practices were also said to be performed by Chinese Christians on other Chinese. The brutal effectiveness of the pamphlet can be judged from this extract:

> During the first three months of life the anuses of all [Christian] infants—male and female—are plugged up with a small hollow tube, which is taken out at night. They call this "retention of the vital essence." It causes the anus to dilate so that upon growing up sodomy will be facilitated. At the juncture of each spring and summer, boys procure the menstrual discharge of women, and smearing it on their faces, go into Christian churches to worship. They call this "cleansing one's face before paying one's respect to the Holy one," and regard it as one of the most venerative rituals by which the Lord can be worshipped.

Chinese were told that missionaries used drugs to enlist converts, made medicines from fetuses, and opened orphanages only to collect infants for eating. Tzu Hsi seems to have believed some of these charges. She told a lady-in-waiting: "Missionaries also take the poor Chinese children and gouge their eyes out, and use them as a kind of medicine." Her comments reflect how very little Tzu Hsi understood about the Christian religion and how much she relied upon her advisers to shape her thinking and attitudes. Although she was curious, she did not have an analytical mind. If told something often enough, she accepted it as true. Her attitudes were normal in China at that time, shared by the Confucian scholar-gentry and

Hanlin scholars like. The brilliant Tseng Kuo-fan had despised all foreigners, Christians in particular. Cooped up all her life in the Forbidden
City or the Summer Palace there was no reason why Tzu Hsi should
doubt what she was told by her ministers and generals. She only saw the
world through their eyes.

The printing and distribution of such pamphlets to far-flung provinces
required significant financial resources. No one knows who was underwriting this propaganda campaign but, stimulated in this way, antiforeign
and anti-Christian fury grew as the nineteenth century ended; missionaries and converts were attacked and murdered and mission property
destroyed. During the 1890s antimissionary outbreaks occurred in all eighteen provinces. Missionaries were accused of being spies, profiteering
merchants, and hedonists.

In 1891 antimissionary riots swept the lower Yangtze Valley, followed
in 1895 by anti-Christian riots in Szechwan, and the massacre later that
year of eleven men, women, and children in Fukien. Great Britain threatened to intervene militarily if the Chinese government failed to punish the
regional officials taken to be responsible. Peking gave in and sacked and
degraded the governor of Szechwan and six other mandarins, executed
thirty-one peasants, and imprisoned or banished thirty-eight others.
Edicts were issued making it clear that further attacks on foreign missionaries, their churches, and their Chinese converts would not be tolerated.
Other edicts warned local officials that they would be held responsible if
there were further incidents. These efforts to placate the West were made
by a government still in the control of moderates. The message was loud
and clear that from here on Christians would be given imperial protection.
Both Emperor Kuang Hsu and the dowager were firm on this point.

The result in places like rural western Shantung was that local officials
became reluctant to risk any confrontation with missionaries or their
flocks, and there was a flood of conversions by Chinese who were seeking
missionary protection from local enemies or trying to avoid prosecution
by local officials for a wide range of crimes. Whole bandit communities
put themselves under the protection of Catholic priests. Village rivals
facing lawsuits had themselves baptized in order to gain legal advantage
in court. Recognizing a golden opportunity for more conversions, Catholic priests defended converts willy-nilly, pressing their cases before government officials, or had pressure applied in provincial capitals and even
through the bishop to legations in Peking. Every demonstration of Christian influence attracted more converts, many of them bad characters.
Shantung's governor, General Li Ping-heng, called them "weed people."
A vicious cycle began in which individual missionaries were encouraged
to abuse their temporal power to increase their heavenly dividends. Confident of the military backing of their home governments, many Catholic

and Protestant missionaries felt smug about their growing influence and superiority to all things Chinese. The Manchu capitulated to a demand that Catholic bishops in China enjoy the same rank as viceroys like Li Hung-chang.

Shantung was becoming a German sphere of influence, and the worst offenders there were German Catholics who represented a powerful voting bloc at home. In 1896 there were widespread attacks on Chinese Christians in Shantung by a group calling itself the Big Swords, which operated in the bandit-ridden southwestern districts bordering Kiangsu. This incensed German Catholics so it became a matter of urgent concern to Governor Li Ping-heng to determine if the Big Swords were a secret society like the White Lotus—a proscribed association dedicated to the ouster of the Manchu—or just a Robin Hood–style village vigilante group. Because Big Swords practiced similar rituals, missionaries thought they were a resurgence of the White Lotus. One of China's oldest secret societies, going back to the twelfth century, the White Lotus had played an important part in opposing the occupation of China by the Mongol khans in the thirteenth and fourteenth centuries. Later it supported the Ming Dynasty against the Manchu and launched two insurrections, in 1774 and 1794, in an attempt to expel the Manchu. In 1813 White Lotus forces tried to seize the Forbidden City and nearly succeeded. Each failure led to grisly reprisals, and by the mid-nineteenth century so many White Lotus leaders had been executed that the organization survived only underground, though its members continued to plot against the dynasty.

The White Lotus became a model for many other secret societies. It was at root a peasant association with strong Buddhist and Taoist underpinnings. Taoism attracted the intelligent and the ignorant; its ambiguity, metaphysics, and serenity appealed to scholars, artists, and poets, while ordinary people took its occult precepts literally as a poor man's guide to immortality. These magical rituals built confidence among impoverished members and attracted recruits during times of hardship. To protect themselves and their families and to attain spiritual harmony, White Lotus members practiced martial arts from Tai Chi to Wushu. Some leaders had extraordinary skill, agility, and power, verging on the supernatural. Others specialized in shamanistic incantations to enlist the help of Chinese gods, casting magic beans to raise spirit armies. Peasant recruits believed they could develop a state of grace if they worked hard, ate the correct foods, conditioned their minds, and recited appropriate incantations. By swallowing amulets they could levitate, become invisible, and be immune to poison or spears.

However, Governor Li Ping-heng discovered that the Big Swords were different from the White Lotus in very important ways. The Big Swords were not conspiratorial, simply a village defense force of farmers and local landlords fighting an epidemic of bandits, many of them posing as Christians to avoid retribution. Instead of being anti-Manchu, they were anti-Christian and antiforeign. They had nothing in common with anti-Manchu cults except the martial arts, which they learned from itinerant masters in village boxing fields and used in the event of bandit attacks or other troubles. This training involved nothing supernatural, only a form of hand-to-hand fighting that toughened the body to make it difficult to penetrate with ordinary knives, swords, and spears. Some incantations and charms were used, but only to create a positive attitude for extreme effort.

Because they had no anti-Manchu political objectives and no link to subversive sects, the Big Swords were tolerated by Governor Li Ping-heng as an unofficial rural militia. The governor had been ordered to exterminate bandits in southwestern Shantung, and delegated the job to a local Manchu official named Yu Hsien. Both the governor and Magistrate Yu Hsien were impressed by the success of the Big Swords in bandit suppression, relieving pressure on the overstretched provincial army. This gave them the idea that they might use the Big Swords as the nucleus for a secret army of irregulars with discreet Manchu approval.

Earlier in his long career, while still a military officer in the mid-1880s, Li Ping-heng had distinguished himself in the Sino-French War, contributing greatly to the Chinese victory at Liangshan. While in Indochina he had observed the operations of an army of guerrilla-partisans, the Black Flags, a triad operating on the border between Kwangsi and Tonkin that made huge profits smuggling. The Black Flags were enlisted by Li's commander, General Tso Tsung-tang, as a secret guerrilla army to help the Chinese fight the French. They infiltrated French positions and operated freely behind French lines, with the aid of Chinese businessmen in Hanoi, striking and vanishing with the ease of a criminal organization, which is what they were. To encourage them the Manchu offered a bounty for every French head. Operating invisibly and outside the law, the Black Flags were able to carry out sabotage and assassinations without provoking international repercussions directly against Peking. They were deniable.

As governor of Shantung during the Sino-Japanese War, Li Ping-heng closely observed the defeat of Chinese regular army forces in his area and gave the lessons much thought. At the time Li was already sixty-five years old, not a hotheaded, inexperienced princeling but a seasoned administrator with considerable organizational skills, scrupulously honest, a man of integrity, efficiency, and commitment. "After twenty-five years of public service," he wrote, "what I have accumulated is a debt of 20,000 taels, but not a single month's food." He had a deep appreciation of the poor farmer who turned vigilante. And his experience with the Black Flags taught him that groups of vigilantes operating as guerrilla irregulars might provide a valuable tool in the Ironhat plan to expel all foreigners. So he found ways through Magistrate Yu Hsien to boost the Big Swords.

Big Swords began collaring bandits and bringing them to local magistrates for prosecution. When the magistrates were swamped with cases, the Big Swords applied summary justice, killing the bandits on the spot. Yu Hsien praised them discreetly. On one occasion he disguised himself as a fortune teller to attend a local fair where he could watch the Big Swords and check on their increasing popularity. Their numbers had grown across the border of Shantung into neighboring provinces, reaching at least thirty thousand—some said a hundred thousand. Quietly Yu Hsien began recruiting the best Big Swords into a special unit of the provincial militia.

One of the biggest bandit gangs in the area was headed by Rice-grain Yue the Second, who commanded three thousand desperately poor peasants preying on local villages. When the Big Swords caught and executed Yue, thousands of his followers immediately became Catholics, whereupon they taunted the Big Swords, claiming that their ability to resist knives, swords, and spears was a sham and that the pagan gods of China were impotent. This turned the quarrel into a pissing contest, which the Catholics were determined to win. They began a campaign of official complaints, alleging Big Sword damage to their churches. The quarrel spilled over into Kiangsu Province, where battles ended in the burning of churches and the sacking of Christian villages. Foreign missionaries were evacuated, and on orders from Governor Li Ping-heng, Magistrate Yu Hsien was forced to intervene. He settled the matter by arresting and beheading the two most prominent Big Sword leaders. He allowed everyone else to go home; no other Big Swords were punished. This sent clear signals down the line that villagers who were not anti-Manchu could organize their own vigilante forces and get away with anything, including persecuting Christians, provided they did not make trouble for Peking by provoking the Foreign Powers. So during the next two years there was a dramatic increase in village defense forces, particularly in the poorest villages along the border with Chihli Province. There in November 1897 a particularly aggressive German priest named George Stenz so outraged villagers in the district of Kuyeh that a band of armed men came one night to murder him and by mistake killed two other German missionaries sleeping in his bedroom. Stenz, who had given his room to these friends and had gone to sleep in the servants' quarters, survived to become the center of an international crisis.

Germany had been seeking a pretext to seize Kiaochow Bay in Shantung as its naval base in China. The German minister in Peking, Baron von Heyking, needed a way to provoke an incident; Bishop Johann Baptist von Anzer, who as luck would have it was in Berlin at the moment, urged the foreign ministry to make an issue of the Kuyeh missionary murders. With telegraphed assurances from Czar Nicholas that Russia would look the other way, Kaiser Wilhelm sent a naval squadron to seize the forts guarding the city of Tsingtao and to occupy Kiaochow Bay. Reinforcements followed in December.

Governor Li Ping-heng urged Peking to fight but was turned down; he found himself the target of intense pressure as the German legation sought to blame him for the missionary murders and to have him sacked from his post. They were aware of his loathing of foreigners and believed that he was encouraging anti-Christian violence across the countryside. Li was also blocking German attempts to secure mineral rights in Shantung and to open factories there, a matter of much greater importance to Berlin than the fate of two missionaries. As compensation for their murders Germany demanded the sole right to construct railways and to open coal mines in the province, the right to build a naval station in Kiaochow, 6,000 taels of silver for the bereaved families, and the dismissal of Governor Li Ping-heng. Peking caved in and granted Germany the concessions she wanted, plus a ninety-nine-year lease on Kiaochow and Tsingtao.

The Germans had won, but in the process unwittingly tipped the balance at court in favor of the hostile Ironhats, by infuriating moderate officials and driving them temporarily into Prince Tuan's ranks.

The throne had planned to reward Li Ping-heng for his very real achievements in Yellow River flood control and his exceptionally honest administration of Shantung by promoting him to viceroy of Szechwan, far to the west. Baron von Heyking insisted that Li must never again be allowed to govern a province. Recalling the recent humiliation by Japan, the court lost its nerve and withdrew Li Ping-heng's well-deserved promotion. The Ironhats intervened to give the old warrior a clandestine assignment at his home province in southern Manchuria, where he was to help train a secret army to support the strike against the Foreign Devils when the time came, but the hero of Liangshan had lost much face. Neither he nor his friends would forget and January 1898 marked the turning point in the Ironhats' dream to kill or expel all foreigners; sooth-sayers began seeking a date. At the end of 1899, Prince Tuan arranged for Li Ping-heng to become supreme commander of all Chinese naval forces on the Yangtze, in the British zone of influence. The soothsayers had now chosen July 1900, only seven months away. The Yangtze allowed Western vessels to penetrate deep into the interior of the empire, leaving that flank vulnerable; when fighting began Li Ping-heng would block all foreign warships at the mouth of the river.

He was replaced as governor of Shantung by Chang Ju-mei, a less orthodox Confucian and a sly administrator who devoted his full attention to building the provincial militia, in which he was assisted by the same Magistrate Yu Hsien who had been Li Ping-heng's agent in promoting the Big Swords and other rural vigilantes. Yu Hsien was named lieutenant governor, and he and Chang Ju-mei became so absorbed in their secret project that they neglected flood control and maintenance of the crucial Yellow River dikes, one of the most important responsibilities of a Shantung governor. Li Ping-heng had devoted six months a year to it alone. After his dismissal, the Yellow River broke through its neglected banks in the summer of 1898, in a disaster of great magnitude. Thousands of square miles of North China were inundated, crops destroyed, and famine followed. Hundreds of thousands of farmers and their families were ruined, a million people made homeless, and western Shantung was set for a cosmic tragedy. Next came a plague of locusts and two years of drought resulting in worse famine. A leaflet advised Chinese that "until all foreigners have been exterminated the rain can never visit us."

Here again was the ongoing anti-foreign propaganda. The ranks of village defense forces swelled and hostility toward missionaries became intense. The success of Catholic priests in the punishment of Governor Li Ping-heng prompted a rush of dubious converts. Weed people and the missionaries backing them grossly exaggerated their protests and demands, extorting larger and larger fines. Non-Christian villagers who lost arguments to converts were forced to serve banquets to the victors inside churches, presenting each course on their knees while the converts jeered and set off firecrackers. Blood debts were being created, and the day approached when they would have to be paid.

"These Chinese Christians are the worst people in China," Tzu Hsi told her lady-in-waiting, Derling. "They rob the poor country people of their land and property, and the missionaries of course, always protect them, in order to get a share themselves."

For his failure to prevent the flood, Governor Chang was removed from office in March 1899, and replaced by Yu Hsien. Here was a man who shared Prince Tuan's intense nationalism, xenophobia, and dream of purging China of all foreign influences. Yu Hsien became the Ironhats' new point man in Shantung, where confrontation with foreigners was becoming explosive. He was not what the Germans wanted: a compliant mandarin giving precedence to their interests. Just the opposite: he was more of a fanatic than Li Ping-heng.

Subtle changes also had occurred in the groups leading Shantung's anti-Christian campaign. One of the problems with vigilantes like the Big Swords was the time and effort required for each recruit to become proficient at hand-to-hand combat. If the anti-Christian campaign was ever to gain mass popularity, it would have to offer easier and quicker results. As if in response a new movement called Spirit Boxing appeared emphasizing the magical aspects of Wushu and downplaying rigorous physical training. Instead of spending months or years practicing the martial arts until they were expert in unarmed combat, Spirit Boxers were taught in less than a week—often in less than a day—to go into a shamanistic trance with the help of charms, rituals, and incantations. During a trance lasting from a few minutes to an hour or more, young men would be possessed by their favorite superheroes from Chinese fiction and village opera and become impervious to knives, swords, spears, and bullets. Exhibiting many of the signs of epileptic seizure, they would go into violent motion, performing the kickboxing movements that every Chinese boy plays at from childhood. Here was instant Wushu that anyone could perform with minimum effort. Boxing was less important than spirit possession, for it was this collective assumption of invulnerability that made the Boxers feel irresistible.

Their instructors were itinerant "masters," dressed as Buddhist or Taoist monks, who appeared out of nowhere and traveled from village to village, some of them highly gifted in shamanistic ritual, including the rudiments of hypnosis. They were adept at feigning possession by demons and equally skilled at enlisting uneducated rural youth, who were easily inflamed by the prospect of taking up the anti-Christian cause. Perhaps the young Spirit Boxers were a spontaneous rural phenomenon, but where the itinerant masters came from, what led so many of them to western Shantung at that moment, and then later toward Peking is another question.

These teachers were sent out as organizers and provocateurs, in the same manner that printed propaganda was being circulated to agitate the countryside. They were probably recruited for the Ironhats by the former bandit chief General Tung Fu-hsiang, through his close ties to underground secret societies of bandits and country fair charlatans; one of Tung's blood brothers later led a hard core of Boxers consisting mostly of these masters. It fits the pattern.

Spirit Boxers first appeared in northwestern Shantung in 1896, about the same time that the most promising Big Swords were being absorbed into the militia. Li Ping-heng and Yu Hsien had encouraged their growth and tried in various ways to guide and control them.

Bertram Lenox-Simpson tells why at the time the legations did not take them seriously:

Duly authorized officers of the Crown have seen recruits, who have performed all the dread rites, and are initiated, stand fearlessly in front of a full-fledged Boxer; have seen that Boxer load up his blunderbuss with powder, ramming down a wad on top; have witnessed a handful of iron buckshot added, but with no wad to hold the charge in place; have noticed that the master Boxer gesticulated with his lethal weapon the better to impress his audience before he fired, but have not noticed that the iron buckshot tripped merrily out of the rusty barrel since no wad held it in place; and finally, when the fire-piece belched forth flames and ear-breaking noise at a distance of a man's body from the recruit's person, they have seen, and with them thousands of others, that no harm came.

There were occasional mistakes, one fellow blown in two by a cannon-ball and others failing to deflect the bullets of firing squads. These lapses were explained as imperfect preparations: the victims had been lax in performing their rituals. Whether or not Westerners believed, most Chinese peasants and many gentry were convinced. With belief came fear. To spread propaganda, Boxers used intimidating chain letters: "If you do not pass on this message . . . you will not be able to escape unnatural death. If, on the other hand, you copy this once and give it to another man, your family will be safe. If you copy it ten times and hand the copies to others, your whole village will be safe."

What was sweeping out of Shantung was a great passion, growing out of desperate poverty, armed only with cudgels and firebrands, and bearing banners with the slogan Protect the Ching, Destroy the Foreign. Under the name Boxers United in Righteousness they began aggressively seeking out Christian converts, mauling them, then looting and burning their homes. Aside from these beatings, few converts were seriously injured till later, but as the incidents multiplied, claims of injury were exaggerated by missionaries into claims of murder, and the legations in Peking were obliged to protest.

London Missionary Society posts were attacked in May, August, and October 1899. In October, General Yuan Shih-kai's cousin was sent to disperse a large band of Boxers who were terrorizing Christian converts. He cornered more than a thousand of them at a temple near the town of Pingyuan and opened fire. Armed only with clubs and a few muskets and antique cannon, the Boxers fought back bravely, putting Yuan's cousin to flight. Government reinforcements soon arrived, killing twenty-eight Boxers, including one of their local leaders. When the battle ended, a village elder who came to plead on behalf of the Boxer youth was shot dead by the soldiers. His killing provoked a powerful reaction from Governor Yu Hsien, who recommended to Peking that General Yuan's cousin be stripped of his command and transferred to another post. In the countryside of Shantung, Yu Hsien's message was clear that the Boxers enjoyed the governor's protection.

With this encouragement, Boxer ranks swelled with a great variety of local youth, farmers, former soldiers, out-of-work bargemen, vagabonds, scoundrels, charlatans, and opportunists. They adorned themselves with red headbands, wristbands, and sashes, bowed to the southeast, burned and swallowed the ashes of written charms, went into theatrical trances, and were possessed by their favorite superhero. Then they scoured the countryside for the common enemy.

In November 1899 a large Boxer band under the famous Red Lantern Chu was making its way home after pillaging a number of Christian villages when they were ambushed by Chinese Catholics. The Boxers counterattacked, wounding three Christians and killing two, burning their town. With these murders the conflict escalated dramatically. Governor Yu Hsien was forced to act to restore order—riot was one thing; killing, another. A few days later, when the Boxer leaders fell to quarreling among themselves, government troops pounced and Red Lantern Chu was captured as he tried to escape, disguised as a nightsoil spreader.

Governor Yu Hsien apparently expected his arrest of Red Lantern Chu to pacify the legations, as had his execution of the two Big Sword leaders several years earlier. Instead, attention suddenly shifted away from Catholic missionaries to American Protestants working nearby. Their protests to the American minister in Peking, Edwin Conger, finally had an effect. At the beginning of December the Tsungli Yamen advised Governor Yu Hsien that Conger had "suggested the necessity and propriety of [the governor's] removal." Since Conger had not been "a habitual meddler" the Yamen thought his protest was not without justification. The following day Yu Hsien was replaced by General Yuan Shih-kai, who (because his loyalties were to Viceroy Li rather than to the Ironhats) immediately set about reversing Yu Hsien's Boxer strategy.

Upon his arrival in Shantung, Yuan issued a proclamation laying down harsh measures to be taken to suppress all bandit gangs and troublemakers, of whatever stripe. Had these measures been put into effect across the board, there is every likelihood that the Boxer movement would have come to an abrupt end. But within a month of taking office Yuan received no fewer than three edicts from Peking, doubtless inspired by Prince Tuan, warning him to be "extremely careful."

The most significant development that December, however, was the arrival from Shansi of a new field commander for the Boxers, someone to take Yu Hsien's place. He was a charismatic bandit named Li Lai-chung, a sworn-brother of Muslim general Tung Fu-hsiang, linked directly through him to Prince Tuan. His arrival in Shantung signaled a new stage of violence. Yu Hsien, meanwhile, was named governor of Shansi to the west of Peking, on the edge of General Tung's frontier domain.

The Boxers flared up immediately. As usual their primary targets were

Chinese Christian converts, but as chance would have it a Western missionary blundered into their path. On the last day of December 1899, the Reverend S. M. Brooks, an Anglican missionary, was returning through the falling snow to his post at Pingyin on the Yellow River when he was surrounded by a band of Boxers armed with swords. Instead of submitting to robbery or other indignities, Brooks fought back and was slashed on the head and arms. The Boxers stripped him to his underwear and dragged him away. In the bitter cold Brooks tried to bargain, offering a ransom for his release. When the gang stopped for lunch at a roadside inn he was tied to a tree. While they ate inside, the innkeeper untied Brooks and the missionary fled, only to be pursued and cut to pieces about a mile from a church run by the Society for the Propagation of the Gospel. His head was cut off and the corpse thrown into a gully.

The Brooks murder provoked a surprisingly unsympathetic reaction from the diplomatic community in Peking. Dr. Robert Coltman, an American medical missionary, wrote to Morrison that "Sir C[laude Mac-Donald] is taking it very coolly and intimating [that Brooks] should not have been travelling in the disturbed state of the country." Edmund Backhouse told Morrison that according to the Anglican bishop of North China "it certainly seems that Brooks deliberately entered a village he had been warned to avoid and refused the offer of a guard."

Nonetheless, the legations in Peking registered strong official protests and demanded that the throne denounce and suppress the Boxers. On January 11, 1900, the court, evenly divided between moderates and hostiles, issued a decree so heavily edited and so full of doubletalk that Conger admitted to "some anxiety as to the effect of its strange wording." The decree read in part:

> Recently in all the provinces brigandage has become daily more prevalent, and missionary cases have recurred with frequency. Most critics point to seditious societies as the cause, and ask for rigorous suppression and punishment of them. But societies are of different kinds. When worthless vagabonds form themselves into bands and sworn confederacies . . . the law can show absolutely no leniency to them. On the other hand, when peaceful and law-abiding people practice their skill . . . for the self-preservation of themselves and their families . . . this is only a matter of mutual help and mutual defense. . . . Let the viceroys and governors of the provinces give strict orders to the local authorities that in dealing with cases of this kind they should only inquire whether so-and-so is or is not a bandit, whether he has or has not stirred up strife, and should not consider whether he belongs or not to a society, whether he is or is not an adherent of a religion.

French minister Stephen Pichon commented that its terms were "vague and elastic" and conveyed a "double meaning." Peking was merely going on record that if the new village defense forces were not subversive (anti-Manchu) they should not be suppressed.

The legations were baffled by the dual nature of the Boxer movement. On the basis of new intelligence from an informant, Edwin Conger wrote in February 1900: "The Empress Dowager is undoubtedly considerably frightened and has been really afraid to move with the necessary force and severity against the 'Boxers' . . . evidently deeming it unwise and unsafe to have at this time, bitterly arrayed against the Government, strong and armed organizations which might be most convenient nucleuses for a general rebellion."

That Tzu Hsi really was frightened is known from what she later told her lady-in-waiting, Derling. "I should have issued an Edict at once to stop the Boxers . . . but both Prince Tuan and Duke Lan told me that they firmly believed the Boxers were sent by Heaven to enable China to get rid of all the undesirable and hated foreigners." Then she added, "I never dreamt that the Boxer movement would end with such serious results for China."

If the legations were mystified, Westerners in the countryside had no doubt that this was all part of a sinister strategy. A month before the murder of Brooks, the American legation was warned in a telegram from missionaries in Shantung that "unless Legations combine pressure, Americans consider situation almost hopeless." Two days before the confusing January 11 edict appeared, British missionaries at Taiyuan, the capital of Shansi, where the coldly fanatical Yu Hsien was now governor, telegraphed Sir Claude: "Outlook very black . . . secret orders from Throne to encourage [Boxers]." But the diplomatic community considered missionaries to be alarmists. As the fateful year 1900 began, Sir Robert Hart wrote: "It is said that Shantung Boxers are really coming into Peking and that we'll yet have a row, started by them here: but there are always rumours of rows circulating!"

Early that January, as if in response to a prearranged signal, itinerant boxing masters began moving from village to village across the North China plain, toward Peking. Contrary to the impression some Westerners had of a wave of Shantung Boxers spreading toward the capital, the masters did not bring Boxers with them but recruited and trained more disciples as they approached the city, which tends to confirm the impression that the masters, not the disciples, were the key to the political strategy behind the campaign and the link between the Boxers and the Ironhats. In a separate but related move, the Shansi bandit Li Lai-chung came up from Shantung with his own handpicked Boxer force, mingled with the local Boxers, and was particularly active in the southern outskirts of Peking near the army of his blood brother, General Tung Fu-hsiang. Li probably was the vital element in the Boxer strategy, perhaps the ringleader. From that point on it is difficult to separate the various groups as they converged on Peking. Whereupon, matters got quickly out of hand.

At the end of January, the British, American, French, German, and Italian ministers sent identical notes of protest to the court demanding a clear-cut decree ordering the complete suppression of the Boxers. Under this pressure, the court instructed officials in Chihli and Shantung to prohibit Boxer activities and to inform the common people that this type of society was forbidden by law. The legations were dissatisfied, and on April 6 raised the alarming specter of armed intervention by foreign warships and troops if their demands for complete suppression of the Boxers were not carried out during the next two months.

In mid-April another decree provided more doubletalk, repeating that self-defense groups would be tolerated but at the same time admonishing people against harassing Chinese Christian converts. The Boxers interpreted this as official recognition of their organization and announced that they could now function under imperial protection.

Early in May the Ironhats proposed that the Boxers be absorbed completely into local militias, where they would be trained, fed, and paid. The court ordered Yu Lu, the new viceroy of Chihli, and Yuan Shih-kai, the governor of Shantung, to consider the Ironhats' proposal and report back. Both officials objected as strenuously as they dared. The elderly Yu Lu, who had developed a close friendship with the British consul in Tientsin, hinted that in his view the Boxers were criminals and charlatans. Governor Yuan, mincing no words, said, "These Boxers, gathering people to roam on the streets and plundering at distances of several hundred miles, cannot be said to be defending themselves and their families . . . plundering and killing the common people and stirring up disturbances, they cannot be said to be merely anti-Christian. . . . The proposal of placing the Boxers under official training is absolutely not feasible."

Yuan's warning fell on deaf ears.

CHAPTER EIGHTEEN

Something Wicked This Way Comes

B y the late spring of 1900 the smell from the open sewer canal running out of the Forbidden City and through the legation quarter was ripening. To the Westerners in the legations it was a normal spring with the usual provincial riots by starving peasants, but most of the foreign staff had learned to ignore peasants and sewage. It was almost time to pack and head for summer retreats at converted temples in the Western Hills, fifteen miles southwest of Peking. Picnics and dinner dances, horse races, tennis, and excursions filled the final weeks with pleasant distraction.

The big event of the month of May was a dinner party at the British legation on the occasion of Queen Victoria's eighty-first (and last) birthday. Of the fifty-nine guests, men outnumbered women two to one, and the radiant Lady MacDonald led Dr. George Morrison and Sir Robert Hart to their places. After dinner there was dancing on the tennis courts beneath bright Chinese paper lanterns, to the music of the I.G.'s new string orchestra.

Two weeks earlier, on May 10, 1900, the North China *Daily News* had carried an anonymous story from "a native correspondent" in Peking, evidently a minor official of good family who had Western friends. The article was extraordinary for its insights and predictions:

> I write in all seriousness and sincerity to inform you that there is a great secret scheme, having for its aim to crush all foreigners in China, and wrest back the territories "leased" to them. . . . The chief leaders of the movement are the Empress Dowager, Prince Ching, Prince Tuan, Kang I, Chao Shu-chiao [Ironhat chief of the Board of Punishments] and Li Ping-heng. . . . The forces to be used [are] the

Peking Field Force (50,000 men) under Prince Ching; the Husheng Corps, or Glorified Tigers (10,000 strong) under Prince Tuan; and the various Banner Corps of the Imperial Guards (aggregating 12,000 men) under Kang I and others. These 72,000 men are to form the nucleus of the Army of Avengers, whilst the Boxers are to be counted upon as auxiliaries to the great fight that is more imminent than foreigners in Peking or elsewhere dream.... All Chinese of the upper class know this, and those who count foreigners among their friends have warned them, but have to my own knowledge been rather laughed at.

This clear warning of impending bloodshed was completely ignored. Yet the danger was a great deal more serious than any foreigner in Peking realized, for the Ironhats were about to strike under the cover of the "spontaneous" anti-Christian uprising of the Boxers. Unrelenting German pressure and more difficulties with Western missionaries and Rice Christians in Shantung and Chihli were provoking such outrage even among moderates in upper levels of the Chinese government that the leverage of the Ironhats was greatly increased.

Prince Chuang and Duke Lan were now the chief and deputy chief of the Peking Gendarmerie, putting them in control of the police and secret police apparatus and enabling them to apply surveillance and intimidation to high-ranking moderate opponents. Prince Tuan was in a similar position within the palace, where his personal influence with the dowager and his control of the inner ring of palace security made it difficult for Jung Lu or any other moderates to interfere. The Ironhats also numbered among their faction the mayor of Peking, the head of the Board of Punishments, the vice-president of the Board of Revenue, the president of the Board of Ceremonies, Grand Secretaries, and Grand Councillors. This inflated the hard-liners' sense of omnipotence, although they did not yet overwhelmingly dominate the court. Moderates could still block them. The target date for the extermination of all Foreign Devils had been set for July 1900, less than two months away, a date chosen by the soothsayers because of an unusual convergence of numerology and calendrics. The fact that the Ironhats had chosen this date did not mean that they had the backing of the dowager and the court. Many moderates were resisting, so the Ironhats would soon have to conduct a bloody reign of terror to silence their opponents.

Despite repeated protests about the Boxers and threats to call in foreign troops, the legations did not take the danger very seriously, preoccupied as they were with fending off what they considered the biggest danger in Peking: boredom. Both Edwin Conger and Sir Claude MacDonald ridiculed the Boxers as "a few fanatics." There was no rain that spring, and throughout North China no corn had been sown. Everything would calm down, they insisted, as soon as there were a few days of heavy rain.

Robert Hart had been predicting disaster for some time. He could not help believing that someday foreigners were going to push the Chinese too hard. As far back as 1894, his thumbs had itched as the undercurrent of Ironhat conspiracy intensified. He was worried about the vulnerability of the foreign community: "Here at Peking we are in a rat-trap and at the mercy of the Chinese: if we could all get together we could hold out against a mass mob, but we are scattered . . . and if there should be a row I doubt if many of us will escape." He added that "I think it quite possible that one of these days [China's] despair may find expression in the wildest rage, and that we foreigners will one and all be wiped out in Peking." Eight months before the siege began he wrote that "all foreigners in Peking are to be wiped out and the golden age return for China." He added that "Tung Fu-hsiang's military rabble (12,000 men) are encamped three miles off and if they break loose we shall have a bad time."

In May 1900 he wrote: "Rumour says the Empress Dowager is herself 'bitten' and in sympathy with [the Boxers]. But really we know very little of official feeling, and see nothing below the surface." If she was bitten that might well be because Westerners were publishing and giving credence to the scurrilous attacks of Kang Yu-wei, Liang Chi-chao, and Lim Boon-keng. This could only have made the old woman more vulnerable to the blandishments of Prince Tuan and Kang I. Humans are notoriously susceptible to jingoism, and Tzu Hsi was no exception. Hart learned later that the best of the Boxer performers had exhibited their techniques first before Prince Tuan, and then before the emperor and the empress dowager, in a command performance arranged by the Ironhats. With skills polished at thousands of country fairs, they easily won over all but the most hardened skeptics. The collective will to be bamboozled takes hold at such moments. Tzu Hsi had no practical experience outside Peking. Before the Sino-Japanese War, she had been persuaded to believe that Viceroy Li's new navy was invulnerable and that his German-designed fortified harbors were impregnable, so why should she not believe in Prince Tuan's magic weapon. She later described how Prince Tuan told her of seeing "a Boxer [shoot] another with a revolver and the bullet hit him, but did not harm him in the least." There is not the slightest doubt that Prince Tuan believed all this. When Tzu Hsi discussed it with Jung Lu, he scoffed at Prince Tuan's foolishness and told her "one foreign soldier could kill one hundred Boxers without the slightest trouble." He told her Prince Tuan was "absolutely crazy" and before they were through, the Boxers were going to cause "a great deal of trouble." In China magic and stagecraft still had tremendous power, however, and Tzu Hsi remained undecided, pulled in opposite directions by her advisers.

The legations took no interest in Hart's worries, any more than they showed interest in the frank warning published in the *Daily News*. No sense of self-doubt plagued the foreign community; they were on God's side, invulnerable as emissaries of civilization to the benighted Chinese, protected by moral superiority. Just as the Boxers were invulnerable to Western bullets. High noon for imbecility.

So nothing was done. Sir Claude did take the precaution of calling for a naval show of force, and two British warships took up station off the Taku Forts, to be joined in mid-April by one American, one French, and two Italian gunboats. In a month there would be twenty-four foreign warships off Taku. Like the appearance of the British squadron in the gulf at the end of the Hundred Days Reform, this alarmed the court, worried moderates, and incensed the Ironhats.

Of the roughly five hundred foreign residents in Peking in 1900, half were missionaries running churches, hospitals, dispensaries, orphanages, and schools; because of their sectarian differences, they rarely spoke to one another. By contrast, the legation quarter was a smug, self-contained world. There were eleven legations representing Austria-Hungary, Belgium, Great Britain, France, Germany, Holland, Italy, Japan, Russia, Spain, and the United States. They were not joined together in a single compound but sprawled over a rectangle roughly three quarters of a mile on a side, tucked under one shoulder of the Forbidden City. On the south the boundary was the wall marking the limit of the Tartar City; and beyond its parapets the stink and clamor of the Chinese City; on the east, the main street leading from the Hatamen Gate; on the north, the outer wall of the Forbidden City; and on the west, the Tiananmen Gate, the main gate into the imperial palace complex. Through the legation quarter ran the foul-smelling sewage canal, filled with fulminating black sludge, with a tree-lined street on either side, which separated the British legation and the neighboring Hanlin Academy from the spacious walled gardens of Prince Su's palace. The British legation had originally been part of Prince Su's compound; it was acquired for the legation after the Allied occupation in 1860.

In addition to the legations themselves, the quarter was full of shops, warehouses, banks, offices, and a hotel, some owned by wealthy Chinese, others by foreign companies. Here were the Hong Kong and Shanghai Bank; the Russo-Chinese Bank; the traders Jardine Matheson; two well-stocked general stores, Imbeck's and Kierulff's; and the Peking Hotel run by a Swiss, Auguste Chamot, with his American wife, Annie Elizabeth MacCarthy. Western employees of Robert Hart's Chinese Customs and

Post Office had their own compound nearby, and there were a few teachers at the new Peking University.

The leader of this isolated community was Sir Claude MacDonald, a tall, thin, canny Scot of forty-eight, with a lovingly waxed mustache and a military bearing gained during England's Egyptian campaigns in the early 1880s. He was a serious man, a good man, stern, reserved, and thoughtful; he was also tenacious, brave, and a solid military commander. He lacked patience and imagination and was not as shrewd in his perception of Oriental motives as his counterpart in Tokyo, Sir Ernest Satow, who, like Hart, had lived in the Far East for the better part of his adult life. While the Spanish minister was the doyen of the diplomatic corps, Sir Claude was the representative of the greatest of the Great Powers, and his legation was the magnetic center of the community. Morrison, who was brutal in his private estimates of friends as well as foes, described Sir Claude as a man who "possesses as little wisdom as judgment."

That May there was a sudden explosion of Boxer activity outside Peking. At the town of Laishui, which was evenly divided between Christians and non-Christians, the Chinese Christians had disrupted a village fair and knocked over the tablets of local deities. In retaliation the village church was ransacked. When Manchu government officials took the side of the Christians, resentment grew; on May 12, 1900, a mob of Boxers burned the church and all the Christian houses, killing thirty Christian families. These Boxers then defeated a punitive force of imperial troops and killed its colonel. Sixty Boxers also died in the battle. A few days later, Boxers burned down a London Mission chapel only forty miles from the capital. Two days later the vicar of Peking, Bishop Favier, warned the French minister, Stephen Pichon, that a date had been fixed for a Boxer attack *inside* Peking. If the Ironhats had their way, Favier wrote Pichon, the Catholic North Cathedral, called the Peitang, would be destroyed first, then the legations. "I implore you . . . to believe me; I am well informed and I do not speak idly. This religious persecution is only a facade; the ultimate aim is the extermination of all Europeans . . . the Boxers' accomplices await them in Peking; they mean to attack the churches first, then the Legations. For us, in our Cathedral, the date of the attack has actually been fixed. Everybody knows it, it is the talk of the town." The bishop pleaded for forty or fifty sailors to protect them. But when the diplomatic corps met to discuss Favier's warning, they decided that a Boxer attack in Peking was inconceivable, so there was no need to send to Tientsin for marines. Sir Claude wrote to the Foreign Office that "little has come to my own knowledge to confirm the gloomy anticipations of the French Father." MacDonald's lack of comprehension was typical of the legations. Further, a representative of Great Britain was hardly going to base his decisions on the rantings of a Frenchman and a Catholic to boot. Prejudices, jealousies, and backbiting in the foreign community would be another hallmark of the Boxer Uprising.

By May 27 one of the main Boxer forces, which had grown to nearly ten thousand men, took control of the city of Chochou, on the rail line fifty-odd miles southwest of the capital, and began attacking and burning railway stations, bridges, and telegraph lines in both directions. The Boxer leaders were determined to force local officials to treat them with respect. Composed as they were of all manner of country people—including more than a few brigands, con men, thugs, and layabouts—they beat and robbed Chochou's mandarins and gentry, who might better have been left alone. There was an immediate outcry in Peking. Senior officials like Jung Lu had grave doubts about the wisdom of the Boxer strategy, not only because it would provoke reprisals from the Foreign Powers but because the Boxers themselves were an unruly mob who could go out of control at any time, possibly overthrowing the government. Incidents like Chochou gave these moderates the courage to raise their voices in imperial councils or to submit memorials of protest to the throne, and Tzu Hsi was sufficiently uncertain to be moved first one way then the other.

Robert Hart picked up the vibrations: "The Court appears to be in a dilemma: if the Boxers are not suppressed, the Legations threaten to take action—if the attempt to suppress them is made, this intensely patriotic organization will be converted into an anti-dynastic movement!" One of Prince Tuan's most effective arguments to the dowager was to threaten that if the Boxers were not backed to the hilt, they would topple the throne. Tzu Hsi later recalled her quandary:

One day Prince Tuan brought the Boxer leader to the Summer Palace and summoned all the eunuchs into the courtyard of the Audience Hall and examined each eunuch on the head to see if there was a cross. [The Boxer leader] said "This cross is not visible to you, but I can identify a Christian by finding a cross on the head." Prince Tuan then came to my private Palace and told me that the Boxer leader . . . had found two eunuchs who were Christians and asked me what was to be done. I immediately became very angry and told him that he had no right to bring any Boxers to the Palace without my permission; but he said this leader was so powerful that he was able to kill all the foreigners and was not afraid of the foreign guns, as all the gods were protecting him. . . . Then Prince Tuan suggested that I hand these two eunuchs supposed to be Christians to the Boxer leader, which I did. I heard afterwards that these two eunuchs were beheaded. . . . The next day I was very much surprised to see all my eunuchs dressed as Boxers. . . . Duke Lan presented me with a suit of Boxer clothes.

She then called in Jung Lu "as I wished to consult with him. . . . Jung Lu looked grieved when he learned what had taken place at the Palace, and said that these Boxers were nothing but revolutionaries and agitators. . . . I told him that probably he was right, and asked him what should be done. He told me that he would talk to Prince Tuan, but the next day Prince Tuan told me that he had had a fight with Jung Lu about the Boxer question, and said that . . . if we tried to turn them [the Boxers], they would do all they could to kill everyone in Peking, including the Court."

Tzu Hsi was badly frightened and began to realize, too late, that she had become a virtual prisoner of Prince Tuan. If she had been a dangerous scheming autocrat she could immediately have had him arrested and executed. But she was way out of her political and intellectual depth in these intrigues and was torn by indecision. Over recent years as she had begun to slow with age, she had allowed Prince Tuan to insinuate himself ever deeper into her private life. At first she liked his attention. It was only when he led the group pressing her with the indictment of Kuang Hsu that she suspected he was a viper coiled around her ankles. When he then bullied her into giving him the bizarre privilege of the Shangfang sword and the entitlement to behead anyone he wished on the spot, she had become frightened by the dark side of his nature, his increasingly obvious paranoia. Unfortunately, there were no royal princes prepared to rally to her side, to defend her from Tuan and his powerful clique. Even Jung Lu had grown wary and was reluctant to confront the Ironhats directly. Jung Lu had lost an argument with Prince Tuan's father back in September 1878 and had been forced into early retirement for seven years, emerging again only when Prince Tun went into decline preceding his death, so he was wary of royal princes. Moderates still dominated most policy debates at court because of their skill at bureaucratic rhetoric and their experience in politics and government, but the palace itself was slipping inexorably into the hands of fanatics.

Another Boxer band struck at the railway station in Fengtai, between Peking and Chochou, burning the depot, the locomotive shed, and the houses of foreign engineers, and blowing up the foreign-built steel bridge over the Peiho River. Because they had no weapons other than spears and swords and a few geriatric cannon, fire was still their chief weapon. In the hills above Fengtai, two American women, Harriet Squiers and Polly Condit Smith, stood watching the black smoke from the ivy-covered terrace of a Taoist temple that had been converted into a summer villa. They could surmise what was happening and they were frightened. Fengtai was the junction where the Peking-Tientsin railway joined the line from Peking to Paotingfu, and it lay smack on the edge of the territory controlled by Muslim general Tung Fu-hsiang. If Boxer mobs—or General Tung's unruly troops—were burning the railway station, what would they do next?

Harriet Squiers's husband, Herbert, was the first secretary of the American legation, and her guest, Polly Condit Smith, was a vivacious young woman from Boston who was on holiday in the Orient and had come to Peking from Japan. With them were the three Squiers children, a German governess, a French governess, and forty frightened Chinese servants. A squad of Chinese soldiers armed with spears had been sent to protect them the previous day, but they had since vanished.

Approaching slowly up the hill from the direction of the smoke was a dusty figure on horseback, and the two ladies were relieved to recognize the correspondent of the *Times*. George Morrison, a close friend of Herbert Squiers who appreciated pretty women, was coming to the ladies' rescue. Earlier that day, when first reports had come of trouble at Fengtai, Morrison had ridden out from Peking to see for himself and to check on the ladies. Herbert Squiers was busy at the American legation and might not be able to leave Peking before its gates were sealed for the night. In the meantime, Morrison set the women to packing and the panicky servants to loading carts for a hasty return to the capital next morning.

Soon after Morrison's arrival, Herbert Squiers rode up with a Cossack borrowed from the Russian legation. Because of a treaty signed with China in 1689, the Russians were the only legation permitted to keep a small permanent guard, seven Cossacks. Squiers was tall, rugged, and handsome with a perpetual half smile and the bearing of a New England man of breeding. He was as comfortable in a three-piece suit as he was now in hacking tweeds with a Mauser rifle in the crook of his arm. Squiers had spent fifteen years as an officer in the U.S. Cavalry before joining the foreign service, and he was an agreeable mixture of gentleman and rogue, at home in boardrooms or saloons. He had political ambitions, a comforting bank balance, a clever wife, and aggressive children, and his valuable collection of Chinese porcelain was known to curators of museums and galleries in America and Europe.

The next morning they set out for Peking, a procession of forty Chinese carts, mules, and donkeys, guarded by the three armed white men on horseback. Five hours later they reached Peking.

That same day a more daring rescue took place. Foreign engineers at a rail station beyond Fengtai were cut off by Boxers and could not escape by rail to either Peking or Tientsin. The Swiss hotelier, Auguste Chamot, and his wife, Annie, rode out at the head of a heavily armed rescue party and brought the refugees to safety in the legations. Other Western families at the station in Paotingfu, fleeing by boat down the Peiho River toward Tientsin, were attacked by mobs and were forced to continue overland, reaching safety only after losing nine of their number.

Conditions in the countryside were deteriorating rapidly, but the legations still exhibited little alarm. The day the Fengtai station was burned, the ministers decided to telegraph Taku for just enough marines to guard the legations. The message was sent, but when the Tsungli Yamen learned of it the marines were forbidden to come. When the legations persisted, the Yamen gave in, as long as only thirty marines came for each legation. With eleven legations, this meant 330 men.

After some difficulty arranging rail transportation, the small international force left Tientsin and made the eighty-mile journey without incident. Between the Peking railway station and the legations six thousand Muslim-Chinese soldiers of General Tung's Kansu Army crowded the narrow streets to intimidate the new arrivals, but they were suddenly withdrawn and sent to protect the emperor and the dowager, who were at the Summer Palace. By removing the Kansu braves from the marines' path, moderates at court were able to lessen the likelihood of immediate confrontation. At 8:00 P.M. the American, British, French, Italian, Japanese, and Russian joint force marched up Legation Street with fixed bayonets—their one act of unanimity that year. All had brought machine guns; the Russians had brought ammunition for their field gun but forgot the gun in Tientsin.

By this time seventeen men-of-war flying various flags were at anchor off Taku, and more were on their way. Sir Claude telegraphed the British fleet's Admiral Sir Edward Hobart Seymour: "No more ships wanted at Taku unless matters become more complicated which I do not think they will." The warships were not there to rescue, they were there to seize. Home governments were taking no chances; if trouble came, no nation wanted to lag behind while others wolfed down huge helpings of Chinese takeaway. In a letter to Seymour following his telegram, Sir Claude said no more British forces would be needed unless the government of China collapsed and it became necessary to compete with Russia and France in an international scramble for spoils. The Peking legations, MacDonald added confidently, "would be the last place attacked."

Bishop Favier had stated flatly that they *would* be attacked, and while nobody believed him the first small units of Boxers in red headbands began to arrive in the streets of Peking at the start of June. On orders from Prince Tuan, guards at the outer gates allowed them to enter only the Chinese City—the lower third of Peking, south of the Tartar Wall. The Ironhats immediately invited them to their palaces as guards. Only now, in June 1900, can it be said that the Boxers and the Ironhats were fully in harness in an operational sense. Previously they had collaborated only in a helter-skelter fashion at a distance through go-betweens such as bandit Li Lai-

Chung. Whatever the Ironhats in moments of nationalistic fervor or megalomania might have dreamed would be the case, this collaboration between princes and peasants lasted in harness less than two weeks and was a disaster for both parties, particularly the Boxers, most of whom were dead before the year was out.

Hundreds of Boxer shrines appeared around Peking, like notices in big character ideographs that a country fair was in the offing, and in the carnival atmosphere local men and boys began to emulate these rustic heroes, practicing Spirit Boxing in the city's streets and parks. Eunuchs in the Summer Palace wore red headbands, wristbands, and sashes (mostly to ward off Prince Tuan's watchdogs), and incense was burned everywhere to demonstrate that there were no Christians present. Wealthy Chinese and Manchu residents of Peking, taking their lead from the Ironhats, decided that it was prudent to hire Boxers as guards, paying them protection money and burning incense to avoid trouble. As other Boxers arrived by the hundreds and then by the thousands, an effort was made to confine them to the Chinese City, beyond the Tartar Wall. In no way did they threaten the legations or even come near them. Many days passed before a single Boxer was seen anywhere near the legation quarter, and then only at a distance.

Venturing out into the Chinese City for a look, Morrison watched one young Boxer demonstrate his skills: "He pretends to receive a spirit from heaven and in a trance slashes the air with sword and knife. He is impervious not only to the foreign bullet and the foreign sword, but the foreign poison . . . with which the foreigner is infecting the native wells." Morrison added that a quick kick from a Westerner (himself) sent the boy sprawling. It was a great jape. Also a needless provocation. Morrison did not see fit to mention in his articles for the *Times* that he was in the habit of kicking and punching Chinese.

The only Chinese military force outside Peking that seemed to be standing in the way of any Boxers was the army of General Nieh Shih-cheng, operating to the east of the capital near Tientsin. General Nieh was a moderate, loyal to commander in chief Jung Lu rather than to the Ironhats. On June 3–4 Nieh's Front Division fought off a Boxer band attempting to blow the vital railbridge at Yangtsun, which would have cut the rail link between the foreign ships off Taku and the legations at Peking. This did not make General Nieh popular with the Ironhats, and he was now a marked man and would shortly be fragged.

On June 3 additional German and Austrian sailors, who had been left behind when the original contingent of marines was dispatched, arrived, bringing the total military force at the legations to 451. Of that total two officers and 41 men were at last sent to protect Bishop Favier and the Peitang Cathedral, leaving 17 officers and 391 men to guard the scattered legations. Everything seemed so tranquil that Lady MacDonald sent her pretty five- and three-year-old daughters, Stella and Ivy, to the newly renovated British legation summer house in the Western Hills, under marine escort. Lady MacDonald's sister, Miss Armstrong, who accompanied them, took a sniff of the air along the way and two days later brought them back. It was June 5 and not a day too soon.

News traveled slowly in the countryside, but shortly after the children returned to the British legation word came that two English missionaries had been murdered four days earlier at Yungtsing, fifty miles south of Peking. Charles Robinson and H. V. Norman were threatened by a mob, sought refuge in a magistrate's office, were forced to leave by the back door, and were caught and cut to pieces. When Sir Claude went with his translator, Henry Cockburn, to the Tsungli Yamen to protest, he noticed that one of the four Chinese ministers present dozed through his presentation. The snoozing minister would later be cited as an example of the callousness of an imperial government that had already committed itself to a policy of exterminating the foreigners lock, stock, and barrel. As Morrison wrote for the *Times*, "while the crisis was impending, the Empress Dowager was giving a series of theatrical entertainments in the Summer Palace."

In fact, during the first week of June, the moderate anti-Boxer faction briefly gained the upper hand at court, due to the excesses of the Boxers during their takeover of Chochou and to the latest fears of foreign intervention stirred up by the arrival of the legation guards. Some people still remembered the Allied invasion of 1860, even if Prince Tuan and his brothers were too young. The North China *Herald* reported that a secret meeting was held at the Summer Palace on June 4 in an attempt to resolve differences between the Ironhats and those senior government officials who were opposed to the Boxer campaign and alarmed at the gathering foreign fleets off Taku and the presence of the marines in the legations. The *Herald* said the militants argued that the Boxers should not be restrained or opposed, since they were loyal to the dynasty and if properly armed would be useful auxiliaries. The *Herald* identified those supporting the Boxers as Prince Tuan, his brother Duke Lan, the elderly Grand Secretary Hsu Tung, Grand Councillor Kang I, and Grand Duke Chung, father of the doomed Empress A-lu-te. The only voices raised in opposition were those of commander in chief Jung Lu and the head of the Grand Council, the aged Prince Li. The *Herald* said Grand Councillor Wang Wen-shao sat silent, and "the empress dowager kept her own counsel." Silence was now Tzu Hsi's only defense against Prince Tuan. Let the moderates talk circles around him and delay the inevitable showdown, and she would tip the balance in their favor wherever she could, but fear made her incapable of defying him openly at an audience. Had there been someone ready to spring to her defense she might have ordered his arrest, but Tuan's confederates were now in so many key posts that only Jung Lu or Yuan Shih-kai might be counted on to protect her. Yuan was far away in Shantung and Jung Lu was alarmed and circumspect, blocking Tuan where he could, but no longer certain of who would come to his own aid in a showdown.

They were afraid to act without Viceroy Li. They had all grown dependent upon Li to handle situations like this; even Jung Lu was waiting anxiously for Li to come to their rescue, to do their thinking for them. But for reasons of his own Li was taking his time down in Canton, waiting for the pot to boil. There was no doubt in anyone's mind meanwhile that direct confrontation with Prince Tuan in the palace would lead to the poisoning of Kuang Hsu and the installation of Pu Chun as the new emperor.

The later efforts of Morrison, Bland, Backhouse, and others to cast Tzu Hsi in the part of the master manipulator behind the antiforeign conspiracy were fabrications that are not borne out by ongoing evidence. Morrison's account of the siege for the *Times* stated: "The anti-foreign, anti-Christian movement . . . was from the outset encouraged and fostered by the Empress-Dowager and by the ignorant reactionaries whom she selected as her advisers."

As we have seen, this simply is not true. The court was split down the middle and the dowager was paralyzed by indecision, shifting one way then the other. Jung Lu was clearly with other moderates in opposing the Boxers. Viceroy Chang Chih-tung, Viceroy Yu Lu, and Telegraph Sheng, the boss of the privately owned Imperial Telegraph Administration, took this occasion to send surprisingly forthright telegrams to the Tsungli Yamen urging the suppression of this so-called "rebellion" staged "on the pretext of anti-Christianity." For the moment, on the Chinese side, sane heads prevailed. But at a delicate moment when the slightest provocation could tip the balance at court in favor of the Ironhats, Westerners seemed to go out of their way to provide it. It is a wonder that the moderates held out as long as they did.

The day of the secret conclave at the Summer Palace, June 4, the foreign ministers decided at a meeting of the diplomatic corps to send identical cables to their governments as a precaution, saying, "We may at any time be besieged here, with the railway and telegraph lines cut" and the commanders of the warships off Taku should be instructed to undertake rescue if that should come to pass. The next day the Boxers cut the Peking-Tientsin railway by removing stretches of track. Worried, Sir Claude went to the Tsungli Yamen for a private conversation with Prince Ching. He came back feeling that the prince no longer had control over events.

On June 8 Boxers set fire to the grandstand of the Peking Racecourse. This was a unique provocation, for the racecourse was the most popular social setting the foreign community had. Here, indeed, was something to shed blood over. The track had been built on a patch of the imperial hunting preserve ten miles south of Peking, where it could be reached easily by train on the short run to Fengtai, or by horseback for the more energetic. The student interpreters saddled up and rode off to have a look at the damage, armed and giddy with excitement. One of them, Lancelot Giles, wrote in his diary:

> We arrived while the ruins of the stand were still smoking, and found a crowd of men from the neighbouring village looting the bricks. . . . We charged them and scattered them right and left. After a rest we decided to proceed yet farther west and see what further damage had been done by the Boxers in their advance. We had not gone more than a quarter of a mile, before we saw the road before us blocked by a dense crowd of Chinese. As soon as they saw us, they began to yell . . . "kill, kill [*Sha, Sha*]." We still advanced till within a hundred yards of them. They then began to dash forward, waving swords and spears which shone ominously in the sun. We promptly wheeled, and galloped off, quickly outdistancing our pursuers, who nevertheless kept up the chase for some time.

Another student interpreter, W. Meyrick Hewlett, added in his own diary that two other students, H. H. Bristow and R. D. Drury, made a second trip to the racecourse later; confronted by the same angry crowd, Bristow took out his pistol and shot a Chinese in the stomach. The first shot had now been fired in Peking, and the first Chinese killed, by an Englishman.

This critical occurence was not noted by a single historian tracing events leading up to the siege and was conveniently left out by Morrison in his account for the *Times* and from Sir Claude's published accounts as well. Morrison reported the incident with the students only as follows: "Students were attacked when riding in the country; our racecourse, grandstand, and stables were burnt . . . Europeans could not venture along the streets outside the foreign quarter without being insulted." He failed to add that Chinese could not insult a foreigner without being shot dead.

That night a gloomy Sir Robert Hart sent the wives and children of his Customs officers to sleep in the British legation.

The burning of the racetrack, Sir Claude remarked, brought home to all Europeans in Peking, as nothing else had, "a sense of the perilous position in which they stood." As Morrison reported, with the burning of the racetrack, "it was now inevitable that we should have to fight." Doubtless the shooting of the Chinese made a very deep impression on the Ironhats, for the advantage gained by the moderates at court the previous week was now lost. A rumor reached Sir Claude that the court had turned around and was now wholly committed to "exterminating" all foreigners. Tzu Hsi later gave her version of these events:

> Matters became worse day by day and Jung Lu was the only one against the Boxers, but what could one man accomplish against so many? One day Prince Tuan and Duke Lan came and asked me to issue an Edict ordering the Boxers to kill all the Legation people first and then all remaining foreigners. I was very angry and refused to issue this Edict. After we had talked a very long time, Prince Tuan said that this must be done without delay, for the Boxers were getting ready to fire on the Legations and would do so the very next day. I was furious and ordered several of the eunuchs to drive him out, and he said as he was going out: "If you refuse to issue that Edict, I will do it for you whether you are willing or not," and he did. After that you know what happened. He issued these Edicts unknown to me and was responsible for a great many deaths.

Prince Tuan's takeover of the palace was now complete. He had dropped any pretense of being filial and submissive to the dowager empress, and like Su Shun at Jehol had brazenly informed her that he was usurping the right of the throne to issue decrees and edicts, without displaying the slightest concern that she might have him beheaded for his presumption. Tuan's men were all around them, and his followers were now in control of the secret police, the gendarmerie, the Board of Punishments, and all the other key elements of internal security. As he had neutralized Kuang Hsu two years earlier, he had now terrorized the court and neutralized Tzu Hsi as well. The once mighty Manchu had fallen so low that nobody dared to defend the throne and the throne was afraid to ask. Everything that happened after this point has to be seen in the context of paralysis by fear. Since he had tens of thousands of troops at his disposal who could have overrun the legations before breakfast, the only thing preventing the prince from declaring his son emperor and going merrily on with his plans, was his own puzzling incompetence. Figuratively speaking, when Prince Tuan galloped off to battle in 1900, he left without a full quiver. Foreigners were ever quick to blame the plain-speaking Jung Lu for the siege, but he was the only Manchu to cut through all the duck fat and pronounce Prince Tuan "insane."

The following day, June 9, the British legation was visited by Lien Fang, an unusually sophisticated Manchu official from the Tsungli Yamen who had served abroad and spoke French, although it was barely comprehensible. He was one of Prince Ching's inner circle, preferring mediation to confrontation. In a dispatch to Lord Salisbury, Sir Claude wrote: "When I spoke to him of the report that was in the air to the effect that the Empress Dowager and her advisers had determined to exterminate all foreigners in Peking and to drive them out of China . . . and that General Tung Fu-hsiang had guaranteed the ability of his Kansu troops to execute the behest of his Imperial mistress in this regard, Lien Fang, instead of deriding the incredible madness of the policy thus ascribed to his superiors, showed unmistakably by his attitude . . . that the report of which I spoke was regarded by him at least as no idle gossip."

Sir Claude then telegraphed Admiral Seymour: "Situation extremely grave; unless arrangements are made for immediate advance to Peking it will be too late." He summoned an urgent meeting of the diplomatic corps to tell them what he had done.

The other ministers chided MacDonald as an alarmist and informed him that news had just come that the empress dowager and the emperor were no longer at the Summer Palace but had returned to the Forbidden City, which they would hardly do if an attack was imminent. They asked Sir Claude to send another telegram to Seymour withdrawing his request for troops. Morrison noted in his diary, "Return of Emperor and Empress has made things a hundred times better."

However, news then came that the dowager had been accompanied by General Tung's cutthroat rabble, whose very presence in Peking made the Europeans' hair stand on end.

There was bad blood between General Tung and the foreign community. During the Hundred Days Reform, Tung had been headquartered in the Southern Hunting Park, the location of the foreign racetrack. On September 30, 1898, some of his men had attacked members of the British and American legations, and the envoys called for marines from each of their China fleets. The following month Tung's men attacked a party of foreign engineers and members of the British legation at the Peking railway station, which was in his military zone in the Chinese City. The legations demanded the removal of his army from the vicinity of Peking, and after great difficulty Tung and his men were moved eighty miles to the east. According to historian Hosea Ballou Morse, this was probably accomplished only "by means which greatly increased the banking account of Tung and his generals." By the end of 1899, however, Prince Tuan had moved Tung and his men back into Peking, this time in close collaboration with those Boxers under the command of Tung's blood brother, the bandit Li Lai-chung. Tung Fu-hsiang was later formally condemned by the Allies for cooperating with Prince Tuan in carrying out "the plan for the destruction of foreigners in China."

The reappearance of General Tung in the streets was cause for alarm. Bertram Lenox-Simpson described the scene: "As it became dark to-day, a fresh wave of excitement broke over the city and produced almost a panic. The main body of Tung Fu-hsiang's savage Kansu braves—that is, his whole army—re-entered the capital, and rapidly encamped on the open places in front of the Temples of Heaven and Agriculture. . . . This settled it, I am glad to say. At last all the Legations shivered."

Had they known that Tzu Hsi and Kuang Hsu were being escorted by General Tung everywhere they went because they were Prince Tuan's hostages, they might have shivered again.

More alarmed than ever, Sir Claude sent a third telegram at eight-thirty that evening, making a blunt appeal for help to Admiral Seymour: "The situation in Peking is hourly becoming more serious . . . troops should be landed and all arrangements made for an advance on Peking at once." Similar telegrams were sent by the other envoys.

Off Taku at eleven o'clock that night, June 9, Admiral Seymour received Sir Claude's last telegram and was galvanized into immediate action. He informed his counterparts in the other fleets that he was leading a force to Peking at once and invited them to join him.

The following morning Sir Robert Hart was sufficiently worried to telegraph Viceroy Li Hung-chang far to the south in Canton, explaining the state of affairs and asking Li, as the "oldest and most trusted" adviser to the dowager, to wire her that the Boxer flirtation was a dangerous policy to pursue. But that very day Prince Tuan was unexpectedly put in overall charge of foreign policy at the Tsungli Yamen, which he was to administer jointly with "the invertebrate" Prince Ching. This bore out Sir Claude's impression that Prince Ching was no longer in control even of his own department.

Before the day ended, a telegram reached the legations saying Seymour was on his way. Then the telegraph lines were cut, isolating Peking from the outside world. All official foreign descriptions of events after this date were composed after the fact and laid blame squarely on the Chinese, ignoring any and all provocative acts by the foreigners. So anxious were diplomats and generals to convey that they had behaved honorably during the crisis that they tailored their accounts to enhance their roles at the expense of the facts. Luckily some uncensored and unedited diaries and personal accounts survive, providing something closer to the truth.

While the legations awaited Seymour's relief force with mounting anxiety, the number of Boxers in the capital increased dramatically, to perhaps as many as thirty thousand. Among them inevitably were many vagrants and criminals who took this opportunity to put themselves under princely patronage and line up for a free lunch. The Boxers were intended to be the outer ring against Seymour and whoever followed, General Tung's twelve thousand Kansu braves would be the middle ring, and the Peking Field Force and the Tiger Hunt Marksmen the inner rings. In practice, this strategy proved to be yet another Ironhat fantasy. The three imperial forces clustered in and around Peking were political armies, whose chief purpose was to provide leverage for their commanders. As such, Prince Tuan and General Tung were not going to squander their men or equipment in set-piece combat. Jung Lu naturally held his big army back in defiance of the Ironhats. The Boxers remained to the bitter end armed only with knives, swords, cudgels, a few antique muskets—and amulets to make them bulletproof.

Tensions were running high. Expecting Seymour's relief force at any moment, Japanese embassy chancellor Sugiyama Akira donned a tailcoat and a top hat on June 11 and set forth with his valet in a Peking wagon to meet the Allied force at the railway station in the Chinese City. He would have been wiser to stay at home, for the Allied relief force was far away having troubles of its own. Outside the Yungtingmen Gate, where Sugiyama entered the Chinese City, he was set upon by General Tung's soldiers, dragged from his cart, and hacked to pieces.

Why Sugiyama was singled out for assassination in this manner has never come to light, although he may have been involved in spiriting the fugitive Liang Chi-chao out of China two years earlier, earning the enmity of the Ironhats. Morrison reported that Sugiyama's heart "was cut out and, there is every reason to believe, was sent as a trophy to the savage General Tung Fu-hsiang himself." Morrison added gratuitously that this was the same General Tung who had escorted the empress dowager and the emperor back from the Summer Palace, and therefore the murder had been committed by "the favorite bodyguard of the empress dowager." Morrison omitted any mention of the edict promptly issued by Tzu Hsi after Sugiyama's murder: "This news has caused us deep and sincere regret. . . . The murderers . . . shall be dealt with, when captured, with the utmost severity."

Walking down Legation Street the day after Sugiyama's murder, forty-seven-year-old Baron Clemens Freiherr von Ketteler, the current German minister—"a man of strong views and impetuous courage"—came upon a covered Peking cart drawn by a mule. Riding in front was a man dressed like a Boxer, red bands tied around his head and wrists, as many ordinary Chinese in Peking were now attired to be fashionable. He was sharpening his knife "insolently" on his boot. This was too much for Baron von Ketteler, who fell upon the man with his lead-weighted walking stick. The man fled, but upon looking inside the covered wagon the baron discovered a young boy of ten or eleven dressed in a similar costume. He hauled the boy out and beat him severely with the weighted cane, after which he dragged the dazed child to the German legation and kept him prisoner. Official demands for his release were ignored. This father and son were the first and only "presumed" Boxers yet seen anywhere near the legations, but the baron's attack on them was to be a major factor in bringing on the siege.

Infuriated by Baron von Ketteler's unprovoked assault on the man and his beating and abduction of the boy, thousands of Chinese, including Boxers and General Tung's Kansu braves, went on a rampage for the next three days, June 13–16. Parts of Peking's Tartar City and a large portion of the Chinese City adjacent to the legation quarter were the scene of rioting, looting, and burning. Boxers poured into the Tartar City through the Hatamen Gate on the first day of rioting, pillaging the shops of Chinese merchants who traded with the foreigners. All this happened at some distance from the legations, not threatening them directly, but the abandoned Customs buildings and Sir Robert Hart's recently vacated home and garden were burned, destroying most of Hart's papers and books. The Roman Catholic East Cathedral and South Cathedral were put to the torch. The South Cathedral, built by Jesuits during the reign of Emperor Kang Hsi and decorated with many works of art, was reduced to a smoldering ruin. Also burned was the Anglican bishop's property, the London Missionary Society, and the Institute for the Blind. The stoutly defended North Cathedral, where Bishop Favier and many of his flock were holed up with their small detachment of marines, came under siege.

Many Western nuns and priests had been brought to the legations the previous day, but around the East and South cathedrals were large communities of Chinese Catholics, who had been abandonned to their own resources. One Westerner recalled: "We could hear the yells and screams of the fiends that were destroying and murdering, and those of their victims too: we learned afterwards that many native Christians had fled to [the South Cathedral] for safety and had been slaughtered or burnt to death within its walls."

Most looting and burning were confined to prosperous districts full of the shops, stores, and homes of wealthy Chinese, including dealers in jewelry and gemstones, silks and furs, embroidery, curios, and precious metals. Old accounts were being squared. In other parts of Peking, including most of the Tartar City, there was no rioting at all; markets and shops stayed open, and neighborhood life continued normally. General Tung's troops and the Boxers evidently were given designated areas to attack.

At the legations, Chinese servants, gardeners, chair-bearers, and interpreters began slipping away. For the foreigners this was not so much a sign of trouble as a great nuisance, for now the burdens of domestic routine, cooking, cleaning, washing, and ironing had to be shouldered by some of the ladies of the legations. All missionaries within reach of Peking had already sought asylum with the diplomats. Others were fleeing overland toward Siberia or the Treaty Ports.

Non-Christian Chinese who lived near the legations fled in terror.

Lenox-Simpson said, "Never have I seen such fast galloping and driving in the Peking streets; never would I have believed that small-foot women . . . could get so nimbly over the ground. Everybody was panic-stricken and distraught. . . . They went on running, running, running. . . . Far away the din of the Boxers could still be heard, and flames shooting up to the skies now marked their track; but of the dread men themselves we had not seen a single one." Not a single Boxer, that is, with the exception of the father and son who had been attacked by Baron von Ketteler.

The baron was intimate only with the Austro-Hungarian minister, Arthur von Rosthorn, so there was similarity in their conduct during these last days before the siege. On June 13 a guard of five Austrians was sent to the Belgian legation, where their machine gun commanded the Customs compound street. During the night some Chinese bearing torches were seen approaching down the thoroughfare—apparently intent upon picking through the ruins of the Customs buildings for anything of value—and were assumed to be Boxers bent on setting more fires. When they were within range, the Austrian machine gun opened fire. "It was a grateful sound," said Morrison with approval. "The torches disappeared. . . . But there was not one dead." Next morning it was found that the Austrians had shot down telegraph lines above the street.

On the afternoon of June 14, Baron von Ketteler was again out hunting, strolling along the top of the Tartar Wall. He observed a group of Boxers about two hundred yards distant, performing their customary exercises in a square of the Chinese City. Von Ketteler hurried down, collected a squad of German marines, and led them to a vantage point atop the wall, where he pointed to the Boxers. Creeping along the wall to get within range without being seen, the Germans fired into the Boxer formation, killing at least seven and wounding twenty. With some satisfaction, Morrison commented, "Ketteler and his merry men have just shot 7 Boxers from the top of the wall. . . . The stalking was excellently done." He did not relate this incident or his opinion to readers of the *Times*.

Reacting to this new provocation, Chinese and Boxers poured like angry fire ants through the Hatamen Gate into the Tartar City. Marines hastily cordoned off all the legations except the outlying Belgian compound, posting sentinels. When more Boxers tried to enter the Tartar City through the Chienmen Gate, they were stopped by Chinese troops and the gates were closed. A silent struggle had begun in which General Jung Lu, as supreme commander of the military district, tried with notable success to keep the lid on the pot, while Prince Tuan and his fellow conspirators tried to make it boil over. Hart wrote: "What a bit of luck for us that the Boxers have only swords, etc. Had they guns, they'd wipe us out in a night, they are so numerous."

On June 15 the dowager and Emperor Kuang Hsu issued explicit orders against the rioters. "All criminals who are found carrying arms and shouting '*Sha*' [kill] are to be immediately arrested, handed over to the gendarmerie, and executed upon the spot. . . . No leniency shall be allowed in the future. . . . The [Boxer] altars erected in the Inner and Outer Cities should all be torn down." They instructed Jung Lu, Prince Ching, Prince Tuan, and Duke Lan to see that these orders were carried out. Once again Tzu Hsi had been persuaded by real events that the Ironhat scheme was sheer folly.

That same day Morrison led a mounted party of Russians and Americans to the South Cathedral, a mile and a half away, to rescue any surviving Chinese Christians. Student interpreter Giles, who accompanied them, said, "Many were found roasted alive, and so massacred and cut up as to be unrecognisable."

The following day Morrison organized another posse to look for other Chinese Christian refugees. They came upon a temple where Boxers were burning incense, chanting, and executing prisoners. After a ten-minute gun battle, forty-six Boxers lay dead and their prisoners were freed. Morrison claimed he killed six Boxers himself. More than two thousand Chinese Christian refugees were now camped beside the sewer in tree-lined Canal Street, which ran in front of the British, Russian, and American legations separating them from Prince Su's walled gardens. This proved to be an embarrassment, for not one of the legations wanted them; there was no room except in the street, where they got in the way. Charity was in short supply. Morrison's rescue of the hated converts, possibly motivated by genuine concern rather than sport, was to backfire tragically.

Lenox-Simpson wrote: "Several of the chefs de mission were again much alarmed at this action of ours in openly rescuing Chinese simply because they were doubtful co-religionists. They say that this action will make us pay dearly with our own lives; that the Legations will be attacked."

No direct assault on the foreign community had yet taken place. In Peking only Chinese had been attacked by Boxers. No Boxer or imperial soldier had yet fired a single shot into the legations. Nobody in the legations had been killed or wounded. All the shooting was going in the opposite direction: foreigners were shooting Chinese. Edwin Conger estimated that by June 15 nearly one hundred presumed Boxers had been shot *without provocation* by marines of various legations. This figure included the Boxers "stalked" by von Ketteler's German guards, but did not include those many Chinese shot by Morrison's marauders, shot individually by student interpreters earlier, and by other flying squads of Western roughriders, numbering in the hundreds. Polly Condit Smith said that one group of fewer than twenty marines said they had killed 350 "thieves, Boxers and Imperial soldiers" by this date. All accounts of the siege have sought to play this down or failed to mention it at all.

By contrast, prior to May 31, when the legation guards arrived from Tientsin, only one foreigner had been killed by the Boxers: the missionary Brooks, who was judged by his peers to have acted foolishly. After the legation guards were summoned, Chancellor Sugiyama had been assassinated by General Tung's soldiers, four French and Belgian railway engineers had been killed in a gun battle while fleeing toward Tientsin, and two British missionaries were slain near Yungtsing. This brought the total of foreign dead so far only to eight. All the rest of the Boxer incidents in Peking and surrounding areas had been directed exclusively against Chinese. (Most Boxer violence in 1900 was concentrated in the small triangle Peking-Tientsin-Paotingfu, although Western accounts make it appear to have swept across all of North China.)

The court still remained sharply divided over policy, thanks to the recklessness of the Boxers themselves. On June 13, the day the Peking riots began, Boxers broke into the mansion of the elderly Grand Secretary Hsu Tung, one of the leading Boxer supporters most hostile to foreigners, and pillaged it. Boxers also assaulted and robbed Grand Secretary Sun Chianai; the chancellor of the Hanlin Academy; a vice-president of the Censorate; and a vice-president of the Board of Appointments. The newly appointed governor of Kweichow was dragged from his sedan chair, forced to kneel in the dirt, and then stripped naked and robbed of his silk garments. Once more this tipped the scales against Prince Tuan. On June 17 Jung Lu was ordered by the dowager and Kuang Hsu to move in troops: "Give energetic protection to the various Legations. Let there be no remissness." However, when Jung Lu asked the legations if they wanted this protection, the diplomatic corps declined, assuming that Jung Lu, being closest to the dowager, planned a massacre. In one of Morrison's telegrams published by the *Times* he stated that attacks on the legations "were ordered by the Empress Dowager and organized by Jung Lu." In the end the fact that almost all Western civilians survived the two-month-long siege unscathed had more to do with Jung Lu's intercession and control of the armed forces than it had to do with the valiant sorties, pickets, and battles waged by the besieged. The potshotting of the legation guards, the galloping gun battles of Morrison's cavalry, his rescue of the converts, and in particular the provocations of Baron von Ketteler were about to pull the rug out from under the moderates.

On the sixteenth Chung Li, the mayor of Peking and one of Prince Tuan's inner circle, came to the German legation personally to ask Baron von Ketteler for the release of the young boy being held hostage. This von

Ketteler was unable to do, because the boy was dead. Apparently during a fit of fury von Ketteler had shot him; this had been covered up by the German legation but was known to the British government, and to Morrison, who discussed it privately with Sir Henry Blake, the governor of Hong Kong, and Lady Blake, but never reported it to the *Times*.

Two days later the Tsungli Yamen appealed to the legations to permit no more armed raids by their roughriders because "it irritated the people." The Boxers still did not attack the legations.

While Tzu Hsi seemed to be in awe of Prince Tuan and to have given in to him increasingly, she was being pressed hard by the moderates as well and leaned first one way then the other. Decades of coalition rule had established precedents that made it difficult for her to act unilaterally, as demonstrated by the undermining of Emperor Kuang Hsu two years earlier. As both Tseng Kuo-fan and Henry Cockburn had discerned, Tzu Hsi was not a strong leader but a figurehead easily influenced. She had maintained her status at court by keeping her own counsel until one group clearly dominated an issue. On the Boxers she reversed course from day to day, waiting to see whose hand was strongest on the tiller. Secrecy obscured this wavering, so the actions of the throne seemed to the legations to be more single-minded than they actually were.

Thanks to so many Western provocations, during the second week of June there was a resurgence of Ironhat control of the court after the return of Kang I and Chao Shu-chiao from their investigations of the Boxers in Paoting and Chochou. The two mandarins had been sent to tell the Boxers southwest of Peking to behave themselves and to disperse, or Jung Lu's troops would kill them. They returned to Peking on June 16 to report that the Boxers were not really planning a rebellion against the government or the dynasty, to whom they pledged their loyalty, and that outrages such as the burning of churches and killing of converts and missionaries were the work of criminal secret society members, not of the Boxers themselves—a subterfuge the Ironhats had maintained all along. Kang I said that when he arrived at Chochou the Boxers all fell to their knees before him with hands clasped in greeting. He blamed all recent excesses and criminal acts by the Boxers on members of the anti-Manchu White Lotus sect, who were said to have taken advantage of the Boxers to infiltrate Peking and launch antigovernment conspiracies. He and other Ironhats assured the dowager and the court that under the circumstances there was no need to repress the Boxers after all, for they were not at fault.

To settle the debate, the throne convened that day the first of a series of extraordinary meetings of all princes, heads of the six government boards and nine bureaus, members of the imperial household—in all, more than a hundred mandarins, princes, and generals. The first meeting was occupied with accounts of the bad behavior of the Boxers, including their attacks on senior officials; debates on how to handle Admiral Seymour's expeditionary force, which was known to have left Tientsin and was expected to appear before the city gates at any moment; and the danger posed by the many foreign warships dropping anchor off the Taku Bar. This first conference concluded with a series of edicts announcing that Jung Lu's imperial troops would bring the Boxers under control in Peking, not only to prevent further looting and manhandling of mandarins but to make it completely unnecessary for Admiral Seymour's force to come to Peking to rescue the legations after all. The dowager again ordered Jung Lu and his army to take responsibility for protecting the legations, whether they wanted protection or not. An edict issued the following day demonstrated the concern of the court: "If amongst the families or staffs in the Legations there are any desiring to proceed temporarily to Tientsin, they should properly receive . . . protection on the way. But at the . . . moment railway communication is interrupted, and if they were to hurriedly proceed by road it would be difficult to insure their safety. They should, therefore, remain quietly where they are until the railway is repaired when the circumstances can be further examined and steps taken as required."

On June 17 a second urgent conference was summoned and Prince Tuan counterattacked, producing an ultimatum supposedly received from the Allies. According to the only eyewitness source we have from this meeting, on the basis of this fake ultimatum the empress dowager told the assembly that the Foreign Powers had made four demands: first, in view of persistent rumors that Emperor Kuang Hsu was still being kept prisoner, a specific palace must be designated as the emperor's residence; second, to eliminate the destructive effects of official corruption, foreigners must be given the right to collect not only foreign customs revenues but all taxes in China on behalf of the government; third, to end corruption in the Chinese armed forces, foreigners must be given authority over all military affairs in the empire; and, finally, Emperor Kuang Hsu must be restored to full power.

There is no evidence of any foreign government's putting such demands forward at this time, so the document had to be a counterfeit. One obvious possibility is that it was an Ironhat forgery designed to upset the moderates and to provoke the empress dowager into approving drastic action. However, it is more likely in retrospect that the counterfeit ultimatum originated with Viceroy Li in Canton, who was trying to provoke an Allied attack.

Ironically, at that very instant, the admirals anchored off Taku did issue an ultimatum—one that would force China into war—but it was nothing like the one Prince Tuan presented to the empress dowager.

As for Admiral Seymour's force of two thousand men who had left Tientsin for Peking by train a week earlier, they seemed to have vanished off the face of the earth. Morrison complained to his diary on June 16, "The Relief party farce. Crawling to our rescue." Sir Robert Hart coined a nickname: "Admiral See-No-More."

CHAPTER NINETEEN

A Mad, Rotten Scheme

Since first dropping anchor beyond the Taku Bar many weeks earlier, the commanders of the foreign squadrons had spent their time disagreeing over what to do. Admiral Sir Edward Hobart Seymour was the senior officer present, and the British squadron was the nucleus around which the men-of-war of other powers anchored. Seymour was the nephew of Admiral Sir Michael Seymour, who laid siege to Canton and Tientsin in 1860, climaxing in the Allied assault on Peking and the sacking and burning of the Summer Palace. As a boy, Edward had served aboard his uncle's flagship and could tell his staff how much the present naval assembly off the Taku Forts reminded him of 1860. On June 6 Seymour called a council of the commanders of France, Germany, Italy, Russia, Austria, the United States, and Japan aboard his flagship, H.M.S. *Centurion,* to arrange details for concerted action, and a plan was worked out for the landing of troops in the event they were needed. The Admiralty cabled Seymour on June 7 and 8 giving him a free hand, but by the time the cables arrived he had already been obliged to seize the initiative. The decision was made for him at 11:00 P.M. on June 9, when he received Sir Claude's urgent telegram asking for troops to march inland immediately. Seymour invited his counterparts to join the force he was leading to Peking. At 1:00 A.M. on June 10—only two hours after reading the telegram—he was ready to disembark nearly five hundred men at Tonghu, the common landing point upriver from Taku. There he commandeered a train, and by 3:00 A.M. they were on their way the twenty-five miles into Tientsin, the first stage of the journey. They quickly overcame resistance at Tientsin's railway station and seized other trains for the next stretch, to Peking. By 9:30 A.M. on the tenth—less than eleven hours after the plea for help—Seymour and his contingent were steaming toward the capital, a distance of less than ninety miles, normally taking four or five hours. Behind them another fifteen hundred troops of eight nations were disembarking to follow.

Seymour had acted boldly and courageously; he fully expected to be in Peking that evening. His officers took their full-dress uniforms, anticipating dinner dances at the legations. Unfortunately, despite having commendable instincts, the admiral was the wrong man to lead troops on dry land, for they quickly ran aground.

He had no reliable intelligence on the situation in Peking or the state of the country between, having obtained information only from the British consul in Tientsin, W. R. Carles, who was in a state of nervous excitement over the danger to British residents in his immediate area of responsibility. Seymour also unwisely left it to others to arrange supply and lines of communication. Worst of all, when he ran into stiff resistance his training persuaded him to stay with his ship—in this case his train—rather than striking out overland as an army officer might have.

All went well in the beginning. At Yangtsun, fifteen miles beyond Tientsin, they reached the steel railway bridge over the Peiho River, guarded by four thousand Chinese regulars under the moderate General Nieh, who had been sent there from Peking by Jung Lu to guard the railway from Boxers and who was one of the few Chinese generals who put up with no Boxer nonsense. Nieh's Chinese troops were friendly and waved Seymour through, exchanging greetings. Seymour pressed on till afternoon, when he had to stop at Lofa, nearly halfway to Peking, to repair tracks torn up by local militia. From that point on they had continual trouble with tracks and bridges, and by the next day, June 11, were only creeping up to Langfang, with forty miles yet to go.

As they approached Langfang they met their first active resistance, when they came under attack from about two hundred local peasants, mostly young boys in red headbands who had only recently become Spirit Boxers, armed with clubs, spears, swords, muskets, and jingals, a huge blunderbuss requiring two people and producing mostly smoke and noise. One of Seymour's men, who had been in China long enough to develop a low opinion of imperial soldiers, said "it was an almost incredible sight, for there was no sign of fear or hesitation . . . they charged until they dropped." Fifty or sixty boys were slain before the rest fled.

The station at Langfang had been destroyed, but Seymour's long delay there enabled the fifteen hundred additional Allied troops that had since debarked to catch up to him in four other commandeered trains.

Other militia attacks followed in greater strength as the local peasants regrouped. Supplies brought for a quick trip ran low. On June 14 the rearmost train, responsible for keeping up a supply shuttle between the expedition and Tientsin, was unable to pass Yangtsun. General Nieh's troops had been withdrawn and the bridge was now in Boxer hands.

Seymour never got farther than Langfang. A party of marines reconnoitered a few miles ahead but found the tracks torn up and the sleepers burned. They were marooned.

Seymour could easily have made the entire journey from Tientsin to Peking on foot in under a week; from Langfang it would have taken only two days. But the admiral had chosen to command trains, and if the trains could not move, he could not move. It was suffocatingly hot and the men were low on drinking water.

The Chinese authorities, although informed of his slow progress, still expected him to continue to Peking overland. Repeatedly, as the days passed, Yamen ministers appealed to Sir Claude to stop the admiral. Again and again, he refused. Memories of Lord Elgin's 1860 occupation stirred panic at court. Four thousand of General Tung's Muslim cavalry were dispatched from Peking to block the oncoming Allied force, which was no longer oncoming.

Unknown to Sir Claude and to the Manchu court, the admiral had decided to turn back. When he returned to Yangtsun he found the bridge had been damaged and was impassable. Whichever direction Seymour went, to Peking or to Tientsin, he was going to have to give up his trains and fight his way overland. So far, he had only to deal with poorly armed peasants and a few teenage Spirit Boxers, but that was about to change. Seymour's German contingent, still at Langfang as rear guard, now came under heavy fire from the Muslim cavalry, who pursued their train for miles. Until June 23 the Muslim cavalry attacks were constant. Unable to recross the bridge at Yangtsun, Seymour reluctantly abandoned his trains to withdraw downriver toward Tientsin. Four junks were seized to transport his guns, provisions, and wounded. The junks had to be towed, while the troops made the journey on foot. They might as well have walked the forty miles cross-country from Langfang to Peking as the thirty miles they now faced from Yangtsun to Tientsin, for the peasants were no happier to see them here. One pretty girl threw herself headfirst down a narrow well rather than be ravished, and it was only thanks to quick action by a German officer that she was rescued in a state of shock. Meanwhile, the situation in Tientsin had worsened: in the distance the men could hear the firing of heavy guns.

In the admiral's absence, Seymour's fellow commanders in their gunboats (each under strict orders to get a slice of the pie) had precipitated a full-scale war with China. On June 14, several days after Seymour had left Tientsin, twenty-four hundred foreign soldiers, seventeen hundred of them Russians, went ashore to guard the foreign concessions outside the old walled city. Nevertheless, on the night of June 15 Boxers burned down most of Tientsin's French Settlement.

Beyond the Taku Bar the Allied commanders were pacing their decks.

Peking was cut off, Seymour had vanished, the French Settlement was in ashes, and at any moment the Chinese might cut the railway connecting Tientsin to the mouth of the Peiho River at Taku where the warships stood twelve miles off, out of artillery range of the forts. Supplies and reinforcements for the forts could be seen arriving, torpedo tubes were being mounted by the Chinese, and it was presumed that mines were being laid in the river channel. Soon the Allied squadrons would be rendered impotent. (In none of this reasoning was the fate of the legations a factor.) Bickering finally stopped, and a majority of the commanders voted to act while they still had the advantage. They would occupy the Taku Forts, by force if necessary. An ultimatum was delivered to the office of the viceroy in Tientsin, setting a deadline of two o'clock on the morning of June 17.

This was a particularly delicate moment and one of those that has been lied about ever since, for no state of war existed between the Allies and China; technically the enemy was Boxer insurgents, not the Chinese government itself. Therefore an attack on the forts by the Allies was nothing less than a unilateral act of war against China. But if the forts were not seized, the commanders argued, the relief of the legations at some future point would become all the more difficult. This was not the only option open to the admirals and generals, for they could have landed three miles to the north in the mouth of the Peitang as they had in 1860, and marched straight to Peking to relieve the legations, making the ultimatum (and the act of war) unnecessary. Human nature being perverse, the plan chosen was the only one on which they could get a simple majority. Thus they showed themselves to be less concerned about rescuing the legations than about seizing and holding territory, a concept they all dimly understood. So at a time when only eight foreigners had been killed compared to well over two hundred Chinese, the Allies took matters into their own hands and opted for war. Their ultimatum demanded only the surrender of the Taku Forts, but that meant war.

There were four forts at the mouth of the Peiho—two on each lip—which had been attacked by the Allies twice during the Opium Wars, the first assault by sea ending in failure waist deep in the mud, the second ending in victory after an approach overland to attack them from behind. Since then the forts had been rebuilt and modernized by Viceroy Li Hung-chang's German engineers and equipped with rapid-fire Krupp guns. So the decision this time to attack head-on again by sea relied more on luck (shall we say) than on cunning. The assault would proceed across the same mudflats set with sharp stakes that had resulted in an embarrassing Allied bloodbath in 1859.

At sunset on the night the ultimatum expired, shallow-draft gunboats bearing nine hundred men took up positions beneath the walls of the forts.

British, German, Russian, French, and Japanese soldiers took part, the Americans abstaining on orders not to become involved militarily in the absence of a declaration of war (a point about to be rendered moot). If the Chinese commander did not surrender by 2:00 A.M. on June 17, there was no question what the Allies intended. Consequently at 12:45 A.M., barely an hour before the deadline, the Chinese opened defensive fire at the approaching force. For six hours the battle raged. The outcome was decided when Allied rounds fell fortuitously into huge powder magazines in the forts on both the north and south sides of the river mouth. The explosions were so colossal that the defenders were stunned. Under cover of the dust cloud, marines stormed the north forts with fixed bayonets. After the second explosion, the forts on the south bank surrendered without a fight. The Chinese commander committed suicide. Upstream, all four German-built destroyers of the Chinese navy were captured intact.

When the Taku Forts were attacked, a de facto state of war came into effect, so Chinese artillery also opened fire on the foreign settlements outside Tientsin; the next day ten thousand imperial troops besieged the settlements. Given the state of war, Washington advised Rear Admiral Kempff that his American troops could now join the engagement, and an international force totaling fourteen thousand men set out from Taku to relieve Tientsin.

This Allied relief column entered Tientsin's foreign settlements on the morning of June 23. Finding it all but impossible to work together, they took another fortnight to capture the old walled Chinese city nearby. While the others watched, the Japanese seized the initiative and set off a huge explosion that destroyed the city's South Gate, whereupon Chinese resistance ceased.

Meanwhile, Admiral Seymour's ragged force, struggling down the shallow Peiho River, had its only success when it reached a point barely three miles from Tientsin and came unexpectedly upon the arsenal at Hsiku, where they were lightly fired upon. Counterattacking, they were surprised to have all resistance melt away and found themselves in possession of a forty-acre arsenal full of machine guns, field guns, rifles, and millions of rounds of ammunition. The few Chinese still in the arsenal fled without another shot. Although they were now less than an hour's walk from Tientsin, Seymour's force was exhausted and remained in the arsenal for five days, missing the battle for Tientsin and completing the final leg of their grand tour only on June 26, as Tientsin was being joyously looted by its Allied conquerors. The last word on the Seymour expedition was had by 29-year-old Commander David Beatty, later admiral of the fleet at the Battle of Jutland in World War I, who called it "the maddest, wildest, damnedest, rottenest scheme that could emanate from the brain on any man." Not necessarily. Worse was yet to come.

The court in Peking did not learn of the Taku Forts ultimatum till June 19, by which time the forts had already been in Allied hands for most of three days. Yu Lu, the viceroy of Chihli, saw no reason to include such disappointing news in messages he sent by dispatch riders. He was an old man anxious for his neck and made no secret of his affection for the British. Before the forts were attacked, Lord Salisbury cabled that Yu Lu was to be offered sanctuary aboard Royal Navy vessels, an offer relayed to him by the British consul.

When Tzu Hsi first learned of the Taku ultimatum (but not that the forts had already fallen), she ordered all viceroys and governors to prepare to defend their provinces from foreign attack. Bland and Backhouse later published a bogus account of what took place at court that day, mixing up dates and events in the process. According to them, this was the day that Prince Tuan showed her the counterfeit ultimatum demanding her abdication. Tzu Hsi was furious: " 'The insults of these foreigners pass all bounds. Let us exterminate them before we eat our morning meal.' " (Backhouse was so irrepressibly clever that he could never resist putting witty expressions into Tzu Hsi's mouth; he seems to have found these colorful phrases while reading Chinese plays and borrowed them for his biographical hoax.)

News reached the empress on the twenty-first of fighting at Taku and Tientsin, but Yu Lu still did not inform her that the forts had long since fallen. All that was known in Peking was that the Allies had issued an ultimatum, their forces had approached the Taku Forts in a threatening manner, and shooting had begun. Accordingly, two days after the Allied attack began the war, she issued an edict acknowledging that hostilities had commenced and that a de facto state of war existed between China and the Allies.

For the better part of a century afterward, most Western histories have insisted that in this edict Tzu Hsi "declared war on the world," implying by the phrasing that she was daft. This was hardly the case. A majority of the Allied fleet commanders had voted to attack the forts, while those who voted against pointed out specifically that the attack would be an act of war. This occurred on June 15 without the knowledge of their home governments, who themselves were informed of the Taku ultimatum only four days later and of the attack and seizure of the forts only on June 21. So the transference of blame to the empress dowager was a deliberate manipulation of the facts that began immediately and has been in place ever since.

In an inspired editorial on June 19, Shanghai's North China *Daily News* proclaimed:

China is at war with all the great powers at once, and she is at war by the choice of the empress dowager and her gang. In their colossal ignorance and conceit they have persuaded themselves that they could safely defy the foreign powers. . . . Whatever happens, this gang, if it does not go of its own accord, must be driven out of Peking. It is to be hoped that it will be possible to get out the emperor Kuang Hsu and replace him [put him back] on the throne. Meantime it should be made perfectly clear to the Chinese that it is the empress dowager who has undertaken the present war, and that we are not fighting China, but the usurping government at Peking.

Despite the dream of Prince Tuan and his group that all foreigners could be expelled from China with the help of the Boxers, the war was over the moment it began. The fall of the Taku Forts and of Tientsin gave the Allies free access to Peking. It was only a matter of time before they regrouped and organized a march to the capital. They were not blocked by Chinese armies, most of them incompetent and poorly armed. Those units that could be considered competent and had modern rifles were political armies, not to be squandered in combat.

Unfortunately for the anxious legations, the Allied commanders in Tientsin could not reach a consensus on a march to Peking for an unbelievable two more months. It was during that needless delay that the siege of the legations occurred, so the quarreling Allied commanders in Tientsin were again as much to blame as anyone for the folly of the siege.

There was still a family quarrel going on in the Manchu court as well; moderates were still finding ways to interfere with the Ironhat strategy. During those long weeks of waiting the Chinese army could have overwhelmed the poorly defended legations at any time, but thanks to Jung Lu and other moderates all punches were being pulled.

On June 17 the first actual exchange of fire occurred, at the instigation again of Baron von Ketteler. Student interpreter Giles recorded the circumstances in his diary:

In the middle of the day [June 17] the Austrians and Germans fired on some of Tung Fu-hsiang's troops who had been throwing stones at the European soldiers. This is most unfortunate, as all wanted to avoid any trouble with the Chinese troops. Bullets began to whiz all over the place, and our picket from North Bridge was temporarily withdrawn. None of our men [the British] fired a shot in return. Later in the evening Sir Claude . . . had a talk with one of the Chinese officers, and both sides agreed to mutually avoid one another, and to look on the incident as a mistake.

Unaware that Admiral Seymour had given up and started back toward Tientsin but anxious to avoid any more shooting incidents, the Tsungli

Yamen tried next to persuade the legations to leave voluntarily. Twelve large scarlet envelopes were brought to the eleven ministers and Sir Robert Hart on June 19. "The Yamen . . . requests that within twenty-four hours Your Excellency will start, accompanied by the Legation's guards . . . and proceed to Tientsin in order to prevent any unforeseen calamity." At the same time the Yamen informed the legations of the Taku ultimatum. Sir Claude was aghast. He wrote bitterly in a note that was to be smuggled to Consul Carles in Tientsin that the Allied commanders had "sounded the death knell of the foreigners in Peking." To the Foreign Office he later described the ultimatum as "premature and needlessly provocative." To the Yamen itself he said that the legation ministers were astonished and knew "absolutely nothing of what had happened with regard to the Taku forts."

All the ministers except the belligerent von Ketteler were now anxious to leave Peking. They debated at length, then sent a message to the Yamen at midnight, asking for a meeting at 9:00 A.M. to work out particulars for their departure. Nobody was looking forward to the journey. One envoy observed sourly that "to stay meant probable massacre, to go meant certain destruction." Speaking of the younger staff, student interpreter Giles said, "We were all dead against [leaving Peking], having regard to the historical precedent of Cawnpore," where the British garrison was massacred during the Sepoy Mutiny. Edwin Conger ordered a hundred carts assembled to move families and their goods to Tientsin. Morrison, who relished a good scrap, said this was to Conger's "everlasting dishonour."

The Yamen responded that "the Princes and Ministers . . . would be very glad to discuss the situation thoroughly, but in view of the excitement that has prevailed during the last few days, it is to be feared that the Representatives might have cause for alarm [security could not be guaranteed] on their way to the Yamen. . . ." Sir Claude maintained in his official report that this message with its veiled warning was not received by 8:00 A.M. when von Ketteler became impatient and decided to make the trip to the Yamen on his own against the advice of his colleagues. Sir Claude recalled that the baron, "a very passionate and excitable man, banged his fist on the table and said 'I will go and sit there till they do come, if I have to sit there all night.'" For von Ketteler it was going to be an unusually long night.

The baron set out about 8:30 A.M. with his legation interpreter, Heinrich Cordes, in two sedan chairs, accompanied by one unarmed Chinese footman ahead and one behind; his sedan chair was hooded in scarlet and green to show his official status. Lenox-Simpson described how von Ketteler was "smoking [a cigar] and leaning his arms on the front bar of his sedan, for all the world as if he were going on a picnic." The two sedan chairs had just passed a small police station on crowded Hatamen Street when Cordes glanced to the left and saw a uniformed Manchu Bannerman, a lance corporal in the Peking Field Force, raise a Sharp's rifle and draw a bead on the baron's head. Cordes shouted a warning at the moment the soldier fired, killing von Ketteler instantly. The sedan chairs were dropped, Cordes jumped out and ran, and was shot through the legs. He was not pursued, and made his way painfully to the Methodist mission.

There is no reason to doubt that the assassination was arranged by Prince Tuan's group in revenge for the aggressive way von Ketteler had been behaving; for his unprovoked beating and imprisonment of the young Boxer boy, ending in the boy's being shot dead; for von Ketteler's repeated use of German legation guards to shoot down unarmed Boxers in the Chinese City's open areas, before hostilities of any kind had commenced against the legations; and for the shooting of General Tung's troops three days earlier by German and Austrian marines. This longstanding pattern of aggressive behavior by von Ketteler had greatly alarmed his diplomatic colleagues. Like many German officials at the time, von Ketteler sought to emulate Kaiser Wilhelm's horseradish arrogance and bombastic manner. The record of his predecessor Baron von Heyking in bringing about the recent German seizure of Tsingtao and Kiaochow Bay also set an aggressive standard that von Ketteler was anxious to emulate. He was quoted by journalists as saying that the best thing for China was to be cut up like bratwurst and swallowed by the Great Powers, with a large slice of North China going to Germany. Of course this irritated the British, Russians, and Japanese, who had in mind the same thing. Sir Claude was so infuriated that at his urging the Foreign Office in London had made a representation to Berlin, and German foreign secretary Count Bernhard von Bülow sent von Ketteler a coded cable reprimanding him on a number of points and warning him of the consequences if the Chinese government learned of his quarrel with other members of the diplomatic corps in Peking. The baron was hated even by normally charitable missionaries, who pointed out that "his imperative manner was at that time particularly obnoxious to the Chinese." Small wonder that he drove the Ironhats to murder.

Von Ketteler's killer, whose name was Enhai, became so celebrated after the assassination that he was later traced by the Japanese, arrested, and executed by the Germans. He told them he had been promised a promotion and seventy taels of silver by his superior but received only forty taels. Just before his head was removed, he was heard cursing the "stupid princes." The message the ministers had received from the Yamen asking them specifically *not* to venture out on the streets was known to Morrison, but he twisted it around and reported in the *Times* "that the Dowager Empress and Prince Tuan . . . had planned a massacre on that fatal morning of all the foreign Ministers."

Not at all, for von Ketteler was a special case. The plan to have the baron murdered must have been agreed on in advance once the Ironhats learned that he had murdered his young Chinese hostage, for (amazingly) the assassination was already being discussed as an accomplished fact in Tientsin and Shanghai days before it actually took place. The murder, which occurred on the twentieth, was reported in London's evening papers on the sixteenth (four days before it happened) and in the *Times* the next morning. As an American missionary in Peking remarked, "It is not often that a crime of this extraordinary character is telegraphed around the world four days in advance." With the telegraph lines cut before von Ketteler's murder, the lag in communications was so great that nobody outside Peking had confirmation of the killing for a full twelve days. Thus, in a particularly Oriental manner, it would take twelve days to learn about something that *had* happened, but you could know a week ahead about something that had not.

A few hours after the shooting, the Yamen sent word to the legations that the time limit for their departure had been extended. But by then von Ketteler's murder had changed the envoys' minds; his fellow diplomats would not leave for Tientsin, no matter how big an escort was provided.

As if the killing was a signal foreigners now poured into the legations from hiding places all over Peking. The total area within the legation quarter defense perimeter was eighty-five acres, two miles around. This was defended by twenty officers and 389 men, of eight nationalities. Also armed were diplomatic staff, student interpreters, and various civilians including a group of self-proclaimed "roughriders" who were regarded with contempt by Morrison. The quarter became jammed with some nine hundred foreign men, women, and children—451 military men, 245 civilians, 149 women, and 79 children. The majority of them eventually were concentrated in the spacious British legation, where different buildings were assigned to each nationality. The British compound covered more than twelve acres and had many buildings, including stables for 150 horses—mostly racing ponies. There were also numerous pack mules, a flock of sheep, and a cow, which was made the exclusive responsibility of Pokotilov, head of the Russo-Chinese Bank. The British legation also had the biggest stock of preserved food, with great quantities of tinned bully beef, and commanded good fields of fire without being directly over-looked by the Tartar Wall. Normally it housed sixty to eighty people. By the afternoon of June 20 it was filled by many times that number. American missionaries and their Chinese converts, including 126 Chinese school-girls, were housed in the legation chapel. Sir Robert Hart and his Customs officers and families moved in with all their food and drink and articles of value. "The place was choked with women, missionaries, puling children, and whole hosts of lamb-faced converts," complained Lenox-

Simpson tongue-in-cheek, "whose presence in such close proximity was intolerable."

Many hundreds of converts milled around in the street outside the British legation and slept by the open sewer, uncertain where else to go. Now that the legations were going to stick it out in Peking, it was decided to do something to clear the great throng of Chinese Christians away, to remove them from the line of fire not so much for their sake but for the sake of the marine guards, and to prevent the enemy from using the converts as cover for a stealthy approach up the canal. Morrison had a bright idea.

Across from the British legation were the palace and grounds of Prince Su, head of one of the eight great Manchu families. These grounds, known as the Fu, consisted of fourteen acres, richly planted with trees and flowering shrubs, filled with pavilions, palaces, and pagodas, thirty buildings in all, surrounded by a twenty-foot-high wall. Sir Claude regarded the Fu as "one of the principal parts of the defence . . . because its loss would render the British Legation almost untenable." The other strategic position was the Tartar Wall: "An enemy holding it commanded easily the entire circle of defence." Marines were in possession of the Tartar Wall.

The Fu, beneath the very eaves of the Forbidden City, was a hereditary Peking estate, passed down through nine generations to the current prince. He was an unusually sophisticated man, not directly involved in the Ironhat conspiracy. No matter how enlightened he was, he would not willingly have abandoned his property, with all its treasures, to a mob of Chinese refugees, Rice Christians at that.

Polly Condit Smith described how the eccentric Professor Huberty James of Peking University, who had participated in Morrison's gunslinging rescue of the converts, acted as interpreter for Morrison during "negotiations" with the thirty-seven-year-old Prince Su:

> They [the Chinese refugees] could not stay in the road; the Legations could not have them. Dr. Morrison and Dr. H. James hit upon one of the happiest of ideas—namely, the seizing of a lovely park belonging to . . . Prince Su. . . . Dr. H. James went personally to Prince Su, and interpreted to him that it would not only be kind, but wise, for him to present his palace and park to his distressed fellow-citizens, who were being massacred by the Imperial soldiers. . . . Dr. James implied that unless he voluntarily gave up his . . . park, we would take it. Prince Su was most suave, and said nothing would give him greater pleasure. There was probably some truth in what he said. He was only too glad to get as far away as possible from these Legation people, notwithstanding he would have to give up his palace. The danger for his life might be very great if he were suspected, even for

a moment, of sympathizing with the foreigners, as might easily have been maintained by his enemies had he continued to live in this palace, which we told him he might do, as it was only his big park we wanted for the Christians.

Morrison reported to the *Times* that Prince Su's palace and gardens had been obtained because of "the influence" Huberty James had with Prince Su. He neglected to mention the threats and intimidation that constituted this influence.

The prince left behind what Polly Smith described as "all his treasure and half of his harem." The palaces were immediately looted by Western-ers. Antiques, artworks, priceless porcelain, and treasures from the prince's library were stolen, and all the silks and satins were ripped down from the walls and taken away to make sandbags. Su's palaces and pavilions were stripped bare of all except their architectural ornamentation. Much money was found hidden in various caches, of which only $34,000 was acknowledged, and part of that was set aside for a memorial to commemorate the siege. There is no record of any of this money being returned to the prince or of any compensation being paid to him later for the looting or damage. The Chinese Christians were then moved onto the grounds, turning them into a refugee camp. This proved convenient, because many of the legation cooks and laundry boys had already fled. The refugees took their places as the domestics of the siege.

The Japanese embassy was directly behind the Fu, so its military at-taché, Colonel Shiba, took responsibility for guarding the palace and gardens and protecting the refugees with twenty-four Japanese marines and thirty-two armed converts. Shiba knew China well, having been there as a student; he spoke Chinese and had served in the Sino-Japanese War with distinction. He had also been a military attaché in London. Almost all the Japanese mission spoke Chinese; no other foreign military officers and few of the diplomatic corps spoke the language.

Throughout the siege, organized Chinese military attacks were concen-trated exclusively on the Fu, against the Chinese Christians there rather than against the foreigners nearby. Once emptied of valuables, there were no white people in the Fu. Morrison and the deputy military commander of the legations' defense, Captain Ben Strouts, and others went on periodic tours of inspection. Western men prowled the gardens at night hunting for unwary girls among the converts, and a number of rapes were hushed up by the diplomatic corps.

At 4:00 P.M. on June 20, firing was heard from the outlying Austrian legation. Panicking, its occupants fled pell-mell to the nearby French legation. From the point of view of the people in the legations, this panic marked the beginning of the siege, although nobody was ever certain why the panic had occurred. Whether a siege ever existed except in their minds is another question.

Morrison was furious at the Austrian retreat because his house was next door. He accused the Austrian commander, Captain von Thomann, a naval officer, of cowardice. Now that their legation had been abandoned, Morrison was forced to pack his prized library and bring it to the British legation, where Lady MacDonald made a place for him at the back of her residence. He stacked his books to the ceiling around a mattress on the floor, where he slept. Soon afterward his empty house was burned to the ground.

On the evening of June 20, after the Austrian legation was abandoned, bystanders idling at the gate of the British legation saw Professor Huberty James come running out of the Fu with a Chinese soldier in hot pursuit. Before he could get across the bridge over the sewage canal, several Chinese sharpshooters appeared from the bushes beyond and shot James in a very deliberate manner, similar to the execution of von Ketteler. As British marines fired volleys in the sharpshooters' direction, James crawled slowly down the bank into the black sewage and died.

His murder made everyone sensitive to the danger now thought to be facing all of them. There had been several isolated incidents of deliberate executions, of people who had earned the special enmity of the Ironhats for one reason or another, beginning with Sugiyama and von Ketteler. Their third target was Dr. James, who had been responsible for the eviction of Prince Su and the looting of his home. But now each person in the legations assumed that he would be next. Nothing whatever had been done to prepare proper barricades at the British legation, which everyone agreed would be the heart of the defense. Only a few sandbags had been tossed by its main gate. That night there was the usual elegant dinner party, presided over by Sir Claude in full evening dress. After dinner he strolled the compound thoughtfully, smoking an Egyptian cigarette.

The next day, windows were sandbagged, leaving firing loopholes, and all the gates were fortified. Looking around the legation quarter's perimeters, Sir Robert Hart observed that for some inexplicable reason he could see only imperial army troops in the brilliant silks of each command. The Boxers with their red headbands had completely evaporated.

CHAPTER TWENTY

The Siege of Peking

What had become of the Boxers? They had ceased to exist. Now that war with the Foreign Powers was a matter of fact, there was no reason to continue the pretense that the Boxers were a peasant uprising for which the government had no responsibility. After their three days of rioting and looting in Peking in mid-June, which challenged the wisdom of letting them run around loose, the court decided to draft many of the younger toughs into units of the imperial army, militia, and police. They were formally placed under the control of Grand Councillor Kang I, Ironhat police chief Prince Chuang, and assistant police chief Duke Lan, all of whom had military commands as well. The older Boxers, many of them uncontrollable troublemakers, were sent out of the capital to the east as a human shield of militia against the Allies. To sweeten their dispositions and encourage them to obey, the court granted the Boxers and the Muslim roughnecks of General Tung 20,000 piculs of rice (more than thirteen hundred tons) and 100,000 taels of silver. The only group of Boxers allowed to continue to function in Peking was the handpicked force attacking the barricaded North Cathedral, refuge of priests, nuns and converts, under the watchful eye of Prince Chuang. Renegade Boxers who resisted these payoffs and enlistment, and continued to riot and loot, were hunted down by government agents. So at the very moment that the famous Boxer siege is said to have begun, the Boxers ceased to have anything to do with it, and ceased to exist.

All the government armies still were represented on the legation perimeter, and could be identified by their brightly colored silks and the banners of their commanders, but the majority of the troops were now those of Jung Lu, under orders from the dowager empress to protect the legations.

Jung Lu was in a political predicament that he found difficult to handle. On the one hand he had to carry out the dowager's edict to protect the legations, while limiting Chinese civilian casualties from Western sharp-shooters. On the other hand, he had to make a convincing display to the Ironhats that his men were earnestly attacking the foreigners, when in fact they were shooting in the air and setting off large quantities of firecrackers. Regrettably the legations failed to understand anything of this. So while Jung Lu's army cordon actually made the legations more secure than they were before, rising anxiety inside the legations made everyone believe that Jung Lu was putting them at greater risk than before. This created a paradox: When the siege began in the minds of the legationers was when it really ended. What they called a siege was a protracted cease-fire.

Not a great thinker or strategist, Jung Lu spent the weeks of the siege maintaining his buffer zone around the legations and waiting helplessly for Li Hung-chang to come back to Peking to save the dynasty. Eventually this is what happened, but not before Viceroy Li had exacted a heavy price from the court, and had the Ironhats in a cleft stick.

In the legations, hysteria was taking over. Although there had been no serious attack, fear of attack made people in the outlying legations extremely nervous, convinced they would be cut off, brutally tortured, and only then hideously murdered. At 9:00 A.M. on June 22, for no apparent reason, there was another panic and guards at the legations of Germany, Italy, France, Japan, America, and Russia all fled into the British legation. No attack came, but some Chinese seized this opportunity to take over an abandoned barricade on Customs Street and to burn the Italian legation to the ground. In the fire the Italian envoy, the Marchese di Salvago-Raggi, and his wife lost everything but their cashbox, which they had the presence of mind to take with them; they were soon elegantly dressed in borrowed finery. The Austrian naval officer, Captain von Thomann, who until then was the senior military officer in the legations, was blamed for this panic and also for the earlier abandonment of the Austrian legation. He was relieved of command, and by unanimous consent Sir Claude MacDonald was named supreme commander for the remainder of the siege. The guards who had panicked were sent back shamefacedly to their positions. The Italians, now homeless, moved into the French compound with the Austrians.

While Chinese troops were occasionally besieging the converts holed up in the Fu, the rest of the legation quarter was subjected only to intermittent harassing gunfire, mostly aimed randomly over the rooftops by General Tung's Muslim soldiers. When they were fired upon by foreign marines at the barricades atop the Tartar Wall or on the outer perimeter, Tung's men fired back; soldiers on both sides were killed or wounded. This was made worse by the fact that as barricade duty on the wall was not popular, American marines and sailors ordered to do duty

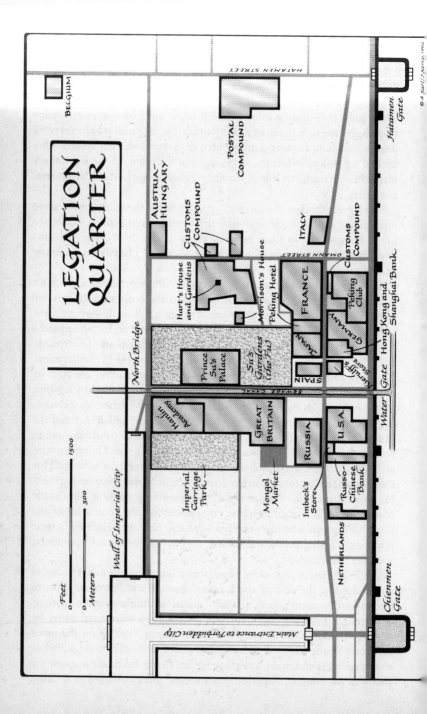

LEGATION QUARTER

Feet 0 — 300 — 1500
Meters

BELGIUM

AUSTRIA-HUNGARY

POSTAL COMPOUND

HATAMEN STREET

Hatamen Gate

CUSTOMS COMPOUND

Hart's House and Gardens

Morrison's House

Peking Hotel

ITALY

CUSTOMS COMPOUND

OMANN STREET

FRANCE

Peking Club

JAPAN

GERMANY

Kierulff's Store

SPAIN

Hong Kong and Shanghai Bank

Water Gate

North Bridge

Prince Su's Palace

Su's Gardens (the Fu)

IMPERIAL CANAL

Hanlin Academy

GREAT BRITAIN

RUSSIA

U.S.A.

Imperial Carriage Park

Wall of Imperial City

Mongol Market

Imbeck's Store

Russo-Chinese Bank

NETHERLANDS

Chienmen Gate

Main Entrance to Forbidden City

© A. Karl/J. Kemp, 1992

there took whiskey bottles with them and stayed drunk most of the time. Morrison sneered in his diary that U.S. Marine Captain Newt Hall "has no control over his men who get blind drunk and insult their NCO with impunity."

Marines and armed civilians manning peepholes and firing points in the legations continued to shoot any stray Chinese they saw, on the assumption that they were Boxers. A number of Chinese were seized, tortured, and then shot dead. Early in the morning of June 24, for example, two brutally beaten Chinese described as "Boxer prisoners" were executed by Englishmen in the north stable of their legation, their bodies thrown into the sewage canal to reincarnate. As the shadows shrank and the day became suffocatingly hot, adding to the overpowering stink of rotting bodies and percolating sewage, a squad of Austrian guards crept toward the ruins of the Italian legation and shot sixty Chinese civilians who were picking through the rubble looking for anything of value. When done by Chinese this was called "looting," when done by Westerners it was called "foraging"; so that same day student interpreter Hewlett was able to say, "This morning they started a system of forage carts working in Legation Street to clear all food from the remaining shops, which was distributed."

Meanwhile, General Jung Lu was trying unsuccessfully to negotiate a cease-fire with the legations. He described his frustration in a message to Viceroy Chang Chih-tung far away on the Yangtze:

> After the death of the German Minister, the British Minister had Prince Su driven out of his palace and ordered thousands of Christian converts to live there. The various legations were united and daily fired their rifles and guns, killing innumerable officials and people.
>
> It was therefore impossible for the Headquarters Army and Tung Fu-hsiang's troops not to defend their positions and make counterattacks. . . . On June 25 I had a notice written in big characters saying that in accordance with the [empress dowager's] Imperial decree we will protect the legations, that shooting is forbidden, and that we should communicate with each other. [The legations] not only paid no attention, but [opened fire]. . . . The difficulty is that there is no way to communicate with [the foreigners].

Jung Lu added that several truce emissaries, both mandarins and imperial army officers, had been shot dead while they waited for a response from Sir Claude. This was typical of the siege folly and occurred the following way: After using binoculars to read Jung Lu's big-character sign asking them to exchange communications, the legations sent a messenger up the road to the north bridge over the sewage canal, but along the way the man panicked and bolted for cover. Mystified by his peculiar behavior, Jung

Lu's truce emissaries—officers and mandarins—stepped out into the open and were shot dead by legation guards. Hewlett tossed it off blithely in his version of events, saying the emissaries were "shot at by the Japs and Italians in the Fu." Nonetheless, Jung Lu finally was able to establish a cease-fire for the next few days.

Young Giles found the cease-fire fascinating: "At 6:15 P.M. some of us . . . picked our way over the ruins to the north end of the Hanlin and had a talk with one of the [Manchu] soldiers who came towards us. . . . Some way behind him . . . were two to three hundred soldiers of all regiments. . . . Their red, green and blue uniforms were very picturesque." Hewlett and Giles busied themselves taking photographs. They planned to write books about the siege, and in the meantime they would send the negatives to Giles's father to place in the British magazines, remembering, of course, to secure the copyright. They spent all their spare time during the siege photographing or "foraging." Hewlett was especially pleased when they found bolts of silk in unoccupied private homes around the Mongol Market, and "annexed" them.

One problem with narratives of the siege is that the authors describe all fusillades as "attacks" even when no attack took place, a cease-fire was in effect, and the Chinese soldiers were partying, shooting into the air, and setting off firecrackers. Some of the "fusillades" were huge strings of firecrackers, which the legations mistook for gunshots. For instance, on the evening of the twenty-fifth, the start of the cease-fire, there was a fantastic "fusillade" from all around that lasted nearly an hour, the Chinese apparently firing into the air because no person or building was hit. This was called "the heaviest firing so far," by people in the legations. One afternoon, Giles wrote, "the alarm was sounded and we dashed to our posts. The attack was severe, but as the Chinese never bother to take any aim, no casualties were reported. One death for every 15,000 bullets fired is a poor percentage." After talking with a few experienced military men, Giles understood: "The Chinese troops . . . fire a tremendous amount, almost entirely without aiming. They crouch behind a wall, load, point their guns over the wall (without raising themselves) and fire—at nothing in particular." He wondered at the point of it all. Once "a fierce fusillade began from the Hanlin. The effect was magnificent. The rifle fire did not last long; but the jingals kept going till four the next morning. The Chinese must be running short of rifle ammunition, having to fall back on these antiquated things." One night the Chinese let loose an estimated two hundred thousand rounds, in the general direction of the moon, killing nobody. It did not occur to the panicky legationers that most of these harmless detonations were merely fireworks.

To be sure, some shooting was very real, at least on the barricades. In the first two weeks of the siege, thirty-eight marines and sailors were killed, mostly in point-blank exchanges at the barricades, and fifty-five people were wounded, mostly by ricochets as they strolled carelessly around the legations. In his diary Morrison observed wryly that, aside from freak shots, few people would have been hit if they had remembered to keep their heads down and stayed out of the open.

It was important for the troops ringing the legation quarter to look good, to expend a lot of ammunition, and to make a lot of noise with firecrackers. Of the five Chinese armies in the Peking region, only the troops under General Tung, who had been mingling with the Boxers earlier, seemed to pose any serious threat to the legations because of Tung's close bond to Prince Tuan. So far it was only a potential threat, because Jung Lu saw to it that they were directly on the legation perimeter at only two or three points. Tung's men were wild but not well trained; some had been given breech-loading rifles but most were armed only with muskets, stink bombs, and jingals. They were as great a danger to the Chinese residents of Peking as they were to the foreign community.

Most of the serious shooting incidents were reciprocal. Many people finding sanctuary in the legations steadfastly refused to take up guns and to participate in sniping at the Chinese, but there were dozens of Westerners who spent their days and nights watching through loopholes and waiting for targets to appear—any targets. For them this was sport. Polly Smith said the Flemish first secretary of the Belgian legation, Merghelynckem, "is a fine shot, but is erratic to a degree. The other day he brought me five long Chinamen's queues, which he had cut off the heads of Boxers he had killed, as a souvenir of a day's work . . . and these trophies hanging up in our living-room for a few days were obviously things of terror to our Chinese servants, although they had been cut from the heads of their dread enemies." How it was certain that these queues came from Boxers, she did not say. Anybody you shot was a Boxer. Some days later a French contingent captured eighteen Chinese in a temple near the legations. Although the Chinese denied being Boxers and gave what Morrison later reported as "much information that was obviously false," every one of them was put to death in the French legation, bayoneted in the stomach by a French corporal to save cartridges. They died slowly.

Not all Westerners in Peking had immediately taken refuge in the legations. On June 27 Edmund Backhouse took advantage of Jung Lu's cease-fire to slip through the Chinese lines and take up sanctuary in the British compound. Edmund kept his work load to a minimum during the siege by claiming to have sprained his knee or ankle. "I doubt whether he was much help to anyone," said one of his relatives, "as I heard that he had managed to shoot his own sergeant major." Lancelot Giles, who was his contemporary, said, "I see Backhouse occasionally. He strained some muscle early in the siege, and has been laid up ever since. He just

manages to crawl about now. He spends his day in a characteristic manner. Every day he reads through from cover to cover Goodrich's Pocket
Chinese-English Dictionary!"

There was work for everyone who wanted it, if only making sandbags
from Prince Su's silks and satins. A thousand were made in a single
morning, the women sewing while the Chinese Christians, now employed
as coolies, filled and carried away the bags. The early days of July passed
slowly in this manner, although there were the sounds of occasional
skirmishes over in the Fu gardens. The whole of July 6 was quiet, with
couples out strolling Chancery Lane, which ran along the west side of the
Russian and British legations from the Mongol Market to the imperial
carriage park, while other couples picnicked on the lawn. It was hard to
tell a siege was under way.

Rummaging through an abandoned foundry near the legations, someone discovered the rusty barrel of an old field gun left from the Allied
expedition of 1860. After a thorough cleaning it was able to fire the
nine-pound ammunition the Russians had brought (while forgetting to
bring their gun). During one of the early panics, before the start of the
siege, they had dropped the useless ammunition down a well to keep the
Chinese from getting it and now had to fish it out. The first round fired
from the old gun, dubbed "Betsy," was shot at the Forbidden City, passing
over the rose-colored wall in the direction of the imperial palace. According to Jung Lu, the palace was hit many times by such shots fired from
the legation quarter.

With so much time on their hands, the besieged were free to speculate
on whatever might have happened to Admiral Seymour and what had
become of the main Allied force storming Tientsin. Tantalizing answers
were provided by a passing Chinese coolie "captured" by legation guards.
Hewlett recounts how the coolie seemed to know a great deal: "Tientsin,
on account of the arrival of foreign troops, was in great disorder . . . Taku
was taken, and 100 men-of-war (foreign) were there. . . . The Boxers and
soldiers yesterday frequently fought in the streets [of Peking] over loot
. . . many of Jung Lu's troops after getting hold of the loot had deserted.
Tung Fu-hsiang was still in the City; affairs were managed by Jung Lu
and [Prince] Tuan. [Prince] Ching had nothing to do with this affair.
Boxer headquarters were at Tuan's palace." The coolie was so well informed that the legations decided he was a spy. He was lucky not to be
thought a Boxer.

At twilight on July 13 the boredom was interrupted by two giant explosions. On the French side of the legation quarter's perimeter there had
been a spate of serious fighting. During the previous week French marines
had shot more than a hundred passing Chinese from the cover of vacant
houses near their legation, pushing the legationers' grand total of Chinese

dead over five hundred. The Chinese were striking back by tunneling under the French defenses. Two kegs of black gunpowder were set off, killing two sailors and badly injuring a number of others.

Boredom soon resumed. The heat was intense and for the first time the smell of rotting bodies was stronger than the smell of sewage in the canal. Giant ravens pecked at the moldering carcasses in the sewer. Marines who bayoneted Chinese prisoners because they could not spare the ammunition to shoot them expended many rounds firing at the ravens for sport and sent the carrion birds to the Chinese Christians to eat.

Morrison was enjoying himself as never before. Others described him as "the best informed person within the Legation . . . a cool judgment, total disregard of danger and a perpetual sense of responsibility to help." Polly Smith thought of him as "the most attractive at our impromptu mess—as dirty, happy and healthy a hero as one could find anywhere."

On July 16 Morrison and Captain Ben Strouts, Sir Claude's deputy commander of the legations' defense, were returning from an inspection tour of the Fu gardens when they were both hit, Morrison superficially, Strouts mortally. The captain had come to be identified by the Ironhats as the prime mover behind British attacks on Chinese soldiers and mandarins so he had to be removed.

Morrison was shot in the rump—or what he chose to describe as the fleshy part of "the right thigh." The undignified wound, too high up in the rear to be ignored or to accommodate a crutch or walking stick, disabled him for the rest of the siege. He was obliged to spend his time prone, which proved ideal for composing his lengthy report on the siege for the *Times*. Bertram Lenox-Simpson, who thought the famous journalist was a stuffed shirt, guessed that Morrison was probably spending his convalescence writing two versions of the siege, a flattering and heroic one for publication in the *Times*, and a second one a bit closer to the truth that would be kept secret. Whatever his failings, the young Lenox-Simpson had a gift for seeing through pretense, for indeed Morrison spent his days alternately composing his falsified newspaper account of the siege while writing a very different version in his private diary.

The mine explosion beneath the French legation and the sniper execution of Captain Strouts were among the isolated incidents in an otherwise quiet stretch from June 25 to July 16, and the day after that (thanks again to Jung Lu) a new cease-fire began that would last ten more days. Not bad for what was to be portrayed as a relentless siege. During this cease-fire, an elderly Chinese messenger brought two communiqués. One, in cipher for Conger from the State Department, was a classic of bureaucratic nonsense; it said only, "Communicate tidings bearer." The second, to Sir Claude from "Prince Ching and colleagues," promised that the Chinese government would "continue to exert all its efforts to keep order and give protection." Prince Ching suggested that if the foreigners would only stop shooting Chinese, the situation might calm down a bit. In retrospect it is obvious the prince was speaking the truth, but the legations were in a state of hysteria inflamed by visions of the Cawnpore massacre, so they had their own definition of truth. The two viewpoints were so far apart that the parallax between was impossible to overcome. What was true for one would always be false for the other. Conger sniffed in retort that from the first "the foreign troops had acted entirely in self-defense and would continue to do so."

A peace offering of vegetables, fresh fruit, and watermelons was brought to the legations and two Chinese soldiers handed over Jung Lu's calling card with a message that he was endeavoring at that very moment to stop all firing. Indeed, at 6:00 P.M. it ceased completely. Unable to get the legations to agree to a formal cease-fire, the Chinese had simply stopped shooting back.

Conger was then invited to cable Washington; the Chinese thought his government might be willing to intercede for peace. However, Conger's message was carefully composed to have the reverse effect: "For one month we have been besieged in the British legation under continued shot and shell from Chinese troops; quick relief only can prevent general massacre."

Taking advantage of the cease-fire to stretch their legs, Chinese-speaking Westerners walked around the barricades, chatting with the Chinese soldiers, offering cigarettes. Lenox-Simpson, who was among them, was reminded that both sides were operating on lies and false assumptions:

Sauntering about, some of the enemy were willing to enter into conversation. . . . The Shansi levies and Tung Fu-hsiang's men . . . had but little idea of why they were attacking us; they had been sent, they said, to prevent us from breaking into the Palace and killing their Emperor. . . . Somebody tried to explain to them that the Boxers had brought it all on. But to this they answered that the Boxers were finished, driven away, discredited; there were none left in Peking, and why did we not send our own soldiers away, who had been killing so many of them. . . . It shows us plainly that not only has something happened elsewhere, but that the Boxer plan is miscarrying in Peking itself. . . . This makes it absolutely plain that this extraordinary armistice is the result of a whole series of events which we cannot even imagine. . . . For all the decreeing and counter-decreeing of the early Boxer days has begun again, and the all-powerful Boxers with their boasted powers are being rudely treated. It is evident that they are no longer believed in; that the situation in and around Peking is changing from day to day. The Boxers, having shown themselves incompetent, are reaping the whirlwind. They must soon entirely disappear. It is even two weeks since the last [Boxer] was shot outside the Japanese lines at night . . . a mere boy of fifteen.

Lenox-Simpson was right on all these assumptions except the Boxers: they had already ceased to exist.

Claude Pelliot, a linguist at the French legation, climbed over the Chinese barricades in Legation Street one day; the soldiers gave him tea and took him to the Tsungli Yamen, where Jung Lu asked him solicitously about food and living conditions in the legations. Pelliot reassured Jung Lu that all the legations needed was fresh fruit. He was fed a splendid twenty-one-course banquet, then was escorted back, his pockets bulging with peaches. He brought news that Viceroy Li Hung-chang was soon expected to arrive from Canton and Shanghai to arrange a settlement.

Aside from not knowing what was going on, and usually jumping to the wrong conclusions, the Westerners bottled up in the legations experienced little hardship. There was never a shortage of food. They had raided every shop, store, and warehouse in the quarter, bringing wagonloads of food and drink into the legations. An abandoned grain shop was found on Legation Street, housing two hundred tons of wheat, with additional rice, corn, and other foodstuffs. Thanks to the liberation of the two general stores, Imbeck's and Kierulff's, alcohol and tobacco were in plentiful supply. There were at least a thousand cases of champagne. Most of the legationers drank champagne every day instead of water. Hewlett confided to his diary that "our mess is always cheerful with our looted champagne and cigars." A typical dinner in July, he said, featured "green peas, (bottled) maize puddings, and 'fizz.' " Sir Robert Hart observed that everyone was in remarkably good condition. The Swiss Auguste Chamot and his wife, Annie, never left their Peking Hotel, where they were baking three hundred loaves of bread a day. They ran a catering service for anyone who could afford it. Lenox-Simpson described the scene at the hotel: "Everybody is at work quite peacefully, milling wheat, washing rice, slaughtering animals."

Some legationers lived very well indeed. The Squiers and their guests, Polly Smith and Morrison (before his wound), had it best. They dined on preserved fruits from California, corned beef, tinned beans, anchovy paste, beef extract, macaroni, endless champagne and coffee. In Lady MacDonald's dining room forty people sat down to every elegant meal, dressed in proper dinner attire—no missionaries allowed.

There was a flourishing black market with the Chinese, as Lenox-Simpson reported and others confirm: "A secret traffic in eggs and ammunition is still going on with renegade soldiery from Tung Fu-hsiang's camp. Great numbers of eggs are being obtained by the payment of heavy sums to some of the more friendly soldiery around us, who steal in with baskets and sacks, and receive in return rolls of dollars, and these eggs are being distributed by a committee. Some people are getting more than others . . . whilst dozens of poor missionary women are suffering great hardships."

To feed the regular soldiers and missionaries, cookstoves were set up in the British legation's ornamental rockeries, and large pots were set on them to boil canned meat and rice, watched over by sweating Chinese Christian cooks in chintz aprons.

There were many thousands of tins of corned beef, but everyone was delighted when the chance came to substitute curried racing pony. On June 24 Lancelot Giles raved: "I was glad to be able to start on some fresh meat for a change, for since last Wednesday we have been living on tinned food. This horsemeat, or rather ponymeat, is really not at all bad; rather like beef, only somewhat tough." For the gourmets among the legations, magpies and sparrows, referred to as "game," supplemented the pony meat. They did not eat the carrion crows that danced and quarreled over the corpses in the canal; those were sent to feed the Chinese Christians.

While the legations complained bitterly about corned beef and champagne, the two thousand converts in the Fu were starving. Abundant stocks of grain reserved by the legations—two hundred fifty tons of wheat, rice, and corn—were not shared with the converts. When the meager supplies they had brought with them ran out, they turned to those ancient staples of Chinese diet: tree bark, leaves, twigs, roots, and finally dirt. Most of the grass and leaves in the Fu already had been eaten by the legation ponies.

Polly Smith explained how "Until now we have been able to give them a certain amount of food daily, but we can only spare this supply a few more days. . . . Every morning when the two horses are shot at the slaughter-house, for distribution to the messes, half of the inedible parts are eaten with relish by these starving people." They ate them raw, she added.

The Fu was of course the focus of intermittent Ironhat attacks. Originally they brought in nine or ten field guns that caused great structural damage when fired at the tops of buildings in the legation quarter during the first five days, but these were removed on Jung Lu's orders before they caused any serious human casualties. Only at the Fu were these field guns fired point-blank to flatten the high garden walls and expose the huddled converts to direct assault. Other guns the Chinese had, including rapid-fire Krupps, were not used during the siege, with one brief exception on the last night.

Much of the tragic mythology of the siege had to be borrowed by the legationers from the agony of these converts. By July 13, after twenty-three days of fighting over the gardens, three-quarters of the Fu was in imperial hands. The courage, intelligence, and stamina of the Buddhist Colonel Shiba and his Japanese marines were what kept Ironhat troops from overrunning the gardens and putting all the native Christians to the sword.

The anxious Westerners across the canal were content to leave that mission to the Japanese because they had other problems. Although 90 percent of them never once saw a Boxer with their own eyes, many of them (men and women) had fits of hysteria behind closed doors, or stayed drunk on various combinations of looted champagne, gin, whiskey, or brandy. The siege was an alcoholic's holiday. Some legationers gave elaborate public displays of calm. Gramophones and music boxes were liberated from Kierulff's store. At the slightest encouragement the wife of the head of the Russo-Chinese Bank, Madame Pokotilov—a former St. Petersburg diva—sang arias. The British played cricket. When rain flooded their compound, the legationers made rafts and paddled about. The German first secretary, Herr von Below, drank schnapps and played the piano. Polly Smith said "during . . . [one] terrifying attack he was seized with the premonition that this was the end. . . . He played . . . in a soul agony, but was rudely awakened some hours later to be told that the attack was all over, and that for this time at least he was not to be massacred in a storm of music." Everywhere there was bitter grousing. It was felt that the diplomats had shirked all responsibility.

Sarah Conger, wife of the American minister and dedicated Christian Scientist, was annoyingly upbeat. "She earnestly assured us," Polly wrote, "that it was ourselves, and not the times, which were troublous and out of tune, and insisted that while there was an appearance of warlike hostilities, it was really in our own brains. . . . There was no bullet entering the room; it was again but our receptive minds which falsely led us to believe such to be the case." Sarah Conger was right, however. The siege *was* largely in their imagination and few bullets came anywhere near; most of the siege passed in truce. So it was less a siege than a standoff.

Herbert Squiers, the acquisitive first secretary of the American legation, came off better than most. Wrote one American missionary: "Had Mr. Squiers been Minister we would never have been in our present terrible situation." After Captain Strouts was killed, Squiers became chief of staff to Sir Claude.

The French envoy, former journalist Stephen Pichon, a large man with a majestic mustache, was frequently heard muttering, "*Nous sommes perdus!*" There was unanimity among the Anglos about Pichon. Lenox-Simpson called him "a poltroon," while Morrison called him "a craven-hearted cur," "the laughingstock of the whole place," and "a horrible coward." Nobody could imagine why the Chinese had chosen to burrow under the French legation, unless they were attempting to destroy its exceptional wine cellar.

At the beginning of the siege, Pichon had legation guards help him burn all his diplomatic papers, while Madame Pichon rushed about stamping on bits that floated away and burned them again. Not to be thought backward, the Russian minister, Baron von Giers, burned his papers the next day. Morrison, who had his own opinion of the relative value of French and Russian diplomacy, offered $5,000 for the French papers and $50,000 for the Russian.

Sir Robert Hart, so recently hale and hearty, had been changed overnight by the disappointment he felt. Now sixty-five and increasingly frail, he put on a brave face. Although invited to don black tie and dine at Sir Claude's exclusive table, he declined, eating instead with his junior assistants. From worry he had lost three pounds the first week, a serious matter for a man of his age and slender physique. Lenox-Simpson said Hart "carried a somewhat formidable armament—at least two large Colt revolvers strapped on to his thin body, and possibly a third stowed away in his hip pocket." Hart refused to join in the looted champagne and cigars. By his order the Customs mess was invariably modest: for breakfast, rice, tea, and jam; for lunch, curried pony and rice; for dinner, curried pony, rice, and jam. Hart was convinced that the Manchu court had been swept by a wave of insanity and all might now be lost. The fact that he was trapped in the legations unable to intercede made him feel impotent and weary.

When it was over, Hart wrote in a letter, "I am horribly hurt by all that has occurred." Outside of his distress at losing his home and a lifetime of mementoes, his self-esteem was badly damaged. On the one hand, Sir Robert could not avoid thinking that the Chinese were trying to murder him, their most trusted and valuable employee. This was only his imagination at work, infected by the widespread assumption in the legations that they were all about to be slaughtered at any moment like the British families trapped in the Sepoy Mutiny. Because he was an insider as no other foreigner had ever been, it was acutely embarrassing that he had not received advance notice. He knew he had not correctly interpreted the many signals that had appeared, like the letter in the North China *Daily News* alerting foreigners. He had taken note of all these omens in his diary, but somehow he had grown complacent over the years, and there had been so many warnings that after a while he became desensitized to them. What did not immediately occur to him was that his protectors at court, including the dowager empress, were not in control of circumstances, so he was being victimized by a situation gone out of control, not by friends who had betrayed his trust. Worst of all, Hart discovered upon moving into the British legation compound that he was much more deeply resented by all the Western diplomats than he had ever suspected. They made it clear that they, not Hart, were now running the show and giving the orders. He was an extra thumb, useless and despised.

The weather did not help. It was midsummer, over 100 degrees Fahrenheit, dusted with sand borne on a hot wind from the Gobi. Flies were everywhere, corpses crawled with maggots. The stench was infernal.

There were many wells of sweet water and others of brackish, so water was never a problem, although the legation wells were foolishly close to the sewage canal and very little of the water was boiled for the requisite half hour before drinking. Dysentery was one thing the legationers all had in common.

During the July cease-fire an old bugler from Sir Robert Hart's band slipped in. He had been struck by a Manchu officer, one ear was cut off because they thought he might be a spy, and he had come because he knew foreign doctors were good. He said the foreign troops had won a big victory at Taku and had occupied Tientsin, and General Tung and the former Boxers had gone to block a further advance on Peking.

On July 18 a message smuggled to the Japanese ambassador, Baron Nishi, said that a mixed force of 33,300 men was to leave Tientsin "on or about July 20th" for the relief of Peking. (Morrison, who was a great admirer of Japan, described Baron Nishi as having "a most curious resemblance to an anthropoid ape.") Everyone was elated by the news, but it was the last they would hear for ten days.

The loss of Taku and Tientsin aroused great fear in the court at Peking, reviving memories of 1860, and presaging a sudden, violent shift to the right in the balance of power. The moderates saw it coming, so the Tsungli Yamen anxiously renewed its request for the envoys to leave the legations. Quarreling immediately began among the foreign ministers; some wanted to go. But because of career rivalry and personality differences they could never agree even on a joint bargaining position for their own escape. Sir Claude replied vaguely to the Yamen without actually refusing and left the moderates with no idea what to try next.

Jung Lu attempted again to convince the legations of his goodwill, sending Chinese merchants into the quarter to open a market of eggs, melons, cucumbers, and other fresh vegetables. A note arrived asking Hart about his welfare.

By July 25 the moderates were becoming desperate to achieve visible results before time ran out, either by successfully persuading the ministers to leave Peking immediately or, failing that, getting them to send uncoded cables to their governments reassuring them of the safety of the legations, so that the Allied rescue operation being mounted at Tientsin could be called off. Only by achieving one result or the other within the next twenty-four hours could the moderates prove the validity of negotiation in preference to war. After that it could be too late.

The Yamen pressed the foreign ministers hard to fix a date for their departure for Tientsin, and urged them to send open messages of reassurance to their governments. The ministers, still waffling, refused to do either. Two days later, on July 27, in a strange final act of supplication, the Yamen sent fifteen carts of flour, melons, and ice, some set aside specifically for Hart, imploring him to negotiate the departure of the envoys. Angry at the way he had been treated by the Manchu and disgusted beyond belief with the foreign diplomatic corps, Hart refused, unaware that he was closing the last door.

The reason for this sudden ominous change in Peking was the arrival the night before of Li Ping-heng, the military idol of the Ironhats and former governor of Shantung who had appreciated the potential of rural vigilante bands years before they had evolved into the Spirit Boxers. While he was hardly responsible for Prince Tuan's grand obsession with the expulsion of all Foreign Devils and a return to glorious empire, Li Ping-heng's absolute conviction that Chinese armies could fight and win gave Tuan confidence that was not justified. So long as Li Ping-heng was around, there was a chance (however remote) that the old general could forge the government armies and officer corps into a reliable weapon. It was his unexpected removal from North China that left the Ironhats adrift to muddle through on their own. After being forced out of office and humiliated by the Germans, Li Ping-heng had been named admiral of the Yangtze. On the river he was far removed from the great debate at court as the Ironhats made their bid for power, and he was unable to counsel and restrain them. Despite their appetite for conspiracy the princes had little real experience of war or politics, and they had botched things royally, mismanaging the Boxers, squandering their momentum, and wasting time in pettifogging arguments with the court moderates. Li had been guarding the Yangtze delta approaches to Shanghai when the Taku Forts fell. He was one of the few senior regional officials to respond vigorously to an imperial edict of July 21 ordering the provinces to rush reinforcements to Peking to help defend the capital against the Allied advance. Three days later another decree summoned him personally to Peking, and characteristically he responded at once.

The return of the old war-horse greatly encouraged the Ironhats and gave them the leverage they needed to defeat their moderate opponents, dooming them to the sword. Challenged to produce results from the legations by the 27th, the moderates had made their last fervent appeals to Sir Claude MacDonald and Sir Robert Hart, and again failed totally. To the Ironhats, this was the ultimate evidence of the failure of compromise, and with Li Ping-heng's support and guidance they counterattacked.

The first the legations knew of this profound sea-change was when the arrival of melons on July 27 was followed shortly by the arrival of field guns. Firing broke out at once, bringing the truce to an end. It was only then, on July 27, that the real siege of the legations began, lasting scarcely a fortnight.

Sir Claude sent a stream of protests to the Yamen, complaining about these violations, of shots being fired overhead, of the field guns being trained on the legations, but it was too late to reach anyone in the Peace party. The War party was now in control. Prince Ching, pirouetting with the new breeze, replied to Sir Claude (this time with considerable irony) that it was "just so much Chinese fireworks."

The impact of the decisive Li Ping-heng on the indecisive court was overwhelming. The Forbidden City had grown unaccustomed to determined and aggressive warriors bludgeoning their way to victory in debate. Rallying conservatives with an appeal to their patriotism and the urgent need for defense of the capital, Li led the Ironhats in a purge of the most prominent moderates, planting terror in the hearts of all those who had collectively thwarted them. Forty-eight hours after his return to Peking, Li oversaw the beheading of two of the court's most cosmopolitan and competent ministers, who had resisted Prince Tuan from the beginning. Hsu Ching-cheng was a former envoy to France, Germany, Holland, Austria, Belgium, and Russia, and Yuan Chang was a leading moderate at the Tsungli Yamen. As vigorous and outspoken leaders of a liberal and pragmatic policy, they had argued since mid-June that the Boxers were nothing but dangerous rebels to be wholly suppressed, that any attack on the foreign legations was a serious breach of international law, and finally that 1860 had proved it was suicidal to resist the foreign troops. As skilled diplomatists and highly trained scholars, Hsu and Yuan had talked circles around Prince Tuan, countering his antiforeign bombast with careful and persuasive arguments in favor of seeking a peaceful solution. As long as these two men were interfering in the conduct of the war, the Ironhats would be hobbled. In Li Ping-heng's opinion, this was a critical moment: "Only when one can fight one can negotiate for peace." On their own, the Ironhats had not dared to attack the moderates directly. But now they produced indictments of their opponents, forced them to admit failure, and rallied enough support to condemn the two peace advocates to death. They were beheaded the next morning. A fortnight later three other leading peace advocates paid with their heads as the Ironhat purge continued, including the president of the Board of Finance, who had refused to pay the Boxers; and the president of the Board of War, who had refused to endorse Prince Tuan's grand strategy. In a final act of vengeance, the Ironhats also arranged the murder at long distance of their old enemy the urbane, fork-wielding Sir Chang Yin-huan who had been in exile in

Sinkiang since the end of the Hundred Days. These executions terrorized the court and put an end to arguments that mediation and compromise might even now save the government from the approaching disaster. High-ranking moderates like Jung Lu were too secure in the Manchu hierarchy, and too close to the dowager empress, to be purged. But even they grew silent. Under these circumstances, the dowager herself was in jeopardy, as was Kuang Hsu.

To give their champion the authority needed to prepare the great defense of Peking, Li Ping-heng was named co-generalissimo with Jung Lu. In an atmosphere of impending doom, he moved the biggest government armies out to the east and south to block the Allied advance and prepared to go out himself to take personal command. Before he left, he ordered two hundred carts and more than six thousand soldiers into the Forbidden City to pack and move the imperial household, and requested that the empress dowager and the emperor prepare to leave for the Summer Palace.

None of this was known to the legations. They were hopelessly confused about developments. A fifteen-year-old Chinese boy had slipped out of the legations unnoticed in early July with a message to Tientsin from Sir Claude. He returned on July 28 with a mystifying reply sewn into the collar of his coat. The message, from W. R. Carles, the excitable British consul at Tientsin, read:

> Your letter of 4 July. There are now 24,000 troops landed and 19,000 troops here. General Gaselee is expected at Taku. When he comes I hope to see more activity. The Russians are at Peitang. Tientsin city is under foreign government and the Boxers' power here is exploded. Do try and keep me informed of yourselves. There are plenty of troops on the way if you can keep yourselves in food for a time, all ought yet to come out well. The Consulate is mended to be ready for you when you come. Almost all the ladies have left Tientsin. Kindest remembrances to all in the Legation.

When this was posted for everyone to read, Morrison flew into a rage: "It was impossible to know whether the troops were on the way to Peking from Tientsin, or to Tientsin from Europe, who were the troops, and how many, or whether the number landed was 24,000 in all or 43,000, while the observation that the troops were coming if our provisions held out seemed to imply that if our provisions failed the troops would return to Tientsin."

Others shared his disgust. "Men moved away," wrote Morrison, "to express their feelings beyond the hearing of the ladies."

Fortunately for the prestige of Her Majesty's Consular Service, an equally opaque communication arrived two days later for Edwin Conger from the American consul at Tientsin. It began, "I had a dream about you last night," contained no news, and ended, "It is my earnest wish that you may all be spared."

Finally, on August 1, coherent information arrived in a message from the Japanese consul at Tientsin: "Your letter of 22nd received, departure of troops from Tientsin delayed by difficulties of transport, but advance will be made in two or three days."

CHAPTER TWENTY-ONE

Chinese Takeaway

When it was finally assembled in Tientsin, the Allied relief force numbered more than sixteen thousand men from eight nations. Blocking their way—but only in a manner of speaking—were upward of twenty-five thousand imperial troops, former Boxers, and local militia. The delay of nearly two months in the organization and departure of this relief force arose from a combination of fear, ineptitude, and rivalry. Fear because the Allies misunderstood why Admiral Seymour's expedition had failed; they assumed there were great dangers lurking in the countryside in the form of hordes of sinister Chinese. As the weeks passed, the number of soldiers thought to be needed to mount the rescue grew and grew. Seymour (who had been afraid to abandon his trains) insisted that at least forty thousand soldiers were necessary. The Japanese, who wanted to be in a position to take control of all North China if the opportunity came, said seventy thousand. America's Rear Admiral Kempff, not wanting to be outdone, advised eighty thousand. It took time for so many soldiers to reach China.

While they dithered, the Allies plotted against one another. If the Manchu regime collapsed as a result of this crisis, each of the powers wanted a piece of the eggroll, and the nation with the largest force would get the biggest piece. Kaiser Wilhelm was able to secure the job of Supreme Allied Commander for Field Marshal Count Alfred von Waldersee, although he would not reach China till the campaign was over.

It was not until Britain's General Alfred Gaselee reached Tientsin on July 27 that anyone seriously considered the need for immediate action to relieve the legations. The Russian commander, General Lineivitch, dragged his feet, while America's General Adna Chaffee, a sour and vindictive Indian fighter who had just come from slaughtering Filipinos, was waiting for his artillery. Compared to them the goodhearted General

Gaselee was a man of unusual compassion and common sense, who rightly felt that the whole idea was to save the legations. He played upon the rivalry of his fellow commanders and let it be known that if they did not rally, the British would set out alone. At last, they agreed to start on August 5, 1900—fifty-seven days after Sir Claude's anxious appeal for rescue.

The largest contingents were the Japanese, Russians, British, and Americans; the French sent a thousand Tonkinese—"the scum of the French army," sneered Royal Navy Lieutenant Roger Keyes. "Even the Russians do not want to have anything do to with them," joked von Waldersee. Small token forces were contributed by Germany, Austria, and Italy, in order to be in on the division of spoils.

The Allies took the same route Lord Elgin had used in 1860—along the towpath beside the Peiho River, followed by a six-mile-long supply train of junks—and met Chinese resistance first at Peitang. Japanese troops formed the Allied spearhead; being of a totally different feudal psychology from the Chinese facing them, they advanced into battle without hesitation. The Chinese were wholly unprepared for this kind of determined assault, as they had not been ready for it during the Sino-Japanese War, and broke off contact immediately. On the second day, the Allies were halfway to Peking at Yangtsun, the farthest point reached by Admiral Seymour's trains, and American and British troops jointly stormed its rustic defenses. By evening Yangtsun had fallen, and the Chinese retreat became a rout; rural militia, former Boxers, and imperial troops all fled helter-skelter, pausing here and there only to steal food from local peasants. After a day's rest among the dusty stubble of millet fields in the terrible summer heat, the Allies struck out again, with Peking only thirty miles away. The small French, Austrian, German, and Italian contingents straggled so far behind that their commanders decided to return to Tientsin to "regroup." Had the Chinese fallen upon them, there would have been a massacre, but nobody fell upon them. Resistance had ceased. After grossly inflating the danger facing them, no Allied commander drew attention to the fact that this danger had evaporated completely. Instead they boasted daily of their boldness and courage and, wherever possible, let the Japanese attack first.

Tungchow was the last city of any size before Peking, and when the Allies reached its sealed gates on August 12, nobody was there. Japanese sappers blew up the main gate to find that the Chinese had already fled. Taking a break from their dusty march, the Allied armies entered Tungchow and began looting. While the court withdrew to relative safety at the Summer Palace, Li Ping-heng set out as commander in chief of four government armies to save the day. His commission was to block the Allied advance at all cost. The old general took his mission very seriously.

But his greatest enemies were his own countrymen—officers and soldiers who attempted halfheartedly to stop the Allies first at Peitang, then at Yangtsun. Had the Ironhats prepared properly for this contingency, Li Ping-heng might have been provided with well-drilled troops and a reliable command chain. Instead his four armies were a mixture of best and worst, in which the noblest intentions were certain to be frustrated. Most of his troops and officers were typical of the ceremonial forces traditionally stationed in and around Peking, with no battle experience, an ancient code of venality, and a visceral fear of risk. Although he was accompanied at first by many of the Manchu princes and high mandarins like Kang I who themselves held commands as adjutants general, both princes and mandarins soon joined the rout to fight another day. The tough Muslim army of General Tung, half of which had remained in Peking as bodyguard to the imperial household, was soon joined by the other half on horses lathered by the flight from the front, and thereafter stuck close to the fleeing court. Prince Tuan's celebrated toy, the Tiger Hunt Marksmen, vanished from the annals without a trace except for its palace guard, which clung to the prince throughout. Thus, sadly, the one heroic figure in the plot of the princes was left to cover their escape.

On August 11, the day before Tungchow fell, General Li wrote a last despairing message to the court:

> I have retreated from Matou to Changchiawan. For the past few days I have seen several tens of thousands of [Chinese] troops jamming all roads. They fled as soon as they heard of the arrival of the enemy. As they passed the villages and towns they set fire and plundered, so much so that there was nothing left for the armies under my command to purchase, with the result that men and horses were hungry and exhausted. From youth to old age I have experienced many wars, but never saw things like these. . . . Unless we restore discipline and execute the retreating generals and escaping troops, there will be no place where we can stand. . . . The situation is getting out of control. There is not time to regroup and deploy. But I will do my utmost to collect the fleeing troops and fight to the death, so as to repay the kindness of Your Majesties and to do the smallest part of a Minister's duty.

The next day, all his efforts having failed, Li Ping-heng swallowed poison. The elderly viceroy of Chihli, Yu Lu, who had arranged to find refuge on a British warship, changed his mind and also committed suicide.

From Tungchow the Allies split into separate prongs aimed at different gates in the outer walls of Peking. General Frey, the French commander who had fallen behind, was trying to catch up. To give these laggards time, the main forces agreed to pause three miles outside Peking to rest overnight. The final assault would begin on the morning of August 14.

Inside Peking the legations still had no definite news on the approach of the relief force. They went about their ordinary routines. A few days earlier, on August 8, there had been a ripple of speculation when they learned that Viceroy Li Hung-chang had been appointed by the throne to start peace negotiations. There was great excitement on August 10, when a note was smuggled in from the British commander, General Gaselee, saying, "Strong force of Allies advancing. Twice defeated enemy. Keep up your spirits." This was followed later that day by a message with more details from General Fukushima, commanding the Japanese vanguard.

For the next two days, the legations came under increasingly heavy fire from completely new troops under banners bearing the names of generals unknown to them. A fresh division had been sent to Peking by the rabidly antiforeign Shansi governor, Yu Hsien, under the command of an officer who swore to storm the legations within five days. Instead he was exposed to gunfire when a barricade collapsed and was shot dead by legation guards, along with twenty-six of his men. From a big-character poster they captured the legations learned that a last-minute bounty had been offered by the Ironhats for the head of any Foreign Devil.

On the night of August 13 while the Allied armies were bivouacked five miles beyond the city walls to wait for the stragglers, the Shansi troops made a final effort to blast the legations. One of China's new two-inch rapid-fire Krupp field guns (which Jung Lu had carefully kept tucked away) was wheeled into position atop the wall of the Forbidden City and began firing directly into the legations. In ten minutes this gun did more damage than the old Chinese smoothbores had in five weeks of occasional bombardment. Sir Claude ordered an immediate response by the American Colt machine gun and the Austrian Maxim. The Krupp was silenced after its seventh round.

The way it was planned, on the morning of the fourteenth the Russians were to head for Peking's Tungchih Gate, the Japanese for the Chihhua Gate, the Americans for the Tungpien Gate, and the British for the Shakou Gate—all advancing simultaneously so no single force would have the honor of being the first to attack Peking. But at midnight before the planned attack rain began to fall and gunshots were heard from the direction of the Tungpien Gate.

The Russians had stolen a march. They said they had heard heavy firing from the legations—the exchange between the Krupp and the Colt and Maxim—and General Vassilievski, the Russian chief of staff, had led a party of scouts through the darkness across the bridge to the gate, surprising the drowsy Chinese guards and killing them all. Seizing their advantage, the Russians brought up two guns before dawn and blew a hole in the gate, whereupon Vassilievski became the first to enter Peking.

Hearing this all the Allies rushed forward. The Japanese assaulted their designated gate. Since the Russians had stormed the gate assigned to the Americans, General Chaffee's troops scaled the wall next to it and made for the legations. The British blew a hole in the Shakou Gate and entered Peking unopposed, also heading directly for the legations. As they neared the inner Tartar Wall, the British vanguard of Sikhs and Rajputs saw atop it three flags: American, British, and Russian. A signaler on the wall semaphored in Morse, "Come in by sewer." He was referring to the foul drainage canal that flowed out of the Forbidden City, through the legations, to exit under the Tartar Wall by a seven-foot conduit blocked with rusty iron bars and jumbled temporary barriers. The bars were hastily cut away, and in minutes Sikhs and Rajputs were wading through the black slime into Canal Street.

Inside the legations the besieged had first heard the guns of the relief force—a series of dull booms, the sound of the Russian attack on the Tungpien Gate—between two and three o'clock in the morning of the fourteenth. It was their first certain knowledge that help had arrived. "The scene in the British Legation was indescribable," Sir Claude said. There was much cheering and shaking of hands. Li Hung-chang's American secretary, William Pethick, who enjoyed deflating his comrades, told everyone not to get hopes up, for the sounds were only Chinese reinforcements coming in. In fact, by this time there were few Chinese soldiers left in Peking except those who had briefly defended the outer gates, and a few household guards at the entrances to the Forbidden City who soon melted away, leaving only a party of eunuchs in charge.

Toward dawn the Chinese volleys around the legations became ragged—"the occasional phut of a bullet and the sustained rasp of the cicadas"—as the last Shansi soldiers slipped away.

Hewlett recalled, "I was asleep in the Hanlin, when I was woken up . . . to say we were relieved. . . . I ran round and saw the welcome sight of the big Black men [the Sikhs and Rajputs] pouring into the Legation."

When Mrs. Squiers and Polly Smith hurried out to greet the Sikhs, General Gaselee jumped down from his horse, took their hands, and with tears in his eyes said, "Thank God, men, here are two women alive." The soldiers thought the Boxers had ravished all the women of the legations and then beheaded them. Polly admitted she had kept a small pistol with her during the siege "to use if the worst happens."

Many of the besieged now appeared in freshly starched shirts with cravats, the ladies in long dresses with parasols. Sir Claude was in immaculate tennis flannels. Lenox-Simpson observed sourly: "People you had not seen for weeks, who might have, indeed, been dead a hundred times without your being any the wiser, appeared now for the first time from the rooms in which they had hidden and acted hysterically."

General Chaffee and the 14th U.S. Infantry reached the legations next about 4:30 P.M., General Lineivitch an hour later, followed by General Fukushima. Lady MacDonald, her pretty face alight with happiness, went from group to group, saying she didn't know who they were but was "simply delighted to see you."

As sieges go it was not half bad. Now the fun would begin. It would have been humane for the victorious Allies to turn their attention at once to the Peitang Cathedral across town, where Bishop Favier had been holding out with a few priests, nuns, converts, and a tiny force of courageous French and Italian sailors guarding more than three thousand refugee men, women, and children—more than all the people in the legations. Nobody even knew whether they were still alive. However, as only a hundred of them were Westerners, they had a low priority. There was celebrating to do and still much champagne to share with the liberators. Mammon was secure; God could wait. Elderly Father d'Addosio, a Catholic priest who had spent the siege in the legations, begged the Allies to liberate the Peitang at once but was ignored. He set out alone on a donkey but got less than halfway when he was murdered.

General Chaffee was bent on storming the Forbidden City before anyone else could. He had been beaten to Peking by the Russians and beaten to the legations by the British. Without consulting his peers, on August 15 Chaffee led his men to the south gates of the Forbidden City and, using battering rams and artillery fired point-blank, smashed through the huge iron-jacketed timber doors into the forecourts. From towers overlooking each courtyard came heavy fire from what Chaffee took to be the Imperial Guard. Actually, the Chinese soldiers had all fled. But unknown to Chaffee, the French, determined to secure the Forbidden City themselves, had mounted their artillery on top of the Tartar Wall opposite the legations and suddenly opened fire on Chaffee's men, imagining them (they said) to be Chinese soldiers. Chaffee galloped over to the French position and had an animated exchange with General Frey and Minister Pichon. Unable to understand what the American was shouting, Frey declared in his own language that they were firing for the honor of France. With fifteen Americans already dead and many more wounded, Chaffee suddenly abandoned his assault on the gates. At a council of commanders the Russians argued that the destruction of the Forbidden City would be pointless, and Chaffee (who had precisely that in mind) reluctantly gave in.

The following day, August 16, it was agreed to do something about the Peitang Cathedral. A mixed force of French, British, and Russians picked their way through empty streets around the Lake Palaces by the western wall of the Forbidden City, only to find that the Japanese had long since taken the initiative and relieved the cathedral on their own.

The cathedral had been defended by two young French officers and forty-one sailors, guarding a sprawling compound that enclosed in addition to the cathedral, an orphanage, the bishop's house, a convent, a dispensary, several schools, a printing press, a chapel, a museum, some stores, stables, and other buildings. Thirty-four hundred Chinese Christian refugees were crowded into this area, with fewer than a hundred Europeans. Food was a great problem. By July 6 the daily rations of rice had been reduced to a pound; three weeks later, to a third of a pound. By August 10 the only mule and the last four hundred pounds of rice had been reserved for the fighting men; the refugees ate bark from the trees and the roots of dahlias and lilies in the convent garden. At least three hundred converts, seventy-five orphans, and sixty Europeans were killed or died of hunger before the Japanese arrived. The Boxers said the reason their magic did not work in storming the cathedral was that the Catholic women inside were flashing their private parts at them out the windows.

In the legation quarter everyone agreed that the siege had lasted fifty-five days. But a review of the statistics is revealing. The only serious fighting was done by marines face-to-face with Chinese soldiers at barricades on top of the Tartar Wall, or by Japanese defending the starving converts in the Fu gardens. Only the first five days, June 20–25, involved heavy or continual Chinese firing, mostly firing for effect at abandoned buildings in the quarter. Although about four thousand artillery rounds were fired in all, most of them were directed only at empty buildings or the walls of the Fu gardens, and all these shellings caused a total of only fourteen casualties. A *de facto* truce followed, with only random sniping and great strings of firecrackers set off for the next three weeks, from June 25 till July 17. The next nine days, July 18–27, there was an official truce, when sellers of fruit and ice were allowed into the legations. So after the first five days the siege was all cease-fire, official or unofficial, with ladies picnicking under parasols and the two sides exchanging jokes. The legations might have called this as a siege, but from the Chinese standpoint it was a case of trying to persuade a bunch of trigger-happy Foreign Devils to leave Peking peacefully, and failing. The day after Li Ping-heng returned, hostilities were resumed, but only in a random manner, completely aimless gunshots off and on for two and a half weeks until the night of August 13, when the Krupp gun was brought up and promptly silenced. The next day the legations were relieved. At no time were Chinese attacks pressed home, despite their vastly superior numbers, and most of the besieged Westerners were aware throughout of this restraint on the part of the Manchu government.

Only sixty-six foreigners, primarily marines of different nationalities exposed at the barricades, were killed and 150 wounded. Two adults and six babies died of illness. No official record exists of the number of Chinese converts in the Fu who were killed or died from hunger and disease, which suggests that the legations thought it wise not to draw attention to the way the converts were neglected and allowed to starve.

In short, the siege was never a siege at all, except in the frenzied imaginations of many of the people in the legations—those who imagined that the end would come at any minute and those like Morrison, Mac-Donald, Squiers, and others whose vanity, ambition, and self-interest required that everything must be seen in operatic terms, with themselves as heroes, "the dowager and her gang" as villains, and everyone else (Chinese and Western) as craven curs. The Allies and legationers now showed their worst qualities as they emptied Peking of everything of value (often beaten to the choicest loot by the diplomats); denounced the hapless dowager and General Jung Lu, who had tried with considerable success to protect them; and produced a falsified and malicious account of what had happened.

Simultaneously with the looting, a horrific bloodbath was conducted against the Chinese out of all proportion to their presumed guilt.

In the Allied assaults on Taku, Tientsin, Peking, and the countryside between, thousands of imperial soldiers and militia were killed and many more were wounded and left to die. Villages were looted and torched, terrible atrocities were committed, and during the next two years Allied armies made continual "punitive expeditions" or "punitive picnics" outside Peking during which no tally of the slain was kept but observers remarked (as they always do) that "the rivers ran red with the blood of the victims." The army of General Yuan Shih-kai killed more than forty-five thousand "Boxers" in Chihli Province alone during the months immediately after the siege; they also killed thousands of rural village Spirit Boxers in northwestern Shantung, where Yuan continued as governor. General Yuan, always very popular with Britons and Americans, carried out this grisly clean-up at their urging.

In Peking itself during the first days of the Allied occupation many mandarins who had backed the Boxers and Prince Tuan's plan to exterminate foreigners committed suicide. Bertram Lenox-Simpson recorded how "Hsu Tung . . . the Imperial Tutor . . . is swinging high now from his own rafters, he and his whole household—wives, children, concubines, attendants, everyone. There are sixteen of them in all, sixteen all swinging from ropes tied on with their own hands, and with the chairs on which they stood kicked from under them."

Many richly appointed palaces and mansions stood empty, their owners fled or hanging like silk bats from the red-lacquered roofbeams. All over Peking, young women were throwing themselves down wells rather than be gang raped.

Individually and in gangs Westerners set out in search of loot. The clever ones from the legations knew exactly where to begin and wasted no time. Leading personalities at the legations, including ministers who had privileged access to areas under constant guard by the occupation forces, competed to steal all they could carry from the Forbidden City, from the Lake Palaces, and from imperial temples. Less privileged but well-informed survivors of the siege, like Edmund Backhouse and George Morrison, immediately ransacked particular Manchu palaces and Chinese mansions, while ordinary soldiers looted temples, stores, workshops, and warehouses, and assaulted girls who could not face wells.

Peking was divided into zones controlled by different Foreign Powers. Three-quarters of the population had fled. Of those who remained, thousands were slain in homes and alleys by the conquering soldiers during the first week. The remainder, said one of the British student interpreters contemptuously, were "grovelling curs." Chinese posted signs on their doors pleading Noble and Good Sirs, Please Do Not Shoot Us.

Student interpreter W. Meyrick Hewlett described his activities:

> I went into all the forbidden places of the Temple of Heaven, the buildings are magnificent, huge grounds and lovely grass . . . we are looting all the silks, furs, and silver, which is being put up to general sale. I can get no private loot, as being the Chief's [Sir Claude's] orderly and interpreter I may not leave the Legation, but I am not forgotten by pals who bring in stuff in secret . . . Organized bands of soldiers [are] sent to loot and bring all the stuff for sale, and equal distribution with a lot of [Western] curs who never raised a finger to touch a gun during the siege, and have got now cartloads of silver and silks and furs.

Lenox-Simpson described how "a transport corps, composed of Japanese coolies . . . belonging to some British regiment, came in hauling a multitude of little carts; and within a few minutes these men were offering for sale hundreds of rolls of splendid silks, which they had gathered on their way through the city. . . . We heard, then, that everything had been looted by the troops from the sea right up to Peking . . ."

> In consequence of this glut . . . a regular buying and selling has set up, and all our armies are becoming armies of traders. There are official auctions . . . where you will be able to buy legally, and after

the approved methods, every kind of loot. The best things, however, are being disposed of privately.

In Prince Tuan's Palace I had seen . . . the incredible sight of thousands of pieces of porcelain and baskets full of wonderful *objets de vertu* smashed into ten thousand atoms by the soldiery who had first forced their way there. They only wanted bullion . . .

There are enormous masses of silver sycee [small ingots] in nearly everybody's hands, and I am certain now that several of our *chefs de mission* are in clover.

He described some looting by young Edmund Backhouse: "One morning, a young Englishman, who has been living in Peking rather mysteriously for a number of years, marched in on me at a very early hour, accompanied by several Chinese. . . . It appeared that the men he had brought with him were . . . Treasury Guards of the Board of Revenue . . . and, according to their accounts, they knew exactly where the secret stores of treasure were hidden in the secret vaults of the Government." When they reached the site, Lenox-Simpson said they discovered that all the treasure had been looted already by the Japanese.

The good people back home were assured by Morrison in the *Times* that the imperial suites inside the Forbidden City had been spared. In his private diary for August 28, 1900, however, he describes his own visit: "This morning Triumphal entry through palace . . . I succeeded in looting a beautiful piece of Jade splashed with gold and carved in the form of a citron, the emblem of the fingers of Buddha. . . . Sat in the Throne of the Emperor . . . everything that could be looted being taken away by . . . ministers and others. . . . So back home very tired with my priceless jade." Morrison noted that Sir Robert Hart was not among the high-ranking looters.

Officially, the palaces in and around the Forbidden City were off-limits. The imperial suites were opened at first only to a select circle of generals, senior diplomats, and their wives, whereupon small curios like Morrison's jade lemon vanished. When dour Sarah Conger, the wife of the American minister, toured the Forbidden City on September 10, she was assured that "not a thing was molested in these halls." All restrictions ceased when it was made possible for anyone to gain entrance to the Forbidden City with permits from the Allied generals, which were easy to get. After a few weeks nothing easily portable remained. Soldiers guarding the palaces were reduced to stealing heavy furniture and large porcelain urns. Lenox-Simpson said soldiers told him how they removed these larger objects from the palaces, taking out " 'vases, small tables, carvings, jars, bowls—everything. We wrap them up in a bundle of great coats and feed bags in the morning, and carry them away: no one's ever the wiser. All round the Palace they are doing the same. The Yankees, the Russians, and all of them are in the same boat. All night they climb the walls to get the swag. Give them another six months and there will be nothing left.' " Sixteen months later Morrison wrote a friend describing how a wealthy Russian "has purchased an immense amount of Palace Curios, tens of thousands of taels worth, and is restoring them to the Emperor and Empress."

Two weeks after the lifting of the siege, Morrison recorded in his diary, "This morning I worked at arranging my silks and furs. . . . I have many of considerable value, also porcelain and bronzes, perhaps 3000 [pounds sterling] in all." (This was a tidy nest egg of stolen goods, representing nearly three years' salary for Morrison.)

To protect their homes and possessions, many Chinese attempted to put themselves under the protection of a Westerner. Chinese women still were not safe. Morrison said "Sir Robert confirmed the story of [his] band-boy. . . . When the Russian soldiers came in ravishing his women folk, in mortal terror he seized the cornet and played the Russian hymn. They sprang to their feet at attention and when the notes were finished saluted and marched out."

Sir Claude was peeved to discover that there were items missing from his quarters, where Morrison had convalesced during the siege. He wrote to Morrison: "Has your boy carried away . . . an inkstand of mine with silver top if so please 'stand and deliver.' "

Great fortunes were made by those like Herbert Squiers, who knew where to find the richest pickings and chose his loot as a connoisseur. So prodigious was his take-home that he made the *New York Times* on September 3, 1901: "H. G. Squiers, Secretary of the United States Legation, started for home to-day on leave of absence. He takes with him a collection of Chinese art, filling several railway cars, which experts pronounce one of the most complete in existence. Mr. Squiers intends to present the collection, which consists largely of porcelains, bronzes and carvings from the palaces, bought from missionaries and at auctions of military loot, to the New York Metropolitan Museum of Art." Needless to say, Squiers had not waited to buy his loot at auction; he and Morrison had been the first to pick through Prince Su's palace.

A reporter for the *New York Times* made inquiries of the Metropolitan about how it would receive such a looted benefaction and was given a frosty reception:

> Curator George H. Story . . . replied: "The Metropolitan Museum of Art does not accept loot. I think it an outrage, however, that such a suggestion should be made in connection with anything which Mr. Squiers has to give. He is a gentleman and has one of the finest

porcelain collections in the country. . . . Now, a man who engages in that kind of work—the collecting of Chinese art—is not apt to be a man who accepts or presents loot. . . . It would be presumed by the Museum that Mr. Squiers' collection had been honestly got, he being a gentleman without question."

Squiers later became the American minister to Cuba and Peru. Morrison said Squiers complained to him that he would have been made minister to Peking except for newspaper coverage of his looting. He told Morrison the articles had also prevented him from running for governor of New York. But he confided that he had made so much money it did not matter. A small portion of it was spent to purchase a 400-ton steam yacht, *Invincible,* that he kept in England, moored at Cowes.

Another who took his booty to America was Auguste Chamot, Swiss proprietor of the Peking Hotel. He and his wife, Annie, had married in San Francisco in 1895 and then headed for China. When they returned eight years later, the thirty-six-year-old Chamot was a rich man. At his hotel in the legation quarter he had been in a superb position to acquire loot. He also obtained a $200,000 indemnity for damage to his building. In 1903 the Chamots used some of this wealth to build a mansion in Inverness, California, in Marin County overlooking Tomales Bay. The three-story villa with a mansard roof was decorated with loot, including a screen made for Emperor Chien Lung and a headdress stolen from the quarters of Tzu Hsi. At the villa Chamot kept a menagerie of pythons, monkeys, bears, and panthers. He consumed destructive quantities of champagne aboard his sailing yacht in San Francisco Bay, at parties that ended with the boat's smashing into the piers. He gambled his assets away in three years, and when his mansion was destroyed in the great San Francisco quake of April 1906, he was forced to part with his remaining loot. On a trip to New York to sell these objects, Chamot fell in love with a manicurist named Betsy Dollar. Divorced by his wife, he married Betsy, and died an alcoholic three years later, in September 1909, leaving fifteen cents to Miss Dollar—a poor rate of exchange.

After the court fled from the Summer Palace it was "unmercifully looted." Even the huge outdoor Buddhas were toppled to get at their true inwardness. The Temple of Five Hundred Buddhas that escaped total destruction in 1860, was torched this time. From Lake Kunming to the summit of the hill stretched scenes of destruction, sparkling galaxies of broken glass, porcelain, and crystal.

The new British minister, Sir Ernest Satow, who arrived from Tokyo to succeed Sir Claude MacDonald, wrote of having tea with General Gaselee: "We talked about the curios in the Summer Palace, which the British and Italian officers want to appropriate and the General thinks that a handsome screen standing behind the throne might be sent to the Queen. I said he had better find out whether Her Most Gracious would be disposed to accept it, and reminded him of the way in which we had denounced the Russians for pillaging."

Americans controlled the southwest quarter of the Tartar City, opposite the legations. General Chaffee made his headquarters in the Temple of Agriculture, a 275-acre cypress-covered compound opposite the Temple of Heaven, which the emperor visited each spring to turn the soil and invoke a good harvest. Chaffee had large holes cut in the walls of the temple and installed plate glass windows.

British military headquarters were in the Temple of Heaven, a magnificent blue-domed building housing ancestral tablets of the Ching Dynasty. There was a giant tablet on the north side, to imperial heaven, and eight cases of tablets to each of the emperors who had reigned during the past 256 years. Every one was broken open and each of the tablets taken away by British officers for transmission to the British Museum.

Count Alfred von Waldersee, the commander in chief of the Allied armies, who arrived after the occupation of Peking, chose to establish his own living quarters in the Forbidden City palace of the empress dowager and his headquarters in Tzu Hsi's office in the Ying-tai pavilion on the South Sea. He had brought from Germany an asbestos camp hut, but relinquished this for Tzu Hsi's private chambers. Von Waldersee purchased an expensive Chinese concubine to amuse him while he was in Peking, and they romped together on the dowager's bed. When winter came, his aides installed potbellied stoves to warm the high-ceilinged chambers of the office and the living quarters. On the night of April 17, 1901, the stoves in the Ying-tai pavilion ignited its silk draperies and the magnificent building was destroyed. Von Waldersee escaped through a window. His chief of staff, who dashed back into his room to rescue some papers, was burned to death.

Churchmen got their tithe. The American Presbyterians and Methodists set themselves up in the mansions of rich Chinese gentry, with the consent of the owners, who sought in this way to avoid losing everything. In the absence of the owners, the missionaries raised money by selling off the furs and clothing they found. The Reverend E. G. Tewksbury occupied the palace of Prince Yu, one of the Ironhat princes and a direct descendant of Nurhachi. When Tewksbury auctioned all the prince's possessions, Morrison was among the buyers. Five years later, he wrote in his diary: "I hurried home in order to welcome the young Prince Yu. . . . He came to receive back the portrait of one of his female ancestors and two ancestral tablets which I purchased at the sale. . . . Came in full costume with a large retinue and must have been well pleased with the service I had rendered him. It would have been given back before only he never came for it. I wished to give it to him direct to avoid any squeezing by the intermediaries."

His own house having been destroyed by fire, Morrison requisitioned the palace of a Chinese prince, "a perfect museum" including a splendid library. "I have left him the glass in the windows, but nothing else." Morrison had all the contents shipped to "a safe place."

Along with the genuine loot from Peking came a flood of forgeries and counterfeits that brought equally high prices and made their way into museums, art galleries, and private collections all over the world. Forgery and copying were accepted practice in China where emperors always had their collections copied and counterfeiting was itself an art. According to experts the traffic in forgeries from China reached a new high during the looting that followed the Boxer Uprising.

Not even the bureaucratic papers of the Chinese government escaped attention, one reason so little is known of the period. An American missionary said "there is nothing whatever left of the documents of any of the six Boards, or of the public offices of any sort with the exception of the Tsungli Yamen. . . . On the night of the 4th of June 1901, a building called the Wu Ying Tien in the southwest corner of the Forbidden City was destroyed by a fire, the origin of which was disputed. . . . Its contents were archives of State, edicts, records, books and blocks of governmental works, and attached to it were the Recording Office and the office of one of the Grand Secretaries."

Thus vanished much of the documentation that would have helped piece together the real details of Tzu Hsi's life. But what need was there for documentation when an entirely new fictional version of history was to be written?

Edmund Backhouse later claimed that during the Allied occupation of 1900–1901 he lived in the mansion of a court official named Ching Shan, who he claimed (incorrectly) was the chamberlain of the imperial household, and found the man's secret diaries, as well as some twenty-five thousand volumes of rare Chinese literary works. These became the basis for his bogus authority on the private life of Tzu Hsi, whom he was to vilify in the coming decade. He compiled the diary himself.

CHAPTER TWENTY-TWO

Forked Tongue

As soon as the siege was lifted, accounts of the ordeal began to appear in print. No one acted faster than Morrison, who had spent his convalescence preparing a day-by-day account for the *Times*. He had it ready to post "within an hour or two of the relief"—the time it took to question General Gaselee and others about events in Taku and Tientsin. This account, published first by the *Times* and then in various adaptations by other newspapers around the world, became the accepted version of events. But it had a dark side of which only a few were aware. One was Bertram Lenox-Simpson, who made a wry observation during the siege that bears repeating here: "Worst of all, our only correspondent, M——, who was shot the other day and is getting convalescent, has been taken under the wing of our commander-in-chief, and his lips will be sealed by the time we get out. . . . With an official history and a discreet independent version, no one will ever understand what bungling there has been, and what culpability."

Morrison's public version, which appeared in the *Times* in two parts on October 13 and 15, 1900, began in a way that was certain to find immediate approval from his peers. He blamed everything on the empress dowager.

One of the ancient sages of China foretold that "China will be destroyed by a woman." The prophecy is approaching fulfillment. When the Empress-Dowager, in September 1898, seized once more the reins of power, who could have foreseen that she was to lead her country with such swiftness to destruction? The anti-foriegn, anti-Christian movement which has now culminated in the occupation of Peking by the allied Powers . . . was from the outset encouraged and fostered by the Empress-Dowager and by the ignorant reactionaries whom she selected as her advisers.

His finger-pointing catered to all the prevailing Victorian and Edwardian prejudices, following the bigoted stance of the North China *Daily News* in demonizing "the dowager and her gang," while unabashedly glorifying the imperial role of Englishmen. This was to be expected, perhaps, but it is a shame because Morrison had all the intellectual equipment needed to make a profound reevaluation of what had taken place in China. Morrison was no longer a detached and independent observer, however; he had a vested interest in boosting the establishment and hiding Western culpability. He had helped to provoke the siege and the Allied reprisals, helped to shape hysteria to his liking, helped to rob private homes and palaces, and now helped to cover up and to assign blame to the most jingoistic target—the aging and increasingly bewildered dowager empress.

Take, for example, his perjured account of the destruction of the priceless Hanlin Library, next door to the British legation, which has continued to be lied about to this day. Historically, and in terms of transcendent human values, this was the most important single Western action during the entire siege. In the *Times* Morrison stated that the Hanlin was burned down by the Chinese themselves in a mindless act of self-abuse.

The Hanlin Academy was in a four-acre compound on the north side of the British legation. Architecturally it consisted of a number of typically ornate Chinese buildings with decorated beams and glazed orange and green tile roofs arranged in rows around courtyards. These housed offices, halls, and blocks of sleeping cubicles for the brain trust of scholar-officials who worked and lived there. Around lotus ponds were gazebos where they could gather and talk, and a large temple, with vermilion columns, jade green eaves, and orange tiled roofs. In the back courtyard, almost butting up against the British legation stables and servants quarters, were several buildings housing the most valuable treasure in the empire—the painstakingly preserved written heritage of thousands of years of Chinese civilization, including ancient tablets, history, literature, poetry, philosophy, and the only copy in existence of the great *Yung Lo Ta Tien*, an 11,095-volume encyclopedia assembled by scholars under the Ming emperor Yung Lo and completed in the year 1408. This was a compendium of all Chinese literature and knowledge that had survived the previous two thousand years. Two hand copies of the original were made under Emperor Chia Ching. The original and one copy were destroyed in the southern capital of Nanking during the Taiping occupation of that city. The copy in the Hanlin was the only one left. The Hanlin Library was in every respect the national archive of the Chinese people.

On the morning of June 21, just after the siege officially began and while everyone was still on the edge of panic, the legations were fired upon from the War Office on the far side of the Carriage Park and from the top of the big temple in the Hanlin complex. Nobody was hit, because as usual the shots were fired only overhead, but the people in the British legation compound were extremely jumpy. They feared that the Chinese would try to burn them out by setting fire to the adjacent buildings.

The following night, after the Italian legation was burned down, the Russians set fire to some abandoned Chinese houses between their legation and the British stables, aggravating these fears of arson. It might be a good idea, someone said, to pull down the nearest Hanlin building, which was very close to the quarters of the British student interpreters and legation servants. (It is usually said that these buildings were only "an arm's length" away, "butted up" to the legation, and "overhung" its servants quarters, but they were actually separated by a distance of about five yards.)

Morrison's account in the *Times* reads as follows:

When it was proposed to pull down an unimportant building in the Hanlin Academy that abuts upon the Legation to the North, the proposition was vetoed. Such desecration, it was said, would wound the susceptibilities of the Chinese Government. It was "the most sacred building in China." To lay hands upon it, even to safeguard the lives of beleaguered women and children, could not be thought of, for fear of wounding the susceptibilities of the Chinese Government! . . .

A strong wind was blowing from the Hanlin into the Legation, the distance separating the nearest building from the Minister's residence being only a few feet. Fire the one and the Minister's residence would have been in danger. Suddenly there was the alarm of fire. Smoke was rising from the Hanlin. The most venerated pile in Peking, the great Imperial Academy, centre of all Chinese learning, with its priceless collection of books and manuscripts, was in flames. Every one who was off duty rushed to the back of the Legation. The Hanlin had been occupied during the night by Imperial soldiers, who did not hesitate, in their rage to destroy the foreigners, to set fire to the buildings. It was first necessary to clear the temple. A breach was made in the wall, Captain Poole headed a force of Marines and volunteers who rushed in, divided, searched the courts, and returned to the main pavilion with its superb pillars and memorial tablets. Chinese were rushing from other burning pavilions to the [Hanlin's] main entrance. They were taken by surprise and many were killed, but they had done their evil deed. Other great libraries have been destroyed by the victorious invader. What can be thought of a nation which destroyed its own most sacred edifice, the pride and glory of its learned men through centuries, in order to wreak vengeance upon the foreigner?

To save the Legation it was necessary to continue the destruction and dismantle the library buildings. With great difficulty, with inadequate tools, the buildings were pulled down. Trees endangering our position were felled. An attempt was made to rescue specimens of the more valuable manuscripts, but few were saved for the danger was pressing. Sir Claude MacDonald, as soon as the fire was discovered, despatched a messenger to the Tsung-li-Yamen, telling them of the fire and urging them to send some responsible officials to carry away what volumes could be rescued, but no attention was given to his courteous communication.

Morrison's account in the *Times* was echoed by other British legationers' narratives, which show signs of having been orchestrated. In a version of his diary edited for publication, Hewlett wrote for June 22: "Sir Claude gave an order to break a hole in the wall to the Hanlin, so as to have a ready communication to put out fire or pull down houses . . ."

Lancelot Giles, whose diary also was edited for publication, noted for the same date: "At night a patrol was sent into the Hanlin, a gap being made in the north wall of the Legation."

All these accounts describe the same events, but there are a number of curious differences among them.

In his highly readable account, *The Siege at Peking*, published in the 1950s, the British author and journalist Peter Fleming chooses to believe Morrison, Giles, Hewlett, and the official British version and presents the story much the same way, adding: "*The Chinese set fire to the Hanlin, working systematically from one courtyard to the next. . . . A few undamaged books and manuscripts were salvaged more or less at random by sinologues* [italics added]." Fleming concludes: "Vandalism so wanton and so decisive would have been hard to forgive if it had been committed in a conquered city as an act of retribution. History affords no comparable example of cultural *felo de se* [that is, of any other culture performing such a wicked act upon itself]."

The fact is, the Chinese did not do it. The truth has been kept hidden for many years. British soldiers in fact entered the Hanlin the evening before the "fire," over the wall, and found no Chinese soldiers inside but only a few women caretakers. Captain Francis Garden Poole, a British soldier sent to Peking to learn Chinese just in time for the siege, was responsible for that section of the defense perimeter and gives the actual dates and movements in his rough unpublished diary:

June 22: At 3 this afternoon the E[nemy] set fire under heavy firing to a house on our S.W. corner [of the legation] near stable. They were trying to set fire to our own Legation. . . . I feared they might fire

[on] us from the Hanlin, so with [Captain] Strouts leave at dusk [with] a party of 15, 10 Marines, 3 Customs, Ben and myself climbed over the wall by ladder. The first European I fancy [ever] to enter the Hanlin was myself. . . . We reconnoitered through the whole place right to the canal road, but found nobody but some Chinese women. . . . Returned, reported place clear to the Chief, impossible to occupy it all night, too few men.

MacDonald ordered them back in the next morning, June 23. As Poole described: "I must take a party inside, clear out E[nemy] and occupy Hanlin. . . . together with 10 B[ritish] Marines, 5 Customs volunteers, Morrison, Barr and myself, make a breach in the Legation wall, and stream quickly through."

Captain Poole said that on entering the Hanlin, he found 250 Chinese Muslim troops only in the "big temple" at the entrance and quickly flushed them out, whereupon in reprisal these unlettered soldiers set fire to the big temple, and this fire spread to the nearest of the several library buildings, which had to be pulled down immediately by Poole's men to get the fire under control. Thanks to a wind shift this fire was completely under control within thirty minutes. It was not repeated.

What actually followed is to be found in the disturbing record of another survivor of the siege, the American missionary Arthur H. Smith, who was among the Westerners of various nationalities who joined in the firefight at the Hanlin. His account, published in 1901 in an obscure small edition, attracted little attention. Smith was not a part of the legation community and had nothing to gain by lying, so his account of the siege and of the Hanlin affair is dry and straightforward.

Smith wrote that "every available man was set to work passing buckets of water from the nearest wells, working the small fire-engines, and cutting down trees with much labour and not a little risk of being crushed beneath the trunks. . . . One of the large halls standing nearest the Legation had to be pulled down for our own safety. It was a difficult and dangerous undertaking for the building was lofty, with large and solid posts and roof-timbers." Meanwhile, many bystanders including Edmund Backhouse were carrying away armloads of priceless Chinese books, scrolls, and manuscripts, like ants swarming over a bowl of sugar. Sir Claude gave orders to bring the books from the library into the legation to prevent their theft, but many had already been stolen and the effort to protect them was abandoned.

Smith continued:

About the time of maximum danger the wind suddenly veered to the northwest, greatly encouraging the firemen and their assistants. The structure next in front of the one pulled down was filled with the bookcases containing some of the choicest volumes in the Hanlin University, particularly a vast work called after its Imperial patron, *Yung Lo Ta Tien*, a cyclopaedia of Chinese literature of immense compass, never printed, but copied by hand. This is supposed to be the sole copy in the Empire. . . .

Scores of the bulky cases were filled with the volumes of the encyclopaedia bound in yellow silk, pasted on the board covers, each book nineteen and a half inches long, twelve wide, and about an inch in thickness, having a strip of bright-coloured silk pasted on one cover with the four characters of its title. To the marines, as well as to many others who worked hard to put out the fire and to clear the building threatened, this was nothing more than a sample of the many unintelligible works thrown about in the greatest confusion on that memorable day. . . .

When it was probable that this building would burn with the rest, the contents of its boxes were unceremoniously tumbled into the yard, where they were soon buried under mounds of other books and lost to sight. An attempt was made to rescue this great cyclopaedia of learning, but although several hundred volumes were collected, many others disappeared. Some, with bushels of other volumes and manuscripts, were thrown into the lotus tank and covered with rubbish to prevent them from taking fire in a mass. At a later period, when they had been thoroughly soaked with water from the fire engines, and by numerous rains, so that they had begun to rot, an order was issued [by Sir Claude] to heap earth upon them to prevent them from infecting the neighbourhood. The execution of this command constituted the formal funeral of all that remained of the ancient Imperial Academy of China!

In the entire area of the Hanlin Yuan the only buildings which escaped the fire were a hall called the Ching I T'ing (now empty except for eleven stone tablets on which are cut the sayings of the sage C'eng-tzu) and others: *the hall containing the cyclopaedia mentioned* [italics added] and three small pavilions behind it. The first, like several others, was stored with Hanlin essays and with the stereotype blocks of numerous Chinese works, especially poetry, which, when once ignited, added greatly to the fury of the flames. Those blocks which remained were scattered about the premises or were used as firewood or as materials for barricades.

The principal literary monument of the most ancient people in the world was obliterated in an afternoon, and the wooden stereotype plates of the most valuable works became prey to the flames, or were used in building barricades, or as kindling by the British marines.

Priceless literary treasures were tumbled into the lotus-ponds, wet with flood of water used to extinguish the fire, and later buried after they had begun to rot, to diminish the disagreeable odour. Expensive camphor-wood cases containing the rare and unique Encyclopaedia of Yung Lo were filled with earth to form a part of the ramparts for defence, while the innumerable volumes comprising this great thesaurus were dispersed in every direction, probably to every library in Europe, as well as to innumerable private collections. Not a few of the volumes were thrown into the common heap to mold and to be buried like the rest.

Thousands of Hanlin essays lay about the premises, the sport of every breeze, serving as fire-wood for the troops. Odd volumes of choice works furnished the waste-paper of the entire Legation for nearly two months; they were found in the kitchens, used by the coolies as pads for carrying bricks on their shoulders, and lay in piles in the outer streets to be ground into tatters under the wheels of passing carts.

Out of twenty or twenty-five halls, but two remained and a few months later [after the siege] every trace of these had been removed from the Hanlin premises, which are now part of the British Legation grounds.

So, as Smith makes painfully clear and others affirm, the main Hanlin Library building was *not* burned down by the Chinese and—thanks to a shift of wind direction—was one of the two buildings still standing when the siege ended, only to be pulled down by the British *after the siege,* when the Hanlin compound was incorporated into the legation. The contents of this great archive, instead of being destroyed by the Chinese, were looted by Britons, Americans, Russians, French, and other Westerners. (The Russians later returned twenty-five volumes of the Yung Lo encyclopedia as a diplomatic gesture.)

This gives an entirely different bite to Fleming's magisterial remark cited earlier: "Vandalism so wanton and so decisive would have been hard to forgive if it had been committed in a conquered city as an act of retribution." (Most scholars and writers have taken the same position as Fleming and assumed, wrongly, that the Chinese were to blame.)

Sir Claude evidently was uneasy about what had occurred during the first hysterical days of the siege, including the Hanlin looting and destruction, so he decided to tell the Chinese government that the library had been burned and its treasures destroyed by the Chinese themselves. As we have seen, Morrison declared in the *Times* that a messenger was sent to the Tsungli Yamen with Sir Claude's message "but no attention was given to his courteous communication." However, Hewlett, who was Sir

Claude's clerical assistant and was later knighted for his service as a diplomat in China, let it slip in his diary that the *plan* was to send a messenger to the Tsungli Yamen but that this was never done because no messenger could be persuaded to go. Thus Morrison's statement that the Chinese ignored Sir Claude's message is not only a lie but one with a gratuitous twist intended to provoke the reader's indignation. None of this would have happened, Morrison suggests over and over, if it were not for the dowager and her gang.

Sir Claude's "Personal Reminiscences of the Siege" carefully skirts the whole episode, saying merely: "There remained only one building entirely intact, the heavy wooden eaves of which overshadowed and almost touched the students' quarters in the Legation."

In his unpublished private diary Morrison admits that the Hanlin Library suffered only slight damage from the fires set to the outer gates by the Chinese soldiers and that the real firing of the buildings, the destruction of the library, and the dispersal of its literary treasures were carried out by Westerners from the legations: "It was decided to dismantle the two buildings nearest us and the combustible books in them, the most valuable in the Empire, were thrown in a great heap into the pond round the summer house, and the building after incredible difficulty was pulled down. . . . Cockburn [the chief British interpreter] thought the Chinese soldiery would come down in force to avenge the destruction of this historic building, the most sacred in the empire."

They did not. The soldiers opposite the Hanlin and on the Tartar Wall at this early stage in the siege were Muslim-Chinese from Kansu and Turkestan who could neither read nor write and could not have grasped the significance of what had happened. It is unlikely that they understood what the Hanlin Academy was. The puzzle is that the Manchu court itself remained unaware of this heinous act, but it was poorly informed about many matters.

Morrison did his best in the *Times* to inflame British opinion against the Chinese and to shift to them (or to the French and Austrians) guilt for everything that had gone wrong during the siege. To emphasize the deprivations suffered by the legations, he lied that "no food supplies of any kind were permitted to pass the Chinese cordon, but on July 18 Chinese Ministers insolently sent some melons, ice and one sack of flour into the British Legation." Morrison neglected to mention that during the riots of June 13–16 the legations hijacked a procession of carts carrying tribute grain to the Forbidden City from Honan Province—two hundred tons of wheat, and similarly huge quantities of white and brown rice, and corn. He also failed to mention the market of fresh vegetables and fruit provided by Jung Lu, the black market in fresh eggs, and the thousands of cases of looted champagne.

Morrison's published account of the murder of the German minister von Ketteler avoids mentioning the baron's harassment and shooting at the Chinese in the days before the siege began or his abduction and killing of the young Chinese boy. Morrison was scolded for this omission in a letter from Edith Blake, the wife of Sir Henry Blake, governor of Hong Kong. "I have just been reading your account of the siege with great interest. Do you not think that Baron von Ketteler having shot the Boxer in the German Legation and making the German Guard fire on the Boxers going through their incantations in the Chinese City . . . had a good deal to say to his murder. I was given to understand Baron von Ketteler had done this before the siege of the Legations began."

In the *Times* Morrison said:

It is also apparent that throughout the Chinese Ministers abroad endeavored to hoodwink the foreign Governments by lying reports that the attacks upon the Legation and the shelling of the compounds, crowded with women and children, were due to lawless rebels, whom the Government was desirous, but powerless, to suppress, whereas the truth is that the attacks upon the Legations were ordered by the Dowager Empress and organized by Yung Lu, Tung-fuh-siang, and Li Ping Heng [sic], high Government officials who were appointed by Imperial decree to reduce the Legations by fire, sword, or famine.

Edith Blake took issue with this as well, telling Morrison, "It seems to me if the Peking Government wished to hoodwink the Powers, they would certainly not let their ministers in London and Washington know the game they were playing in Peking."

Lumping General Jung Lu and the dowager empress together with the Ironhats was not the result of ignorance on Morrison's part but typical of the malice taking hold of his imagination that would enable him to endorse and publish Backhouse slanders in the *Times* repeatedly during the next ten years. When his siege narrative appeared, Morrison was acclaimed far and wide as one of the heroes and was christened "Chinese" Morrison, and "Morrison of Peking." He was lionized by his journalistic peers. Fellow correspondent H. A. Gwynne wrote from South Africa: "I read . . . your splendid account of the Peking affair. It was really a first-class account of things and it was above all things correct. For one could see so easily that every fact had been verified and everything had been most carefully described without exaggeration or fine writing. Anyway that is the impression it gave me and all the other fellows who read it."

If the editors of the *Times* had any doubts about Morrison's version of events, they restrained themselves. They praised Morrison's "clear eye and cool judgement," and went on to defend him against his critics:

His statements have been often officially questioned and sometimes officially contradicted. They have almost invariably proved to be absolutely correct, in small matters as in great. . . . What he relates is in the main what he has seen with his own eyes while fighting for his life in the British Legation. Mistake is impossible. Neither the competence nor the credibility of the witness can be impugned. His statement more than justifies the worst suspicions entertained of the Dowager-Empress and her party. He affirms that she and they are personally responsible for all the blackest crimes perpetrated by the "Boxers."

By patting Morrison's back they patted their own, and enshrined his malice as gospel for most of a century to come.

Morrison condemned commander in chief Jung Lu for "following the Dowager's orders" to attack the legations and was criticized by his Japanese friends, who told him he had it backward. The harm had been done, but he tried to placate the Japanese by sprinkling his later reports with positive remarks about the man who (with Tzu Hsi's support) had more than likely saved them all. He wrote to Bland: "Was I right in saying a word for Jung Lu. . . . The Japanese are very strongly of opinion that we should support Jung Lu, and affect to believe the assurances of Yuan [Shih-kai], Chang [Chih-tung] and Liu [Kun-i, viceroy of Kiangsu, Kiangsi, and Anhwei] that he played a part in favour of the foreigner when the final struggle came."

Apparently Morrison was led to believe that if he made his account of the siege sufficiently favorable to Great Britain he could reasonably expect a knighthood. While there is no direct evidence that Sir Claude made such an offer in so many words, it was believed to be true by others in the legations.

Robert Hart had no illusions about Morrison's malicious reporting: "It would be interesting to get a really reliable Chinese account of palace doings—and Peking doings—during 1900. As it is, we are all guessing and inferring and putting this and that together, but we have not got the facts yet."

While Hart had been charmed by Morrison's urbane manner and sophisticated wit in the beginning, he soon discovered that Morrison was a lazy, self-indulgent man, intolerant, racist, and unprincipled. What Hart observed of Morrison and others at the British legation during the siege soured him. But he was loyal to Great Britain. Although he wrote extensively afterward about the Boxer affair, Hart never referred in any way, public or private, to the looting and burning of the Hanlin. His reaction to Morrison's articles in the *Times* was carefully noncommittal: "I think his own sufferings have made him take a more revengeful tone than he would otherwise have held: it is not the time for sentiment—*common sense* is what is most wanted." Nor did Hart address the circumstances leading to the killing of von Ketteler, the seizure and looting of Prince Su's palace, or the neglect of the Chinese converts in the Fu, episodes he found too painful to discuss. He did remark sharply that if Admiral Seymour had abandoned his trains and marched the last thirty miles to Peking, it would have changed history. Hart rightly laid the blame for the siege squarely on the Allies. He was puzzled that the Chinese never stormed the legations: "That somebody intervened for our semi-protection seems . . . probable: attacks were not made by such numbers as the Government had at its disposal—they were never pushed home, but always ceased just when we feared they would really succeed . . . its curiously half-hearted character not only gave us the chance to live through it, but also gave any relief forces time to come and extricate us." He concluded that the Boxers' motives were fundamentally patriotic. "In fifty years' time there will be millions of Boxers . . . below the surface is the seed, and sooner or later will follow the crop." In this as in many other judgments about China he was correct.

Morrison's vilification of the dowager in his articles for the *Times* became part of history. In his 1901 book Lim Boon-keng spoke of her "complicity in the anti-foreign crusade," as "the soul of the traitorous cabal," who "was quite able to control all the Manchus and the soldiers under them."

All biographies of Tzu Hsi but one take the Morrison line. Charlotte Haldane's 1965 biography, for example, says, "On 13 June 1900, the wolves of China, at last unleashed by the Motherly and Auspicious Empress dowager, descended on their enemies and launched their vicious attack on the Legations of Peking, determined to wipe them out." Sheer nonsense. However, even *The Cambridge History of China* says that the dowager decided that it was necessary for there to be "an all out attack on the legations."

Perhaps the most damaging distortion by Western writers was to blame Tzu Hsi for the grisly murders of forty-five foreign missionaries, including wives and children, at Governor Yu Hsien's mansion in Taiyuan on July 9, 1900. It was only after the Allied invasion and seizure of Tientsin, and consequent state of war that serious and grotesque atrocities were committed against foreigners elsewhere in China, not by Boxers but by angry and vengeful Manchu and Chinese officials, particularly Yu Hsien—one of the two men who had first encouraged the Boxers in

Shantung and who had kept up a running battle with foreign missionaries there before being transferred to Shansi. In cold fury he ordered all missionaries in the province brought to the capital, allegedly for their protection, and then personally supervised their beheadings, husbands, wives and children. Much of the horror associated in Western minds with the Boxers and with the siege of Peking is traceable to this ghastly event far to the west of the capital. An eyewitness described the executions:

The first to be led forth was Mr. Farthing. His wife clung to him, but he gently put her aside, and going in front of the soldiers knelt down without saying a word, and his head was struck off with one blow of the executioner's knife. He was quickly followed by Mr. Hoddle and Mr. Beynon, Drs. Lovitt and Wilson, each of whom was beheaded by one blow of the executioner. Then the Governor, Yu Hsien, grew impatient and told his bodyguard, all of whom carried heavy swords with long handles, to help kill the others. . . .

When the men were finished the ladies were taken. Mrs. Farthing had hold of the hands of her children who clung to her, but the soldiers parted them, and with one blow beheaded their mother. The executioner beheaded all the children and did it skillfully, needing only one blow. . . . Mrs. Lovitt was wearing her spectacles and held the hand of her little boy, even when she was killed. . . .

When the Protestants had been killed, the Roman Catholics were led forward. The Bishop . . . asked the Governor why he was doing this wicked deed. I did not hear the Governor give him any answer, but he drew his sword and cut the Bishop across the face one heavy stroke; blood poured down his white beard, and he was beheaded.

The priests and nuns quickly followed him in death. . . .

On that day forty-five foreigners were beheaded in all. . . . The bodies of all were left where they fell till the next morning. . . . Some of the heads . . . were placed in cages on the city wall. All were surprised at the firmness and quietness of the foreigners, none of whom except two or three of the children cried, or made any noise.

Three weeks later, at the end of July, a proclamation *was* issued in Peking as the Allied armies approached, ordering the beheading of all foreigners. These extermination orders were issued personally by the Ironhat Prince Chuang under his seal, not the empress dowager's.

The outside world did not learn of these mass murders until many weeks after the siege of the legations was lifted. When Morrison and others in the legations eventually heard about the Shansi massacre, they conveniently identified themselves from then on with that spectacular atrocity to reinforce their claim to having barely survived.

In evaluating what had taken place in Shansi, Sir Ernest Satow put all the blame squarely on Governor Yu Hsien, as did all of the other legation ministers. There was no attempt by any of the envoys to suggest that this was the work of Tzu Hsi; Governor Yu Hsien was acting on his own.

However, by sleight of hand after Tzu Hsi's own death she was blamed personally for the atrocity. The *Times* made this a matter of record when it stated in its obituary of the dowager: "It is almost beyond doubt that the Empress Dowager approved of the horrible massacre of Europeans in Shansi, and that she could have prevented it with a word." This obituary, although credited to J.O.P. Bland, Shanghai correspondent for the *Times*, was written for him by Edmund Backhouse.

When Backhouse and Bland published their first biography of the empress in 1910, they quoted at length from the Ching Shan diary. According to the diary, during the early days of the Boxer siege Tzu Hsi finally had enough of foreign interference and declared at a secret council meeting: " 'The foreigners are like fish in the stew-pan. For forty years have I lain on brushwood and eaten bitterness because of them.' " She personally directed "Prince Chuang, as head of the city gendarmerie to issue a proclamation offering taels 50 for every head of a male barbarian brought in, taels 40 for that of a woman, and taels 30 for that of a child." According to the Bland and Backhouse book it was Tzu Hsi, not Governor Yu Hsien, who personally ordered the missionary beheadings in Shansi. " 'I command that all foreigners—men, women, and children, old and young—be summarily executed. Let not one escape, so that my empire may be purged of this noisome source of corruption.' " The diary claimed that on June 24, Tzu Hsi sent a secret decree to Yu Hsien: " 'Slay all foreigners wheresoever you find them; even though they be prepared to leave your province, yet must they be slain.' " Unable to resist one last gruesome bit of fiction, Backhouse added that Yu Hsien memorialized the throne, "reporting that he cunningly entrapped all the foreigners, cast them into chains, and had every one decapitated in his yamen. Only one woman had escaped, after her breasts had been cut off [a typical Backhouse touch], and had hidden herself under the city wall; she was dead when they found her."

These outright lies were allowed to stand as a matter of record by foreign diplomats in Peking (many of whom knew they were not true) and their governments. Not a single Western official ever challenged these assertions although their private papers indicate that they did not hold the dowager responsible. Thanks to Morrison, Tzu Hsi was blamed entirely for the siege. Thanks to Backhouse, she became a mass murderess.

CHAPTER TWENTY-THREE

The Dragons Flee

While Peking was being looted, the empress dowager's frightened entourage was fleeing seven hundred miles overland to presumed safety, escorted by thousands of the red-uniformed Muslim troops of Prince Tuan's faithful ally, General Tung.

Part of the myth of the Boxer siege—to justify the gross excesses of the conquering Allies—is that Peking was heavily defended to the bitter end and that Tzu Hsi did not flee until late on August 14, and then did so in a disreputable and murderous fashion. As it is usually told by mythmakers and historians alike, at the hour of yin in midafternoon in the Forbidden City, when the Allies had just reached the legations, the dowager supposedly ordered her chief eunuch, Li Lien-ying, to bring disguises. She put on the rough black cotton muslim jacket and trousers of a Chinese woman, cut her very long fingernails, tied up her hair in a simple bun like a peasant, then summoned Emperor Kuang Hsu. When Kuang Hsu appeared, the story goes, he was accompanied by Chen Fei, his Pearl Concubine, who threw herself down and begged the dowager to let them stay behind to carry out negotiations. The dowager became enraged and (again according to the Western version) commanded her eunuchs to get rid of this little slip of a girl. They picked up the struggling Pearl Concubine, carried her to a well in a small courtyard by the Palace of Peace and Longevity, turned her upside down in her layers of silks, and flung her into its depths. This evil deed done, the dowager fled in a donkey cart like a common criminal out the back exit of the Forbidden City, the Gate of Divine Pride.

This story first appeared in an article in the *Times* written after the dowager's death, credited to "Our Shanghai Correspondent," Bland, but was drafted for Bland by Edmund Backhouse. Bland was too sick with the flu to write anything. By 1910 Backhouse had embellished the story, claiming the details came from the secret Ching Shan diary. The dowager, according to Backhouse, ignored Kuang Hsu's pleas for the Pearl Concubine, ordering, " 'Throw this wretched minion down the well!' " In his second book, Backhouse claimed that new diaries corroborated and expanded on the death struggle. He said the eunuchs threw heavy stones down on top of the Pearl Concubine and "mocked the Emperor in his grief." There is no evidence at all to support this dark fable. The pungent details and witty dialogue are pure Backhouse.

As to the real fate of the Pearl Concubine, nobody knows. There may have been animosity between her and Tzu Hsi. The girl was spirited in the same way the dowager had been as a girl, and after she entered the palace she got into trouble for influence peddling. Some sources insist that she and the emperor were intimate and that she gave Kuang Hsu contrary advice, as a lover might, encouraging him to defy the dowager on various matters. But this does not fit more believable medical and other evidence that Kuang Hsu strictly avoided his empress and both his concubines because of his embarrassing impotence and nervous state. It is possible that on her own the girl chose to stay behind and was done in by the eunuchs on their own initiative, or flung herself down a well. Many young women committed suicide when the Allies arrived. As Lenox-Simpson reported, "The wells near the Eastern Gates, have you seen them, where all the women and girls have been jumping in? They are full of women and young girls." Chen Fei's chubby sister, the Lustrous Concubine, Chin Fei, continued to be an enthusiastic part of the dowager's retinue for years afterward, suggesting that nothing sinister had occurred. In any case the well in question is too narrow to take even the body of a six-year-old.

Because of the destruction and looting of court archives very little is known about what really happened during those last days in Peking, but what is known points to an entirely different sequence of events. For one thing, Tzu Hsi and Kuang Hsu were not even in the Forbidden City on August 14, because they had left it many days earlier. This would have become obvious to anyone making a careful study of the evidence that is commonly available, but everyone was so taken in by the Morrison, Backhouse, and Kang Yu-wei portrayal of Tzu Hsi as the central villain and became so complacent about it that no reexamination of this episode was ever undertaken.

Diaries of the siege state that more than two weeks earlier, back on July 27, a Chinese soldier told people in the legations that two hundred carts and sixty-five hundred soldiers, among them forty-eight hundred of Tung's Kansu braves, had gone into the Forbidden City, "which all points to the Emperor and Empress Dowager preparing for flight." By this point, General Li Ping-heng had taken over military operations around

Peking. Quickly assessing the gravity of the situation, he requested the exodus of the court to the Summer Palace, removing them from immediate danger and lessening the likelihood that they might become hostages of the Allies. General Li then left Peking in his doomed attempt to block the Allied advance. Lenox-Simpson noted on August 8 that there were completely new troops surrounding the legations. Accordingly, sometime between July 27 and August 8 the troops of General Tung, of Jung Lu, of Prince Ching, and of Prince Tuan, including the Peking Field Force and the Marksmen for the Tiger Hunts—all the inner rings of defense for the throne—left the center of Peking and were replaced by provincial troops from Shansi sent by Governor Yu Hsien. The departure of these armies confirms that the empress dowager and the emperor had already gone, at least to the Summer Palace. Two days later, on August 10, people watching through binoculars from the legations observed "Chinese soldiers going in and out of the Chien men [the main gate leading to the Forbidden City], and carts going out in great numbers, and people moving furniture, very interesting to watch." The carts were hauling away the most important imperial treasures and personal effects.

This was the same day that commander in chief Jung Lu, Grand Councillor Kang I, Grand Secretary Hsu Tung, and Grand Duke Chung were ordered to remain behind to take charge of governmental affairs after the court's escape to the north and west. So it would appear that the dowager left the Forbidden City no later than the eighth—a full week before the Allies arrived, going to the Summer Palace for two days, possibly to designate what was to be removed for safekeeping—and left Peking entirely during the night of the tenth, four days before the Allies marched in. Thus the story of her hastily donning a disguise on the fourteenth is a fanciful invention based on a misunderstanding of the chronology of events. Tzu Hsi had been through all this before in 1860; this time she was a pawn of the Ironhats, then it was the Gang of Eight.

As Tzu Hsi later told a lady-in-waiting, when Prince Tuan learned that the foreign troops were approaching, "He was so frightened that he made us all leave Peking." She then talked about letting herself be bullied by Prince Tuan, and started to cry, saying, "You need not feel sorry for me for what I have gone through; but you must feel sorry that my fair name is ruined. That [giving in to Prince Tuan on the Boxer affair] is the only mistake I have made in my whole life and it was done in a moment of weakness."

As Lady MacDonald had discovered, Tzu Hsi was a woman at the mercy of her advisers, swayed first one way then the other. This impression was confirmed by the senior interpreter at the British legation, Henry Cockburn, who had accompanied Lady MacDonald to the dowager's tea and had all his previous ideas of her strength, power, and cunning over-turned, summing up Tzu Hsi's true character as "amiability verging on weakness."

The dowager's recollections to Derling continued:

Prince Tuan and Duke Lan suggested that we should go at once. They also suggested that we should go in disguise, which made me very angry, and I refused. After the return of the Court to Peking [a year later], I was told that many people believed that I did go in disguise and said that I was dressed in one of my servant's clothes, and rode in a broken cart drawn by a mule, and that this old woman servant of mine was dressed as the Empress Dowager, and rode in my sedan chair. I wonder who made that story up? Of course every-one believed it, and such a story would get to the foreigners in Peking without any trouble. . . .

The Young Empress [her niece] was the only one of my family who went with me. A certain relative of mine, whom I was very fond of . . . refused to go with me. I knew that the reason she would not go was because she thought the foreign soldiers would catch up . . . and kill everyone.

I had a very hard time, traveling in a sedan chair, from early morning, before the sun rose, until dark. . . .

The Emperor went all the way in a cart, drawn by a mule, also the [Young] Empress. . . . One day something happened. It rained so much and some of the chair carriers ran away. Some of the mules died suddenly. It was very hot, and the rain was pouring down on our heads. . . .

I cannot tell you how fatigued I was, and I was of course worrying very much, which made me quite ill for almost three months. So long as I live I cannot forget it.

These quotes recorded in Mandarin and then translated into English by the lady-in-waiting, Derling, accurately portray what we know of Prince Tuan and Jung Lu. Derling was too young to have known either of them personally, and in any event she was not in Peking from 1899 to 1903. This supports the conclusion that her narrative of Tzu Hsi's remarks, while perhaps losing a lot in clumsy translation, is essentially true. Tzu Hsi's chagrin about the Boxer business was remarked upon by many who observed her in the months following the debacle. For Tzu Hsi, it was the low point in her life. She and Kuang Hsu both blamed Prince Tuan, who had terrorized them and brought this disaster upon them all. Tzu Hsi had been made to look like a fool, a coward, and worse. Members of her own family were afraid to accompany her during the escape for fear that they would be pursued and slain. On the journey northwestward along the Great Wall, she was forced to endure great hardships, aggravating the humiliation. That she survived at all at her age speaks well of her remaining strength of character.

Prince Su, whose palaces and gardens had been commandeered by the legations to house the unwanted Christian converts, fled with the dowager and left a detailed description of part of the journey.

From the Summer Palace they traveled first to Kuanshih, twenty miles north of Peking, escorted by three thousand soldiers of various commands. Other troops had gone ahead. There mule litters were supplied, and from then on the procession covered twenty miles a day. Reaching the Great Wall on the road to Jehol, they climbed to its broad masonary roadway, where six horses or more could gallop abreast, and followed it to the west, away from Jehol, snaking through the mountains to the palace at Hsuanhua, a fortified city on the wall 120 miles from Peking. There a halt was made till the last days of August. The hardships of the journey and the humiliation by the Allies proved too much for Grand Councillor Kang I, who died along the way. The court still feared pursuit and capture by the Allies, so they resumed their flight on August 25, again following the Great Wall to Kalgan, another fortified city on the edge of the Mongolian plateau, and reached Tatung in Shansi at the end of the month. According to Prince Su, the dowager did little during the long journey but weep and condemn those she thought responsible for the disaster. Emperor Kuang Hsu, he said, "reviled everyone." The Ironhats had wrecked his attempt to reform the government, beheaded his reform advisers, and humiliated him personally, then—gaining control of the throne by intimidating Tzu Hsi—had foolishly miscalculated and brought the Ching Dynasty to its darkest defeat. The economic and other consequences of the Boxer folly, the Allied invasion and occupation of Peking, the looting and division of spoils made all previous confrontations between China and the Foreign Powers seem small by comparison. The dynasty would never recover.

As the procession crept slowly northwest, its nucleus grew as fleeing Ironhats and their remaining troops caught up to the main body. At Tatung they turned south down the length of Shansi Province, shielded from the Allied armies in Peking by a range of mountains, and stopped on September 10 at the provincial capital, Taiyuan, the post of the murderous Governor Yu Hsien, the former Shantung magistrate who had encouraged the Big Swords and the Spirit Boxers from idea to uprising. Here Tzu Hsi was lodged in the governor's mansion, under heavy guard; in its courtyard, nine weeks earlier, Yu Hsien had supervised the mass beheading of the Western missionaries and their wives and children. Prince Tuan's son, the heir apparent Pu Chun, is said to have pranced around the courtyard brandishing one of the swords used.

During their three-week stopover at Taiyuan, Prince Tuan showed his continued hold over the court by having himself named Grand Councillor to succeed the late Kang I. Here in Governor Yu Hsien's isolated provincial capital, in an area controlled militarily by General Tung, Prince Tuan remained pre-eminent despite the calamitous failure of his policies. The fact that the prince remained in control and was able to intimidate his opponents for months to come and then to evade all punishment for his folly, illustrates how powerless Tzu Hsi really was. General Tung's army guarded the throne but also held it captive. He owed his wealth and power as warlord of northwestern China to Prince Tuan's family. So long as Prince Tuan retained Tung's military support and the instruments of power, including the Shangfang sword, nobody dared challenge him. He still had the support of the conservative Manchu aristocracy, who blamed the Allies and not the Ironhats. A failed Manchu hero was nonetheless a hero. As in 1860 their escape from Peking was seen as a strategic withdrawal. The lightning collapse of the Ironhat strategy had come so recently that the thunderclap of consequences had not caught up. Reality was hundreds of miles away. Incredible as it may seem the hard-liners still argued for a continuation of the war; they insisted that the fall of Tientsin and Peking was due to the betrayal of traitors and that if Tung's army was increased to fifty thousand men the Allies could be expelled.

This was the first time that Tzu Hsi had been in the interior of the empire. By her own account she was in a mild state of shock. She and the emperor had no choice but to go where they were led; she was now an uncertain old woman approaching seventy, while Kuang Hsu's wishes carried no weight whatever with the Ironhats.

On October 1 the court left Taiyuan, traveling westward for nearly a month to Sian in neighboring Shensi, which had been the capital a thousand years earlier during the Tang Dynasty. Nearby was a hot spring called Lin-tung, surrounded by palaces and pavilions. This move to Sian became necessary when the Allies learned about Yu Hsien's massacre of the missionary families and it was thought that they might mount a punitive expedition to Shansi. Sian was well into the Muslim wastelands controlled by General Tung; here they could hold out indefinitely. According to one source, Tung had the court under continual surveillance at Sian, where "not only has he stationed a special and devoted guard of troops, but where his spies and emissaries are located in such numbers that the most minute occurrences are reported to him. The Empress Dowager apparently has not been able to consult with any of her advisers without Tung knowing all about what happens. . . ."

Tung was able to control the empress through his men. "While there is a body of Manchu of military rank—about 250 in number—who are called by courtesy 'Imperial Guardsmen,' who take turns holding the great gates of the Governor's yamen, which now does duty as an imperial palace for the Empress Dowager and the Emperor . . . the real guards of the palace are furnished by a Kansu battalion composed entirely of Gen. Tung Fu-hsiang's fellow-townsmen and clansmen from Ninghsia, who are devoted heart and soul to him and recognize no authority but his."

In Sian Tzu Hsi continued to be deeply troubled. Tears welled in her eyes whenever she discussed the situation. She often got up in the middle of the night, sighing with anxiety. She was conspicuously kind to Emperor Kuang Hsu, who often cursed the Ironhats bitterly. Their fate was out of their hands.

It was now the turn of the Allies to make demands. Their instrument was Viceroy Li Hung-chang, giving him the opportunity he craved to complete his revenge on the Manchu. How Li took advantage of the Boxer crisis by manipulating the news coming out of Peking, creating shock and horror in the West and precipitating the Allied invasion, is a completely unknown part of the siege. It is reconstructed here for the first time.

For Li the conspiracy to cripple Emperor Kuang Hsu's reform initiatives in 1898 had been only a partial victory. Li had failed to regain his lost post as viceroy of Chihli; instead, he was given as a sop the lesser post of viceroy at Canton, far away to the south, where his brother had been viceroy previously and where Li would be less of a threat to the Ironhats. His departure for Canton left his northern financial empire vulnerable from Mukden and Tientsin to Shanghai. Grand Secretary Hsu Tung and Grand Councillor Kang I immediately proposed the government takeover of many of Li's holdings, including the China Merchants Steam Navigation Company, the Imperial Telegraph Administration, and the Kaiping Mines. They complained that Li had been permitted by the throne to start a number of Western-style enterprises on the proposition that they would benefit China and bring much-needed revenue to the government, while not a single coin from his profits had ever reached Peking. In Canton Li fought back, working through his lieutenants, and a settlement was reached to pay the Manchu court 20 percent of the corporate earnings of these enterprises instead of zero. Kang I, who was referred to behind his back as "the Great Extortionist," groused that this was completely inadequate, but for the moment Li had staved them off.

Before the siege of the legations began, Tzu Hsi cabled Viceroy Li to return to Peking. She realized that Li was the one man in China who could talk the foreigners into leaving the capital willingly before Prince Tuan made serious trouble, and with Li back in Peking there would be no need to worry about Allied reprisals. She also hoped that Li could bring enough indirect pressure to bear on the Ironhats to neutralize their growing power at court. He had worked miracles in the past. But Li had his own agenda.

Eleven other urgent appeals were sent to Li in Canton. He found one pretext after another to delay the journey north. If he was going to go to their rescue, the Manchu would first have to meet his price.

After the Peking telegraph wires were cut, Tzu Hsi's telegrams were taken by courier on horseback to the telegraph office in Shantung, which continued to function throughout under the watchful eye of Li's protégé, General Yuan Shih-kai.

Meanwhile Li was making good use of the time he gained by these delays to lobby the foreign consuls in Canton, and to circulate among journalists he had cultivated the first of many false stories designed to inflame the world against the Ironhats. He also had time to contrive the counterfeit ultimatum of June 17.

On June 18, 1900, one day after the Taku Forts were attacked, Li was bluntly commanded to go to Peking at once. He arranged for one of the steamers of his shipping line to be sent to Canton to take him north. Learning of the fall of the forts, he changed his destination to Chinwang-tao, where he said he planned to take a train to Peking, although he knew the railway had been cut. It was all a dodge. By June 21 he had reversed himself again and decided to stay where he was till he received further word from Peking.

Li obviously had mixed feelings about helping Tzu Hsi if it also meant helping the Manchu out of the oncoming catastrophe. They had undone much of what he had accomplished in his life. He told the American consul in Canton that during the years he had been viceroy in Chihli "that place was in peace and prosperity and there was no rebellion. Now it is infested with robbers [Boxers] and I must go to clear them out."

Since becoming viceroy at Canton Li had formed a new bloc with four other powerful Chinese—Chang Chih-tung, now the viceroy of Hupeh and Hunan; Liu Kun-i, the viceroy of Kiangsu, Kiangsi, and Anhwei; his protégé Yuan Shih-kai, governor of Shantung and head of the most modern of the five northern armies; and Telegraph Sheng, head of Li's Imperial Telegraph Administration. Together they controlled most of China's vital organs, and refused to involve themselves or their troops in Prince Tuan's plot, discreetly concluding a separate peace with the Foreign Powers.

They manipulated the news coming out of Peking through Shantung, with devastating effect. This was done through Li's control of China's telegraph system. Despite its bureaucratic name the Imperial Telegraph Administration was actually a private company set up by Li as part of his financial empire. It was centered in Shanghai and directed by Telegraph Sheng. All news from Peking came out by dispatch rider to General Yuan in the governor's office in Shantung, then through the telegraph office there to Telegraph Sheng's headquarters in Shanghai.

Sheng's cronies called him "the Old Fox." As a young man he had been one of Li's most promising lieutenants, becoming chief executive and largest stockholder of Li's China Merchants Steam Navigation Company. Over the years he set up many other enterprises for Li, gaining valuable experience dealing with foreigners; his biggest achievement was in 1880, when he organized the joint stock company that strung China's first telegraph lines. It was Sheng's (and Li's) personal preserve for the next twenty-two years and they found mischievous use for it.

During the Boxer affair, as all messages wired from north to south passed through Sheng's hands, he was able to manipulate every bit of news before it reached the outside world. He kept in constant touch with Li.

At the start of the crisis, Telegraph Sheng wired Li suggesting that he should urge the throne to use force to put down the Boxers: "The Grand Councillors Jung Lu and Wang Wen-shao understand the situation well, but they need the support of the provincial authorities in order to break the erroneous views [of the Ironhats] and to convince the supreme authority [Tzu Hsi]." In his reply Li hinted broadly that it might not be a bad thing to let them stew in their own juice for a while.

This attitude came to be shared by the other members of Li's power bloc. Yuan Shih-kai was their eyes and ears in the north. As his governor's mansion in Shantung was the main link with the isolated court, he was the best-informed man in the empire. He and Li were in constant contact also. Li sent his telegrams to the dowager through Yuan, who sent them on by ten separate couriers carrying identical messages to Peking. When news of the June 11 murder of the Japanese embassy chancellor, Sugiyama Akira, reached Shantung, Yuan promptly advised General Jung Lu either to protect the legations or to evacuate all diplomats. This marked the beginning of Jung Lu's security perimeter efforts. When Yuan heard that Admiral Seymour's relief expedition had set out, he wired Telegraph Sheng: "About 8,000 foreign troops near Tientsin and Peking; 10,000 more on their way. Dare not surmise what will happen. Please advise me. Do Viceroys Liu K'un-i and Chang Chih-tung have any good suggestions?"

As the crisis worsened, the southern viceroys urged Li to do something to save the day. Li was unmoved, "It is futile to memorialize," he replied. He knew that Tzu Hsi had become uncertain and powerless as the struggle between moderates and Ironhats intensified.

All along Li and Sheng were secretly taking advantage of journalists in Shanghai to bring more pressure to bear. The grimmer the news, the wider the international coverage it received. Everyone was expecting the massacre of the legations. On June 17, before the siege even began, newspa-

pers in London and New York carried reports that "all the Peking legations have been destroyed." The same day reports came that "the German
Minister, Baron von Ketteler, has been killed," although that was yet to
happen. On July 3 the *New York Times* headlined: LITTLE HOPE FOR ENVOYS
AT PEKING. And on July 5 the same paper announced: ALL FOREIGNERS IN
PEKING DEAD. All these reports originated in Shanghai, supposedly from
legation servants who escaped the massacre. "They report that all the
foreigners, about 1,000 in number . . . held out, till their ammunition was
exhausted, in the British legation. The legation was finally burned, and
all the foreigners were killed." The sources described how food and
ammunition ran low and "the rooms of the legation were filled with sick
and wounded, the killed lying unburied in heaps."

Some Western observers remained skeptical till July 16 when the worst
was confirmed in a story originating in the London *Daily Mail* and picked
up by newspapers around the world. The version carried by the *New York
Times* was headlined: FOREIGNERS ALL SLAIN AFTER A LAST HEROIC STAND.
Below that was a chilling subhead: SHOT THEIR WOMEN FIRST—THEY HAD
FORMED A SQUARE ROUND THEM AND THE CHILDREN—HEADS CARRIED ON
RIFLES.

The story went on:

An official telegram received [July 15] from Governor [Yuan Shih-kai]
states that a breach in the wall (of the British Legation in Peking) was
made, after a gallant defense and all the ammunition had given out,
and that all the foreigners were killed.

The Shanghai correspondent of the *Daily Mail* says: "I can assert
positively that the Chinese authorities [in Shanghai] had the dreadful
news from Peking a week ago, and that [Telegraph Sheng] knew that
all the foreigners in Peking were dead. . . . At 6 o'clock in the evening
of July 6," says the correspondent, "fire was opened with artillery
upon the British Legation where the foreigners were concentrated.
For two hours the walls were battered with shot and shell, and huge
breaches were made in them . . . the legationers formed a square with
the women and children in the centre. . . . The foreigners went mad
and killed all their women and children with revolvers. . . . The
Boxers rushed upon them and hacked and stabbed both dead and
wounded, cutting off their heads and carrying these through the
streets on their rifles."

This ghastly image held the world transfixed with horror. Kaiser Wilhelm swore revenge, the British organized a memorial service at St. Paul's
Cathedral, and generals planned reprisals. The *Times* published long obituaries of Sir Robert Hart, George Morrison, and Sir Claude MacDonald.

The *Illustrated London News* printed pictures of Sir Claude's pretty wife and, separately, their two angelic daughters. The somber accompanying text read:

> Five years ago, Sir Claude MacDonald became Minister at Peking. Thither went with him his devoted wife, who had early served an apprenticeship to suffering. She was already a widow and childless, her husband, Mr. Craigie Robertson, of the Indian Civil Service, and her two children having all died together in one day from cholera. Fate has repeated itself strangely. Two children also she had in her second marriage, Ivy and Stella MacDonald, the last-named a child of three born in Peking: and again husband and two children perish together, but in companionship with the wife and mother.

Readers were invited to dwell on their agony. For more than two weeks, newspapers and magazines everywhere in the world reviewed the sickening details over and over, and published dire warnings. Thousands of soldiers embarked for China to carry out a great vengeance for something that had not happened.

The reporter who wrote the original massacre story, from details fed to him by Telegraph Sheng, was the *Daily Mail*'s Shanghai correspondent, an American named F. W. Sutterlee, also known as W. F. Sylvester. "This man," Morrison later advised his editors at the *Times*, "was manager of the firm of Kern Sutterlee & Co. of Philadelphia who in January 1896, after the failure of the firm, sold thrice over by means of forged warehouse certificates, the same stock of wool, and then skipped with the proceeds to Tientsin . . . [where he] went into partnership with Louis Spitzel . . . who had been in trouble with the police in England for being in possession of goods knowing them to have been stolen. . . . At the outbreak of the war between the United States and Spain [1898] the two . . . engaged in a lucrative trade selling arms to the Philippine insurgents."

Li's rumor mill in Shanghai did not confine itself to just one or two hoaxes. On July 5 Telegraph Sheng provided the *Daily Mail* correspondent with a story that Emperor Kuang Hsu and Empress Dowager Tzu Hsi had both been poisoned, compelled by Prince Tuan to swallow a fatal brew. The emperor succumbed, according to this story, while Tzu Hsi was "insane from the effects of the drug." Next day another story appeared quoting two anonymous Manchu "who have arrived at Shanghai [and] certify to the truth of the statement that Prince Tuan visited the palace and offered the Emperor and the Dowager Empress the alternative of poison or the sword. The Emperor, they say, took poison, and died within an hour. The Dowager Empress also chose poison, but craftily swallowed only a portion of what was offered to her, and survived."

Meanwhile, back in the real Forbidden City, fear of foreign intervention grew, and the court tried to get Governor Yuan to send his troops from Shantung to Tientsin to block the foreign invasion. Yuan made a show of sending three thousand men—but recalled them before they crossed the provincial border, claiming disciplinary problems. Two days later Viceroy Chang sent a token force to Peking, arguing that one of them had to make a demonstration of loyalty.

Throughout the crisis Li and his power bloc consistently and truthfully maintained that all this trouble was provoked by the Ironhats not by the empress dowager. When the Taku Forts were attacked, Li cabled Chinese diplomats abroad that "fighting at Taku was not ordered by the Throne" and asked them to convey this to their host governments and request a truce, so the crisis could be settled by negotiation (in which Li would be chief negotiator). Li advised Telegraph Sheng that even if an edict declaring war existed, he would not recognize it as authentic, for it could only have been issued without proper authorization from the throne, meaning by Prince Tuan. (This supports Derling's account of Tuan's telling Tzu Hsi that if she did not cooperate he would issue edicts himself.)

Li's bloc was convinced that the dowager was not acting of her own free will but was being manipulated. To extricate her from this predicament, Telegraph Sheng proposed that Yuan should march on Peking at the head of his superior army, provide protection for the dowager and the emperor, and purge the court of Prince Tuan's faction. But Yuan was too cagey to commit himself, replying, "It is an internal disease, and it has to be treated internally." It would not be prudent for a Chinese general to intervene in a Manchu quarrel. As Li had said, better to let them stew. Five days later the Japanese foreign minister sent a message to Yuan asking him to intervene. But again Yuan refused: "If I lead my troops to save the foreign ministers at Peking without Imperial orders, I am afraid that on the way I shall be defeated. This I really cannot do."

Li's bloc wanted commander in chief Jung Lu to take charge, but Jung Lu had his own problems, as he explained in a telegram to the southern viceroys in mid-June: "Half of the entourage of Their Majesties and the princes belong to the Boxer societies, as do the majority of Manchu and Chinese troops. They [the Boxers] swarm in the streets of the capital like locusts, several tens of thousands of them, and it is extremely difficult to re-establish order." He could not deal with the Boxers, the Ironhats, and the legations simultaneously.

When the Allied armies seized Tientsin, the throne demanded that Li come to Peking "without a moment's delay." Three days later he was commanded again to start at once. In desperation on July 8 the Manchu finally gave him what they thought he wanted. Li was reappointed viceroy of Chihli and Superintendent of Trade for the Northern Ports, the posts he had held for twenty-five years from 1870 to 1895 and was deprived of after the Sino-Japanese War.

Still Li did not budge. The court had given him only half of what he wanted. More telegrams were sent, ordering him to come at once.

On July 16 Li left Canton for Shanghai, but only to work more closely with Telegraph Sheng. Although the throne pleaded and demanded, he remained in Shanghai for the next two months at the home of the wealthy organizer of the White Pigeon Lottery on Bubbling Well Road. He told Telegraph Sheng that he would remain there until the Ironhats awakened from their dreams. He could hardly arrange a truce with the Allies when he had not been given full authority to negotiate. He knew that the Ironhats would give in eventually. All the time Li was in Shanghai, he and Telegraph Sheng met secretly each day with foreign diplomats identified only as "certain members of the consular body."

Li's counterfeit ultimatum to the Ironhats and his phony massacre stories in the international press were classic examples of the kind of disinformation recommended two thousand years earlier by the master strategist Sun Tzu, and they had achieved results for Li by bringing about the Allied invasion of China. Now, to prepare the way for negotiations, Li arranged for a little truth to leak out. The legations, it seemed, had not been massacred after all. On August 2 editors everywhere began publishing apologies and retractions. The *New York Times* said:

> . . . nothing more hideous and appalling than this picture [of the massacre] had been presented to the public within a century. . . . The definite statements of the correspondents, especially in Shanghai, practically destroyed doubt that all these had been slaughtered in circumstances of the most revolting cruelty. . . . The Cabinets of nearly every Government were considering how the swiftest and most impressive punishment could be inflicted on China. The feeling thus aroused was the more intense, because the reports were spread instantaneously over the whole globe. . . . Now it turns out that almost every statement sent out from China, and especially from Shanghai, was essentially false, and the details were wholly so.

Every one of these reports, of course, had been passed to the Western press in Shanghai by Telegraph Sheng, who in turn had been getting his information from Yuan Shih-kai in Shantung and his instructions from Li Hung-chang in Canton.

Li finally got what he wanted. As the court fled Peking, he was appointed to negotiate with a completely free hand. When the Allies marched into Peking on August 14, Li completed the last stage of his triumphant return to his longtime base at Tientsin, putting himself back in charge as China's real boss, the chairman of the board.

Li knew that Germany would want the Ironhats surrendered for punishment before peace talks could begin. He also realized that it was one thing for the Manchu Clan Court to decree punishment and another entirely to turn the emperor's own cousins and high Chinese mandarins over to the Foreign Devils for torment and humiliation. Chinese were stoic about cruelty within their own society, but they came unglued at the prospect of torture by aliens. This primal fear Li turned ingeniously to his advantage to force the Ironhats and the Allies into a compromise.

Before leaving Shanghai for Tientsin, Li got the jump on the Germans by sending the dowager empress his own list of five men he thought must be punished—among them his own personal enemies, Prince Tuan and Grand Councillor Kang I (whose death had not yet been reported). The others on his list were Prince Chuang; Ying Nien, vice-president of the Board of Revenue; and Chao Shu-chiao, president of the Board of Punishments. Li suggested to the throne that these five should be removed from their posts immediately pending a decision by the Clan Court on their precise punishment. He pointed out that it would be better for the throne and the Clan Court to exact punishment on Manchu princes than for it to be left up to the Foreign Devils.

Here was a golden opportunity to sweep the court clean of the most militant and inflexible Manchu and Chinese, a grand opportunity to settle old scores, and Li was an old man of seventy-seven whose health was failing. There was little time to waste.

No record survives of how the court reacted when Li's list of culprits arrived in Taiyuan, but it must have been a memorable moment. Four of the men listed were present and in full voice. Only Kang I was missing, having died on the Great Wall during the flight from Peking.

Nobody could argue with Li's point that it was better to be punished by their own peers than by the barbarians. Li was shrewdly giving trapped men a way to escape. He did not underestimate the wiliness of General Tung in helping Prince Tuan. On September 25 the throne issued its first edict of punishment. In addition to the five men listed by Li, it included four others. All were deprived of office and handed over to the appropriate boards for sentencing.

Three days later the throne also dismissed the bloodstained Governor Yu Hsien. Two days afterward Viceroy Li advised the throne that the Allies demanded the death penalty for nine ministers in all, plus General Tung Fu-hsiang and former Governor Yu Hsien.

Sir Ernest Satow was determined "that the Court should be made to understand the heinousness of the attempt to destroy the Legations."

Satow had talked with everyone from Sir Robert Hart to Colonel Shiba. During his meeting with the colonel he learned that while everyone else was busy looting, Shiba had removed from the Forbidden City several trunks full of documents implicating a large number of officials in the Boxer conspiracy but would not publicize the names because it would "do much harm." Shiba identified only a few to Satow. The rest were kept secret and the documents removed to Tokyo, where they would be useful to Japan in the future.

Viceroy Chang urged Li to pin all the blame on General Tung Fu-hsiang. Li replied that punishing the old Kansu bandit alone would not satisfy the Allies. Plus it would be awkward to demand Tung's head while the emperor and the dowager empress were inside Tung's territory surrounded by the general's army.

At the end of October, more mind-boggling details of Yu Hsien's missionary massacre were inflaming foreign hostility. By then the Allies had identified Yu Hsien as a moving force behind the Boxers from the beginning. Edwin Conger called Yu Hsien and General Tung "the worst of all." Morrison (with his usual absolute certainty) declared that the origin of the Boxers could be traced to "one man, Yu Hsien." Sir Ernest said that during a meeting with Viceroy Li on October 29, he (Satow) "nearly broke down at one place when the idea of the murdered women and children came into my mind, but kept it back and so recovered my self control." In December, Satow was hard-pressed by Li when it came to dickering about punishment:

Showed [Li] the proclamation . . . offering graduated rewards for the capture of [Western] men, women, and children, which was issued under the responsibility of Prince Chuang, Duke Lan and [Prince Tun II]. Did not such people deserve death? [Li] replied they did not accomplish their purpose. I said 60 people were killed and 160 . . . wounded in the Legations. He said these were nobodies [meaning mostly marines]. I replied that any Englishman was as good as any Chinaman. He added that [the Ironhats] were all cousins of the Emperor. I said what would you think if the Prince of Wales and cousins of the Queen had headed an attack on the Chinese minister in London. He replied they [the Ironhats] were foolish people. He asked me to write him a letter enclosing a copy of this proclamation, and he would memorialize the throne.

The dowager's predicament as a virtual prisoner of the Ironhats was altered by the arrival in Sian of her chief protector, Jung Lu, at the head of his own army. Earlier when Jung Lu had been ordered to remain in Peking to negotiate a truce, he had prudently withdrawn to the nearby city of Paoting, where his main army had been moved to avoid direct confrontation with the Allies. He remained in Paoting until he was warned by Viceroy Li that his life was in danger there, whereupon he headed west with his troops. He arrived in Sian on November 11, altering the military equation, and was immediately named a Grand Councillor by the dowager, displacing Prince Tuan.

His arrival brought Tzu Hsi great relief after months in the clutches of General Tung's wild horde. Even now extreme tact had to be exercised not to force a showdown between the two armies. As commander in chief, Jung Lu took over security for the throne and the court. General Tung was instructed to move his troops south to the area between Shensi and Honan. He had no alternative. Two weeks later another decree instructed Tung to reduce his troop strength by 2,500, followed by another to cut a second 2,500. Once the Muslim army was at a safe distance, Jung Lu became the principal intermediary in persuading the Clan Council to accept the terms of peace agreed to by Viceroy Li and the Allies. Long unappreciated in the West and usually portrayed as a villain, Jung Lu thus emerges from the Boxer episode with greater stature than any other Manchu official. Many in the legations owed their lives to him.

On November 13, an edict from the dowager announced punishments: Prince Tuan and his cousin Prince Chuang were to be imprisoned for life at Mukden in Manchuria. His eldest brother, Prince Tun II, was to be placed under house arrest. His younger brother, Duke Lan, was to be degraded one degree in rank and lose all his privileges. Ying Nien was to be degraded two degrees. Kang I's punishment was waived because he had died. Yu Hsien was to be banished for life to the most remote frontier in Turkestan and condemned to hard labor. Two other princes were to be imprisoned by the Clan Court.

However, this decree did not placate the Allies, who considered the punishments inadequate. Another decree three months later assigned stiffer sentences, but also failed to impress the Allies. They were wasting their breath, for whatever punishments were assigned on paper had nothing to do with what happened in fact. In the end only two Ironhats were actually seen to have paid with their lives.

In February 1901 Morrison attended the public executions at the vegetable market on Greengrocer Street of two Ironhats who did not get away. Chi Hsiu, president of the Board of Ceremonies, had been a leader of the purge against moderates and had boasted that "the foreigners in Peking and the interior will be all driven out or exterminated by the patriotic people." Hsu Cheng-yu, son of Grand Secretary Hsu Tung, was held responsible for the beheading of the purged moderates. His clan hired an expert executioner.

Morrison wrote in his diary:

Hsu [was] apparently deeply narcotised [and] was led along to the execution at the hands of a common headsman. Chi Hsiu behaved with much dignity. He drove up in a cart escorted by Japanese, having been brought from the Japanese prison. . . . While seated in his cart he raised the curtain to receive a letter which he read with composure. A young man did [the beheading] whom I hadn't seen before, though the old man [the official headsman] . . . who draws the head away as the neck is divided was there in his bloody apron. The executioner was not the bloody looking ruffian whom all photographed, but an amiable looking artisan with a good knowledge of his profession. . . . It is impossible to know what large fee was paid to the executioner. Two mats were laid down. There was a great crowd, a multitude of correspondents, and photographs by the score were taken. Rarely has an execution been seen by so many nationalities. . . . One slice in each case was sufficient.

The Allies had demanded the execution of twelve ringleaders in all, but these two deaths were the only ones witnessed. Prince Chuang, Ying Nien, and Chao Shu-chiao were said to have been given the honor of committing suicide, but whether they did is not certain; Hsu Tung had hanged himself earlier, of course, and Kang I had died during the flight into exile.

The real fate of Yu Hsien is a total mystery. In late October 1900, viceroys Li Hung-chang and Chang Chih-tung reported to the Allied ministers that Yu Hsien had committed suicide. Robert Hart wrote in a letter on November 1, 1900, that Yu Hsien had "already died off." But it was reported from Shansi that when Yu Hsien was sentenced in the first punishment edict to spend his life at hard labor in Turkestan, he left to begin the journey on November 13—after his alleged suicide. Three months later in the second edict of punishment Yu Hsien was sentenced to execution, so he was still alive when that edict was published. Years later Backhouse and Bland asserted that Yu Hsien was beheaded by imperial order before the citizens of Lan-chou, capital of Kansu. However, Lan-chou was controlled by General Tung, Yu Hsien's ally and protector, who had also wriggled completely off the hook by then, and Bland and Backhouse are completely unreliable as a source for anything. It was one of Yu Hsien's policies as a magistrate in Shantung to let Big Sword leaders disappear for a while, instead of decapitating them, after which they could resume activities under a new nom de guerre. There is a good chance that "the butcher of Taiyuan" spent the rest of his life in pleasant exile somewhere in Tung's vast domain.

The fate of General Tung himself was argued back and forth. Although the Allies originally had demanded Tung's execution, they finally grasped that it would be rash to press the matter. He was too dangerous. At the end of November 1900, Edwin Conger wrote to Washington that Tung's name should be left off Allied demands for punishment, "so that he might carry out the imperial order for the execution of others." A fanciful idea, but hardly a reasonable expectation. Satow wrote in his diary, "As to Tung Fu-hsiang, his government has expressed opinion that it may be impolitic to demand death penalty . . . I found [Morrison] also is a little disposed to think Tung might be let off." A cautious decree from Tzu Hsi deprived the general of his official ranks but allowed him to remain the warlord of Kansu provided he went back there immediately. Before he went, he was given a large part of the nearly four hundred thousand taels of silver delivered to Sian at that time by Yuan Shih-kai "for the use of the throne." So in the end Tung was paid off, retaining his army and his properties.

The departure of General Tung had a salutary effect on Tzu Hsi, as Sir Ernest learned from a Chinese official who had been to Sian to see the dowager. The official found her once again "the man of the situation." Far from being the mastermind manipulating generals and princes, she had been, like Kuang Hsu, the frightened pawn of ambitious princes and the uneasy houseguest of a warlord.

From Sian, General Tung and the emperor's first cousins Prince Tuan and Duke Lan, and probably Yu Hsien as well, journeyed together to the farthest reaches of Turkestan. Rather than to a prison in Manchuria, as one edict stipulated, Prince Tuan went to a palace outside Urumchi, the provincial capital of Sinkiang, near the border of Russia, a region of magnificent desolation, dominated by the twenty-thousand-foot peaks of the Celestial Mountains or Tien Shan. He shared this remote but luxurious exile with his brother, Duke Lan. Thanks to General Tung, they had all the comforts of home.

The old bandit Tung lived in luxury at his Ninghsia palace until February 1908, when he died of natural causes at age sixty-nine.

The Foreign Powers were unable to decide what to do about Prince Tuan's son Pu Chun, the designated heir to the throne, although they agreed that he should be removed for his father's crimes. Pu Chun behaved so boorishly in Taiyuan and Sian that he infuriated both the emperor and the dowager. Prince Su told Sir Ernest Satow that "the heir apparent had been severely beaten by the emperor and Empress-Dowager." At the end of November 1901, he was sent to join his father in exile, but grew bored with Turkestan and in 1904 was reported living in Peking "in honorable captivity."

When North China was picked clean, the Allies turned their attention to indemnities and put the finishing touch to a sorry episode. Li and the Allies concluded final negotiations for peace, the Boxer protocols, at Peking on September 7, 1901. The terms included apology missions to Germany and Japan for the murders of Sugiyama and von Ketteler, the permanent razing of the Taku Forts, the occupation of twelve points along the coast by Allied military forces, and payment of the huge sum of 450 million taels of silver in indemnity to the Allies for the cost of their military expeditions and the destruction of the personal property of foreigners during the uprising.

Here was a last opportunity to profit from the disaster. Government archives the world over are filled with claims from the Boxer Uprising, like one submitted by an American who charged for books lost from his library: *Uncle Tom's Cabin*, $2.50; *Bound Babyland*, $2.00; *Robert's Rules of Order*, $.75; *Jungle Book*, $1.00; *Diseases of the Rectum*, $1.00. He claimed reparations also for the loss of three toothpick holders, five pounds of vermicelli, two-thirds of a bag of sugar, four tins of corn beer, one dozen Vienna sausages (large); four door springs, one hot water bag, and four lemon drops.

Morrison, who had looted thousands of pounds' worth of furs, books, manuscripts, and precious objects, demanded £1,500 for his house, £515 for a collection of photographs, £484 10s. for books, £417 for furniture and fixtures, £7 for six Chinese costumes, and £2,625 for "pain . . . shock and mental anguish" suffered from his wound.

Morrison was grossly inflating his claim. He was in the habit of making an annual evaluation of his assets at the start of each year and had fixed his total worth at the end of 1899 as £1,249 10s., listing the value of his house as only £250 (not £1,500), his books at £250, and miscellaneous personal possessions at £200, the balance of his assets being in a London bank account. But this was not the last time he would cook the books.

CHAPTER TWENTY-FOUR

"That Odious Woman"

Once the peace treaty was signed, the court began the seven-hundred-mile journey back to Peking with an overland leg to the railhead at Chengtingfu, a great procession of covered wagons decorated with flags and streaming banners, the dowager and the emperor escorted by the remaining Manchu princes and a vast bodyguard of cavalry in brilliant silks. After the hasty exodus from Peking fourteen months earlier, every effort was made to regain face by making the return journey seem elegant. Provincial officials saw to it that every inch of road was cleared of stones by hand; gangs of men swept the path and sprinkled yellow chalk. Morrison (so busy recently looting the Forbidden City and the Hanlin Library) sniffed in the *Times* that the cost of preparing the dirt road was "1000 pounds a mile" and "quite useless, of course, for the ordinary traffic of the country."

At Chengtingfu, Tzu Hsi boarded a train for the first time in her life, a locomotive pulling twenty-one gaily festooned cars. Two thousand princes and mandarins were at the Peking station to greet them, a swarm of silks and furs. When the emperor appeared, the crowd prostrated itself until he took his place in a palanquin lined with yellow silk and sable. His procession moved off at a trot, cavalry at the head, followed by a phalanx of officials on shaggy ponies, uniformed ranks of Bannermen, umbrella bearers, and spearmen. The empress dowager followed in an identical entourage. Behind her palanquin rode the graying Jung Lu, his title now changed from head of the Grand Council to prime minister—part of the effort to put a new face on the regime. Soldiers lining the route knelt, rifles at present, while buglers sounded Manchu fanfares.

As always the streets were cleared of citizens, but for the first time thousands of Chinese were permitted to climb onto rooftops to watch, a revolutionary change from usual Chinese practice. A serious effort was being made to de-mystify and humanize the court, now that Prince Tuan's hard-liners had been expelled. Greater opportunity was provided to foreigners to witness the event than would have been the case at most European courts. The horseshoe wall around the Chienmen Gate was crowded with European diplomats, army officers, missionaries, women, photographers, and correspondents. The envoys of Great Britain, France, Russia, and America refused to attend, but all the ladies of the legations were on a balcony overlooking the cortege.

As Tzu Hsi was borne past the balcony where the legation ladies stood, she leaned forward in her chair to look up at them and returned their salutations with a warm smile, a nod of her head, and a slight wave. It was not what they had expected. Sarah Conger found the show exhilarating: "This was a wonderful day."

The gate was draped with banners and silks to hide the damage done by Allied artillery. But other evidence of destruction and looting was not so easy to disguise, as Tzu Hsi remarked: "I had another dreadful feeling when I saw my own palace again. Oh! it was quite changed; a great many valuable ornaments broken or stolen. All the valuable things at the Sea Palaces had been taken away, and someone had broken the fingers of my white jade Buddha, to whom I used to worship every day." Her pavilions had been used by von Waldersee and his concubine and her Ying-tai office burned.

She moved to the northeast corner of the Forbidden City to live in Emperor Chien Lung's palace, a group of low-lying pavilions that foreigners had not violated.

A few days after the court's return, six foreign envoys presented their credentials to Tzu Hsi and Emperor Kuang Hsu in an unprecedented audience inside the Forbidden City. This was the first time foreign diplomats had ever entered the Forbidden City with an invitation; previous audiences had all been staged outside its walls. During the court's exile at Sian, foreigners had toured every room and posed for photographs on the imperial thrones, helping themselves to anything portable. Under the Boxer Protocols the emperor henceforth was required to hold audiences in a proper throne hall. Morrison, who was not invited, collected impressions of Tzu Hsi from Colonel G. F. Browne, the British military attaché: "She [is] strong, powerful [and] masterful, fit to be the ruler of a nation, seated on the throne untouched by art, looking 50 not her real age of 65 and seated below her . . . the Emperor . . . who could never command admiration or devotion . . . looked . . . round as a schoolchild might to his mistress afraid of reprimand. It was a pitiful sight but there can be no doubt who is the ruler."

Colonel Browne may have been impressed by Tzu Hsi's sitting on the raised throne in her full regalia, capped by the ornate Manchu headdress, but the Ching Dynasty was fatally wounded and dragging itself into the undergrowth.

Sir Ernest Satow noted that Tzu Hsi "appeared to me to be under the influence of strong emotion, but mastered [it] and began to speak. . . . She went on to say she was very sorry . . . and wound up by saying . . . happiness and health to the Ministers and then dismissed us with a gracious nod."

How could she possibly explain to these assembled diplomats and military officers what she could not explain to anyone: That for nearly a decade the palace had been in the grip of a power struggle climaxing first in the crushing of the Hundred Days Reform, then in the Boxer theatrics and the siege of the legations. Since 1893 when Prince Tuan had first begun insinuating himself into her inner circle, she had known no peace. Relentlessly, he and his brothers, cousins and followers had moved in, taking advantage of her confusion after the Sino-Japanese War, tricking her into resuming the regency and in the process neutralizing poor Kuang Hsu. Growing bolder they had named Pu Chun heir-apparent, set up their own secret police in the palace, brought the Boxers into the Forbidden City, frightened her into submission and usurped the right to issue edicts in her place. Her good name had been ruined by Wild Fox Kang in 1898 and by Morrison in 1900. Her whole world had been destroyed by the Ironhats and the Allies. There seemed to be no way she could put things right. All her attempts to make amends produced the reverse effect. Sir Robert Hart grumbled, "The Audiences have all gone off so well that critics consider them too sweet and so suspect insincerity."

Thanks to the sinister image propagated by Morrison and Wild Fox Kang, everyone was wary, assuming that the empress dowager was a dangerous woman. The diplomats were not likely to change their preconceptions, but their wives were more adventurous, as they had shown in 1898 and early in 1900 when they had tea with Tzu Hsi in the Sea Palaces. When she now invited them to tea again, this time at the Summer Palace, Morrison expressed contempt: "That odious woman," he wrote in his diary.

This time the severe Sarah Conger took the leading role previously played by Lady MacDonald and as the tea party began addressed the dowager for all those present: "[We] heartily congratulate you and the Imperial Court that the unfortunate situation which led you to abandon your beautiful capital has been so happily resolved." Tzu Hsi replied, explaining that there had been a "revolutionary" disagreement in the palace, which had brought about the tragic circumstances that "compelled our hasty departure." Formalities over, the ladies were led into an antechamber and—according to Morrison's account in the *Times*—were astonished to see the dowager following them, holding Mrs. Conger's hand while tears spilled down her cheeks. Trembling and weeping openly, Morrison wrote, she exclaimed with some difficulty that the attack on the legations had been a terrible mistake, for which she was bitterly sorry. When Sarah Conger reassured her that the past would be forgotten, Tzu Hsi removed some bracelets and rings from her own hands and placed them on Mrs. Conger's wrists and fingers.

According to Sarah Conger, Morrison invented this whole tearful scene. There had been a poignant moment, certainly, but Morrison had exaggerated the bathos to ridicule the dowager and Mrs. Conger. "The Empress Dowager did not weep upon my neck. . . . There was nothing said by either of us about forgiving and forgetting." She blamed Morrison's manipulation of the truth on a nasty prevailing attitude among Western men in Peking. "There were sharp and bitter criticisms of the ladies' acceptance of the Imperial invitation. Individual bitterness still has its poison and would keep the breach open [between China and the West] and even widen it if possible." Typical of this hostile male chauvinism was a letter that Bland wrote to Morrison complaining, "To me the taking of gifts by the Legation women was as undignified as it was unnecessary. There is no doubt whatever as to the Empress Dowager's complicity in the Boxer business. . . . The address which Mrs. Conger incongruously read strikes on the mind like a cold douche of imbecile fatuity."

Morrison invariably drew his malicious accounts of these tea parties from the same catty source. Since Sir Ernest Satow was not wedded to an Englishwoman (he had a Japanese wife and two children in Tokyo) the British legation was represented at the dowager's tea parties by Lady Susan Townley, whose husband was first secretary. Lady Susan, a tall, pretty woman, was a fin-de-siècle airhead and dedicated gossip, on whom Morrison relied for what passed in his perception as feminine insights. Her narrative of social life in Peking and of these parties at the Manchu court was contrived to win male approbation over cigars and brandy. Emperor Kuang Hsu, who had once been a handsome youth with bright, nervous eyes but whose neurasthenia made him unable to face such occasions without strong sedatives, she described as a virtual idiot, slack-mouthed with "glazed eyes and a fixed expression . . . due to his opium-sodden condition. He was kept by order [of the dowager] under the influence of the drug." This was an exaggeration put about by Wild Fox Kang, which Lady Susan borrowed to spice up her authority.

Lady Susan ridiculed Mrs. Conger as "a funny old lady" who "bade us all curtsy to Her Chinese Majesty, and strongly recommended that we should all wear white embroidered under-petticoats, so that, in the event of our tripping over our feet in the performance of these curtsys, no undue display of stockinged leg should offend the susceptibilities of the surrounding Chinese dignitaries!" Tzu Hsi sat on a divan wearing a loose coat of pale blue silk. "Her piercing dark eyes when not engaged looking at the ladies roved curiously about her surroundings. . . . her appearance is that of a much younger woman." So that they would feel at home, the ladies were given a choice of tea, beer or champagne at a Western table, and this time Tzu Hsi sat with them to eat Chinese delicacies. Emperor Kuang Hsu stayed throughout but, in keeping with the Chinese custom of segregating sexes, sat away from the table and chain-smoked European cigarettes.

A more intimate party was thrown on February 27, 1902, again in the Summer Palace. Sarah Conger said, "We were taken into the most private room, Her Majesty seemed greatly pleased and waved her hand toward a richly draped and cushioned kang [bed] that reached across one end of the long room. At the back of the kang there was a shelf filled with beautiful jade and other ornaments, and seven rather small clocks, all running. . . . Her Majesty got upon the kang and motioned for me and others to do the same. She took a small jade baby boy from the shelf, tucked it into my hand, and with actions interpreted her unspoken words, 'Don't tell.' " This secrecy was prompted by the bad reaction of the legations and the foreign press to earlier presents Tzu Hsi had given the ladies. It was customary in China to make such gifts, but Westerners predisposed to despise the dowager construed this as an attempt to wheedle. The old woman, so determined to be open and friendly, was merely being a bit giddy in the enthusiasm of the moment.

The only time Morrison ever saw Tzu Hsi, even at a distance, was late in April 1903 as the court returned from a pilgrimage to the Western Tombs, after which he recorded this sole impression: "Uncoloured with missing teeth." When Lady Susan told him about a private audience later that year, she made a point of saying that Tzu Hsi was "disfigured by a slight goitre." Then, after having done all she could to flesh out Morrison's caricature, she asked the dowager for the one souvenir she fancied most: a dish from which both Tzu Hsi and Emperor Kuang Hsu had eaten.

Thereafter, the ladies were regularly entertained at the Summer Palace for teas and picnics. More often than not these occasions were soured by games of one-upmanship among the foreign ladies. An American woman was appalled by the behavior of her contemporaries. "Each seemed to watch the other with a jealous eye, in constant fear that some one might overstep her place. Some did not hesitate, even, to show their private animosities on the steps of the Throne, or before their hostesses at the table. They seemed to act on the principle that the Chinese, not understanding the language, would not understand anything else."

Tzu Hsi was annoyed when one guest arrived wearing a heavy tweed traveling suit with enormous pockets, into which she thrust her hands as though it were extremely cold, and wore a cap of the same material. Later

Tzu Hsi asked a lady-in-waiting if she had noticed the woman with the clothes made out of "rice bags." The empress thought she might be a gate-crasher, but it was only Alicia Little, champion of Wild Fox Kang.

Horrified, Tzu Hsi resolved to exercise more discretion in issuing her invitations, to keep the missionary element out, "as well as other undesirables." She was not insensitive to the contempt some Western women had for China, or for her, remarking: "They seem to think we are only Chinese and do not know anything, and look down upon us. I notice these things very quickly and am surprised to see people who claim to be well-educated and civilized acting the way they do."

As her parties became less extraordinary, some Western ladies began to snub invitations. The wife of the Austro-Hungarian minister, Madame von Rosthorn, daughter of a dentist in Vienna, sniffed that she would not have tea with the empress dowager of China "because it is so common."

These gatherings, superficial as they may seem, were the first informal social contact the Manchu throne ever had with foreigners. They helped to dispel some Manchu fears, and might have had a historic benefit if they had taken place forty or fifty years earlier. As to Western perceptions of the dowager, sadly it was now too late. Morrison's portrayal, built upon the lies of Wild Fox Kang and encouraged by the bigotry of Bland and others, had become the conventional wisdom of the West—embodied in the continual rantings of the English-language press in Shanghai about "the dowager and her gang." No contrary impressions were welcome, especially those of women.

Mrs. Conger was "indignant over the horrible, unjust caricatures of [Tzu Hsi]." So that the world might see her "more as she really is," she asked the dowager's permission to have her portrait painted.

It was arranged for American artist Katherine Carl to paint her for the Louisiana Purchase Exposition in St. Louis. She remained in Tzu Hsi's suite at the Summer Palace from August 1903 to May 1904. When Morrison heard of the plan he wrote to Valentine Chirol, foreign editor of the *Times,* that Mrs. Conger was "on terms of considerable intimacy with that infernal old harridan." In the opinion of fellow correspondent Bland, Tzu Hsi twisted the "simple-minded wife of the American Minister" around her little finger.

Kate Carl was in her late forties, daughter of a German soldier of fortune and an Irish girl who had met while traveling in Mississippi in the 1850s and settled there. Kate had an older brother, Francis; she was the Carls' second child, born in New Orleans. Her father, Captain Augustus Carl, organized a company of soldiers for the Confederacy and was killed in the Civil War. His widow found a job teaching at the Tennessee State Female College in Memphis, eventually becoming its "lady president." Kate graduated from the college in 1882, then made her way to Paris to study art at the Julien Academy. She was only modestly talented, receiving honorable mentions in Paris exhibitions.

Kate's mother was a Bredon, related to Lady Hart, and Francis worked for the Chinese Customs. The Harts met her during one of their visits to Paris, and Sir Robert called her "very breezy—quite a tornado in fact." In the winter of 1902 Kate traveled to China on the Trans-Siberian Railway with her mother, who was convinced that she was dying and wanted to visit her son. Indeed, within a month of their arrival in China she contracted pneumonia and expired.

Kate was five feet tall, built like a fireplug, face freckled like a cake of barley soap, hair paper white since birth. At the Summer Palace she was given a studio and suite of rooms where she could rest while working on the portrait, spending her nights in the nearby palace of Emperor Kuang Hsu's father, the first Prince Chun.

When Kate arrived for the dowager's first sitting in August 1903, she was surprised to find "a charming little lady, with a brilliant smile." With her entered the emperor, "almost boyish in appearance." Not the opium sot seen by Lady Susan Townley.

"I had heard and read so much of her . . . and nothing . . . had at all prepared me for the reality. . . . She was so considerate and tactful, and seemed so really kind in her relations with those who surrounded her. . . . She was at once a child and a woman with strong, virile qualities."

As the portrait progressed Kate found herself obliged by officials to adjust it to Chinese artistic conventions, with minimum detail, no perspective, and no shadow. "The Empress Dowager, however, knew nothing of my discouragement, and seemed perfectly contented with the progress of the portrait then on hand."

The final painting was to contain all the emblems of her office: ceremonial fans, a three-fold screen, nine phoenixes, stalks of bamboo, and pyramids of an aromatic citrus fruit called Buddha's Hand, on which was modeled the jade and gold citron that Morrison had stolen. For it she wore a winter gown of stiff satin with a sable lining, fringed with pearls; in her Manchu coiffure a tassel of pearls, and ceremonial jewels. The pose was stiff and symmetrical, and everyone at court interfered, so there was much repainting.

The dowager was pleased with the results, except that her face was shaded on one side and light on the other, not in keeping with Chinese convention. "I had explained that this was the shading," said Derling, Tzu Hsi's lady-in-waiting, "but Her Majesty insisted on my telling Miss Carl to make both sides of her face alike. This led to a pretty hot discussion between Miss Carl and myself but she finally saw that it was no use going against Her Majesty's wishes." When it was done, the portrait was static and unrevealing. Its significance lies in the fact that it gave Kate Carl access to Tzu Hsi, preserving one of the few records of her mannerisms, once again showing her to be an ordinary human.

Carl was paid well for the four portraits she did during the next year and did not intend to write about her experience. "After I returned to America, I was constantly seeing in newspapers . . . statements ascribed to me which I never made. Her Majesty was represented as having stood over me in threatening attitudes, forcing me to represent her as a young and beautiful woman! It was reported that she refused to give me any compensation for the portraits, and a number of other statements, equally false, were daily appearing in the papers."

Morrison had written of the dowager in the *Times*: "Some one has said 'she has the soul of a tiger in the body of a woman,' and Miss Carl found the old lady shrewd and tempestuous."

Kate was furious. "The latter statement, which I never made, seemed to me enough to have on my shoulders, but the article was copied in American papers." She decided to set the record straight. "I am the only European who has ever had a chance to study this remarkable woman in her own milieu, or to look upon the facts of her life from a standpoint within her own circle." Her memoir, *With the Empress Dowager of China*, was published in 1905 and dedicated to Sir Robert Hart.

She was not an experienced writer, and reviewers were put off by her breathlessness. The *New York Times* said, "Unfortunately, Miss Carl is not an observer or a writer. . . . The part relating to the Empress, like the portrait, is without perspective . . . [although] one gets occasional sights of comparatively unvarnished facts . . . however much we should have liked a more balanced judgment on the ruler of China and her Court, we cannot blame Miss Carl for her enthusiasm."

Perhaps what bothered reviewers most was that Carl did not corroborate the devious, reptilian image of Tzu Hsi that they had been led to expect. While a man would have perceived an Oriental Lucrezia Borgia with a poisoned chalice, Carl gave them an elderly female version of the harmless Wizard of Oz.

During her stay in the Summer Palace, Carl's conversations with the dowager were conducted mainly through the lady-in-waiting, Derling. She had first met Carl in Paris while her father was minister to France. Her family background was a bit unsavory, and even Hart was puzzled by it. "The Yu Keng family are not well thought of anywhere," he wrote, "but the old man himself has powerful backing—I don't know why. Mrs. Yu is the Eurasian daughter of a small American storekeeper who used to be at Shanghai, and, as far as Yu was concerned, the marriage, I believe, was a love affair."

Presumably Yu Keng owed his status to dirty work he had done for Viceroy Li; there was a saying in China: "Every dog that barks for Li is fat." This off-color reputation attached to Derling as well, because she conducted her private life by Zolaesque standards in an empire that had never heard of Emile Zola. A pretty, bright-eyed girl in her early twenties, she was too worldly for Peking. Educated at missionary schools in China and a convent in France, she spoke English and French fluently and was no stranger to liaisons. Morrison alleged in his diary that she was having an affair with a "grandfatherly" Italian military attaché. Prince Ching's eldest son, Tsai Chen, a connoisseur of young women, was one of her early protectors. And it was Prince Ching who arranged for Derling, her mother, her sister, and two brothers to attend the dowager in the Summer Palace beginning in 1903, to provide Tzu Hsi with more cosmopolitan interpreters during her audiences with Western women, so that she would not miss nuances.

Like the books of Sarah Conger and Kate Carl, the memoirs of Derling have been unfairly derided. She made herself vulnerable by using the title "Princess Derling" when her books were published in the West, apparently being encouraged to do so by her American friends. Nevertheless, Derling's recollections of the dowager provide valuable glimpses of Tzu Hsi's private life. Critics condemned her artless writing and the banality of Tzu Hsi's nature as it emerged from Derling's pages. Behind the exotic trappings of an Oriental potentate how could there be only a dowdy matriarch, a Jewish mother, a bridge-club granny who liked flowers, lapdogs and overelaborate clothing and of late had been inclined to weep. Where was the menace? Obviously all these women had failed as observers. Or had they?

One of Derling's brothers did electrical installations at the Summer Palace while another piloted Tzu Hsi's steam launch on Lake Kunming. The electrician was also a competent photographer using the glass-plate cameras of the day, and it is to him that we owe the photographs of Tzu Hsi between 1903 and 1905, the first ever taken of her and her court. Every book with pictures of imperial China uses his images. But court photographer Yu has never been recognized as Derling's brother. Serious scholars ignored Derling's book, as they did those of Conger and Carl, because they were the works of silly women, while they made use of her brother's photographs without knowing who he was. They all reveal the same person, but the photos allow you to project an evil personality onto the subject.

Tzu Hsi became fascinated by the photographic process and examined Yu's camera closely, displaying the same interest and understanding that she had of Western clocks. "After the method of taking the photograph had been fully explained to her," Derling said, "she commanded one of the eunuchs to stand in front of the camera so that she might look through the focusing glass, to see what it was like. Her Majesty exclaimed: 'Why is it your head is upside down?'"

From then on she was delighted to be photographed, making many changes of clothing, dressing in theatrical costumes like the traditional regalia of the Goddess of Mercy, Kuan Yin, and insisting that her chief eunuch, the weary old Li Lien-ying, also dress up and join her in these set pieces, although he appears ill at ease, glowering at the lens. Tzu Hsi watched the developing of the plates and the printing. She told Derling, "Whenever I have been angry, or worried over anything, by dressing up as the Goddess of Mercy it helps me to calm myself, and so play the part I represent. . . . By having a photograph taken of myself dressed in this costume, I shall be able to see myself as I ought to be at all times." What Westerners preferred to see in the photos was Morrison's "infernal old harridan" and her "false eunuch," and a "shrewd and tempestuous woman."

While Derling was in her service, Tzu Hsi suffered a stroke that partially paralyzed the right side of her face. She was nearly seventy. The stroke interfered with the normal mobility of her face, so in Yu's photographs her expression seems slack and dull—exactly opposite the vivacity commented upon by virtually all those who met her.

While Carl was in the Summer Palace, there were three crises: a rebellion in Kwangsi Province, the refusal of the Russians to withdraw from Manchuria, and the outbreak in Manchuria of the Russo-Japanese War. Telegrams and dispatches were rushed in to Tzu Hsi outside of normal audience hours. They were brought to her throne room, or during her walks in the gardens, or were sent over from the new Foreign Office, the Wai-Wu-Pu, which had replaced the Tsungli Yamen after the Boxer troubles. She continued to share with Kuang Hsu the official duties of the throne, but he avoided as many of these responsibilities as possible, having recognized that the exercise of imperial power in Manchu China was strictly ceremonial and the throne powerless, leaving it to his aunt to uphold the dynasty's formal position. She seemed to take these crises heavily. Carl noticed much sighing, listlessness, and solitude.

Tzu Hsi was old and tired. Thanks to the stroke her once beautiful face was flaccid and simian. Her body was a sack of millet. Her vitality and energy had been sapped by the strain of surviving decades of disaster. Constantly under the scrutiny of eunuchs and courtiers, she had acted out the role given her in 1861. For more than forty years she had lived on a dais, obliged to be exemplary by men who needed her to hide their own corruption and incompetence. While they played their games and departed, she remained to take the blame. No one since Empress Wu had been so viciously maligned. But her skirts were very large. There was room behind them for everyone.

In 1905, after both Carl and Derling had left the court, their guileless impressions of Tzu Hsi were confirmed when a Western male gained access to the dowager for a few days. The fine artist Hubert Vos executed two portraits, one of Tzu Hsi as a young woman of twenty-five that hangs today in the Summer Palace, the other done entirely for his own interest, showing Tzu Hsi as she was at seventy. This "old" painting was never seen in China and today hangs in the Fogg Museum at Harvard University.

Hubert Vos was a tough and engaging man, a perceptive observer and a gifted raconteur. His letters from Peking provide a refreshingly different encounter with Tzu Hsi.

Vos was a product of the Dutch school, studied at leading academies in Paris, Rome, and Brussels, became friends with James Abbott McNeill Whistler, and helped found the Society of British Portrait Painters. In 1893 he settled in America. Fascinated by racial differences, he traveled all over the world painting classic ethnic types: Sioux and Chippewa Indians in the Dakotas, South American Indians in British Guiana, Oriental archetypes in Korea, Hawaii, Japan, Java, and Tibet. When Vos visited China for the first time in 1899, he tried to get permission to paint Tzu Hsi's portrait but failed. However, during that trip he did exceptional portraits of Viceroy Li Hung-chang, Prince Ching, and General Yuan Shih-kai. These brought a new summons to China in 1905. He was told only to submit a bid for several portraits of officials of the Foreign Office. It was not till June, when he took a room in the newly rebuilt Peking Hotel, that he learned his subject was to be the empress dowager. "If I had known," he said, "I might have doubled my price." She was to sit for him in one of the Sea Palaces next to the Forbidden City, coming in from the Summer Palace for three days for that purpose.

He was told to be at the foreign minister's mansion at 4:30 A.M. on June 20 with all his paraphernalia, because the dowager would begin posing at 5:00 A.M. Vos took it all in good humor: "This beats any early rising I have done so far! . . . Just fancy taking a photograph at 5 A.M." Because many of his subjects were busy, it was his habit to take photographs so that he could continue painting in his hotel room between sittings, and he planned to do this with Tzu Hsi. "The worse is it must be done in ten minutes for she wants to pose afterwards for ten minutes and I may get one more, perhaps two more sittings of half an hour each. I shall take a small canvas and paint the head from life in two sittings and paint the larger canvas afterwards from that and with the help of the photographs. . . . I shall have headaches from worry and no end of difficulty."

Luckily, Vos discovered that Tzu Hsi's photograph had been taken by a Japanese, Yamamoto, with copies distributed to all the diplomatic missions and foreign royal houses, and the negative destroyed. "I have been able to get one on a secret loan from the Dutch minister. I am going to make a drawing on a small canvas in order to paint right away without having to draw, and to get familiarized with the subject before I will be allowed to gaze upon her countenance."

He ate an early dinner the night before, set out his evening dress with all his decorations pinned on, a perfumed handkerchief in the pocket, and—so he could pile up his paraphernalia—hired the only open Victoria carriage in Peking for 3:30 A.M. But when he woke he was horrified to find the hotel dead asleep and no carriage waiting. No rickshaws were to be seen, and only a sleepy Chinese boy was there to give him tea.

"I was in a terrible state of excitement and used my choicest swear words which unhappily were mostly lost on the Chinese boys but something in my looks and tone of voice must have been understood for they ran . . . into the Chinese City to get some rickshaws; at last after 20 minutes a couple came, we overloaded and ran at top speed to Wu Ting-fang's house where that gentleman was impatiently waiting after having dispatched one of his . . . runners to look for me."

Racing across town they were met by Prince Ching's son, Prince Tsai Chen, who would take Vos into the dowager's presence.

"Prince Tsai Chen is minister of Commerce and is the most favored of the younger set with the empress . . . a fat jolly fellow . . . beautifully dressed, does not speak any foreign language, so we could only grin at each other, but we did exchange cigarettes." They hurried into the grounds of the Sea Palaces, where Vos was "dumbfounded of the beauty and the cleanliness . . . and there before us is a great big lagoon covered with lotus . . . forbidden ground!" Vos was led to a covered courtyard, where he was allowed to set up his gear. At one end was a throne, with a backdrop representing a bamboo grove. On either side of the throne were potted plants, symbolic pyramids of fruit, and two Pekingese dogs, their hair done up in back with gold peacock clasps.

Tzu Hsi entered.

"Really I was struck very strongly by her appearance," Vos said. "I had seen the picture [by Kate Carl] in the St. Louis exhibition [which] told nothing. I saw a photograph taken by the Japanese photographer in Peking . . . but I found her absolutely different; erect and a tremendous will power, more than I have ever seen on a human being, hard firm will and thinking lines, and with all that a bow full of kindness and love for the beautiful. I fell straight in love with her."

He set to work taking photos. "My first photograph was a failure. I dared not make her look at me, no one may ask her anything. . . . I made her favored eunuch stand behind the camera so that she could look at him and I snapped par hazard without looking at her several more pictures. I took six of her. By that time I was told her majesty was tired, so I had to stop, my shutter refused to work once and I couldn't focus well." Vos had to promise to keep the photos secret and to destroy them afterward.

The next day he returned for the second sitting.

> I painted away until she got tired and I was told to stop after about three-quarters of an hour. She came and looked at my work and talked and pointed at different parts of my picture and Wu Ting-fang translated and told me I had to make the eyes go up, no shadows under or above the eyes, the eyes wide open, the mouth full and up, not drooping, the eyebrows straight, the nose no shadows, no shadows, no shadows, no wrinkles!
>
> I bowed and she went out and we ... discussed the matter at length. Eunuchs everybody full of excitement and full of merriment. Finally I began to understand that I was not allowed to paint realistically. I had, I was told, "to paint her as she told me." ... I got home by 9:30 and after a cold bath and a whiskey and soda I began with a new head, this time young and beautiful with very light shadows. ... I worked until 4 P.M. when my sketch was finished, drawn and painted; the empress at [age] twenty-five.

Vos was obliged to paint Tzu Hsi as she wanted to be remembered, as she was in the 1860s, a young dowager empress, mother of the boy emperor, the high point in her life—not as an old woman.

> The next morning at 5 en route again. ... I with my two sketches, the first and the new. ... When I showed my new sketch the eunuchs and Prince [Tsai] Chen and Wu Ting-fang were immensely impressed. ... I suppose her majesty and her ladies in waiting [also] had a good look at the picture, when finally we were told to enter. ... I was told that her majesty was pleased. So I altered as little as I dared, merely going for the general color. I asked permission to take some notes in my little note book. Her majesty showed me the eyes more up, more slanting—they are evidently stuck on their characteristic irregularities. I drew some notes from mouth, eyes, and nose and the Empress stood up and came near me and took my pencil and made a line on my notebook while I held it. This is the closest ever a white man has been to her.
>
> When she went out that day she turned round and smiled to me. The first smile I got, I will get more!—In the waiting house I was told that her majesty had said she liked me. During this third sitting,

she smoked two pipes, and had a gorgeous cloak brought, feeling cold, it was I believe coquetterie to show off.

It was the only recorded instance of the dowager's flirting.

The next day was his last sitting.

"I saw through the glass her majesty sitting at breakfast surrounded by heaps of beautiful young princesses and everywhere the most gorgeous curios. . . . I picked out the place for her to sit and unpacked my picture. She bowed very gracefully when she came in and I began to work . . . after the sitting she asked Wu Ting-fang how to say in English very good. Which she said to me with a smile 'very good!' "

Vos labored in his hotel room through the hot summer to finish the young portrait. Morrison had a look at the canvas and was enthusiastic. He told Vos he would like to keep the picture as it was, "the finest he has ever seen." Whatever it was that appealed to Morrison's romanticism, it did not alter his thinking.

Vos returned to America exhausted. In his New York studio he went to work on his other portrait, the realistic Tzu Hsi begun in Peking and then put aside. It probably comes closest to the essence of the woman, neither old nor young, capturing her strength and bearing.

Sir Robert Hart was the only other Western male to experience anything approximating intimacy with Tzu Hsi. So completely was she isolated that, surprisingly, until 1902 Hart had never had a single audience with her and had seen her at a distance only once when she returned to the Forbidden City from Sian in 1901.

This restraint was required because Hart occupied a unique position in Peking. As "Our Hart," he was not a foreigner but a servant of the throne. Therefore protocol separated him from the dowager like a solid wall. It was not until well after the Boxer affair—in February 1902, when the court had greatly relaxed its traditional isolation—that Hart had his first private audience with her. By then he had worked for Tzu Hsi for forty-one years, providing the one consistent and reliable source of revenue for the throne. Paradoxically, her rigid isolation from someone like Hart reveals not strength but weakness, behind the great barrier of bureaucratic etiquette. Had she been running the Manchu regime the autocratic way that Empress Wu once ruled the Tang court, she could have bent the rules at whim and seen Hart as easily as Emperor Chien Lung saw Lord MacCartney. As it was, rigid court etiquette prevented even a private meeting. Nor was Hart permitted to attend foreign diplomatic audiences with Emperor Kuang Hsu. All his dealings had to be through third parties: Prince Kung, Prince Ching, or Viceroy Li.

However, in the altered circumstances immediately after the court returned to Peking, Tzu Hsi and Emperor Kuang Hsu arranged a special audience as a way of making up to Hart for his suffering and disillusion during the siege of the legations. He was now a frail sixty-six, the same age as Tzu Hsi, and was given the unique honor of being allowed to sit in a chair in her presence. The audience lasted only twenty minutes, but the passage of time was different because Hart spoke excellent Mandarin, and no time was wasted on translations or formalities. Tzu Hsi wept openly in his presence. She repeatedly told him that the Boxer business was "all due to ignorance." She followed by saying, "We have long wished to see you and to talk with you but that has not been possible."

There was an embarrassing moment when she asked Sir Robert about his house: "Where are you living and how is your house?" She did not know that his prized bungalow had been burned by the Boxers along with all his working papers and mementos of nearly half a century in China. (In his diary he had written: "My poor band like everything else lost and destroyed.") After the siege he had set up a temporary Customs office in a small temple under the city wall. For his own accommodations he rented two small rooms behind Kierulff's store, and this remained his home till a new house was built later in 1902. But when Tzu Hsi asked the innocent question, Hart was still living in the two rooms behind Kierulff's, and a mortified silence fell over the audience chamber.

Before Hart could compose himself to reply, Prince Ching fell to his knees: "It is all gone with the others." Tzu Hsi wiped away some tears. "It is terrible," she said, "but it was all due to ignorance."

What else could she tell Hart—that she too had lost everything and was presiding over an empty shell? Maintaining appearances had been her whole career. The life-force of her dynasty, the power and strength of the Manchu, was dissipated long before she entered the Forbidden City as a pretty sixteen-year-old concubine. No vitality had been left for her husband's brief reign. It was all a thieves' banquet. In 1644 the last of the Ming emperors had carelessly left the door unlocked and the Manchu had moved in like gypsies, not believing their luck. Chinese resistance was silenced by a reign of terror that had never ended, and was stronger now than ever. In these borrowed palaces the Manchu had gorged, splurged, and squandered until—sometime during the last years of the prodigal Emperor Chien Lung—it was all gone except the hangover. Along with China's wealth they had misspent their own juices, breaking all the rules on self-restraint until their yang was gone. Unable to stand up to Taipings or Foreign Devils, they were reduced to quarreling among themselves while Chinese mercenary armies protected them for a heavy price. At Hsien Feng's death in Jehol, Tzu Hsi had been chosen by the gods to preside over a funeral procession, not the one that reached Peking in December 1861 but a much longer state funeral that was only now reaching its end in the first decade of the twentieth century. There was nothing left now but to see to her tomb and a tomb for Kuang Hsu. They would be in them soon enough.

Afterward, still in the grip of intense emotion, Hart was extremely terse in recording his account of the audience in his diary. He was struggling to cope with contradictory emotions of love and hate for China and his own homeland. For China because his loyalty and dedication had been tarnished by the folly of the Ironhats. For Great Britain because he had seen the deceit of his compatriots in their falsification of the record, and their greed during the Allied occupation. He had soured on Morrison, and there were barriers between them, yet he could not resist, after the audience, telling Morrison that he now had observed for himself that Emperor Kuang Hsu was "not an imbecile. He is clever and bides his time." The empress dowager, he let it be known, "spoke in a sweet feminine voice." But in his bitterness he said no more.

Two years later Sir Robert was summoned again by the throne and found that "the empress looked very young, not more than 40. Emperor thinner than last [time]."

In March 1905 he was called in again so that Tzu Hsi could present him with a scroll of her own calligraphy for his seventieth birthday. This time, he noted, she was "looking aged."

After many years of delaying his retirement because he did not want to leave China, in April 1908 it was time at last for Hart to go home. A farewell audience was arranged, where he found Tzu Hsi looking better than the previous year but older. Kuang Hsu "uttered never a word; looked bright and intelligent." Tzu Hsi gave him some "keepsakes." Overcome with emotion, Hart was struck dumb, completely forgetting the proper formula for returning thanks. All he could do was to mutter the Chinese words for "thank you" devoid of proper flourishes. Beside him a minister of the court flung himself to his knees to recite the ritual courtesies, but neither Hart nor Tzu Hsi noticed. This was the last time he would see her. Although technically he was only taking home leave—as a way of saving face—he was in fact leaving China forever.

He had often daydreamed of the countryside of Ulster. It brought tears to his eyes. "I don't like the thought of passing away here alone . . . so far from friends. . . . I should prefer to go to Heaven . . . via London."

"The morning of his going," wrote his niece Juliet Bredon, "I remember, broke fine and clear and the I.G.'s own band had come of its own accord to play 'Auld Lang Syne.' As the I.G. stepped from his sedan chair at the end of the [railway] platform his face wore an expression of bewilderment, but only for a moment. Then he turned to the commanding officer, and saying 'I am ready,' walked steadily down the lines of saluting troops while the bands all played 'Home, Sweet Home.' " He was spared the grief of observing the dowager's end.

CHAPTER TWENTY-FIVE

Hunting Snipe

I t was the beginning of the end for all of them. Having swept the palace of his worst enemies, seventy-eight-year-old Viceroy Li Hung-chang once again became the most important man in China; but he was to savor his triumph only briefly before being struck down. In the autumn of 1901, after signing the Boxer Protocols agreeing to pay the Foreign Powers hundreds of millions of dollars in indemnities and to make other concessions of China's sovereignty, Li fell ill. He sent a message to the throne graphically describing his condition:

On the night of the nineteenth, I suddenly vomited half a spittoon of blood; the color was purple black with some lumps in it. Cold sweat appeared and my head became dizzy, and my condition became critical. I immediately summoned a Western physician and took medicine to stop the vomiting. For the past two days, I fortunately have not vomited, but at present I cannot rise or sit. When I try to sit up my head becomes dizzy. The doctor says a small blood vessel has broken in my stomach. I must lie quietly and recuperate in a peaceful way for some time. I eat only milk, chicken soup, lotus root powder, and thin gruel. I am forbidden to eat hard and dry foods for fear that the broken blood vessel will not close. . . . I will pay special attention to recuperation hoping for an early recovery.

At the time, the court was still on its way back to Peking from Sian and had paused for a break in the mountains of northern Hunan Province when a telegram arrived announcing the death of Viceroy Li on November 7, 1901. Li's genius and cunning had made him a formidable presence in China for half a century, coinciding with Tzu Hsi's time at court. While she had gradually become a fixture on the throne, the chief symbol of authority and the main target of growing anti-Manchu hatred, Li had wielded the real economic, political and military power of the empire in a way that was largely invisible. By comparison to the dictatorial Manchu regime, Li was feared rather than hated—a velvet hand in the iron glove. His was the unseen hand that outmaneuvered the Ironhats during the succession crisis of 1875, that had drawn Tzu Hsi reluctantly into resuming the throne during the reform crisis of 1898. Through Yuan Shih-kai it was Li who subverted Emperor Kuang Hsu. Similarly it was Li who manipulated the foreign press to enrage the West with false atrocities, to bring about the Allied invasion of 1900. So, while he did more than anyone else to sustain the dowager and the dynasty as a means to continue his own unique privileges, Viceroy Li was one of those most responsible for blackening the dynasty's standing and the dowager's reputation historically. When he died he left the Manchu court lying there like an empty handpuppet unable to perform. It was a mailed fist, to be sure, but it functioned only at the touch of the master.

Li had risen to power with the help of Marquis Tseng and on his death he passed the wand to Yuan Shih-kai. Unfortunately, the apprentice was unlike the sorcerer in important ways: Where Li had been coldblooded and dispassionate, Yuan was vain and perpetually in heat, dangerously driven to trip himself up.

The same day Li died General Yuan was designated to succeed him as viceroy of Chihli and Commissioner of Trade for the Northern Ports. Yuan received the news of his promotion in his usual cagey fashion. He regretfully declined the appointment, saying he felt it was unwise to leave the governorship of Shantung without completing all of the public works, schools, and other civic undertakings that he had begun, not to mention the rich veins he had tapped and the empire he was building. When Telegraph Sheng urged him to take the new and greater post, Yuan replied, "My waning health and confused mind do not permit me to do as I am commanded. If I go, Shantung will certainly fall into chaos like Mukden. How can Chihli look after itself if both Shantung and Mukden are in turmoil. My departure . . . can only harm the delicate situation." If this sounded strangely like Marquis Tseng and Viceroy Li doing a duet from their favorite Chinese opera, Yuan had taken voice lessons from them.

Telegraph Sheng was quick to grasp Yuan's hidden message. He initiated a proposal to the throne that Yuan's responsibilities as the new viceroy of Chihli be expanded to include his present overlordship of Shantung Province, in effect giving him both posts. Prime Minister Jung Lu seconded the proposal, and by November 17, 1901, Viceroy Yuan had all of northeast China in his pocket.

During the months of Allied occupation, Yuan had shone like a bright penny. "All praise highly the work done by Yuan Shih-kai already," wrote Morrison grandly from Peking. He commended "the excellent good order of the people due to the military police of Yuan Shih-kai." He did not call Yuan a ruthless oppressor because he admired the man's prefascist style. Yuan admitted to having exterminated more than forty thousand "Boxers" throughout the north, which was a bit odd as there had never been much more than twelve thousand of them, mostly hungry country boys, the rest being out-of-work toughs. However, so long as Yuan was mopping up Boxers and putting things in order, there was no reason to be squeamish about butchering an extra twenty-five or thirty thousand unemployed. See it as famine relief and labor mediation.

George Morrison had his first formal interview with the sly, manipulative forty-three-year-old viceroy in March 1902. They talked through translators for nearly two hours, over hot green tea and iced champagne. Yuan was skilled at cultivating people he wished to impress. So impressed was Morrison (as he confided to his diary) that when he wrote his report for the *Times* he had to comb out the excessive praise, fearing that otherwise "people will say I have been 'got at' by Yuan." Hart had warned him that Yuan had "a shifty eye." But there was nothing Morrison admired more than a man of panache, wit, cunning, and absolute power, even if he happened to be short, fat, and Chinese. The famous journalist became one of Yuan's most important conquests, and the viceroy—although genuinely liking Morrison—played him expertly in the years to come, doing the Australian favors so often that they became addictive, until Morrison ceased to be fully independent and finally quit the *Times* in 1912 to become Yuan's public relations man, at a handsome salary. It was Yuan's way.

From 1902 to 1912 Morrison was quick to defend the viceroy in his *Times* articles, to see his side in every political argument, and to discount all slurs. When he heard that Yuan had a Japanese wife, he told his diary, "I don't believe it." In fact, the viceroy had a prodigious sex life, with a harem full of concubines and thirty legitimate offspring. It was one of those moments of history when the prejudice of the observer created a pronounced double standard: Morrison could find countless subtle ways to poison the empress dowager's reputation, while uncritically advancing the imperial ambitions of one of the most unscrupulous men in China. By a trick of the mind, he could praise Yuan's brutal suppression campaigns while condemning Tzu Hsi's imaginary evil. He saw what he wanted to see. In this, to be fair, he was only reflecting British policy and popular Western opinion, which regarded Yuan as the strongman who could put things right.

Yuan always went out of his way to ingratiate himself with Westerners. He also worked hard to cultivate the empress dowager, seeing to it that she received large sums (squeezed from provincial officials, gentry, and businessmen) for use on pet projects. He showered her with gifts. The plundering of the palaces during the Allied occupation had left her in reduced circumstances, relatively speaking. Many Manchu nobles were no longer in a position to compete financially with Yuan for her affection. His access to the revenues of Chihli, Shantung, and the Northern Ports gave him a deep pocket.

Among his little *cadeaux* he gave Tzu Hsi an automobile fitted with a throne. (She never went for a drive, because there was no way a chauffeur could sit down in her presence.) When she traveled to the Western Tombs in April 1903 to perform ancestor worship, Yuan built a twenty-five-mile railway line especially for her trip. Along the way he entertained her in a palace redone for the occasion, including fantastical gardens with stuffed birds, squirrels, and monkeys attached to the trees, and miniature boats on miniature lakes. She was delighted with Yuan's courtly attentions and his gifts, happy to be hustled by someone with style. He seemed genuinely anxious to please the old lady and to be her champion, putting himself to endless trouble in her behalf while helping himself to the treasury.

All the while he was relentlessy enlarging his power base. Nobody understood better than Yuan how meaningless an army was unless the troops were competent. He devoted much of his attention to army modernization and by 1905 had expanded his Northern Army to six full divisions. That same year, when he was pressing the government to let him reorganize and modernize the national police, which would bring it under his control, a terrorist's bomb was thrown at the Imperial Constitutional Commission. In the excitement a frightened Tzu Hsi asked Yuan to lead a thousand men to the Summer Palace to guard her and to investigate the entire affair personally. The upshot was that the nervous court approved his takeover of a new Board of Police, more than he had asked for. Rumors circulated that Yuan had arranged the explosion to win his point, for timely terrorist bombs and assassinations were his signature. His role as the new boss of China's national police and secret police doubled his leverage and tangible assets. Even Morrison observed (in his diary, not in print), "The secret service of [Yuan] is a most disreputable body—blackmailing and predacious." But that was okay, because Yuan he understood.

When Tzu Hsi's old friend and protector, Prime Minister Jung Lu, died of old age in the spring of 1903, she appointed Prince Ching ("the invertebrate") as her new prime minister. Some saw this as a setback for Viceroy Yuan, as Prince Ching was assumed to be his "enemy." However, they had both been in bed with Li Hung-chang for so many years that their performances under the coverlet, while different in style, were entirely complementary. Their invisible partnership held the regime together a decade longer than could be explained by the laws of physics. While Prince Ching was now the top pencil, Yuan was its sharp end. To congratulate the impoverished prince on his appointment (the Boxer fiasco had left him flat broke) Yuan sent him 100,000 taels of silver. From then on no man became a governor unless he was a Yuan man. With Prince Ching's silent approval Yuan promoted his followers into all ranks of the military and civil administration.

Clever as he was, Yuan did not grasp what Li had seen all along: being emperor was not as good as being chairman of the board. Early in life Li had recognized the impotence of the throne because of the impossible constraints of court etiquette and the endless scheming of princes and mandarins. Figurehead is merely another word for target; Li had used Tzu Hsi as a lightning rod, drawing criticism away from himself. But Yuan was imprudent, and failed to see that if he became emperor he also became vulnerable. As far back as 1897 Robert Hart had written that Yuan "will not be last in the race should a scramble for the throne come about." By 1906 Morrison had "acquired the conviction that Yuan Shih-kai was bidding for the throne. All power was gradually passing into his hands. . . . The Viceroy controls all the best forces in China."

There were those at court who had not forgiven Yuan for betraying Emperor Kuang Hsu in 1898 and who foresaw that his unquenchable ambition might one day tempt him to seize the throne and start his own dynasty. His chief enemies were a new generation of young Manchu firebrands led by a Japanese-trained officer in his mid-twenties, General Liang Pi, and by the brother of Emperor Kuang Hsu, twenty-year-old Prince Chun II, whose infant son, Pu Yi, was now the secretly designated heir to the throne. They tried to undercut Yuan by removing four of the six army divisions from his command, transferring them to General Liang Pi. In August 1907 they succeeded in having Yuan removed from his posts as viceroy of Chihli and high commissioner of military and foreign affairs. But a few days later, after a private audience with the empress dowager in which he poured on all his charm, Yuan was named foreign minister and appointed to the Grand Council. There seemed to be no holding him back. Tzu Hsi needed a protector. Yuan had been created for this very purpose by the farseeing Li Hung-chang, to guard the dying dynasty like a stone demon on the way to the Western Tombs. Yuan was her palace guard, the lion dog at her door like her favorite black Pekingese, Shadza. She need not worry about whether he was housebroken. Yuan was going to wait till she was gone before he got up on the furniture.

At this fateful moment the dowager's three most powerful cabinet ministers or Grand Councillors were Prince Ching, former viceroy Yuan Shih-kai, and former viceroy Chang Chih-tung. Prince Ching was already in Yuan's pocket, and he neutralized Chang Chih-tung by persuading the empress dowager to arrange the betrothal of Yuan's son to Chang's daughter.

The British legation was delighted with Yuan's latest promotion. Morrison rationalized privately that Yuan's only faults were "over copulation and overeating without any exercise whatever except stepping in and out of his carriage and seeing out officials. In the palace [as a Grand Councillor] he will at least have to kowtow."

Every mandarin worth his button attended Yuan's fiftieth (by Chinese reckoning) birthday party in September 1908, a two-day celebration staged at the Peking palace previously occupied by Viceroy Li. Morrison was out of town, but the affair was described to him in a letter from Walter Hillier, a legal adviser to the Chinese government:

> I certainly have never seen any gathering like it . . . the whole of the entrance courtyards and the inner corridors as well as the reception rooms . . . were packed with . . . every official of prominence in Peking. . . . The street was packed with carts and carriages and lined with troops, and while I was there a long line of yellow chairs arrived in which were presents of various sorts from the Empress Dowager, the Emperor and Empress. These were escorted by a band and met at the gate by Yuan who prostrated himself . . . and repeated the obeisance 27 times. . . . I do not think that any official in China has ever celebrated his fiftieth birthday under circumstances of greater distinction, and to my mind no more convincing proof could be given of the high place which Yuan holds in Imperial favour.

Tzu Hsi's susceptibility to Yuan's attentions is hardly surprising. He was clever, charming, competent, and followed through. And he handled foreigners with unusual skill. A perfect cabinet minister. But Morrison's infatuation with Yuan was part of a dangerous trend. Although he was at the zenith of his prestige at the *Times*, his professional behavior and judgment were becoming careless. Editors in London could not read the minds of their correspondents nor could they control (or even know about) the people their journalists depended upon as sources or assistants.

Loneliness made Morrison crave intellectual and emotional companionship. Solitary though he was, he did not apply himself seriously to locating a wife. He was obsessed by the idea that Western wives were "hysterical, neurotic [and] faithless." As a devout racist he could not follow the course Hart and Satow had pursued, of taking a Chinese or a Japanese wife. Nor could he do as Hart and so many others had done and make a trip home to find a proper white woman. Meeting Lady Hart during one of her rare visits to Peking, Morrison was horrified: she "talked in one continuous stream with a strong brogue and without any expression. The I.G. wants her to go. He cannot work when she is here. . . . She must bore the I.G. damnably."

To sublimate, Morrison went on longer and longer bird-hunting expeditions; in August 1907 he jotted that he had bagged 229 snipe that month alone.

Because of his solitude and his urgent need to stay informed in a capital where he was uniquely isolated by language and etiquette, Morrison had become dangerously dependent upon Edmund Backhouse. It was never a formal or full-time arrangement, just a convenient friendship, but one that had a seductive, insidious effect. Edmund had the peculiar ability to change himself into whatever Morrison wanted: intellectual companion, sexual raconteur, adviser on rare Chinese manuscripts, translator, interpreter, news source, journalistic stringer, editor, and consultant on all things Chinese or Manchu.

Like Morrison, Edmund had helped loot the Hanlin Library early in the siege. Then while Morrison recovered from his rump wound, Edmund had avoided participating in the defense, claiming a strained muscle, and was seen haunting the buildings and grounds of the Hanlin, collecting as discreetly as possible all the books and manuscripts he could. After the siege, he and his roommate, G. P. Peachey, had ranged as far afield as Chochou, where they were arrested for looting, blackmail, and robbery. On his release, Edmund had obtained permission to occupy part of a house in the British sector of Peking, inside the Tartar City. This proximity made it more convenient for Morrison to use him for translations and court gossip.

Morrison's envy was aroused when Edmund's father was made a baronet, the title to be inherited by the eldest son upon his father's death. During the Boxer business, Morrison's aspirations for knighthood and a political career had moved forward a giant step, when his daring made him the darling of the legations and his account of the siege was falsified to flatter his countrymen. Apparently he was encouraged to think that this would assure him of a knighthood and backing for his political ambitions. When he went to Australia on home leave in 1902, he was given a warm reception in Melbourne by leading members of the ruling party. He was flattered by their attention and had "curious dreams" of "my premiership of Australia." But nothing immediately came of either knighthood or premiership, and on his return to Peking he drifted slowly into careless habits and the gravitational field of Yuan Shih-kai. These careless habits allowed Backhouse to play a larger and larger role as his editor and adviser, as a servant takes over his master. Backhouse "read my narrative critically and suggested many alterations." Edmund did more reporting and more of Morrison's legwork: "Court returned to Peking. . . . Backhouse present. . . . Empress having need of operaglasses." "Backhouse writes me Chang Chih-tung . . . [is] too weak to remain in Metropolis and take on new duties." "Backhouse came in. Thinks Prince Ching [is] in a bad way. Says Yuan Shih-kai is hated and regarded as the most oppressive viceroy the province has ever had." "Backhouse writes me that Prince Ching [is] really ill—hemorrhages and may not recover. Thus recurring illnesses probably not a sham." "Backhouse has just left 11:15 P.M. after very pleasant and instructive evening. Says . . . Li Lien-ying the Chief Eunuch is the murderer of Shen Chin [a journalist]. He is known as . . . Treacherous Smile Li. . . . Everyone condemns the Empress for executing Shen Chin but Li Lien-ying." Morrison had no way of knowing whether any of this was true. Edmund took pains not to be too extravagant and to suit his gossip to Morrison's prejudices. The last thing he wanted was for Morrison to realize that he was being manipulated.

In the spring of 1902 Morrison caught Backhouse lying about a personal matter and their friendship briefly soured. Now the charming Edmund is referred to in Morrison's diary as "the brilliant but mendacious." It was Morrison's first glimpse of Edmund's carefully hidden streak of insanity. For a while they saw each other less and less. In November 1902 Morrison tried to patch things up by making a significant gift to Backhouse: "I gave him a good present of one of the volumes of the Great Encyclopaedia"— the *Yung Lo Ta Tien*, the Ming Dynasty encyclopedia stolen from the Hanlin; Morrison possessed at least fourteen of its volumes. The gift did no good, for Edmund was deep in one of his paranoid withdrawals in which he was overcome by loathing. Six months later, in April 1903, Edmund was protesting that he had been "incommoded" by a visit from his old friend. When Morrison saw him riding by in a cart "he passed me as if I had been the pestilence. This morbid sickness must be increasing."

Like many bachelors, Morrison was a bit of an old hen: cranky, selfish, egocentric, flustered by falling acorns. Writing to Backhouse he tried to discover the source of the problem, and Edmund responded: "I feel pained that you should think the reason for my not going round to see you should be due to any other reason than the long hours . . . and the impossibility to get a moment to myself. It is not likely, while you are so good as to be willing to see me, that I should ever wish to keep away! I shall be very glad to come round tonight after dinner."

Morrison was not the only one making use of Edmund's linguistic abilities. By 1903 Backhouse had mastered Manchu and Mongol as well as Mandarin and was employed by the British minister, Sir Ernest Satow, as an occasional free-lance spy. Satow considered sending him on a secret mission to Mongolia in the fall of 1903, but Edmund stalled, pleading that his duties as a part-time teacher of languages at the imperial university would not allow him to leave on short notice. He also claimed his health was not good. Satow wanted an agent at Mongolia's capital, Urga, to keep him informed of Russian activities there, and wrote to Lord Lansdowne, the foreign secretary, that he intended to employ Backhouse in this capacity. In May 1905 Edmund agreed to make the trip, but it never came off.

Morrison also was interested in what the Russians were up to. Across all of Asia, Russia was seen as England's nemesis, and Japan benefited from their rivalry. Morrison was trying to discredit Russia by exposing in the *Times* a czarist plot to absorb Manchuria through a secret deal with the late Viceroy Li. He became obsessed with forcing the Russians completely out of Asia, by encouraging, then openly advocating, and finally provoking Japan to attack the Russians in Manchuria. So successfully did he pursue this policy, privately and in the *Times*, that the Russo-Japanese War of 1904–1905 was christened "Morrison's War." When the Japanese made a surprise torpedo boat attack on Russian ships in Port Arthur, Morrison was elated. Russia was quickly defeated, and he was sent by the *Times* to cover the peace conference hosted by the United States at Portsmouth, New Hampshire. In America he found himself a celebrity.

During the nine months Morrison was away, J.O.P. Bland moved up from Shanghai to cover Peking for the *Times*. Recognizing an easy mark, Edmund immediately fell in with him, and soon Bland saw himself as the protector of this "fearfully timid" young man whose assistance was so useful.

When Morrison returned to Peking in mid-April 1906, he had lost all interest in being a China correspondent. Journalism had soured. China had soured. He soon soured on Japan as well. He was able to make longer snipe-hunting trips, leaving Bland at the helm in Peking, with Edmund to aid him. Bland reassured him: "Go in peace! I shall be on hand here for some time to come, and in the event of the Old Buddha dying, or any other interesting event, will keep the *Times* informed. May you shoot 100 snipe, and not get a sunstroke doing it."

In October 1908 Morrison was about to leave for another hunting trip but hesitated when news came that Emperor Kuang Hsu was seriously ill. On October 11 his diary notes that two Western-trained doctors had seen the emperor but "are not permitted to make a thorough examination." The legations all knew that Kuang Hsu had been chronically ill with kidney disease and related neurasthenia for a very long time. There was no real mystery, and no conspiracy, but they were in a typical diplomatic tizzy. On October 25 the emperor failed to perform the Winter Sacrifices. "The absence of the Emperor," Morrison scribbled, "renews fears that he is dying." Annoyed at this interference with his long-planned hunting trip, he wrote with a contemptuous flourish in his diary on November 9, "The Emperor is suffering from constipation and the Empress Dowager from diarrhea . . . the Imperial balance is struck. Through the Empress dowager the Emperor even defecates vicariously."

Morrison encountered Prince Kung's son, Prince Kung II, at a reception in the British legation and was assured by him that the emperor's illness was "nothing." But the head of the Chinese Foreign Office, who was also at the party, said, "You'd better not go away. I have had bad reports about the Emperor."

Morrison decided to go anyway and was happily bagging snipe with friends on the mudflats of the Yellow River delta at Kwantai when the emperor died on November 14. The next afternoon Empress Dowager Tzu Hsi also died. Morrison knew nothing of either event until his return to Peking that evening, November 15.

A dispatch had already been sent to the *Times*:

DEATH OF THE EMPEROR AND EMPRESS-DOWAGER
(From Our Own Correspondent Peking November 15).

It is officially announced that the Emperor died yesterday evening.

Countless rumours are rife regarding the nature of the Emperor's final illness and the manner of his death. No scientific medical opinion is obtainable, but a general description of the symptoms indicates neurasthenia as the direct cause of death. The Palace officials report that the Emperor had been in a state of coma since Thursday evening, with a period of consciousness yesterday, when the Empress-Dowager sent the Chief Eunuch Li Lien-ying to attend him. They state that his Majesty declined to allow himself to be removed to the Pavilion of Peaceful Longevity, thus violating the precedents which prescribe the death-place of the rulers of China. Eventually, he expired without having donned the robes proper to the occasion in the same quarter of the Palace where he was confined after the coup d'état of 1898, his relations with the Empress-Dowager remaining strained until the last.

Reports, confirmed from several quarters . . . , state that the Empress dowager collapsed this morning [November 15] and died at 3 P.M. A decree issued at noon announced her impending death.

This scurrilous dispatch, larded with mischievous innuendo, was written neither by Morrison nor his deputy Bland. Morrison was still on the mudflats south of Tientsin and Bland had the unfortunate luck to be confined to bed with a high fever when news reached him of the deaths. Unable to leave his room he sent an urgent message to Backhouse, who rose to the occasion. With his facile grasp of Chinese etiquette (and having posed for years as a man with intimate inside knowledge of the secrets of the court), Edmund was able to draft the whole dispatch on the spot without need for further investigation. All the bedridden Bland had to do was to read over the dispatch to be sure that the language was up to his own standard; he did not see anything wrong in its statements. Edmund's outright lie about "strained" relations between the emperor and the dowager *persisting to the very end* and the insinuation that the emperor had long been kept her prisoner merely confirmed prejudices that Bland himself had been certain about since he had been duped by the fugitive Wild Fox Kang in Shanghai in 1898. In signing Edmund's dispatch as his own, the foolish Bland felt only that he was guilty of plagiarism. He poured out his thanks to Backhouse and wrote to the *Times* praising Backhouse by name. Edmund would accept no payment, but his generosity in handling the emergency for Bland forged an unwholesome bond that would become the most famous coauthorship of Chinese history. Bland was not as wary as Morrison, so there would be countless ways Edmund could use him as he might not have dared use Morrison. Soon after the dowager's death Edmund wrote to Bland in priceless understatement, "I cannot help feeling that the Empress Dowager's decease, however lamentable in other respects, was a lucky event for me, in that it gave me the chance of being privileged to make your acquaintance."

The moment Morrison arrived in Peking by railway on November 15 and learned what had happened in his absence, he "hurried over to Backhouse's and there concocted . . . a message which I sent off." The next morning he was up early: "Working all day . . . trying to retrieve my blunder of being away from Peking during the Crisis. Backhouse helped me and I sent off three messages."

This was not the first time, to be sure. Edmund had been the real author of many of Morrison's dispatches for some years, particularly those dealing with the supposed inner workings of the court. For his authority in such matters, he always had special, privileged, secret sources, unidentified mandarins or *ming-shih* who gave him incomparable insights into what was really happening behind the throne. He professed to have such sources whenever and wherever the need arose—all of them equally imaginary or at least bogus in their authority. He fed Sir Ernest Satow tips from a "friend" who supposedly was a prominently placed Mongol; it was the nonexistence of this Mongol that made him refuse Satow's offer of a job spying in Mongolia. Now Edmund developed a new friend, a prominent Manchu near the throne, presumably a lover who produced all sorts of colorful details of court life and Manchu intrigue and became one of Edmund's chief claims to authority. He did not reveal the identity of this source, but a businessman who employed Backhouse to arrange deals with the Manchu insisted that the source "proved right all along, except when it came to dates and some small matters." Edmund may have had numerous sexual liaisons with members of the *ming-shih* and their patrons, who could have shared gossip of the court with him. In his unpublished memoirs he claimed, of course, that his secret lover was in fact the elderly empress dowager herself.

Accordingly, the articles Morrison was "concocting" with Backhouse from this point on show what appear to be an insider's confidential knowledge of the court. Whenever additional details were needed to liven up dreary facts, such as Kuang Hsu's failing to die in the right robes or in the correct pavilion, Edmund could oblige, and Morrison and Bland were profoundly grateful.

Morrison wrote in the *Times* with astonishing certainty:

Her Majesty's illness dated from November 1, when the court was terrified by a burst of uncontrollable temper, and on November 12 her Majesty suffered a paralytic stroke upon being informed of the precarious condition of the Emperor. . . . A high official says that the Empress died of apoplexy and was able to talk up to within a few hours of her demise. Both their Majesties awaited death in their full official robes, surrounded by hundreds of Court officials and followers.

So soon as it was known throughout the Palace that their Majesties were dead, a condition of panic ensued. The widow of Tung Chih attempted to commit suicide on perceiving that she would not be Empress Dowager. There was an outbreak of wailing and general pandemonium. Many of the Palace eunuchs fled, carrying away such valuables as they could lay their hands on.

Not a word of this was true, but who was to know? Certainly not Morrison. The idea that Tzu Hsi died having a fit of anger that caused a blood clot in her brain must have appealed to him, and it kept Edmund chuckling up his sleeve.

When the dowager and Kuang Hsu died, the *Times* was embarrassed to find that it had no canned obituaries of them. Normally, these were done months or years in advance for prominent individuals. For some reason, the *Times* had overlooked the assignment, and Morrison had failed to anticipate the need. *Times* editor Moberly Bell wrote to him angrily, "We were put to a good deal of inconvenience by the absence of an obituary of either the Emperor or Empress of China—and we think that you ought some time ago to have let us have them. . . . May I beg you to keep us up to date with any obituary of any very prominent person in the Far East about whom you can furnish. . . . Your letters and articles are always more interesting. . . . Your telegrams are always excellent but they can never be expected to give us the information available from such a vast and almost unknown field."

Bell had seen through Morrison's cobble of hasty dispatches and obviously felt that Morrison had been lax in his reporting over recent years, dashing off 200-word telegrams based on Backhouse translations of news events from the Chinese press, fleshed out with colorful Backhouse inventions, which readers mistook for arcane knowledge. Morrison was deeply stung and replied, "I am sorry that you had no obituaries. . . . I do not wish to evade responsibility but I am not to blame. . . . How could I possibly have known that you wanted obituaries when no one ever told me so."

The *Times* did not publish an obituary of Tzu Hsi until December 29, 1908, six weeks after she died, because it was too long to cable and had to be mailed. It was credited not to Morrison but to "Our Shanghai Correspondent," Bland. It was actually written by Edmund Backhouse, while Bland remained sick with the flu.

It is tragic that Tzu Hsi's obituary should have been written by Backhouse, for in it appeared for the first time much of his innuendo and black propaganda that have since become the accepted version of her life. As a concise review and summary of the life of the deceased, the obituary gave Edmund a chance to assemble in the pages of a trusted newspaper all the basic elements of what would become his bogus portrait of an evil dowager, his counterfeit masterpiece. It was a tour de force in the art of fraud. Thereafter he would be able to quote the *Times* as his source, as would Chinese and Western scholars who were unaware of the identity of the obit's real author. The fact that these biographical statements appeared in the *Times*, the world's leading newspaper of record, made all these details official, while in fact they were false.

From the beginning of her career—referring to the Jehol Coup in 1861—Tzu Hsi was identified by the obituary as the force behind all events in the court and in China. "She was able to turn the table on [the Gang of Eight.]" Speaking of events in 1875, when Emperor Tung Chih died, the obituary said that "the Empress Dowager his mother declined to call in proper advice . . . being given out that he was suffering from smallpox," implying that she had allowed her son to die. Of the death of Tung Chih's pregnant wife, A-lu-te, the obit said, "It is commonly believed . . . that poison was administered to the unfortunate woman by Tzu Hsi's orders: a conclusion inevitable under the circumstances." On the appointment of Kuang Hsu as the new emperor: "Her Majesty saw in the physical deficiencies of the new Emperor further promise of power for herself in the years to come, since it was unlikely that he would ever become a father"— implying that even as an infant of three, Kuang Hsu was a physical freak, lacking normal reproductive organs, recalling an earlier Chinese slander that he had two pupils in each eye. At the end of the Hundred Days Reform, "there seems no doubt that [Kuang Hsu's] death had been decided upon." For her part in the Boxer Uprising, the obit said that her chief eunuch, Li Lien-ying, "convinced the superstitious Empress Dowager of the invulnerability of the Boxers, and he more than any man, is therefore responsible for that movement and all its consequent bloodshed." The obit blamed her for the missionary massacre in Shansi, and for the purge and beheading of moderates in Peking, although Backhouse insisted that she put them to death by having them "sawn asunder." According to the obit this was not a surprise, as a "Manchu official, who knew [her] well, describes her as liable to sudden paroxysms of rage." It described Tzu Hsi's fleeing Peking during the Allied advance in 1900 "dressed as a peasant woman, and with her hair arranged in the Chinese fashion. . . . Even in this moment of disorder and danger, however, she found time and means to play the vindictive autocrat. Her last act before departing was the murder of the Emperor's favourite concubine (against whom she had long cherished a grudge) by having her thrown down a well." "As regards her private life, the Empress Dowager revived the worst traditions of the Ming Dynasty in the dignities and power accorded to eunuchs." Summing up: "It is by her public record that she must be judged."

The obit went on to note that Alicia Little, the fervent supporter of Wild Fox Kang who had included his most vituperative slander against the dowager in her 1901 book *Intimate China*, "has expressed the belief . . . that future ages will hold the Empress Dowager in even greater horror than the Empress Wu."

Inevitably, after a decade of such dark allegations about her character, never discredited by a countercampaign, the nearly simultaneous deaths of Tzu Hsi and Kuang Hsu inspired intimations of foul play. Among Peking residents, foreign and Chinese, there was intense suspicion. Readers of the *Times* were led to believe that Tzu Hsi, determined that Kuang Hsu would not survive her, had sent her chief eunuch to his bedside to ensure that the emperor breathed his last before she did, an idea planted in the first brief death notice dispatch by Backhouse and Bland. At this point, Edmund was content to imply the use of poison. Later he "revealed" that Tzu Hsi had her eunuch strangle the emperor.

The truth is that many senior officials visited the emperor during the hours before his death, but only the visit by chief eunuch Li Lien-ying was singled out by Edmund, because that made it possible to suggest that he was sent to commit murder. Actually Tzu Hsi appears to have sent the eunuch to reassure the dying Kuang Hsu that in keeping with the long-standing agreement between them (since 1901), she was announcing immediately the formal designation of his brother's child, Pu Yi, as heir to the throne. Morrison and Bland might have learned this if they had done any serious reporting on their own, but their minds were closed to the subject.

The British government knew very well that neither the emperor nor the dowager had been murdered. There were two medical reports that contradicted this assertion. One was composed in October 1908 by Dr.

G. Douglas Gray, physician at the British legation, and sent to London as an intelligence analysis. The other was published some thirty years later, in 1936, by a Western-trained Chinese, Dr. Chu Kwei-ting, who attended Emperor Kuang Hsu just prior to his death. This Chinese report must be considered first, because it reveals how the emperor's illness was understood by the court in the weeks just preceding his death.

Dr. Chu's report stated that early in September 1908, during an audience for senior military advisers, Kuang Hsu doubled up in pain. Tzu Hsi said, "The emperor has been sick for such a long time, why don't you ministers recommend a good doctor to treat him?" Prince Ching suggested Dr. Chu, who had successfully treated his own recent illness, and Tzu Hsi gave her approval. Yuan Shih-kai was delegated to bring the doctor from Tientsin. Chu arrived on September 10 and was met by Prince Ching, who told him, "You must go ahead. Just do your best. If there is any danger, let me know. I can advise the empress dowager in secret." Chu was taken first to Tzu Hsi, who interrogated him about his methods; then he was allowed to examine Kuang Hsu. His symptoms included seminal emissions, headache, fever, backaches, and no appetite, with indications of kidney disease—much as Dr. Dethève of the French legation had found in 1898. His lungs were not good, with the possibility of tuberculosis, but this could not be established without a more careful examination. His face was pale; his pulse and heartbeat were very weak. His constitution had never been strong, and he was very neurotic. Any stimulus, stress, or loud noise caused him to ejaculate. Dr. Chu gave the emperor a Western prescription. Chu did not identify it but said it could be taken orally or applied externally. Because of famous incidents of poisoning during the Ming Dynasty, no prescription could be given to the emperor without copies going immediately to all members of the Grand Council and the imperial household.

Dr. Chu came each morning, and Kuang Hsu took his medicine very carefully, always examining it closely. After many days, his breathing became normal, and the kidney pain lessened.

On the eighteenth of October, Kuang Hsu had a sudden relapse, doubling up with severe stomach cramps, rolling over and over in his bed, crying, "My stomach is in terrific pain!" Only two eunuchs were in attendance. "Since the Empress Dowager was also very sick," Chu recalled, "the whole court was in a terrible mess. I examined the Emperor. He could not sleep all night, constipation, heartbeat fast, very feeble, face color was black, the color of the tongue was yellow and black." He could see little hope. It was only a matter of time. Four weeks later Kuang Hsu was dead.

Dr. Gray did not examine the emperor or the dowager, before or after they died. He compiled his medical intelligence report on the basis of what he learned from Western-trained Chinese doctors in Peking, including senior Chinese military doctors, all of them intensely interested in the signs and symptoms of both the emperor and the dowager.

Morrison, Backhouse, and Bland all knew that Dr. Gray had considered the possibility of poisoning and after exhaustive investigation had ruled it out. Douglas Gray was a close friend to Morrison, Backhouse, and Bland and was their personal physician; his wife, Lucy, was one of Morrison's favorite gossips.

Dr. Gray counted among his other patients a number of Chinese, and he was particularly interested in the problems of eunuchs, resulting from their leaky plumbing, which gave him unusual familiarity with defects and diseases of the male reproductive and urinary organs. In his intelligence analysis for the British Foreign Office, he first addressed himself to the emperor's medical history, challenging the basic assumption of kidney disease made in 1898 by Dr. Dethève and again in 1908 by Dr. Chu:

Since birth he had never been of robust constitution. There seems little doubt that he suffered from . . . a congenital condition in which there is absence of some part of the floor of the urethra. It is a surgical fact that in almost all these cases there is some degree of arrested development of the testicles and scrotum [affecting] ability to procreate. The local irritation caused by this [condition] is capable of setting up spermatorrhea, or rather a false spermatorrhea in which there is a discharge of seminal like fluid, destitute of spermatozoa. The presence of this complaint would serve to keep him in a more or less debilitated condition—a lack of virility—all his life. The heavy duties of court life, from which there was never any respite, with Grand Council meetings beginning at 4 A.M. and all the worries of his peculiar position, would appear to have brought him into a condition of neurasthenia. From time to time he suffered from attacks of insomnia. The never-ending press of work in an individual in whom the capacity for work was limited, and the general history of the case, were causes such as give rise to neurasthenia. . . . The progressive weakness of neurasthenia was accompanied, as is the case in its latter stages, by cardiac weakness and general loss of tone of the circulatory, intestinal and sexual systems from which he respectively suffered in the last stages of his illness (1) swelling of the lower limbs (2) pronounced constipation (3) increased spermatorrhea. The "vicious circle" thus established by which the weaker his constitution became the more these symptoms were aggravated and vice versa give quite a reasonable explanation of how he came by his death.

Simply put, after his lifelong illness became worse, the emperor died of exhaustion. Yet in the *Times* Morrison, Bland, and Backhouse repeatedly implied murder.

Next Dr. Gray turned to the dowager:

At the recent Audience . . . it was remarked by those of us who were present that while Her Majesty was looking well, she had aged in appearance, and for some time previous to that there were reports that she had not been in good health. At the beginning of October she suffered from an attack of weakness and the Chinese said she had caught cold. . . . There was a good deal of influenza in Peking about that time from which a great many Chinese suffered and it is quite possible she had had that as there were no definite symptoms that they could put a name to beyond general body weakness. On her birthday, and by all accounts, she ate more than usual and took some fruit which was over ripe. By next day she was suffering from dysenteric symptoms, and the acute diarrhea with loss of blood very soon brought her into a debilitated state. Dysentery in elderly people is always much more dangerous than in earlier life. . . . In any case it seems certain she never really rallied from this attack and felt herself getting steadily weaker. While in this state she sent Prince Ching to see about her tomb and during his absence on hearing of the Emperor's grave condition her anxiety became acute and so no doubt made her worse. A few hours after Prince Ching's return, the Emperor died—about 8 P.M. This in itself, having regard to the unsettled state of the succession, coupled with the absence of any proper treatment, sedative or otherwise, must have strained her to the utmost. She held a Grand Council meeting at 2 A.M., after a long and anxious day, and later on, in the early morning when they returned to again consult with her she could only wave them aside saying she was too weak to speak. She died next afternoon—her dysenteric symptoms persisting to the end. On reviewing the circumstances of these deaths with a view to rumours which have been bruited abroad as to foul play (poisoning), while, in the Emperor's case there is *no evidence of it* [italics added], the sudden appearance of acute intestinal disease in the Empress Dowager might be said to be suspicious. But *I do not think so* [italics added] for the following reasons: Poisons all fall into the three main classes of (1) corrosives (2) narcotics (3) irritants. Unless there was a widespread collusion to hide the truth she had none of the symptoms of the two former classes. Those of corrosives are marked and unmistakeable and narcotics are equally excluded— there was no sudden death as by prussic acid, nor coma as by a narcotic nor sudden rapid suffocating sensations as by strychnine.

She might have been given an irritant poison: in the absence of all opportunity for analysis it would be difficult to say definitely but from her symptoms it is improbable that such was the case. There is no mention of her having had nausea, violent vomiting, great pain and her illness did not steadily increase in severity till collapse and death occurred. As far as can be gathered though the treatment may have left much to wish for and if properly carried out might have tided her over this attack, *her death was a natural one* [italics added], my diagnosis being dysentery accentuated by overfatigue in a senile condition.

In short, the dowager was old, weak, and grief-stricken, and died of flu complications. What pushed her over the edge was her grief at Kuang Hsu's death, and her determination to keep her promise to order the succession of his nephew Pu Yi. She could not leave such important things to ministers or to quarreling princes.

Despite this comprehensive testimony by Dr. Gray and (later) by Dr. Chu, court sources at the time (eager to make everything seem rosy) foolishly insisted after Kuang Hsu's death that the emperor "had enjoyed excellent health and had seldom been sick in his life," which fueled rumors that his death was sudden and unexpected, which is nonsensical. Despite the availability of both British and Chinese medical reports, scholars have preferred the Backhouse versions. Historian Immanuel C. Y. Hsu writes: "Legend reveals that he [Kuang Hsu] secretly, if imprudently, rejoiced over the dowager's impending death. The Imperial Woman then vengefully vowed: 'I cannot die before him!' *Indications point to the possibility that she poisoned him the day before she died* [italics added]." Even the *Encyclopaedia Britannica* says that Kuang Hsu died "presumably from poison."

In his entry on Kuang Hsu in the biographical volumes *Eminent Chinese of the Ching Period,* which frequently cite Backhouse as a source, Arthur Hummel concluded: "Whether he died a natural death, or was murdered, has never been determined."

The British and Chinese medical reports and other evidence of the emperor's and empress dowager's natural deaths have been available for many decades to any reasonably diligent researcher, so these assertions cater to the worst instincts. In her seventy-third year Tzu Hsi was a very sick old woman, and the notion that she posed a threat to anyone would be laughable were it not given credence by so many scholars.

At the time everybody seemed to have a pet theory. Those who did not blame Tzu Hsi for Kuang Hsu's death blamed Yuan Shih-kai.

The Headlands, missionary doctors to many ladies in the imperial court, discussed the two deaths in a book they published the following year, *Court Life in China* (1909). They pronounced the death of Tzu Hsi "undoubtedly nature's own work." But they had been told by "enemies of Yuan Shih-kai . . . that the Emperor had 'had a Chinese doctor,' to whom the great Viceroy paid $33,000 for his services." The Headlands' implication is that the doctor was paid this money to poison the emperor, but from Dr. Chu's own account he was brought in by Yuan in response to a majority decision of the Secret Military Council, authorized by Tzu Hsi. Dr. Chu remained silent about his role till 1936 to avoid being unfairly associated with the rumors of poisoning.

Hong Kong newspaper editor Philip Sergeant, whose remarkably fair and balanced biography of the empress dowager appeared the following year, 1910, discussed the Headlands' poisoning theory: "To make the [poisoning] story probable it is necessary to imagine a huge palace conspiracy, in which not only Yuan Shih-kai was implicated, but . . . a crowd of lesser people." Sergeant's biography, since it refused to cater to the cravings for dowager intrigue, was ignored and forgotten.

Kuang Hsu's successor as emperor, his nephew Pu Yi, relates how he was told by an old eunuch about the "suspicious circumstances" of Kuang Hsu's death:

> According to his story Kuang Hsu was fairly well on the day before his death and what made him seriously ill was a dose of medicine he took. Later it was discovered that this medicine had been sent by Yuan Shih-kai. . . . I was later told by a descendant of one of the Household Department officials that before his death Kuang Hsu was only suffering from an ordinary case of flu; he had seen the diagnosis himself, and it had said that Kuang Hsu's pulse was normal. Moreover he had been seen in his room standing and talking as if he were healthy, so that people were very shocked to hear that he was seriously ill. What was even stranger was that within four hours of this came the news of his death. All in all, Kuang Hsu's death was very suspicious. If the eunuch's story is true it is further proof that there was a conspiracy, and a deep-laid one at that, between Yuan Shih-kai and Prince Ching.

Why were so many people pushing the idea of foul play? The answer is politics. Rivalry always occurred during a succession; therefore much of the conspiracy talk derived from the selection of Pu Yi as the new emperor. After the dismissal of Pu Chun as the heir apparent in 1901 there was no immediate replacement officially, but with the Ironhats out of the way it was decided secretly that the future offspring of Kuang Hsu's brother, the teenage Prince Chun II, and his consort, the daughter of Jung Lu, would succeed to the throne. This appears to have been an effort on

Tzu Hsi's part to make up to Kuang Hsu for the dismal events of his reign and his humiliation by the Ironhats. Prince Chun II did not produce a son till 1906. Nevertheless, Tzu Hsi's deathbed designation of the child as heir apparent two years later was not a last-minute thing but was the old woman's last gesture of loyalty and affection for her nephew and the promise she had made him in 1901. Accordingly, at the end of 1908 the three-year-old Pu Yi became emperor, with his young father as regent. As usual the succession caused a game of musical chairs in Peking, as various officials lost their jobs and others took their places, which explains a lot of the character assassination during the months following the deaths of Kuang Hsu and Tzu Hsi. The rival camps were those allied with Pu Yi's family and those in favor of putting Yuan Shih-kai on the throne instead. The rumor that Yuan had poisoned Kuang Hsu was a powerful weapon in the hands of his rivals. It is hardly surprising that as he grew up, Pu Yi was willing to assume the worst of Yuan. Nor is it surprising that Morrison sought every opportunity to advance Yuan's cause by shifting guilt to the dowager.

The story took a grotesque turn when Edmund Backhouse wrote his intimate memoirs of his private life in China, "Decadence Mandchoue." Nothing else so clearly reveals the mind of the man who drafted the dispatches innocently published by the *Times*—and who wrote (with Bland's collaboration) the primary texts on which historians depend.

> The palace eunuchs . . . had purchased . . . by the Empress Dowager's command, four ounces of P'i Shuang or arsenic crystals on . . . November 5, 1905. . . . The original plan was to poison the emperor gradually by inserting small . . . doses in sponge cakes. . . . But the British Legation physician [Dr. Gray] had been instructed through Sir Edward Grey, the Foreign Secretary . . . to ask permission to see Kuang Hsu and to diagnose his malady . . . hence her abandonment of the poisoning programmes for the simpler and quicker method of strangulation.

After having the emperor strangled, Backhouse wrote, Tzu Hsi was confronted by Yuan Shih-kai and the Manchu general Liang Pi. They demanded that she abdicate and appoint them regents for the infant Pu Yi. When Tzu Hsi refused, Backhouse wrote, Yuan "fired three shots . . . at point blank . . . hitting her 'au bas ventre.' [in the lower belly]" This last was a typical Backhouse touch, for where else would you want to shoot a hated woman but in the womb.

CHAPTER TWENTY-SIX

Hatching the Dragon Lady

Tzu Hsi was now history, but absurdly little was known about her life. The *New York Times* printed a long, error-filled obituary calling her Tzu An, the title of her coregent who had died twenty-seven years earlier. A photograph of an entirely different woman, neither Tzu Hsi nor Tzu An, appeared with the obituary; it was one of Tung Chih's surviving concubines. If the editors of America's leading newspaper were not certain of the dowager's simplest title, Tzu Hsi, it is hardly surprising that they were uncertain about the elementary facts of her life. How, for instance, had she come to reign over China for half a century, and (more to the point in light of all the scandal surrounding her) how had she gone about murdering her husband, her son, his wife, her coregent, and the emperor she had kept cruelly imprisoned for ten years, not to mention numerous others.

What was needed was a fair and balanced review of her life by a Western scholar who understood the inner workings of the Manchu court.

Exactly that was conceived by Edmund Backhouse and produced by him in 1910, in collaboration with J.O.P. Bland, a book of 525 pages titled *China under the Empress Dowager.* It was not by a recognized China scholar, but it was the next best thing: a book by a well-known China correspondent (Bland) and a well-informed Western sinologue (Backhouse) based on the secret diary of a Manchu official with inside information.

George Morrison might have been Edmund's natural choice as collaborator, but he was absent from Peking so much of the time (and was so suspicious by nature) that Backhouse formed the literary partnership with the gullible and pompous Bland instead. Bland had just authored *Houseboat Days in China,* published by Edward Arnold in London, and he wrote a letter to Arnold describing his new undertaking: "I am now preparing in collaboration with a very noted Chinese scholar, who possesses exceptional sources of information and many unique documents, a life of the late empress dowager, intended to throw light on many unexplained incidents in Chinese history. . . . My collaborator is a student and a man of laborious days, and . . . my part is only to revise and put the thing into an attractive form."

For the book Backhouse came up with impressive Manchu and Chinese court documents and memoirs that he claimed to be translating. He was amazingly quick. Four months after the dowager's death, he was well into drafting the book. Bland refined and polished the language, putting it all in elegant prose. By April 1910 the book was done. Arnold backed out, but a contract was signed with William Heinemann, who saw promise in the book that others failed to grasp. He was intrigued by the long extracts Backhouse had taken from a hitherto unknown source, "The Diary of His Excellency Ching Shan," a Manchu courtier who provided an unprecedented look at secret activities inside the court, especially during the Boxer summer of 1900. Ching Shan's diary was exactly the sort of document that Westerners had always dreamed of, providing a clear understanding of the Manchu and the Boxers. Made to order, as it were. Here was the first insider's view of the deep divisions between the anti-Western Ironhats who thought the Boxers were invincible and those moderate and sensible mandarins favoring reform of the empire and compromise with the West. The diary revealed all these conflicts, and although the leaders of these factions were now dead or in remote exile, the legacy of their quarrel was still a potent force in China and in the minds of Western observers. In essence the Ching Shan diary confirmed and amplified all the nasty little intrigues that Morrison had intuited (with the help of Backhouse) from the very beginning, in his own accounts of the siege and its background.

In a long letter Edmund Backhouse described how he came to possess the diary. He claimed that in 1900 Ching Shan had held the office of comptroller of the imperial household. His eldest son had become involved with the Boxers and during the siege had murdered his own father. After the lifting of the siege, while the Allies occupied Peking, Backhouse said he had been given permission to live in Ching Shan's house inside the British sector. (He did not mention that he and his roommate Peachey had been jailed for looting, blackmail, and robbery.) A Captain Rowlandson "authorized me to take any books and papers for my own use, requesting that I should inform him if I found any Boxer documents or evidence of the Boxers' occupation of the house," Backhouse claimed.

> I returned to my new quarters and . . . entered . . . what had been Ching Shan's private study. It contained a table, chairs, and two large

cupboards. On the brick floor were several boxes, the contents of which had been rifled. I then proceeded to examine the papers. . . . The first thing that struck my eye was the date on a long sheet, because it was very recent. On examining further I perceived that it was a record of the Court's departure [from Peking]. . . . The more I looked into the litter of papers, the more convinced I became of their interest. As the handwriting tallied with that on various documents of another nature bearing Ching Shan's signature, I came to the conclusion that the records were undoubtedly by him. I at once informed Captain Rowlandson of the discovery, which greatly interested him. . . . When, a few days later, the eldest son [of Ching Shan] was arrested, reference was made at the Court Martial to the charge made by his father against him. He was found guilty of murder and of harbouring Boxers. The sentence of death by shooting was carried out under the wall of the Imperial City. . . .

When Sir E. Satow arrived in Peking, I informed him of the document at my first visit to him. . . . He strongly advised publication but recommended that it be deferred till after the Empress's death.

Satow had long since retired and could hardly be expected to recall such minor details. There is no record of this discussion in his meticulous private diaries. Edmund waited nearly ten years to make these assertions, by which time no Westerner was in a position to check his claims, and no Chinese or Manchu official was remotely aware of what he was up to. In Peking the government had been turned upside down, the diplomatic corps had been recycled, the emperor and the empress dowager were dead, and by 1910 the Ching Dynasty was in a state of near collapse. In any case, Ching Shan had been only a lowly assistant secretary of the imperial household and not, as Backhouse claimed, the comptroller. But more about that later.

"After the Empress's death in November 1908," Backhouse continued, "I began to think of publishing my find. . . . I was naturally much pleased when Mr. Bland, whose acquaintance I had recently had the privilege of making, offered to collaborate with me in writing a biography of the Empress, whom, like myself, he greatly admired and reverenced."

The Ching Shan diary confirmed everyone's worst suspicions about the corruption of China and the reptilian nature of its female ruler, so Backhouse was not introducing evidence of anything Westerners were not already predisposed to believe. Everyone had heard of ghastly atrocities, beheadings of missionary children, poisonings in the palace, false eunuchs; here was corroboration. To throw off doubters, Edmund feigned admiration for Tzu Hsi, a rhetorical device maintained throughout the book. He decorated every passage with so much obscure lore, detail, names, and atmospherics that readers were bemused, the way an audience is lulled and then bamboozled by a gifted magician. The Backhouse style is so ornate with these mischievous digressions that after a while it can be recognized immediately when another writer uses his material without attribution. (For example, the first report of the deaths published in the *Times* and quoted earlier has ornamental details about which chamber the emperor should have died in and the robes he should have been wearing.)

China under the Empress Dowager was published in October 1910, the authors' names listed according to Heinemann's notion of their marketability: J.O.P. Bland and E. T. Backhouse. Here was the first highly readable account of the entire reign of Tzu Hsi, compiled from "authentic" Chinese sources. Curiously, Bland, although fluent in Chinese himself, never once looked at the original documents, only at Edmund's "translations." A complacent man, Bland never questioned his own assumptions.

The book's virtues were immediately obvious. It had great authority because it contained what appeared to be original Chinese state papers. Here were the secret diaries of Chinese officials and private interviews with them, all produced by Edmund like a conjurer. Here were intimate revelations of palace politics and extraordinary insights into Oriental personalities, all written in a style that was relaxed, agreeable, and urbane, the hallmark of self-assured Edwardian gentlemen. The intelligent Western reader found it, as he will still find it, both instructive and delightful reading. Reviewers were unanimous in their praise. The book came "as near as any book could to explaining the enigmatic character of the Dowager Empress Tzu Hsi. That character is unquestionably impressive. Tzu Hsi was guilty of both cruelty and licentiousness, but her environment and the traditions of her race explain much which could not possibly be condoned according to English standards." The *Spectator* commended the authors for publishing for the first time "documents which but for the diligence of the authors would probably never have come under the English eyes." A few years later, when Sir Claude MacDonald addressed the Royal United Service Institution, he referred his audience to the book, calling it "one of the most fascinating works ever written on things Chinese." He might more accurately have called it "one of the most fascinating works of fiction," but of course the Ching Shan diary supported the assertion that the Chinese had burned the Hanlin, for which Sir Claude must have been grateful.

In the first eighteen months the book went through eight printings and was translated into several languages, including Chinese, so that it became a treacherous source even for Chinese scholars. Because of the destruction or theft of so many of China's state papers and archives in 1900, Chinese were deprived of documentary assets and thus were in no position to challenge what Backhouse published—nor were they inclined to, in the

revolutionary mood of the day. The People's Republic continues to produce movies for domestic consumption in which Tzu Hsi has her ministers beheaded or sawed into pieces and stuffed down wells, as a symbol
of the evils of imperialism.

As though anxious to protect the dowager empress from groundless
innuendo, Backhouse and Bland began the book by denouncing Tzu Hsi's
critics. They condemned the "many unfounded and ridiculous stories
[that] have been circulated in recent years. . . . Many of these are nothing
more than the fruit of Yellow Journalism. . . . Others, however, undoubtedly owe their origin to the envy, hatred and malice of Palace intrigues,
to the initiative of the Iron-capped Princes and other high officials of the
elder branch of the Imperial family, many of whom were addicted to
besmirching the family and character of Tzu Hsi."

They went on to pan their Western competition.

Equally valueless, for purposes of historical accuracy, are most of the
accounts and impressions of the Empress recorded by those Europeans (especially the ladies of the Diplomatic Body and their friends)
who saw her personality and purposes reflected in the false light
which beats upon the Dragon Throne on ceremonial occasions, or
who came under the influence of the deliberate artifices and charm
of manner which she assumed so well. . . . and the apparently artless
bonhomie of her bearing, all combined to create in the minds of the
European ladies who saw her an impression as favourable as it was
opposed to every dictate of common sense and experience.

Having thus discredited all other sources, ridiculing even those who
had become acquainted firsthand with their subject, they set about con-
tructing their own vision of Tzu Hsi. Put to rest were the troublesome
mysteries about her early life, her husband, her son, and others who
perished for disagreeing with her. It was no longer necessary to look for
other explanations. With this book and its sequel, *Annals and Memoirs of
the Court of Peking*, Backhouse and Bland transformed Tzu Hsi and her
court from a subject of historical inquiry into a historical tradition, tied
in a neat bundle. The many conundrums of Manchu history could be
explained by ascribing all cause and effect to Tzu Hsi. She alone was "the
mastermind of the Forbidden City."

Page after page they evoke "the far-seeing intelligence" of the young
Yehenara, her "ambitious and magnetic personality" and "virile and untir-
ing energies." In order to "play one opponent off against another" she
"speedily laid her plans" until her "lust for vengeance" and her "love of
power" made her the "defacto ruler of the Empire."

Her enemies feared her because "they were speedily to learn by bitter experience that Tzu Hsi was not to be opposed, and that to live peacefully with her in the Palace was an end that could be attained only by complete submission to her will." This resulted from "her inability to brook any form of opposition and her absolutely unscrupulous methods for ridding herself of anything or anyone who stood in the path of her ambition." She was "too determined to retain her position and power to allow any weight to attach to sentimental, religious, or other considerations." Her "only possible motive was personal ambition," so she "gained an easy and complete victory."

Once victorious, "this masterful woman" matured into a ruler of "enormous personal influence and fertility of resource." She had "the courage of masculine intelligence that enabled her to overcome all obstacles." While she was masculine in intellect, she was feminine in mood, "Souvent femme varie, and the mind of Tzu Hsi never ran consistently for long in the same groove."

How would Marquis Tseng Kuo-fan have reacted to this portrait? Backhouse and Bland might be presenting a caricature of Empress Wu, but they certainly were not talking about the dowager the marquis had known.

Having now led readers to believe that Tzu Hsi was a uniquely powerful woman—a Manchu Margaret Thatcher who intimidated friends and foes alike—they introduced the Shakespearean theme of murder as an everyday practice in her court.

Europeans, studying the many complex and unexpected phases of her extraordinary personality from the point of view of Western moralities, have usually emphasized and denounced her cold-blooded ferocity and homicidal rage. Without denying the facts, or extenuating her guilt, it must, nevertheless, be admitted that it would be unjust to expect from her compliance with standards of morals and conduct of which she was perforce ignorant, and that, judged by the standards of her own predecessors and contemporaries, and by the verdict of her subjects, she is not to be reckoned a wicked woman.

Years of research produce no support for this paragraph. No Europeans "emphasized and denounced her cold-blooded ferocity and homicidal rage" before Wild Fox Kang fled into exile at the end of 1898 and began inventing this image. Between 1898 and the dowager's death, the only Westerners who pushed that image were Alicia Little and others of her circle taken in by Kang—and Morrison's own small group, including Bland and Backhouse themselves. It was only after the publication of *their* book that the image of "cold-blooded ferocity and homicidal rage" became the conventional wisdom.

"Tzu Hsi played her royal part in the great game. . . . When she sent a man to death, it was because he stood between her and the full and safe gratification of her love of power," wrote Backhouse and Bland. "Her methods, in fact, were Elizabethan rather than Florentine. . . . She appeared to be the born and inevitable ruler of the degenerate Dynasty, and if she became a law unto herself, it was largely because there were few about her fit to lead or to command." She acted "in a manner which brings forcibly to mind Queen Elizabeth's methods of dealing with similar remonstrances." "She had, moreover, a Bismarckian way of guiding public opinion, of directing undercurrents of information through the eunuchs and tea-house gossip, in a manner calculated to appeal to the instincts of the literati and the bourgeois." She had "a keen natural aptitude for State affairs (similar to that of Queen Victoria, whom she greatly admired from afar)." Also, "the picture brings irresistibly to the English mind memories of another strong-minded Queen and her inspection of another garden, where heads were insecure for gardeners and Cheshire cats."

In this Backhouse version of history, Prince Kung and his coalition hardly exist. History, to him, was one woman's wickedness. But Edmund was not writing history, he was writing fiction. He had learned from years of observing George Morrison and doing much of his work that nobody would be in a position to challenge. As Moberly Bell of the *Times* had reminded Morrison, China was "a vast and almost unknown field." When it came to such an obscure place, fiction, if well informed and well written, was just as good as history and involved a great deal more art. Had not Napoleon defined history as "tricks we play on the dead"?

"Tzu Hsi died, as she had lived, above the law. . . . She died, as she had lived, a creature of impulse and swiftly changing moods, a woman of infinite variety" "This personal charm, this subtle and magnetic emotion, was undoubtedly the secret of that stupendous power with which, for good or evil, she ruled for half a century a third of the population of the earth."

Morrison was visiting England when *China under the Empress Dowager* was published, and he exchanged letters with Edmund on the subject. It was a curious exchange, with spite, envy, and disbelief lurking behind every word. Morrison was dismayed and puzzled that Backhouse had never once mentioned to him his discovery of this sensational Ching Shan diary.

Edmund feigned modesty. "With regard to Bland's and my attempt at collaboration, I am very grateful for your kind words. My name ought not really to appear at all," he wrote, "indeed, I had decided to withdraw it, but found that it was too late to do so. . . . The diary was found by me in the house which I occupied after the siege—you probably remember the insolence of the man En Chu, the son of old Ching Shan and his arrest and subsequent execution for harbouring Boxers? It was he whose ears you boxed so violently! . . . I never regarded it as important until . . . Bland strongly advised its publication. . . . In any case what credit there may be in the book belongs to Bland, and my part is merely mechanical."

Morrison responded: "You are far too modest about your book. It is a splendid book and does you the greatest honour. Chirol [foreign editor of the *Times*] wrote a most flattering review of the book and of you in the *Times* weekly edition."

There was more of the same posturing, but behind this doffing of hats the letters danced around a bitter and startling accusation. Something was very wrong with the book by Backhouse and Bland, and the first to spot it was the ever suspicious Morrison. He evidently had read the galleys of *China under the Empress Dowager* when he saw Bland in London in August 1910, just before the book was published and immediately denounced it to Bland as counterfeit. Bland was astonished by Morrison's violent reaction. Morrison seemed "sick at [the book] and damned Backhouse freely," telling Bland that he had been duped and that Backhouse had invented the Ching Shan diary. Morrison maintained that Ching Shan had not died in 1900 as Backhouse claimed but two years later, so how could Edmund possibly have obtained the diary of a dead man when the man was not dead? It was all a hoax perpetrated by the "brilliant but mendacious" Backhouse. In a letter to Bland, Backhouse defended himself, insisting that obviously Morrison had confused the diarist Ching Shan with another man of similar name. In the introduction to the book Edmund tried to deflect suspicion by drawing the reader's attention to this issue: "It should be explained that Ching Shan must be distinguished from Ching Hsin, who died about 1904."

Eventually, Bland found a more comforting explanation for Morrison's fury. He concluded that Morrison was angry because "he will never forgive Backhouse for having kept the diary from him all these years." He kept Edmund informed of Morrison's continued backstabbing in England, which was approaching the level of criminal libel, and eventually Backhouse confronted Morrison by letter.

Morrison, who was on dangerously shaky ground himself when it came to defrauding readers with Edmund's assistance, backpedaled furiously:

Some anonymous person had told [Heinemann, the book's publisher] that I had said that Ching Shan's diary was a fake. I have never said any such thing. Bland himself has spoken so wildly about the diary that I believe it is he himself who has created an impression, if such an impression has been created, that he had some doubt himself. . . . If there is one man in the world of whom I have always spoken with extraordinary admiration it is you. You are a genius with powers

. . . that have been given to no other man of my acquaintance, and I have always said this to every man to whom I have ever spoken about you.

Edmund had him by the Thrice Precious.

Morrison knew that he could not easily prove the diary a fake and make the charge stick in a British court. Once the book had been published by Heinemann, the reputation of the publisher was at stake, not just that of Backhouse and Bland. Morrison would have to face involvement in a major scandal, legal expenses, and red tape. He had long ago tumbled to the dark side of Edmund Trelawny Backhouse. This put the journalist in an awkward position. He had entered into a variety of incriminating intrigues with Backhouse. In the course of a counterattack, Edmund could easily prove that he had written many of Morrison's most famous reports while Morrison was away hunting snipe. The editors of the *Times*, who were considering Morrison as a successor to Chirol as foreign editor, would be horrified to learn that he had depended for ten years on an assistant he knew all along was a liar, a thief, and a counterfeiter. If this was to become public knowledge, the graver embarrassment would be to the *Times*. And of course, there was Morrison's falsification of the Boxer siege, which had never been exposed and was still seen as the authoritative account. To reveal the sorry truth of the heroic defense of the legations would be to make a spectacle of England herself. So to expose Backhouse, Morrison would have to drop his own pants.

When he returned to Peking and saw Backhouse on March 11, 1911, Morrison noted, "He blushed badly when he spoke of Ching Shan's diary." They understood each other all too well. Privately, Morrison continued to condemn the Ching Shan diary as a fraud but he never pressed the issue home.

There was another painful reason that Morrison could not afford to reveal Backhouse as a con man and counterfeiter. For many years Morrison had been buying, looting, and otherwise acquiring rare Chinese books and manuscripts, building a unique collection that one day would be sold to pay for his retirement. He felt compelled to have such a library as a journalistic totem. In the course of assembling this library, he had bought Chinese manuscripts from Backhouse that he later realized were of dubious origin.

Morrison had also relied on advice from Backhouse to purchase Chinese curios, artworks, and scrolls, many of which might be counterfeits produced by a circle of Chinese art forgers with whom he knew Backhouse associated. So if Morrison revealed what he knew about Edmund, he would jeopardize his own collection. By 1910 Morrison was hard-pressed financially, having lavished so much money on books, scrolls, and curios;

he had to weigh his moves carefully. "My financial position is bad—damned bad. . . . I have bungled my affairs badly."

He had black suspicions that Backhouse had stolen more than one genuine manuscript from him while helping to catalogue the library. He described Edmund in his diary as "wonderfully clever but morally unsound and I am afraid of his stealing my books." Other disquieting bits of information confirmed the hint of insanity. A former classmate of Edmund's told Morrison that "Backhouse was regarded as mad at Winchester. He used to borrow money and not repay pretending he smoked opium . . . [he was] a liar, a kleptomaniac and regarded as unclaimable."

Morrison was not alone in these suspicions. Sir John Jordan, the new British minister to Peking, also believed the Ching Shan diary was a fake, as did the Italian diplomat Daniele Vare. In his own popular biography of Tzu Hsi, Vare quoted the diary extensively but declared openly that Morrison had believed the work to have been forged by Backhouse with the aid of his Manchu teacher. Vare also noted, not altogether correctly, that "Mr. J.O.P. Bland did not enter into the controversy, but, as proprietor of the original document, he deposited it in the British Museum so that Sinologues might examine it, a facility of which many scholars have availed themselves."

J.J.L. Duyvendak, a Dutch sinologist, undertook an examination of the manuscript in 1924 and pronounced it genuine. Reginald Johnston, who became the tutor to Emperor Pu Yi, also declared it authentic. Johnston pretended to dislike Edmund Backhouse, but during his years as British magistrate in Weihaiwei had made trips into Peking where he and Backhouse were commonly seen together making the rounds of popular theaters on the back streets of the city. Johnston maintained that he did not meet Backhouse until 1914; however, they were both interpreters at one of the British legation entertainments for the Manchu court ladies in 1903. The opinions of Duyvendak and Johnston gave Edmund increased stature as a sinologist, but Johnston, at least, was lying.

Many others challenged the judgment of Duyvendak, and in 1936 a devastating argument that the Ching Shan diary was fake was put forward by the British journalist and China scholar William Lewisohn. He studied the diary while preparing an article on the Boxer siege and found many instances where the diary was both inaccurate and incredible. Many phrases in it, he discovered, were quotes from well-known Western figures like Talleyrand, and there were passages lifted verbatim from a contemporary account by Grand Secretary Wang Wen-shao. Evidently Edmund did not limit himself to plagiarizing clever lines from Chinese plays, but borrowed whole passages wherever he saw fit. Lewisohn sent copies of his article to Bland and Backhouse, and Bland was deeply distressed, but Backhouse merely thanked Lewisohn for sending him the article and did not respond to the issues raised.

Professor Duyvendak (who had pronounced the diary authentic) was outraged and, after failing to stop the publication of Lewisohn's article, stepped into the fray once again. He planned to vindicate his original opinion by obtaining from Backhouse other portions of the diary that Edmund had said he had with him in Peking. Unfortunately, Backhouse now informed Duyvendak, he had been forced to sell these sections, and the original purchaser had sold them to other clients and had since been murdered, making it (conveniently) impossible to trace them.

Edmund tried to cover his tracks by claiming that he had lent the Ching Shan diary to Grand Secretary Wang Wen-shao and that Wang must have plagiarized passages from it—not the other way around. In the end, Duyvendak was forced to agree with Lewisohn that the diary was a fake. But Duyvendak hedged by asserting that Backhouse had been taken in by the actual forgers and had nothing to do with the falsification himself.

Bland's faith was shaken, but his own credibility depended upon the credibility of Backhouse, so he persisted in affirming the authenticity of the diary and continued to describe Edmund as "one of the greatest Oriental scholars." Privately he had serious doubts. When at age seventy Bland began writing his memoirs, which were never published, the name Edmund Backhouse was not mentioned once.

Argument went on over the authenticity of the Ching Shan diary, but no one ever questioned the image it presented of Tzu Hsi and the events it described in which she supposedly figured. Nobody ever wondered what motivated Edmund to concoct the diary. The fact that Edmund bitterly hated his mother, blamed her for his misery and his long exile from England, and later railed at her in his private diaries in a way oddly similar to his railing at Tzu Hsi, was never noted. Despite these challenges to the authenticity of the diary, Edmund's books became the basic source on the Manchu throughout the world. Few ordinary readers were ever aware that his authority was in doubt. Lewisohn's challenge had no perceptible impact on sinologists and their assumptions about the value of Backhouse as a source. They all continued to use him.

In their first book Backhouse and Bland made veiled references to a sexual liaison Tzu Hsi supposedly had with Jung Lu, but for the most part restrained themselves. In their next collaboration they devoted many pages to Tzu Hsi's supposed secret life, for which (as we have seen) there was no evidence whatever.

In June 1911 Backhouse wrote to Morrison that he was thinking of writing a second book, a "Defence of the Manchus." He said he had found various diaries and memoirs that would make an interesting framework for the book, which would trace the history of Manchu China from the fall of the Mings to the collapse of the Chings. When the second collaboration, *Annals and Memoirs of the Court of Peking*, was published in 1914, the byline was reversed to read "E. Backhouse & J.O.P. Bland," apparently because Bland was weary of explaining that the most titillating material originated with Backhouse.

Again reviewers were full of praise. One in the *New York Times* wrote, "The book is one which no student of Chinese affairs can afford to miss." Indeed. He added, however, that much of the book was "repellent and even shocking." Edmund had slyly seen to that. He was now much more confident of what he could get away with.

He and Bland avoided the delicate question of good taste by quoting from "the recent work" of four Chinese writers "in order that the reader may form an impression of the opinion in which the great Empress Dowager was held during her lifetime . . . a lamentable picture of the inner life of the Forbidden City, where corruption festered around the foundations of the Dragon Throne."

With the help of these anonymous sources—seen only by Backhouse and doubtless concocted by him from the pornographic "secret histories" he had collected since early 1899—the two authors expanded their historical caricature of Tzu Hsi to include the whole range of nymphomania, debauchery, and perversion associated traditionally with Empress Wu. *Annals* established beyond doubt that when all else failed, Tzu Hsi resorted spontaneously to murder, and its analogue: if murder occurred, Tzu Hsi was the probable reason. Hereafter it became customary for historians who cut their teeth on Bland and Backhouse to draw the same conclusion at every turn.

From the success of *China under the Empress Dowager* and *Annals and Memoirs of the Court of Peking* Edmund Backhouse gained an international reputation as a China scholar. And why not? When Morrison challenged the Ching Shan diary, it was not because he disagreed with the point of view it supported, for he too had found it convenient to falsify the record. Nevertheless, it was one thing for George Morrison to distort facts in the interest of empire and another entirely for Edmund Backhouse to make them up for his own amusement. Despite his occasional lapses, Morrison was a fundamentally moral and ethical man whose distortions were Olympian in their motivation. Edmund, on the other hand, was falsifying an entire period of history, motivated only by mischief. Nearly a century later, such a fine distinction is blurred.

The Backhouse legacy of a venomous female serpent eating her young remains unchanged to this day. His ghost still looms over Peking, high on Prospect Hill, built of spoils dredged to create the Lake Palaces beside the Forbidden City, an artificial man-made hill of debris that goes by the Chinese name Ching Shan. It was the kind of pun Edmund enjoyed most.

Dynasty's End

While Bland and Backhouse were becoming the chief Western experts on the empress dowager, Morrison was turning his back on journalism to risk everything as a political adviser to Yuan Shih-kai. The *Times* had invited him to succeed Valentine Chirol as foreign editor in London, a handsome offer bringing with it extraordinary influence and prestige, but he turned the job down. He had spent too much time in the permissive Orient to function happily in the constraints of London society. In Peking, Morrison was a law unto himself; in London, he would face intense competition and continual cross-checking. His professional conduct had become much too lax for that. Finally there was a clash of wills with his editors. When he championed the Japanese cause against Russia in 1904–1905, he was in tune with British policy, but then he did an unexpected turnabout and began exposing Japanese excesses in China. This was contrary to the pro-Japan policy of the Foreign Office, which was endorsed by the *Times*. When Morrison refused to toe the line, his dispatches were altered by his editors to reverse their political viewpoint. Morrison was furious.

His apprehensions about leaving China were deepened by a disturbing encounter with Sir Robert Hart during Morrison's protracted visit to England in 1910–11.

Hart had not left Peking a forgotten man. In addition to honors from the Chinese government, he had decorations from thirteen countries and the Vatican, and honorary doctoral degrees including one from his alma mater, The Queen's College in Belfast. He was far from poor. Morrison calculated that Hart's salary and awards, plus his Boxer indemnity, had netted him close to half a million pounds for his years in China. Morrison also noted ungraciously that salaries Hart had arranged for members of his family in the Customs Service totaled another quarter of a million sterling. Prudent investments in British real estate early in Hart's career had increased his wealth, including what was assumed to be the "family estate" of Kilmoriarty in Northern Ireland, which he subsequently sold at a handsome profit, the proceeds going to his wife and son. He and Lady Hart took up residence at Great Marlow in Buckinghamshire, where they were close to London. Hart's wealth and honors galled Morrison, who was deep in debt and feeling cheated of his own knighthood.

In his diary Morrison described his meeting with Hart bitterly: "Sir Robert looked exceedingly shaky and frail, shattered in mind and body. He hopes to return [to Peking] in April, is still clinging to the shekels. . . . It was very painful speaking to him. Wretched feeble animal, he has caused infinite suffering in his time and has been singularly unjust. Apparently he cleaves to the hope that he will return to China and finish his life there. He was almost lachrymose and shrill." A few months later, on September 20, 1911, Sir Robert Hart died in England, three weeks before the dynasty he had spent his life supporting was overthrown.

While still in London, Morrison hired a private secretary to work for him in China. Dark-haired Jennie Wark Robin was a stunningly beautiful twenty-two-year-old New Zealander. Jennie knew French and German and had been private secretary to Lord Balfour of Burleigh. She was twenty-seven years Morrison's junior. According to him, he hired her to "help me put in order all the papers and documents I have accumulated during the last 15 years."

Once back in Peking, it did not take long for all the Western swains to rush her. She soon had two proposals of marriage and was briefly engaged to Herbert Philips, assistant Chinese secretary of the British Consular Service. Morrison had to act quickly or lose her. By mid-May 1912 he confided to his diary, "I am in love." They paid a call on Edmund Backhouse, and Jennie thought Backhouse was "most agreeable and polite." In late August, after returning to England and obtaining her parents' consent, she and Morrison were married.

It was all very romantic, and like the blurb on a romantic novel, they fell in love while all about them the once great Ching Dynasty was collapsing in ruin. Unwisely, Morrison chose this moment to become involved in political conspiracy and was soon in over his head.

After the nearly simultaneous deaths of Kuang Hsu and Tzu Hsi, the rudderless Manchu court divided in the classic manner into rival factions determined to control the new child emperor. On one side of the throne was an executive faction dominated by Prince Ching and Yuan Shih-kai. Opposed to them was a monarchist faction led by the new regent, Prince Chun II, and the Japanese-trained General Liang Pi, who commanded the Imperial Guards; their aim was to reassert Manchu hegemony over China, with Japanese assistance.

The monarchists were convinced, as were their Japanese allies, that Yuan intended to seize power at the first opportunity and set up a military dictatorship. Prince Chun II, a younger brother of the late Emperor Kuang Hsu, was determined to avenge Yuan's betrayal during the Hundred Days Reform of 1898. Although the Japanese offered to arrange Yuan's assassination, the monarchists feared reprisals by Yuan's military protégés, who commanded elements of the Northern Army. Instead, they tried to get rid of Yuan politically. In January 1909, two months after Tzu Hsi's death, they thought they had found an ingenious way to remove him from office. It had long been Yuan's habit to duck unattractive assignments by pretending illness, a ruse his enemies now turned against him. A decree from the regent, Prince Chun, commanded Yuan to take sick leave from all official duties on the pretext of a nonexistent injury to his foot. He was ordered to convalesce until the throne decided his foot was better.

Yuan's dismissal annoyed Westerners, who had come to rely upon him as their man on the Grand Council. Sir John Jordan, who had succeeded Sir Ernest Satow as British minister, complained to Morrison: "Why can't Yuan Shih-kai put himself at the head of 10,000 men and sweep the lot out." Yuan bought a country estate and made a pretense of living the life of a retired official. Behind this charade he was busier than ever politicking, working through his protégés.

The means to strike back at the monarchists were readily available to him. With the twentieth century, times had changed in China. In Shanghai, Chicago-style mobsters took over the drug trade, prostitution, and financial rackets, led by the Green Gang. Where once political murder meant a poisoned hanky or a silk bowstring, now homemade bombs and gun-toting professional killers were commonplace.

All Yuan had to do was wait because events were moving in his favor. By the summer of 1911 the monarchists were foundering. Bankrupted by the Boxer settlement, the dynasty was trying unsuccessfully to negotiate emergency loans with a consortium of foreign banks. South China was on the verge of rebellion, agitated by the troublemaking of Sun Yat-sen's republican revolutionaries. Among China's upper classes, hatred of the Manchu was running at an all-time high.

In Wuhan on the Yangtze, on October 9, 1911, a cell of discontented army officers was plotting an uprising when one of their homemade bombs accidentally exploded. Police locked the city gates and surrounded the army barracks. Panicking, the dissident military officers decided to risk everything and proceed with their insurrection. Under their leadership, four battalions mutinied and seized the city on October 10—the auspicious tenth day of the tenth month, or "Double Tenth." These mutineers in Wuhan were complete unknowns with no ties to Sun Yat-sen, but they had achieved by accident what other revolutionaries had failed to accomplish in decades of effort. By October 12 a provisional republican government had been formed in Wuhan, and province after province joined the rebels, declaring themselves independent of Manchu authority.

In a desperate effort to preserve the dynasty, Prince Ching persuaded the young prince regent to recall Yuan Shih-kai from retirement. Yuan said his foot was still troubling him. After repeated appeals, he submitted a list of conditions, including complete control of the military. The desperate Manchu gave in and on October 27, 1911, Yuan was named imperial high commissioner of all military forces to fight the republicans. The throne also convened a provisional parliament and named Yuan to replace Prince Ching as prime minister with a new cabinet full of his cronies. Yuan launched carefully orchestrated military assaults on the disorganized republican forces, always stopping short of victory. His object was to gain the upper hand for himself, without really strengthening the Manchu position, till both republicans and Manchu were exhausted. Viceroy Li would have been proud.

Unable to cope, Prince Chun retired as regent, leaving General Liang Pi to save the dynasty, if he could, from Yuan and from the republicans. On January 26, 1912, Liang Pi was mortally wounded by a bomb-throwing assassin, one of those surgical removals that Yuan practiced with the same flair as Viceroy Li. Nobody of substance stood any longer in Yuan's path. Manipulating negotiations between the throne and the republicans, he traded the forced abdication of the child emperor Pu Yi for the resignation of Sun Yat-sen as provisional president of the republic, in favor of Yuan himself. He emerged the sole victor: President Yuan Shih-kai.

By always portraying him favorably in the *Times*, Morrison had done much to create the impression in Western minds that Yuan was China's great hope. He failed to see that Yuan was using him and that, clever and ruthless as he was, Yuan had neither the political skill nor the patience to rule China.

Morrison urgently needed money, however, and Yuan was beckoning. All around him people were raking it in. He wrote in his diary, "I am determined to leave the *Times*. . . . The Chinese talk of giving me employment and of never allowing me to leave China. The British minister promises me, but I need hardly say that I count nothing upon this, that he will make every effort to obtain for me a knighthood." What the Chinese had to offer was the highly paid job of political adviser to Yuan Shih-kai, in this case a euphemism for press secretary or public relations man.

In September 1912, one month after marrying Jennie, Morrison left the *Times* to work for Yuan at more than triple his salary, plus lavish expenses. Fellow Australian journalist W. H. Donald, then representing the New

York *Herald* in Peking, said Morrison "asked me . . . why I did not enter the service of the Government. My reply was that once a man entered the paid service of a Chinese his influence was gone. Morrison scoffed—now he admits it. Bitter proof. As *Times* correspondent he had twice the prestige and three times the influence." Money, or the lack of it, had affected Morrison's normally patrician judgment, but in a famine even the devil eats flies.

It took Morrison a while to realize he had blundered badly. Yuan did his own decision making, and his foreign advisers found themselves isolated, and soon stupefied by lack of work. Within three months Morrison was complaining, "My job is becoming an impossible one. I am really heartily sick of it and will leave as soon as I am out of debt."

The president was too busy outwitting rivals to spare time for Morrison. At Yuan's invitation, Sun Yat-sen established a branch of his Kuomintang (KMT) political party in Peking and left the popular politician Sung Chiao-jen in charge. Sung's growing popularity was a direct challenge to Yuan's dictatorship, and on March 20, 1913, as he prepared to board a train in Shanghai, Sung was shot twice in the stomach, dying two days later. Documents turned up implicating Yuan and his cabinet.

Sung's assassination began a reign of terror that Morrison unhappily found himself obliged to defend on a hasty trip to England in June 1914, jeopardizing his own remaining credibility to make a dictator seem worthy. His detractors grew in number.

The way was clear now for Yuan to declare himself emperor. After four centuries of Manchu rule, there would be a Chinese on the throne. Morrison, either willfully ignorant or not taking it seriously, encouraged Yuan's fantasy by gilding his public image, giving Yuan a false impression of the strength of his position. Yuan's eldest son, excited about the idea of a dynasty's one day making him emperor, too, urged his father on.

A grass-roots Yuan-for-Emperor Association was launched, followed by a unanimous vote in the National Assembly and a petition campaign making it "impossible" for Yuan to refuse the mandate of heaven. On December 11, 1915, Morrison wrote in his diary: "Yuan Shih-kai today accepted the Throne. Quite a surprise!!! Such is the silly make-believe."

Morrison was not present for the dress rehearsal of Yuan's coronation, but he heard about it: "Yuan was sitting with his Crown; 3 thrones at his side for the 1st, 2nd, and 3rd wives on descending levels. First wife came in annoyed; kow-towed, took her proper seat. Long delay and 2nd wife, the Korean wife, failed to come. Sent for peremptorily. She came in but refused to take her seat, saying Yuan had promised her a throne on the same level as the No.1. Hearing this No. 1 jumped down from the Throne and went for No. 2 with her fingers. The Master of Ceremonies . . . did not lay impious hands upon the struggling Empresses, whereupon Yuan waddled down from the Throne and tried to separate the 2 combatants. Order was finally restored but the rehearsal was postponed." Not an auspicious portent.

Yuan's dynasty started officially on January 1, 1916, under the reign name Hung-hsien, the "Grand Constitutional Era." Protest was loud and long; Yuan had miscalculated public opinion badly. Unaware of the irony in his remark, Morrison wrote in his diary, "Surrounded by sycophants the Emperor does not hear the truth." Military leaders in Yunnan sent an open telegram denouncing Yuan and proclaiming the independence of their province. Other provinces followed.

As the crisis grew, obese and unwashed Emperor Yuan schlepped around the palace in an old velvet coat, which Morrison called a "hoary garment that . . . has been in use summer and winter since early in 1912." In desperation Yuan grudgingly took off his crown near the end of March 1916 and resumed the presidency. He had been emperor of China for eighty-three days.

Morrison saw him late the next month and was startled. "Marked change since I saw him last. Has lost weight; his face somewhat drawn. . . . suffering from tooth-ache and rubbed his teeth with alcohol using a chopstick and cotton wool as a cleaner. He said . . . he was tired in the head and in the body. He would like to retire and have some rest and he looked like it."

One month later President Yuan was too sick to conduct business. The medicines he was given had a salutary effect on his bowels:

> Yuan's belly was rumbling fiercely and he was calling at the top of his voice to be helped out of bed to the privy. If he had been a southerner, this would have been simply a matter of going to a commode in a corner of the room, but . . . being a native of Honan he was . . . accustomed to squat on his haunches in an outhouse. He was supported to this place—not without difficulty for he was grossly corpulent—but as soon as he got there, he fell down head first, and when the servants raised him to his feet he was not an agreeable sight. Hearing the outcry, all the concubines came running, but they stopped short and covered their noses.

Here was a sign of celestial displeasure. Yuan Shih-kai, the eighty-three-day wonder, died at 3:00 A.M. on June 6, 1916, at age fifty-six, the cause officially uremic poisoning. On his deathbed Yuan chided his ambitious son Yuan Ko-ting, so recently the heir apparent: "It is you who have brought me to this." The great man's last words were: "He destroyed me."

Although his patron was gone, Morrison continued to collect his annual Chinese government salary of £3,500 plus expenses and witnessed a brief comic-opera restoration of the Ching Dynasty. On July 1, 1917, the citizens of Peking awoke to find themselves again the subjects of a Manchu emperor, the eleven-year-old Pu Yi, who had abdicated in 1912 to make way for Yuan. People again scurried about the streets in court costumes from another age, sporting false Manchu queues fashioned out of horsehair, and tailors sold dragon flags as fast as they could make them.

The restoration lasted only twelve days. A month later Morrison sold his library to a wealthy Japanese for £35,000 and considered returning to Australia. Before he and Jennie could reach a decision, he was sent to Paris to help China prepare for the Versailles peace talks. She joined him there.

Despite his rugged frame, Morrison's health was not good, and suddenly deteriorated with alarming speed. For years he had struggled to keep his weight down; now it was falling off. He had difficulty carrying his briefcase, describing himself as "appallingly ill" and "yellow, emaciated and ghastly." A doctor diagnosed jaundice. The Morrisons went to England to seek treatment. After a diagnosis of acute pancreatitis, he entered an expensive nursing home where patients dressed for dinner. By October 1919 he was down to ninety-seven pounds. Desperate, he moved with Jennie and their two sons to a house in Devon in March 1920, "in the hope that a balmier air . . . may enable me to recover sufficient strength to return to China." Had his final meeting with Robert Hart occurred now, Morrison might not have been so brutal with the epitaph: "Wretched feeble animal, he has caused infinite suffering in his time and has been singularly unjust."

After spending most of his career cultivating the British at the expense of the Chinese, if he was going to die Morrison wanted it to be in China, "among the Chinese who have treated me with such consideration for so many years." Jennie went to London to make arrangements for their return to Peking but received an urgent telegram and hurried back to Devon, where she was at his side when he died. She was so devastated that she succumbed to grief herself three years later, at age 34.

Backhouse outlived them all. He was a young man when Tzu Hsi died, and he survived Morrison and Bland to become the guru of Peking. Around him from time to time clustered the curious and the sincere, charmed or conned by this genial eccentric. As he became more of a recluse, they had to seek him out.

Now and then he was nearly exposed as a swindler but he always eluded his victims. In 1915 the British minister in Peking, Sir John Jordan, commissioned the forty-two-year-old Backhouse to procure arms from his "secret Chinese sources." After arranging for £2 million sterling to be wired to a bank in China as payment for the weapons, negotiations dragged on for months until it became clear that Backhouse was running a scam. Prudently, Edmund took this moment to make one of his discreet periodic trips to England, to check on his gifts of "rare and valuable" Chinese manuscripts to the Bodleian Library at Oxford. Over the years Backhouse provided the Bodleian with some twenty-seven thousand Chinese volumes and scrolls. Many were only copies or crude forgeries, but the library was taken in and had his name added to its marble honor roll along with Paul Mellon and the Rockefeller Foundation.

In 1916 Edmund offered his services to the American Bank Note Company of New York, agreeing to procure, through his excellent connections in Peking, the contract to print money for China. He produced signed contracts and received nearly £6,000 in commissions, plus expenses. When the contracts were presented to Chinese officials, they protested that they did not know any Backhouse and that the documents and signatures were forgeries. Edmund fled to Canada till the scandal subsided.

During this same period he offered to sell an American executive rare Chinese curios that he had acquired over the years, along with pearls that had previously belonged to Empress Dowager Tzu Hsi. The curios were phony, the pearls imaginary.

Edmund inherited his father's baronetcy in 1918, becoming Sir Edmund Backhouse, which added to his appearance of legitimacy. But that was all he inherited.

In 1921 he went completely native. He lived away from any Westerners on the far side of the Forbidden City at 19 Shih Fuma Street, in the Tartar City. He dressed in a long white silk Chinese gown and let his beard grow long and full—it eventually turned white as well—until he resembled a venerable sage. If he went out, he sent his Chinese boy ahead to warn him if any Westerners were about. If he passed them in a rickshaw, he hid his face with a handkerchief. He declined all social invitations. Two Anglican bishops kept an eye on him and administered his allowance.

Backhouse was a recluse, but he was always available to tell gamy stories to anyone who wanted to listen. Hope Danby, a painter and writer who lived in Peking from 1926 to 1942, regarded him as a benevolent, absent-minded professor, with an "intimate knowledge of Chinese history." Others who tracked him down were Maurice Collis and Harry Hussey, whose works were among the most malignant and damaging to the historical image of the empress dowager. Libraries are full of them.

With the outbreak of the Pacific war in December 1941, Edmund was liable for internment by the Japanese, but in view of his age and infirmity he was allowed to live in a room of a house in the British legation compound, coming back to the scene of his early swindles. There he came under the care and protection of Switzerland's honorary consul, Dr. Reinhard Hoeppli. The German-born Hoeppli had been a doctor in the kaiser's navy before becoming a Swiss citizen. A bachelor fond of travel, he had roved the world till 1930, when he joined Peking Union Medical College. When Switzerland took over responsibility for American, Dutch, and British interests in Japanese-occupied territories, Hoeppli was given the Swiss consul's job in Peking.

Hoeppli was fascinated by the eccentric Englishman in the British legation, spending many hours listening to Edmund's stories. His first impressions were of "a distinguished looking old scholarly gentleman . . . who had a definite charm and spoke and behaved with exquisite slightly old-style politeness," he said.

> His long white beard gave him a venerable aspect, his walking was slow and somewhat unsteady. . . . His eyes were remarkable for the very different expressions they were able to show in rapid succession. . . . They might at one moment have the quiet look of an old scholar, quite in line with beard, dress and refined politeness; suddenly they became the eyes of a monk in religious ecstasy, to change again into the eyes of an old salacious profligate with a very clever cunning look. . . . It was his eyes which betrayed the fact that the first and dominant impression of an old scholar represented only a part of his personality. Gradually after somewhat closer contact one obtained an entirely different aspect, that of a person who notwithstanding age and ailments, still harboured a strong sexuality and who, after some external inhibitions had been overcome, revealed with lascivious pleasure the erotic part of his personality. In such moments, he presented occasionally the very picture of an old satyr enjoying happy memories.

In April 1943 Sir Edmund entered the French St. Michael's Hospital in Peking, where he spent the final months of his life. Hoeppli found him irritable and gloomy, preoccupied with his impending death, and came up with the idea of giving his patient something to occupy his time and earn a bit of pocket money. (Sir Edmund's remittances had been cut off by the war.) Hoeppli commissioned two manuscripts: "The Dead Past" and "Decadence Mandchoue." Hoeppli said that he alone was "responsible for their existence. . . . Both represent essentially collections of the various stories which Sir Edmund told [me] on [my] frequent visits during the first year of the Pacific War. Whatever the historic value of these stories may be, it seemed regrettable that they should be lost."

"The Dead Past" was a nonstop outpouring of hatred and loathing toward everyone Backhouse had known in his childhood and student days before coming to China, with particular emphasis on his mother. "Decadence Mandchoue," completed in May 1943, was nearly one hundred fifty thousand words and catalogued his relations, sexual and otherwise, with the Manchu court from his arrival in Peking in 1899 until the looting of the imperial tombs in 1928.

The most curious sections of these two memoirs were the passages in which he described the long sexual liaison he claimed he had with Tzu Hsi after she turned sixty-seven years old. He had been regaling gullible people with the stories for decades. He also found many opportunities in the narrative to denounce and ridicule his former friends and acquaintances for the last time, including George Morrison, "that arch-liar . . . (now howling in the deathless flames of Hell)." Bland was a "detestable personality."

Whether or not Sir Edmund used the *Venice Letters* as a model, his memoirs closely follow the tradition of Victorian pornography, except that his characters were Chinese and Manchu mandarins and British prime ministers instead of Venetian stevedores and gondoliers. Hoeppli had no way of knowing whether the stories were true or imaginary, but he knew Sir Edmund's reputation as a distinguished sinologue and eminent historian and rightly grasped that these memoirs would be of value to scholars. Just how they would be of value did not matter so long as they were preserved for study.

Hoeppli believed both works contained elements of great historical significance, such as the circumstances of the deaths of Emperor Kuang Hsu and Empress Dowager Tzu Hsi. "Both Kuang Hsu and Tzu Hsi according to this work were murdered. . . . When [I] mentioned the old rumour that Kuang Hsu had died after having eaten poisoned tarts, Sir Edmund declared that such an attempt had been made but had failed. A scholar with access to the Archives of the British Foreign Office will have no difficulty to verify Sir Edmund's statement in 'Decadence Mandchoue' as he personally told [me] that he at that time had fully informed the British Government."

Hoeppli intended to publish the memoirs in a small private edition for scholars, but doubts were cast on their authenticity by the French consul, Roland de Margerie, to whom Hoeppli showed the manuscripts. Just as Lewisohn and other critics of the Ching Shan diary had found many inaccuracies in the early Backhouse and Bland biographies, similar inaccuracies blemished "Decadence Mandchoue." Hoeppli was prepared to overlook such things, as Sir Edmund had worked without references or notes.

Among the many bizarre episodes in "Decadence Mandchoue" was a visit Sir Edmund claimed he made to the tomb of the empress dowager to pay his last disrespects, as it were.

In the summer of 1928, the tombs of Emperor Chien Lung and Tzu Hsi were broken into and looted by Nationalist Chinese troops. Generalissimo

Chiang Kai-shek made no effort to apprehend and punish those responsible for the desecration of the tombs, and some of the jewelry taken from the bodies—gold, pearls, rubies, sapphires, emeralds, and diamonds—ended up in the possession of the Chiang family while some of Tzu Hsi's pearls were used to decorate Madame Chiang's shoes.

The twice-dethroned Emperor Pu Yi received an official account of a commission of Manchu nobles and ladies who put the tombs back in order. The site was a scene of desolation; not a pine tree was left, and the open crypt of Chien Lung had been flooded by recent storms. Gathering their courage they crawled "like snakes" down a tunnel to reach the burial chamber of Tzu Hsi. By lantern light they saw her empty coffin on end against a wall. The room was stripped bare of ritual furniture, and the lid of the outer casket was upside down in a corner. A plank had been thrown across the upended casket itself, and when they pulled this away they found themselves looking, after twenty years, upon Tzu Hsi. She was lying on her face, left hand behind her, hair disheveled, naked to the waist with only pantaloons and stockings remaining, stripped of her richly decorated funereal garments and gems.

"Very gently," said the commissioners, "we turned the Jade Body on its back. The complexion of the face was wonderfully pale, but the eyes were deeply sunken and seemed like two black caverns. There were signs of injury to the lower lip." The Manchu ladies took over, cleaning and wrapping the body in rolls of silk. Tzu Hsi was then returned to her coffin and the lid resealed.

In "Decadence Mandchoue" Sir Edmund claimed he went with a Chinese friend to see firsthand what damage had been done. It comes as no surprise that his physical description of the scene bears no resemblance to the Manchu account, since his was entirely imaginary.

We were horrified to see huddled on the pavement in that blistering sun . . . an uncomely shape of tiny dimension which was of human form, stark naked and ghastly . . . lying before us, her glorious raven hair shockingly disheveled, half-rust half-ruined ebony, her face drawn and ghastly but with familiar features as recognizeable as when I had last seen her . . . twenty years ago; her mouth wide extended and set in a horrible grin, eyes partially open and glazed with a yellowish film, her breasts covered with thousands of hideous black spots, body distorted and transmuted to a leathery or parchment hue, the left side of the abdomen presenting a different colour from the rest of her body, probably due to the hemorrhage after Yuan's fatal shot, her once beautiful pudenda which I had formerly (to her pleasuring and mine own) so playfully fondled . . . displayed before us in their full sacrilegious nudity, the pubic hair still abundant.

Like everything else he had ever written about her, his final words were pornographic fiction.

"With difficulty (for everything had been looted) we obtained a strip of matting and covered up Her Majesty's secret parts from the gaze of the vulgar."

NOTES

The scene at Hart's garden party is drawn from the letters, diaries, and published works of many Westerners who attended these affairs. Morrison relentlessly recorded in his diaries the foibles of these foreign residents. Hart also kept diaries but was the soul of discretion. Hart's huge correspondence includes published and unpublished materials that are at The Queen's University, Belfast, Northern Ireland. Hart's handwriting deteriorated over the years, requiring any researcher to spend many difficult hours decoding his writing. When we began research for this book, the only Hart letters that had been published were his correspondence with his London agent James Duncan Campbell, published by Harvard in two volumes as *The I. G. in Peking, Letters of Robert Hart/Chinese Maritime Customs, 1868–1907* (1975) edited by John K. Fairbank, Katherine Frost Bruner, and Elizabeth MacLeod Matheson. All Hart correspondence listed in these notes is from this two-volume set, except where otherwise noted. Later, Harvard published a first volume of the Hart diaries as *Entering China's Service: Robert Hart's Journals, 1854–1863* (1986) edited by Katherine F. Bruner, John K. Fairbank, and Richard J. Smith. But much remains.

Morrison's correspondence includes published and unpublished materials. The largest collection of his published letters is a two-volume set edited by Lo Hui-men, *The Correspondence of G. E. Morrison* (1976, 1978), including letters written to and by Morrison. Lo's encyclopedic work provides many biographical details about Morrison and his contemporaries and is an invaluable reference tool. Because of space constraints, Lo had to omit certain passages from the correspondence, and in many cases we have used the full texts from the original letters, some of which are housed in the Mitchell Library, Sydney, Australia.

Like Hart, Morrison kept an elaborate daily diary during his nearly twenty years in China. These diaries are preserved at the Mitchell Library, and we scoured them all. Fortunately, Morrison had a clear hand. In 1928 a portion of his diaries covering the years 1899–1901 was edited by the *Times* journalist John

B. Capper. When Capper's manuscript was finished, publication was prevented by the trustees of the Morrison Papers (among them Sir Miles Lampson, then British minister in China), who considered the documents as politically sensitive. In the mid-1960s author Cyril Pearl saw the original diaries and included many quotes from them in his book, *Morrison of Peking* (1967). Apparently some of the more salacious remarks quoted by Pearl offended the trustees, for we discovered certain entries were now missing from the originals. Except where noted, we are quoting directly from the original diaries.

p. 4 "Crafty and inconstant": Sir Claude MacDonald writing to Morrison, [September] 1898, quoted in Lo Hui-men.

"The two curios of Peking": Stanley Bell, *Hart of Lisburn*, p. 73.

Programs for these parties are in the Hart Collection at The Queen's University Library, Belfast.

5 "Ironclad autocrat": Paul King, *In the Chinese Customs Service*, p. 246. King was one of Hart's employees, with a long career in Customs from 1874 to 1920.

6 "When in doubt": an article in the *Times*: "For a quarter of a century, at least the final instructions given successively to every British Minister on his appointment to Peking might be summed up in half-a-dozen words: 'When in doubt, consult Sir Robert Hart,' " quoted in Pearl, p. 83.

"I rarely meet the I.G.": Morrison letter to J.O.P. Bland, 26 May 1897, from Lo Hui-men.

7 "Poignant regret": Morrison diary, 7 January 1899.

"Thanks to [Morrison]": *China Mail*, 8 September 1899. Morrison pasted the clipping in his diary.

"The intelligent anticipation of events": Peter Fleming, *The Siege at Peking*, pp. 61–62.

"Fat and gushing": Pearl, p. 121.

The anecdote about Jack the Ripper: ibid., p. 83. The real identity of Jack the Ripper is still debated. Recent books attempt to implicate Lord Salisbury in a conspiracy to protect the throne, of which Jack the Ripper was a part, but the evidence so far does not survive serious scrutiny. Morrison was jesting.

8 Di Martino's mistress is in Pearl.

Viceroy Li once served future president Hoover a glass of champagne. Hoover gagged and discovered that Li had served the same wine to others and poured their dregs back into the bottle for the next occasion. Hoover was part of a consortium that acquired Li's Kaiping Coal Mines. Hoover's shady dealings in China are detailed in Ellsworth Carlson, *The Kaiping Mines*, and George Nash, *The Life of Herbert Hoover*.

Published sources avoid calling Juliet the daughter of Robert Bredon, specifying that she was the daughter of Lily Bredon. In his diaries Morrison stated, "Juliet Bredon is the offspring of the adultery of Charlie Begg and Lady Bredon. This explains why she has never married." Morrison diary, 19 April 1909.

Morrison's caddish sniping about Lily Bredon's love affairs can be found in many places in his diary. See especially the entries of 8 May 1900 and 19 September 1907.

"Very Welsh": Morrison diary, 28 July 1899.

Pearl includes many anecdotes about Nestegaard from the Morrison diaries. Pearl, p. 121.

The conversion figures are from Morrison's *An Australian in China*, which notes that some fifteen hundred Protestant missionaries gathered only slightly more than three thousand Chinamen into the fold (few of whom were genuine converts) at a cost of £350,000 sterling.

p. 9 "Pushing Englishman": Hart to Campbell, 17 December 1899.

"That awful woman": Morrison diary, 7 and 17 May 1903.

The bare pubes anecdote is from Nigel Cameron, *Barbarians and Mandarins*, p. 368.

11 "Kang Yu-wei has shown the cloven foot": undated entry in the 1898 volume of Morrison's diaries.

12 "As near as any book": *The Book Review Digest*, 1910, p. 37.

"That the work is authoritative": the *New York Times*, 26 November 1910.

"Rarely is a book": *The Spectator*, 22 October 1910.

13 The Backhouse Chinese manuscripts at the Bodleian Library have been called into question in various ways over eighty years. Doubts arise mainly over the authenticity of particular works, some thought to be forgeries, others only recent copies. Backhouse always was prudent in mingling real and fake material. Serious questions also exist about the manuscripts' provenance—how they came into his hands before going to the Bodleian. Many rare and priceless manuscripts were looted by Westerners from Peking's great Hanlin Library before it was burned down during the Boxer siege, an atrocity that they craftily blamed upon the Chinese.

ONE: *Lady Yehenara*

18 Bland and Backhouse popularized the notion that Yehenara's milk-name was Orchid, but there is no real evidence to support it and every reason to believe that Backhouse made up things as he went along.

19 Anti-Manchu propagandist Wen Ching repeats (then denies) the Canton sex slave story, a rhetorical device he and Backhouse frequently used—to publish a slander and then deny its truth, knowing that the slander will endure.

Harry Hussey invented details about her ne'er-do-well father and repeats the Russian story, then denies its authenticity.

"Her father" is from *China under the Empress Dowager*, p. 2. Hereafter this book will be referred to as *CUED*.

20 "Her father was honest": Marina Warner, *The Dragon Empress*, p. 16.

p. 20 "A lady of great ability": *CUED*, p. 7.

Yehenara's mother as a great beauty is from Maurice Collis's play, *The Motherly and Auspicious* (1944). The play is cited as an example of falsified biography only because Collis makes extravagant claims for authority in his introduction to the play, claiming many hitherto unknown sources about the empress dowager's life.

21 "Bearing the mark of the fox": Harry Hussey, *Venerable Ancestor*, pp. 11–12, 23. There is a remarkable similarity in the claims of Backhouse, Collis, Hussey, and other writers as to their sources for these stories. Hussey describes one of his key sources as being "an old Manchu scholar," whom he fails to identify; in fact, all these writers are really referring to Backhouse as their source.

"It is not certain": Daniele Vare, *The Last Empress*, p. 5. Vare repeats much of the Backhouse gossip, but he was one of the first to challenge in print the authenticity of major portions of *CUED*, especially the Ching Shan diary.

"Slim bodies": Hussey, pp. 55–56.

"Apparently [he] was": ibid., p. 50.

She put her own name on the list: Hussey, p. 59.

22 "On the day of her examination": Frank Dorn, *The Forbidden City*, p. 202.

" 'The odor of the fox' ": Hussey, pp. 172–73.

The British author is Collis, the source for the sexual anecdote.

23 Haldane provides the detail about purchasing a male baby.

25 "I have had a very hard life": Princess Derling, *Two Years in the Forbidden City*. Derling was denounced as a fake by Reginald Johnston, the tutor to Emperor Pu Yi, so her books have been ignored. In fact, Derling did live in the Forbidden City for nearly two years, acting as an interpreter for Tzu Hsi, and Derling's sister and brothers were also at court during this time. The closeness of Derling and her siblings with Tzu Hsi is irrefutable—her brother took a series of photographs of the dowager and her court, showing them together on many occasions. Many of these photographs appear as illustrations in Derling's memoirs. Johnston's motive in denouncing her is obvious: he was an intimate friend of Backhouse, and Derling's picture of Tzu Hsi challenged the Backhouse caricature.

27 In the melee Bandit Li escaped to Peking, where out of spite he murdered General Wu's father, the concubine, and everybody else in the family. Eluding capture, Li sought refuge in Hupeh Province, but peasants caught him stealing food and clubbed him to death.

28 Prince Kung's birthname was I Hsin.

Many biographical details about the Chings are taken from Arthur Hummel's *Eminent Chinese of the Ching Period.* Despite the fact that Hummel relied in some instances on the works of Bland and Backhouse, his work remains valuable for this period of history. Because of the ease with which Backhouse inventions can be spotted, stylistically, Hummel's usefulness is not diminished.

In all, Emperor Tao Kuang had ten daughters and nine sons, three of whom died in infancy. Hummel, p. 576.

I Tsung was the birthname of Prince Tun.

p. 29 Married to a girl from the Niuhuru clan. This is also the clan of Hsien Feng's mother. The Niuhuru clan gained enormous prestige when its leader was slain by his own son for acting arrogantly toward Nurhachi, the dynasty's founder. In appreciation, Nurhachi gave the Niuhuru boy high station and military rank, to pass on from generation to generation. The Niuhuru and the royal Aisin Gioro clans were thereafter intertwined by marriage. Hummel, pp. 221–22, 286. Prominent Niuhuru included Emperor Chien Lung's mother, and his infamous favorite, Ho Shen. Ibid., pp. 288, 369.

Nowhere were women: Little has changed since the third century, as shown by a court case in Confucian South Korea in 1989: in the course of resisting rape by two men, a young woman bit off a piece of one man's tongue; the court found her guilty of "excessive self-defense."

The poem is from Alasdair Clayre, *The Heart of the Dragon*, pp. 68–69.

31 "Some were as young as fifteen." Tzu Hsi's son, Emperor Tung Chih, left behind several ladies who were thirteen when they married him and were widowed two years later. In 1924, thirteen years after the establishment of the republic, concubines of former emperors were still living inside the Forbidden City.

32 She entered: The date 1852 is from Luke Kwong, *A Mosaic of the Hundred Days*, p. 31. The year's preparation outside the Forbidden City is from Reginald Johnston, *Twilight in the Forbidden City*. Kwong has carefully reconstructed Tzu Hsi's true status at court during her rise from concubine to empress. See his "Imperial Authority in Crisis," p. 235.

"Learned to paint skilfully": *CUED*, pp. 7–8.

"Almost, if not quite, illiterate": Wen Ching, *The Chinese Crisis from Within*, p. 74. This statement (one of the few Wen Ching made that was accurate) has been corroborated by scholar Luke Kwong, who has done much to challenge the image of Tzu Hsi as an evil mastermind.

33 The four tribes of the Nara clan were the Yehe, Ula, Hada, and Hoifa, of which the Yehe were most warlike. Yehe is Mongol for "great tribe." According to tradition, the Nara got their name when the clan's founder repulsed a Mongol attack. Amazed at his prowess, the Mongols shouted, asking him what his name was. He answered with the challenge, "Nara," meaning "Come and get it." The Mongols decided it was wiser not to. The Yehenara and Ulanara were originally enemies of Nurhachi, resisting his attempts to buy them off with women. Nurhachi became angry when one of the girls he gave the Ulanara was used for target practice with whistling arrows; he brought them to heel in 1620. Hummel, pp. 17–18.

The proper number of imperial bedmates is from Robert van Gulik, *Sexual Life in Ancient China*, p. 17. He cites the appropriate numbers of concubines, with the ranks and roles of the various ladies.

p. 34 Details of Taoist sexual customs and attitudes are from Reay Tannahill, *Sex in History;* Eric Chou, *The Dragon and the Phoenix;* and Gulik.

Gulik provides the precoitus routine, pp. 18, 190.

36 Brief mentions of Princess Jung An are in Hummel, p. 380.

Rules for a healthy conception and pregnancy are in Miyazaki Ichisada, *China's Examination Hell,* p. 13; Gulik, p. 17; and Tannahill, p. 173.

37 "When I arrived at Court": Derling, p. 251. This statement, while it flatters Tzu Hsi, is more or less borne out by the recent research of Luke Kwong.

Yehenara's son was given the name Tsai Chun, but reigned as Tung Chih, which is how we refer to him in this volume for the sake of simplicity. See "Tsai Chun" in Hummel, bearing in mind that the account is tainted by Backhouse.

38 Yehenara's lack of leverage is confirmed by Kwong.

39 "As has always": Derling, p. 252.

40 "I was lucky": ibid., p. 251. This quote, published in 1911, is borne out by revisionist scholars Kwong and Sue Fawn Chung.

"I had . . . quite a lot of trouble": Derling, p. 252. Doubtless it grated on Tzu Hsi that she had to take second place to Tzu An when Tzu An was two years younger.

The second son is mentioned in Kwong, "Imperial Authority . . ." p. 235; and Hummel, p. 380.

TWO: *Foreign Devils*

42 Christopher Hibbert gives the British view in *The Dragon Wakes;* the classics are John Fairbank's *Trade and Diplomacy on the China Coast* and H. B. Morse's *The International Relations of the Chinese Empire.* But the most balanced is Shen Wei-tai's *China's Foreign Policy, 1839–1860.*

In nineteenth-century England and France opium was no more evil than alcohol; fashionable for medication and meditation, in its raw form for smoking or eating and as the kicker in tonics like Godfrey's *Cordial* and Dalby's *Carminativa.* Upright Britons grew plots of poppies at home. In China, opium had been cultivated for centuries, but the trade was monopolized by powerful families.

43 "How, alas!": Shen Wei-tai, p. 63.

Commissioner Lin Tse-hsu had such an unclouded reputation that he was nicknamed "Blue Sky." See Arthur Waley on the opium war.

45 "After a long period": Ssu-yu Teng and John Fairbank, *China's Response to the West,* pp. 24–25. Lin thought that if he cut off rhubarb supplies to England, Britons would die of constipation. He persuaded the emperor to issue an edict obliging the West to pay for rhubarb with silver, reversing the outflow of precious metal.

"Unjustifiable imprisonment": Shen Wei-tai, p. 72. Lin dissolved the opium in lime and flushed it into the sea, after apologizing to the Sea Spirit.

A committee of the House of Commons concluded that opium trafficking was done "with the sanction, implied, if not openly expressed . . ." of the British government. Ibid., p. 73.

"To discover the perpetrators": ibid., p. 78. Privately Elliot thought opium was "staining the British character with deep disgrace," no better than piracy, but it was his job to protect it. Ibid., p. 86, note 104. As the *Times* of 6 April 1843 pointed out: "morality and religion, and the happiness of mankind, and friendly relations with China, and new markets for British manufactures were all very fine things . . . [but] the opium trade was worth . . . 1,200,000 pounds a year . . ."

p. 46 "A war more unjust": Shen Wei-tai, pp. 87–88.

The tragicomic confrontation at Ningpo is described by Pei in Waley.

China's treaty with the U.S. was negotiated by Caleb Cushing, who got the job by chance during musical chairs in the last months of the Tyler Administration. Cushing bought a formal diplomatic uniform with gold braid because "a people who in time of war, expect to repel an invading army by terrific pictures of wild animals . . . must place great reliance on the importance of external appearances."

Tao Kuang's poignant end is described by William Speer in *The Oldest and the Newest Empire*, p. 368.

China had been in the hands of a good man who could do nothing right. He had not even built himself a proper tomb. Modestly he had set aside only a small sum, and the builders had produced a cut-rate vault that leaked so badly it had to be abandoned. A tomb that did not leak was built at a different location.

Unless specified, we use Western ages. By Chinese reckoning, Hsien Feng was twenty years old (sui generis) from conception.

The French Orientalist Henri Cordier (1849–1925) opined, "Hsien Feng had not a single quality to redeem his defects, too unintelligent to realize that the Manchu dynasty, foreign in a land which was hostile to it, was running towards destruction if the trend of its policy was not completely changed; profiting in no way from the lessons of the past, unconscious that the rebellions breaking out in his empire were only precursory signs of a storm which would sweep away his race . . . [he] let his ship wander according to the current of events, incapable of directing it through the channel, strewn with rocks, in which it sailed." Better to say events were moving faster than the ship, rendering its rudder useless. Quoted in Shen Wei-tai, p. 137.

47 Hummel and Miyazaki deal with these currency scandals.

48 In 1861, after the Peking debacle, Bowring was reposted to Italy, where he died in 1872, his dream unfulfilled.

Our appraisal of Parkes is based on Hart. See his journal, 20 March 1858, for a firsthand description.

49 "Mainly by never giving in": Stanley Lane-Poole, quoted in Shen Wei-tai, p. 137.

p. 49 Portuguese kidnapped many thousands of Chinese (rich and poor) and sold them as slaves or indentured coolies in all parts of the world. The inhumanity of this trade was beyond belief.

Best accounts of the *Arrow* are in J. Y. Wong, "The Arrow Incident," and in Shen Wei-tai.

50 "Laughed at me": Wong, p. 378.

"On British soil": Shen Wei-tai. British investigators determined that the *Arrow* was a fence ship for pirates, that the Chinese marines had behaved correctly, and that Parkes was in the wrong. But the damage had been done.

Michael Seymour was the uncle of Edward Seymour, who in 1900 answered MacDonald's plea to save the legations. The nephew served under his uncle in the early 1860s. Admiral Sir Michael Seymour, *My Naval Career and Travels*, p. 115.

"You have turned a consul": Shen Wei-tai.

The French used as their excuse the murder of Abbé August Chapdelain, in February 1856.

51 Lord Elgin's voyage from England was interrupted by the Sepoy Mutiny, obliging him to divert troops to Calcutta. Atrocities committed by the Sepoys on British men, women, and children inflamed public opinion in England against "Asiatics" in general. When the Sepoys were put down, Elgin resumed his China mission with fresh orders to take Canton by force.

U.S. envoy William Reed, a Philadelphia politician, was instructed by President Buchanan to say that America had no territorial or political designs on China but wanted whatever was granted to Britain and France. W.A.P. Martin said Reed was a man of "no fixed principles." Reed wrote to the secretary of state (May 16, 1857) that "all the consequences of (the first Opium War) . . . were favorable to the commerce of the world . . ."

According to Reed's son, who accompanied his father, Commissioner Yeh "was caught [by Harry Parkes] climbing over a wall. [Imprisoned on H.M.S. *Inflexible*] he was now a most unpleasant guest . . . drank three bottles of champagne every day, [and] never washed nor changed his clothes." Diary of William Reed, Jr., Manuscript Collection, Library of Congress. Yeh was shipped to Calcutta, jailed at Fort William and Tolly Gunge, where he died of boredom at fifty-one. Epitaph by a Chinese essayist: "He did not fight, he did not keep peace; he did not defend the city; he did not surrender; neither did he escape when he was in danger, nor did he die when he was made prisoner; . . . such equanimity is unparalleled . . .": Shen Wei-tai, p. 148.

"A scene of great desolation": young William Reed, Jr.'s, diary. "Where the Factories once stood, nothing remained but ruins; no one could ever have imagined what Canton had been."

Colonel Thomas Holloway and Captain F. Martineau des Chavez ruled with Parkes.

Chihli Province protected Peking's eastern approaches from the sea; its main city, Tientsin, was the chief port of North China, entrepôt for rice and other tribute from South China.

p. 52   The Allies knew the Chinese guns were fixed in masonry and could not be turned. Britain made the same mistake in Singapore. Young Reed says, "Preparations for the attack made a brilliant scene. . . . From every ship went strings of boats, loaded down with men, sailors and marines, with their white caps and helmets, French and English all mixed up together, tricolor and red ensigns . . . all towed by the British gunboats."

Chief negotiator was Grand Secretary Kuei Liang, seventy-three, father-in-law of Prince Kung, "stooped with age, and a little deaf . . . but the lustre of his dark eye indicates that he retains much of his mental vigor . . ." *New York Times*, 23 September 1858. He was helped to his chair by Hua-sha-na, a jolly man with a big nose and a taste for wine. Hummel, p. 430. With them was Kiying, who had negotiated the Treaty of Nanking and who was now gravely ill and half-blind. Hummel, p. 133.

At the time, Lay was employed by China as head of Customs in Shanghai, but at Elgin's urging took time off to harass his employers in Tientsin. His ability to serve two masters made Lay slippery as an amphibian. The inability of Allied leaders to speak Chinese gave Lay leverage, and he became, in one mandarin's words, "discourteous to the extreme." When Kuei Liang pleaded that he would lose his head if he accepted Allied demands, Lay said, "The more I make it appear that you act under compulsion, and in order to prevent an advance on the capital, the more sure will be your personal immunity."

Lay's methods shocked some Westerners. Reed and Admiral Putiatin implored Elgin to restrain him. Elgin told Reed to mind his own business, believing the end justified the means. "Though I have been forced to act almost brutally, I am China's friend in all this." John Lyle Morison's biography, *The Eighth Earl of Elgin*, contains many such fragrant quotes.

53   Frederick Bruce was asked to take an overland route to Peking from Shanghai. Annoyed by this inconvenience, he sailed north to anchor off the Taku Forts, provoking trouble.

"It grieves me" and "Accounts from China": Shen Wei-tai, p. 169.

Commodore Tattnall, who had accompanied John Ward, sent neutral American forces to assist the British, roaring, "Blood is thicker than water" and that he was "damned if he'd stand by and see white men butchered before his eyes": Shen Wei-tai, p. 169, note 113. The *New York Times*, 26 September 1859. reported: ". . . the mud on landing being up to the knees . . . of one thousand men who landed, barely one hundred reached the first of the three wide and deep ditches . . . scarcely twenty had [kept] their rifles or ammunition dry."

54   Elgin was gloomy about his "unwelcome errand." The punishment he was to exact would be excessive and unconscionable. "Can I do anything to prevent England from calling down on herself God's curse for brutalities committed

on another feeble Oriental race? Or are all my exertions to result only in the extension of the area over which Englishmen are to exhibit how hollow and superficial are both their civilisation and their Christianity?" Theodore Walrond, ed. *Letters and Journals of James Eighth Earl of Elgin*, p. 325. The French were under General Cousin de Montauban, a capable but ill-tempered officer. The British commander, Sir James Hope Grant, was a genial man and an accomplished cellist, whose success grew from extreme caution and great popularity with his troops. The British naval commander was the sour-natured Admiral Hope who had (in the words of Karl Marx, then London correspondent of the New York *Daily Tribune*), "so gloriously buried the British forces in the mud" at Taku.

p. 54 This time the Allies attacked from the rear. General Seng, ordered not to put his own life at risk, left a deputy commanding a solid wall of Mongol cavalry. They were cut to pieces by Armstrong field guns, the little Mongol ponies knocked aside by massive Irish chargers. Allied gunners hit the powder magazines, and the battle was over. China lost fourteen hundred men; the Allies, thirty-four. See Hibbert, p. 262.

Taku's surrender was arranged by Harry Parkes, standing in for Horatio Lay, who remained in Shanghai not daring to risk another appearance in the north with Allied armies. Lay was knifed by assailants hired by vengeful Shanghai gentry. Jack Gerson's book, *Horatio Nelson Lay and Sino-British Relations*, is useful and entertaining.

Capture of Tientsin was followed by months of looting and vandalism by French and British troops. English accounts condemn French behavior. The French said that after the British finished "you cannot find so much as a nail . . ." They all drank too much sam-shoo local brew; see Colonel Garnet Wolseley's memoirs. Elgin was exasperated. The Chinese foolishly delayed negotiations long enough to allow an Allied force of nineteen thousand men to assemble. "Here we are, then, with our base established in the heart of the country . . . and these stupid people give me the snub, which obliges me to break with them." Obviously, "a little more bullying" was needed to make Peking "come to its senses." Elgin ignored all peace overtures till he reached Tungchow, five miles east of Peking. See campaign maps in Morse, volume 1.

55 General Seng placed his army as a shield for Peking, fearing that the barbarians might launch a surprise attack to capture the emperor. Two forces of equal size but unequal armament met on a broad plain of sunbaked clay, dotted with kilns and tombs of local gentry. In addition to twenty thousand Mongols, there were eighty-six thousand Manchu Bannermen in and around Peking. Mongol crossbowmen captured Parkes and his party, including Bowlby of the *Times*.

"bad faith of the Chinese": Shen Wei-tai, p. 176.

Chien Lung's improvements to the Summer Palace were financed by the flood of British silver in payment for China's silks and teas, before silver was replaced with opium. Intrigued by tales of the Vatican, Chien Lung filled the northern corner of the palace with Italian Renaissance buildings designed by Jesuit Giuseppe Castiglione, in gardens laid out by Jesuit Michel Benoist.

p. 56 Count d'Herrison said "there was at the entrance of the bridge a Tartar of gigantic size . . . holding an immense yellow banner . . ." Bows and arrows were futile against grapeshot fired between the legs of the Mongol ponies. "The enemy was in full retreat . . . but this Tartar still stood there alone, abandoned by his comrades . . . The shells burst and the bullets whistled around him, but he remained immovable; his courage was sublime, and General Montauban exclaimed: 'Save him!' . . . but at this moment the hail of grape . . . cut him down, and the great banner flew away, carrying with it attached to its pole the arm which had sustained it." (Montauban became the Count of Palikao.)

58 "Nothing like it": Hibbert, p. 272. Soldiers' accounts are sanguine, but American missionary William Speer was horrified: "Into these great depositories of Oriental wealth, which had been multiplying for centuries, the regiments of European and Hindu soldiers, maddened by liquor, utterly beyond all restraint of their officers, profanely plunged, to gorge themselves with what pleased their drunken fancy, and to destroy an equal amount out of the pure love of destruction. . . . Low and vile men made themselves rich with the secret treasures of royalty." Army chaplains cut short Sunday services to loot with their men.

In the Summer Palace the soldiers found imperial lion dogs later christened Pekingese. One called Looty was presented to Queen Victoria, who put a different ribbon around his neck each day of the week. Looty lived to age twelve and had his portrait painted by court artists including Sir Edwin Henry Landseer.

"War is a hateful business": L. Carrington Goodrich and Nigel Cameron, *The Face of China as Seen by Photographers & Travelers*, p. 117.

THREE: *The Palace Coup*

59 The court left the Summer Palace September 22, reaching Jehol October 2. Luke Kwong has reexamined the circumstances of the coup in "Imperial Authority . . ." Tony Teng's study of Prince Kung also is valuable. A splendid map and paintings from MacCartney's journey along the same route in 1793 are in Alain Peyrefitte, *L'Empire Immobile*.

Chien Lung kept Mongols under control by building Lamaist monasteries in Jehol. Since Mongol Lamaism obliged at least one male member in each family to become a celibate monk, this reduced rebellious manpower by half. Chien Lung quipped: "Better a monastery than ten thousand troops."

60 "One of the most melancholy decades": Mary Wright, *The Last Stand of Chinese Conservatism*, p. 7.

"The timid and dissolute emperor": Hibbert, p. 265.

61 "Dreaming as usual": Shen Wei-tai, pp. 174–76.

"Unusually good Confucian monarch": Paul Cohen and John Schrecker, eds. *Reform in Nineteenth Century China*, p. 89.

p. 61   "After a childhood": Wolseley, p. 287.

"Is not such a fool": Walrond, p. 372.

62   She was galvanized: The reconstruction of these events is based on an imperial edict which is quoted later in this chapter on page 77.

63   "The prince is not very clever": Hart letter to Charles Hannen, 9 August 1861. Quoted in Morse, vol. 2, p. 53, note 16.

64   For a description of Kung's palace, see H. S. Chen and G. N. Kates, "Prince Kung's Palace and Its Adjoining Garden in Peking."

During the first five years of Hsien Feng's reign, Prince Kung assisted his brother in many ways, exacting huge "donations" from wealthy Chinese to help pay for defense against Western incursions and Taiping depredations. As the Taipings threatened Peking, the twenty-year-old prince was appointed to the Grand Council and made a lieutenant general. Since then the emperor and his half-brother had fallen out, through the influence of Su Shun. When his mother died in 1856, Kung was reprimanded for negligence in mourning, deprived of all posts, and ordered to return to school to brush up on filial piety. Freed of duties, he wrote poetry, read history, and tended his garden.

Sheng Pao, who was Prince Kung's personal bodyguard, had served under Seng-ko-lin-chin against the Taipings and later the Niens.

65   Sappers were given: Charles "Chinese" Gordon thought the task was easy because the wall was of inferior masonry. But Wolseley, the youngest lieutenant colonel in the British army, was uneasy. As the deadline drew near, he said, "I held my breath . . . we were playing a game of brag. For . . . with the number of rounds we had with us, no effective breach could be hoped for."

Parkes was outraged: U.S. envoy John Ward said, "Parkes . . . was only humiliated by being made to enter Peking in rather a different style from what he had anticipated, having been first bound and thrown into a country wagon and made to perform the kowtow and rub his face in the dirt whenever he passed a Mandarin. An occasional bambooing added to this was all the punishment inflicted upon him, 'tis not considered harsh treatment by those familiar with his history in China and the wrongs and injuries inflicted by him upon the Chinese": National Archives. Record Group 59. There was nothing Kung could do about the twenty other prisoners, taken to the Summer Palace and tortured. Bowlby of the *Times* so infuriated the Gang of Eight that he was given the Death-of-a-Thousand-Cuts and his body fed to imperial pigs. Prince Kung agreed to pay three hundred thousand taels of silver in compensation to their families. An account appeared a few weeks later in the *New York Times*, under the headline HORRIBLE TREATMENT OF THE ENGLISH PRISONERS.

Elgin, viewing the Forbidden City from the top of its walls, saw "a large enclosure crowded with yellow-roofed buildings . . . a few trees dotted among them. It is difficult to imagine how the unfortunates shut up there can ever have any exercise. I don't wonder that the Emperor preferred [the Summer Palace]": Walrond, p. 369. Wolseley argued: "The very gorgeousness [of the Summer Palace] . . . has been one great promoting cause of the luxury and effeminacy which have served to debase the late rulers of China, causing the descendants of fierce warriors to degenerate into mere enervated debauchees": Wolseley, p. 287. Wolseley was the embodiment of militant Victorian morality at midcentury, already becoming the most celebrated officer in the British army, which he eventually led as field marshal and commander in chief.

"Upon the 18th October": Wolseley, p. 278.

The destruction: On a bright October afternoon three years after the looting and burning of the Summer Palace, Anson Burlingame, America's new envoy in Peking, went picnicking with his wife among the ruins. She wrote home on October 11, 1863, that "enough remains to show its former splendor, which must have equaled anything we read of in the Arabian Nights . . . I cannot describe its beauty, even now, and what it must have been in its palmy days, filled our imaginations with wonder." Burlingame Papers, Manuscript Collection, Library of Congress.

p. 66 The day the Peking convention was signed, October 24, 1860, Prince Kung was escorted to the southern part of the Imperial City by Sheng Pao and four hundred horsemen; then, taking only twenty men, he entered the main hall of the Board of Rites. Elgin made it a point to be three hours late, entering Peking with two thousand men in a display of pomp, riding in a sedan chair decorated like the emperor's own but in crimson rather than yellow, borne by sixteen men (a privilege reserved for the emperor). Despite these affronts, Prince Kung made an effort to be gracious, bowed, slightly, clasped Elgin's hands and shook them in the Chinese style. But his feelings could not be concealed. Wolseley said the prince looked "upon the assembled 'Barbarians' almost with a scowl; but this supercilious sneering expression may have partly resulted from his most strangely set eyes. [His] youthful air . . . was contradicted, upon examining him more closely, by a worn-out expression indicative of debauchery, so very common with Asiatic potentates": Wolseley, p. 293. After the signing Prince Kung felt obliged to invite the Western delegation to a banquet, but Elgin declined, fearing they would all be poisoned.

The Tsungli Yamen was established March 11, 1861. Prior to the 1840s, ceremonial contacts with tributary states were handled by the Board of Rites; Russian and frontier affairs, by the Court of Colonial Affairs; and trade with Western countries by the governor-general at Canton. Between the Opium and Arrow wars, 1842–56, the governors-general at Canton and Nanking acted as China's unofficial foreign ministers. The acceptance of foreign diplomatic residence in Peking in 1860 created a need for a foreign office to receive diplomats, allocate quarters, pay indemnities, open Treaty Ports, etc. It functioned as a subcommittee of the Grand Council. In theory it concerned itself only with the execution of foreign policy, not the making of it; policy decisions rested with the emperor and his Grand Council. In practice, under Prince Kung, recommendations of the Yamen were usually approved by the throne. Immanuel C. Y. Hsu, *The Rise of Modern China*, p. 325; S. M. Meng, *The Tsungli Yamen: Its Organization and Functions*, p. 27.

p. 66 "If we do not restrain our rage": Teng and Fairbank, *China's Response*, pp. 47–48.

"A dirty, cheerless, barren building": Meng, p. 25.

"A donkey with a heavy load": ibid., p. 75.

Cavorting with female impersonators: Chou, p. 91. That winter of 1860 the emperor ordered the entire company of the Imperial Recreation Bureau to perform in Jehol. Tony Teng, p. 69.

67 The last attempt to arrange an audience with Emperor Hsien Feng was in 1859 by John Ward, the U.S. envoy who had agreed to come to Peking by road. A modified protocol was suggested, in which Ward would merely touch a knee to the ground and then his fingertips, but Ward, a genteel Southerner, rejected this compromise, saying that he bowed only to God and Woman. His audience was canceled.

"During the last year": Derling, pp. 251–52.

68 China had a long history: The first Manchu emperor who tackled this problem head-on was the great Kang Hsi, the third son of Emperor Shun Chih. Becoming emperor when he was barely seven years old, Kang Hsi was guided by several advisers, dominated by a Manchu named Oboi who tried in various ways to usurp imperial power. After eight years of Oboi's meddling, when he reached his majority Kang Hsi immediately deposed Oboi, threw him in prison, and took power for himself. Under Kang Hsi the grip of eunuchs on the imperial household was broken. He used harsh measures to dispose of corrupt officials and established his own secret service by sending trusted Chinese into the field as his personal spies.

He was succeeded by his son Yung Cheng, the most tyrannical of all the Manchu emperors. It was said that Kang Hsi had chosen another son as his heir, but the conspiratorial Yung Cheng grabbed the throne for himself by staging a coup with the help of ambitious princes and the Banners. Yung Cheng then proceeded to kill or imprison both the princes, eliminating the chance that another ambitious man might repeat his power grab. Through a campaign of extraordinary terror, Yung Cheng rid the empire of all opposition. He was so successful that for most of the next century no rival prince or faction challenged the throne, making life easy for his son and successor Emperor Chien Lung.

During Chien Lung's reign, China enjoyed peace and relative prosperity, largely due to the police state his father had installed. Luxury was real, but brilliance and good management were illusions. His unparalleled extravagance was underwritten with the silver that was flooding into China in payment for exports to the West of tea, silk, porcelain, and other exotic goods. He grew accustomed to having a bottomless purse.

By 1780, Chien Lung began to exhibit the insanity that flawed his reign. At age sixty-six he developed a grand passion for a young Manchu cavalry officer, Ho Shen. According to popular tradition, the dashing twenty-five-year-old bore a strong resemblance to a beautiful Moslem princess who had been the emperor's lost love in his youth. Chien Lung decided that Ho Shen was his lover reincarnated, and named him vice president of the Board of Revenue, putting him in control of all taxes. He was also made a Grand Councillor, a minister of the Imperial Household, and was allowed to ride his horse inside the Forbidden City. Ho Shen appointed his friends to key posts and persuaded the emperor to wed a royal princess to his son, tying him directly to the imperial family. Thereafter, he openly engaged in extortion of the richest men in the empire acquiring property worth one and a half billion dollars. It infuriated the princes that an interloper like Ho Shen had such power and wealth, but their hands were tied.

Only with Chien Lung's death in 1799 was Ho Shen at last vulnerable. The new Emperor Chia Ching, with the help of his brothers, had Ho Shen arrested and forced him to commit suicide. His treasure and properties were distributed among the princes and grandees as a reward for their service and to guarantee their future loyalty. But Chia Ching made a basic mistake. Unlike Kang Hsi and Yung Cheng, he did not purge all those who might undermine his exclusive control. Chia Ching and every emperor who followed failed to grasp the essentials of Manchu politics.

p. 69   Empresses had been forced to commit suicide: When dynasty founder Nurhachi died at age sixty-seven, a struggle began among his sixteen sons. The mother of Dorgon was forced to commit suicide to clear the way for the seizure of power by his older brother, Abahai. When Abahai died, he too failed to name a successor and the selection of six-year-old Shun Chih was made by a state council. Dorgon got his revenge by having himself named regent during the boy's minority. When Shun Chih died of smallpox at age twenty-three he had eight sons but failed to designate an heir. The choice went to seven-year-old Kang Hsi, guided by four regents. The next four emperors were mature when they gained the throne but succeeded only after conspiracy. Thus conspiracy was the rule rather than the exception.

70   The edict announcing Hsien Feng's death is in Tony Teng, p. 78.

71   "What is to be done": Derling, pp. 251–52.

"His mothers": see edict on page 77.

"I would not wish": Derling, p. 252.

Hsien Feng had stymied: The Gang of Eight did not want Yehenara's son on the throne and tried to substitute a different prince. Their choice was limited by Manchu house rules; to avoid challenges before the Clan Court, they had to pick from the proper generation. A deal apparently was worked out with a black sheep named Tsai Chih to make him a puppet emperor instead of Yehenara's son. While he was the right generation, Tsai Chih was not a royal by blood: he had been adopted by Emperor Tao Kuang's oldest son, who had long since died. Now fifty years old, Tsai Chih was at best a willing pawn. His son, Pu Lun, was twice suggested in 1875 and 1908 as a potential emperor.

72   There are many theories about the seals and who possessed which one. Tony Teng says, "One imperial seal, bearing the characters 'His Majesty has read,'

was placed in the custody of the Gang of Eight; the other, bearing the characters 'The Imperial Hall of Tung-tao' (Hall of the Common Way), was in the custody of Hsien Feng's widowed empress, Tzu An."

p. 74 According to Tony Teng there was a difference of about twenty-four hours in the namings of Tzu An and Tzu Hsi to the position of empress dowager. While Palace Daily Records do not explain this, Teng assumes there was a sharp argument between Su Shun and Yehenara about the granting of honors following Hsien Feng's death. It is likely that Tzu An chimed in on Yehenara's behalf and that Su Shun capitulated in the face of the two women. Tony Teng, p. 79. Until late in life, Tzu Hsi lived in the western sector of the Forbidden City, Tzu An in the east—hence the titles West Empress/East Empress. During the Allied occupation in 1900, these pavilions were looted and damaged by Westerners. Only the chambers of retired concubines in the northeastern sector were spared. When Tzu Hsi returned to Peking in 1901, she took up residence in this northeastern sector, the only area that had not been desecrated/polluted. This is why later maps show her living in the east instead of the west.

Among high officials who began sending memorials to Jehol were Grand Secretaries Chia Chen and Chou Tsu-pei; Censor Tung Yuan-shan made this petition. Mary Wright, *The Last Stand*, p. 17.

76 "No sooner had he approached the body": Tony Teng, p. 85.

77 "More appropriate and convincing": Tony Teng, pp. 87–88. The edict also stated: "Even though the list of Special Regents includes loyal and learned men, your humble servant thinks that it could be more appropriate and convincing to select one or two more from the close members of the Imperial Clan to be appointed as Imperial Regents to guide the Emperor and advise the empress dowagers on national affairs."

"There has never been in our nation's history": ibid. p. 89.

80 "To sow seeds of discord": Tony Teng, pp. 101–102.

Ching Shou, who had been a spy for Prince Kung, was married to Kung's elder half-sister, but she had since died, so her sensibilities were not at issue when it came to determining Ching Shou's guilt or innocence in the Jehol plot.

81 "She put into execution": *CUED*, p. 32.

"Prince Kung . . . in secret correspondence": ibid., p. 36

Collis is just one of many writers who insist that Yehenara was sexually insatiable. Wen Ching claims that the emperor became suspicious of Su Shun, who was "too ardent an admirer of [Yehenara]." Dorn and Haldane made up yarns about her love life with Jung Lu, embroidering upon rumors originating in Bland and Backhouse. Hussey tells us that at Jehol, "Hsien Feng was fast growing weaker. It was evident to everybody that he had only a few weeks, perhaps only days, to live. To relieve him of pain he was kept almost continuously under opium or other drugs. While in this condition Su Shun gradually poisoned his mind against [Yehenara] . . . He accused [Yehenara] of improper relations with [Jung Lu]. How far the conspirators succeeded in convincing the Emperor of this is not known, but [they] did succeed in getting the Emperor to sign a decree appointing them regents . . . still further they induced the Emperor to write a decree to force [Yehenara] to commit suicide on his death": Hussey, p. 115. This is fiction based on drinking-party backbiting decades later.

The idea that Yehenara destroyed the emperor by poison was popularized by Collis, who says a court physician prescribed two small spoons of elixir, but on Yehenara's advice the emperor was taking two bowls each day. When the physician discovered this massive dosage, he was petrified. Collis says eunuch Li Lien-ying appeared with another bowl of the elixir and forced this on the emperor, saying, "[Yehenara] cooked it herself . . . Your Majesty knows Her Highness is a wonderful cook." The emperor soon expired, but Collis says the doctor was so afraid of Yehenara that he ruled it a natural death. Collis obviously knew nothing of the intricate safeguards designed to prevent poisoning at court. Silly as it is, the Collis approach is typical of writing about Tzu Hsi. Communist Chinese movies have Tzu Hsi cutting her enemies into pieces to drop down wells.

The decree supposedly giving Tzu An full power to have Yehenara executed was popularized by Gustav Detring, Hart's Customs commissioner at Tientsin and Viceroy Li's cat's-paw, who was planning to write a dynastic history. His idea is not contemporary with the succession of 1875, but grew out of anti-Manchu gossip two decades afterward. Hart jotted down what Detring said without comment.

p. 82 Lady Jane Grey: The intrigues of the Tudor Court during the English succession crisis of 1553 give some insight into the perilous business of monarchy and regency. On his deathbed, the fifteen-year-old tubercular King Edward VI was persuaded by his powerful adviser, John Dudley, Duke of Northumberland, to denounce his half-sister Mary as a bastard. Ignoring the English laws of inheritance and the will of his father, King Henry VIII, Edward named as his successor his cousin Lady Jane Grey. The fifteen-year-old Lady Jane Grey (who was also Northumberland's daughter-in-law) collapsed in a faint when she learned the news, but nonetheless was proclaimed Queen of England. Her reign was one of the briefest in history. Nine days later, Queen Mary, the legitimate heir to the throne, and her supporters won the day and Lady Jane Grey was imprisoned in the Tower of London. Betrayed by the unscrupulous politicians who had forced her to accept the crown, the reluctant little queen pleaded guilty to the charges of treason and was sentenced to death. Because of the extenuating circumstances, no one really blamed Lady Jane and the sentence was commuted. Unfortunately Lady Jane's father saw this as a sign of weakness on the part of Queen Mary and chose this moment to launch his own rebellion. It was too much for Queen Mary to brook yet another outrage from this unreliable branch of her family and Lady Jane Grey was beheaded on February 12, 1554, four months after the celebration of her sixteenth birthday.

p. 83 "There has been a court revolution": National Archives, Record Group 59.

FOUR: *Behind a Gauze Curtain*

In recent years scholars Luke Kwong and Sue Fawn Chung have been among the pioneers in reassessing the personal character of Empress Dowager Tzu Hsi. Those who rose to her defense after the turn of the century, like Sarah Conger, Derling, and Katherine Carl, were dismissed as imbeciles by contemporary "experts" like J.O.P. Bland. But their perceptions are now being vindicated.

85 "Hazardous and troublous times": Kwong, *Mosaic*, p. 19.

87 The bare facts are that Wu was born in A.D. 625, shortly after the Tang Dynasty was established. At age thirteen she became one of 120 official concubines of dynasty founder Emperor Tai Tsung. Of hundreds of emperors during two thousand years, only a dozen were great men of explosive passions, ruling with an iron fist, reshaping the empire and setting it on a new course that would endure for generations afterward. Emperor Tai Tsung was one of them. Unifying China, he set the stage for a renaissance, a flowering of creativity many scholars believe has not since been equaled. Much of the credit for carrying out these changes, and institutionalizing them, must be shared with Wu, who took power after his death and ruled China for half a century. Those are the few surviving hard biographical details. Thereafter, her story becomes an opera scored for falsetto voices, filled with sexual depravity, murder, and conspiracy—revealing less about Wu than about Chinese men and how they look upon women, especially successful women. Charles Fitzgerald's famous biography, *The Empress Wu*, fails to distinguish between fact and male fantasy.

88 After disposing of female rivals, Wu eliminated meddlesome elder statesmen. In a country where cruelty is an art form, Wu's methods were considered extraordinary. She hounded them to death and purged their families for good measure. It was not unusual for male rulers to do this, but Wu was female. If she did the same things, she was evil and perverse.

"Abase her body": Fitzgerald, p. 44.

Chinese sex games are amusingly detailed in Chou, Gulik, and Tannahill among others.

89 In keeping with the tradition of Chinese anecdotal history, her lovers were prodigiously endowed, particularly a young gambler. Wu supposedly offered to let one of her ladies-in-waiting sample his wares, but the woman balked, exclaiming, "It must be a mule's. I beg to be spared the ordeal." Instead she was permitted to observe the empress exercising her mule: Chou, p. 29. One of Wu's "white faces" was said to have been a traveling salesman named Hsueh, who specialized in aphrodisiacs and gave live demonstrations. Grateful Wu supposedly made this holy man abbot of the White Horse Monastery. The story goes on interminably in Fitzgerald, pp. 129–35.

So powerful did the Changs become that satraps of the court vied to win their favor. One shameless mandarin swooned that the younger Chang must be a reincarnation of a famous sage of the Chou Dynasty, who ascended to heaven on the back of a crane. So taken was Empress Wu with this image that she staged a pageant in which Chang was dressed in feathers and ascended to heaven on the back of a mechanical crane. Fitzgerald, pp. 163–67.

p. 90 The poem is in Hilda Hookham, *A Short History of China*, p. 51.

Tseng's comments are from Kwong, *Mosaic*, pp. 36 and 37.

93 "The infinite resource": J.O.P. Bland, *Recent Events and Present Policies in China*, p. 66.

See Kwong, *Mosaic*, p. 21, about the dowager's literacy.

95 The definition is Webster's.

The North China *Herald* in Shanghai reported at the end of November 1861 that Tzu An was "beautiful, courageous, able and pro-foreign," though on what these appraisals were based is not clear. Although Robert Hart mentions Tzu An briefly in his diary, he makes no mention of her whatever in his voluminous business correspondence with London, except a passing reference to her funeral in a letter dated 30 October 1881. Hummel, p. 297, has a brief biography.

97 Tzu Hsi's craving for fresh air is in Katherine Carl, *With the Empress Dowager of China*, p. 36.

98 "I don't . . . talk about these places": Derling, pp. 320–21.

101 The most reliable record of these daily routines, and their flavor, is preserved by Carl and Derling, who lived in proximity with Tzu Hsi for many months. While their observations were made after the turn of the century, physical details of the Forbidden City and Tzu Hsi's pavilions never altered significantly.

FIVE: *Two Men on a Horse*

105 I. J. Roberts, who had tutored Emperor Hung, wrote: "I [now] believe he is crazy, especially in religious matters. . . . He calls his son the young savior of the Word, and himself the real brother of Jesus Christ": Li Chien-nung, *The Political History of China*, p. 81.

As one historian put it, when Hung failed to become a bureaucrat, he "began to think": Archibald Forbes, *Chinese Gordon*, pp. 32–33. As to being a younger brother of Christ, the idea is not nonsensical. Jesus did have a younger brother, according to *Jesus, the Evidence*, but this was erased along with other biographical details when the Jesus legend was rewritten by the Council of Nicaea in A.D. 325 et seq; thereafter it became illegal for a newly divine Jesus to have a mortal brother, not to mention an Oriental one.

Traditionally, Chinese gentry survived catastrophic upheaval by switching their support to the victor at the last moment, providing him with an intact administrative machine. The great mistake of the Taipings was to frighten the gentry by challenging their survival as the accepted bureaucracy. If out of expediency the Taipings had shown willingness to preserve the Confucian system for the time being, they might have gained gentry backing till the Manchu were ousted. But the Taipings were too sincere.

p. 106 Much of the Tseng material in this chapter is drawn from the excellent study by Jonathan Porter, *Tseng Kuo-Fan's Private Bureaucracy*.

Exceptional Hunan also was the home of Mao Tse-tung.

Yung Wing, the first Chinese student to study in America, described Tseng: "His face was straight and somewhat hairy. He allowed his side whiskers their full growth; they hung down with his full beard which swept across a broad chest and added dignity to a commanding appearance. His eyes though not large were keen and penetrating. They were of a clear hazel color. His mouth was large but well compressed with thin lips which showed a strong will and a high purpose." Yung Wing, *My Life in China and America*, pp. 145–46.

While still green, Tseng's Hunan Army suffered defeats as well; these setbacks made Tseng so despondent he tried to drown himself twice, but was saved both times by his men.

107 In the West most discussion of the inner workings of the Manchu court is superficial, appearing in larger works about China by Westerners who show little interest in the Manchu themselves. A study by Hsieh Pao-chao in 1925 sheds important light on how Manchu policy was developed, and is recommended.

The term "regent" here is being used by the translator, and should not be taken literally.

About Tseng's skill as a manager a Chinese said, "Talent coursed to him as spokes to the hub of a wheel." Another compared him to "a great carpenter: from fine woods, to odds and ends of scraps, there were none that he did not collect. Forming it, first he measured it with standard rules, next he chiselled and shaped it, and finally he rubbed and polished its grain. Using it, then as pillar, rafter, eave, and wedge, all positioned in the best manner, each man went forth as he had intended." Both Porter, pp. 32–33.

Tseng lived according to the precepts of Sun Tzu, who remarked, "The general must be the first in the toils and fatigues of the army. In the heat of summer he does not spread his parasol nor in the cold of winter don thick clothing. In dangerous places he must dismount and walk. He waits until the army's wells have been dug and only then drinks; until the army's food is cooked before he eats; until the army's fortifications have been completed, to shelter himself."

108 Li Hung-chang's grandfather and great-grandfather purchased scholarly degrees of the kind General Tseng was selling to raise money for his campaign against the Taipings. Li's own father, however, was a scholar of serious merit and passed the top *chin-shih* exam the same year as Tseng Kuo-fan. A special bond existed among men of what amounted to the same graduating class.

p. 109 "I am the son of a poor man": Liu Kwang-ching, "The Confucian as Patriot and Pragmatist," p. 24.

Tseng would employ four Li brothers in all. Stanley Spector, *Li Hung-chang and the Huai Army*, p. 17.

"Too shallow a beach": ibid., p. 18.

Tseng rose before dawn to breakfast with his assistants while Li lingered in bed. In exasperation, Tseng sent a messenger to say the general could not eat till all his staff was present. Li hurried to the mess tent, where the meal proceeded in silence. At the end Tseng growled, "Around this place, what we most honor is the word 'sincerity,' and that is all." Eventually Tseng relieved him of duty. Miffed, Li stayed away more than a year. Tseng had to woo him back by writing a plaintive letter: "I am sick within and without. . . . If you bear me no ill feeling, I hope that you will come back to me." Li returned in the autumn of 1861.

Chinkiang lay forty miles east of Nanking on the confluence of the Yangtze and the Grand Canal, upon which the central government depended for shipment of tribute and taxes. Shanghai also was crucial, fast becoming the funnel for coastal trade and waterways linking the Yangtze delta with the interior, dwarfing Canton as a center of tea and silk. Ibid., pp. 27–28.

Tseng was reluctant to defend Shanghai because the city represented everything he hated about foreigners and the Chinese who coupled with them in business and pleasure. He blamed Westerners for the Taiping Rebellion, because they brought Christianity to China. Ibid., p. 28.

110 Quoth a Shanghai resident: "Men of prominence fled their native places and came there to take up refuge. And through gambling and drinking, conversation and poetry, they almost forgot the ravages of war." Paul Cohen, p. 34.

Governor Hsueh's army were "ruffians and rascals of the street whose fighting ability was negligible": Spector, p. 31.

"The rabbit runs": ibid., p. 36.

Like Tammany Hall counterparts in New York, Boss Wu and Boss Takee knew how to squeeze the bureaucracy. Boss Wu had foreign friends whose loyalty was secured by regular emoluments.

111 Sungkiang fell July 16, 1860, but was soon back in Taiping hands. For an Ever Victorious campaign map, see Morse, vol. 2.

"The first and best item": ibid., p. 71, note 27.

112 "Is it more important": Spector, p. 53.

Li's army grew to forty thousand men, ten thousand with Sharp's rifles. His headquarters near the foreign settlement made him keenly resentful of Western leverage in Shanghai and the fact that Chinese groveled to them. He was alarmed by suggestions that after the Taipings were defeated, Shanghai and its revenues should be put under Western control. Much mischief was afoot. "We are treading on frost over ice," he wrote, "there is indeed a hidden danger." Liu Kwang-ching, p. 18.

p. 112 "Devilish governor": Burlingame Papers, Manuscript Collection, Library of Congress.

Ward's being shot in the back is in Mrs. Archibald Little, *Li Hung-chang*, p. 15. Ward was given full honors of a Chinese general. His dog, "a great shaggy black and white creature," conveniently died a few days later and was buried beside him.

"Chinese" Gordon described Burgevine as a "man of large promises" and said he was "subject to violent paroxysms of anger, which rendered precarious the safety of any man who tendered him advice that might be distasteful. He was extremely sensitive of his dignity." Jonathan Spence, *To Change China*, pp. 79–80.

113 Gordon took command on March 23, 1863.

The reader is cautioned about elements of Charles Trench's biography, *The Road to Khartoum: A Life of General Charles Gordon*, in which his appraisals of Li are based largely on memoirs counterfeited by William Mannix in *Memoirs of Li Hung Chang*. While these memoirs were proved fake in 1923, Trench mentions fifty-five years later only that their "authenticity is not above suspicion."

Gordon was an exotic: Although he could not swim, Gordon had the eccentric habit of periodically throwing himself into a convenient body of water so that he could be rescued by concerned bystanders. Richard Smith, *Mercenaries and Mandarins*, pp. 125–26.

Gordon noted that the men of the Ever Victorious Army "were very touchy as to precedence and apt to work themselves about trifles into violent states of mind. . . . One half of them were usually in a violent state of quarrel with the other." Spence, *To Change China*, p. 82.

When Burgevine was pressing his case for reinstatement with U.S. minister Burlingame, he went to Peking where he was the guest of the Burlingame family. "He came laden with presents," Mrs. Burlingame wrote. "He brought for me two Sedan chairs . . . some books, and pictures, for Gertie [their daughter] a beautiful box, containing French candy, for Anson, six boxes of California wine, a globe and a large Atlas . . . Gertie takes a great fancy to General Burgevine and is now sitting with him . . . while he is making a dress for her doll." Mrs. Burlingame's letters of 11 and 24 May 1863, Burlingame Papers, Manuscript Collection, Library of Congress.

114 "Premeditated treachery": Richard Smith, p. 161.

The Yorick anecdote is in Juliet Bredon's biography, *Sir Robert Hart*, which includes her uncle's recollection of these events.

Gordon's portrait in the Imperial Yellow Riding Jacket hangs in the Royal Engineers mess room at Chatham. Li received his yellow jacket in February 1864. Little, *Li Hung-chang*, p. 38. For the jacket and its significance, see A. C. Scott, *Chinese Costume in Transition*, p. 25.

Alicia Little wrote in 1904: "It has been said of Li Hung-chang that at more than one period of his career, especially during the Taiping rebellion, he cherished secret ambitions to the throne. Gordon referred to this rumour in letters written from China in 1863, but does not appear to have attached more importance to it than it deserved." See also Bland, *Li Hung-chang,* pp. 99–100.

In May 1864 the Ever Victorious was paid off with 100,000 taels and disbanded. In its last two years of existence it had cost nearly three million U.S. dollars. Its contribution to the defeat of the Taipings was peripheral, but its existence gave Li unassailable authority.

"Smoke and flames": Hookham, p. 287.

"White like snow": ibid., p. 286.

Li was not permitted to join the final battle. Tseng wanted his brother alone to savor victory and its spoils. Li was busy squeezing money from Shanghai merchants to underwrite this last act of butchery. Tseng was desperately short of cash, and the plundering of Nanking was the only way to ensure his soldiers would disperse peacefully. Spector, p. 95.

p. 115 "Looking back in our history": Tony Teng, p. 134.

The secret message is mentioned in Hsu, p. 302.

The Nien were active on the borders of Shantung, Kiangsu, Anhwei, and Honan. Famine and higher taxes to pay for campaigns against the Taipings produced a surge in Nien popularity. Li had recruited the nucleus of his private army from the same Anhwei bandit gangs and secret societies. Jean Chesneaux, *Secret Societies in China,* p. 40.

For his failure to stop Lord Elgin, the Gang of Eight stripped General Seng of rank and titles. After the Jehol coup, Prince Kung rallied to his defense, saw that he was made a prince of the second degree and again became a favorite at court.

Tseng and Li's men were supposed to cooperate with Seng, but he was unable to control them. Their commanders would not follow Seng's orders unless they were cleared with Tseng and Li, which took many days. Spector, p. 110.

Some of Hart's assistants went to Seng's funeral in Peking. Hart wrote: "By law, it is forbidden to bring a corpse into Peking, but on special occasions, to do honor to some highly deserving man, the regulation is relaxed . . . the coffin carried by 124 bearers was led [by] the deceased's horse, and behind it came his son as chief mourner, followed by the chairs and carts in use while alive." Hart journal, 13 July 1865.

116 Tseng let it be known that he would be happy to go back to Nanking but meantime an official named Ma had been given that job. Shortly thereafter, Viceroy Ma was walking to his office when an assailant knifed him. Suspicions were aroused that others had been involved, including one of Li's lieutenants named Ting (later Admiral Ting). Although Ting was exonerated, he prudently took a four-year leave of absence to mourn his mother's death. Mourning and sick leave were convenient excuses. Ailing officials were miraculously cured after only a brief change in political climate. Ting was richly rewarded by Li, though whether for a part in Ma's assassination or many other services

is open to conjecture. Ma's murder enabled Tseng to resume his post as viceroy of Nanking and Li to become viceroy of Chihli.

SIX: *Life in a Yellow Mist*

Our account of palace life for a child emperor is drawn in part from the autobiography of Pu Yi, *From Emperor to Citizen*. In the Forbidden City things changed glacially, if at all, particularly with respect to the raising of child emperors. Other details were gleaned from a variety of sources. Another perspective on Pu Yi's childhood comes from the memoirs of his tutor, Reginald Johnston. Sources on eunuchs are G. Carter Stent, "Chinese Eunuchs", Tannahill; and Mitamura Taisuke, *Chinese Eunuchs*. Photos of a "tonsored" eunuch are in Warner. That Tung Chih was feckless seems beyond question; but there is still much about his life, particularly about his death, that needs investigation.

p. 117 An entry for Wo Jen is in Hummel, but a more complete source is Chang Hao's *The Anti-foreignist Role of Wo-jen*.

118 Hibbert and many others tell the story of Chien Lung's love affair with Ho Shen.

119 "The primary instrument": Shen Han-yin, "Tseng Kuo-fan in Peking," p. 70.

To force Wo Jen into contact with foreigners, Prince Kung appointed him to the Tsungli Yamen. Chang Hao describes how Wo Jen threw himself off his horse to injure his foot, pleaded illness, and was relieved of all duties except as Tung Chih's tutor. Years later Yuan Shih-kai simply invented a bad foot.

120 "A 'good spanking' ": letter of Mrs. Anson Burlingame, 18 January 1863, Burlingame Papers, Manuscript Collection, Library of Congress.

"He is said to be childish": The *New York Times*, 3 November 1872.

121 "Whenever I think of my childhood": Pu Yi, vol. 1, p. 39.

George Carter Stent joined Hart's Customs in 1869 and made a landmark study of eunuchs a decade later. An abbreviated version was sent to the secretary of state and is preserved in the National Archives, Record Group 59. In spite of the "rough mode in which the operation is performed," death rarely occurred.

122 "Semi-men" was the term of Matteo Ricci, Jesuit adviser in the Forbidden City from 1601 to 1610.

Hsi Tsung was known as "the carpenter emperor" because he passed his days whittling wood. Eunuch Wei purged hundreds of officials for annoying him with the grievances of the people.

Mitamura and Tannahill have background on eunuch society.

123 Osbert Sitwell (*Escape with Me*) encountered these withered creatures after the collapse of the Ching Dynasty. See also James Burke, "Eunuchs of Peiping."

No "potential": Kwong, *Mosaic*, pp. 42–43.

p. 124 "Always fooling around with eunuchs": memorial of 1874 that Prince Kung sent Tung Chih about his demeanor. Kwong discusses the power struggle, but the standoff between Tung Chih and Prince Kung is our own interpretation of events. Tony Teng's dissertation is one of the few sources that give exclusive attention to the role of Prince Kung at the court. Kung has yet to receive adequate attention by researchers.

126 Tsai Cheng is mentioned in Kwong, *Mosaic*, pp. 43–44. Kung's sons were always getting into trouble. Robert Hart noted on 15 July 1880 that one son had kidnapped a girl. Tsai Cheng died childless in his early twenties.

"He appears to have been living awful fast": Hart journal, 11 January 1875. Hart rarely included gossip and rumor in his diaries, and never idle gossip of a sexual nature. So he rated this report beyond gossip. China's fate depended on the boy.

This novel was *P'in Hua Pao Chien*. See Henry McAleavy, *Wang T'ao*.

127 "Rabbits": see Chou. Eric Chou was a Chinese journalist who worked for Brian Crozier, for many years China correspondent of *The Economist*. He knew the blue world firsthand, and after retiring from journalism, gathered material on Chinese sex life and compiled fact, rumor, and speculation in *The Dragon and the Phoenix*. Informative, taken with salt. I knew a reed-slim Chinese newspaper publisher in Vientiane who visited Thailand regularly and was always provided with two girls of less than twelve years of age by the manager of a leading Bangkok hotel.

129 For the conciliatory gesture, see U.S. minister Frederick Low to Secretary of State Hamilton Fish, 25 March 1872. National Archives, Record Group 59.

130 According to contemporary diplomatic observers, Tung Chih told the dowagers he wanted their regency to end with his wedding, but they refused. Confidential memo, Low to Fish, 5 June 1872. National Archives, Record Group 59.

The quarrel was downplayed by the dowagers in a edict on June 2, 1872, scolding an official for criticizing the emperor's behavior. "On the 19th of this month [an official] presented a memorial to the Throne begging his Majesty to be more regardful of filial duty ... and [to] live in happy concord with their majesties the Empresses. What bold language is this! From His Majesty's infancy ... during the eleven years he has occupied the throne he has been most faithful in his duties to ourselves. At all times his exercise of filial duty has been unchanged. That he has always been constant in the practice of filial duty any of the court ministers can testify. [The official] in his memorial begs his Majesty in his relation to ourselves to be more gentle in remonstrance, and less indifferent to our wishes. . . . We are at loss to find the aim of such language as this. It appears to be the ranting of one who has conjured up something in his own mind—language altogether false and evil. Let [the official] be handed over to the proper board for the severest punishment. His memorial is returned to him with contempt." The Peking *Gazette*, 2 June 1872.

132 "His Majesty expresses": Low to Fish, 10 July 1873. National Archives, Record Group 59.

p. 132 "The ceremony passed off to everyone's satisfaction," wrote Hart to Campbell on 5 July 1873, "and although this is still far from putting ministers in Peking in the position they would occupy in Paris, still it is another step, another point scored in favour of progress. Things are already looking slightly more promising, and having made the plunge, they [the Manchu] don't find the water half so cold as they had dreaded."

"You consider work too burdensome": Tony Teng, pp. 178–79.

133 Avery reports to Fish on the emperor's illness, 22 December 1874. National Archives, Record Group 59. A decree appeared in the Peking *Gazette*, 18 December 1874, describing the illness. "During the present month, We having . . . experienced the felicity of the heavenly flowers, the Prince Imperial Tun and others came to Us with an earnest and united request, that in order to compose our mind We should awhile throw off the cares of state. . . . We have Ourself repeatedly solicited both their Imperial Majesties, the Empress Dowagers, to take into consideration the necessity of now attending to our health and requested that they will condescend to look over all the reports and memorials which may come up from any officers in the capital and provinces, and decide or revise them as they deem best."

SEVEN: *Suicide of a Phoenix*

Events relating to Tung Chih's death—the Manchu cabal in selecting a successor, the death of Empress A-lu-te, and the interplay among the elder Aisin Gioro princes (Tun, Kung, and Chun)—are the author's deductions, based on sources listed below. By piecing together scattered evidence of events in Peking from December 1874 to the end of March 1875, a new picture emerges of the court and the role of Empress Dowager Tzu Hsi.

136 The documents in question: Kwong, *Mosaic*, p. 256, note 12.

See *Encyclopaedia Britannica* for basic medical data on syphilis.

137 "The pox": Lady Antonia Fraser discusses this in her biography, *Mary Queen of Scots*, referring to Mary's second husband, Lord Darnley, whose skull was found to be pitted by virulent syphilis. See also W. Armstrong Davison, *The Casket Letters;* Fraser, p. 339 footnote.

"Mysterious": The *New York Times*, 21 October 1875.

Motive was everywhere: Dissatisfaction with Tung Chih's reign was reported by the U.S. minister to Washington: "The late Emperor . . . had little if any influence in practical affairs, nor did his brief period of nominal authority give promise of the ultimate development of qualities befitting a ruler of China at this epoch, when the elements of decadence and dissolution can be neutralized only by the infusion of a fresh and vigorous motive into the central government, under the prudent leadership of an original mind. His only independent and characteristic acts were exhibitions of temper against Prince Kung. . . . He had established no claim to the affection of his subjects, and the traditional veneration due to his position is apparently too weak to inspire more than ceremonious grief anywhere." Avery to Fish, 27 January 1875. National Archives, Record Group 59.

p. 138 Some sources claim that Emperor Tung Chih *had* designated an heir, Prince Tun's child, nineteen-year-old Tsai Lien. It is unlikely that so many emperors "neglected" to designate an heir.

Morse says the decision against Pu Lun was made by "the dowagers," but this was his assumption, since many powerful Manchu nobles were at the meetings. There may have been an entirely different reason. Tzu Hsi once made a cryptic remark about a "wicked" nephew of Tzu An who had coveted the throne at Jehol in 1860, and this could refer only to Pu Lun's father, Tsai Chih. Thus the rejection of Pu Lun may have been necessary because of his father's involvement with the Gang of Eight.

139 If the rules: British minister Sir Thomas Wade advised the Foreign Office of bits of intelligence that were deleted from the Blue Books: "Hsien Feng is believed to have been properly not the fourth son [of Tao Kuang] but was born some days later than Prince Tun." When Hsien Feng was designated heir, Prince Tun was removed from the succession by being given in adoption to his uncle. Wade said, "It was thought by some that one of [Tung Chih's] uncles, Prince Tun, Prince Kung or Prince Chun, would succeed. But against this it was urged that Prince Tun, a great drunkard withal, was removed by his adoption . . . that Prince Chun who is simply a man of violence would certainly not be pre-favored to Prince Kung." Some thought that a son of Prince Tun would be chosen, but Kung outfoxed his half-brother. "It is considered that Pu Lun has been unduly set aside, and that the son of Prince Chun has been brought in by an intrigue of his mother's sister [Tzu Hsi]." Wade says Prince Kung excluded all members of his own family from the succession, moved [by] "a desire to let at rest the jealousy of his brother Prince Chun . . ." So in the end, Kung cut a deal to maintain his control of the government by backing Prince Chun against Prince Tun.

140 " 'This is your emperor!' ": Avery to Fish, 27 January 1875. National Archives, Record Group 59.

141 In order to satisfy traditionalists, Kuang Hsu became, in a sense, Tung Chih's clone. When Kuang Hsu had a son, the boy would be recognized as Tung Chih's son.

An emergency meeting: Hart noted in his diary that Prince Kung's supporters insisted on "sending for Li and summoning a meeting of high officials to decide the succession." During his three years in Shanghai, 1862–65, Li had built his Huai Army, brought the revenue of the city under his control, including Customs, Likin taxes, and Salt Gabelle. He entrenched his private bureaucracy and became China's strongest governor. When his Huai Army became the core of the new Northern Army, he also became one of China's most powerful military leaders. Thus his role in backroom haggling was incomparable.

142 Matters were suddenly reversed: Li had a history of disclosing the deaths of people who were not yet dead, as in the case of Baron von Ketteler in 1900,

suggesting at the very least that he knew somebody intended to have them killed. When he made such advance disclosures Li usually did so through third parties to exert political pressure in the press, and sometimes his timing went awry because of bad communications. Li told Hart privately that A-lu-te killed herself by swallowing gold leaf.

p. 142 Our account of the selection of the new emperor and the death of Empress A-lu-te is drawn from Hart's unpublished journals, with which most scholars seem unfamiliar. See Hart's journal for the first two weeks of January 1875 and a brief mention in Hart to Campbell, 10 February 1875.

"Within the past month": Avery to Fish, 29 March 1875. National Archives, Record Group 59.

143 "The circumstances": The *New York Times*, 18 May 1875.

144 That Tzu Hsi became deathly ill with a severe liver ailment at the same time Tung Chih died and A-lu-te "committed suicide" is very suggestive. Luke Kwong in *Mosaic* talks about Tzu Hsi's ill health. He does not say when the illness began, but refers to it as a lengthy illness lasting until 1883. However, we found diplomatic documents that date the beginning of her illness.

EIGHT: *"Our Hart"*

Our portrait of Robert Hart is drawn from many sources, chiefly his diaries and letters. His only substantial biography, *Hart and the Chinese Customs*, was written by Stanley Wright, but it ignores the more intimate and lively details provided by his niece, Juliet Bredon. A short sketch of Hart appears in Spence's *To Change China*. A cameo by Bell provides useful background on the Hart family.

146 "She has temper": Hart journal, 9 January 1875.

147 In the eighteenth century, Ningpo's popularity with Western ships rivaled Canton's. Fearing that Foreign Devils would soon be trading up and down the coast unsupervised, avoiding Customs and unloading contraband, Peking increased Customs duties everywhere except Canton. When Western skippers ignored the hint, all ports but Canton were closed, remaining closed for eighty years till the end of the First Opium War in 1842, when China was forced to reopen Ningpo and other Treaty Ports. When Hart arrived to work for the British consul, Ningpo had been open eleven years.

Details of Hart's early life come from Bruner et al.; Bell; Stanley Wright; Spence; and Fairbank et al., *The I.G. in Peking*.

148 "Never venture into the sun": Bredon, *Sir Robert Hart*, pp. 24–25.

149 "Quite like those of a maniac": Hart journal, 19 October 1854.

The British consulate, where Meadows lived and worked, was in a renovated Chinese building set back from the river opposite the north gate of the city. Hart lived upstairs, opposite Meadows and his Chinese concubine. Soon Hart had tiny bachelor accommodations. When he had guests, Hart slept on the floor. Ibid., 20 November 1854.

"I happened to have a pretty rose": ibid., 2 May 1855.

The Portuguese were notorious for disguising ships as British or Dutch vessels; the Dutch were notorious for tipping the Chinese off to British and Portuguese smugglers; Americans were not above lending their flag as cover.

Marques's description is in Hart's journal, 20 October 1854.

Dragged into the paddy fields and beheaded: Bredon, *Sir Robert Hart*, pp. 41–42; Bruner et al., p. 160.

p. 150   "A queer looking old fellow": Hart journal, 21 October 1854.

"The language is so very peculiar": ibid., 29 December 1854.

"Here is a great temptation": ibid., 29 October 1854.

"He rather surprised me": ibid., 28 August 1854.

"He treats the Chinese": ibid., 2 December 1854.

151   "That sinister eye!" Waley, p. 233—a fine profile of Gutzlaff. When Britain seized Ningpo, Gutzlaff became magistrate; his rude justice astonished the Chinese. A local bard wrote a poem calling him "Daddy Kuo": "Up to his high dais / Daddy Kuo comes. / If you are in trouble / He'll get things straight, / If you have been wronged / He'll come to the rescue, / If you have got into difficulties / He'll arrange things for you. / He's a master at speaking the Chinese language, / There is not an ideogram he cannot read. / Daddy Kuo is nothing short of a genius!" Always unorthodox, Gutzlaff employed wicked characters to run Ningpo. His police chief was a man who sold girls and furnished names of rich people who could be squeezed for money. At the signing of the Treaty of Nanking, Gutzlaff was one of three interpreters. He then sold Bibles to Chinese at a small but not insignificant profit through peddlers recruited from opium dens. Gutzlaff said he translated the Bible into Chinese, a claim many were making. As an evangelist he was a fraud. His real talent was manipulation.

The second Mrs. Gutzlaff was Harry Parkes's cousin. When she died in 1849 the widowed Gutzlaff went off to England to promote his missionary work. While in England he met his third and last wife, Dorothy Gabriel. Wedded bliss was short, Gutzlaff dying in China less than a year later, when his gout turned into dropsy.

For Horatio Lay, see Spence, *To Change China*, and Gerson.

Lay's father, George Tradescant Lay, was a linguist, a musicologist, a naturalist, an agent of the British and Foreign Bible Society in China, and an interpreter during the First Opium War. Unlike Gutzlaff he was a mild man who got on so well with the Chinese that he "proved incapable of pounding the tables of the Mandarins." See Fairbank, *Trade and Diplomacy*, p. 162.

152   "Lay is the most crafty": Spence, *To Change China*, p. 99.

p. 152 During the Second Opium War in 1858, Robert Hart was transferred from Ningpo to Canton to serve as Parkes's secretary during the Allied occupation of the city.

For the knifing, see Gerson, pp. 123–24 and pp. 298–99, notes 150, 151.

In the beginning Hart dealt mostly with Wen Hsiang, whom he found shrewd, capable, and the driving force of the Yamen. Hart praised him as "one of the ablest, fairest, friendliest and most intelligent Mandarins ever met by foreigners." Meng, p. 52. In talks lasting sometimes the entire day, Hart (always prepared with documents and statistics) put before Prince Kung the essential facts of every commercial situation; he could explain without lecturing.

153 " 'Our Hart' ": Spence, *To Change China*, p. 106.

Hart's remarks to Rennie are in Bruner et al.

154 "Covetous anxiety": Spence, *To Change China*, p. 111.

"I saw [Prince Kung] frequently": Hart to Hannen, 9 August 1861. Morse, vol. 2, p. 53, note 16.

Lay insisted that the fleet be run by his personal choice, Captain Sherard Osborn, a British naval officer. If Lay's scheme had gone through, his flotilla would have been present at the fall of Nanking and would have been entitled to 30 percent of the plunder by agreement with Prince Kung. Tseng Kuo-fan's brother would have forfeited much money and plunder. Even Li was not allowed to join the siege because the plunder was to be the sole property of Tseng's brother.

"The Inspectorate of Customs": Spence, *To Change China*, p. 112.

155 The British consul who complained was E. L. Oxenham.

In 1864 a member of Hart's harbor staff got £240–600 sterling a year, which compared well to London wages. Indoor staff began as student interpreters earning £400 a year, including room. A man who thrived on the language and the life could earn £600 his second year, and if he worked hard could be a port commissioner within eight years, earning as much as £3,000. Leave came every five years, with twelve months on half-pay. Stanley Wright, pp. 267–68, 275.

"Unfinished experiments": Hart to Campbell, 1 September 1871.

"I want to make China strong": ibid., 16 October 1881.

Hart wrote to Campbell in London about his difficulties trying to settle his Chinese children in life: "In 1866 I sent home my three wards (Anna, Herbert, and Arthur Hart), and Smith Elder & Co. committed them to the charge of their book-keeper's wife, Mrs. Davidson. . . . I have put off longer than I ought the duty of arranging for the future of these youngsters . . ." The boys were to be trained for the Indian civil service; Anna was sent to school in Vevey, near Montreaux. School was not a great success and by 1879 Hart was desperate, asking Campbell to apprentice the boys to any trade possible—"make a druggist of one, a woollen-draper of the other." Hart was worried that his brother-in-law, James Maze, who had been badgering him for money, might get wind of his illegitimate Chinese children and try blackmail. "I will never pay a penny to shut any man's mouth." However, six weeks later he "lent" Maze £700 and agreed to employ Maze's sons in the Customs; nevertheless, Maze continued to plague him. Hart to Campbell, 15 September 1895. Hart called him a "lunatic." Hart to Campbell, 12 February 1899. Wright avoids confronting the subject. Eventually Hart reached a settlement with a solicitor named Foss in behalf of his children. In the diary entry for August 19, 1905, he wrote "regarding [my] connection with Ayaou (1857–1866) and her children Anna, Herbert, and Arthur. I was not married to Ayaou and her children . . . are illegitimate. I was only married once—in 1866 to Hester Jane Bredon and my only legitimate son is Edgar Bruce: he is the legitimate heir of the Baronetcy." Hart journal, 19 August 1905.

p. 156 "One of the most amiable": Hart to Campbell, 23 November 1875.

"I feel rather lonely": Hart journal, 6 March 1865.

Marco Polo Street was later renamed Rue Hart.

157 The Harts' separation was broken only briefly in March 1906 when Hester and Nollie returned to Peking for a visit.

"You shall not have the chance": Bredon, *Sir Robert Hart,* pp. 144–45.

158 "He wants occupation": Hart to Campbell, 13 June 1897.

Hart's efforts did not go unnoticed. He was decorated by Belgium, Sweden, Austria, and France. But he was Inspector General for sixteen years before Britain acknowledged the value of his work. Even then he got only a Companionship in the recently reconstituted Order of St. Michael and St. George (C.M.G.)—the lowest honor possible. This was a calculated insult that he took gracefully. "I have officially written to tender my most respectful thanks, but I have added a private note in which I say that while I appreciate the honour individually, as an individual I must admit that it (a simple C.M.G.) will very generally be looked upon as no compliment to my work, my position, or the Government [of China] I serve." Hart to Campbell, 11 October 1879. A higher honor had been recommended but vetoed by Sir Thomas Francis Wade, the minister in Peking. Hart to Campbell, 5 October 1879. Under pressure from friends in London and Peking, the insult was rectified three years later in April 1882, when Hart was given the rank and title of Knight Commander of the Order of St. Michael and St. George, becoming Sir Robert Hart. Stanley Wright, pp. 425–26.

In his unpublished diaries, Hart said Hessie wrote about the offer of the Peking diplomatic post, "I am not a bit glad: and I should really have been glad had it been the announcement of the appointment of another." Hart journal, 25 June 1885. Surprisingly, all published sources insist Lady Hart wanted him to take the appointment. See Fairbank et al., *The I. G. in Peking,* p. 592, note 1.

"What self-assertion": Hart journal, 7 May 1865.

"The Yamen thinks": Hart to Campbell, 8 April 1888.

p. 158 For Detring, see Morse, vol. 2, pp. 368–72.

"He seems a pleasant, intelligent young fellow": Hart journal, 22 October 1865.

Hart's fears for the Customs Service under Viceroy Li are aired in his letter to Campbell, 29 August 1885. As Stanley Wright put it, "All during July, Li . . . kept sedulously pushing the claims of his candidate Detring . . . Rumours flew thick and fast. Detring's merits and great abilities were fully recognised, but the general opinion was that he could not be relied on to stand up against his patron Li if the interests of the Service were at stake. Some went so far as to say that an understanding had been reached between Li and Detring regarding the staffing and maintenance costs of the Service. Prince Ching, too, as head of the Yamen had no desire to add to Li's influence and authority, believing that Detring would most probably be more loyal to his patron Li, than to the Yamen."

NINE: *A Hostage to Etiquette*

For medical details about the physical and psychic problems of Emperor Kuang Hsu, readers should refer to Chapters 14 and 25, in which medical examinations and reports are discussed.

160 Kuang Hsu was born August 14, 1871. It is Hart who identifies Tzu An as the official adoptive mother of Kuang Hsu, and Tzu Hsi only as the boy's aunt: Hart journal, 25 February 1875.

161 "She was a devout Buddhist": Pu Yi, pp. 23–24. We are the first to establish that it was Kuang Hsu's biological mother and not Tzu Hsi who terrorized the boy.

163 "He is said . . . to be passionate and self-willed": U.S. minister Charles Denby to Secretary of State Thomas F. Bayard, 11 January 1889. National Archives, Record Group 59.

Kuang Hsu's nephew became Emperor Pu Yi. The disciplining of both of these boys was in the hands of their fathers, Princes Chun I and Chun II, respectively. Pu Yi recalled that the eunuchs used this method on him. But this strange cure was not an invention of the eunuchs, it was a family tradition that the eunuchs were explicitly instructed to observe.

Kuang Hsu's dread of thunder: Kwong, *Mosaic*, p. 50 and p. 259, note 60.

"The diet of the emperor": Denby to Bayard, 28 December 1891, National Archives, Record Group 59.

164 "To settle his stomach": Pu Yi also had this method used on him.

"He was so thin and weak": Derling, p. 253.

"Downfall of the Tang": Kwong, *Mosaic*, p. 48.

He ordered them beaten: ibid., pp. 48–49.

"For the last month or more": The *New York Times*, 20 October 1878.

The story from *Empire* was quoted in the *New York Times,* 22 October 1879. This probably was from the Shanghai newspaper, *Celestial Empire.* For more about *Celestial Empire* and similar publications, readers can consult Frank H. H. King and Prescott Clarke, *A Research Guide to China-Coast Newspapers, 1822–1911.*

p. 165 "Prince Tun is amiss": Kwong, *Mosaic,* p. 52. Much of the research into the upbringing of Kuang Hsu by Weng has been done by Kwong.

166 These medical reports are quoted at length in Chapters 14 and 25.

"The emperor has been carefully educated": Denby to Bayard, 11 January 1889. National Archives, Record Group 59.

"It is said that he has a remarkable memory": ibid. 28 December 1891.

167 Falling snow: Kwong, *Mosaic,* pp. 53–55 and notes.

The edict announcing the death of Tzu An is in a dispatch to the State Department, 11 April 1881. National Archives, Record Group 59.

"Vague rumors": ibid.

"Tzu An fell ill": *CUED,* p. 152.

168 "Tzu Hsi made up her mind": This version is from Edmund Backhouse and J.O.P. Bland, *Annals and Memoirs of the Court of Peking,* pp. 482, 487–88. Backhouse covered his tracks by attributing these remarks to an unnamed Chinese source, a tactic he frequently employed.

"Devoted to her": Denby to Bayard, 11 January 1889. National Archives, Record Group 59.

"How wonderfully the Empress has held out": Hart to Campbell, 22 December 1886.

169 When the central government tried to draw on Chinese domestic customs revenues (distinct from Hart's foreign customs), Li refused to part with the funds, saying the needs of his immediate area required that he, not the government, receive the money. He cooked his account books, the way he had been taught by Tseng Kuo-fan, remaining vague about revenues and expenditures so nobody could take him to task. Spector, pp. 217, 219.

171 The founding father of the Pure party was the same ultraconservative tutor, Wo Jen, who (always putting form before substance) had been one of the two tutors responsible for the disastrous education of Emperor Tung Chih. When the showdown came in 1884, the attack on Prince Kung was led by Censor Sheng Yu, from the Ironhat family of Prince Su. Joining in were Chinese scholar-officials, known as the Four Admonishing Officials, who made it their business to break Prince Kung's grip on decision making. Taking advantage of the rumormongering and carping criticisms of Censor Sheng Yu, of the Pure party, and of the Four Admonishing Officials, Prince Chun waded into the argument against his brother. He had three private audiences on the matter with Tzu Hsi, in an effort to win her over. Kwong, *Mosaic,* p. 34 and p. 254, note 90.

172 The edict of dismissal is in Tony Teng, pp. 191–95.

p. 172   "Roundly denounced her for depraved morals": *CUED*, p. 154.

173   Not only did Li survive, he prospered, and subverted the officials who had led the campaign of criticism against him. He planted his agents on the newly reorganized Grand Council and in the Tsungli Yamen. He bought over Censor Sheng Yu, who had led the attack on Prince Kung, and won over one of the Four Admonishing Officials to such a degree that he married Li's daughter. Far from falling from grace, Li remained the most powerful Chinese official in the empire. It would take more than a few hectoring militants to bring him down.

Our physical description of Lung Yu may seem unkind, until one sees her photographs in Derling, and a sketch done by Kate Carl that appears in Carl's memoirs.

Kuang Hsu's concubines, from the Tatala clan: Denby to Bayard, 11 February 1889. National Archives, Record Group 59. The two concubines were cousins of Chih Jui, a Hanlin scholar. Both Derling and Kate Carl knew the chubby Lustrous Concubine, and photos and portraits of her are to be found in their memoirs.

Denby noted: "There were reports that [the empress-elect] had serious objections to the marriage": ibid., 8 March 1889.

The *New York Times* alleged that Kuang Hsu refused even to see his empress-elect, and was supported in this by tutor Weng Teng-ho. The *New York Times*, 24 November 1889.

174   "Nothing could be more honourable": Hart to Campbell, 25 February 1889. (Mormons confer religion on their ancestors.)

175   The smoking anecdote is from Kate Carl. She and Derling show genuine sympathy and appreciation for Emperor Kuang Hsu.

"Praying hard for rain": Hart to Campbell, 24 July 1890.

"He has the appearance now of a delicate youth": Denby to Bayard, 10 March 1891. National Archives, Record Group 59.

"He has a hesitation in his speech": ibid., 11 January 1889.

Despite his impairments, Kuang Hsu was unstinting in meeting his obligations as emperor, although the demands of the job would have drained a much more vigorous man. His days were long and arduous. Denby reported: "He is possessed of considerable firmness and determination. I suppose that he does more work than any other sovereign in the world. His day commences at [midnight]. He first sees the members of his Privy Council; then he devotes an hour to the study of the Manchurian language; then he studies English; then receives one or more members of the various Boards, and then the Governors, Viceroys, and other officials who have come to Peking . . . for instructions. The Emperor receives them alone. . . . After the receptions are over the emperor rides on horseback and practices shooting with the bow and arrow. These exercises . . . are prescribed and cannot be avoided. . . . The emperor retires about 2 p.m." (Obviously, he was not a wimp.) Ibid., 28 December 1891.

Few China scholars have devoted much attention to the internal power struggles of the Manchu princes. Too often they fix on the prominent role of Chinese viceroys, in particular Li Hung-chang, leaving readers with the impression that after Emperor Chien Lung's reign the Manchu court became powerless, a pawn of Chinese viceroys (until the "evil" Tzu Hsi appeared). In fact, Chinese viceroys and Manchu princes were interdependent, in symbiosis; neither could survive without the other, as illustrated by Marquis Tseng. Long after their armies became impotent, the Manchu maintained their power by intense and constant fear of denunciation—not unlike the Catholic Inquisition, the Nazis, the Bolsheviks, the Japanese militarists, and the House Un-American Activities Committee—a form of terror by intimidation and dread that can immobilize generals and saints. Foremost in maintaining this terror were the archconservative princes and their Chinese sycophants, including a number of so-called Princes of the Iron Helmets, or Ironhats. To keep things simple, we have lumped them together under the generic term Ironhats, a metaphor for their state of mind. The best scholarly study of the Manchu power elite is Hsieh Pao Chao's *The Government of China (1644–1911)*, published in 1925. (See note for page 182, top of page 501.)

p. 177 Fate hung on how Viceroy Li handled Japanese provocations: A few months after Kuang Hsu ascended the throne, on August 8, 1889, Li's brother (Li Han-chang) was made viceroy of the southernmost provinces at Canton (remaining in this post until April 1895). Between them the Li brothers controlled nearly the entire China coast, from Vietnam to Korea, their power extending far into the interior, including the agricultural heartland, the most vigorous cities, the most profitable ports, and taxes and commerce between them. One year later, on September 9, 1990, Li's adopted son was appointed minister to Japan, the most important diplomatic post in terms of immediate threat to China, and the most lucrative in terms of bribes, kickbacks, commercial or industrial contracts. Called "Lord Li," he was the viceroy's nephew as well as adopted son (Li's only natural son was born retarded). Lord Li remained in Tokyo until 1892, when relations with Japan reached the danger point and his father replaced him with one of his shrewdest operators. Lord Li's withdrawal from Tokyo in 1892 was made under the pretext of undertaking mourning on the death of his adoptive mother. The man who replaced him as ambassador to Japan was Li's point man in Tokyo, forming a triangle of intrigue with Li in Tientsin and Yuan Shih-kai in Seoul. The fact that they failed to outwit the Japanese is what made war inevitable. (In 1895 Lord Li reappeared as Li Hung-chang's associate in negotiating the Shimonoseki Treaty.)

The regent of Korea was seized by Yuan Shih-kai's forces and exiled to Paoting, where he was held until the summer of 1885.

The 1884 coup: At a dinner party celebrating the opening of the first post office in Seoul, attended by all foreign envoys except the Japanese minister, the coup attempt took place. The American envoy described the scene: "As the dinner drew to a close an alarm of fire was given, and nearly all the guests withdrew from the table and went out of doors to view the fire, which seemed near at hand. A moment later [the Korean deputy foreign minister] entered, his face and clothing covered with blood which was streaming from seven or eight ghastly wounds." Assassins posing as dinner guests had struck. Michael Montgomery, *Imperialist Japan*, p. 126.

p. 177   Both countries continued Korean intrigues under the table: To strengthen China's hand, Yuan busied himself training Korean troops as royal guards and police forces.

178   A Chinese gunboat took Kim's body to Korea, where it was hacked to pieces and put on display, enraging Japan.

The truth of the Kim murder plot emerged when Chinese scholars found the original drafts of letters that Viceroy Li wrote to his chief agent in Japan, the chief of legation in Tokyo, regarding the assassination. This was a rough draft, and the final version that was actually sent did not include the revealing passage. See Chow Jen Hwa, *China and Japan*, p. 181 and p. 294, note 174. This is a valuable source on the Manchu court's ministers in Japan.

Toyama, head of the Genyosha, announced the formation of a Society of the Friends of Mr. Kim. See Michael Montgomery for more.

"Go and extinguish the fire": E. Herbert Norman, "The Genoyasha," p. 281.

Six days after Yuan slipped out of Korea, Japanese troops forced their way into the palace and obliged King Kojong to order the expulsion of all Chinese troops and to appoint a new cabinet headed by his father, the pro-Japanese former regent.

179   Both John Rawlinson (*China's Struggle for Naval Development*) and Michael Montgomery discuss the *Kowshing* incident.

"China is keeping quiet": Hart to Campbell, 27 July 1894.

Japan already had obtained: Richard Storry, *Japan and the Decline of the West in Asia*, p. 23.

For the ambivalent role of Weng Tung-ho, see Kwong, *Mosaic*.

180   The most complete study of Li Hung-chang and the Chinese navy is Rawlinson.

181   The total cost of the Summer Palace reconstruction, begun under Tung Chih and resumed under Kuang Hsu, has been placed as high as 100 million taels. In 1894 Robert Hart wrote that the Admiralty Board should have had 36 million taels in assets, but was flat broke. It was charged that 8.5 million taels were diverted from the board to rebuild the palaces, but what happened to the navy's remaining 27.5 million taels? Nobody seems to know. This is hardly surprising given the awesome venality of the men on the navy board. Hart was told by Viceroy Li that they (Li and the two ruling princes) had "allowed" the dowager to squander the money on various projects, but this remark is self-aggrandizing. Li and the others lavished money on the dowager

to win favor, disguising where it came from. Li was a master of duplicity, and everything he said was seasoned with cunning, for the paths of patronage are devious in the extreme. Rawlinson gives statistics and describes the "secret funds," then incredibly ends up blaming the dowager. We are not at all convinced of her complicity. It is unlikely, given the humiliation of her armed forces at the hands of the French, that she would have knowingly agreed to the diversion of new naval funds. This is borne out by her subsequent behavior, when she personally canceled costly plans for her sixtieth birthday celebrations in distress over further naval defeats.

Despite the advent of steamships, as late as 1905 British men-of-war still had sword and cutlass drills and boarding exercises. Naval strategists were not yet willing to relinquish the melee and the ram, to rely on big naval guns.

p. 182 Li added to his profits by having his naval vessels double as passenger ships and tramp steamers. They carried cargo manifested as luggage. Rawlinson, p. 144.

"There can hardly be a doubt": Denby in Rawlinson, p. 163.

"Li's boasted fleet": Hart to Campbell, 2 September 1894.

"Some very big folk": ibid., 11 November 1894.

War profiteering: navy munitions were the responsibility of Viceroy Li's nephew. In November, Li's son-in-law, Chang Pei-lun, was cashiered and tried for embezzlement. He and Li's nephew were found guilty of having supplied the fleet with defective ammunition. Hummel, p. 49; Fairbank et al., *The I.G. in Peking,* p. 996, note 3.

"Coast is now literally clear": Hart to Campbell, 23 September 1894.

183 In her biography of Li Hung-chang, Alicia Little tells us that Li was divested on 17 September.

"I should not be surprised": Hart to Campbell, 9 December 1894.

184 Prince Kung was called out of retirement on September 29.

185 "Had it been done": Hart to Campbell, 11 November 1894.

"One day a force": ibid., 4 November 1894.

Prevented by his Ironhat advisers: Morse, vol. 3, p. 38.

Admiral Ting made no pretense of being a sailor. As he told one subordinate: "Here, I am Admiral of the Fleet. Do I pretend? Do I assume to know anything about a ship or navigation? You know I do not; so take an example from me and pretend no more." Rawlinson, p. 166.

Li Hung-chang was dismissed as viceroy in the fall of 1895.

"Peace can only be got": Hart to Campbell, 24 February 1895.

186 "I am afraid we are tinkering a cracked kettle": Hart in W.A.P. Martin, *A Cycle of Cathay,* p. 411.

"I fear": Hart to Campbell, 3 November 1895.

"How can I bear": Kwong, *Mosaic,* p. 58. Hart wrote: "It is said the Emperor wants to retire." Hart journal, 5 June 1895.

p. 186 "There is something curious going on": Hart to Campbell, 8 December 1895.

Ironhat princes were removed from direct participation in executive and military power more than a century earlier during the reign of the tyrant Yung Cheng. To prevent any rival from striking at him, Yung Cheng neutralized the princes, leaving them their titles and estates but divesting them of traditional Manchu military commands and executive appointments at court. Thereafter they were blocked from serving as Prince Advisers or as members of the Grand Council. For more than a hundred years, no Ironhat and no royal Aisin Gioro prince had been named to the Grand Council, until Prince Kung. Instead, they spent their time in idle pursuits, looking for ways to amuse themselves, raising goldfish and songbirds, hawking in the deserts, playing war games with comrades, toying with flowers in the back garden. As a way of wielding indirect power, they engaged in court intrigue and led informal power blocs that conspired endlessly in the manner of Renaissance princes. While they had the power of denunciation, fear, and political murder—the power of terror—generations had passed since they had commanded armies in battle, and they had no idea what was required to become serious statesmen. Their brief experience of executive power under the Gang of Eight had shown them able to intrigue and intimidate but unable to win battles against either the Taipings or the Foreign Devils, who were not vulnerable to intimidation because neither was within the system. The fact that the Ironhats were born into the nobility made it impossible for them to accept their own incompetence. Despite their patriotism, this proved to be their fatal flaw.

188 Tuan as a reactionary: Robert Hart commented on this in his work, *These from the Land of Sinim*. He trusted that in time Tuan would see reason.

189 Lord MacCartney saw imperial troops dressed in tiger skins during his trip to China in 1793. The costume also was used by imperial troops during the opium wars. The object was less to frighten the enemy than to encourage one's own men.

Sue Fawn Chung talks about the Tiger Hunt in *The Much Maligned Empress Dowager*, p. 93.

190 Tung Fu-hsiang's story is little known. We pieced together the fragmentary evidence from W. L. Bales, *Tso Tsungt'ang*; H. B. Morse, *The International Relations*; Lo Hui-men; Hummel; Hart journals; J. K. Fairbank et al., *The I.G. in Peking*; Morrison journals; and Satow's diaries. He is another important character who has been neglected by scholars.

192 "No doubt about the murder": George Lensen, *Korea and Manchuria between Russia and Japan*, p. 92.

ELEVEN: *The Wild Fox*

Traditional views of Kang Yu-wei, which glorified his role in the Hundred Days Reform, are to be found in the works of Lo Jung-pang (*Kang Yu-wei: A Biography and a Symposium*, 1967), Hsiao Kung-chuan (*A Modern China and a*

New World: Kang Yu-wei, Reformer and Utopian, 1975), and Jonathan Spence (*The Gate of Heavenly Peace*, 1981). This image is debunked by Luke Kwong in his landmark work, *A Mosaic of the Hundred Days*, which is recommended. What all these works (including Kwong's) overlook, is that Kang and his clique were responsible for spreading the first slander about the empress dowager, which became the fountainhead for Backhouse and a root cause of the distortion of history. So the discovery that Kang Yu-wei was a fraud, a poseur, a plagiarist, and a liar is fundamental to any understanding of imperial *and* modern China. Kuang Hsu himself condemned Kang Yu-wei.

p. 194 "A lot of quicksilver": The elusive nature of Kuang Hsu's power as emperor was remarked upon by Hart two years earlier. Hart to Campbell, 12 January 1896.

195 "One of their ideas": ibid.

Other unsettling rumors: "Years ago," Hart continued, "I heard that there was a young fellow who claims to be the son of Tung Chih and gets some recognition: but he cannot be the son of the Empress Alute, for although said to be enceinte that poor girl had to die when the Empress Dowager placed Kuang Hsu on the throne. But who was the mother? I recollect that an A-ko of 18 was sold off for the little emperor when he reached the age of puberty in 1870 or thereabouts, being then about fifteen." Hart journal, 22 May 1897.

"Yuan will not be the last": Hart to Campbell, 13 June 1897.

196 He spent most of his time and energy avenging himself: "Prince Kung," wrote Hart, "seems to be clearing out all who superseded himself and party." Ibid., 11 August 1895.

199 Intolerance of scholars: The emperor who built the Great Wall to keep out barbarians had all books but those dealing with medicine, pharmacy, divination, and agriculture destroyed, and even *The Analects of Confucius* was proscribed during his reign; possession of a banned book was punished by branding with a hot iron and a life sentence at hard labor. Five hundred scholars were put to death in his purges and thousands more banished.

For more about the *ming-shih*, see Kwong, *Mosaic;* Miyazaki; and McAleavy's *Wang T'ao.*

On Peking theater: Only the stars received salaries; young boys apprenticed to the theater by destitute parents earned money by "attending the banquets of the Chinese men about town: when they are not actually playing [on stage], they go up into the private boxes to the richer visitors, whom they amuse with the latest gossip": A. B. Freeman-Mitford, *The Attaché at Peking*, pp. 347–55.

Kang Yu-wei's youth is described in Lo Jung-pang; Spence, *Gate;* and Howard Boorman, *Biographical Dictionary of Republican China.* Hsiao contains much about the philosophical contortions of Kang Yu-wei.

Kang boasted that he came from a family of scholars and teachers, but most of his ancestors were merchants.

200 Offend local custom: After a traditional marriage was arranged for him, Kang refused to bind his daughter's feet, scandalizing the whole village. This later

led to his profitable connection with the British antifootbinding leaguers, most important among them being indefatigable Mrs. Archibald Little.

p. 200 Kang's biographer Hsiao described his subject as having "intense self-confidence bordering on self-conceit." One of Kang's students said, "He refuses to adapt his views to fit facts." Hsaio, pp. 18–19.

"The elegance": Spence, *Gate*, p. 3.

On the finer things in life: Hsiao said of Kang: "A man of robust desires and stout emotions, he was inclined to regard the enjoyment of sensuous pleasures and creature comforts as a legitimate element of the good life."

A girl of seventeen: Hsiao, p. 10.

201 As "evidence" of . . . reform: See Kwong, *Mosaic*, pp. 84–85.

In his preface Kang acknowledged the assistance of his pupils in a general way, but he did not acknowledge that he had lifted this "discovery" and other material directly from their papers. It was left to seem as if he deserved the credit exclusively. See ibid., pp. 87–88.

In the puritanical America of 1891, an equivalent scandal might have been caused by the public assertion that the basic facts of Christianity had been altered by the Council of Nicaea in A.D. 325 and the Council of Chalcedon in A.D. 451, something that would not surprise a serious Biblical scholar but would horrify and outrage religious fundamentalists.

Dubbed a naughty "wild fox": Kwong takes a close look at the relationship of Weng Tung-ho and Kang Yu-wei.

202 As Kwong puts it, "Kang's subsequent claim that he should have scored the first place at all three levels of the examination is too boastful to deserve serious attention." Kwong, *Mosaic*, pp. 90–91.

"I was not going to bend my back": Lo Jung-pang, p. 67.

"The empress dowager": ibid., p. 66.

203 While still in Peking, Kang joined a Society for the Study of National Strengthening. Unable to shine in Peking's intense intellectual circles, Kang went to upstart Shanghai to organize a branch of the society there and was able to exercise autocratic control over this splinter group. The newspaper in which Kang insisted on dating from the death of Confucius caused an uproar, but the issue involved was not of any real significance. As one scholar summed up Kang's career to that point, he was defeated by a "combination of the banality of his reform ideas and his overestimation of their power." Kwong, *Mosaic*, p. 103.

For more on Sir Chang Yin-huan, the parlor lion and favorite of the foreign community in Peking, see Hummel, pp. 60–63. Sir Chang had known Kang Yu-wei since 1894. For Chang's patronage of the Wild Fox, see Kwong, *Mosaic*, p. 138.

204 Drawing on his foreign friends, Kang also prepared a potted history of reform in other countries, focusing on the methods of Russia's Peter the Great. Both the history and the memorial were passed to the emperor as part

of the flood of memorials the emperor was reading and passing on to his viceroys and governors for comment.

p. 205 Kang's version of the story appears in Lo Jung-pang, p. 91.

He visited every few days: Chung, *Much Maligned*, pp. 29–30. Sue Fawn Chung's work, along with that of Luke Kwong, has done much to correct the false impression that Tzu Hsi opposed reform from the beginning,

"It will not be denied": Denby in Cohen and Schrecker.

A compilation of the decrees issued by Kuang Hsu during the Hundred Days appears in Morse, vol. 3, pp. 137–39.

TWELVE: *The Puppet Show*

Many questions about the "heroes" and "villains" of the summer of 1898 can be traced directly to the writings of Kang Yu-wei and Yuan Shih-kai. Both men of huge vanity and ambition, their self-serving accounts made a caricature of the Hundred Days Reform and became the basis for almost all subsequent studies of the crisis. Scholars Luke Kwong and Sue Fawn Chung have begun the long overdue reexamination of this period, but much work remains to be done, particularly on the role of Japan during these critical months in China's history.

207 This characterization of Weng as the archetypal Confucian bureaucrat is contained in a letter from Denby to Bayard, 11 January 1889. National Archives, Record Group 59.

A tyrannical Tzu Hsi: Kang later claimed that Weng told him " 'the emperor has really no power. The empress dowager is extremely suspicious and keeps a close watch over him. When the emperor has pastries served to the princes . . . she opens each piece to see whether it contains a secret message or not.' Thus," wrote Kang, "I came to know about conditions in the palace." Quoted in Lo Jung-pang, p. 70. Lo's notes, especially those expanding upon Kang's autobiographical account, make interesting reading.

208 For a profile of Kang I, see Kwong's *Mosaic*.

209 "Fussy conservatism": Hart to Campbell, 19 June 1898.

"The Edicts of the 15th" and "talk of dethronement": Hippsley to Morrison, 20 June 1898. Lo Hui-men, p. 87.

210 "Pity": Hart to Morrison, 18 June 1898. Ibid., p. 86.

211 Anger the dowager: Kwong, *Mosaic*, p. 179.

Jung Lu: After his early successes setting up a security ring around Peking for Prince Kung at the time of the Allied invasion of 1860 and participating in the arrest of the Gang of Eight in 1861, Jung Lu pursued police and security work as a commander of the Banners guarding Peking. From 1879 to 1887 he withdrew from public life. It was alleged that he offended Tzu Hsi by having an affair with one of her ladies-in-waiting and withdrew to escape punishment, but this is the kind of excuse employed by courtiers to remove a man who is becoming too powerful. Jung Lu simply ran afoul of Prince Tun.

p. 212 Biographers Stephen MacKinnon and Jerome Chen see Yuan as something of an innocent in matters leading up to the Hundred Days.

213 Chung Li was coincidentally the father-in-law of Emperor Kuang Hsu's brother, Prince Chun II.

Tzu Hsi did not let either appeal goad her into interfering: Both Chung and Kwong argue convincingly that the empress dowager and Kuang Hsu were not at odds over reform or other political issues. After being obliged by the Ironhats to resume overseeing the administration, Tzu Hsi did not rescind Kuang Hsu's reforms.

Kang's friend in the Censorate was Sung Po-lu.

Kang dragged his feet: Although Kang was only a minor player in a much larger drama, if he had gone when the opportunity first presented itself, Ironhat tempers might have cooled and the reforms might have been given a fair chance. They were modest reforms, not in themselves of great substance or of revolutionary impact. It is likely that not one of these reforms would have been rejected if they had been presented without the accompanying gibes, insults, and provocations that were part of Kang's campaign to draw attention to himself. Therefore, his absence would have removed the most irritating element. During his stay in Peking, Kang submitted a total of eleven memorials to the throne, with no appreciable effect. Despite his later claims, he was not the leader of the reform movement nor even *one* of its leaders; he was simply the loudest and most insulting. Kuang Hsu was interested in collecting a broad range of opinions and did not focus on any individual as a main source of inspiration. The infatuation of scholars with Kang has other causes.

214 Viceroy Chang Chih-tung was an old rival of Viceroy Li's. In 1884 Chang had headed the Pure party that had worked with the princes to oust Prince Kung. Chang Chih-tung was born in 1837 in Kweichow but was considered a native of Chihli Province, where his ancestors had settled in the fifteenth century. He was unusually precocious as a student, passing his first exams at age thirteen and finishing all at age twenty-six in 1863, when he became a compiler at the Hanlin, and was promoted in 1879 to tutor at the Imperial Academy. After that success Chang was rewarded with his appointment as viceroy of Hunan and Hupeh, where he remained for eighteen years, much longer than the normal three-year tenure. Pursuing a career parallel to Viceroy Li's, Chang became a supercomprador, opening the first modern mint in China and launching its first iron- and steelworks. He ordered a smelter from England but knew so little about the process that he failed to locate it near a coal-mining area. This exposed him to ridicule, but he went on to become a leader in introducing Western science and technology to China, encouraging the development of schools, newspapers, and translation bureaus, hiring talented young scholars. Ultimately it was this that led to his briefly becoming a patron of reform.

Tan Ssu-tung's father was a widower who served in many official capacities, taking his son everywhere, finally becoming governor of Hupeh in 1889. See Cohen and Schrecker for more.

p. 215   Tokyo was watching developments in Peking: At the beginning of 1898 three officers of the Japanese general staff, Kamio Mitsuomi, Kajikawa Jutaro, and Utsunomiya Taro, came to China ostensibly to see Viceroy Chang Chih-tung, to discuss Japanese training for a new army, a concept newly in vogue. Unlike Tan, the viceroy was no provincial naïf when it came to appreciating the motives underlying offers of Japanese help. He insisted on first discussing a moratorium on war reparations. This the officers rejected.

Yang Jui was virtually adopted by Viceroy Chang Chih-tung and had been on his secretariat for more than ten years. When Yang Jui became one of the emperor's reform secretaries, Chang paid his living expenses in Peking. William Ayers, *Chang Chih-tung and Educational Reform in China*, p. 142.

Liu Kuang-ti had been a secretary of the Board of Punishments for more than ten years. Cohen and Schrecker, p. 299.

216   "The great man": Hart to Campbell, 3 January 1897.

217   Li's Russian friends: Hart to Campbell, 25 September 1898. Hart was absent from Peking during the summer of 1898, but his letters shed light on the events during those months.

218   We do know that the Genyosha were watching Ito closely during this trip, either to protect their assets or to take advantage of openings resulting from Ito's Peking audiences.

Yamagata was pursuing a grand strategy in which the Japanese army was responsible for seizing North China, Manchuria, and Russia, and the navy was responsible for South China, Indochina, and the Pacific archipelagoes. He was born in 1838 to a family of low samurai rank opposed to the military dictatorship that had ruled Japan since the seventeenth century. Educated at a private school, he began his career as a police informer and joined the movement that overthrew the shoguns and restored the emperor. Early on, Yamagata discovered that professional soldiers were no match for spies, agitators, and irregulars. By 1871 he had organized the Imperial Guard and was promoted to vice minister of military affairs, then chief of the general staff. In 1889 he became the first prime minister of Japan and thereafter devoted himself to Japan's takeover of Asia, as a confidential adviser to the emperor. In 1900 Yamagata sent the largest contingent of troops to lift the siege of the Peking legations. After Ito's assassination in 1909, Yamagata became virtual dictator of Japan. In 1921 he meddled in Hirohito's marriage plans and was publicly censured, dying in disgrace on February 1, 1922. See Michael Montgomery.

Pornographic pictures: Norman, pp. 278–79.

219   "Tokyo's unofficial ambassador": Michael Montgomery, p. 143.

This is the sequence according to Sue Fawn Chung. Luke Kwong says this draft of the memorial was written on September 14 and presented on September 18.

THIRTEEN: *The Betrayal*

The bloody climax of the Hundred Days Reform has been greatly confused by the fact that a number of the primary sources—Kang Yu-wei, Liang Chi-chao, and Yuan Shih-kai—tailored their memoirs, diaries, and autobiographies to make themselves look good after the fact. In Yuan's case he hid his sordid betrayal of the young emperor to make himself seem the hero of the hour. When Kang and Liang discovered how eager Westerners were to believe the worst about the empress dowager, they portrayed themselves as the "imprisoned" emperor's champions and dined well in exile. In order to strip away nearly a century of voguish disinformation, the authors drew upon a wide variety of sources to reconstruct a computerized chronology of events, revealing many interesting coincidences. Certain of these remarkable coincidences suggest how Yuan's betrayal actually came about and how Kang, utterly ignorant of the palace coup, took unscrupulous advantage of Western gullibility to build a career as a self-styled martyr. However, much work remains to be done in tracing the mischievous role of the Japanese in this story.

p. 221 The secret decree appears to be another of Kang's many fabrications. Scholars who examined Kang's holographic copies of this and five other so-called secret edicts in his possession concluded that they were counterfeit. Lo Jung-pang, p. 164, note 63.

222 The first he knew about the decree: ibid., p. 125.

Second private meeting: Chung, *Much Maligned*, p. 65.

He made his way there: Chung says this happened on September 17 or 18. Kwong says September 18.

223 Holding a secret audience: Satow, British minister to Tokyo at the time, said, "Ito had seen the Emperor on the 18th and another meeting was to take place on the 20th when the conservative party under the Empress-Dowager was prompted into action." See Lo Hui-men, vol. 1, p. 91.

Censor Yang Chang-i's role is described in Kwong, *Mosaic*. Yang's daughter was married to Viceroy Li's grandson. Yang was a witch-hunter and a leading opponent of the *ming-shih*, considering them to be a subversive influence. In 1896, when Viceroy Li had come under strong *ming-shih* attack for the peace terms ending the Sino-Japanese War, Yang led an assault against the *ming-shih*, including the censure of Wen Ting-shih. In September 1898, by playing a leading role in the Ironhats' denunciation of the emperor's unilateral actions and the ominous involvement of Japan, Yang may have been hoping to discredit the *ming-shih* as a group and to bring about a full reinstatement of Li Hung-chang.

224 Yang was not arguing against reform but in favor of collective decision making. We know the details of Yang's report to the dowager because a summary was prepared after the audience with Tzu Hsi, from notes taken during the discussions. See Kwong, *Mosaic*.

Chung says Jung Lu had learned that Yuan was in Peking and summoned him to Tientsin on the pretext that war had broken out between Russia and Britain. Chung, *Much Maligned,* p. 66.

p. 227 "The Hanlin [scholars]": Hart to Campbell, 8 December 1895.

Intriguing with dissident scholars: Hart to Campbell, 12 January 1896.

Morrison reported Kuang Hsu's secret audience with Ito in a letter to Valentine Chirol on 20 September 1898. Additional information about this meeting is in Lo Hui-men, vol. 1, pp. 90–91, note 2.

228 "There is no statesman": Morrison to Chirol, 20 September 1898, Lo Hui-men.

229 Kang's version of these events is from his autobiography. See Lo Jung-pang.

Yuan had played them all for fools: "I heard," wrote Kang later, "that Yuan knew of [the conservatives' plans for] the coup d'état and therefore refused to obey the emperor's orders." Lo Jung-pang, p. 127.

230 Yuan's version of the conversation with Tan is in his memoirs. Readers will find these quoted extensively in Jerome Chen's *Yuan Shih-kai.* The memoirs allegedly were composed by Yuan at his headquarters in Hsiaochan on October 10, 1898, but were not published (in Chinese) until 1926. Other versions appeared in Yuan's private diary, again published many years later. It is generally accepted that Yuan contrived these accounts long after the events and backdated them. It seems likely that Yuan's version benefited from long conversations he had with an admiring George Morrison, who was helping Yuan with his image building. According to Yuan, Tan told him, "Our worries lie at home, not abroad . . . His Majesty is in grave danger, and you, Mr. Yuan are the only one who can help!" Tan continued: "Jung Lu has recently proposed to dethrone and murder the Emperor. Did you know that?" Yuan responded that this was doubtless nothing but a groundless rumor. Tan persisted, saying, "If you really mean to help His Majesty out of the present difficulty, I have a plan." In his memoirs Yuan wrote: "Mr. Tan then produces a piece of paper . . . on which are these words: 'Jung-lu plans to dethrone and murder H.M. Traitor! Must be done away with as soon as possible—else H.M.'s position is untenable. Yuan leaves for Tientsin on the 20th. Give him a mandate in the Vermilion Pencil, ordering him to arrest and execute Jung Lu. Yuan takes over the viceroyalty and the commissionership. Make known Jung-lu's treachery . . . Yuan and his troops should then come to Peking to guard the Forbidden City and besiege the Summer Palace. Commit suicide in H.M.'s presence if plan rejected.'" The last sentence must have given Yuan food for thought if the other comments had not. Unfortunately, all the sources are suspicious.

231 Without offending her: Here again, the long-established myth of enmity between the empress dowager and Kuang Hsu is disproved. Kwong, *Mosaic,* p. 214.

p. 231 The conventional account charging Yuan with betraying the emperor was told by Bland and Backhouse in *CUED*. According to their version, Yuan was summoned on September 20 to the emperor to discuss army reform, but instead the emperor in the private audience ordered Yuan to go immediately to Tientsin and there to put Jung Lu to death. Then he was to lead his troops to the capital to seize and imprison Tzu Hsi. By this story Yuan left on the morning train, arrived at Tientsin at noon and told Jung Lu of the plot; Jung Lu rushed to the Summer Palace and revealed the plot to Tzu Hsi, who hurried to Peking and took over. See also Lo Jung-pang, pp. 168–69, note 64. We can now see from a straightforward chronology that this is all codswallop. There was a betrayal, but not in this manner.

There has been a great deal of controversy over whether Jung Lu actually made this trip or whether he did or did not convey news of the plot to Tzu Hsi in some other way. Kwong argues that Jung Lu did not inform the dowager of the plot until he saw her on the twenty-seventh, which he believes explains why the Six Martyrs were not charged with sedition till that date. However, U.S. minister Conger cabled the Department of State on the twenty-fourth, saying that it was definitely the conspiracy against the dowager that had provoked the arrest of the Martyrs, which occurred on that date. "It is also authoritatively stated and believed that the Emperor was planning for the arrest and imprisonment of the Empress Dowager . . . Jung Lu, who is really the Commander in Chief of all the military in the capital province, is a strong friend and supporter of the Empress Dowager, as are also most of the army officers under him." National Archives, Record Group 59. There has to be some other explanation why the charge of sedition was not made from the outset. The most plausible explanation, we believe, is that Tzu Hsi was reluctant to act on hearsay based only on General Yuan's report and that she waited till Jung Lu and others were able to carry out an investigation to confirm the details, which they were able to do only on the twenty-seventh. She had previously shown reluctance to act on the basis of hearsay in the charges made to her by Censor Yang on the eighteenth, and Yang was obliged to concede that many of his charges were indeed based on hearsay and rumor.

233 It is important to remember that the empress dowager was not hiding herself for sinister reasons by sitting behind a curtain. Etiquette demanded that she observe this protocol, which is not unlike the Muslim practice of women in purdah.

The conversation between Ito and Kuang Hsu is from Teng and Fairbank, *China's Response to the West*, p. 180.

234 Edict of September 21 is quoted from British *Blue Books*.

235 Despite rumors she heard of the emperor's imprisonment, Sarah Conger turned out to be a staunch supporter and defender of the empress dowager.

Kang's version of Tan's attempt to rescue the emperor is found in Lo Jung-pang, p. 134.

236 He also went back to sitting beside her: Chung, *Much Maligned*, p. 72.

The exact circumstances of Tan's arrest have not emerged. None of the other six men arrested that day had felt any reason for alarm, so there would appear to be no reason for Tan himself to have anticipated danger. Regrettably, many people later felt it necessary to invent heroic scenarios, including one in which Tan planned to rescue the "imprisoned" emperor from the Ying-tai pavilion with the help of ninja-style swordsmen. In another he refused help from the Japanese and faced certain death alone.

"Collusion": Kwong, *Mosaic*, p. 220.

p. 237   Kwong maintains that this is the first time during that turbulent week that Jung Lu met with Tzu Hsi. The viceroy arrived in Peking on the twenty-seventh bearing further details of the plot from his investigators, and conferred with Tzu Hsi.

Edict ordering the executions: Chung, *Much Maligned*, p. 151.

Yang Shen-hsui was a follower of Viceroy Chang Chih-tung. Born in 1849, he was a native of Shansi, a *chin-shih* of 1889, and had served on the faculty of Viceroy Chang's Ling-te Academy in Shansi. In Peking he was one of the Censors who submitted reform memorials (prepared by Kang and other *ming-shih*) to the emperor.

Kuang-jen's body: North China *Herald*, 10 October 1898, quoted in Morse, vol. 3, p. 148, note 56.

This translation of the decree was sent to Washington on September 30, 1898. National Archives, Record Group 59.

238   "Something untoward" Lo Jung-pang, p. 172 note 69.

Tung's appearance in Peking: H. B. Morse, vol. 3, pp. 151–52.

Robert Hart accurately described the designated role of Tung's troops at this time: "The Chinese think we are afraid of Tung's men and so say to themselves 'just the men we ought to keep here!' Tung and his men . . . are now so many daws in the peacock's feathers." Hart to Campbell, 13 November 1898.

On the plan to rescue Sir Chang, see letter of Sir Claude MacDonald to Morrison in 1898. Lo Hui-men. Sir Chang was exiled to Urumchi, capital of Sinkiang Province. Both Russia and England attempted to establish control of this area. Urumchi has always been a Muslim stronghold.

Hsu Chih-ching remained in jail until he was released when Allied troops entered Peking in 1900, during the Boxer affair. He died soon afterward.

239   "The issue of reform": Hsu, p. 449.

"The emperor found himself at war": John Fairbank and Edwin Reischauer, *China: Tradition and Transformation*, p. 375.

"The Empress Dowager found her entire world threatened": ibid., p. 376.

"Executed the radicals": John Fairbank, *The Great Chinese Revolution*, p. 135.

240   Edict of November 16 quoted in Cohen and Schrecker, p. 104.

p. 240 After the Hundred Days many of Kuang Hsu's reforms remained in place. Only the ones most onerous to the Ironhats, and to the scholar-gentry, were rescinded. Tzu Hsi introduced additional reforms of her own but stopped short of making radical revisions in the structure of the government or in the special privileges and pensions that the Manchu had enjoyed for two centuries. By contrast, after the assassination of President John F. Kennedy, Lyndon Johnson immediately rescinded most of Kennedy's radical foreign policy initiatives, including moves to reach détente with Russia and Cuba and to withdraw all U.S. troops from Vietnam. There are many interesting parallels between the two palace coups. See Jim Marrs's *Crossfire* (New York: Carroll & Graf, 1989).

Cockburn's appraisal of the dowager is from the unpublished records of the Foreign Office. Public Records Office, London.

241 "Since 1897 and 1898": Chung, *Much Maligned*, p. 262.

Two women: see Derling and Carl.

"Their relations": Carl, p. 68.

242 "The situation here has changed": Hart to Campbell, 25 September 1898. Hart, like most members of the Western community, had escaped the summer heat of Peking.

Agreeing with Hart was Yeh Chang-chih, a Chinese scholar at the time who was acquainted with some of the actors in the tragedy: "Kang and Liang in their reform movement had the intention of an alliance with Britain and Japan to give them support, and the return of the empress dowager to power was actually prompted by the Russians. This was why the coup was carried out so suddenly and [why] Britain and Japan dared not intervene.": Lo Jung-pang, p. 156, note 41.

The Hundred Days Reform was over. But some things never change. Nearly a year after the beheading of the Six Martyrs, Morrison of the *Times* wrote a letter from Peking to his counterpart in Shanghai, J.O.P. Bland. In it Morrison quoted some information he had just received from W. V. Drummond, sometime Acting British Crown Advocate in Shanghai: "There is a conspiracy on foot to overthrow the empress Dowager and restore the Emperor and the Reform party. The Japanese are to seize the opportunity to occupy Peking and drive back Russia. . . . Japan is to act with England if possible." Morrison to Bland, 14 July 1899. Lo Hui-men.

FOURTEEN: *The Fugitive*

Kang Yu-wei's alleged intimacy with Emperor Kuang Hsu gave great weight to his remarks about the empress dowager, which came to be accepted by foreigners and overseas Chinese as gospel. Almost without exception, historians and biographers have treated the direct observations of the Western ladies as sentimental dross, while preferring to accept Kang entirely at face value.

p. 243 About Kang's escape, he himself gave a number of different versions, including the conversations reported to the *Times* by its Shanghai correspondent, J.O.P. Bland, another to a journalist in Hong Kong, and his own "official" (embellished) account, which appears in the work by Lo Jung-pang. He was also interviewed by several British diplomats, including Byron Brenan and Henry Cockburn, who were not taken in. Their cool appraisals were kept in British diplomatic traffic, so did not see the light of day.

"Is this a photograph of you?": Kang's account of his escape in Lo Jung-pang.

244 "On the morning of the 23rd": This portion of Brenan's report to MacDonald appeared in *The Blue Books, China No. 1,* 1899, pp. 307–8.

245 On the "red pills" see Chung, *Much Maligned,* p. 175 and p. 197, note 86.

The rumored marriage and honeymoon trip of Tzu Hsi and Li Hung-chang appeared in the *New York Times,* 21 October 1898. One wonders if the original source did not say "the dowager and the viceroy"—meaning Jung Lu—but was misunderstood to mean Li Hung-chang. Casting Jung Lu would have conformed to the canard that he had a long-running secret affair with Tzu Hsi. The substitution of Viceroy Li turns it into a real howler.

247 "Thrust through his bowels": The *New York Times,* 2 October 1898. Somebody was having fun at the *Times's* expense. No doubt this and the honeymoon story originated with Telegraph Sheng.

248 Bland's dispatch was quoted in the *New York Times,* 26 September 1898.

Cockburn's report is contained in the unpublished records of the Foreign Office. Public Records Office, London. It was not included in the official *Blue Books.* See also Lo Hui-men for other assessments of Kang by Bourne and Cockburn.

Prince Yin is from the *New York Times,* 2 October 1898.

249 For more on Sir Robert Hotung see Boorman, vol. 2, p. 75.

Kang made contact with the Japanese consul in Shanghai, Ueno Suesaburo. The assurances of Okuma are found in Lo Jung-pang, p. 173, note 73.

250 This is how Kang's interview with the *China Mail* appeared in the North China *Daily News* of 15 October 1898.

No source mentions Kang's ever actually seeing the dowager. Only Kang Yu-wei himself makes that assertion.

For Kang's "disclosures" to the foreign ministers, see Foreign Office 223/122, Public Records Office, London. Letter from Kang Yu-wei to Sir Claude MacDonald written from Hong Kong about October 15, 1898. An almost identical letter was sent to the U.S. mission. National Archives, Record Group 59.

251 On Kang's attempts to murder Tzu Hsi, his conversation with Miyazaki is included in Hsiao Kung-chuan, pp. 238–39 and note 162. Other sources men-

tioning Kang's murder plots include: The *New York Times* 23 June 1904, and Chung, *Much Maligned*, p. 267.

p. 252 "The old lady is furious": Hart to Campbell, 23 October 1898.

"Should there be any persons": edict quoted in *Blue Books*.

Morrison tried to get the assignment for himself: MacDonald to Gwynne, 16 October 1898. Lo Hui-men.

Dethève was accompanied by an interpreter, M. Vissiere.

The original diagnosis of Dr. Dethève was forwarded by the foreign ministers to their home governments. Our copy came from Conger to Hay, 19 October 1898, National Archives, Record Group 59. See also Kwong, *Mosaic*, p. 259, note 79, for comments on the emperor's health, and Chung, *Much Maligned*, p. 177.

254 Digitalis has, among other things, a diuretic effect.

255 "Six youths": Hart to Campbell, 16 October 1898. Readers should recall that just as breaches in etiquette were grounds for dismissal of an official, ill health was another time-honored pretext that allowed officials to retire or to be removed from their position. That this might be applied to the emperor himself is not out of the question.

A dark-horse candidate: This situation was described by Morse, vol. 3, p. 150. Morse says Jung Lu led the opposition to Prince Ching's son. But at the time Jung Lu was not, as Morse says, in the Tsungli Yamen council; the only man who seems to come close to Morse's description as leading the opposition would be Chung-li, although he was not an Imperial Clansman.

Figuring out Manchu or Chinese family trees is a strenuous exercise. We have spared the reader many of these digressions in the text but include one here as an example: Pu Chun was the son of Prince Tuan. When he became heir apparent, it is argued that the other candidates in the direct imperial succession included twenty-five-year-old Pu Lun (and Pu Lun's brother Pu T'ung). But Pu Lun, and therefore his brother, had been rejected once before in 1875 because they were in the imperial family only through the adoption of their father. The other possibility was Pu Wei, grandson of the late Prince Kung, son of Tsai Ying. By order of the empress dowager, Pu Wei was made the adopted son of Prince Kung's eldest boy, Tsai Cheng (1858–85), who had died childless. Accordingly, Pu Wei eventually became Prince Kung II and was helpful to the Japanese in the 1930s when they set up the puppet empire Manchukuo under the last Manchu emperor, Pu Yi. Another possibility (according to Liang Chi-chao) was Tsai Chen, son of Prince Ching, but he was of the same generation as Tung Chih and Kuang Hsu, ruling him out. In addition, Prince Tsai Chen was a notorious gadabout. Among other conquests, he kept as a concubine Yang Tsui-hsi, a courtesan celebrated both as a singer and for her tiny bound feet. Whether Kuang Hsu had it in mind to retire when Pu Chun reached his sixteenth birthday is not clear. For the genealogy of Pu Chun, see Lo Hui-men, p. 99, note 1. For background on Prince Tuan, see Chung, *Much Maligned*, and Hummel.

In a legalistic sense, Pu Chun was Tzu Hsi's nephew, her niece being the wife of Prince Tuan, although the boy's biological mother was a concubine.

The man appointed chief tutor to heir apparent Pu Chun was Grand Duke Chung, father of Empress A-lu-te. He was now one of Prince Tuan's most ardent supporters.

Morse is the source for the Shangfang sword.

p. 257 Prince Heinrich's audience at the Summer Palace on May 15, 1898, is mentioned in the North China *Herald* of 6 June 1898. Isaac Headland, *Court Life in China*, p. 155; Morse, vol. 3, p. 110; and Kwong, *Mosaic*, p. 148. Hart described Prince Heinrich as "winning all hearts by his sympathetic face and charming unaffectedness." Hart to Campbell, 22 May 1898. Before the audience, the prince was said to have been asked by Lady MacDonald to persuade the dowager to grant an audience to the foreign ladies. Philip Sergeant, *The Great Empress Dowager of China*, p. 198.

"Some good may result": Conger to Hay, 14 December 1898. National Archives, Record Group 59.

"First they were not ready": Hart to Campbell, 4 December 1898.

258 "The Empress was very curious": Lady Ethel MacDonald, "My Visits to the Dowager Empress of China." All quotes from Lady MacDonald in this chapter are from this source unless otherwise indicated. Sarah Conger's commentary is from her book, *Letters from Peking*. A photograph of the ladies and interpreters appears in this book.

Lady MacDonald's address is from Foreign Office 223/122, Public Records Office, London.

260 "I feel very strongly": Chirol to Morrison, 16 December 1898. Lo Hui-men.

261 "Her Majesty was especially gracious": The *Times*, 16 December 1898.

"The Empress Dowager made a most favorable impression": *Blue Books.*

" 'Amiability verging on weakness' ": is from Ethel MacDonald, *Empire Review.*

FIFTEEN: *Poisoned Pen*

The historical impact of the black propaganda against the empress dowager is addressed in later chapters, which discuss biographical works of Backhouse and his relationship with both G. E. Morrison and J.O.P. Bland.

263 The ideograph is from Joseph Levenson, *Liang Chi-chao and the Mind of Modern China*, p. 33.

The acting consul was Hayashi Gonsuke. Lo Jung-pang, p. 171, note 67.

Just before Kang left Peking in September, a new Chinese minister was appointed to Tokyo. Li Sheng-to was a thirty-eight-year-old native of Kiangsi and member of the Hanlin Academy who became an imperial Censor in 1895. During the early part of the reform movement, Censor Li had been closely aligned with Kang Yu-wei but suddenly changed his loyalty from reform to antireform, possibly because of the involvement of Japan. In May 1898 he was one of three Censors to impeach Kang to the throne, which suggests a dramatic turnaround. During the September crackdown Li was suddenly given the ambassadorial appointment to Japan, replacing an envoy who had held the position for only six weeks. This was highly irregular, as envoys were generally appointed for terms of three years. When Kang was considering the Japanese invitation to go to Tokyo, he expressed fear of Minister Li. It was generally believed that Minister Li received the appointment due to the influence of Jung Lu, who was one of the targets of the plotters. Less than a month after arriving in Tokyo, Li received orders from Peking to arrest Kang Yu-wei. For some reason he chose to ignore the order, and turned out to be Kang's good fairy. He may have been bought over by the Japanese, who were able to reassure Kang that he was utterly safe in Japan.

p. 264 "A very valuable present": quoted in Levenson, p. 55.

Biographical background on Liang Chi-chao comes from Levenson, Boorman, Lo Jung-pang, and Spence, *Gate*.

Governor of Hunan at the time was Chen Pao-chen.

265 Takahashi Kichitaro was the member of the foreign ministry.

Miyazaki was a Genyosha agent involved in a variety of intrigues including selling weapons to Filipino *insurrectos*. He and Hirayama were the personal secret agents of Inukai Takeshi, the lieutenant of Foreign Minister Okuma.

The Genyosha served as a bridge over troubled waters. Sun Yat-sen repeatedly suggested that he and Kang Yu-wei join forces. Hirayama served as chief intermediary between them.

Among the prime movers in Japanese intrigues to bring all East Asia under their domination were Sugawara Den, Miyazaki Torazo, Inukai Ki, Okuma Shigenobu, and Soejima Taneomi. Inukai Ki backed the Genyosha strategy to support Kang in North China, Sun in South China, and Emilio Aguinaldo in the Philippines. Carrying out these plots in the field was left to the Genyosha mastermind Toyama Uchida and his field agents, backed by the Japanese army and navy, government agencies, and the great commercial houses, or *zaibatsu*. Toyama's association with Inukai Ki began before the turn of the century when they jointly took Sun Yat-sen under their wing. Inukai was eventually assassinated by Toyama's mobsters in the 1930s after a disagreement.

Okuma Shigenobu did much to modernize and reorganize Japan's fiscal system after the Meiji Restoration. An English-speaking liberal who favored a parliamentary system, he started the Progressive party and served as foreign minister until an attack by a nationalist fanatic nearly cost him his life and did cost him a leg. The attack was arranged by the Genyosha—or Dark Ocean Society—which opposed Okuma's policy of negotiating with foreign nations. After reaching an understanding with the Genyosha, Okuma served again as foreign minister in 1896 and thereafter as prime minister briefly. He became prime minister again at the start of World War I. He died in 1922.

Sue Fawn Chung examines *China Discussion* and Liang's propaganda machine in considerable detail, along with the reaction to this black propaganda inside the Forbidden City.

p. 266 "A tortoise cannot grow hair": Liang Chi-chao, "Why the future of China depends on the emperor," 22 March 1899. Translation from the original by Clio Whittaker.

267 Viceroy Chang Chih-tung had good reason to exhibit zeal in pursuit of the exiles. Several reform secretaries beheaded in September 1898 had been recommended to the emperor by him. As a consequence, Chang nearly lost his post as governor-general of Hupeh and Hunan. His closest associates in the Hunanese reform movement (Governor Chen Pao-chen and his son) were cashiered. Why Chang himself was spared has never been explained, but some suggest that only a close friendship with Tzu Hsi kept his head on his shoulders. To save his hide, Chang quickly changed sides, turning on the reformers with such vigor that this alone did him credit in the eyes of the Ironhats. In disgust the surviving reformers christened Chang "the weathercock mandarin." Lim said Chang was "a sort of patriot" but "a traitor towards his rightful Sovereign"—meaning he betrayed the emperor to support the dowager, which was Kang Yu-wei's party line. "In the last two years," Lim went on, Chang "is scarcely the same honest man whom we admired years ago. He has changed considerably for the worse : . . his subordinates secretly despise him . . ." See Wen Ching's *The Chinese Crisis from Within*.

268 In 1899 Okuma presented Liang Chi-chao with the handsome sum of 7,000 taels for a trip to Hawaii. Liang wrote in his diary, "Truly, in Japan, I have the feeling that here is my second home." Liang returned to China to take part in the Hankow uprising but arrived too late. Resuming his sanctuary in Japan, he settled into his life role as a leading critic of the Manchu.

269 "The reach of the Manchu knife is long": Wen Ching, p. xiii.

"Somewhat bumptious": Morrison diary, 23 December 1901.

"Distinguished": Johnston, p. 92.

The associate of Sun Yat-sen was Huang Nai-shang.

Boorman makes the mistake of saying that Lim Boon-keng's book, *The Chinese Crisis from Within*, was published in the 1930s. It was published in 1901. Interestingly, Wen Ching (Lim Boon-keng) had direct ties to the Manchu and once played host to Prince Su's son when the boy was sent to Singapore to study English. He also had connections to the American community in Singapore through family links with the American Methodist Church.

All the quotes on pp. 266–68 are from Wen Ching.

272 "Her private character has been spotless": Denby to Bayard, 1889, reviewing events since 1875. National Archives, Record Group 59.

SIXTEEN: *The Sly Pornographer*

Only brief excerpts of Morrison's diaries have been published, and most of these are in Cyril Pearl's biography. While some of the Morrison-Backhouse correspondence was published in Lo Hui-men's excellent two-volume work, the unedited original correspondence at Sydney's Mitchell Library contained fascinating additional information. In Australia we examined both the correspondence and the diaries in detail and have made extensive use of both in following chapters. In London, Sir Edmund Pickering generously arranged for us to have access to the archives of the *Times*, where we found a number of valuable unpublished letters and cablegrams to and from Morrison. While our portrait of Morrison is darker than those of Lo Hui-men and Pearl, we feel that the umber lends depth and complexity to what had been only a heroic caricature.

p. 273 "Do you consider it conceivable" and "the best solution": Morrison to Bland, 12 October 1898. Lo Hui-men.

276 "Skill in extracting the truth": Morrison diary, 18 May 1899. Whenever he was praised, Morrison recorded the puff in his diary. With Li Hung-chang's death in 1901 and Pethick's own death soon afterward, Morrison lost a unique source; to stay on top of the news he had to reorient himself toward Yuan Shih-kai.

He almost met Prince Ching: ibid., 14 January 1904.

"A very good candidate": Hart to Campbell, 26 February 1899.

"E. Backhouse to breakfast": Morrison diary, 3 March 1899.

277 "We have had in our employ": Morrison to R. Nicholson, Manager, the *Times*, 7 July 1911. Archives of the *Times*.

278 "Don't bother to get me any chocolate": Backhouse to Morrison, 8 May 1903. Mitchell Library.

279 "Many thanks for the jam": ibid., 14 May 1903.

"I was lunching": Backhouse to Morrison, 23 January 1900. Lo Hui-men.

"The only maidens": Morrison diary, 30 May 1899.

Masturbation: ibid., 9 June 1899.

"G. came in smelling": ibid., 1 June 1907.

The affair with Maysie and related quotes from Morrison's diary appeared in Pearl's highly readable 1967 biography. But when we examined the original diaries in 1986, these pages were missing. It is not clear who purged the gamy entries during the intervening decades. Robert Hart took no chances and destroyed the diaries he kept during his liaison with his Chinese mistress.

280 "The longest pair of horns": Morrison diary, 3 January 1908.

"Lily has syphilis": ibid., 8 April 1900.

"Like nothing but": ibid., 15 April 1900.

"An independent fast woman": ibid., 22 June 1899.

" 'Get out Sir' ": ibid., 13 September 1900.

"Married an American hooker": ibid., 1 August 1907.

"And what about Casenave": ibid., 29 April 1909.

"She loves beautiful women": ibid., 22 June 1899.

"She was a notorious lesbian": ibid., 29 January 1903.

"Furtively I find them together": ibid., 17 July 1905.

"She employs the Japanese": ibid., 4 February 1908.

"I.G. till very late": ibid., 11 April 1899.

"Dined with the I.G.": ibid., 23 April 1900.

p. 281 Backhouse looked as innocent as an acolyte: Backhouse's raunchy nature was well described toward the end of his life by Reinhard Hoeppli.

While Morrison kept Backhouse informed of the latest sexual gossip from the legations, Edmund responded in kind with tales of Manchu decadence. The tantalizing charges of sexual misconduct made by Wild Fox Kang against the dowager fascinated both men as voyeurs. As a raconteur Backhouse was skilled. Hoeppli recalls how "it was very fascinating to hear him speak of the past, he brought back scenes of bygone days with many details and when on winter afternoons, sitting in half-darkness in his arm chair, he spoke of people dead since long, they seemed as if by magic to return to life and to reveal some of their secrets, charming, scandalous and even horrible as they may have been." Hoeppli notes to Edmund Backhouse, "Decadence Mandchoue," p. 439.

"Drawing on a typically Babu store": *CUED*, p. 477. The scathing reference is, of course, to the stereotypical Western-educated, bumbershooted Bengali, in the days of the Raj.

282 He complained bitterly of his parents: The quotes about his family are from Edmund Backhouse, "The Dead Past," p. 124 et seq.

A friend of Alfred Douglas: Morrison diary, 16 October 1908.

Hugh Trevor-Roper's book, *The Hermit of Peking*, is recommended to any reader who wishes more detail about the life and cons of Edmund Backhouse.

283 "A love affair . . . with a prime minister": Lord Roseberry was prime minister from March 1894 to June 1895.

"He took me": Backhouse, "The Dead Past."

Corvo is a phallic metaphor based on the Latin genus *Corvus*, to which crows and ravens belong. Toward the end of the 1880s Rolfe went up to Oxford as an unofficial student or tosher, who sat in on various lectures. A fancy dress ball was planned for a visit by the Prince of Wales, and Rolfe came as a raven. When the prince reached the receiving line at the top of the stairs, Rolfe edged up, looking at him first with one eye and then with the other, bird fashion, then emptied a pint of whitewash through a hole in his tail. "The Many Lives of Frederick Rolfe, Alias Baron Corvo," *The Observer*, 1975. A novel Rolfe wrote titled *Hadrian the Seventh*, about a poor boy who becomes

Pope, was ambiguously commended by D. H. Lawrence, who called it "a clear and definite book of our epoch," but Rolfe's earnings from it came to only eleven shillings three pence. See Cecil Woolf, *Baron Corvo's Venice Letters*, and Donald Weeks, *Corvo*.

p. 283   Fox lived till 1935, evidently circulating copies of these letters to friends. In the 1920s there was a privately printed edition. It is likely that Edmund Backhouse saw them during trips to England until 1921. But the *Venice Letters* were only one example of a tradition of homosexual pornography that Backhouse apparently had been steeped in since childhood; it is to this tradition that his own memoirs revert.

286   "My intercourse . . . in 1902": quotes are from Backhouse, "Decadence Mandchoue."

SEVENTEEN: *Weed People*

In 1987 Joseph W. Esherick published a landmark study, *The Origins of the Boxer Uprising*, which earned the Fairbank Prize in East Asian History. Esherick's book is the first major reexamination of the Shantung Boxer movement at the grass roots level since the pioneering work of Chester Tan, *The Boxer Catastrophe* (1958) and Victor Purcell, *The Boxer Uprising* (1963). He shows clearly that the individual Boxers themselves were a spontaneous manifestation of anti-Christian, antiforeign outrage in rural areas of North China. Unfortunately, in concentrating on the grass roots, Esherick did not also reexamine the parallel role of the Manchu Ironhats, who tried to take advantage of the Boxers, and his book presents the established image of an evil Tzu Hsi based on the counterfeit Backhouse biographies.

287   It is foolhardy to see conspiracy in terms of grand design, for chance and opportunity always play major roles in the most determined plot. "I hate these absolute systems," Alexis de Tocqueville said, "which make all the events of history depend on first great causes by a chain of fatality, and which, as it were, exclude man from the history of mankind." Similarly, A.J.P. Taylor remarked, "I discovered, or thought I discovered, that Hitler, though no doubt resolved to make Germany a world power, had no clear-cut plan how to do it and moved forward with the changing situation." Nowhere is this truer than in the Boxer affair, which has always been seen as part of a conspiracy backed by the empress dowager. The point is that Prince Tuan and his faction *aspired* to expel all foreigners and turn the clock back, making use of the Boxers and various other means, but for many reasons failed. Their bad luck and incompetence do not alter their aspiration, which from the Manchu viewpoint was essentially patriotic.

289   "Take away your missionaries and your opium": Morse, vol. 2, p. 220; and Hart, *Sinim*, p. 158. British trade in opium remained legal until 1917. Thereafter it came under the control of the Red and Green gangs based in Shanghai. Big Eared Tu Yueh-sheng and Generalissimo Chiang Kai-shek benefited immensely from drug traffic, as did their Japanese business partners, and

Nationalist Chinese continue to dominate the drug trade out of the Golden Triangle. Recently the People's Republic has been confronted with a resurgence in domestic opium trade and addiction. There had been a long series of collisions over missionaries. In 1870 at Tientsin, French Sisters of Charity offered to buy sick Chinese orphans in order to baptize them before they died. Rumors spread that the infants were being procured for evil purposes. A mob gathered and was fired upon by the French consul, who was immediately torn to pieces. The enraged mob then killed twenty other foreigners, including ten nuns, and destroyed the Catholic mission. When Tseng Kuo-fan was ordered to investigate the Tientsin Massacre, he discovered that the sisters were not involved in kidnapping children and there was no substance to the bizarre rumors. The French, for their part, demanded the decapitation of two local officials who were suspected of complicity in the riots and threatened to go to war against China should she fail to meet these terms. But strains of the Franco-Prussian War left the French unable to muster the firepower to press these demands, and they had to be satisfied with the dismissal and degrading of the two mandarins. It did not always turn out that way.

p. 290   Anti-Christian propaganda: Peter Fleming, *The Siege at Peking*, p. 41; and Cohen, "The Anti-Christian Tradition in China." Cohen is the source for the quoted materials. The author of this Chinese propaganda pamphlet is thought to have been one of Tseng Kuo-fan's private employees *(mu-fu)* who contrived it at Tseng's instruction.

"Very clever . . . a queer mixture": Hart to E. B. Drew, 12 October 1870, quoted in Morse, vol. 2, p. 235, note 57.

"Missionaries also take the poor Chinese children": Derling, p. 177.

292   The Manchu capitulated to a demand: In 1899 the throne granted Roman Catholic bishops the right of certain trappings and privileges: the mandarin's button; the appropriate retinue of chair-bearers, outriders, and footmen; the umbrella of honor; the discharge of a cannon on arrival or departure; and a rank equivalent to governors-general. The impact on Chinese opinion can be gauged by imagining nineteenth-century British reactions to the announcement in a court circular that African witch doctors were to have equal precedence with Lords Lieutenant. Six months later a conference of Anglican bishops in Shanghai passed the following resolution: "We cannot view without alarm, both on behalf of our own flock and of the Chinese population generally, the rapidly growing interference of French and other Roman Catholic priests with the provincial and local government of China." There was genuine concern for the dangers implicit for all missionaries in the self-aggrandizement of Roman Catholic clergy. When the antiforeign storm broke, there is evidence that Roman Catholics were seen as a more important quarry than Protestants. Fleming, pp. 40–43. It is all relative.

For more on White Lotus, see Chesneaux, *Secret Societies*.

293   Yu Hsien was a Manchu from Kwangtung in South China. Purcell suggests that Li Ping-heng, Yu Hsien, and others aimed to divert the ever growing

popular discontent and agitation away from the Peking government and against the foreigner.

p. 293 This strategy of deniability was the brainchild of General Tso Tsung-tang. The Black Flags were brought into the Manchu service by him in the same way he had cut a deal back in 1869 with the Muslim renegade Tung Fu-hsiang. Tso's genius for organizing these kinds of irregular forces makes him in a sense the philosophical godfather of the Boxer movement. Unfortunately for the Manchu, Tso died in 1885 at the age of seventy-three.

When the Japanese drove the remains of China's northern fleet into the naval base at Weihaiwei in Shantung, Governor Li Ping-heng did everything he could to help. When he telegraphed Peking for assistance, his messages arrived during the New Year holiday, and it was a week before a reply was sent. By then Weihaiwei had fallen, and Admiral Ting had killed himself with an overdose of opium. Rawlinson, pp. 189–90 and p. 240, note 109.

"After twenty-five years": Tan, pp. 104–5.

294 Rice-grain Yue was killed in 1895. It was said that the head of the Big Swords was rewarded with a mandarin's button. Esherick, p. 113.

296 "These Chinese Christians are the worst": Derling, p. 179.

297 "Duly authorized officers": B. L. Putnam Weale, *Indiscreet Letters from Peking*, p. 9.

298 "If you do not pass on this message": Purcell, pp. 224–25.

One of the many forms of kickboxing in Shantung was called the Plum Flower school, after the spring festivals at which its disciples performed before the community; when its practitioners took up the struggle against the Christians they adopted the more militant name Boxers United in Righteousness. Missionaries who contributed reports to newspapers in Shanghai called them simply Boxers, and thereafter the nickname was applied mistakenly to any group in China that practiced the martial arts. (The generic sobriquet "Boxers" was first applied by one or two missionaries in the interior who acted as local correspondents of the North China *Daily News* of Shanghai.)

Pingyuan: See Esherick, pp. 249–50; and Purcell, p. 200, for two versions of the fracas. The magistrate of Pingyuan reported: "Previously boxing teachers from elsewhere boasted of their talents and bravery, and young villagers, being ignorant, were moved by them to gather in groups and study boxing. Their intent was to protect each other. This magistrate observed the situation and had the strong enrolled in the militia, in order not to lose the aspect of self-protection. The weak would respectfully keep their station. They would not themselves do anything to cause unexpected offense." Esherick, p. 230.

The Boxers enjoyed the governor's protection: Purcell remarks the pro-Ching slogan and pro-Ching Boxer movement "has a somewhat synthetic air about it. Even after its adoption by the Boxers it was never fully integrated with the Boxer programme." He goes on to suggest that the pro-Ching policy of the Boxers was "an afterthought" or overlay. The last of the anti-Manchu White Lotus leaders to be captured in Shantung, Chu Heng-ten, was immediately put to death by Yuan Shih-kai when he took over as the new governor. Purcell concludes that "it is from this [October 1899] that we must date the beginnings of the ascendancy of that element of the Boxers which decided to throw in their lot with the Manchus." Perhaps it would be better to say that as of that date the Ironhats were successful in preempting the Boxer movement, by purging from it the last of the hard-core antigovernment activists, rendering the Boxers harmless. They were wrong in this assumption, as they were in so many things, and became alarmed by the danger the Boxers posed inside Peking. In the summer of 1900 as many Boxers as possible were incorporated into government forces, and Manchu princes were given command of them. Others were driven out of the city. Those who survived the Allied invasion were later exterminated by Yuan Shih-kai.

p. 299 Yuan ordered the immediate execution of Red Lantern Chu, the captured Boxer leader whose spirited defense at Pingyuan in October 1899 had caused the cashiering and humiliation of Yuan's cousin. Here was his revenge. Esherick, pp. 224–25.

300 "Sir C is taking it very coolly": Coltman to Morrison, 16 January 1900. Lo Hui-men.

"It certainly seems that Brooks": Backhouse to Morrison, 23 January 1900.

The edict is in Tan, pp. 60–61.

301 "The Empress Dowager is undoubtedly considerably frightened": Conger to Hay, 22 February 1900. National Archives, Record Group 59.

"I should have issued an Edict": Derling, p. 357.

"Unless Legations": Fleming, p. 63.

"It is said": Hart to Campbell, 6 January 1900.

302 Early in May: see Chung, *Much Maligned*, p. 209.

"These Boxers": Tan, pp. 61–63.

EIGHTEEN: *Something Wicked This Way Comes*

Like the Hundred Days Reform, the legend of the 1900 Boxer siege is highly colored, confused, and contradictory. Only after exhaustive comparison of contemporary sources, private journals, diaries, and unexpurgated records of the British Foreign Office (those not sanitized for inclusion in the official *Blue Books*) do the events of June 1900 begin to make sense. It becomes obvious that nobody in the legations wanted the real story to be known, because it was too disreputable; in addition, vanity, arrogance, and other human foibles made it impossible for the leaders in the legations to grasp what was really happening: they were as unseeing as the Six Blind Men of Hindustan who grasp various parts of an elephant's anatomy—trunk, tusk, ear, leg, belly, and tail—and imagine it to be everything but an elephant.

303 The warning in the North China *Daily News:* The date for the article warning Western residents of an imminent uprising is given as 10 May 1900

in Roland Allen's contemporary work, *The Siege of the Peking Legations*, but L. K. Young dates the article 16 May 1900, in *British Policy in China, 1895–1902*. The article is quoted in A. H. Smith, *China in Convulsion*, pp. 222–23. Later it was reported that this courageous *Daily News* correspondent "died in Peking during the troubles"—evidently murdered for his indiscretion.

p. 305   "A few fanatics": Mary Hooker, *Behind the Scenes in Peking*, p. 20. Hooker was the pen name of Polly Condit Smith, an American woman who was visiting in the legations during the siege and later published her diary.

"We are in a rat-trap": Hart to Campbell, 27 July 1894.

"I think it quite possible": ibid., 28 October 1894.

"All foreigners in Peking": ibid., 23 October 1899.

"Tung Fu-hsiang's military rabble": ibid., 13 November 1898.

"Rumour says": ibid., 20 May 1900.

Hart learned later: Hart, *Sinim*.

"A Boxer [shoot]": Derling, p. 358.

"One foreign soldier could kill": ibid., p. 361.

Prince Tuan was "absolutely crazy": ibid., p. 360.

Sir Robert's peers were trigger-happy and, because of his caution, regarded him as an old maid. One young British officer called him "an awful old footler." Another upgraded that to "an awful old funkstick." Poole diary, Manuscript Collection, British Library.

306   A fear of isolation drove MacDonald to action. There was tension between the Manchu and his legation over its role in the escape of Wild Fox Kang. While Kang was in Hong Kong, the court offered a reward for his capture or assassination, which was denounced as a violation of British colonial sovereignty. (The British did not see their rescue of Kang outside Shanghai as a violation of Chinese sovereignty.) MacDonald sympathized with Peking in the Kang matter but was instructed by his government to protest, which caused resentment at court. There also was disagreement about the imprisonment of Sir Chang, British disapproval of Pu Chun as heir apparent, and MacDonald's personal irritation at the lack of firm action against the Boxers. He advised the Foreign Office in London that the only way to settle the matter was to order a naval demonstration off Taku. Lord Salisbury, the prime minister, restrained Sir Claude during the months from October 1898 until April 1900. When MacDonald sounded out his Peking colleagues on the naval demonstration, Lord Salisbury was irritated, snapping: "It was stupid of him to do this without asking me." Quoted in L. K. Young, p. 115. When Yu Hsien was named governor of Shansi Province, MacDonald carried out his threat and the first two British warships were sent to Taku, but with instructions to confine themselves to protection of British life and not to join ships of other powers in the use of force. Ironically, the effect of the two British warships was to encourage the dispatch of warships from other nations and in this way to aggravate the court's fears of foreign aggression, contributing to greater tolerance of the Boxers. Ibid.

p. 307 "Possesses as little wisdom as judgment": This cutting remark was typical of Morrison backbiting. He enjoyed the MacDonalds' hospitality and was their well-fed houseguest as an invalid during the siege. Characteristically, Morrison was as hard on his friends as he was on his enemies.

At the town of Laishui: Esherick, pp. 283–84.

"I implore you": Fleming, p. 64.

"Little has come to my own knowledge": Morse, vol. 3, p. 195.

308 "The Court appears": Hart to Campbell, 27 May 1900. The fact that 1900 had an eighth intercalary moon prepared the Chinese mind not only to expect, but to help along, untoward occurrences. The year of twelve lunar months contains 354 or 355 days, and the discrepancy from the solar year is rectified by inserting an extra or intercalary month in seven out of every nineteen years. To confound matters, 1900 was a Kengtze year, which occurs in ten-year cycles. This was the first time that an intercalary month had occurred in the eighth month in a Kengtze year since 1680. The Chinese were fascinated by astrology, numerology and the more arcane aspects of calendrics, so they expected a great upheaval to occur in 1900, approximately during the period of July/August, and felt compelled to do everything possible to help it along. The character Keng had always been regarded as a bad omen for the Ching Dynasty. Morse, vol. 3, p. 183.

The dowager's difficulties are from Derling, pp. 357–60.

310 Morrison's rescue is recounted by Hooker.

Details about Auguste and Annie come from a variety of sources, including *"Notes sur la carrière d'Auguste Chamot."*

311 Thirty marines came for each legation: Things went awry, as Morrison explained: "As usual in these conjoint international expeditions, there had been serious blunders. In the first place, the British force numbered, when leaving Tientsin, 100 men, not one too many; but Russia was sending only 75 men. Accordingly the British Consul detrained 25 of his men in order that the number of British might correspond with the number of Russians." The *Times*, 13 October 1900.

"No more ships": Fleming, p. 69.

"Would be the last place attacked": ibid., pp. 69–70. In his famous report for the *Times*, Morrison left out the endless vacillation and changing of signals by the foreign ministers in Peking, as it would give the impression, rightly, that no one in the legations really understood what was going on, or could find common cause.

On orders from Prince Tuan: *The Yi Ho Tuan Movement of 1900*, p. 32.

312 Hundreds of Boxer shrines: ibid., p. 33. See also Putnam Weale's account, and Chung, *Much Maligned*.

"He pretends": Pearl, pp. 109–10.

313 The commentary and quotes from the *Herald* are from Morse, vol. 3, pp. 200–201.

p. 314 "We may at ar time": ibid., p. 201.

Sir Claude finally came to the conclusion that his last resort was to make representations directly to the emperor and empress dowager. The Foreign Office lifted its restrictions on his actions and placed control entirely in his hands as the man on the spot. L. K. Young, p. 118. For the next few critical weeks, decisions were being made in the field by MacDonald and Admiral Seymour without prior consultation with London. Ibid., p. 131.

The student confrontation with the Boxers: Lancelot Giles, *The Siege of the Peking Legations*, p. 107 and p. 180, note 5. Another student interpreter, W. Meyrick Hewlett, also reported the event in his published diary.

315 "A sense of the perilous position": Pearl, p. 112.

316 "Matters became worse": Derling, p. 361.

317 "Situation extremely grave": Morse, vol. 3, p. 201.

"Return of Emperor and Empress": Morrison diary, 10 June 1900.

General Tung's men were moved to Kichopei.

"By means which greatly increased": Morse, vol. 3, p. 152

The plan for the destruction": Tan, p. 217.

"As it became dark": Weale, p. 22. Bertram Lenox-Simpson wrote under the pen name Putnam Weale.

318 "The situation in Peking": Fleming, p. 72. It has been suggested that Sir Claude overreacted, precipitating a tragic shooting war. Many of the personal accounts in which these charges were laid were written by people given to backbiting. Refusing to accept any responsibility themselves, they all blamed Sir Claude. The diplomatic corps occupied a privileged position, resented by merchants, military, missionaries, Customs officers, and journalists. All blamed the diplomats for getting them into this mess and singled out Sir Claude for caricature because he was the most conspicuous target. Nevertheless, aside from Colonel Shiba, MacDonald was the only one competent to command.

"The invertebrate": ibid., p. 203.

319 Tensions were running high: On June 10 the British "Summer Legation" in the Western Hills was burned down. A student interpreter noted in his diary: "Lady MacDonald is very wroth about it, as many of her priceless treasures (those of sentimental value) were out there." Giles, p. 109. Morrison's report gives a better idea why Lady MacDonald was angry. "Soldiers sent to guard the summer residences . . . left their posts during the night. The buildings had been . . . placed under the protection of the Imperial Government. In the pre-arranged absence of the [Imperial] soldiers the buildings were attacked by Boxers and entirely burnt to the ground; the soldiers witnessed if they did not assist in the burning."

Murder of Sugiyama Akira: Sarah Conger, wife of the American minister and one of the besieged, said that Sugiyama was stoned to death, not hacked to pieces. Culpability and details were hard to assign, as Morrison himself noted in the *Times:* "No attempt was ever made to recover the body" of Sugiyama. One cannot help supposing that Sugiyama was a marked man (like von Ketteler) because of previous dark deeds, perhaps a role in the 1898 Japanese rescue of Liang Chi-chao.

Heart "was cut out": The *Times*, 13 October 1900.

"This news has caused us": edict quoted in *Blue Books*, 13 June 1900.

The von Ketteler episode was difficult to untangle, but once the basic elements were incorporated in a computerized chronology the sequence of cause and effect immediately became obvious. No one previously has made the connection between the abduction of the "Boxer" boy, the city riots, and von Ketteler's execution.

"A man of strong views and impetuous courage": Fleming, p. 92.

p. 320 "We could hear" are the words of H. J. Macoun of Hart's Customs, quoted in Morse, vol. 3, p. 205, note 51.

321 "Never have I seen": Weale, 11, 12, and 14 June 1900.

"Kettler and his merry men": Fleming, p. 98.

"What a bit of luck": Hart in ibid., p. 98. Elsewhere, Boxers went on a two-day rampage in Tientsin, killing Chinese Christians, burning mission chapels and the French cathedral. Unlike Peking, Tientsin's foreign settlements were outside the old walled city; the Boxers attempted to storm the settlement with spears and swords but were cut down by breech-loading rifles. They replied with firebrands, and most of the French Concession burned down on June 15. Morse, vol. 3, p. 206.

322 "All criminals": edict printed in *Blue Books*.

Morrison claimed he killed six: Fleming, p. 95.

The Yi Ho Tuan Movement, p. 80, attributes this estimate to Conger.

One group of fewer than twenty marines: Hooker, p. 41.

Boxer attacks on high officials are in Tan, p. 94.

323 "Give energetic protection": *Blue Books*.

Diplomatic corps declined: Giles, p. 119.

"Were ordered by the Empress Dowager": The *Times*, 12 September 1900.

Release of the young boy: Morse, vol. 3, p. 217.

324 The situation inside the court is dealt with in Tan and Sue Fawn Chung. Esherick writes from the Shantung perspective and does not deal with the drama inside the Forbidden City.

325 "If amongst the families": *Blue Books*.

The only eyewitness was Yun Yu-ting, who may have had ulterior motives. Yun claimed that around midnight on June 16, a man named Lo, who was a lowly grain superintendent in Kiangsu Province, sent his son to Jung Lu to inform him about four demands made by the foreign powers. Again according only to Yun, early the next morning Jung Lu supposedly rushed to see the dowager, and she immediately decided to declare war on the foreign powers. Sue Fawn Chung considers Yun a prejudicial witness with regard to the role of the empress dowager. We conclude that Yun's version of events is completely destroyed by the timing and actions of Allied commanders, which are incontrovertible facts. Ergo, if the Allies started the war, then the dowager did not. And by Admiral Seymour's own admission, the Allies started it.

p. 325   There is no evidence: According to some accounts, several members of the Tsungli Yamen went to the British legation to find out from Sir Claude whether the four demands were legitimate. They supposedly avoided asking him directly but were satisfied that they were not legitimate when Mac-Donald made no mention of any such demands. This is extremely ambiguous and based entirely on supposition. MacDonald reported the meeting but made no mention of any demands. Still, the "four demands" became part of the Boxer fable, a basis for the false assertion that they caused Tzu Hsi to declare war on the Foreign Powers. Tan, p. 74.

The decision to attack the Taku Forts was reached only after days of discussion among the Allied admirals and generals, with the foreign consuls. There was nothing ambiguous about it. One consul advised, "If you take the forts, you will be signing the death warrant of every foreigner in the interior." The admirals did not heed the warning. Morse, vol. 3, p. 211.

NINETEEN: *A Mad, Rotten Scheme*

Journalist Peter Fleming wrote his celebrated account of the siege of Peking in the late 1950s. It is fast-paced and a good read but very selective in its reconstruction and unabashedly flattering to British readers. A very different picture emerges on reexamining contemporary sources, many of which Fleming apparently chose to ignore, taking only the parts of sources that fit his narrative while ignoring other passages in the same books. A case in point is the eyewitness account of missionary A. H. Smith, which Fleming cites but which directly challenges his rendition. Peter Fleming was, however, given access to many of Sir Claude MacDonald's private papers. Unfortunately, MacDonald's heirs were dismayed at Fleming's portrayal of Sir Claude so that the estate resisted our attempts to review this important collection.

326   The Admiralty cabled Seymour: Morse, vol. 3, p. 201, note 35.

For Seymour's expedition we have taken details from Morse and cross-checked them with Seymour, p. 341 et seq. Some details were added from L. K. Young, pp. 120–22.

Among Seymour's officers were Captain John Jellicoe, later Admiral Sir John of the Battle of Jutland, and Commander David Beatty, later 1st Earl of Beatty.

328   General Nieh was one of the best generals in China, but his opposition to the Boxers earned him the enmity of the Ironhats; on July 9, one month after allowing Seymour's force to pass, Nieh was reported killed in battle, probably

fragged on orders from Peking. Some sources say he was killed by Boxers; others, by the foreign troops. In view of what was done to other officials opposed to the Boxers during the purges of late July, largely at the instigation of Li Ping-heng, it is likely that Li had Nieh assassinated. Tan, pp. 99–100.

"It was an almost incredible sight": Captain Clive Bingham, one of Seymour's intelligence officers. Bingham is quoted in Fleming, p. 77, and identified in Morse, vol. 3, p. 215.

p. 329 He could not move: The besieged made the following remarks. U.S. minister Conger: "We cannot understand why . . . they do not . . . march directly here." Robert Hart: "Had his force left the train and marched straight across the country . . . it could have been with us on the 13th or 14th and so changed history, for opposition was not yet organized." Morse, vol. 3, p. 213.

Memories of Lord Elgin's 1860 occupation: Finally, the court issued a decree. "We have received a report . . . saying that more than one thousand foreign troops will come to Peking by train. Now that the bandits have stirred up disturbances around the metropolitan area, we are handling a difficult situation. . . . If the foreign detachments still come one after another, the consequences would be unthinkable. Let [Viceroy] Yu Lu order the whole army under [General Nieh] back to the railway area near Tientsin to guard the strategical points there. If again there are foreign troops attempting to go up north by train, it is Yu Lu's responsibility to stop them." Tan, p. 71.

One pretty girl: Admiral Sir Edward Seymour, *My Naval Career and Travels*, p. 350.

330 A unilateral act of war: "Of course our attacking the forts, held as they were by the Government's troops, was nothing more nor less than an act of war against China." Ibid., p. 347.

331 After the second explosion: Ironically, the capture of the forts in 1860 had been facilitated by a similar great explosion of a powder magazine, which had startled and demoralized the defenders.

A forty-acre arsenal: Morse, vol. 3, p. 214.

332 The court did not learn that shooting had commenced until June 21. Viceroy Yu Lu in Tientsin saw no reason to include this disappointing news in his messages carried by dispatch riders to Peking. He was an old man anxious for his neck and made no secret of his affection for the British. (Before the attack on the Taku Forts, Lord Salisbury cabled orders that Yu Lu was to be offered sanctuary aboard Royal Navy vessels, an offer relayed to him by the British consul. He declined.)

"The insults" and "exterminate them" are from the "Diary of His Excellency Ching Shan," a Backhouse forgery that was the centerpiece of his first collaboration with Bland, *China under the Empress Dowager*.

News reached the empress: Tan, pp. 74–75.

She issued an edict: Sue Fawn Chung has pointed out that the so-called declaration of war edict supposedly issued on June 20 first appeared in the diary of Ching Shan, a Backhouse forgery. Chung also notes that in his September 1900 review of the events, Sir Claude MacDonald was not aware that the Ching court had ever declared war. Nor does Morrison mention the declaration of war edict in his contemporary newspaper story about the siege.

p. 332 A majority of the Allied fleet commanders: Seymour, pp. 347–48.

"China is at war": North China *Daily News*, 19 June 1900, quoted in Morse, vol. 3, pp. 218–19.

333 "In the middle of the day": Giles, p. 119.

334 "The Yamen . . . requests": Fleming, p. 101.

"Sounded the death knell": MacDonald to Carles, 19–20 June 1900, L. K. Young, pp. 128–29.

"Premature and needlessly provocative" and "absolutely nothing": *Blue Books*.

"Asking for a meeting": Fleming (p. 104) says the meeting was for 9:30 A.M. *Blue Books* say 9:00.

"We were all dead against": Giles, p. 120.

"Everlasting dishonor": Fleming, p. 104.

The timing of von Ketteler's departure is important, and both Giles and Hewlett maintain that word of his death was received in the legations at 9:00 A.M.—not later, as asserted in other sources.

"Smoking [a cigar]": Weale, p. 67.

The two sedan chairs: Hewlett, p. 11.

335 Killing of von Ketteler: Fleming, p. 108. Ernest Satow in his diaries records that the Belgian minister Joostens said von Ketteler "was killed by a soldier of Prince Ching." Satow diary, 21 October 1900. PRO 30/33, Public Records Office, London.

See Egbert Kieser, *Als China Erwachte*, for the recent German reappraisal that confirms our portrait of von Ketteler. Claus Terheggen helped locate additional material on Baron von Ketteler.

"His imperative manner": Fleming, p. 108.

He drove the Ironhats to murder: They were uniquely placed to arrange his surgical removal. The chief of police in Peking and head of the secret police was Prince Chuang, one of the most hostile Ironhats; the assistant chief of police was Duke Lan, Prince Tuan's brother. Both Prince Chuang and Duke Lan made it their daily duty to be out in the streets observing what was happening, often accompanied by Chao Shu-chiao, head of the Board of Punishments, and at times they were accompanied by Prince Tuan himself, who had the inarguable right to behead anyone anytime. They were well informed of the baron's aggressive behavior. Chung Li, another of Prince Tuan's hard-liners whose job was a cross between mayor of Peking and commissioner of police, had gone to the German legation to persuade von Ketteler to release the kidnapped "Boxer" boy, only to discover that the boy was dead, and Chung Li was roundly insulted by the baron in the process. This must have been the last straw. Bear in mind that, from the Chinese viewpoint, von Ketteler had committed murder and had ordered his marines to shoot dead scores of young Boxers before the confrontation began.

"Stupid princes": see Pearl, p. 116, and Fleming, p. 108. According to one version put about by the Tsungli Yamen, from inside his sedan chair von Ketteler himself fired a pistol into a crowd of Chinese, and only then was he shot in self-defense. This might be disinformation, but the baron probably was armed and did have a history of shooting people. Fleming, p. 109.

"Planned a massacre": The *Times*, 12 September 1900.

p. 336 The plan to have the baron murdered: Morse, vol. 3, p. 224.

"It is not often": Fleming, p. 107.

"The place was choked": Weale, p. 78.

337 Strategic importance of the Fu: Sir Claude MacDonald, "Some Personal Reminiscences."

"They . . . could not stay in the road": Hooker, pp. 40–41.

338 Much money was found hidden: Hewlett, p. 66.

Rapes in the Fu gardens: "There have been a number of attempts on the native girl converts, which have been hushed up." Weale, p. 132.

339 Death of Huberty James: Weale, p. 77. Fleming says three Chinese cavalrymen jumped down after him and dragged him away, still alive and kicking because he had been singled out for special treatment; three days later, after being tortured, Fleming says he was beheaded. However, Fleming got this from the diary of Ching Shan, which was completely fabricated by Edmund Backhouse. Weale (Lenox-Simpson, an eyewitness) is a much more reliable source.

Only a few sandbags: Weale, p. 76.

TWENTY: *The Siege of Peking*

In gathering material for this chapter, it was interesting to see that the younger people in the siege (those on the fair side of thirty) were relatively frank and unguarded in their journals. On the other hand, officially sanctioned accounts of the siege written afterward by various foreign ministers are prudently contrived histories. Morrison, of course, did both a forthright secret diary and a falsified public account. Historians have used the official histories and Morrison's account in the *Times*, ignoring the personal diaries of Giles, Hewlett, Hooker, and Weale (Lenox-Simpson). By ignoring them, historians have missed many important twists that contradict the sanitized histories. Sir Claude, for one, was greatly distressed when he learned of the publication of the Weale book in 1905–6. The word went out that Weale was "way over the top"— unrestrained, exaggerated, and inaccurate—so that his work, among others, has never been given the studied examination and credit it deserved. Following the

Foreign Office line, the *Times* condemned his book and effectively doomed it to poor sales. The account of Hooker (Polly Condit Smith) was published in America, where it was regarded as a piece of feminine fluff. Unlike the foreign ministers, Lenox-Simpson, Hewlett, and Giles were all fluent in Chinese and thus were able to converse with the "enemy" during cease-fires and lulls in the siege. Lenox-Simpson, having grown up in China, comprehended much more of the nuances, ironies, and absurdities of the siege and was by nature a brash and witty iconoclast. Hewlett and Giles present a special case, because they clearly attempted to sanitize their diaries as they wrote them, to conform with Sir Claude's position in all matters. But being young and inexpert at bowdlerizing and doublethink, they made a mishmash of it, blurting out embarrassing details then pausing to insert the official line. Luckily, they did not go back later to rewrite their diaries, as diplomats usually do. Other eyewitness sources such as A. H. Smith have been out of print for many decades and were sorely neglected by scholars. Ultimately, the trick has been to feed all the contrary data into a computer and painstakingly sort out the dates, details, and contradictions. What then emerges is a very different story. The discovery of Morrison's secret confession to having helped loot and destroy the Hanlin confirms our conclusions.

p. 340 To sweeten their dispositions: In Chinese armies men often went long periods without pay and were expected to forage off the land, seizing food from local people, encouraging banditry by soldiers. Commanders kept their troops' pay for themselves and dispensed it grudgingly only to ward off mutiny. The Boxers themselves were dependent ultimately upon their patrons, the Ironhats, whose generosity had its limits. They preferred to have the Boxers paid out of the imperial treasury, but there was sharp disagreement over this; the president of the Board of Finance, Li Shan, was opposed to the Boxers, while the vice-president of the Board of Revenue, Ying Nien, was one of the leading Boxer supporters. This dispute was conveniently resolved by putting Li Shan at the top of a list of men to be executed in the near future.

341 Kieser says von Thomann was a frigate commander.

343 "Has no control": Fleming, p. 142. Hall was second-in-command of the American contingent. He was the only serviceman of any rank or nationality accused of cowardice during the siege. He was tried and acquitted.

Early in the morning: Hewlett, p. 18, and Giles, p. 129.

"When done by Chinese": Hewlett, p. 21.

"It was therefore impossible": Tan, pp. 113–14.

344 Hewlett tossed it off blithely: Hewlett, p. 19.

This series of quotes about the "attacks" is from Giles, pp. 130, 131, 133, 135.

To be sure, some shooting was real: Serious Chinese assaults were directed exclusively at the Chinese converts in the Fu gardens, which Morrison and Huberty James confiscated from Prince Su under duress. These converts generally were despised by the legation personnel, and they were shoved off into the Fu gardens and left to starve. So Chinese attacks directed at these converts cannot be rationalized as attacks on the legations. Other Chinese attacks were directed at the marines behind barricades on the Tartar Wall, or along outlying streets on the perimeter of the legation quarter. Duty on the wall was resented, as the American Captain Myers reported to Conger: "It is slow sure death . . . The men all feel that they are in a trap and simply await the hour of execution." To fortify their courage, they consumed prodigious quantities of whiskey and brandy and fired indiscriminately at any Chinese who showed his head above opposing barricades. To be sure, the Chinese fired back, initiating many exchanges. There were many casualties at the barricades on both sides. But here again these gunbattles were isolated from the crowded legations, where few were injured except by ricochets.

p. 345   "Five long Chinamen's queues" Hooker, p. 117.

Bayoneted . . . by a French corporal: Morrison in the *Times*, 15 October 1900.

"I doubt whether he was much help": Trevor-Roper, p. 52.

"I see Backhouse occasionally": Giles, p. 163.

346   The first round fired: Hewlett, p. 38.

With so much time on their hands: Because of the anarchy of the Boxers, the Yamen's idea of escorting the diplomats to Tientsin was frightening, for "we should be very apprehensive of misadventure." The legation ministers were requested to proceed in small groups to the Yamen "but at the time of leaving the Legations there must on no account whatever be taken any single armed foreign soldier, in order to prevent doubt and fear on the part of the troops and people, leading to untoward incidents. This is the only way of preserving relations that we have been able to devise in the face of innumerable difficulties. If no reply is received by the time fixed, even our affection will not enable us to help you. Compliments." Fleming, p. 159. This letter was a genuine, if misguided, attempt by Jung Lu and Prince Ching to avoid further trouble by getting the diplomats out of the capital. Telegraph Sheng had declared this to be true as early as July 3, in talks with the Belgian consul at Shanghai. Five days later, July 19, the offer was renewed with a specific promise to send them under armed escort to Tientsin. If the ministers refused to leave, the Chinese government, having "faithfully given warning in advance, cannot accept the responsibility." Morse, vol. 3, p. 257. With the memory of Baron von Ketteler's fate so fresh in their minds, the ministers declined. Whether or not the offer was sincere, the Chinese army was so notoriously incompetent and unreliable that nobody was willing to take the risk. The defect in traditional accounts is that they refuse to accept the offer as sincere.

348   "For one month": Conger in Morse, vol. 3, p. 254. It was sent July 17, received July 20. Ibid., p. 263.

"Sauntering about": Weale, pp. 157–59, 163.

349   He brought news: Giles, p. 157.

"A secret traffic" and other quotes about black market foodstuffs are from Weale, pp. 165, 173, 178.

p. 350 Abundant stocks of grain . . . were not shared with the converts: The pretext
was that the grain might be poisoned, although that would seem preferable
to carrion crows. However, this poison excuse was contrived to protect the
legations from criticism. This was grain taken from a nearby warehouse,
which they knew was untainted and which Chamot used to bake bread for
the Europeans. Hundreds of tons more were hijacked by legation guards from
a wagon train of tribute being delivered to the Forbidden City. Although the
legations already had plenty of grain for themselves they would not send any
of this hijacked grain across the canal to the Fu. However, this surplus grain
was used to feed the ponies in the legations (ponies that were then eaten with
great relish by the ministers) and the horses of the Allied relief forces that
arrived in mid-August.

Most of the grass: Giles, p. 128.

Conditions for the converts: Hooker, p. 162. Weale recorded that "babies are
dying rapidly . . . The native children, with hunger gnawing savagely at their
stomachs, wander about stripping the trees of their leaves . . . Some of the
mothers have taken all the clothes off their children on account of the heat
and their terrible water-swollen stomachs and the pitiful sticks of legs elo-
quently tell their own tales . . . To the babies we give all the scraps of food
we can gather up after our own rough food is eaten . . . The Europeans still
have as much food as they need . . ." Hewlett remarked on August 9: "Two
days ago, the Ministers asked the Yamen for provisions for the converts in
the Fu, who are supposed to be starving. No answer sent yet, so 9 dogs were
killed in the Legation for them . . . only pony meat left for four days and
tobacco almost run out—an awful state of affairs." (There was still a lot of
tinned beef.) Early in July, before he was wounded, Morrison, who was
primarily responsible for bringing the converts to the Fu, went for an inspection and found the refugees crowded "like bugs in a rug" . . . "stinking and
insanitary . . . Children ill with scarlet fever and small-pox, with diphtheria
and dysentery." It was on his return from one of these visits that he was
wounded. Morrison and others made many other visits to the Fu to loot the
prince's private quarters.

351 The anxious Westerners: Fleming, p. 149.

Diplomats shirked all responsibility: "The men often make some trifling
ailment an excuse to shirk all work for the common defence, and spend their
time groaning over the situation, and becoming more hateful daily to the men
and women upon whom the real responsibilities of the siege are resting; while
the women who have collapsed simply spend their hours, day and night,
behind the nearest closed door, and await each fresh attack to indulge in new
hysterical scenes. I can honestly say there are more men to the bad than
women." Hooker, pp. 129–30.

"She earnestly assured us": ibid., p. 62. During one bombardment, Mrs.
Conger found Polly Condit Smith lying on her mattress on the floor, not
bothering to dress for her beheading. "Do you want to be found undressed
when the end comes?" she asked. Polly told her "as it was absolutely of no

benefit to anyone my being dressed during these attacks, I was going to stay in bed unless something terrible happened, when I should don my dressing-gown and, with a pink bow of ribbon at my throat, await my massacre."

p. 352 Morrison . . . offered $5,000: Hewlett, p. 51.

From worry he lost three pounds: Giles, p. 126.

The Customs mess: Hooker, p. 108.

"I am horribly hurt": Hart to Campbell, 8 September 1900.

355 The Ironhats launched a bloody purge: Besides Hsu Ching-cheng and Yuan Chang, the men beheaded in mid-August were Hsu Yung-I, president of the Board of War; Lien Yuan, subchancellor of the Grand Secretariat; and Li Shan, president of the Board of Finance. These executions were ordered *not* by Tzu Hsi but by Prince Tuan. When the Boxers had first crowded into Peking in the spring and summer of 1900, their ranks were infiltrated by some anti-Manchu White Lotus agents, apparently intending to take advantage of the confusion to topple the Manchu court. Denis Twitchett and John Fairbank, *The Cambridge History of China*, p. 118. Two thousand White Lotus conspirators assembled secretly in Peking, vowing to get "one dragon, two tigers, and three hundred lambs"—the emperor, Prince Tuan and Prince Chuang, and three hundred lesser Manchu nobles and court mandarins. Hsu, p. 467. Their strike was set for September 8. Hsu cites Purcell as his source. The White Lotus plot was uncovered in late July, and nearly two hundred sect leaders and followers were arrested. Of them, seventy-eight men and women were executed on August 15, seventy more on the twenty-fifth, and thirty more on the thirty-first, at Greengrocer Street. Purcell, pp. 220–21, 260.

356 Hewlett is among those to comment on these strange messages from the consuls in Tientsin.

TWENTY-ONE: *Chinese Takeaway*

The imperial loot stolen from Peking in 1900 graces many Western museums to this day. In fact, between the looting by Westerners in Peking in 1860 and 1900 and the removal of other treasures by Generalissimo Chiang Kai-shek's secret police chief from the mainland to Taiwan in 1948–49, the Forbidden City today is nearly as empty as the Palace of Versailles. Many of the details about these postsiege days are from missionary A. H. Smith, *China in Convulsion*, an excellent source that was largely ignored in the preparation of books like Fleming's *Siege at Peking*.

358 Sixteen thousand and twenty-five thousand: Figures vary; we have used Morse, vol. 3, pp. 268, 273.

361 The legations learned: This order was issued by Prince Chuang, head of the Peking Gendarmerie, and was *not* authorized by the empress dowager or by the emperor.

362 "Come in by sewer": Fleming, p. 204.

p. 362 "The scene . . . was indescribable": ibid., p. 205.

"Thank God, men": Hooker, p. 176.

Polly admitted she had kept a small pistol: ibid., p. 128.

Immaculate Sir Claude: MacDonald, "Personal Reminiscences."

363 Father d'Addosio: The *Times*, 16 October 1900.

364 Flashing their private parts: Esherick, p. 297.

365 Yuan's campaigns of terror: see Esherick and Purcell.

366 Westerners set out in search of loot: Giles and Hewlett both record some of their experiences in the free-for-all, as do Morrison in his diary, and Weale.

367 "Our *chefs de mission* are in clover": Weale, p. 276. Remarks like this made him extremely unpopular with British officialdom when his book was published.

"Not a thing was molested": Conger, p. 171.

Soldiers guarding the palaces: A. H. Smith, *China in Convulsion*, p. 529.

368 "Has purchased an immense amount": Morrison to Bland, 25 January 1902. Lo Hui-men.

"This morning I worked": Morrison diary, 30 August 1900.

To protect their homes and possessions: Morrison recorded that he had "an amusing interview . . . with the aged widow in my boy's shop who has untold wealth which she desires to place under my guardianship." Morrison diary, 31 May 1901.

"Sir Robert confirmed the story": ibid., 6 September 1901.

"Has your boy carried away": MacDonald to Morrison, 22 August 1900. Lo Hui-men.

369 "Mr. Squiers' collection had been honestly got": In his diary, Morrison described his friend's gentlemanly methods: "Squiers buying for a drink of gin carved ivories worth 200 taels and for 4 dollars a lacquer table worth 400." Morrison diary, 31 August 1900. Much of the Squiers collection of purloined porcelain was acquired secretly with the help of Pethick, the private secretary of Viceroy Li Hung-chang, who had intricate connections through Li with wealthy Chinese on the edge of the underworld. Viceroy Li himself took advantage of the black market in stolen Chinese art to sell "antiques" whose provenance only he knew—"it being well known that he would sell anything he owned, provided the amount offered was large enough, from the Russian sable coat in his own wardrobe to the fine latest antique, delicate-tinted rose vase he had procured." Hooker, p. 164. When Yuan Shih-kai became emperor, impoverished Prince Ching became a major international dealer in stolen and/or counterfeit antiques out of Tientsin.

400-ton steam yacht: Pearl, pp. 208–9.

The Summer Palace: ibid., p. 533.

"We talked about the curios": Satow diary, 15 November 1900. PRO 30/33, Public Records Office, London. He went on to note that "Jamieson it seems arranged with [Captain Mortimer] O'Sullivan that Ching-ming's house was to be looted, and that he was to have part of the furniture. Capt. Selwyn came to me to say that it seemed hard to turn the women out of the house, with no place to go. Expressed my surprise at the confiscation of the goods, and refused all participation on side of the Legation." Ibid., 27 November 1900. Sir Ernest Satow was appointed to replace Sir Claude MacDonald in Peking before the siege but was interrupted. After the dust settled, they changed places, with MacDonald going to Tokyo. The two men continued to send each other advice from time to time. "The looting," Sir Claude wrote, "of abandoned private houses and the looting of the Palaces of the gentlemen in your list of punishment is I think excusable . . . [however] with the mandarin class be just, but by the Lord Sir Harry, put the screw on, the higher the mandarin, the tighter the screw." Sir Claude to Sir Ernest, 1 January 1900. PRO 30/33, Public Records Office, London. One wonders if Sir Claude was invoking Sir Harry Parkes, who was knighted for his special aptitude in putting the screws on high mandarins.

p. 370 Chaffee's headquarters in the Temple of Agriculture: Michael Hunt, "The Foreign Occupation."

Installed plate glass windows: A. H. Smith, *China in Convulsion*, p. 546. Chaffee and his second-in-command were assisted by five Chinese, including the grandson of Marquis Tseng—Tseng Kuang-luan—a friend of Welsh missionary Timothy Richard. Tseng's home in the legation quarter was destroyed during the siege and one of his brothers killed. He took up residence in the American occupation sector in late August and for the next two months worked closely with Chaffee handling cases against Chinese looters, acting as a translator to smooth troubles between Chinese civilians and occupiers. When Tseng then left for his home in Hunan with his large family and dependents, traveling under a U.S. Army escort, his place at Chaffee's headquarters was taken by thirty-seven-year-old Yun Yu-ting, a Hanlin official who had attended many of the court's deliberations during the summer of 1900. With Chaffee's approval Yun set up a police force to help control the city and arranged shelters and charity kitchens to aid the homeless—that is, Chinese made homeless by the looting Allies (as in the Vietnam War's famous phrase, "We had to destroy them to save them"). Yun raised funds by collecting a special house tax but was thought to be raking some of it off for himself. See Hunt, "Foreign Occupation."

Every one was broken open: A. H. Smith, *China in Convulsion*, p. 548.

Von Waldersee set up his residence in the I-luan Tien, Tzu Hsi's pavilion in the Forbidden City. Tan, p. 145. Because von Waldersee had defiled her private apartments, Tzu Hsi moved to Emperor Chien Lung's favorite pavilion in the northeastern corner of the Forbidden City on her return from Sian.

His chief of staff . . . burned to death: A. H. Smith, *China in Convulsion*, p. 531.

In the absence of the owners: ibid., p. 538.

p. 370 "I hurried home": Morrison diary, 21 March 1905.

371 "A safe place": Trevor-Roper, p. 54.

Along with the genuine loot: For some disturbing insights into Oriental forgeries and how to hustle them in the international art trade today, see Carl Nagin, "Paper Dragons."

"Nothing whatever left of the documents": A. H. Smith, *China in Convulsion*, p. 545.

TWENTY-TWO: *Forked Tongue*

Although Cyril Pearl had access to Morrison's diaries when he wrote the famous journalist's biography in the late 1960s, he did not reveal the true fate of the Hanlin—perhaps not realizing the significance of those passages. Already sensitized to the matter because of other sources, we nonetheless were startled by the discovery of the damning entries in Morrison's diary, because they provided the final confirmation. Even without the Morrison diaries, historians long have had access to A. H. Smith's *China in Convulsion*, published in 1901, no matter how obscure and out of print, and also to the works of Weale (Lenox-Simpson), Giles, and Hewlett. Despite this, no Western historian ever seems to have doubted that the Chinese themselves destroyed this irreplaceable repository. Not one scholar protested when Fleming condemned the Chinese for this atrocity in his *Siege at Peking* in the 1950s, or when Marina Warner blamed Tzu Hsi explicitly in *The Dragon Empress* in the 1970s. In general, the whole story of the Hanlin has been ignored by Western scholars.

372 "Within an hour or two of the relief": Morrison to Bland, 4 November 1900. Lo Hui-men.

"Worst of all": Weale, p. 173.

373 Our description of the physical layout of the Hanlin comes from Adam Yeun-chung Lui, *The Hanlin Academy*. He is one of the few sources of information.

375 In reading the relevant passages from Poole, Giles, and Hewlett, it must be remembered that all three were working for Sir Claude and were obliged to keep official policy in mind when describing what occurred, which accounts for the many peculiar contradictions and juxtapositions in their journals; in the case of Giles and Hewlett—very young men embarking on careers in the diplomatic service—it may never have occurred to doubt or challenge Mac-Donald's interpretation of events. (If Sir Claude said the Chinese burned the Hanlin, then that was the prevailing gospel.) However, Poole's telegraphic style allows certain details to slip through that are at variance with the official history. And in Giles and Hewlett many odd details are blurted out that do not jibe with each other or with the official line. Poole makes it clear that Tung Fu-hsiang's red-uniformed soldiers (not Boxers) set fire to the outer gates of the Hanlin and that the strong wind spread the flames to other gateways nearby, but that a windshift made it possible to bring these fires

under control quickly. After that there were no more fires to endanger the library buildings in the rear of the grounds, and no more Chinese entered the Hanlin compound. Hewlett (June 23) reveals that the fire started at 11:15 A.M. and was under control within half an hour. During that afternoon "we began pulling down houses which were a danger to our North defence." The next day so many books had been stolen by people in the legations and so many others were being thrown indiscriminately onto the ground or into the lotus ponds that "Sir Claude gave orders that an attempt should be made to save the valuable books and prevent stealing them (many of the good ones have been stolen) and that all be brought to the Central Hall of the Legation; but, of course, many have been destroyed and only a minimum saved. They wanted (no messenger could be got to go) to send a message to the Yamen, to ask some civil authorities to come and see for themselves that the Chinese soldiers had set fire to the Hanlin (as hundreds of cartridges bore witness) and that we were trying to save the library." He thereby makes it clear that contrary to Morrison's account in the *Times* nobody actually took a message to the Yamen. His friend Giles (June 23) makes an effort to put the blame on the Chinese by asserting that "the Chinese [set] fire to the various buildings all through the day," which both Poole and Hewlett explicitly deny. Then Giles claims: "The Library was almost entirely destroyed: an attempt was made to save the famous *Yung Lo Ta Tien* but heaps of volumes had been destroyed, so the attempt was given up." Both Poole and Hewlett have stated very clearly that the fire was put out in only half an hour, and that far from being damaged by fire the main library buildings were only pulled down over the next few days on orders from Sir Claude as a preventive measure. Having made this effort to fix blame on the Chinese, Giles proceeds to tell us that "I secured volume 13,345 for myself, merely as a specimen. The pages are one foot by one foot eight inches and the volumes vary from half an inch to one inch in thickness. Each page has eight columns, each column contains two rows of twenty-six characters. I also picked up a couple of the essays written by some candidate for one of the great examinations. Within the next few days we completed the work begun by the Chinese and razed the Hanlin to the ground." Giles, p. 126. In other words, Westerners emptied the main library buildings at the rear of the Hanlin (closest to the British legation) and then began tearing them down. The most important library building actually was not torn down till *after* the siege; whereupon the entire Hanlin compound was leveled, all the damaged books buried, and the whole area incorporated into an expanded British legation. As Morrison's unpublished diaries confirm, Smith and Lenox-Simpson had it right all along.

p. 378 The contents of this great archive: "The Yung-lo Ta-Tien: An Unrecorded Volume," an article in the *British Museum Quarterly*, describes the museum's acquisition of Poole's stolen volume of the great encyclopedia in the 1960s; his widow was paid a meager £50 sterling for the volume that today, according to members of the museum staff, is worth over £10,000. The volume is in fact the property of the People's Republic and by accepted international standards is a stolen masterpiece. Lenox-Simpson accurately anticipated the fate of these looted volumes: "It is possible that missing copies of China's literature may be some day resurrected in strange lands." Weale, p. 9.

p. 378 Most scholars and writers have taken the same position: In the 1970s Warner assured us that Tzu Hsi demonstrated "how truly superficial her vaunted respect for learning was" when she rewarded the Boxers after the burning of the Hanlin on June 24. This alleged event simply did not occur; by June 21 there were no Boxers to be seen anywhere in Peking, and anyway the Hanlin was looted and destroyed by Westerners, not by Chinese.

379 Tribute grain: Smith recalled some years later: "When, early in June, the Boxers were revelling in an orgy of fire and slaughter they set alight to a street up which was coming a long procession of carts bearing the annual tribute of grain to the Court from the Province of Honan. The procession was consequently deflected into the Legation quarter, and quietly annexed, as 'bread sent from Heaven.' This little help consisted of 200 tons of wheat, besides mountains of rice, white and yellow, and Indian corn." It was this entirely surplus wheat, rice, and corn that was withheld from the starving Christian converts in the Fu and later fed to the relief force horses. Smith is quoted in *The Journal of the Royal United Service Institution*, August 1914.

380 "I have just been reading": Lady Edith Blake to Morrison, 7 December 1900. Lo Hui-men.

"It seems to me": ibid.

"I read . . . your splendid account": H. A. Gwynne to Morrison, 19 December 1900. Ibid.

381 "Clear eye and cool judgement": The *Times*, 12 September 1900.

"Was I right": Morrison to Bland, 25 January 1902. Lo Hui-men. The role of Jung Lu, his guilt or innocence in in the siege, continues to be debated to this day. We conclude that he was innocent and tried hard to protect the legations.

"It would be interesting": Hart to Smith in Trevor-Roper, p. 75. When Lenox-Simpson's version of the Boxer siege appeared in 1906, Morrison seemed sanguine: "Lunch with the objectionable Simpson . . . very clever." Morrison diary, 7 April 1906. But Morrison learned that Sir Claude was taken aback by some of the frank passages in the book: "Sir Claude has written an agitated letter to Sir John [Sir John Jordan, then the British minister in Peking] about Simpson's 'Indiscreet Letters.' " Morrison diary, 1 August 1906. The book was spicy and irreverent and did a lot of finger pointing, but Lenox-Simpson was careful to identify people only by an initial, to dodge libel laws in the manner of the day. His book was derided by the *Times*, because it disputed the official version. About his *Indiscreet Letters*, *Times* foreign editor Valentine Chirol wrote to Morrison: "They are sensational to a degree, but I doubt whether even so they will attract very much attention here, as the British public has a very short memory, and the story is now from its point of view a chestnut. On the whole you come off better than most people, though there is a nasty insinuation that because when you were wounded the MacDonalds took charge of you, you were therefore 'got at,' and the only chance extinguished of an impartial account of the siege. Altogether it does not seem to me a very creditable publication. What good can all this flinging of mud do now anyhow? Moreover some of the incidents which the writer admits to have taken part in himself, are not particularly creditable to him, and do not increase one's confidence even in his veracity. I am told that 'Putnam Weale' himself played a very shady part after the occupation, and was once very nearly laid by the heels when he organised a looting expedition of his own with the help of some friendly Russians. The diary, or what purports to be such, I take to be a mere literary formula." Chirol to Morrison, 2 February 1907. Lo Hui-men.

p. 382 "That somebody intervened": Hart, *Sinim*, p. 39.

Lim Boon-keng wrote under the pen name Wen Ching.

383 The eyewitness account of the executions is from Sterling Seagrave, *The Soong Dynasty*, pp. 132–33.

In evaluating what had taken place: Morse, vol. 3, p. 238 and notes 48–51.

384 The counterfeit Ching Shan diary was a major section of *China under the Empress Dowager*, by Backhouse and Bland.

TWENTY-THREE: *The Dragons Flee*

386 "Throw this wretched minion down the well!": *CUED*, p. 301. "Mocked the Emperor": Backhouse and Bland, *Annals and Memoirs*, p. 440.

"The wells near the Eastern Gates": Weale, p. 252.

For one thing: There are many contradictory Chinese accounts, which appear to have been heavily edited after the fact. Some of these are given in Tan. It is apparent from these contradictions that none of the sources in question was really certain and that for various reasons they choose to fudge and settle on the commonly held notion that the court—after first planning to leave in the early hours of August 11—put off its departure until the early hours of the fifteenth, staying in the Forbidden City overnight *after* the foreign armies had taken control of the city. This may have been the popular assumption at the time, but it is absurd on the face of it. Bland and Backhouse fixed this date in the popular imagination.

"Which all points": Hewlett, p. 56.

387 Lenox-Simpson noted: Weale, p. 183.

"Chinese soldiers going in and out": Hewlett, p. 68.

This was the same day, August 10: Tan, p. 116 and p. 118, note 9.

Tzu Hsi later told a lady-in-waiting: The dowager's account is from Derling, pp. 357–62, 181–83.

389 Prince Su's account: The *New York Times*, 8 January 1902.

The mass beheading of Western missionaries: In all about two hundred fifty missionaries (including more than fifty of their children) were murdered in China during the year 1900.

p. 390 Tung had the court under continual surveillance: The *New York Times*, 13 January 1901.

391 Left [Li's] northern financial empire vulnerable: See Albert Feuerwerker, *China's Early Industrialization*, for a full treatment of Li Hung-chang's quarrel with Kang I.

392 After the Peking telegraph wires were cut: The last telegram Hart managed to send before the wires were cut also was to Li. Hart wrote: "You have killed missionaries: that is bad enough. But if you harm the Legations you will violate the most sacred international obligations and create an impossible situation." Hart's telegram is from Fairbank et al., *The I.G. in Peking*, vol. 2, p. 1234, note 5. Paul King, who was employed by the I.G. in Canton, received a wire from Hart on June 10 that said: "All Legations apprehend attack and Chinese Government considered helpless if not hostile. If anything happens, or if the situation does not quickly improve, united foreign intervention on a large scale certain and end of Empire possible. Beg [Li] from me wire Empress Dowager to make Legation safety paramount and disregard all counsellors who advise hostile action. Urgent." Paul King, p. 142.

"That place was in peace and prosperity": McWade to Hill, 17 July 1900, quoted in Spector, p. 267.

Liu Kun-i: Another Li loyalist was the governor-general of the provinces adjoining Shanghai on the north, Viceroy Liu Kun-i, who was also a target of the Ironhats. Liu Kun-i was the fifth spoke in the wheel. A native of Hunan, his first job was as an officer in Tseng Kuo-fan's Hunan Army fighting Taipings and bandit groups. As a reward he was made governor of Kiangsi from 1865 to 1874. In 1875 he became acting governor-general of Liang-Kiang and Superintendent of Trade for the Southern Ports, occupying approximately the same position in the south that Li Hung-chang then held in the north. He then served as viceroy of Kwangtung and Kwangsi before returning to Liang-Kiang, where he was successful in keeping a lid on anti-Ching and antimissionary activity along the Yangtze in the early 1890s. When Kang I was appointed as imperial commissioner to Liang-Kiang to investigate why half the imperial revenues were disappearing into the pockets of middlemen, the ailing Viceroy Liu was vulnerable. Beginning in January 1899, Liu sent repeated requests to the throne asking to be relieved of his duties because of failing health, hoping to delay Kang I's inspection tour. He was called to Peking for a special audience with Tzu Hsi, during which she assured him that for his hard work in the past and his ability to deal with rebels and bandits, he would not be made to suffer personally by Kang I.

Telegraph Sheng: When Viceroy Li suffered his political setbacks at the end of the Sino-Japanese War, Sheng outwardly shifted his allegiance to Viceroy Chang Chih-tung, whose leverage in Central China was crucial. But behind the scenes he remained loyal to his original patron, Li. Telegraph Sheng was Li's chief agent in the Yangtze Valley and in dealing with foreign diplomats and businessmen or journalists in Shanghai. He provided a link between Viceroy Li and Viceroy Chang, helping Chang get loans from Japanese sources to pay for mining enterprises, military arsenals, and railroads. With the backing of both viceroys Telegraph Sheng was appointed director-general of the Imperial Railway Administration in 1896, giving him control over the three most important communications links in China—telegraphs, railways, and steamships. He also organized the first modern bank in Shanghai, becoming China's first tycoon. He and Viceroy Li were both targets of the Ironhats, who had only recently tried to sieze control of the telegraph company, the shipping company, and Li's Kaiping Mines and failing that had squeezed vast sums from Sheng and Li to fatten the depleted Manchu purse. See Boorman, vol. 3, p. 117, and Feuerwerker, *China's Early Industrialization*.

p. 393 Carrying identical messages: Paul King, p. 147.

Advised Jung Lu: This was on June 12.

394 "About 1,000": Jerome Chen, p. 48.

"All the Peking legations have been destroyed": The *New York Times*, 17 June 1900.

The *Daily Mail* story appeared also in the *New York Times*, 16 July 1900.

395 The obituary for Sir Claude and Lady Ethel is in the *Illustrated London News*, 21 July 1900.

"This man": Morrison to Moberly Bell, 20 October 1900. Lo Hui-men.

"Insane from the effects" and "who have arrived at Shanghai": The *New York Times*, 5 and 6 July 1900.

396 Yuan made a show: Jerome Chen, p. 51.

Two days later: Tan, p. 80.

Throughout the crisis: One very real problem was that the Ironhats had appointed the firebreathing former governor of Shantung, Li Ping-heng, as admiral of the Yangtze, to prevent foreign navies from seizing the great cities along the river; he had threatened to fire on the first foreign warship encountered, so he had to be neutralized before the shooting war spread inland. Li's strategy was to reach an accommodation with the Foreign Powers through their consuls in Shanghai and Canton, in which the southern viceroys guaranteed the security of the Yangtze, while the Foreign Powers guaranteed the security of Shanghai, avoiding any confrontation along the river itself. On June 24 Sheng telegraphed viceroys Li Hung-chang, Liu Kun-i, and Chang Chih-tung, and they agreed that Sheng and the Shanghai *taotai* should propose to the Foreign Powers that the interior of the Yangtze Valley would be protected by the viceroys, while the foreign settlement in Shanghai should be protected by the powers. They pulled strings in Peking to have the throne recall Li Ping-heng to assist in the defense of the capital—why should he not go to the rescue of the Ironhats instead of one of them? This ploy worked, and on June 30 the man who had first adopted the Boxer irregulars was called to save Peking from the consequences.

When the Allied armies: on July 3.

397 All the time Li was in Shanghai: Bland, *Li Hung-chang*, p. 204.

p. 397 "Nothing more hideous and appalling": The *New York Times*, 2 August 1900.

398 He [Li] pointed out: On September 18 Germany did propose that the Foreign Powers should make it a condition prior to entering into negotiations with the Chinese that the guilty princes and mandarins should be surrendered to the Powers for punishment.

"That the Court": Lensen, p. 12.

399 Shiba had removed . . . several trunks: Satow diary, 22 October 1900. PRO 30/33, Public Records Office, London.

"One man, Yu Hsien": Lo Hui-men, vol. 1, p. 9.

"Nearly broke down": Satow diary, 29 October 1900. PRO 30/33, Public Records Office, London.

"Showed [Li] the proclamation": ibid. 13 December 1900.

Meanwhile Hsu Tung and his entire family hanged themselves from their own lacquered rafters. Despairing of his own role in the conspiracy, Duke Chung (father of the ill-fated Empress A-lu-te) also committed suicide. Lenox-Simpson tells of the Hsu family suicides.

400 Jung Lu was immediately named a Grand Councillor: The Grand Council was reduced to only three men: Wang Wen-shao, Lu Chuan-lin, and Jung Lu. Lu Chuan-lin, former governor of Kiangsu, had agreed with Li Ping-heng that it was necessary to prevent by force Allied warships from entering the Yangtze. Tan, p. 135.

The second decree of punishment was issued February 13, 1901.

401 Morrison's account of the executions is from his diary, 23 February 1901.

"Already died off": Hart to Campbell, 1 November 1900.

402 On the fate of Tung Fu-hsiang: "So that he might carry out": Conger to Hay, 20 November 1900. Record Group 59, National Archives. "As to Tung Fu-hsiang": Satow diary, 13 November 1900. PRO 30/33, Public Records Office, London. The Allies eventually agreed that "For Tung Fu-hsiang, the Representatives of the Powers take note of the assurances you have given them on the subject of the [death] penalty to be ultimately inflicted on him. They are of opinion that in view of the execution of this penalty, it is necessary to deprive him as soon as possible of his [military] command." Tan, pp. 219–20.

"He was given a large part": From the very beginning of the court's exile, Yuan Shih-kai was busy sending large sums of tax money for its support. During the first month of exile Yuan sent nearly four hundred thousand taels to the court, much of it extracted from the gentry and intercepted from revenues being sent to occupied Peking from other provinces. His first payment was dispatched on August 29, an amount of 260,000 taels. A few weeks later another 137,000 taels. MacKinnon, *Power and Politics in Late Imperial China*, p. 34.

He shared this remote but luxurious exile: Lo Hui-men, vol. 2, p. 491, note 2. Prince Tuan remained in Sinkiang for the next ten years while tempers cooled, then moved to Tung Fu-hsiang's own province of Kansu, to be closer to friends. Hummel, p. 733. His elder brother, Prince Tun II, was reduced to the rank of commoner.

The Foreign Powers were unable to decide: Fraser to Morrison, 17 July 1901. Lo Hui-men. Morrison wrote in his diary that there was a theory that "the attack on the foreigners was an episode in a general disturbance devised by Prince Tuan to put him on the throne." Morrison diary, 29 September 1901.

"The heir apparent had been severely beaten": Satow diary, 20 February 1901. PRO 30/33, Public Records Office, London.

"In honorable captivity": Lady Susan Townley, whose husband was first secretary in the British legation with Satow. Townley, *My Chinese Notebook*, p. 89.

p. 403   The huge sum of 450 million taels of silver in indemnity: Conger was horrified when Secretary of State Hay ordered him to demand $25 million for American damages; this would have come to $46 million under the long-term installment plan accepted by the Manchu throne. Conger felt that the sum was far in excess of real damages and military costs, but he followed orders. Under pressure the Roosevelt Administration ultimately returned the funds, on the condition that they be used as the United States wished. Hunt, "The American Remission of the Boxer Indemnity."

Government archives: The National Archives and Records Service in Washington, D.C., has many hundreds of pages of such bizarre listings of items that people claimed to have lost in the siege. This is from one of the more detailed accountings.

Morrison wrote: "I have presented a claim for compensation for [pounds sterling] 5804 11s. 3d. but my claim has been referred to me for revision on the ground that it is flippant. I had made use of the expression 'Their Majesties the Empress and Emperor whom God preserve! (till this claim be settled)' and other things were objected to especially the description of my house [he claimed it had twenty-six rooms] which I got from an Auctioneer's notice on the back page of the *Times.*" Morrison to Bland, 4 November 1900. Lo Hui-men. See also Pearl, pp. 133–34.

His assets at end of 1899: Morrison diary, 31 December 1899.

TWENTY-FOUR: *"That Odious Woman"*

404   Tzu Hsi and Kuang Hsu rode in separate railway carriages decorated with yellow silk, each with its throne and reception room. Tzu Hsi's sleeping chamber, prepared under the personal supervision of Telegraph Sheng, was furnished with a European bed. The young empress and Lustrous Concubine shared another car. A first-class carriage was provided for chief eunuch Li Lien-ying, and two of second class were packed with ordinary eunuchs. Nine freight cars followed, crammed with servants, palanquins, wagons, cavalry ponies and mules, guarded by Bannermen clinging to the sides and roofs, grinning from ear to ear, almond eyes streaming with tears in the wind.

The descriptions of the royal progress back to Peking comes from various sources including Pearl, Conger, Morse, and the *New York Times*, 1 November 1901 and 8 January 1902.

p. 405 A slight wave: Conger to Hay, 7 January 1902. National Archives, Record Group 59.

"This was a wonderful day": Conger, pp. 215–16.

"I had another dreadful feeling": Derling, pp. 182–84. Tzu Hsi was apparently referring to her personal quarters in the Forbidden City, which had been lived in by von Waldersee and his concubine, as well as the Ying-tai pavilion, her office in the Sea Palaces, which had been damaged in a fire started by von Waldersee's potbellied stove. After returning to Peking she took up residence in a palace built by Emperor Chien Lung that was in the northeast corner of the Forbidden City, the only area that was not opened to the Westerners during the occupation of Peking, apparently because this was the refuge of a number of aging concubines and someone, perhaps Robert Hart, interceded. The lady-in-waiting, Derling, described how she later accompanied Tzu Hsi to the Summer Palace and visited the Marble Barge: "Whilst we were looking at the ruin, she said: 'Look at those colored glasses in the windows and these beautiful paintings. They were all spoiled by the foreign troops in 1900." Derling, p. 76.

"She [is] strong, powerful": Morrison diary, 28 January 1902.

406 "Appeared to me": Satow diary, 28 January 1902. PRO 30/33, Public Records Office, London.

"The audiences have all gone off so well": Hart to Campbell, 9 February 1902.

"That odious woman": Morrison diary, 13 January 1902.

Morrison's account of the audience is in the *Times*, 3 February 1902.

407 Sarah Conger's rebuttal to Morrison's claims appears in her book, pp. 222, 236. The source of the tears could also have been the British language officer C. W. Campbell, a close friend of Bland's, who had served as Admiral Seymour's translator during his misbegotten "expedition" to Peking in June 1900. Campbell mentioned the tears in his report, but backed off saying he had not himself observed the dowager weeping. He noted sourly that "the empress Dowager is reputed for her ability to shed tears appropriately." Foreign Office 17/1520, Public Records Office, London.

"To me the taking of gifts": Bland to Morrison, 12 February 1902. Lo Hui-men.

Morrison, who frequently used Lady Susan's gossip, told his editor she was "a pattern of indiscretion and communicativeness, most charming." Morrison to Chirol, 7 July 1902. Lo Hui-men. But he referred to her in his diary as "the cold-blooded Lady Susan." Morrison diary, 25 November 1902.

Lady Susan's quotes are from her two books: *"Indiscretions" of Lady Susan*, pp. 86–87, and *My Chinese Notebook*, p. 272.

408 "We were taken": Conger, p. 224.

It was customary in China to make such gifts: Tzu Hsi's secrecy about the gift was later explained by American portrait artist Katherine Carl: "When the ladies of the Legation were first received at the Palace, the Empress Dowager naturally followed the Chinese Imperial custom of giving each lady a present. Unfortunately this act was construed into a desire on her part to wheedle the foreigners . . . After the first few Audiences (when the presents were really of value) Her Majesty gave [only] small and unimportant presents at the garden parties, which [also] were made the subject of ridicule. Her Majesty had heard that the ladies did not wish to receive such handsome presents as she had first given, and she hence gave inexpensive souvenirs. Finally, the Ministers asked the Chinese Foreign Office to request the Empress Dowager to give no more presents [of any kind] at the Audiences . . . though Her Majesty continued to give presents in private." Carl, pp. 232–33.

"Uncoloured": Morrison diary, 29 April 1902.

"Disfigured by a slight goitre": ibid., 15 June 1902.

The ladies could not have Tzu Hsi to tea in return, as her advisers refused to allow it, but they did invite the court princesses. Sarah Conger persuaded her husband to make the American legation available, and eleven princesses accepted. Eleven Western hostesses were on hand when the princesses arrived in sedan chairs, with an entourage of 481 servants. After lunch they retired to the drawing room for tea, piano duets, songs, and a peek at Sarah's picture albums. The princesses reciprocated by throwing a banquet at the Summer Palace where the American ladies and the Japanese ambassador's wife, Mrs. Uchida, were each presented with one of Tzu Hsi's favorite black Pekingese dogs, seated in red satin-lined baskets wearing collars with solid gold bells, silk tassels, and gold buckles. Conger, pp. 226–28, 233.

"Each seemed to watch": Carl, p. 170.

p. 409 "As well as other undesirables": Derling, pp. 366–67.

"They seem to think": ibid., pp. 52–53.

"Indignant": Conger, pp. 247–48.

"On terms of considerable intimacy": Morrison to Chirol, 7 September 1903. Lo Hui-men.

"Simple-minded": *CUED*, p. 290, note 1.

Like many women at the time, Kate Carl was vague about her age; her death notices in 1938 mention that she was in her eighties while her death certificate gave her age as eighty. This would have made her between forty-five and fifty at the time she went to paint Tzu Hsi's portrait. Her father, Captain Francis Augustus Carl, married Mary Breadon sometime in the 1850s. Her maiden name Breadon is sometimes spelled Bredon, and she seems to have been related to Lady Hart (Hester Bredon). Kate's mother claimed that she was related to Sir Garnet Wolseley. Carl biographical data is based on *Who Was Who;* her obituary in the *New York Times* and Memphis, Tennessee, newspapers; and documents obtained from the Smithsonian Institution.

p. 409 Kate's brother did well, leaving on his death in 1930 an estate of nearly $300,000. The value of his estate was given in the *New York Times*, 12 February 1932.

410 "Very breezy": Hart to Campbell, 6 March 1904.

Carl's quotes and conversations with the dowager come from her book.

"I had explained that this was the shading": Derling, p. 352.

When Sir Ernest Satow saw Carl's portrait he had to ask who it represented. At the exposition the portrait was hung in the fine arts building between one of Queen Victoria and another of Pope Leo. When the exposition ended, the portrait was presented to the U.S. government by Sir Chentung Liang-cheng, the Chinese minister to Washington. During the lifetime of Katherine Carl there was controversy over the copyright of photographs made of the portrait in St. Louis. Although the portrait had been presented as a gift to the U.S. government by the Chinese minister in 1904, Kate Carl felt that she retained the copyright and objected vigorously when the Smithsonian Institution distributed photos of the portrait, which thereafter ran in publications, Miss Carl receiving no compensation. The issue was not decided in her favor. Perhaps more distressing is the fate of the portrait. When we were researching Carl's life and the history of her project, we were provided by the Smithsonian with a number of letters and news clippings about the artist and her portrait, including those written by Miss Carl objecting to violations of her putative copyright. However, during the administration of President Lyndon Johnson, the portrait was loaned to the Taiwan government and consigned to a dingy corner in the National Museum of History in Taipei. As the Smithsonian had no color record shots of the portrait on file and the National Museum of History in Taipei failed to respond to our letters, we had to arrange privately for a researcher to travel to the museum, where he was only able to photograph the portrait under very poor conditions on exhibit. It was hanging in a dark corner, dirty and neglected and in need of the attention of a competent conservationist. The Smithsonian noted in a letter to us in 1985 that there were no plans to recall this outstanding loan from Taiwan despite the passage of decades and the miserable conditions. The end of Kate Carl was also sad. She remained single till the end of her life in December 1938. It appears that she had no exceptional means of livelihood, having received only a $2,000 annuity from her brother upon his death in 1930. She had been living in Manhattan for the last five years at 170 East 78th Street. Her obituary reported: "At about noon Wednesday a maid found her in a bathtub at the apartment burned by running hot water which apparently had given her so great a shock that she was unable to turn it off. A physician gave her first-aid and ordered her sent to [Lenox Hill] hospital," where she died at 8:00 P.M. Her death certificate mentions that the scanty biographical data was provided by Robert Elkins, a friend of thirty-five years, and gives cause of death as "Second degree scalds of the trunk, thighs and right upper extremity; Pending investigation."

411 "Unfortunately": the *New York Times*, 4 November 1905.

"The Yu Keng family": Hart to Campbell, 14 September 1902. Of her father Derling writes that he was a member of the Manchu White Banner Corps, had entered the army young and served in the Taiping Rebellion and the Formosan war. Yu Keng was minister to Japan from 1895 to 1898 and to France from 1899 to 1902. He died in 1905. See Hummel, p. 300, and Chow. Yuan Shih-kai's first wife was from the Yu family, suggesting a hidden and valuable relationship for Lord Yu. When the Yu Kengs returned from Paris in 1903, they were greeted in Tientsin by Viceroy Yuan Shih-kai. Boorman, vol. 2, p. 24. Yu and his family lived in one of Li's fine Peking properties, the mansion of a duke, with 175 rooms and pavilions scattered over ten acres. When it was burned down during the Boxer affair, the family moved to the Temple of the Loyal and Virtuous, where Li's American secretary, Pethick, stayed when he was in Peking.

"Every dog": Spector, p. 115.

p. 412 It is possible that Derling and her brothers were working for the Japanese, as their eyes and ears in the Summer Palace.

For reasons he does not make clear, Trevor-Roper concurs with Bland's assessment that Derling was bogus and so were her memoirs, which is surprising. Roper writes: "There were the memoires of the bogus 'Princess Der Ling,' whose claims to have been a member of the Empress Dowager's court he [Bland] was at this moment, in alliance with Sir Reginald Johnston, exposing." Johnston, who in 1919 became the tutor to Emperor Pu Yi, was outraged by an entirely different book published by Derling in the 1930s dealing with the life of Emperor Kuang Hsu. It was not a good book by any measure. But there is no relationship between it and her court memoirs published in 1911. Johnston was in Peking only infrequently before 1919, so his insistence that Derling was counterfeit is based primarily on what he was told by Bland and by Backhouse, who had their own reasons for wanting to build themselves as definitive sources on the dowager, and to derogate rival Derling's firsthand observations. Although Johnston denied knowing Backhouse, they had been intimate cronies since working together as translators in 1898; after 1900, whenever Johnston was in Peking or Backhouse in Tientsin, they wined and dined and went to Chinese theaters together. Johnston insisted that Derling was a fraud and that he felt pretty sure "that she never entered the Forbidden City during those years." See Trevor-Roper, pp. 244–45. However, as we have shown, Derling and her brothers *were* in the Forbidden City and Summer Palace, were in intimate contact with Tzu Hsi, and while Derling foolishly allowed her American friends to persuade her to use the title Princess Derling as a byline, her father was in fact Lord Yu and she was a member of the nobility if not necessarily a princess; the rendition of Chinese and Manchu titles into English allows a lot of latitude. Her presence at court is confirmed by Hart and Carl, who saw her frequently. Her sister Yung Ling published her own memoirs in Chinese in 1957 under the title *Miscellaneous Notes of the Ching Court (Ching-kung so-chi)*. See Fairbank et al., *The I.G., in Peking*, pp. 1328–29, note 2; Lo Hui-men, vol. 2, p. 524, note 4, and Sue Fawn Chung.

Derling eventually married an American soldier of fortune and became a U.S. citizen. Her husband, Thaddeus C. White, was, according to Lo Hui-men, "an American adventurer, who had worked as marshal of the American Court in Shanghai. He subsequently undertook many shady dealings as a commercial agent, and was involved in the attempted sale of Palace treasures from the Manchu Palace in Mukden." Lo Hui-men, vol. 2, p. 524, notes 3 and 4. They settled in Los Angeles and she appeared in the social columns of the Los Angeles *Times*, which described how she met her future husband when she was dancing in a fund-raising performance to aid an American singer who had gone broke in Shanghai; Derling said she had studied under Isadora Duncan in Paris. In the early 1940s she taught Chinese at the University of California in Berkeley and died November 22, 1944, when she was struck by an automobile.

p. 412   In none of the many picture books on China have scholars deduced who court photographer Yu was, which is puzzling since many of the same photos by brother Yu illustrate Derling's book. Perhaps this is an effect of the long-standing prejudice against using Derling as a source. So we are the first to identify the man who took these wonderful photos of the dowager and court.

413   Derling described how "Her Majesty was taken slightly ill, and complained of suffering from severe headaches . . . She, however, got up as usual in the morning, and held audience, but was unable to take her luncheon, and very soon had to retire to her bed . . . After her illness Her Majesty was indisposed more or less for quite a long time, and doctors were constantly in attendance . . . Her nerves became absolutely unstrung, as she was unable to sleep during the day." (It had been her custom, as it was of most senior officials, to sleep from midafternoon till midnight, then begin her day.)

414   The artist's grandson, Hubert D. Vos of Santa Barbara, California, provided us with copies of the Vos letters and a number of articles and clippings on his grandfather. He owns seven of his grandfather's excellent portraits, including one of Prince Ching, one of Yuan Shih-kai, and one of Li Hung-chang. Other information was obtained from the Smithsonian Institution.

According to his memoirs, Vos was introduced to Yuan Shih-kai by Colonel J. W. Norman Munthe, a Norwegian formerly employed by Robert Hart in the Customs Service who had since gone to work for Yuan's New Army as a cavalry instructor. Munthe, wrote Vos, "took me all the way inland to the principal Chinese military camp, strictly guarded . . . The sittings [with Yuan] were in the morning, in the afternoon we used to play Poker with the Chinese army Doctor and another Chinese Secretary and interpreter, who were both graduates from American universities; in the evening . . . a dinner of thirty-three courses, with the military band playing outside, sometimes playing Chinese and sometimes Sousa marches, sometimes they gave us a great display of Chinese fireworks; and at night we barricaded ourselves securely in Mr. Munthe's little house with loaded revolvers and guns close at hand, for we felt, although the Chief was our friend, the common soldier might like to send us to Kingdom Come."

Although Vos later wrote in his autobiographical letter that he had been summoned by the empress dowager to paint her portrait, his personal letters to his wife and friends indicate that he was first approached to paint portraits of some of the officials of the Foreign Office.

p. 417 When the "old" portrait was exhibited for the first time in 1910, Vos told an interviewer, "I have been gathering facts about the career of the Empress Dowager, most interesting. Even her ministers know very little or nothing about her. The book of a reigning dynasty is a secret closed book and comes only to light when she dies and only then when her dynasty ends." Vos letter, 29 August 1905. According to an article from the *Mexico Daily Record*, 7 March 1910, "had Mr. Vos shown publicly anything that he had painted in the Sacred City during the late Dowager Empress' lifetime, he would have been guilty of a gross betrayal of confidence. The death of [the Empress Dowager] . . . left Mr. Vos at liberty to do as he pleased with his portrait of her Imperial Majesty." The "old" portrait includes two inscriptions in Chinese, one over the head of the dowager that reads "The Great Ching State, Tzu Hsi, Empress Dowager Kuang Hsu reign, [1905]." To the dowager's right the inscription "Respectfully painted by Hua-shih Hu-po" (Vos Hubert). Fogg Art Museum, Memo for Accession number 1943.162. Letter to authors, 30 October 1989, Phoebe Peebles, Archivist. (Mrs. Peebles asked Robert Mowry, Associate Curator, Department of Asian Art, to translate the inscriptions.)

Hart's first audience with the dowager was on February 23, 1902, which he described to Morrison and Campbell. Morrison diary, 24 February 1902; Hart to Campbell, 8 March 1902.

419 "The empress looked very young": Hart to Morrison. Morrison diary 22 February 1904. "Looking aged": Hart to Morrison. Morrison diary, 15 March 1905.

"Uttered never a word": Hart to Morrison. Morrison diary, 11 April 1908.

"I don't like the thought": Hart to Campbell, in Spence, *To Change China*, p. 120.

"The morning of his going": Bredon, *Sir Robert Hart*, p. 248.

TWENTY-FIVE: *Hunting Snipe*

420 Li's report on his illness: Spector, pp. 268–69, note 30.

421 "My waning health": Jerome Chen, p. 54.

422 "All praise highly": Morrison diary, 28 September 1901.

"The excellent good order": ibid., 27 September 1901.

Over hot green tea and iced champagne: ibid., 2 March 1902.

p. 422   There is a detailed biography of Yuan Shih-kai in Boorman, vol. 4, p. 89. Other major sources include Jerome Chen and Stephen MacKinnon, though we dispute their portrayal of relations between Yuan and Li Hung-chang.

Yuan always went out of his way: Yuan took pains to entertain the wives of important foreigners, seeing, for example, that the chatterbox Lady Susan Townley (wife of the British first secretary) enjoyed her visit to Paotingfu. Lady Susan rushed back to tell Morrison that it was "a glorious time . . . Yuan Shih-kai gave her a dinner. She was the guest of the viceroy and was treated with much distinction." Morrison diary, 9 April 1903.

423   For other gifts to the dowager, see Carl, pp. 290–91. See MacKinnon, *Power and Politics,* about Yuan's gifts to Tzu Hsi, including a troupe of dancers from India and an elaborate tricycle. On her birthdays he gave her fox fur gowns, a pair of filigree and pearl phoenixes, and a branch of coral as tall as a man for a choice spot in her courtyard. Ibid., p. 64.

When she traveled to the Western Tombs: Townley, *My Chinese Notebook,* pp. 273–77.

A palace redone: ibid., p. 378.

Yuan began army modernization in 1895 with the backing of Prince Ching and Jung Lu. Now it was no longer necessary for him to share the game with other senior generals. Military reform was overseen by a commission nominally headed by Prince Ching, but actually under Yuan's thumb.

"The secret service": Morrison diary, 22 July 1907.

424   Yuan sent him 100,000 taels: Yuan also paid for the prince's birthday party, that of his wife, and for the wedding of their son, jolly Prince Tsai Chen, who introduced Derling and Hubert Vos to the dowager. Prince Ching's estate near the Summer Palace had been looted and destroyed by the Allies in 1900, and Lenox-Simpson wrote that he was "so miserably poor, they say, and has so little of the things he most needs, that he has been forced to borrow looted [silver] from the [Allied] corps Commanders." Weale, p. 298. Sir Robert Hart helped Prince Ching get a personal loan from the Hong Kong and Shanghai Bank. Hart to Campbell, 12 September 1900.

He promoted his followers: A severe disciplinarian, Yuan was nevertheless popular with his officers and men, because he made sure they were paid regularly.

"Will not be last": Hart to Campbell, 13 June 1897.

"Yuan Shih-kai was bidding for the throne": Morrison diary, 20 May 1906.

It is often asserted that Pu Yi was Tzu Hsi's grandnephew. However, Pu Yi himself confirms that he is not the blood nephew of the dowager. See Pu Yi's autobiography.

425   "Over copulation and overeating": Morrison diary, 5 September 1907.

Yuan's fiftieth birthday party: Hillier to Morrison, 14 September 1908. Lo Hui-men.

"Hysterical": Morrison diary, 18 September 1907.

"She must bore": ibid., 18 April 1906.

p. 426 After the siege: ibid., 4 February 1901.

"Curious dreams": Lo Hui-men, vol. 1, p. 203.

"Read my narrative": Morrison diary, 11 November 1902. "Court returned": ibid., 23 April 1903. "Backhouse writes me": ibid., 20 May 1903. "Backhouse came in": ibid., 30 May 1903. "Prince Ching [is] really ill": ibid., 4 June 1903.

427 "Backhouse has just left": ibid., 24 August 1903. "The brilliant but mendacious": ibid., 8 May 1902. "I gave him good present": ibid., 8 November 1902.

Morrison tried in January 1909 to sell thirteen volumes of the encyclopedia to the Newberry Library in Chicago, for a price of four thousand Mexican dollars. The offer was declined.

"This morbid sickness": Morrison diary, 25 June 1903.

"I feel pained": Backhouse to Morrison, 21 November 1903. Mitchell Library. Lo Hui-men included many Morrison/Backhouse letters in *The Correspondence of G. E. Morrison,* but they were often edited, because Lo was not particularly interested in the personal nature of the material. We obtained the original texts, which did much to fill in the details about the personal and professional relationship.

428 "Fearfully timid": Bland in Trevor-Roper, p. 65. "Go in peace!": ibid., p. 63.

"The absence of the Emperor": Morrison diary, 25 October 1908. "The Emperor is suffering": ibid., 9 November 1908.

429 "You'd better not go away": ibid., 9 November 1908. This second Chinese was the diplomat Lui Yu-lin, who would later become the Chinese minister in London.

430 Edmund would accept no payment: Trevor-Roper, p. 65.

"I cannot help feeling": ibid., p. 66.

"Hurried over to Backhouse's": Morrison diary, 15 November 1908. "Working all day": ibid., 16 November 1908.

Now Edmund developed a new friend: Trevor-Roper, pp. 67–68.

431 "Her Majesty's illness": The *Times,* Peking dispatch 19 November 1908.

"We were put to a good deal of inconvenience": Bell to Morrison, 24 November 1908. Archives of the *Times.*

432 "I am sorry that you had no obituaries": Morrison to Bell, 14 January 1909. Lo Hui-men.

434 Gray was at the legation from 1902 to 1920. Dr. Chu had treated Viceroy Li, Prince Ching, Viceroy Yuan, and other prominent people and in 1908 served as director of the Tientsin Department of Health. In 1936 he revealed that he had attended the emperor shortly before his death, in recollections published in a Chinese work titled *The Secret Record of Treating Emperor Kuang Hsu.* He said he was the last Western-trained doctor to examine Kuang Hsu before he died, traditional court physicians attending him thereafter. Dr. Chu's narrative was translated from the Chinese by Polly Juen Chow.

p. 435 Gray's Report from Peking Legation, 19 November 1908. Foreign Office 228/2243, Public Record Office, London.

437 "Legend reveals": Hsu, p. 499.

438 After the dismissal of Pu Chun: Satow wrote as far back as November 1902: "The 'grandson' of Jung Lu . . . is the child who it is hoped will be born of the marriage between Prince Chun . . . and Jung Lu's daughter. But he is not yet in existence. If such a son is born, he would be capable of being adopted as the heir to the late Emperor Tung Chih, and it is quite possible that an attempt might be made to set aside the present Emperor Kuang Hsu." Satow diary, 12 November 1902. PRO 30/33, Public Records Office, London.

439 As to the death of the empress dowager, Pu Yi wrote: "Another tradition is that when Tzu Hsi realized that her illness was fatal she murdered Kuang Hsu rather than die before him. This is possible, but I do not believe that she thought herself fatally ill on the day she proclaimed me successor to the throne." Pu Yi, p. 18.

The much-feared Yuan was placed in charge of the funerals of both the empress dowager and the emperor and was made senior guardian of the infant emperor Pu Yi, an honor similiar to that bestowed on Li Hung-chang during Tung Chih's infancy. By making the current strongman Lord Protector of the child emperor, his interests and those of the child were entwined, which was thought to improve the boy's chances of survival. In this case it failed.

TWENTY-SIX: *Hatching the Dragon Lady*

440 For *CUED*, Backhouse provided the "inspiration of the work." Trevor-Roper, p. 70.

441 "I am now preparing": Bland in ibid.

In a long letter: Backhouse to Bland, April 1937, in Purcell, Appendix A, pp. 280–84.

443 Bland looked only at Edmund's translations: Trevor-Roper, p. 225.

"As near as any": *The Book Review Digest,* 1910, p. 37. And a review from *The Spectator,* 22 October 1910.

"One of the most fascinating": Sir Claude MacDonald, "Some Personal Reminiscences."

444 All quotes on pp. 444–7 are from *CUED.*

446 "With regard to Bland's": Backhouse to Morrison, 5 October 1915. Mitchell Library.

447 "You are far too modest": Morrison to Backhouse, 22 October 1911. Lo Hui-men.

"Damned Backhouse freely" and "he will never forgive Backhouse": Bland in Trevor-Roper, pp. 95–97.

"Some anonymous person": Morrison to Backhouse, 2 January 1911. Mitchell Library.

p. 448   Morrison had himself become involved in a memoir, the "authoritative life of Yuan Shih-kai incomplete and badly written but capable of much improvement." This was given to him in late May 1911 by Tsai Ting-kan, Yuan's English-language secretary, who had been among the first hundred Chinese students sent to study in America in the 1870s. Tsai acted as liaison between Yuan and Morrison long before the famous journalist became Yuan's public relations adviser. Lo Hui-men, vol. 1, p. 480, note 1.

They understood each other all too well: There was a curious incident in May 1911, when Morrison wrote to D. D. Braham, then editor of the *Times*, complaining about the obituary of Tzu Hsi's chief eunuch, Li Lien-ying, which had appeared on April 11. "It was based upon notes sent to Bland . . . by Backhouse, who was careful to point out, so [Backhouse] tells me, that what he sent was newspaper gossip, for the accuracy of which he could not vouch. He is somewhat shocked to find his simple statements so exaggerated. Are there readers of the *Times* credulous enough to believe that in the hands of the Chief Eunuch lay the making or marring of Chinese dignitaries— Grand Councillors, Viceroys and Governors—and that from Kalgan to Canton men went in fear of his displeasure? The story reads well, but is imagination not fact . . . It is curious to find the *Times* gravely publishing a statement that the fortune of the Chief Eunuch amounted in 1908 to two and a half millions sterling. Two and a half million cash [the practically worthless common coins of China] would be a more probable estimate . . . why is it necessary to formulate our condemnation in such picturesque exaggerations?" Here was a case in which Morrison caught Backhouse up to mischief, called him on it, and Backhouse quickly demurred, claiming that he had warned Bland that this was all unreliable gossip. This reveals quite clearly how the gullible Bland was used by Backhouse.

He had bought Chinese manuscripts from Backhouse: In December 1905, while Morrison was on a brief trip to England, Backhouse wrote to him announcing an important purchase. He recently had "obtained," he said, "an interesting scroll. It is a specimen of the calligraphy of the Buddhist priest whose name in religion was Hsui Su. His grass characters were famous in the Tang dynasty and men like the great Li Tai Po were anxious to get specimens of his work. This scroll is dated 746 and is of great value. I have been offered a large sum for it in the [Peking book market]. It came from a Shansi family of official rank now reduced in circumstances . . . I got it through a Shansi man who took refuge with me after the relief of Peking." Backhouse to Morrison, 24 December 1905. Morrison did not immediately bid for the scroll, but two years later Backhouse again offered to sell it; Morrison's greed overcame good judgment, and he became a partial owner, agreeing to try to arrange for its sale and to split the profit with Backhouse. Ibid., 6 January 1908. Offering the scroll to various connoisseurs in London, Morrison was shocked when an art expert told him it was not an original but a copy. He wrote to Backhouse: "I have received the enclosed letter from Voynich with regard to our Scroll . . . What I would now like to be able to tell him is that it was you who described the scroll . . . If a copy, it is a very early and interesting copy, but I myself believe it to be genuine. At any rate let us hope Voynich may be able to sell it." Morrison to Backhouse, 23 September 1911. Backhouse responded: "If you like to mention my name, pray do so, but I fear that even your generous recommendation and certificate of my Chinese knowledge will not suffice to convince people at home . . . If only I were Lionel Giles [Keeper of Oriental Books and Manuscripts at the British Museum] . . . the scroll would find a ready market." Backhouse to Morrison, 23 September 1911. Morrison approached Charles Freer, whose gallery of Asian antiquities in Washington, D.C., recently had been given to the U.S. government. Ibid., 10 March 1912. By 1913 most scholars who had examined the scroll believed it to be a forgery, and a recent one at that. Still defending its authenticity, Backhouse proposed to Morrison that they draw straws, with the winner buying the loser's share for $175. Morrison became its sole owner. Backhouse also whetted Morrison's appetite for rare books by telling him that a book he acquired for eleven taels of silver was seen by Lionel Giles, who "pronounced it unique . . . irreplaceable and old Giles bought it for the Cambridge University for 40 pounds." Backhouse boasted to Morrison of selling one eighth of his personal library for more than the entire collection had cost. Morrison diary, 14 December 1909. Morrison's library was famous in Peking. Robert Hart came to see it in April 1908 and, recorded Morrison in his diary, "Praised my library and asked me how much I would take for it. I said I would be sorry to part with it. He said that so valuable a library ought never to leave Peking, that it ought to be purchased for the [Chinese Foreign Affairs Office]." Ibid., 11 April 1908.

p. 449 "My financial position": ibid., 13 January 1912. In 1905, after a trip to England, he wrote to Backhouse: "I have been living at a ruinous rate . . . bought a lot of valuable books and have practically bought every book on China which I did not previously possess . . ." Morrison to Backhouse, 9 November 1905. Mitchell Library.

In April 1903 Backhouse wrote to Morrison protesting that he could not possibly have "mislaid a volume" from Morrison's collection. "I have taken the greatest care of them, as being your property." Backhouse to Morrison, 26 April 1903. Mitchell Library. Morrison's library eventually included four hundred early manuscript dictionaries and grammars, twenty thousand printed volumes, four thousand pamphlets, and two thousand maps and engravings.

"Wonderfully clever but morally unsound": Morrison diary, 8 October 1908.

"Backhouse was regarded as mad": ibid., 11 July 1905.

Vare's feelings are revealed in a footnote on p. 215 of *The Last Empress.*

Backhouse and Johnston: *Diary of a Plague Fighter* mentions Backhouse and Johnston together at these theaters. Trevor-Roper talks about meetings between Johnston and Backhouse.

450 "One of the greatest Oriental scholars": Bland in Trevor-Roper, p. 254.

The name Edmund Backhouse was not mentioned once: Trevor-Roper, p. 265.

p. 451 "Repellent and even shocking": The *New York Times*, 31 May 1914.

Ching Shan: On Prospect Hill there was an enclosed area where the bodies of emperors lay in state. There was also a school and buildings that were sometimes used as prisons. Emperor Yung Cheng locked up two of his brothers there. It was on Prospect Hill that the last Ming emperor hanged himself.

EPILOGUE: *Dynasty's End*

452 Morrison was a law unto himself: He had long coveted the post of Great Britain's minister to Peking, but his views had become too inflexible for a sensitive diplomatic post.

A list of honors conferred on Hart appears in Morse, vol. 3, Appendix E, pp. 470–71.

Morrison also noted ungraciously: Morrison to Braham, 26 September 1911. Lo Hui-men.

453 "Family estate": Hart to Campbell, 6 March 1904.

"Sir Robert looked exceedingly shaky": Morrison diary, 29 July 1910.

"Help me put in order": Pearl, p. 209.

Backhouse was then living in a palace compound that had once belonged to one of the Ironhats. Morrison diary, 16 May 1912.

Their first child, Ian, was born on May 31, 1913. He became a journalist and was killed during the Korean War. It is thought that one of the protagonists in *Love Is a Many-Splendoured Thing* by Han Su-yin is modeled on Ian Morrison.

454 "Why can't Yuan": Jerome Chen, p. 85.

Behind this charade: Yuan and his family were given British protection.

455 "I am determined to leave the *Times*": Morrison diary, 7 July 1912. Morrison wrote to fellow Australian journalist W. H. Donald, representing the New York *Herald* in Peking: "Statements that I have been appointed advisor are, to say the least, premature for no communication of any kind has reached me that could be so interpreted. I have been sounded that is all . . . Lots of men are here cadging for jobs."

In 1928, Donald himself took the plunge and became a special adviser to Marshal Chang Hsueh-liang and in 1934 to Generalissimo Chiang Kai-shek.

456 Stupefied by lack of work: An average work week totaled four hours. Pearl, p. 279. Morrison's photograph appeared on the cover of the *Illustrated London News* (31 August 1912), his head pasted over that of a figure standing behind President Yuan: the power behind the throne. Hardly.

"My job is becoming an impossible one": Morrison diary, 18 December 1912. Furthermore "Jennie fears that I will lose all energy and ambition and think only of my salary," quoted in Pearl, pp. 278–79. Much of his time was spent handling job applicants who wanted to board Yuan's gravy train as he had.

p. 456 Sung's assassination: The reign of terror climaxed in the sacking of republican Nanking by Yuan's army.

A hasty trip to England: In June 1914 Morrison made a brief visit to England, where he tried to "remove false impressions due to incorrect statements published in the European press with regard to China and to the policy of the President." He gave interviews, took speaking engagements, and sought to influence opinionmakers through his personal connections. Lo Hui-men, vol. 2, p. 196.

Yuan-for-Emperor Association: "It is two months today since I was summoned to see my august master," Morrison complained to his diary in the summer of 1915. "What devilment is he up to? It is ominous this rumour of his raising himself to the throne." Morrison diary, 11 August 1915. Yuan failed to take Japan into account. With the outbreak of World War I in Europe in the autumn of 1914, Japan was free to grab Germany's concessions in Shantung Province. Britain, France, and Italy, to win Japan's support against Germany, secretly promised Tokyo that it could keep Shantung after the war. With this encouragement, Tokyo put before Yuan a list of "21 Demands" that would make China its vassal. Unwilling to commit his precious Northern Army to war against Japan and always assuming that he could triumph in the end through greater cunning, Yuan acquiesced to the "21 Demands" ultimatum. It was a calculated gamble that he lost.

"Yuan Shih-kai today accepted the Throne": ibid., 11 December 1915.

Yuan's coronation: ibid., 17 April 1916. Morrison learned of this only after Yuan had already restored the republic on 22 March 1916.

457 "Surrounded by sycophants": ibid., 13 January 1916. Morrison added: "Yuan has lost his grip—not the same Yuan."

Yuan miscalculated badly: A National Protection Army began to advance on Szechwan, and before the end of January, Kweichow had declared independence, followed by Kwangsi in mid-March. Morrison wrote in his diary that Peking had grown dangerous: "Suppression of opinion. Men disappear daily. Taken across the River and not seen again . . . average 2 daily. Executed after military trial by N.C.O. shooting with revolver." Ibid., 20 January 1916.

"Hoary garment": ibid., 8 March 1916.

"Marked change": ibid., 29 April 1916.

Yuan was too sick: Morrison learned that Yuan was being attended by a doctor from the French legation, and three Chinese traditional physicians. As a doctor himself, Morrison noted that "the evil is that each of his three eldest sons recommends a Chinese native physician and apparently the old man, not to cause jealousy, had to take decoctions from all three and such decoctions!" Ibid., 5 June 1916.

"Yuan's belly": Pearl, p. 326.

"It is you who have brought me to this": Morrison diary, 14 June 1916. "He destroyed me": Pearl, p. 326. The allusion is to Yuan's ambitious eldest son, who had nagged his father to make himself emperor, despite Yuan's apprehensions and misgivings.

p. 458 A comic-opera restoration of the Ching Dynasty: Wild Fox Kang came back from exile to support the restoration, along with the same Ironhats, Prince Tuan and Duke Lan, who had brought about the Boxer affair and the beheading of Kang's brother. Wild Fox Kang, after spending the better part of seventeen years in exile, living off the proceeds of his Save the Emperor Society, was at last where he had always wanted to be: inside the Forbidden City, as deputy director of the emperor's advisory council, fixing the imperial chop to edicts. But he was not there long. The restoration lasted only twelve days. After the Forbidden City was bombed by anti-Ching airplanes, the Wild Fox sought refuge at the American legation; from there he fled to Shanghai, where he established a Society for the Study of Celestial Peregrination. He died in March 1927 and was buried on a hill above Tsingtao. For more details, see Spence, *Gate,* pp. 71–76, 102–3, and Boorman.

Morrison sold his library: The wealthy Iwasaki Hisaya bought Morrison's library. Lo Hui-men, vol. 2, p. 622, note 1, and *Memoirs of the Research Department of the Toyo Bunko.* These books, pamphlets, and maps formed the largest, most comprehensive collection dealing with China and the Chinese in all languages. *Far Eastern Review,* September 1917. Morrison retained three thousand volumes in English. Pearl, p. 344. Fifty-seven crates were shipped to Tokyo, where they became the core of the Oriental section of the National Diet Library.

Morrison's health was not good: Morrison diary, 30 September 1915. Pearl spends many pages on this fatal illness.

459 Edmund's many scams are covered in detail in Trevor-Roper.

Edmund's father left him only a life interest in his house, the Rookery in York, and the trustees of the estate were given wide powers that would protect it against any claim he tried to make. As his father put it in his will, "I have reason to believe that he is amply provided for outside any legacy from me by his own consistent hard work, conduct and industry in China for which I wish to express to him my most sincere gratitude and appreciation." Edmund complained bitterly that it was a "most unjust will" and that he had been forced to make do with a limited allowance since before he arrived in Peking.

He lived . . . in the Tartar city: Trevor-Roper, p. 269. Just before hostilities began between Japan and Great Britain, Edmund moved into the former Austrian legation, fearing to remain in his house in the Tartar City. When the Japanese occupied Peking there was an active propaganda campaign against Westerners, but there was no violence during this early period. Edmund's papers and library, which he inexplicably left behind when he fled to the legation—or claims that he left behind—he said were lost in a fire. He maintained that the papers were destroyed by the Japanese, who suspected him of some mischief, but others speculate that he arranged to have his papers destroyed to obscure his trail. With Edmund nobody could be certain.

p. 459 Reinhard Hoeppli, 1893–1973. We discovered many new details about Hoeppli's life. He knew China well and among others befriended Morrison's second son, Alastair. Alastair Morrison, like his two brothers, studied at Trinity College, Cambridge. After university he became an administrator and student of Malaysia. After many years with the British Colonial Service in Sarawak, he joined the Australian Government in Canberra. Lo Hui-men, vol. 2, pp. 83–84.

460 "A distinguished looking old scholarly gentleman": Hoeppli's notes appended to the Backhouse manuscript, "Decadence Mandchoue," pp. 437–38.

"Detestable personality": Trevor-Roper, p. 330.

His characters were Chinese and Manchu mandarins: It may be that Backhouse did have a sexual liaison with some mid-level mandarin in the Manchu court; perhaps he was a prototype for the fictitious Ching Shan, for the court *was* dissolute and there were doubtless a few mandarins who could have found it amusing to have the pale-skinned young Backhouse as the object of their sexual attentions. We conclude that Backhouse modeled his account of his imaginary affair with the empress dowager on some ongoing sexual liaison with a mid-level court mandarin. He claimed in his memoirs that he had been Prince Ching's lover.

461 "Both Kuang Hsu and Tzu Hsi": Hoeppli notes on "Decadence Mandchoue," p. 452. Hoeppli prepared four typewritten copies, which he intended to deposit with the Bibliothèque Nationale in Paris, the Harvard College Library, the British Museum, and the Bodleian Library (along with the original manuscript and first typed copy with Backhouse's personal corrections). Ibid., p. 461. Another copy was sent by Hoeppli to the Australian National Library.

Hoeppli intended to publish the memoirs: Trevor-Roper, pp. 286–87.

Looting of the imperial tombs: Pu Yi described in his memoirs how "Sun Tien-ying, an ex-gambler, opium peddlar and former subordinate of Chang Tsung-chang's who was now an army commander, brought his troops to this area and began to carry out systematic tomb robbery. First he posted notices announcing that he was going to carry out military manoeuvres and cut all communication. Then he set his troops to digging and after three days and nights they cleared out all the treasure that had been buried with Chien Lung and Tzu Hsi." In London the *Times* ran a brief article on August 6, 1928, reporting: "Suspicion was aroused by the selling of large quantities of valuable pearls, precious stones, blocks of jade and gold ornaments at Tientsin and Peking. One newspaper states that certain Chihli troops spent two weeks in breaking into the tombs, where they opened 14 coffins, and after robbing the bodies, tumbled the bones back into the coffins and reclosed the tombs." According to Pu Yi, "The funerary objects of Tzu Hsi mostly comprised pearls, gems, emeralds and diamonds, and her phoenix crown was made of enormous pearls and gold wire. On her coverlet was a peony consisting entirely of jewels, and on her arm was a bracelet of dazzling brilliance in the form of a large chrysanthemum and six small plum blossoms all set with diamonds of various sizes. In her hand was a demon-quelling wand over three inches long made of emerald, and on her feet she wore a pair of pearl shoes. Apart from all this the coffin contained seventeen strings of pearls and gems strung together as prayer beads and several pairs of emerald bracelets." Pu Yi, p. 195. A more sensational account of the riches looted from the tombs appeared in the *Times* on November 13, 1928, from "our Shanghai correspondent." The source for this fabulous account allegedly was the diary of chief eunuch Li Lien-ying—a total fabrication by Edmund Backhouse. By then the *Times* had forgotten Morrison's warning regarding earlier fanciful stories from Bland and Backhouse that they had run about Li Lien-ying. Now they devoted the better part of a column to the dowager's burial as described in the Grand Eunuch's bogus secret diary: "Before the Dowager Empress was laid in the coffin, the bottom was spread with a mattress of gold thread, seven inches thick, in which was woven an embroidery of pearls. On top of the mattress was laid a silk embroidered coverlet strewn with a layer of pearls. In the pearl layer was a lace sheet of pearls, into which was woven a figure of Buddha. At the head there was placed a jade ornament resembling lotus leaves and at the foot a similar ornament of jade in the shape of a lotus flower . . ." etc., etc. The *Times* gave the total value of these bogus treasures as £6.25 million sterling. The differences between Emperor Pu Yi's account and this account are typical of Edmund Backhouse. Once again the *Times* had been duped. Backhouse assured Bland that Grand Eunuch Li's memoirs confirmed all their own judgments of Tzu Hsi.

The *Times* carried a brief report describing how "A party of Manchu nobles recently visited the [tomb] and reported that the coffin of the famous Empress dowager was open with her naked body lying on the lid, half-covered with a dilapidated yellow dragon robe. The hair had not rotted and the face was lifelike, but the colour of the body was purple." This is pure Backhouse. The *Times*, 10 September 1928.

BIBLIOGRAPHY

Aitchison, Margaret. *The Doctor and the Dragon.* Basingstoke, Hampshire: Pickering & Inglis, 1983.

Allen, Bernard M. *Gordon in China.* London: Macmillan, 1933.

Allen, Roland. *The Siege of the Peking Legations.* London: Smith, Elder, & Co., 1901.

Axelbank, Albert. *Black Star over Japan.* London: George Allen & Unwin, 1972.

Ayers, William. *Chang Chih-tung and Educational Reform in China.* Cambridge: Harvard University Press, 1971.

Backhouse, Edmund. "The Dead Past." Unpublished manuscript.

———. "Decadence Mandchoue." Unpublished manuscript.

———, and Bland, J.O.P. *Annals and Memoirs of the Court of Peking.* Boston: Houghton Mifflin, 1914.

Bales, W. L. *Tso Tsungt'ang: Soldier and Statesman of Old China.* Shanghai: Kelly and Walsh, 1937.

Bays, Daniel H. "The Nature of Provincial Political Authority in Late Ch'ing Times." *Modern Asian Studies,* no. 4 (1970).

Beers, Burton F. *China in Old Photographs: 1860–1910.* New York: Charles Scribner's Sons, 1978.

Behr, Edward. *The Last Emperor.* New York: Bantam Books, 1987.

Bell, Stanley. *Hart of Lisburn.* Lisburn, Northern Ireland: Lisburn Historical Press, 1985.

Benkovitz, Miriam J. *Frederick Rolfe: Baron Corvo.* London: Hamish Hamilton, 1977.

Bergamini, David. *Japan's Imperial Conspiracy.* London: Heinemann, 1971.

Berridge, Virginia. "Victorian Opium Eating." *Victorian Studies,* Summer 1978.

Biggerstaff, Knight. "The Official Chinese Attitude toward the Burlingame Mission." *American Historical Review,* July 1936.

Blakeslee, George H. *China and the Far East.* New York: Thomas Y. Crowell and Co., 1910.

Bland, J.O.P. *Li Hung-chang.* Freeport, N.Y.: Books for Libraries Press, 1971 (first published in 1917).

———. *Recent Events and Present Policies in China.* London: William Heinemann, 1912.

———, and Backhouse, E. *China under the Empress Dowager.* London: William Heinemann, 1910.

Bodard, Lucien. *La Vallée des Roses.* Paris: France Loisirs, 1977.

Bohr, Paul Richard. *Famine in China and the Missionary.* Cambridge: East Asian Research Center, Harvard University, 1972.

Boorman, Howard L., ed. *Biographical Dictionary of Republican China.* 5 vols. New York: Columbia University Press, 1979.

Borel, Henri. *The New China: A Traveller's Impression.* London: T. Fisher Unwin, 1912.

Bourne, Peter. *Twilight of the Dragon.* New York: G. P. Putnam's Sons, 1954.

Bozan, Jian, et al. *A Concise History of China.* Peking: Foreign Languages Press, 1981.

Brackman, Arthur. *The Last Emperor.* New York: Charles Scribner's Sons, 1975.

Bredon, Juliet. *Peking: A Historical and Intimate Description.* Shanghai: Kelly and Walsh, 1931.

———. *Sir Robert Hart: The Romance of a Great Career.* London: Hutchinson & Company, 1910.

Britton, Roswell S. *The Chinese Periodical Press.* Shanghai: Kelly and Walsh, 1933.

Bruner, Katherine F.; Fairbank, John K.; and Smith, Richard J., eds. *Entering China's Service: Robert Hart's Journals, 1854–1863.* Cambridge: Harvard University Press, 1986.

Buck, Pearl S. *Imperial Woman.* New York: John Day Co., 1956.

Burke, James. "Eunuchs of Peiping." *Life,* 21 February 1949.

Cahill, Holger. *A Yankee Adventurer.* New York: The Macauley Co., 1978.

Cameron, Nigel. *Barbarians and Mandarins: Thirteen Centuries of Western Travelers in China.* New York: Walker and Weatherhill, 1970.

Cammann, Schuyler. *China's Dragon Robes.* New York: Ronald Press Co., 1952.

Carl, Katherine A. *With the Empress Dowager of China.* 2d ed. Tientsin: Société Française de Librairie et d'Edition, 1926.

Carlson, Ellsworth C. *The Kaiping Mines.* Cambridge: Harvard University Press, 1971.

Chang Hao. "The Anti-foreignist Role of Wo-jen." *Papers on China*, 14: 1–29. East Asian Research Center, Harvard University: 1960.

———. "Liang Ch'i Ch'ao and the Intellectual Changes in the Late Nineteenth Century." *The Journal of Asian Studies*, November 1969.

———. *Liang Ch'i Ch'ao and Intellectual Transition in China, 1890–1907.* Cambridge: Harvard University Press, 1971.

Chang Hsin-pao. *Commissioner Lin and the Opium War.* Cambridge: Harvard University Press, 1964.

Chang Te-chang. "Economic Role of the Imperial Household in the Ch'ing Dynasty." *The Journal of Asian Studies*, February 1972.

Chen, Gideon. *Tseng Kuo-fan: Pioneer Promoter of the Steamship in China.* Peking, 1938.

Chen, H. S., and Kates, G. N. "Prince Kung's Palace and Its Adjoining Garden in Peking." *Monumenta Serica* #5 (1940).

Chen, Jerome. *Yuan Shih-kai.* 2d ed. Stanford: Stanford University Press, 1972.

Chesneaux, Jean. *China from the Opium Wars to the 1911 Revolution.* New York: Pantheon Books, 1976.

———, ed. *Popular Movements and Secret Societies in China, 1840–1950.* Stanford: Stanford University Press, 1972.

———. *Secret Societies in China.* London: Heinemann Educational Books, 1971.

Chi Hsi-sheng. *Warlord Politics in China: 1916–1928.* Stanford: Stanford University Press, 1976.

"The Chinese Reform Movement of the 1890s: A Symposium." *The Journal of Asian Studies*, November 1969.

Chou, Eric. *The Dragon and the Phoenix.* New York: Arbor House, 1970.

Chow Jen Hwa. *China and Japan: The History of Chinese Diplomatic Missions in Japan 1877–1911.* Singapore: Eurasia Press, 1975.

Christman, Margaret. *Adventurous Pursuits, Americans and the China Trade: 1784–1844.* Washington, D.C.: Smithsonian Institution Press, 1984.

Chu Wen-djang. *The Moslem Rebellion in Northwest China, 1862–1878.* The Hague: Mouton & Co., 1966.

Chung Sue Fawn. *The Much Maligned Empress Dowager.* Ann Arbor, Mich.: Xerox University Microfilms, 1975.

———. "The Much Maligned Empress Dowager." *Modern Asian Studies* 13, no. 2 (1979).

Clayre, Alasdair. *The Heart of the Dragon.* London: Harvill Press and William Collins Sons & Co., 1984.

Clubb, O. Edmund. *China and Russia: The Great Game.* New York: Columbia University Press, 1971.

Cohen, Paul A. "The Anti-Christian Tradition in China." *The Journal of Asian Studies*, February 1969.

————. *Between Tradition and Modernity: Wang T'ao and Reform in Late Ch'ing China.* Cambridge: Harvard University Press, 1974.

————. *China and Christianity: The Missionary Movement and the Growth of Chinese Anti-Foreignism, 1860 to 1870.* Cambridge: Harvard University Press, 1963.

————, and Schrecker, John E., eds. *Reform in Nineteenth Century China.* Cambridge: Harvard University Press, 1976.

Collis, Maurice. *The Motherly and Auspicious.* New York: G. P. Putnam's Sons, 1944.

Conger, Sarah Pike. *Letters from Peking.* Chicago: A. C. McClurg & Co., 1909.

Covell, Ralph R. *The Life and Thought of W.A.P. Martin.* Ann Arbor, Mich.: University Microfilms International, 1986.

Coye, Molly Joel, and Livingston, Jon, eds. *China Yesterday and Today.* New York: Bantam Books, 1979.

Denby, Charles. *China and Her People.* Boston: L. C. Page & Co., 1906.

Derling, Princess (Yu Derling, Mrs. Thaddeus White). *Two Years in the Forbidden City.* New York: Moffat, Yard and Co., 1911.

Dickens, A. G., ed. *The Courts of Europe.* New York: McGraw-Hill Book Co., 1977.

Donahue, William J. "The Caleb Cushing Mission." *Modern Asian Studies* 16, no. 2 (1982).

Dorn, Frank. *The Forbidden City.* New York: Charles Scribner's Sons, 1970.

Douglas, Robert K. *Li Hungchang.* London: Bliss, Sands and Forster, 1895.

Drake, Belle Vinnedge. "A Visit to the Empress Dowager." *The Century Magazine,* September 1902.

Earle, James E. "Playing at Clouds and Rain in Chinese Literature." Master's thesis, Eckerd College, 1973.

Eastman, Lloyd E. "Ching-i and Chinese Policy Formation During the Nineteenth Century." *The Journal of Asian Studies,* August 1965.

————. "Political Reformism in China before the Sino-Japanese War." *The Journal of Asian Studies,* August 1968.

————. *Throne and Mandarins: China's Search for a Policy During the Sino-French Controversy, 1880–1885.* Cambridge: Harvard University Press, 1967.

Esherick, Joseph W. *The Origins of the Boxer Uprising.* Berkeley: University of California Press, 1987.

Fairbank, John K. *The Great Chinese Revolution.* New York: Harper & Row, 1986.

————. *Trade and Diplomacy on the China Coast.* Stanford: Stanford University Press, 1969.

————; Bruner, Katherine Frost; and Matheson, Elizabeth MacLeod, eds. *The I.G. in Peking: Letters of Robert Hart/Chinese Maritime Customs, 1868–1907.* 2 vols. Cambridge: Harvard University Press, Belknap Press, 1975.

————, and Reischauer, Edwin O. *China: Tradition and Transformation.* New York: Houghton Mifflin Co., 1973.

Felber, John E. *The American's Tourist Manual for the People's Republic of China.* Newark, N. J.: International Intertrade Index, 1974.

Fernald, Helen E. *Chinese Court Costumes.* Toronto: Royal Ontario Museum of Archaeology, 1946.

Feuerwerker, Albert. *China's Early Industrialization.* New York: Atheneum, 1970.

————. *Rebellion in Nineteenth-Century China.* Ann Arbor: Michigan Papers in Chinese Studies, no. 21, 1975.

Fitzgerald, Charles P. *The Empress Wu.* 2d ed. London: The Cresset Press, 1968.

Fleming, Peter. *The Siege at Peking.* New York: Harper & Brothers, 1959.

Foord, John. "The Root of the Chinese Trouble." *North American Review,* September 1900.

Forbes, Archibald. *Chinese Gordon.* New York: John B. Alden, 1884.

Franke, Wolfgang. *A Century of Chinese Revolution, 1851–1949.* Columbia: University of South Carolina Press, 1970.

Freeman-Mitford, A. B. *The Attaché at Peking.* London: Macmillan and Co., 1900.

Gerson, Jack J. *Horatio Nelson Lay and Sino-British Relations, 1854–1864.* Cambridge: Harvard University Press, 1972.

Giles, Lancelot. *The Siege of the Peking Legations, A Diary.* ed. L. R. Marchant, n.p.: University of Western Australia Press, 1970.

Gillen, Donald G. *Warlord Yen Hsi-shan in Shansi Province: 1911–1949.* Princeton: Princeton University Press, 1967.

Goodrich, L. Carrington, and Cameron, Nigel. *The Face of China as Seen by Photographers & Travelers: 1860–1912.* Millerton, N.Y.: Aperture, 1978.

Grant, General Sir Hope. *Incidents in the China War of 1860.* London: Henry Knolly, 1875.

Greenberg, Michael. *British Trade and the Opening of China 1800–1842.* Cambridge: Harvard University Press, 1951.

Gregory, John S. "British Intervention against the Taiping Rebellion." *The Journal of Asian Studies,* November 1959.

Griffith, Samuel B., trans. *Sun Tzu: The Art of War.* Oxford: The Clarendon Press, 1963.

Grousset, René. *The Empire of the Steppes.* New Brunswick, N.J.: Rutgers University Press, 1970.

Guide to the Papers of George Ernest Morrison in the Mitchell Library. Sydney, Australia: The Library Council of New South Wales, 1977.

Gulik, Robert H. van. *Sexual Life in Ancient China.* Leiden: E. J. Brill, 1961.

Haldane, Charlotte. *The Last Great Empress of China.* New York: Bobbs-Merrill Co., 1965.

Harem Favorites of an Illustrious Celestial. Taiwan: Chung-t'ai Printing Co., 1958.

Harrison, John A. *China since 1800.* New York: Harcourt, Brace & World, 1967.

Hart, Robert. "China and Her Foreign Trade." *North American Review,* January 1901.

———. *These from the Land of Sinim.* London: Chapman and Hall, 1901.

Headland, Isaac Taylor. *Court Life in China.* New York: Fleming H. Revell Co., 1909.

Hedin, Sven. *Jehol: Die Kaiserstadt.* Leipzig: Brodhaus, 1932.

Herrison, Count d'. "The Loot of the Imperial Summer Palace at Pekin." *Smithsonian Institution Annual Report 1900.* Washington, D.C.: U.S. Government Printing Office, 1901.

Hewlett, W. Meyrick. *The Siege of the Peking Legations.* Published as a supplement to the *Harrovian* of November 1900, by the editors.

Hibbert, Christopher. *The Dragon Wakes.* Harmondsworth, Middlesex: Penguin Books, 1984.

Hogarth, Peter, and Clery, Val. *Dragons.* New York: Viking Press, 1979.

Hooker, Mary. *Behind the Scenes in Peking.* London: John Murray Publishers, Ltd., 1910.

Hookham, Hilda. *A Short History of China.* New York: New American Library, 1972.

Hsiao Kung-chuan. *A Modern China and a New World: Kang Yu-wei, Reformer and Utopian, 1858–1927.* Seattle: University of Washington Press, 1975.

Hsieh Pao Chao. *The Government of China (1644–1911).* Baltimore: Johns Hopkins Press, 1925.

Hsu, Immanuel C. Y. *The Rise of Modern China.* London: Oxford University Press, 1970.

Hummel, Arthur W. *Eminent Chinese of the Ching Period.* 2 vols. Washington, D.C.: Government Printing Office, 1943.

Hunt, Michael H. "The American Remission of the Boxer Indemnity: A Reappraisal." *The Journal of Asian Studies,* May 1972.

———. "The Foreign Occupation: Peking, 1900–1901." *Pacific Historical Review,* November 1979.

———. *The Making of a Special Relationship: The United States and China to 1914.* New York: Columbia University Press, 1983.

Hunter, Bluebell. *The Manchu Empress.* New York: Dial Press, 1945.

Hunter, William C. *Bits of Old China.* London: Kegan Paul, Trench & Co., 1855.

Hussey, Harry. *Venerable Ancestor: The Life and Times of Tzu Hsi, 1835–1908, Empress of China.* Garden City, N.Y.: Doubleday & Co., 1949.

Johnston, Reginald F. *Twilight in the Forbidden City.* London: Victor Gollancz, 1934.

Kaempffert, Waldemar. "The World's Most 'Cultured Criminals.'" *Saturday Review,* 3 June 1944.

Kahn, Harold. "The Politics of Filiality." *The Journal of Asian Studies,* February 1967.

———. "Some Mid-Ch'ing Views of Monarchy." *The Journal of Asian Studies,* February 1965.

Kates, George N. *Chinese Household Furniture.* New York: Dover Publications, 1962.

Kennedy, Malcolm D. *A History of Japan.* London: Weidenfeld and Nicholson, 1963.

Keown-Boyd, Henry. *The Fists of Righteous Harmony.* London: Leo Cooper, 1991.

Kieser, Egbert. *Als China Erwachte: Der Boxeraufstand.* Munich: Bechtle Verlag, 1984.

King, Frank H. H., ed., and Clarke, Prescott. *A Research Guide to China-Coast Newspapers, 1822–1911.* Cambridge: Harvard University Press, 1965.

King, Paul. *In the Chinese Customs Service.* London: Heath Cranton, 1930.

Kuhn, Philip A. *Rebellion and Its Enemies in Late Imperial China.* Cambridge: Harvard University Press, Harvard East Asian Series 49, 1980.

Kwong, Luke S. K. "Imperial Authority in Crisis: An Interpretation of the Coup d'Etat of 1861." *Modern Asian Studies* 17, no. 2, (1983).

———. *A Mosaic of the Hundred Days.* Cambridge: Council on East Asian Studies, Harvard University, 1984.

Lane-Poole, Stanley. *The Life of Sir Harry Parkes.* London: The Macmillan Company, 1894.

Latourette, Kenneth S. *The Chinese: Their History and Culture.* New York: Macmillan Co., 1947.

———. *A History of Modern China.* London: Penguin Books, 1954.

Lee En-han. "China's Response to Foreign Investment in Her Mining Industry (1902–1911)." *The Journal of Asian Studies,* November 1968.

Lensen, George Alexander, ed. *Korea and Manchuria between Russia and Japan 1895–1904: The Observations of Sir Ernest Satow.* Tokyo: Sophia University, 1968.

Levenson, Joseph R. *Liang Chi-chao and the Mind of Modern China.* Cambridge: Harvard University Press, 1953.

Levy, Howard S. *Chinese Footbinding: The History of a Curious Erotic Custom.* New York: Walton Rawls, 1966.

Li Chien-nung. *The Political History of China, 1840–1928.* Stanford: Stanford University Press: 1967.

Li Dun, J. *The Ageless Chinese: A History.* New York: Charles Scribner's Sons, 1965.

Liang Ch'i-chao. *Intellectual Trends in the Ch'ing Period.* Translated by Immanuel C. Y. Hsu. Cambridge: Harvard University Press, 1959.

Library for the School of African and Oriental Studies. *Papers Relating to the Chinese Maritime Customs, 1860–1943, in the Library for the School of Oriental and African Studies.* 1973.

Lin Yutang. *A History of the Press and Public Opinion in China.* London: Oxford University Press, 1937.

Little, Mrs. Archibald (Alicia Bewicke Little). *Intimate China.* London: Hutchinson & Co., 1901.

———. *Li Hung-chang: His Life and Times.* London: Cassell & Co., 1903.

Lo Hui-men, ed. *The Correspondence of G. E. Morrison.* 2 vols. Cambridge: Cambridge University Press, 1978.

Lo Jung-pang, ed. *Kang Yu-wei: A Biography and a Symposium.* Tucson: University of Arizona Press, 1967.

Lui, Adam Yuen-chung. *The Hanlin Academy.* n.p.: Archon Books, 1981.

Lui Junwen. *Beijing: China's Ancient and Modern Capital.* Peking: Foreign Languages Press, 1982.

Lui Kwang-ching. "The Confucian as Patriot and Pragmatist: Li Hung-chang's Formative Years, 1823–1866." Offprint from *Harvard Journal of Asiatic Studies*, 30 (1970).

McAleavy, Henry. *A Dream of Tartary: The Origins and Misfortunes of Henry P'u Yi.* London: George Allen & Unwin, 1963.

———. *That Chinese Woman.* London: Allen & Unwin, 1959.

———. *Wang T'ao: The Life and Writings of a Displaced Person.* London: China Society, 1953.

MacDonald, Sir Claude. "Some Personal Reminiscences." *The Journal of the Royal United Service Institution,* August 1914.

MacDonald, Lady Ethel. "My Visits to the Dowager Empress of China." *Empire Review,* April 1901.

Mackerras, Colin. *Modern China: A Chronology from 1842 to the Present.* London: Thames and Hudson, 1982.

MacKinnon, Stephen R. "The Peiyang Army: Yuan Shih-k'ai and the Origins of Modern Chinese Warlordism." *The Journal of Asian Studies,* May 1973.

———. *Power and Politics in Late Imperial China: Yuan Shi-kai in Beijing and Tianjin, 1901–1908.* Berkeley: University of California Press, 1980.

McNair, Harley Farnsworth. *Modern Chinese History: Selected Readings.* Shanghai: Commercial Press, 1911.

Mannix, William Francis. *Memoirs of Li Hung Chang (with the Story of a Literary Forgery by Ralph D. Paine).* Boston: Houghton Mifflin Co., 1923.

Martin, W.A.P. *A Cycle of Cathay.* Edinburgh, 1900.

Memoirs of the Research Department of the Toyo Bunko. Tokyo: Toyo Bunko, 1967.

Meng, S. M. *The Tsungli Yamen: Its Organization and Functions.* Cambridge: Harvard University Press, 1970.

Michael, Franz. *The Taiping Rebellion.* Vol. 1, *History.* Seattle: University of Washington Press, 1966.

Miner, Luella. "The Flight of the Empress Dowager." *Century Magazine,* March 1901.

Mitamura Taisuke. *Chinese Eunuchs.* Tokyo: Charles E. Tuttle Co., 1970.

Miyazaki Ichisada. *China's Examination Hell.* New Haven: Yale University Press, 1981.

Montgomery, Michael. *Imperialist Japan.* London: Christopher Helm, 1987.

Morison, John Lyle. *The Eighth Earl of Elgin.* London: Hodder & Stoughton, 1928.

Morrison, George E. *An Australian in China.* London: Angus and Robertson, 1895.

Morse, H. B. *The International Relations of the Chinese Empire.* 3 vols. London: Longmans, Green, 1910–1918.

———. *In the Days of the Taipings.* Salem, Mass.: The Essex Institute, 1927.

Nagin, Carl. "Paper Dragons." *Art & Antiques,* November 1988.

Nash, George H. *The Life of Herbert Hoover: The Engineer, 1874–1914.* New York: W. W. Norton & Co., 1983.

Needham, Joseph. *Science and Civilisation in China.* Vol. 5, *Chemistry and Chemical Technology, Part Seven.* Cambridge: Cambridge University Press, 1986.

Nevius, John L. *China and the Chinese.* New York: Harper & Brothers, 1869.

Nivison, David S., and Wright, Arthur F., eds. *Confucianism in Action.* Stanford: Stanford University Press, 1959.

Norman, E. Herbert. "The Genyoasha: A Study in the Origins of Japanese Imperialism." *Pacific Affairs,* September 1944.

"Notes sur la carrière d'Auguste Chamot." *Revue Historique Vaudoise* (Lausanne, Switzerland: March, 1955).

Nye, Gideon. *The Morning of My Life.* Canton, 1872.

The Opium War. Peking: Foreign Languages Press, 1976.

"Orientalia." *The Quarterly Journal of the Library of Congress* 21, no. 4 (April 1964).

Paulsen, George E. "The Szechwan Riots of 1895 and American Missionary Diplomacy." *The Journal of Asian Studies,* February 1969.

Pearl, Cyril. *Morrison of Peking.* Sydney: Angus & Robertson, 1967.

Peyrefitte, Alain. *L'Empire Immobile ou Le Choc des Mondes.* Paris: Fayard, 1989.

Pong, David. "The Income and Military Expenditure of Kiangsi Province in the Last Years of the Taiping Rebellion." *The Journal of Asian Studies,* November 1966.

Porter, Jonathan. *Tseng Kuo-fan's Private Bureaucracy.* Berkeley: Center for Chinese Studies, China Research Monograph no. 9, 1972.

Pratt, Julius W. "Our First War in China: The Diary of William Henry Powell, 1856." *American Historical Review,* July 1948.

Price, Don C. *Russia and the Roots of the Chinese Revolution, 1896–1911.* Cambridge: Harvard University Press, 1974.

Pu Yi, Aisin Gioro (Henry). *From Emperor to Citizen.* 2 vols. Peking: Foreign Languages Press, 1979.

Purcell, Victor. *The Boxer Uprising: A Background Study.* Cambridge: Cambridge University Press, 1963.

Rankin, Mary Backus. "Public Opinion and Political Power: 'Qingyi' in Late Nineteenth Century China." *The Journal of Asian Studies,* May 1982.

Rawlinson, John L. *China's Struggle for Naval Development.* Cambridge: Harvard University Press, 1967.

The Reform Movement of 1898. Peking: Foreign Languages Press, 1976.

The Revolution of 1911. Peking: Foreign Languages Press, 1976.

Richard, Timothy. *Forty-five Years in China.* New York: Frederick A. Stokes, 1916.

Rockhill, William W. *Diplomatic Audiences at the Court of China.* London: Luzac & Co., 1908.

Rosenbaum, Arthur Lewis. "The Manchurian Bridgehead: Anglo-Russian Rivalry and the Imperial Railways of North China, 1897–1902." *Modern Asian Studies* 10, no. 1 (1976).

Savage-Landor, A. Henry. *China and the Allies.* London: William Heinemann, 1901.

Schafer, Edward H. *Ancient China.* New York: Time, 1969.

Schrecker, John. "The Reform Movement, Nationalism and China's Foreign Policy." *The Journal of Asian Studies,* November 1969.

Schurmann, Franz, and Schell, Orville, eds. *The China Reader.* New York: Vintage Books, 1967.

Scott, A. C. *Chinese Costume in Transition.* Singapore: Donald Moore. n.d.

Seagrave, Sterling. *The Soong Dynasty.* New York: Harper and Row, 1985.

Sergeant, Philip W. *Dominant Women.* 1929. Reprint. Freeport, N.Y.: Books for Libraries Press, 1979.

———. *The Great Empress Dowager of China.* London: Hutchinson & Co., 1910.

Seymour, Admiral Sir Edward H. *My Naval Career and Travels.* London: Smith, Elder & Co., 1911.

Shen Han-yin. "Tseng Kuo-fan in Peking." *The Journal of Asian Studies,* November 1967.

Shen Wei-tai. *China's Foreign Policy, 1839–1860.* New York: Columbia University Press, 1932.

Shih, Vincent Y. C. *The Taiping Ideology.* Seattle: University of Washington Press, 1967.

"Short-Sighted Chinese: Dr. G. E. Morrison's Unequalled Library of Books on China is allowed to leave China for Japan." *The Far Eastern Review,* September 1917.

Shu Chao Hu. *The Development of the Chinese Collection in the Library of Congress.* Boulder, Colo.: Westview Press, n.d.

Sitwell, Osbert. *Escape with Me.* New York: Harrison-Hilton Books, 1940.

Smedt, Marc de. *Chinese Erotism.* New York: Crescent Books, 1981.

Smith, A. H. *China in Convulsion.* Edinburgh: Oliphant, Anderson & Ferrier, 1901.

———. "The Contribution of Foreigners to Chinese Discontent." *Outlook,* 15 December 1900.

Smith, Richard J. *Mercenaries and Mandarins.* Millwood, N.Y.: KTO Press, 1978.

Soothill, William E. *Timothy Richard of China.* London: Seeley, Service & Co., 1924.

Spector, Stanley. *Li Hung-chang and the Huai Army.* Seattle: University of Washington Press, 1964.

Speer, William. *The Oldest and the Newest Empire.* Hartford, Conn.: S. S. Scranton & Co., 1870.

Spence, Jonathan. *The Gate of Heavenly Peace.* New York: Viking, 1981.

———. *To Change China: Western Advisers in China 1620–1960.* Boston: Little, Brown, 1969.

———. "The Seven Ages of K'ang-hsi." *The Journal of Asian Studies,* February 1967.

Stent, G. Carter. "Chinese Eunuchs." *The Journal of the North China Branch of the Royal Asiatic Society,* New Series 11 (1877).

Storry, Richard. *Japan and the Decline of the West in Asia, 1894–1943.* London: Macmillan Press, 1979.

Strachey, Lytton. *Eminent Victorians.* London: Chatto & Windus, 1918.

Summerville, John. *Fodor's People's Republic of China.* London: Hodder and Stoughton, 1981.

Swallow, Robert W. *Sidelights on Peking Life.* Peking: China Booksellers, 1927.

Swinhoe, Robert. *Narrative of the North China Campaign of 1860.* London, 1863.

Tan, Chester C. *The Boxer Catastrophe.* 1958. Reprint. New York: Octagon Books, 1975.

Tannahill, Reay. *Sex in History.* New York: Stein and Day, 1980.

Taylor, A.J.P. *Essays in English History.* Harmondsworth, Middlesex: Penguin Books, 1976.

Teng Ssu-yu, and Fairbank, John K. *China's Response to the West: A Documentary Survey 1839–1923.* Cambridge: Harvard University Press, 1979.

———. *Research Guide for China's Response to the West.* Cambridge: Harvard University Press, 1954.

Teng Tony Yung-yuan. *Prince Kung and the Survival of the China Rule, 1858–1898.* Ann Arbor: University Microfilms International, 1986.

Teng Yuan Chung. "The Failure of Hung Jen-k'an's Foreign Policy." *The Journal of Asian Studies,* November 1968.

"The Tientsin Massacre." *The Nation,* 22 September 1870.

Tompkins, Peter. *The Eunuch and the Virgin.* New York: Clarkson N. Potter, 1962.

Townley, Lady Susan. *My Chinese Notebook.* London: Methuen & Co., 1904.

———. *"Indiscretions" of Lady Susan.* London: Thornton Butterworth, 1922.

Trench, Charles C. *The Road to Khartoum: A Life of General Charles Gordon.* New York: W. W. Norton & Co., 1978.

Trevor-Roper, Hugh. *The Hermit of Peking: The Hidden Life of Sir Edmund Backhouse.* Harmondsworth, Middlesex: Penguin Books, 1978.

Twitchett, Denis, and Fairbank, John K., eds. *The Cambridge History of China.* Vol. 2, *Late Ching, 1800–1911, Part 2.* Cambridge: Cambridge University Press, 1980.

Vare, Daniele. *The Last Empress.* Garden City, N.Y.: The Sun Dial Press, 1936.

Waldersee, Alfred Count von. *A Field-Marshal's Memoirs.* London: Hutchinson & Co., 1924.

Waley, Arthur. *The Opium War through Chinese Eyes.* Stanford: Stanford University Press, 1958.

Walrond, Theodore, ed. *Letters and Journals of James Eighth Earl of Elgin.* London: John Murray, 1872.

Wang, Y. C. *Chinese Intellectuals and the West, 1872–1949.* Chapel Hill: University of North Carolina Press, 1966.

Warner, Marina. *The Dragon Empress: The Life and Times of Tz'u-hsi, Empress Dowager of China 1835–1908.* New York: Macmillan Co., 1972.

Weale, B. L. Putnam (Bertram Lenox-Simpson). *Indiscreet Letters from Peking.* 2d ed. London: Herst and Blackett, 1906.

Weeks, N. Donald. *Corvo.* London: Michael Joseph, 1971.

Wen Ching (Lim Boon-keng). *The Chinese Crisis from Within.* London: Grant Richards, 1901.

Wesley-Smith, Peter. *Unequal Treaty 1898–1997: China, Great Britain and Hong Kong's New Territories.* Oxford: Oxford University Press, 1980.

Williams, S. Wells. *The Middle Kingdom.* New York: George Palmer Putnam, 1848.

Williams, Frederick Wells. *The Life and Letters of Samuel Wells Williams.* New York: G. P. Putnam's Sons, 1889.

Wilson, Verity. *Chinese Dress.* London: Victoria and Albert Museum, Far Eastern Series, 1982.

Wolseley, G. J. *Narrative of the War with China in 1860.* London: Longmans, Green, Longman and Roberts, 1862.

Wong, J. Y. "The Arrow Incident: A Reappraisal." *Modern Asian Studies* 8, no. 3 (1974).

Wood, Minnie Norton. "Summer Splendor of the Chinese Court." *The Century Magazine*, August 1904.

Woolf, Cecil, ed. *Baron Corvo's Venice Letters*. London: Cecil Woolf, 1974.

Worswick, Clark, and Spence, Jonathan. *Imperial China: Photographs 1850–1912*. n.p.: Pennwick Publishing, 1978.

Wright, Mary C. "The Adaptability of Ch'ing Diplomacy." *The Journal of Asian Studies*, May 1958.

————, ed. *China in Revolution: The First Phase 1900–1913*. New Haven: Yale University Press, 1968.

————. *The Last Stand of Chinese Conservatism: The T'ung-Chih Restoration, 1862–1874*. 2d printing with additional notes. Stanford: Stanford University Press, 1962.

Wright, Stanley F. *Hart and the Chinese Customs*. Belfast: Mullan, 1950.

Wu Lien-teh. *Plague Fighter: The Autobiography of a Modern Chinese Physician*. Cambridge: University of Cambridge Press, 1959.

Wu Yung. *The Flight of an Empress*. Translated by Ida Pruitt. New Haven: Yale University Press, 1936.

Yang Lien-sheng. "Female Rulers in Imperial China." Paper prepared for Conference on Political Power in Traditional China, September 1959, at Laconia, New Hampshire, sponsored by the Center for East Asian Studies, Harvard University.

Yao Hsin-nung. *The Malice of Empire*. London: George Allen and Unwin, 1970.

The Yi Ho Tuan Movement of 1900. Peking: Foreign Languages Press, 1976.

Young, Ernest P. *The Presidency of Yuan Shih-k'ai*. Ann Arbor: University of Michigan Press, 1977.

Young, L. K. *British Policy in China, 1895–1902*. Oxford: Clarendon Press, 1970.

Yuan Chung-teng. "Reverend Issachar Roberts and the Taiping Rebellion." *The Journal of Asian Studies*, November 1963.

Yung Wing. *My Life in China and America*. New York: Henry Holt and Co., 1909.

"The Yung-lo Ta-Tien: An Unrecorded Volume." *British Museum Quarterly*, no. 25.

UNPUBLISHED DOCUMENTS

Diary of Lieutenant Francis Gordon Poole, Siege of the Legations, held by the British Library Manuscript Collection, London. Correspondence between Mrs. F. G. Poole and the British Library, concerning the acquisition of a copy of the *Yung Lo* encyclopedia.

Diaries of Sir Ernest Satow, held by the Public Records Office, London.

Letters of Hubert Vos, held by his grandson, Hubert D. Vos, in Santa Barbara, California.

Diaries and correspondence of G. E. Morrison, 1895–1918, held by the Mitchell Library, Sydney.

Diaries and correspondence of Robert Hart, 1864–1911, held by The Queen's University, Belfast.

Letters of Mrs. Anson Burlingame, held by the Library of Congress Manuscript Collection, Washington, D.C.

Manuscripts of Edmund Backhouse, "Decadence Mandchoue" and "The Dead Past," held by the British Library, London.

Diary of William B. Reed, Jr. Voyage to China 1857–1859, held by Library of Congress Manuscript Collection, Washington, D.C.

Consular and Ministry Records of the United States, National Archives and Records Service, Washington, D.C., especially Record Group 59.

Foreign Office Records of Great Britain, Public Records Office, London.

Backhouse Family Letters, held by the University of Durham, England.

ACKNOWLEDGMENTS

Work began on this book in the National Archives in Washington, D.C., in the summer of 1980, and continued in China, Australia, Northern Ireland, England, and the Continent over eleven years, with a few interruptions. Wherever possible, we did the research ourselves. But we were extraordinarily fortunate during the later years to have the help in London of Elizabeth Murray, who tracked down all manner of books, articles, documents, and experts to unravel the tangled story of the Ching Dynasty.

While he was busy pursuing research of his own, Carl Nagin found and photographed for us in Taipei the Katherine Carl portrait of the Empress Dowager. (The Smithsonian, responsible for the loan to Taiwan, was unable to provide color transparencies.) Thanks also to Carl Nagin for insights into Chinese counterfeiting and art forgeries. Polly Juen Cheo translated Chinese medical reports on Emperor Kuang Hsu, and secret histories of the Ching Court. Clio Whittaker helped with translations and Chinese periodicals.

Particular thanks to R. G. Tiedemann, Lecturer in the History of the Far East, School of Oriental and African Studies, London University. And to Beth McKillop and Hamish Todd, Curators, British Library Oriental Collection, for invaluable help on a range of questions.

Others who were most helpful were: Hubert D. Vos, of Santa Barbara, California, who graciously provided copies of his grandfather's correspondence with family and friends. Phoebe Peebles, Archivist of Fogg Art Museum at Harvard University, and Robert Mowry, Associate-Curator of its Department of Asian Art. Gordon Wheeler and Mary Kelly of The Queen's University Library, Belfast, who made Hart's diaries and correspondence available. Warren Horton, Director General of the National Library of Australia, in Canberra, and Manuscript Librarian Graeme

Powell, for their help on Morrison and Hoeppli. The Mitchell Library in Sydney, for access to Morrison's papers. Margaret Aitchison, whose grandfather was a physician to Sir Edmund Backhouse, for answering many questions. M. S. McCollum, Assistant Keeper, Department of Palaeography and Diplomatic, University of Durham, for Backhouse family correspondence. The Brooks Museum of Art, Memphis, Tennessee; the Memphis Shelby County Public Library & Information Center, and Memphis State University, for details about Katherine Carl. The National Museum of American Art, Smithsonian Institution, Washington, for assistance on Katherine Carl and Hubert Vos. Sir Edmund Pickering, for permission to peruse Morrison correspondence at the *Times;* and Archivist Melanie Aspey of the *Times* for her help. Jenny Watson of New Hampshire, who traced obscure copies of books long out of print. Silke and Claus Terheggen in Hamburg, who found answers to questions about Baron von Ketteler. John Brereton, who helped on the British Cavalry.

Other libraries that were most helpful: British Library Reference Section, Department of Printed Books; British Library Official Publications Library; British Library Newspaper Library, Colindale; The London Library, St. James's Square; Westminster Central Reference Library, London; Library of the School of Oriental and African Studies, London; Public Records Office, Kew, London; The British Museum; Royal United Services Institute for Defense Library, Whitehall; Verity Wilson at The Victoria and Albert Museum; Registry of the Family (Wills & Administration), Somerset House, London; General Register Office, St. Catherine's House, London; George Mason University Library, Fairfax, Virginia.

INDEX